2003

A SENSE OF VALUE

A Sense of Value

A THEMATIC READER

Ann Jeffries Thaiss

Christopher Thaiss

George Mason University

Mayfield Publishing Company

Mountain View, California

London • Toronto

LIBRARY OF CONGRESS CATALOGING-IN-PUBLICATION DATA
Thaiss, Ann Jeffries.
    A sense of value : a thematic reader / Ann Jeffries Thaiss, Christopher Thaiss.
        p.   cm.
    Includes index.
    ISBN 1-55934-203-X
    1. College readers.   2. English language—Rhetoric.   I. Thaiss, Christopher.
    II. Title.
PE1417.T46   1993
808'.0427—dc20   93-28683
                                                                       CIP

Manufactured in the United States of America
10 9 8 7 6 5 4 3 2 1

Mayfield Publishing Company
1280 Villa Street
Mountain View, California 94041

Sponsoring editor, Janet M. Beatty; production editor, April Wells-Hayes; manuscript
editor, Loralee Windsor; text and cover designer, David Bullen; cover image, David Toy;
art director, Jeanne M. Schreiber; manufacturing manager, Martha Branch. The text was
set in 10/12 Bembo by Thompson Type and printed on 45# New Era Matte by the
Maple-Vail Book Manufacturing Group.

Acknowledgments and copyrights appear at the back of the book on pages 606–608,
which constitute an extension of the copyright page.

To Ma and B, Jeff, Jimmy, Christopher,
Flannery, and Ann Louise

PREFACE

We look at *A Sense of Value* as meeting people at a crossroads, at that time in life when students realize that profound choices must be made about their careers, the people to whom they will commit their lives, and the personal and public principles that will guide their future decisions. This is an unabashedly hopeful book, because it assumes both that the reader accepts the challenge to decide how to live and that these personal decisions will make differences in the reader's personal happiness and the good of society.

A Sense of Value is a book of tools for making decisions. First, it offers more than 60 writings in which famous and not-so-famous individuals from many walks of life tell the stories of the choices they have faced and made. Included among these selections are well-crafted student essays (one in each thematic section) that help illustrate how other students have dealt with critical choices. Second, it surrounds each reading with questions that challenge the reader to probe the writer's assumptions and positions, to see connections and dissimilarities with his or her own experience, and, ultimately, to make better-informed decisions.

Third, *A Sense of Value* is designed to help teachers help their students succeed as reasoned thinkers and communicators. Part of the fear, even shock, that students experience in college is the realization that they are now expected to speak and write from knowledge; moreover, they are expected to develop informed positions that they must be able to argue in a reasonable, logical way. No longer is it enough just to tell one's story. Now one's story must make a point, and that point needs to be supported with evidence beyond one's feelings, however passionate. Perhaps even more shocking to many students is that even a well-supported point isn't good enough; one has to become able to appreciate many points of view, to argue several sides of a question, to understand how to see in many different ways.

It's no wonder that many students in such an environment come to see their prior experience as inadequate. Some become silent, feeling that they have nothing to say. Others resent college culture's insistence on diverse points of view and constant questioning of assumptions; they become vehement defenders of the values they've brought with them to school. Still others give unquestioning respect to the opinions in textbooks or other printed materials; they put together papers filled with unexamined quotes from published writers. Even worse, some students feel so unable to join this questioning, debating culture that they steal the essays of others and submit them as their own.

In building *A Sense of Value* we have tried to find writings that can help people bridge this gap between personal experience—life before or outside school—and the demands of college culture. Most of the essays, though not all, include an element of personal history, and most of these stories are about crucial decisions either that the writers or the people who are the subjects of the essays have made. But what turns these stories into powerful essays is that these actors don't see their decisions as simple or obvious; they see decisions as having consequences; they weigh alternatives; they study to make better choices; they are sensitive to how one person's life touches others, and how one person's joy may mean another's pain. In short, as editors we have tried both to appreciate the personal story and to show how it functions in the larger world of issues.

The questions and projects that surround the readings reinforce this integrating of the personal and the public. Questions often try to enlarge the context of the reading; we often ask the reader to compare one essay with another, or we provide a piece of additional information that can help the reader see the essay in a new light. Questions frequently ask the reader to explore a personal experience that relates to the experience described in the essay. Other questions and projects suggest ways to add to one's knowledge of the subjects of the essays.

The readings and questions follow two introductory chapters that give detailed instructions and examples of ways to accomplish the critical inquiry and persuasive writing that college demands. These two chapters address the interrelatedness of reading and writing, offer strategies to build critical reading skills, supply down-to-earth suggestions for writing effectively, and provide a structured sequence of techniques for turning writer-based essays into reader-based essays. Like the readings and the questions, these chapters are dedicated to helping people join the questioning, debating college environment without casting aside the passions, stories, and personal strengths that they see as defining themselves.

We suggest that in using this book's various tools, students (and teachers) experiment with the sequences in which they read the chapters. (Teachers should consult the Instructor's Manual for detailed suggestions about various possible syllabi.) The reader will note that the first two chapters make frequent references to specific readings that illustrate particular points. We suggest that a person practicing the research-based essay described in Chapter 2 may want to study two or more of the readings to which we refer. We also suggest strongly that the reader proceed slowly through the first two chapters, doing the exercises described. Just reading these two chapters without practicing the techniques will not be very effective (in the same way that reading a computer manual without hands-on practice is not particularly valuable).

Although we have had to put the chapters in some order, we see them as of equal importance and usable in any order a teacher may choose. We'll be delighted to learn from teachers using *A Sense of Value* the various ways in which they've ordered the works for their classes.

It's never possible to acknowledge all who should be recognized; there's nothing like writing an acknowledgments section to teach us how wide our net of debts and influences spreads. But to name a few:

Thanks to the students of George Mason University—those brand new, those emerging as versatile readers and writers, and those now long graduated into careers and communities—whose needs and ambitions give purpose to this text. Students Karen Browne, David Flory, Stephen Getlein, Donté Cornish, Carol Mullen, Andrew Myers, Jeffries Thaiss, and James Wasley deserve special thanks for allowing us to use their essays in this volume.

Thanks to the dedicated and ingenious composition faculty at George Mason University, whose idealism even in the last week of the semester brings sunshine to the soul. Special thanks to the Composition Committee of the English Department: Mark Farrington, Ruth Fischer, Don Gallehr, Jim Henry, Wilkie Leith, Virginia Montecino, John O'Connor, Ashley Williams, and Terry Zawacki, for many things, including their boundless enthusiasm for discussing theories and practices in teaching.

Thanks especially to Carolyn Barrett, Louisa Enright, Robert Karlson, Ellen Nunnally, Amelia Rutledge, Tricia Snell, Patrick Story, Ashley Williams, and Terry Zawacki for suggesting student and professional essays for the collection. Ashley Williams and Terry Zawacki deserve particular thanks for their ongoing suggestions for the book and for their insights and revelations about teaching, reading, and writing. Working day by day with such people convinces us that you can't talk about literacy without also talking about values.

Thanks go to Sharon McLaughlin, R.N., A.C.C.E., registrar extraordinaire of the Washington, D.C. chapter of ASPO/Lamaze for her cheerful listening, week by week, to the many ups and downs of our writing; to Winifred Coulter, Ph.D., for her understanding and her wisdom in "sorting it all out"; to Mary Ann Schmitt for her always generous heart and brilliant reasoning on all of the tough issues; to the staff of Miller's Office Products in Vienna, Virginia, our home away from home, for their always gracious assistance with the photocopy and fax machines; and to Jan Howard and Dorothy Zalaskus for their years of friendship, superhuman patience, and always being there.

For their careful, helpful reviews of the manuscript, we'd like to thank Wendy Bishop, Florida State University; Richard Bullock, Wright State University; Kay Halasek, Ohio State University; Nancy L. Joseph, York College of Pennsylvania; Joyce Kinkead, Utah State University; James C. McDonald, University of Southwestern Louisiana; James C. Raymond, University of Alabama; Judith A. Stanford, Rivier College; and Dennis Young, James Madison University.

Thanks to Nancy Peck of Mayfield Publishing Company for her exemplary representation of the company and for her support of this project. Special thanks to Jan Beatty, Senior Editor at Mayfield, for her faith in this project, her creative suggestions, her careful choices and guidance in the review process, and her tactful insistence on big and little ways to make this book better. It's wonderful to work with an editor who knows and cares about the book she's helping the writers create.

To Andella and Virgil Jeffries, the best parents and grandparents that any family could have—thank you for your love, daily support, babysitting, and dinner every night to make our lives so much easier. You are the foundation of this family's values.

Finally, thanks to Jeff, Jimmy, Christopher, Flannery, and Ann Louise Thaiss for more joy than we can describe. Thank you, Jeff, for your honest, careful prose, your confidence in all that you do, and your discipline to your noble art. Thank you, Jim, for your drawings of imagination and beauty, the Jakal Jam Band, ten years of All-Star baseball, and for all the baseball years to come. Thank you, Crink, for being the anchor in our home, for always being interested in what we are doing, and for your patience and being able to fix anything, especially our computer. Thank you, Flann, for always being ready to "Play Ball," for your sense of humor, and for being everyone's best friend. Thank you, Ann Louise, for your laughter, your singing and dancing "like a 'rincess," and for your love of your brothers. Each of you, every day, sharpens and smooths our sense of value.

CONTENTS

Part One

ACHIEVING A
SENSE OF VALUE

Think about different meanings people attach to the word *value*.

"Eggs are a good value at the store this week."
"I value your friendship."
"You don't value me as much as you should."
"I'll vote for the candidate with the right values."
"The value of the stock changes from day to day."
"What is the value of *n* in this equation?"

In each of these uses of the word, *value* seems to be either a quality that's part of a person or thing ("Eggs are a good value . . ." "the value of the stock") or an idea that a person holds about someone or something ("I value your friendship" ". . . the candidate with the right values"). But what all these uses of the word share is a quality of change. How "valuable" something is changes with the situation and the viewpoint. We value a warm coat on a cold day, but we can't shed that coat fast enough when we walk into a hot room. Similarly, if a person views an object closely and for a long time and from different angles, it's likely that the person attaches more "value" to that object than someone who walks by it without a glance. Is the object valuable in itself? Or is it meaningless to talk about *value* unless we consider the situation and the viewer?

As the writers of much of this book and the collectors of the readings that make up the rest of it, we define "a sense of value" as having two goals. Both are goals that we seek to achieve and to help our readers achieve.

The first "sense of value" is an appreciation of more of the world. We are continually struck by the persistence of mass media in broadcasting an astonishingly narrow range of experiences and points of view—astonishing, given the potential of communication technology to give all of us windows on many worlds. The same few dozen "star" faces beam at us from commercial to commercial; the same few politicians occupy news broadcasts; the same products are hawked hour after hour; the same point of view—more is better, so buy, buy, buy—comes across not only in commercials but also in the programs they surround. It may be that no book can counteract the multimedia power of mass communications with its message of sameness; still, by presenting writers who appreciate the value of many different ideas, places, people, and events, we hope to help ourselves and our readers appreciate diversity. We strongly value the notion that by appreciating more, we promote our own happiness and the happiness of those we've learned to respect.

The second "sense of value" is the more careful evaluation of ideas, people, and things. This goal complements the first. If we allow ourselves to appreciate more widely and deeply, we increase our ability to make wise choices of what to believe and do. We do have to make such choices because none of us is capable of honoring all ideas equally. (That capability is one definition of divinity!) So how do we choose? How do we give fair value to the great diversity of things we can experience?

This book follows the path of "rational, literate inquiry," that is, asking and answering questions through reading and writing. Ours isn't different from most books in this regard; books by definition must be written and read. Moreover, it's common for books used in college courses to include questions for study, because rational, literate inquiry is the standard method by which students have been prepared to make life choices since the days of Socrates. What we feel makes this book somewhat different from the others is our emphasis:

- We've tried to select readings that show the writers trying to understand and make decisions, that is, attempting to achieve a sense of value.
- We've created questions about each reading that focus on the process of achieving the goals of greater appreciation and more careful evaluation. The questions probe the readings from many angles; we persistently ask readers to study their own reactions and convictions and ask them to question why they believe as they do.
- We continually urge readers to go beyond their own thoughts. Questions and assignments push readers to share their views with others, ponder issues in group discussions, and go out into the broader com-

munity to learn. We feel that the twin goals of appreciation and careful evaluation demand these ventures.

We readily admit the limitations of the rational, literate approach to achieving a sense of value. Words can do a lot, but they can't do everything. Ironically, much of the power of these writings comes from the nonliterary work of the writers. We've included, for example, whole chapters on athletics, art, the pain and struggle of warfare, and the many mysteries of sexual experience. There are many ways to wisdom, as the following pages reveal, and the questions before and after each selection offer a variety of rational, literate ways to inquire into these many modes of experience. In the next two chapters we present a detailed system for making reading and writing central methods in achieving your own sense of value.

CHAPTER ONE

Reading for Insight and Understanding

BECOMING A BETTER READER: A LIFELONG PROCESS

This is a book about people's lives. More than that, it is a book of people telling us their most important life stories: the events that led them to their most valued possessions—the principles that give their lives direction.

At another level this is a book about reading and writing. Like every other written artifact, it proves the power of the written word to shape our thinking and change our lives. Every person whose life and struggles are presented in this collection has been shaped by reading. Sometimes the writer makes the debt explicit, as Annie Dillard does in her many references to other writers, or as Malcolm X does in his autobiography, when he describes the great changes brought about in him by his voracious reading while in prison. Sometimes the influence is implicit: Aldo Leopold can see history in the rings of the tree struck by lightning only because he has read the history of environmental law in the Midwest.

As you read selections in the book, keep in mind the influence of reading on these writers; look not only for the clear references to books, articles, and stories, but also for ideas that could only have come through something read. And beyond that, look for the way that a person's story takes shape because that person has read the stories of others. A writer's "style" doesn't just emanate naturally from within; no one is born a writer. We learn to make stories because we grow up hearing them, often in conversation, or on TV, but also sometimes from people, usually our parents, who are reading them from books. As we listen and gradually learn to decipher letters, words, and sentences, we learn many things about stories—things that no one ever tells us but that we learn because we've heard and read so much.

We learn, for example, that people tell stories for many different reasons: to impress us, make us think a certain way, include us in what they know (or to exclude us from it), make us feel better (or worse), make themselves feel better, make a sharper memory of something they don't want to forget, and so on. We learn that it isn't always easy to know those reasons. We learn early to recognize many different kinds of stories, including fairy tales, stories about how the world began, historical stories, gossip, sermons, tall tales, wishes, confessions, dreams, weather forecasts (and other predictions), instructions, rules, and lots of different kinds of jokes. Moreover, we hear and read so many stories of each type that we need very little information to tell us what kind of story to expect: "Once upon a time," "Do you know what I heard?", and "Wouldn't it be great if . . ." each give us definite expectations of the type of story to come.

These types and these words become so much a part of us, even as small children, that as adults we fail to appreciate just how amazingly complex this knowledge—our ability to read—is. We tend to think of it as something natural rather than as something we have slowly and steadily learned.

Moreover, we never stop becoming better readers. One thing we learn more and more deeply as our lives progress is that no story means exactly the same thing to everyone who hears it. The same joke that drew gales of laughter from a close friend may draw a puzzled stare from a new acquaintance and anger from someone else. "Once upon a time" signals "fairy tale" to most native English speakers, but it means nothing to a person who does not know the language. John Hinds, a linguist who compares the structures of writing in different cultures, contends that a piece of writing that is "normal" in one culture may be "wrong," "immoral," or "crude" in another. For example, Hinds says that in the United States it is considered good form for a newspaper editorial to get right to the point, that is, to state its point of view in the first paragraph. In Japan, on the other hand, getting to the point in an editorial is poor writing, both because it may insult the person who does not share that point of view and because it insults Japanese readers in general, who expect writing to offer different possible meanings that it is the reader's responsibility to discover (Hinds 99–100). Just as small children learn to distinguish in ever finer ways among stories of different types, we adults grow as readers by learning the ever more subtle distinctions among messages from different people. We learn many possible meanings of even single words.

LEARNING TO READ FOR POSSIBILITIES RATHER THAN RIGHT ANSWERS

A major purpose of this book is to present many ways to read the selections and, by extension, any other piece of writing you encounter. As authors we take the position that real reading requires the reader to become ever more adept at seeing the possibilities within the material. The educated, mature reader is able to ask many different questions about any writing, to think about it from diverse perspectives, and to appreciate the difficult craft of the writer. To us, *A Sense of Value* refers not only to the values of the people whose writing we present here; it refers also to this process of reading. To read anything with an appreciation of its complexity, with an appreciation of the art of the writer, proclaims its value. Many economists say that anything is worth only as much as people will pay for it. The corollary to this is that all of us will at times disregard things, including books and sometimes even people, only because we have not yet learned how to "read" them—to see their possibilities.

The definition of reading we present here confronts a definition of reading that often predominates in schools, largely because of the influence of standardized tests. Under this influence, students come to see reading as a search for a single "right" meaning, rather than as an act of imagination and a challenge to their creativity. Standardized test*takers* can't look into their reading for personal meanings because a reading test*maker* gives them all the questions to answer and all the possible answers. It's no wonder that many beginning college students are unable to respond to a teacher's open-ended question about a reading assignment: "What do you want to say about the reading?" Students used to multiple-choice or fill-in-the-blanks reading tests aren't prepared to think about their own responses to reading, and they've come to disregard their own opinions as they try to guess what will be "on the test."

Similarly, students are sometimes not prepared to create their own questions to ask about a reading because the emphasis on standardized tests has taught them that other people ask the questions. In fact, such students are often impatient with teachers who don't ask "right answer" questions but persist in demanding that students develop their own questions and responses. If we look at this conflict from a values perspective, we can say that such teachers place a high value on the growth of students as independent thinkers, whereas multiple-choice testing places a high value on the students' conforming to the agenda set by the testing agency.

Another thing that students often "learn" about reading by taking reading tests is that what they read seems to have come from nowhere, was written by no one, and isn't connected to anything else they might read. Students might be told that the play *Hamlet* was written by someone named William Shakespeare in England in about the year 1600 and that it was one of several tragedies written by the same person. And a reading test might ask students to give back such information. But does this information help us understand the play? Would it help us use the play for some purpose that's important to us? A more useful question to ask about *Hamlet* might be "What about the play suggests where it might have been written?" Such a question probes our ability to read the play, but it is not likely to show up on a multiple-choice test because it has no easy answer.

A reader looking for possibilities might ask the following open-ended questions about the author of the play and its connections with other works: "From reading the play, what ideas do I have about the sort of person (or people) who wrote it? What other plays or stories remind me of *Hamlet*? What are the similarities? How are they different?" Questions such as these make us better readers by forcing us to look into the work and how it relates to our other experiences.

Finally, if you regard what you read as possessing many possibilities rather than simply the right answers to questions that other people ask, you avoid making lots of wrong assumptions as you read. For example, it's convenient for testmakers to have you assume that William Shakespeare wrote *Hamlet;* it's inconvenient for you to learn that the authorship of *Hamlet* has long been disputed and that Francis Bacon and Edward de Vere, among others, have been proposed as authors of the play. If you read with a sense of the possibilities, you would even be open to the speculation that the *Hamlet* you know is the work of many people over many years in many countries. Indeed, literary historians—people who have learned to read with a sense of possibilities—tell us that whoever wrote the play about the Prince of Denmark that was performed in London sometime around 1600 was working out of a long tradition of similar stories and may simply have revised an earlier play based on those stories. We also know that this play from around 1600 existed in several versions and that virtually every company that has produced it has changed it to suit its performers, financial backers, and audiences.

If you learn to read with a sense of the possibilities of texts, you aren't stuck with anyone else's simple ideas about what you read; you aren't just consumers of the text, but people who are free to *use* the text for your own purposes. Reading then becomes an important tool in your own efforts to achieve a sense of value.

SOME TOOLS FOR EFFECTIVE READING

At the heart of effective reading is the ability to create questions to ask yourself and others about what you are reading. The best tools we can give you for effective reading are diverse, provocative questions that others have already created, and some methods for you to use in generating further questions.

Questions for Effective Reading

Think of a question as a way to look at something. The more questions you can ask about anything, the more ways you have to regard it and the more information you can create. One reason many students have trouble talking and writing about what they read is that they lack questions to ask about reading. Without questions to focus their act of reading, it's hard for them to do anything with the words that pass before their eyes.

The four questions below provide different ways to focus reading. They give you ways to say different kinds of things about what you've read.

- Do you like this essay?
- *What* do you like about it?
- If you could talk with the author, what would you ask her or him to write more about?

- If you had one minute to summarize this essay for a friend, what would you say?

The number of possible questions is infinite, yet creating questions takes some imagination and some knowledge of the many kinds of questions that others have asked.

Some examples of questions and types of questions follow. Feel free to use some or all of them as you reflect on the readings in the chapters. You will notice that the questions before and after each reading tend to fit into the categories listed here or to blend several categories.

Exercise

Try adding another question in each category after you've read the examples below. Pool your questions with those of others doing this exercise and compare your results.

- Questions about emotional reaction
  What do you like about the piece? What don't you like so well?
  How do you think the writer is trying to make you feel? What words or passages provoke the strongest emotional reaction in you?
- Questions about the main point or key ideas
  As you read, look for the main points that the writer is trying to make. Can you find sentences that openly express these main points? Can you find sentences that imply a main point without stating it openly?
  Do you find ideas in this piece that seem to contradict one another?
  What ideas or pieces of data in this piece are new to you? How do they change your thinking?
- Questions about sequence and organization
  How does the piece begin? What effect does that have on you? Try starting the piece with something else from the text. How does the effect change?
  How does the piece end? Try changing the ending or cutting off the last paragraph. What happens?
  What is the sequence of ideas? Make an outline or flowchart of the piece, with a few words about each paragraph in the sequence. What would happen if you changed the order of ideas?
- Questions about difficulty
  What words or sentences do you find difficult to understand? Reread as much of the piece as it takes to resolve your confusion. Could you substitute some clearer wording?

If you could talk with the writer, what would you ask her or him to write more about to improve your understanding?

Why is this text difficult for you? What experiences or education would you need to make it easier to understand or more useful to you?"

- Questions about the author or authors

What else do you know about the writer or writers of this piece? Does this knowledge in any way affect your response to this piece?

Does the writer tell you anything directly about himself or herself in this piece? Note these data. Does the writer imply some personal information that isn't stated openly?

If you have read something else by this writer, how does that affect your reading of this text? What's different here? What's the same?

- Questions about the writing process

Does the writer say anything in the piece about how she or he wrote it? Does she or he say anything about changes that might have occurred during the writing?

Where does the information in this writing come from? Are sources listed or noted in the piece? Where else would you look for information on these topics?

Is the text you are reading the same text that the author wrote? How have others, such as editors, translators, or printers, changed the text?

- Questions about you as a reader

What happens to you as you read this piece? Do your expectations and feelings change as you go on? What causes this to happen?

What kinds of things do you like to read? What kinds of reading do you try to avoid? How do these prejudices affect your reaction to this piece? How could the writer (or you) change it to make it more attractive to you?

What knowledge or other personal experience do you bring to this reading? What do you already know or think about these topics? How does that prior experience affect your reading of this text?

- Questions about intended audience

What kinds of knowledge or what beliefs does the writer assume about the person reading this piece? Where, if anywhere, does the writer state these assumptions?

Where does the writer use technical language or strange terms that you don't understand? Who would understand them?

Does the writer seem to be addressing more than one type of reader? How do you know? Who are these different readers?

- Questions about genre

What type (genre) of writing does this piece seem closest to (for example, personal story, fiction, technical description, advertising, proposal, political speech)? How is it like something else in this genre? How is it different?

How does the writer use different genres in this piece (for example, personal anecdote, argument, conversation)? What would you add or take away? Why?

- Questions about tone or mood

What mood is created in you by this piece? Cite words and passages that are especially powerful in creating this feeling.

Try reading the piece aloud in several different voices as you try to create different tones. Does one voice sound more appropriate than the others? Try revising the piece to make it fit a different mood.

- Questions about culture

Are there cultural events mentioned in the piece but not explained, because the speaker assumes that explanation is not necessary (for example, holidays, customs, religious or patriotic figures)? Is knowledge of these references important for understanding the piece? How?

Is anything described in the piece that seems foreign or strange to you? Is there anything that seems illogical or irrational about the speaker's thoughts or behavior? Can you account for this strangeness or seeming irrationality on the basis of cultural difference? (Chapter 9 includes many examples of the clash of cultures, though each chapter explores this phenomenon to some extent.)

- Questions about values

Where, if anywhere, does the writer state a principle or an idea that he or she believes in? Does this belief seem deeply held? How can you tell this from the text?

What values or principles are implied by this piece but not stated? Mark passages that imply these values.

If values are stated in the piece, where in the piece do you see how the writer (or the person written about) came to those beliefs?

What ideas (or people or sources of information) seem to be devalued in the piece? How do you feel about this? How would you change the piece to reflect different values?

Questions Used throughout the Book

We surround each selection in the book with questions, not to limit the types of inquiry into the readings, but to suggest a few ways to look at the work. Because this volume focuses on people's values and how they achieve them and on better reading and writing as tools for achieving a sense of value the questions tend to be about values, how the piece was written, and the reader. Thus every selection is accompanied by questions (and exercises) that ask you to

- analyze and evaluate the principles stated or implied in the piece: for example (from chapter 7), "What gives Junko Tabei her drive to conquer mountains? What does the article suggest about her motivation?

What questions remain for you? If you were to interview her about her drive, what would you ask?"

- study features of the writing—such as organization, genre, language—and imagine different ways of doing these things: for example (from chapter 10), "Write a short essay on any topic of your choice. Use Annie Dillard's style. Mobilize metaphors. Is it easier to write when you have a style to imitate?"

- put yourself in the place of the writer or compare your experiences with those of the writer or the main subject: for example (from chapter 7), "How have your behavior, dreams, and ambitions been influenced by athletes or their portrayal in the popular media?"

- add to your knowledge by seeking information outside the text and outside your prior experience: for example (from chapter 3), "Go to your local government offices and find out the local process by which land is zoned for particular kinds of use, such as high-rise office buildings, private homes, and factories. Find out where in the zoning process citizens' opinions about zoning can be heard."

Many of the questions and assignments require you to write, talk with people, read further, and share your findings with others. We believe strongly that the process of "achieving values" goes on through life, and that by questioning and exercising in these collaborative ways we achieve authentic *values*—principles of worth, not momentary impressions or ideas that we claim to "believe in" just because we've heard them many times or because somebody attractive has told us to believe in them.

Some Ways to Create Questions

Our questions before and after the selections imply a principle we'd like to make explicit: We hate to leave any piece of writing "as is," to venerate it as an object. We believe that any writing is effective only if people use it for something, and using it means that each reader turns it into something different. Our questions therefore tend to ask you to think about the reading as something that can be changed—made useful through modification. To return to the *Hamlet* example: Every age has made of the Prince of Denmark story something different, and every theatre or film director and every good actor has made it his or her own. Inevitably this means that these people have asked of *Hamlet* questions that were important to them—their own questions, not someone else's. The kinds of questions listed earlier are useful models, but if you are ever to become a *mature* reader, you must become able to ask your own questions of whatever you read. Mature readers find all texts interesting because they have learned many ways to look at texts, they always find something to engage the imagination. It's the poor reader who finds texts "boring," because the poor reader has very few ways to "hook" onto a text.

CONDUCT A DIALOGUE WITH THE TEXT: READ WITH PEN IN HAND   For centuries, experienced readers have treated reading as a conversation between writer and reader. If you read for possibilities rather than for right answers, you read with pen (or pencil or computer) in hand, not to mark all the stuff that you think might be "on the test" but to ask questions about the text or to make comments about the reading that reflect your thinking as you read. The sample below shows the kinds of questions and comments you might write.

> On that first day, Don Collins and I had gone down to the bank *worth how much?*
> in the city square and had withdrawn fifty (rand) for the week; the
> *which?* second was a holiday; on the third I was taken down to the farmer's
> supply where I bought a pair of black rubber boots and stiff green
> overalls. And on this, the fourth morning, we were starting later than
> I thought we should. *Will he explain this?*
>
> (from David Flory, "One Day, South Africa," in chapter 4)

You don't need to mark on the text, if you fear that marking it will reduce its value or if you are using someone else's copy, but you need a method and materials for catching your thoughts as you read. We personally like paperback books (which we feel less guilty marking in) with large margins that allow much questioning and commenting.

Looking back through a text you've marked is a great way to find a focus for a paper or an idea you'd like to develop in some other way, because marginal comments (or page-by-page comments or questions in a notebook you keep as you read) often reveal your freshest insights.

KEEP A READING-RESPONSE NOTEBOOK   Margins let you catch insights in shorthand, but a reading-response notebook lets you think on paper (or on a computer screen) about your reading. The notebook can be as serious or light-hearted as you wish to make it. You can use it for systematic explorations of your reading (using, for example, any of the questions from the twelve categories listed earlier in the chapter), for "discovery drafts" of papers you are writing (see "Writing for Others" in chapter 2), or for brief notes as you read. One of the major benefits of such notebooks (also called "reading-response logs" or "reading journals") is that the act of think-writing (a shorthand way of saying "writing as you think") generates fresh observations and questions.

Like any log or journal, the reading-response notebook provides a private, familiar place for your observations, reflections, experiments, and speculations. For the notebook-keeper, rereading the entries is a major pleasure and source of inspiration. An idea that seemed to go nowhere when it was written may spark an insight later, or you may find a brilliant connection between two entries written weeks or months apart.

KEEP A DOUBLE-ENTRY NOTEBOOK   Some log-keepers like to combine the value of text markings with the notebook's power to enable extended thought. They use a double-entry version of the notebook, in which the notebook page is divided lengthwise. On one side, the reader copies brief bits of the text (a word or a phrase) or makes a brief comment. On the other side of the page, the reader writes longer comments that connect two or more of the brief notes. When setting up the double-entry notebook, you should leave enough space between the brief notes for later explorations.

To illustrate notebook and double-entry notebook entries, here is the first paragraph of our selection from Diane Ackerman's *The Moon by Whale Light* in chapter 3, plus notebook entries about it:

> One winter evening, I took a seat in a natural amphitheater of limestone boulders, at the bottom of which was the wide, dark mouth of Bracken Cave. Nothing stirred yet in its depths. But I had been promised one of the wonders of our age. Deep inside the cavern, Mexican free-tailed bats were hanging up by their toes, twenty million of them. They were the largest concentration of warm-blooded animals in the world. At dusk, all twenty million would fly out to feed, in a living volcano scientists call an emergence. They would flow into the sky with their leathery wings and ultrasonic cries, and people fifty miles away, in cities like San Antonio and Austin, would, without realizing it, rarely be more than seventy feet from a feeding bat.

Sample Notebook Entry

I wonder how she can be so sure that this is the "largest concentration of warm-blooded animals in the world." How can the scientists know? Do they count them? Do they look at small concentrations, count them, and then multiply by what they estimate is the size of the cave? There's so much hard work—tedious, mind-numbing work—behind every confident statement like that, and it's so hard to know when reading statistics or claims whether the research backs up the statement! I hope the rest of the article goes into the kind of research they did to come up with those claims about the Bracken Cave.

Sample Double-Entry Notebook Entry

took a seat . . . amphitheater	builds expectations of a show; compares nature to something built by humans
wide, dark mouth	builds suspense, fear; again, nature compared to human form
wonders of our age	more built suspense
bats hanging by toes	grotesque—more suspense
living volcano	neat image—something natural to be feared, and even worse because it's

a-li-i-ive! The whole paragraph makes
you feel like you're in a vampire/
disaster movie.

DRAW INSPIRATION FROM OTHER READERS If you learn to
read for possibilities, your imagination can be sparked by the comments and
questions of fellow readers. Teachers often discourage students from reading
published interpretations or reviews of books, plays, and so on, because they
fear that the scholars' views will be taken as absolute truth—the right answer—
by readers who haven't learned to read imaginatively. But reading takes place
in a community of readers and writers; people who love to read love to share
their ideas and feelings about what they read. Consider the times that you
have been inspired to read a book or article by the enthusiasm of a fellow
reader.

To get the most out of published interpretations and reviews, we recommend that you read more than one interpretation of any work. If you read
one of the thousands of articles about *Hamlet,* for example, you'll get a narrow
view of the play. If you read several, you'll begin to see the possibilities, and
your own reading of the play will be enriched.

The same goes for discussions with fellow readers. Talk about what you
read with others. Such discussions will force you to think about why you feel
as you do, so you will come to understand yourself a little better, as well as
what you have read.

REFERENCES

Hinds, John. "Inductive, Deductive, Quasi-Inductive: Expository Writing in Japanese,
Korean, Chinese, and Thai." *Coherence in Writing.* Ed. U. Connor and A. Johns.
Alexandria, VA: Teachers of English as a Second Language, 1990.

CHAPTER TWO

Writing Effectively

THE READING-WRITING CONNECTION

Be sure you have read chapter 1 before proceeding here. Early in that chapter we stressed the need for all writers to be avid, questioning readers. We included many questions that a reader can apply to any text. These questions will generate successful topics for writing about your reading. Later we showed ways by which regular, thoughtful writing can help you become a more successful, sophisticated reader. One of these ways was to keep a reading-response notebook, which can help you mature as an independent thinker.

The reading-response notebook and the variations on it described in chapter 1 represent one of the two kinds of writing—writing for yourself—that we stress as necessary for students of values and for college students in general. We will devote part of this chapter to another example of writing for yourself—writing about values. The chapter will also explore the second kind of writing—writing for others—which students are frequently asked to practice in college. This part of the chapter will include sections about writing personal essays and reading-based papers.

WRITING FOR YOURSELF

Writing about Values

Sometimes when I come across an old photograph of myself, particularly one of those taken when I was ten or twelve or thereabouts, I stare at it for a while trying to locate the person I was then, among all the persons I've been, trying to see stretched out down the years the magnetic chain linking the onlooker and the looked at, the gay expectant child and the sober near adult. If I am successful, and very often I am, the two merge and I recall little snatches of life. Running through the wet grass in the dusk of early evening. My father's vulnerable smile as I walked down the aisle on graduating from kindergarten. A wet kiss on my cheek from a stranger brother on an Atlanta street. Being called *nigger* and straightening my shoulders and lifting my head because I would not let it be known that I was hurt though

I didn't fathom the complexities of why I was hurt and why I had to be brave.

Joan Frances Bennett, in "Members of the Class Will Keep Daily Journals," in
A Day at a Time: Diary Literature of American Women, ed. Margo Culley (New
York: Feminist Press, 1985) 279

My father did not want a girl. My father was over-critical. He was never satisfied, never pleased. I never remember a compliment or a caress from him. At home, only scenes, quarrels, beatings. And his hard blue eyes on us, looking for flaws. When I was ill with typhoid fever, almost dying, all he could say was: "Now you are ugly, how ugly you are.". . . Yet I had a hysterical sorrow when he finally abandoned us.

Anaïs Nin, *Diary, 1931–1934* (New York: Swallow Press, 1966) 76

I find incessant labor with the hands, which engrosses the attention also, the best method to remove palaver out of one's style. One will not dance at his work who has wood to cut and cord before the night falls in the short days of winter; but every stroke will be husbanded, and ring soberly through the wood. . . . I have often been astonished at the force and precision of style to which laboring men, unpracticed in writing, easily attain when they are required to make the effort. It seems as if their sincerity and plainness were the main thing to be taught in schools,—and yet not in the schools, but in the fields, in actual service, I would say.

Henry David Thoreau, *A Writer's Journal,* ed. Laurence Stapleton (New York:
Dover, 1960) 10

The questions and exercises throughout this book ask you to talk and write about what you value and why. One reason for keeping a diary or personal journal is to put statements about value on paper. In that way you can

- think more clearly about what you believe by putting your beliefs into words
- document the "here and now" of belief—what you believe at this moment
- think through important decisions by weighing alternatives and imagining consequences
- comment on the values of others (including characters in books) and compare your own situations with those of others
- test your values by rereading your diary to see if your values persist through time and experience

In a sense, all writing says something about the writer's values. Even the most seemingly neutral "fact" statement ("I got up at 6:40 this morning") asserts something that you believe to be true. When you put such a statement in writing, you are affirming it much more emphatically than if you merely kept it "in mind." Nothing shows how value-laden all statements are better than trying to write down exactly what happened and then comparing what you wrote with another observer's version. No two witnesses ever see exactly the same thing. What you see in any scene or event reveals what you do and do not value:

> "He drove away in a red car; I don't know the kind. Sort of small. But he was wearing Panache jeans—I'd know that label anywhere."
> "I think he had a reddish car, and he was dressed casually—I don't notice clothes. Oh, yeah, he had the state U. symbol on his rear windshield—you know, the Spouting Whales—I remember that because my sister goes there."

To write regularly for any of the purposes listed above should help you strengthen and broaden your sense of value. But the writing will work only if it helps you see more than you saw before. That's why it's useful to practice different types of seeing, and you can do this by using your writing to practice looking for different types of things. In chapter 1, we listed 12 types of questions you can ask about anything you read (a mere fraction of the infinite number of questions that might be asked), and we listed several questions within each type. If you exercise your mind by asking these diverse questions, you will become a more observant—better—reader. You will become more proficient still by cultivating the ability to create your own questions. The same principle applies to any other type of thought: The more different exercises you practice, the richer your thinking becomes.

IMPROVING YOUR ABILITY TO SEE   The first goal, then, is to write, since all your writing forces you to see who you are. The second goal is to write with the express purpose of improving your ability to see yourself and everything around you. And that is where diverse questions and exercises come in, because you can't improve your seeing by continuing to look in the same old way.

To Achieve a Fuller Sense of Value

Goal One: Write regularly for and to yourself.

Goal Two: Write for the purpose of improving your ability to see.

Method: Practice with different questions in mind. For starters, use the questions in chapter 1 (pages 8–12) and the questions that come before and after each selection in chapters 3–10.

PRIVACY, FEAR, AND FREEDOM   We can't overstress the need for every writer to have a place and time for private writing. You can't do the serious creative work (or fun) of thinking if you're always aware of someone looking over your shoulder, if you're always preoccupied with meeting dead-lines, or if you spend all your leisure time letting someone else entertain you.

You may have difficulty writing for yourself because you have been taught by your schooling that writing is something you do only for a teacher. You haven't learned the joy of playing with sentences and the sounds of words, of watching ideas take shape, of setting down memories to keep safe as a legacy for loved ones.

For another thing, it's not easy to look yourself square in the eye through the mirror of your words. Once you start to grapple with your thoughts you may find yourself letting loose some strange creatures that you'd just as soon keep locked up. It does take some courage to write, even just to yourself.

> I haven't written for a few days, because I wanted first of all to think about my diary. It's an odd thing for someone like me to keep a diary; not only because I have never done so before, but because it seems to me that neither I—nor for that matter anyone else—will be interested in the unbosomings of a thirteen-year-old schoolgirl. Still, what does that matter? I want to write, but more than that, I want to bring out all kinds of things that lie buried in my heart.
> Anne Frank, *Diary of a Young Girl* (New York: Doubleday, 1972) 12

You may believe that you don't write well, so you don't write because you don't want to be reminded of a source of embarrassment.

The beauty of writing for yourself is that you control the situation. There is no teacher or boss telling you what to write, how to write, or when to write. If your writing unearths feelings that you'd rather not deal with at the moment, you don't have to. If someone has criticized your writing in the past, well . . . they're not around now. Once you begin writing for yourself, you'll experience tremendous freedom. You can do anything you want to, and writing is a quiet enough and small enough thing that you won't be trampling on anyone else's turf or disturbing their rest.

Some Suggestions for Writing about Values

There are no rules you must follow in writing for yourself—if you feel that there are rules and you're not following them, you're not writing for yourself. In the previous chapter and in this, we give you many suggestions for ways we and others have found to make writing for yourself a rich, productive activity. We suggest that you try some of them or all of them; we hope they will inspire you; but don't by any means feel limited by them.

READ AND ASK DIFFERENT QUESTIONS ABOUT YOUR READING See chapter 1.

KEEP A DIARY OR JOURNAL Both *diary* and *journal* literally mean "daily," but you needn't write every day. Just write one entry at a time. Don't start with the idea that you'll keep this up forever, or even that you'll fill an entire book.

You needn't write in a book, either. One of us keeps several diaries, off and on, in several series of blank-page and spiral-bound books; the other intermittently keeps a journal on the computer. Some diarists write on anything that comes to hand, including backs of envelopes and grocery slips.

But the diary or journal isn't just random writing. The key idea seems to be that the writer keeps the work together so that he or she can find and come back to it. Since there is nothing like a diary for capturing the here and now of our thinking, keeping the work where you can find it lets you go back and learn from your earlier writing.

Many diaries and journals have become famous; we have selected excerpts from some of them for this book because of the candor and freshness that diary writing retains, even after centuries. If you are interested in keeping a diary, we suggest that you read other diarists to see how many different purposes and styles there are. You might even try some of them out in your own diary.

Here's a short list of published diarists:

John James Audubon	Henry David Thoreau
Charles Darwin	Colette
Anne Frank	Charlotte Forten
Anaïs Nin	Daniel Defoe
Dorothy Wordsworth	Dag Hammarskjöld
Samuel Pepys	Andy Warhol
Meriwether Lewis and	Sylvia Plath
William Clark	Katherine Dunham
Robert Falcon Scott	Thomas Jefferson
George Washington	Janet Flanner
Tobi Gillian Sanders and	
Joan Frances Bennett	

For a sampler of diary styles across two centuries and many cultures, we recommend Margo Culley's collection *A Day at a Time: The Diary Literature of American Women from 1764 to the Present* (New York: Feminist Press, 1985).

USE QUESTIONS AND EXERCISES   The more you write, the more ideas you'll discover to vary your thinking and keep it fresh. Here are some suggested questions and exercises:

Question: What do I value?
  • Exercise: Make a list of ideas, people, and things you value. Keep the list so you can add to it. Try to be honest with yourself. (No one's watching.) List quickly and then come back and try to put

the items in order of importance. Then write about your list, especially anything that surprised you.
- Variation: Choose one item from the list. Write about the process
by which you came to value this item. What events or other people's opinions influenced you?

Question: What is my position on (a current issue in the news)?
- Exercise: Choose a controversy and write about it. Force yourself
to take a stand. (For example, if you find yourself vaguely "for" or
"against" gun control, specify someone who definitely should or
should not be allowed to possess a gun.) List as many reasons as you
can for thinking this way. Look back at your reasons, and write
briefly about the source of each one. Are you basing it on an
opinion you heard? Something you read? A personal experience? A
moving story of someone else's experience?
- Variation 1: Imagine yourself in a dialogue on this issue with a
person who continues to disagree with you. Write some of this
dialogue. What reasons do you give? What counterreasons does he
or she give? Try hard to keep thinking of this person as someone
you like and respect. That way you'll do a better and fairer job of
reporting that person's point of view.
- Variation 2: Create a story about the hypothetical person with
whom you are disagreeing. Write this story so that it seems reasonable for this person to think as he or she does.

Question: What do I see?
- Exercise: Describe a place from several different angles and with
several different focuses. Every description should focus on something different in that specific place such as
1. only what you see
2. only what you hear
3. only what you feel through your skin
4. only what you smell
Study the place for one minute, then go away and describe it as
fully as you can; then return and note ten things you didn't see, feel,
hear, and smell, and ten that you described incorrectly or incom-
pletely. Write about yourself as an observer: Why did you see some
things and ignore others? How has the exercise changed you as an
observer?

USE OTHER MODES OF EXPRESSION   We should add that in
doing these and other exercises you might consider using other modes of
expression to intensify your sense of dealing with values. If you like to draw,
for example, consider augmenting your writing with sketches.

While most of the exercises above lend themselves most easily to writing
in sentences and paragraphs, free yourself to try other modes:

VERSE   MUSIC   CARTOONS
      SONGS   STORIES

Feel free to spread your thinking out over the page, as we have in the previous sentence. Some people are comfortable think-writing (a shorthand way of saying "writing to think") in some form of "clustering" or "mind-mapping," whereby a focal idea, such as "things I ignored in the room," is put in the center of a page and subsequent ideas are placed around it.

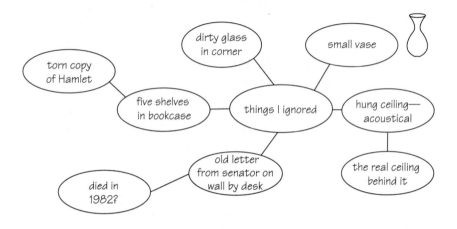

Remember, these are suggestions. You make up the rules.

WRITING FOR OTHERS: A PROCESS

Most college writing begins with a teacher's assignment, so writing to meet others' demands occupies much of your time as students. If you realize that you can begin the assignment by writing for yourself, you can eliminate much of the anxiety that often accompanies writing for someone else's approval. Indeed, we can picture the process of writing to meet an assignment as follows:

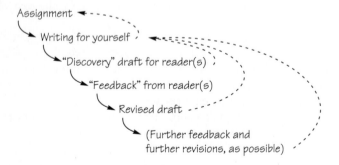

Don't think of this scheme as a step-by-step process in one direction. Though you'll start by writing for yourself, you can continue to use this tool at any stage of your writing, to help you sort out new ideas and solve problems that arise in thinking about the task.

THE ASSIGNMENT Once you've received an assignment, always be prepared to ask your teacher for clarification of anything that puzzles you. Sometimes a good question won't come to you until after you've had a chance to do some writing in your diary or journal about the assignment, so feel free to ask the teacher for more information at any point.

If the teacher gives a writing assignment orally rather than in writing, quickly record the details. Don't hesitate to ask the teacher to repeat these details so that you can record accurately. If your writing reveals details that you don't understand, ask for clarification.

WRITING FOR YOURSELF Use writing as a tool of thought at every stage of the process. For example, you might quickly write your understanding of the assignment and any questions that come to mind. You can use think-writing to brainstorm the idea that you really want to make the center of your research and writing:

> . . . he wants us to write about an event that changed our thinking about something important. One event? A series of events? Like a story? Does he want it to be mostly story with a little analysis of what it all means? Or does he want us to talk about the idea we had and how we changed it, with a little about the event thrown in the middle?
>
> What to write about? Tracy's accident? Losing the house in the hurricane? Does it have to be one big event, or could it be something that changed us over time? I think I'd really like to write about my computer stuff, but that's not one event, but it sure has changed me.

You can use writing to "dump" onto the page everything that you already feel you know about the topic; you can use writing to jot down everything you'd like to know, but don't. With most college writing assignments, you'll be writing to take notes on print sources, interviews, and so on. You can even use writing to speculate about how you think you should go about completing the assignment. You'll find that using writing to solve problems that arise in the writing process will save you time and eliminate some of your anxiety.

DISCOVERY DRAFT FOR READER(S) Professional writers always have "helping readers" they trust to give them good feedback on drafts of their work. Especially in the computer age, when word processing has made revising so easy, there's no good reason to suffer the anxiety of trying to get a draft "perfect" the first time. (Even before computers, the pros still knew that the best way to write was to show drafts to helping readers and then revise.)

When you have written for yourself through the early stages of the process and feel that you've acquired enough material to begin a draft of the assigned paper, think of that first draft as a means of discovery. Use the draft to experiment with beginnings and endings, the sequence of ideas, the tone, and the messages you want to get across. Write fairly quickly. Don't allow yourself to get stymied trying to come up with the perfect phrase. Remember, you're trying to get the feel of the language by trying things out, so write down what sounds good at the moment, and plan to revise later.

> Maybe a really important event for me was my learning how to use e-mail on the computer. It didn't change my life overnight (as a matter of fact, I thought it was a waste of time when I started), but I think I can say it's changed me for the better. . . .

FEEDBACK FROM READER(S)   Ideally you should be able to get feedback on your draft from the person who assigned the work, and we strongly recommend that you take drafts of papers to your teachers for their comments before you must submit the papers for grades. Our colleagues continually tell us that they offer students the chance to get such feedback, but very few students take them up on the offer. These are opportunities wasted. We admit that we ignored these opportunities frequently when we were in college, because we feared that the teachers would criticize what we wrote. Instead we sweated out countless hours wondering what to write and countless other hours waiting for the grade. Bad bargain.

If you take your draft to the teacher, or other helping readers, always attach a brief note with a few specific questions about particular problem areas. This will save your reader time and get you a quicker, more useful response. Make sure that your questions always ask for information, such as,

> *What do you think my most important idea is here?*

Never just ask for a yes or no judgment, such as

> *Do you like this?*

It's too easy for a reader to say, "It's fine." This may make you feel good, but it won't help you.

If you have nothing more specific to ask your reader, two good all-purpose questions are

> *What's not clear enough to you? What would you like me to write more about?*

If you fear that your helping reader will hesitate to give you suggestions for change because he or she doesn't want to hurt your feelings, you might start out with a "feel good" question, such as

> *Tell me the things you like best about my draft.*

When your helping reader has given you a little praise, he or she may feel freer to answer your other questions.

REVISED DRAFT Use the feedback as the basis for revision. Keep in mind that you may want to repeat the feedback—revision cycle more than once, if you want your reader's opinion on the changes you've made. It's not uncommon for important documents, such as master's theses and doctoral dissertations, to be commented on and revised several times. Generally speaking, the more important the writer believes a document to be, the more time he or she spends getting feedback and making changes. The stories writers tell about their work are almost always revision stories.

Sample Draft–Feedback–Revision Sequence

Draft: Maybe a really important event for me was my learning how to use e-mail on the computer. It didn't change my life overnight (as a matter of fact, I thought it was a waste of time when I started), but I think I can say it's changed me for the better. . . .

Feedback: I really like how honest you come across here, especially admitting you thought it was a waste of time at first. But I wonder if you might want to get rid of the "maybe" at the start. Are you still not sure if the e-mail was important? It sounds as if you really are sure. I think you should sound more confident.

Revision: Learning how to use e-mail on the computer has really changed me. Not only have I learned a useful skill, but I feel that the experiences I've had as an "e-mail junkie" have made me a different, and perhaps better, person. . . .

WRITING A PERSONAL ESSAY

While following the process outlined above will help ensure that all your writing brims with your ideas and your personality, the term *personal essay* has come to denote a particular kind of writing that is becoming ever more popular in schools and in magazines, newspapers, and books. In brief, the personal essay tells a story about you, the writer, and uses that story to make a point.

Sometimes the writer begins with the personal story:

When I went to kindergarten and had to speak English for the first time, I became silent.
> Maxine Hong Kingston, "A Song for a Barbarian Reed Pipe," *The Woman Warrior* (New York: Random House, 1977) 191

Sometimes the writer begins with the issue about which the story will make a point:

> I went to the woods because I wished to live deliberately, to front only the essential facts of life, and see if I could not learn what it had to teach, and not, when I came to die, discover that I had not lived.
> Henry David Thoreau, "Where I Lived and What I Lived For," *Walden* (New York: Norton, 1966) 61

Frequently personal essays move back and forth from story to point, with the writer describing events, reflecting on their meaning, going further into events, and so on. Because this book is made up mostly of personal essays, you can easily find examples that will illustrate this story-point-story-point structure.

We believe that to learn to write personal essays, you must not only read them but also study them for what they can teach you as a writer. One of our major intents is to present essays that will help you become an able writer of the personal essay. The questions in chapter 1 and the questions that surround the reading selections throughout the book will help you become a personal essayist. Writing for Yourself, as detailed in this chapter, will give you systematic practice in combining story and point.

The Challenge to the Personal Essayist

Everyone has a story to tell; everyone tries to make points. Everyone, in daily conversation, uses little personal stories to try to make a point to someone else. A crying child runs into the room: "She stole my toy—punish her!" Story, point. But the parents aren't convinced: They need more information. "Did you steal her toy?" they ask the accused child. And so on. The challenge to the personal essayist, in this case the crying child, is to make the story so good that it answers all the doubts of the reader, in this case the parents. If you've ever found yourself in a similar scenario, you know how difficult that can be.

How does one make a story that good?

Keep in mind that the power of the story you need to tell depends on at least a couple of factors: the reader you're trying to convince and the size of the point you're trying to make. This situation isn't unique to the personal essayist; it applies to any situation where one person is trying to persuade another: legal cases, scientific experiments, advertising, and so on. (Note that lawyers, scientists, and advertisers all use personal stories as part of their strategies for making points, but they also rely on other types of evidence.)

A person who knows you well and agrees with your views on most issues might very well accept a sweeping claim based on your personal story. Chances are that your professor won't, because scholars in all fields are trained to be skeptical of claims that aren't supported by strong evidence. For example, your honest, vivid recollection of an especially good or poor teacher would not justify, to most faculty, any claim about all teachers. You would have to augment that story with other evidence, such as

- additional stories from others
- detailed descriptions of your careful observations or detailed descriptions by others
- strong opinions from recognized authorities
- statistical data from studies, surveys, and experiments
- the clear demonstration of *your own authority*, such as being able to show that you have studied this question for a long time.

Exercise

Read one of the pieces in chapters 3–10. As you read, mark if, where, and how the writer uses the five types of evidence listed above in addition to the writer's own personal story. Are there other ways in which the writer establishes authority to make claims?

Educated readers tend to be especially doubtful about sweeping or emphatic claims—"There is no good reason for abortion," "No private citizen should be allowed to own an automatic weapon"—unless the evidence is very strong and of different types. If your primary evidence is your personal story, the educated reader will be looking for a very tentative claim. For example, instead of asserting, "My experience shows that it's a waste of time for people to try to change local laws," the educated reader will prefer a less ambitious claim, such as, "I expected the process of getting a law changed to be much easier than it turned out to be. I'd advise anyone contemplating a similar act to do several things in preparation: . . ." and so on.

The scholar's experience indicates that any issue can be debated and that the authoritative writer is one who is aware of different viewpoints. To the scholar, then, the strong writer is one who makes tentative claims and shows awareness of different ways to see any question. Ironically, the scholar judges the person who makes sweeping, assertive claims to be a weak writer, unless the evidence is especially varied and carefully gathered.

Exercise

Reread the same selection you used in doing the previous exercise. Mark the points or claims that the writer makes. Do you feel that the evidence supports the claims? Note the writer's use of words that make the claim tentative rather than assertive or sweeping. If you feel that a claim is still too great for the evidence to support, revise the claim to fit the evidence.

What kinds of evidence do you feel would be needed to support the greater claim?

_____

Why Can't I Just Write What I Believe?

Many writers lose patience with good scholarly writing because it is tentative and careful. But good writing of any kind requires patience; if you want to set down your opinions loudly and entertain no dissenting views, do it in your diary. (All of us need a place where we can spout off without hurting anyone, and that's one thing a diary's for.) Then come back a week or 10 or 50 weeks later and see if your opinions still suit you.

If you want to turn your personal writing into a personal essay for an educated reader, you'll have to learn and follow the values described in the previous paragraphs about claims and readers. This doesn't mean that you need to douse your fire as a writer. The selections in this book burn brightly. But if you want to write so that people are warmed and enlightened by your story, you have to provide evidence powerful enough to ignite that fire in your reader's mind.

_____

Exercise

Create your own personal essay by following the process outlined in "Writing for Others: A Process" (pages 22–25). Focus on telling the story, then use that story to make a point. In asking for feedback on the draft of the essay, ask your reader to suggest how the evidence can be strengthened or how the point should be restated to suit the story. Revise.

_____

WRITING A READING-BASED PAPER

Many, if not most, college writing assignments will ask you to work in some way with written material. Usually the assignment will require you to evaluate the reading in some way. This doesn't mean a thumbs up or down review such as a critic would give a new novel. In the professional disciplines, evaluating a written source means showing how the writing is valuable by using it in some way in your own writing. For example, psychology students doing experiments with rats in mazes will have to read many articles about previous experiments; they will need to evaluate those articles to compare the findings of the various researchers and to design their own experiments. The more they read and the more they try to use what they read, the more adept they will become at evaluating the quality of the research.

Evaluating Written Sources

Students new to college frequently misunderstand what it means to use written sources in their writing. Students assigned to do what are commonly called research papers, or term papers, often just collect written material on a topic and then quote it in large chunks. Such writers don't use their reading; they are used by it, because they just copy what they've read without thinking about its value.

HINTS FOR EVALUATING SOURCES   The exercises and assignments throughout this book are meant to strengthen you as an evaluating reader who systematically questions what is read and compares one piece of reading with another. The questions and techniques described in chapter 1 begin this process and are intended as strategies that can be used with reading of any type. The following are two other strategies to use when you're evaluating your reading:

- Seek advice. In compiling this collection of essays, we not only read widely through magazines, biographies, autobiographies, and other collections of essays, we also sought the advice and recommendations of fellow teachers, librarians, students, writers, and editors. Especially if you are investigating a topic for the first time, you need the advice of people familiar with the subject to learn about authoritative sources to use and unreliable sources to avoid.
- Ask whether your sources make tentative claims and cite varied evidence. The principles about claims and evidence discussed in "The Challenge to the Personal Essayist" (pages 26–27) also apply to the sources you're evaluating. Use the exercises on pages 27–28 and 30–31 to help you decide the usefulness and reliability of a source.

WAYS TO CITE READING IN YOUR WRITING   The best way to learn how to refer to your reading in your essays is to observe how other writers do it. We suggest that you select pieces from this collection and mark how the writers blend references to other works into their own prose. The two main things to look for are paraphrase and direct quotation.

The most common way in which one writer refers to another's work is the paraphrase. When writers paraphrase, they don't stop the flow of their writing, but they give credit to those from whom they've borrowed. In the following example, rather than using Leakey's own words, the writers blend his ideas into their own prose:

> . . . a British anthropologist, Dr. Louis S. B. Leakey, is displaying some fossil bones—a foot, part of a hand, some jaws, and skull fragments. On the basis of these, Dr. Leakey has said it's time to rewrite completely the history of man's origin.
>
> Malcolm X and Alex Haley, *The Autobiography of Malcolm X* (New York: Ballantine, 1965) 181.

Of course, the writer must paraphrase as accurately as possible, taking extreme care not to misrepresent or oversimplify the ideas. This is never an easy task, because paraphrasers are literally changing the words of other writers into their own. Anytime writers paraphrase, they need to read for possibilities, being aware that any passage might be interpreted, hence paraphrased, in different ways.

Because writers need to take care when they paraphrase, it's often important to use direct quotation as well. Remember to use direct quotations from another text for two reasons only: (1) to be scrupulously careful about getting the other person's words right, when there might be controversy, or (2) to cite wording that is particularly beautiful or powerful. Never quote another writer just to save yourself the time and effort of paraphrasing. Here's an example of direct quotation for the purpose of accuracy:

> I spread my contract out before me on the table and turned to the morals clause.
> ". . . Provided, however, that in the event that at any time in the future . . . First Party shall be charged with adulterous conduct or immoral relations with men other than her husband, and such charges or any of them are published in the public press, the waiver herein contained shall be null and void and of no force and effect. . . ."
> Gloria Swanson, "The Greatest Regret of My Life," *Ever Since Eve,* ed. Nancy Caldwell Sorel (New York: Oxford, 1984) 244

Note that Swanson quotes only the part of the legal contract most pertinent to the point she is making. She uses ellipses (. . .) to indicate that her citation is part of a larger statement.

Caution: In citing any source, even when you quote directly, you need to take care not to quote "out of context." The words you cite must be as much as possible in keeping with the spirit of the work from which you've taken them. Never just skim a source until you find what you think might be "the perfect quote" to use in your essay, because you'll very likely be quoting our of context.

Double Caution: When you quote directly from any source, you must place the quoted material in quotation marks or set it apart from your words in some other way to indicate that the words belong to someone else. If you do not do this, you will be guilty of plagiarism. You must also in some way indicate the source you are using (see "Avoiding Plagiarism," below).

Exercise

Read quickly through several of the selections in the book to locate examples of paraphrase and direct quotation. Note diverse ways in which writers use each strategy, including instances in which the writer uses both paraphrase and quotation in referring to a work. Can you tell from the reference whether or not the writer is paraphrasing accurately? Can you tell if the writer is quoting out of context? What factors in the writing lead you either to trust the writer or to question the writer's accuracy and fairness?

Avoiding Plagiarism

Give credit in your essay to your sources for any information that you found in a source. If you didn't need a source for a particular bit of information, you don't need to cite one.

This rule pertains to paraphrases as well as to direct quotations. Some student writers think that they need to cite sources only when they use direct quotation. This is not so. Most charges of plagiarism are based on uncredited paraphrases.

Giving credit for paraphrases is easy, but styles of citation differ. Popular writing, such as that found in newspapers, magazines, and books for the general public, tends to give a quick reference to the source where it is actually used:

> According to Chief Architect Melissa Jones in a March 17th article in *City Art News,* the art center should be completed by summer 1995, "unless the City Council makes us redesign the whole project."

Popular writing does not employ lists of sources or references at the end of the essay.

Scholarly writing, such as that found in professional journals in any field—and in the research-based writing you do in college—cites sources both at the point of use and in a list of sources at the end of the essay. At the point of use, the source reference is quick; the list at the end of the essay gives more information, so that other researchers can find the sources if they wish to read them. At the point of use one method of citation is to put the author's last name and the page of the reference in parentheses.

> A recent estimate by Melissa Jones, Chief Architect of the project, indicates that the art center will be completed by summer 1995 (Jones, 35).

The same reference expanded in the list of sources at the end of the essay would include more information.

> Jones, Melissa. "A Personal Response to the Art Center Controversy." *City Art News* 17 Mar. 1992: 12.

For detailed information on the method used above, see Joseph Gibaldi and Walter S. Achtert, *MLA Handbook for Writers of Research Papers,* 3rd ed. (New York: Modern Language Association, 1988). For another method, see *The Publication Manual of the American Psychological Association* (Washington, DC: American Psychological Association, 1983). You will find that the *MLA*

Handbook is used mostly in humanities and literature courses, while the *APA Manual* is used mostly in the social sciences, natural sciences, and other technological fields. But always ask your teacher to recommend which "style guide," as these books are called, to use in the particular course.

Blending the Personal Essay and the Reading-Based Paper

Earlier in the chapter we noted that as you write a personal essay you become more convincing to educated readers by being able to use other evidence besides your personal stories. Such evidence frequently comes from reading. The strong personal essay requires the writer frequently to be an *evaluating reader:* one who can use written sources to good effect in the essay. This book includes many such pieces; indeed, one premise of the book is that worthwhile writing about values always blends the writer's respect for personal experience—the personal story—with respect for the experiences and reflection of others often found through reading.

Exercise

Read several of the many personal essays in this volume that blend the personal story with other kinds of evidence (for example, the selection from Annie Dillard's *Pilgrim at Tinker Creek* or John McPhee's *Pieces of the Frame* in chapter 3; Walt Harrington's "The Mystery of Goodness" in chapter 4; the selection from Patricia Williams's *The Alchemy of Race and Rights* in chapter 5; and Victor Villanueva, Jr.'s "Whose Voice Is It Anyway?" in chapter 9). How does their work blend personal and reading-based writing? Note how the writers refer to other writers without losing the flow of their own prose. Observe how they paraphrase others so that their experience of reading becomes part of the experience that they are communicating to you, the reader.

To achieve this blending of personal and reading-based writing in your own work, it's essential that you come to view your reading as part of your own search for meaning. That's one reason we recommend that you try out some version of the reading-response notebook we described in chapter 1. Keeping such a notebook will help you become as comfortable with describing and reflecting on your reading as with describing and reflecting on any other type of experience. If you achieve some ease with writing for yourself about your reading, the task of writing about your reading for professors and other educated readers will become much easier.

Following the Reading-Based Essay Process

In writing this paper, you can usefully follow the same PROCESS we outlined in "Writing for Others: A Process" earlier in the chapter.

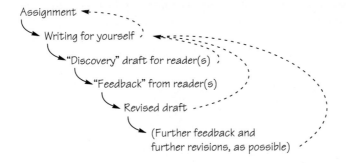

In the feedback stage, the questions you ask of your helping readers might focus on how you use sources of further evidence:

> Which references to other documents and works are most effective?
> What seems to be my strongest source? My weakest?
> Where in my draft do you see the need for further references?
> Note my uses of paraphrase and direct quotation. Where should I add information? Where would other direct quotes be helpful? Where can I delete or shorten quoted material?

Practicing the Reading-Based Essay: Some Sample Assignments

A COMPARISON OF TWO OR MORE READINGS ON THE SAME ISSUE   This book brings together works that can be compared easily and usefully. Indeed, the questions before and after the readings frequently ask for a comparison. Select one such question or develop your own. (Use the questions in chapter 1 to get started.) This assignment will require frequent and accurate paraphrase and quotation for you to make your point about the essays you're comparing.

Study the following brief comparison of two readings. Observe how the writer begins with the point of the comparison and then uses evidence from each reading to support the point. Imagine that you are this writer's helping reader; point out what you like about the essay, then offer suggestions for strengthening the evidence or any other part of the writing.

Two "Voices" of War: Beirne Lay, Jr., and John Saddic

W AR INSPIRES writing in different styles and for different pur-
poses. Even personal writings about wartime experiences can show great differences in style as the writers try to achieve specific purposes for very different readers. For example, Beirne Lay, Jr.'s "I Saw Regensburg Destroyed" (*The Saturday Evening Post* 6 Nov. 1943) shows a writer trying to paint a vivid, inspiring portrait of war for U.S. citizens "back home." By contrast, Henry Berry's version of his interview with Marine John Saddic, a veteran of the Korean War, shows a writer trying to convey a former soldier's anger about a war long past.

Lay, a bomber pilot flying missions over Germany in World War II, creates the image of a dedicated soldier fulfilling his orders. In addition, he strives to paint a vivid picture of the environment of war, so that his faraway readers can share his sensations: "After the briefing, I climbed aboard a jeep bound for the operations office to check up on my Fortress assignment. The stars were dimly visible through the chilly mist that covered our blacked-out bomber station, but the weather forecast for a deep penetration over the Continent was good. In the office, I looked at the crew sheet, where the line-up of the lead low and high squadrons of the group is plotted for each mission. . . ." His description is clear, but not flowery; we can feel the "chilly mist over the blacked-out bomber station," but he doesn't get so preoccupied with the scenic details that we lose sight of his top priority, his official mission.

Almost four decades after the U.S. intervention into the Korean conflict, Henry Berry's *Hey, Mac, Where Ya Been? Living Memories of the U.S. Marines in the Korean War* is not concerned with keeping up the spirits of the wartime reader. Berry strives to capture the anger of Marine veterans who, like their counterparts who served in Vietnam, felt unrewarded and unremembered by the American citizens they felt that they had served. In presenting his version of his interview with Sergeant John Saddic, Berry makes this anger vivid through using "tough" language—fitting the Marine stereotype—and lots of movie-like dialogue (short speeches):

> "Are you off your rocker? Haven't you had enough of all that killing? There's bound to be another war, and you'll be the first one called up."
>
> "Oh, no, not with all my experience," I told her, "me, a Purple Heart machine gunner. I'll spend the war training kids."
>
> Well, I trained kids all right. On the ship going to Korea we had some machine gunners who had never fired a machine gun. We tied a wooden duck to a line we had hanging off the fantail. I showed these kids the score off the ass end of our ship. And it was the same with the mortar men. We must have scared the hell out of the fish.

Like Lay, Berry does take care to give a precise picture of the scene: "We tied a wooden duck to a line we had hanging off the fantail." Also like Lay, Berry presents an idea of "the G.I." that fits a popular stereotype. But Berry's "tough-talking Marine" is strikingly different from Lay's "dedicated man of few words."

YOUR POSITION ON A CONTROVERSIAL ISSUE In this assignment you want to make a point about something you believe, why you believe it, and why others should agree. In deciding what to say and how to support it, study the part of this chapter on claims (pages 25–28).

Use this assignment to practice working with a personal story and with other types of evidence derived from your reading. Follow the process outlined in "Writing for Others: A Process." Also practice different types of beginnings for your draft. One time begin with your story. For example,

> When I read *No Turning Back,* I kept thinking about my aunt Sharon, who was always great to me and my brother when we were growing up, but who was absolutely hated by some of our relatives. I remember asking my Mom—I was about ten, I guess—why Aunt Sharon never seemed to be invited to our house when Aunt Carol was, and my Mom telling me to "never mind." Not till last year did Mom finally let the cat out of the bag. Aunt Sharon had had an abortion.

Another time begin with your *point.* For example,

> When I read *No Turning Back,* I found myself getting angry with the church officials who seemed unthinkingly to stand behind "the rules," rather than to take into account the reasoning and the convictions of Ferraro and Hussey. I can't definitely say that I agree with their position on abortion (I'm studying the various arguments), but I have come to some definite conclusions—through painful experience—about how administrators should handle subordinates who disagree on principle with organization policies.

A third time begin with a strong paraphrase or quotation. For example,

> ". . . Uneasily, I did tell her that I would not choose to have an abortion if I were pregnant.
> During the day of the abortion, while Tony and I kept an anxious vigil by the telephone, I thought about what I had told Cheryl, and I realized it wasn't true."
> With these words (from Barbara Ferraro and Patricia Hussey's *No Turning Back*), a nun realizes how a crisis can show us how empty our so-called "beliefs" can be.

YOUR RESPONSE TO ONE OF THE PIECES IN THIS BOOK
Begin the process with your strong reaction to one of the essays in the book (for example, your intense enjoyment of the writer's style, your identification with the writer's story, your strong agreement or disagreement with the writer's viewpoint). Use your reading-response notebook to explore this reaction and note all the passages that have sparked it. (Remember to read for possibilities and strive to be fair and accurate in citing the text.)

In making your point about the work, practice using your own personal story (if relevant) plus other evidence from reading. (Good examples of "reaction" essays are Victor Villanueva, Jr.'s "Whose Voice Is It Anyway?" and Donté Cornish's essay about *The Autobiography of Malcolm X,* both in chapter 9.)

Part Two

READINGS,
QUESTIONS,
AND PROJECTS

CHAPTER THREE

Respecting the Environment

We went to Southdale today,
We went to the Zoo,
We bought some things,
We came home about 4:00.

On September 30, 1957, Ann Jeffries wrote this in her childhood diary. The Southdale to which she refers opened in 1956, "the first temperature-controlled shopping mall" according to Joel Garreau, whose "Earthmover" is one of the seven pieces in this chapter. In her four simple lines describing a memorable day, Ann notes at least four of humanity's great conquests of the environment of which we are a part: conquest of weather (the temperature-controlled mall), conquest of other animals (the zoo), conquest of distance (the ability to transport goods to markets), and conquest of time. *Southdale, Zoo, bought things, home,* and *4:00* each represent the drive of humans to dominate wilderness, to manipulate nature for our comfort.

Each of the writings in this section shows humans thinking about their relationship to the world in which they move and breathe. Each, some more extensively and explicitly than others, contends with the human drive to control. All see this relationship with the land, the water, the plants, the animals, and the air as something that human beings have power to determine. None sees humanity at the mercy of natural forces: We've included no stories of humans swept away by tidal waves, buried by volcanic ash, frozen in winter, parched in the desert. We've been convinced by these and other writers that the most compelling environmental force is humanity. Could we think otherwise, when the things that dominate the senses in the lives of most Americans—car traffic, machine noise, packaged food, and treated water—are manufactured?

These readings represent a very short range of human experience, less than 200 years. All the writers are Americans writing about places in the United States. But we feel that even this narrow selection shows a wide diversity of perspectives. What these pieces also show, we trust, is the power of looking closely at the nature most people miss. In choosing what to write about, each has chosen what to look for and at and into; each has also chosen not to see, to avoid seeing, what others spend most of their time looking at and thinking about. What we humans devote our time to observing says much about what we value.

Thinking about the Issues

1. Write about an environment in which you spend a substantial portion of your life. Describe it in as much detail as you can. As you read the selections, note the kinds of details that the writers have seen that you would have ignored. Think about how you might revise your description.

2. Write about your powers to control environment. List as many technologies that you have at your disposal as you can. If possible, compare your list with those of others.

3. Focus on one of the powers that you listed above about which you have an ethical concern. What are your fears? What has influenced you to feel this concern? How have you modified your use of this technology in response to your concern? If you have not modified your use, how have you justified this course of action to yourself?

ANNIE DILLARD

from *Pilgrim at Tinker Creek*

"*Unfortunately, nature is very much a now-you-see-it, now-you-don't affair. A fish flashes, then dissolves in the water before my eyes like so much salt. Deer apparently ascend bodily into heaven; the brightest oriole fades into leaves.*"

Annie Dillard was born April 30, 1945, in Pittsburgh, Pennsylvania. She received her B.A. from Hollins College in 1967, and her M.A. in 1968.

Her first published work of prose, Pilgrim at Tinker Creek, *won her a Pulitzer Prize for general nonfiction in 1974. Says Dillard, "People want to make you into a cult figure because of what they fancy to be your lifestyle, when the truth is your life is literature! You're writing consciously, off of hundreds of index cards, often distorting the literal truth to achieve an artistic one. It's all hard, conscious, terribly frustrating work! But this never occurs to people. They think it happens in a dream, that you just sit on a tree stump and take dictation from some little chipmunk! . . . If you're going to think or write seriously, you have to be intelligent. You have to keep learning or die on your feet." (From an interview by Mike Major, quoted by Deborah A. Straub in* Contemporary Authors).

The following excerpt is one chapter of Pilgrim at Tinker Creek. *For more of Dillard's work, see chapter 10, in which we have reprinted a portion of her book about her craft,* The Writing Life.

Before and as You Read

1. Consider the word *see*. List as many meanings and uses of this word as you can think of. When you get stuck, check a thesaurus for synonyms or trace the Indo-European roots of the word through the *American Heritage Dictionary*.
2. In the training of visual artists, it's common for a teacher to have the student observe an object for a long period of time; to draw it, sometimes several times from different angles; and perhaps to sculpt it, write about it, or work with it in other ways. The training of scientists is similar, in its attention to patient and systematic observation. Try an experiment. Look at an object steadily and try to draw it in as much detail as you can. Don't worry about the quality of your drawing, but be honest about what you see. What does your drawing teach you about the object? What will you see in the future when you look at this object?
3. What does the word *pilgrim* mean to you? As you read, think about why Dillard calls herself a pilgrim.

SEEING

W HEN I was six or seven years old, growing up in Pittsburgh, I *1* used to take a precious penny of my own and hide it for someone else to find. It was a curious compulsion; sadly, I've never been seized by it since. For some reason I always "hid" the penny along the same stretch of sidewalk up the street. I would cradle it at the roots of a sycamore, say, or in a hole left by a chipped-off piece of sidewalk. Then I would take a piece of chalk, and, starting at either end of the block, draw huge arrows leading up to the penny from both directions. After I learned to write I labeled the arrows: SURPRISE AHEAD or MONEY THIS WAY. I was greatly excited, during all this arrow-drawing, at the thought of the first lucky passer-by who would receive in this way, regardless of merit, a free gift from the universe. But I never lurked about. I would go straight home and not give the matter another thought, until, some months later, I would be gripped again by the impulse to hide another penny.

It is still the first week in January, and I've got great plans. I've been *2* thinking about seeing. There are lots of things to see, unwrapped gifts and free surprises. The world is fairly studded and strewn with pennies cast broad-side from a generous hand. But—and this is the point—who gets excited by a mere penny? If you follow one arrow, if you crouch motionless on a bank to watch a tremulous ripple thrill on the water and are rewarded by the sight of a muskrat kit paddling from its den, will you count that sight a chip of copper only, and go your rueful way? It is dire poverty indeed when a man is so malnourished and fatigued that he won't stoop to pick up a penny. But if you cultivate a healthy poverty and simplicity, so that finding a penny will literally make your day, then, since the world is in fact planted in pennies, you have with your poverty bought a lifetime of days. It is that simple. What you see is what you get.

I used to be able to see flying insects in the air. I'd look ahead and see, *3* not the row of hemlocks across the road, but the air in front of it. My eyes would focus along that column of air, picking out flying insects. But I lost interest, I guess, for I dropped the habit. Now I can see birds. Probably some people can look at the grass at their feet and discover all the crawling creatures. I would like to know grasses and sedges—and care. Then my least journey into the world would be a field trip, a series of happy recognitions. Thoreau, in an expansive mood, exulted, "What a rich book might be made about buds, including, perhaps, sprouts!" It would be nice to think so. I cherish mental images I have of three perfectly happy people. One collects stones. Another—an Englishman, say—watches clouds. The third lives on a coast and collects drops of seawater which he examines microscopically and mounts. But I don't see what the specialist sees, and so I cut myself off, not only from the total picture, but from the various forms of happiness.

Unfortunately, nature is very much a now-you-see-it, now-you-don't *4* affair. A fish flashes, then dissolves in the water before my eyes like so much salt. Deer apparently ascend bodily into heaven; the brightest oriole fades into leaves. These disappearances stun me into stillness and concentration; they say of nature that it conceals with a grand nonchalance, and they say of vision that it is a deliberate gift, the revelation of a dancer who for my eyes only flings away her seven veils. For nature does reveal as well as conceal: now-you-don't-see-it, now-you-do. For a week last September migrating red-winged blackbirds were feeding heavily down by the creek at the back of the house. One day I went out to investigate the racket; I walked up to a tree, an Osage orange, and a hundred birds flew away. They simply materialized out of the tree. I saw a tree, then a whisk of color, then a tree again. I walked closer and another hundred blackbirds took flight. Not a branch, not a twig budged: the birds were apparently weightless as well as invisible. Or, it was as if the leaves of the Osage orange had been freed from a spell in the form of red-winged blackbirds; they flew from the tree, caught my eye in the sky, and vanished. When I looked again at the tree the leaves had reassembled as if nothing had happened. Finally I walked directly to the trunk of the tree and a final hundred, the real diehards, appeared, spread, and vanished. How could so many hide in the tree without my seeing them? The Osage orange, unruffled, looked just as it had looked from the house, when three hundred red-winged blackbirds cried from its crown. I looked downstream where they flew, and they were gone. Searching, I couldn't spot one. I wandered downstream to force them to play their hand, but they'd crossed the creek and scattered. One show to a customer. These appearances catch at my throat: they are the free gifts, the bright coppers at the roots of trees.

It's all a matter of keeping my eyes open. Nature is like one of those 5
line drawings of a tree that are puzzles for children: Can you find hidden in the leaves a duck, a house, a boy, a bucket, a zebra, and a boot? Specialists can find the most incredibly well-hidden things. A book I read when I was young recommended an easy way to find caterpillars to rear: you simply find some fresh caterpillar droppings, look up, and there's your caterpillar. More recently an author advised me to set my mind at ease about those piles of cut stems on the ground in grassy fields. Field mice make them; they cut the grass down by degrees to reach the seeds at the head. It seems that when the grass is tightly packed, as in a field of ripe grain, the blade won't topple at a single cut through the stem; instead, the cut stem simply drops vertically, held in the crush of grain. The mouse severs the bottom again and again, the stem keeps dropping an inch at a time, and finally the head is low enough for the mouse to reach the seeds. Meanwhile, the mouse is positively littering the field with its little piles of cut stems into which, presumably, the author of the book is constantly stumbling.

If I can't see these minutiae, I still try to keep my eyes open. I'm always 6
on the lookout for antlion traps in sandy soil, monarch pupae near milkweed, skipper larvae in locust leaves. These things are utterly common, and I've not seen one. I bang on hollow trees near water, but so far no flying squirrels have

appeared. In flat country I watch every sunset in hopes of seeing the green ray. The green ray is a seldom-seen streak of light that rises from the sun like a spurting fountain at the moment of sunset; it throbs into the sky for two seconds and disappears. One more reason to keep my eyes open. A photography professor at the University of Florida just happened to see a bird die in midflight; it jerked, died, dropped, and smashed on the ground. I squint at the wind because I read Stewart Edward White: "I have always maintained that if you looked closely enough you could *see* the wind—the dim, hardly-made-out, fine débris fleeing high in the air." White was an excellent observer, and devoted an entire chapter of *The Mountains* to the subject of seeing deer: "As soon as you can forget the naturally obvious and construct an artificial obvious, then you too will see deer."

But the artificial obvious is hard to see. My eyes account for less than one percent of the weight of my head; I'm bony and dense; I see what I expect. I once spent a full three minutes looking at a bullfrog that was so unexpectedly large I couldn't see it even though a dozen enthusiastic campers were shouting directions. Finally I asked, "What color am I looking for?" and a fellow said, "Green." When at last I picked out the frog, I saw what painters are up against: the thing wasn't green at all, but the color of wet hickory bark.

The lover can see, and the knowledgeable. I visited an aunt and uncle at a quarter-horse ranch in Cody, Wyoming. I couldn't do much of anything useful, but I could, I thought, draw. So, as we all sat around the kitchen table after supper, I produced a sheet of paper and drew a horse. "That's one lame horse," my aunt volunteered. The rest of the family joined in: "Only place to saddle that one is his neck"; "Looks like we better shoot the poor thing, on account of those terrible growths." Meekly, I slid the pencil and paper down the table. Everyone in that family, including my three young cousins, could draw a horse. Beautifully. When the paper came back it looked as though five shining, real quarter horses had been corraled by mistake with a papier-mâché moose; the real horses seemed to gaze at the monster with a steady, puzzled air. I stay away from horses now, but I can do a creditable goldfish. The point is that I just don't know what the lover knows; I just can't see the artificial obvious that those in the know construct. The herpetologist asks the native, "Are there snakes in that ravine?" "Nosir." And the herpetologist comes home with, yessir, three bags full. Are there butterflies on that mountain? Are the bluets in bloom, are there arrowheads here, or fossil shells in the shale?

Peeping through my keyhole I see within the range of only about thirty percent of the light that comes from the sun; the rest is infrared and some little ultraviolet, perfectly apparent to many animals, but invisible to me. A nightmare network of ganglia, charged and firing without my knowledge, cuts and splices what I do see, editing it for my brain. Donald E. Carr points out that the sense impressions of one-celled animals are *not* edited for the brain: "This is philosophically interesting in a rather mournful way, since it means that only the simplest animals perceive the universe as it is."

A fog that won't burn away drifts and flows across my field of vision.   *10*
When you see fog move against a backdrop of deep pines, you don't see the
fog itself, but streaks of clearness floating across the air in dark shreds. So I see
only tatters of clearness through a pervading obscurity. I can't distinguish the
fog from the overcast sky; I can't be sure if the light is direct or reflected.
Everywhere darkness and the presence of the unseen appalls. We estimate now
that only one atom dances alone in every cubic meter of intergalactic space. I
blink and squint. What planet or power yanks Halley's Comet out of orbit?
We haven't seen that force yet; it's a question of distance, density, and the
pallor of reflected light. We rock, cradled in the swaddling band of darkness.
Even the simple darkness of night whispers suggestions to the mind. Last
summer, in August, I stayed at the creek too late.

Where Tinker Creek flows under the sycamore log bridge to the tear-   *11*
shaped island, it is slow and shallow, fringed thinly in cattail marsh. At this
spot an astonishing bloom of life supports vast breeding populations of insects,
fish, reptiles, birds, and mammals. On windless summer evenings I stalk along
the creek bank or straddle the sycamore log in absolute stillness, watching for
muskrats. The night I stayed too late I was hunched on the log staring spell-
bound at spreading, reflected stains of lilac on the water. A cloud in the sky
suddenly lighted as if turned on by a switch; its reflection just as suddenly
materialized on the water upstream, flat and floating, so that I couldn't see the
creek bottom, or life in the water under the cloud. Downstream, away from
the cloud on the water, water turtles smooth as beans were gliding down with
the current in a series of easy, weightless push-offs, as men bound on the
moon. I didn't know whether to trace the progress of one turtle I was sure of,
risking sticking my face in one of the bridge's spider webs made invisible by
the gathering dark, or take a chance on seeing the carp, or scan the mudbank
in hope of seeing a muskrat, or follow the last of the swallows who caught at
my heart and trailed it after them like streamers as they appeared from directly
below, under the log, flying upstream with their tails forked, so fast.
But shadows spread, and deepened, and stayed. After thousands of years   *12*
we're still strangers to darkness, fearful aliens in an enemy camp with our arms
crossed over our chests. I stirred. A land turtle on the bank, startled, hissed the
air from its lungs and withdrew into its shell. An uneasy pink here, an unfathomable blue there, gave great suggestion of lurking beings. Things were going
on. I couldn't see whether that sere rustle I heard was a distant rattlesnake, slit-
eyed, or a nearby sparrow kicking in the dry flood debris slung at the foot of
a willow. Tremendous action roiled the water everywhere I looked, big action,
inexplicable. A tremor welled up beside a gaping muskrat burrow in the bank
and I caught my breath, but no muskrat appeared. The ripples continued to
fan upstream with a steady, powerful thrust. Night was knitting over my face
an eyeless mask, and I still sat transfixed. A distant airplane, a delta wing out
of nightmare, made a gliding shadow on the creek's bottom that looked like a
stingray cruising upstream. At once a black fin slit the pink cloud on the water,

shearing it in two. The two halves merged together and seemed to dissolve before my eyes. Darkness pooled in the cleft of the creek and rose, as water collects in a well. Untamed, dreaming lights flickered over the sky. I saw hints of hulking underwater shadows, two pale splashes out of the water, and round ripples rolling close together from a blackened center.

At last I stared upstream where only the deepest violet remained of the cloud, a cloud so high its underbelly still glowed feeble color reflected from a hidden sky lighted in turn by a sun halfway to China. And out of that violet, a sudden enormous black body arced over the water. I saw only a cylindrical sleekness. Head and tail, if there was a head and tail, were both submerged in cloud. I saw only one ebony fling, a headlong dive to darkness; then the waters closed, and the lights went out. 13

I walked home in a shivering daze, up hill and down. Later I lay open-mouthed in bed, my arms flung wide at my sides to steady the whirling darkness. At this latitude I'm spinning 836 miles an hour round the earth's axis; I often fancy I feel my sweeping fall as a breakneck arc like the dive of dolphins, and the hollow rushing of wind raises hair on my neck and the side of my face. In orbit around the sun I'm moving 64,800 miles an hour. The solar system as a whole, like a merry-go-round unhinged, spins, bobs, and blinks at the speed of 43,200 miles an hour along a course set east of Hercules. Someone has piped, and we are dancing a tarantella until the sweat pours. I open my eyes and I see dark, muscled forms curl out of water, with flapping gills and flattened eyes. I close my eyes and I see stars, deep stars giving way to deeper stars, deeper stars bowing to deepest stars at the crown of an infinite cone. 14

"Still," wrote van Gogh in a letter, "a great deal of light falls on everything." If we are blinded by darkness, we are also blinded by light. When too much light falls on everything, a special terror results. Peter Freuchen describes the notorious kayak sickness to which Greenland Eskimos are prone. "The Greenland fjords are peculiar for the spells of completely quiet weather, when there is not enough wind to blow out a match and the water is like a sheet of glass. The kayak hunter must sit in his boat without stirring a finger so as not to scare the shy seals away. . . . The sun, low in the sky, sends a glare into his eyes, and the landscape around moves into the realm of the unreal. The reflex from the mirrorlike water hypnotizes him, he seems to be unable to move, and all of a sudden it is as if he were floating in a bottomless void, sinking, sinking, and sinking. . . . Horror-stricken, he tries to stir, to cry out, but he cannot, he is completely paralyzed, he just falls and falls." Some hunters are especially cursed with this panic, and bring ruin and sometimes starvation to their families. 15

Sometimes here in Virginia at sunset low clouds on the southern or northern horizon are completely invisible in the lighted sky. I only know one is there because I can see its reflection in still water. The first time I discovered this mystery I looked from cloud to no-cloud in bewilderment, checking my bearings over and over, thinking maybe the ark of the covenant was just 16 passing by south of Dead Man Mountain. Only much later did I read the explanation: polarized light from the sky is very much weakened by reflection, but the light in clouds isn't polarized. So invisible clouds pass among visible clouds, till all slide over the mountains; so a greater light extinguishes a lesser as though it didn't exist.

In the great meteor shower of August, the Perseid, I wail all day for the shooting stars I miss. They're out there showering down, committing hara-kiri in a flame of fatal attraction, and hissing perhaps at last into the ocean. But at dawn what looks like a blue dome clamps down over me like a lid on a pot. The stars and planets could smash and I'd never know. Only a piece of ashen moon occasionally climbs up or down the inside of the dome, and our local star without surcease explodes on our heads. We have really only that one light, one source for all power, and yet we must turn away from it by universal decree. Nobody here on the planet seems aware of this strange, powerful taboo, that we all walk about carefully averting our faces, this way and that, lest our eyes be blasted forever. 17

Darkness appalls and light dazzles; the scrap of visible light that doesn't hurt my eyes hurts my brain. What I see sets me swaying. Size and distance and the sudden swelling of meanings confuse me, bowl me over. I straddle the sycamore log bridge over Tinker Creek in the summer. I look at the lighted creek bottom: snail tracks tunnel the mud in quavering curves. A crayfish jerks, but by the time I absorb what has happened, he's gone in a billowing smokescreen of silt. I look at the water: minnows and shiners. If I'm thinking minnows, a carp will fill my brain till I scream. I look at the water's surface: skaters, bubbles, and leaves sliding down. Suddenly, my own face, reflected, startles me witless. Those snails have been tracking my face! Finally, with a shuddering wrench of the will, I see clouds, cirrus clouds. I'm dizzy, I fall in. This looking business is risky. 18

Once I stood on a humped rock on nearby Purgatory Mountain, watching through binoculars the great autumn hawk migration below, until I discovered that I was in danger of joining the hawks on a vertical migration of my own. I was used to binoculars, but not, apparently, to balancing on humped rocks while looking through them. I staggered. Everything advanced and receded by turns; the world was full of unexplained foreshortenings and depths. A distant huge tan object, a hawk the size of an elephant, turned out to be the browned bough of a nearby loblolly pine. I followed a sharp-shinned hawk against a featureless sky, rotating my head unawares as it flew, and when I lowered the glass a glimpse of my own looming shoulder sent me staggering. What prevents the men on Palomar from falling, voiceless and blinded, from their tiny, vaulted chairs? 19

I reel in confusion; I don't understand what I see. With the naked eye I can see two million light-years to the Andromeda galaxy. Often I slop some creek water in a jar and when I get home I dump it in a white china bowl. After the silt settles I return and see tracings of minute snails on the bottom, a planarian or two winding round the rim of water, roundworms shimmying 20 frantically, and finally, when my eyes have adjusted to these dimensions, amoebae. At first the amoebae look like muscae volitantes, those curled moving spots you seem to see in your eyes when you stare at a distant wall. Then I see the amoebae as drops of water congealed, bluish, translucent, like chips of sky in the bowl. At length I choose one individual and give myself over to its idea of an evening. I see it dribble a grainy foot before it on its wet, unfathomable way. Do its unedited sense impressions include the fierce focus of my eyes? Shall I take it outside and show it Andromeda, and blow its little endoplasm? I stir the water with a finger, in case it's running out of oxygen. Maybe I should get a tropical aquarium with motorized bubblers and lights, and keep this one for a pet. Yes, it would tell its fissioned descendants, the universe is two feet by five, and if you listen closely you can hear the buzzing music of the spheres.

Oh, it's mysterious lamplit evenings, here in the galaxy, one after the other. It's one of those nights when I wander from window to window, looking for a sign. But I can't see. Terror and a beauty insoluble are a ribband of blue woven into the fringes of garments of things both great and small. No culture explains, no bivouac offers real haven or rest. But it could be that we are not seeing something. Galileo thought comets were an optical illusion. This is fertile ground: since we are certain that they're not, we can look at what our scientists have been saying with fresh hope. What if there are *really* gleaming, castellated cities hung upside-down over the desert sand? What limpid lakes and cool date palms have our caravans always passed untried? Until, one by one, by the blindest of leaps, we light on the road to these places, we must stumble in darkness and hunger. I turn from the window. I'm blind as a bat, sensing only from every direction the echo of my own thin cries. *21*

I chanced on a wonderful book by Marius von Senden, called *Space and Sight.* When Western surgeons discovered how to perform safe cataract operations, they ranged across Europe and America operating on dozens of men and women of all ages who had been blinded by cataracts since birth. Von Senden collected accounts of such cases; the histories are fascinating. Many doctors had tested their patients' sense perceptions and ideas of space both before and after the operations. The vast majority of patients, of both sexes and all ages, had, in von Senden's opinion, no idea of space whatsoever. Form, distance, and size were so many meaningless syllables. A patient "had no idea of depth, confusing it with roundness." Before the operation a doctor would give a blind patient a cube and a sphere; the patient would tongue it or feel it with his hands, and name it correctly. After the operation the doctor would show the same objects to the patient without letting him touch them; now he had no clue whatsoever what he was seeing. One patient called lemonade "square" because it pricked on his tongue as a square shape pricked on the touch of his hands. Of another postoperative patient, the doctor writes, "I *22* have found in her no notion of size, for example, not even within the narrow limits which she might have encompassed with the aid of touch. Thus when I asked her to show me how big her mother was, she did not stretch out her hands, but set her two index-fingers a few inches apart." Other doctors reported their patients' own statements to similar effect. "The room he was in . . . he knew to be but part of the house, yet he could not conceive that the whole house could look bigger"; "Those who are blind from birth . . . have no real conception of height or distance. A house that is a mile away is thought of as nearby, but requiring the taking of a lot of steps. . . . The elevator that whizzes him up and down gives no more sense of vertical distance than does the train of horizontal."

For the newly sighted, vision is pure sensation unencumbered by meaning: "The girl went through the experience that we all go through and forget, the moment we are born. She saw, but it did not mean anything but a lot of different kinds of brightness." Again, "I asked the patient what he could see; he answered that he saw an extensive field of light, in which everything appeared dull, confused, and in motion. He could not distinguish objects." Another patient saw "nothing but a confusion of forms and colours." When a newly sighted girl saw photographs and paintings, she asked, "'Why do they put those dark marks all over them?' 'Those aren't dark marks,' her mother explained, 'those are shadows. That is one of the ways the eye knows that things have shape. If it were not for shadows many things would look flat.' 'Well, that's how things do look,' Joan answered. 'Everything looks flat with dark patches.'" 23

But it is the patients' concepts of space that are most revealing. One patient, according to his doctor, "practiced his vision in a strange fashion; thus he takes off one of his boots, throws it some way off in front of him, and then attempts to gauge the distance at which it lies; he takes a few steps towards the boot and tries to grasp it; on failing to reach it, he moves on a step or two and gropes for the boot until he finally gets hold of it." "But even at this stage, after three weeks' experience of seeing," von Senden goes on, "'space,' as he conceives it, ends with visual space, i.e., with colour-patches that happen to bound his view. He does not yet have the notion that a larger object (a chair) can mask a smaller one (a dog), or that the latter can still be present even though it is not directly seen." 24

In general the newly sighted see the world as a dazzle of color-patches. They are pleased by the sensation of color, and learn quickly to name the colors, but the rest of seeing is tormentingly difficult. Soon after his operation a patient "generally bumps into one of these colour-patches and observes them to be substantial, since they resist him as tactual objects do. In walking about it also strikes him—or can if he pays attention—that he is continually passing in between the colours he sees, that he can go past a visual object, that a part of it then steadily disappears from view; and that in spite of this, however he twists and turns—whether entering the room from the door, for 25 example, or returning back to it—he always has a visual space in front of him. Thus he gradually comes to realize that there is also a space behind him, which he does not see."

The mental effort involved in these reasonings proves overwhelming for many patients. It oppresses them to realize, if they ever do at all, the tremendous size of the world, which they had previously conceived of as something touchingly manageable. It oppresses them to realize that they have been visible to people all along, perhaps unattractively so, without their knowledge or consent. A disheartening number of them refuse to use their new vision, continuing to go over objects with their tongues, and lapsing into apathy and despair. "The child can see, but will not make use of his sight. Only when pressed can he with difficulty be brought to look at objects in his neighbourhood; but more than a foot away it is impossible to bestir him to the necessary effort." Of a twenty-one-year-old girl, the doctor relates, "Her unfortunate father, who had hoped for so much from this operation, wrote that his daughter carefully shuts her eyes whenever she wishes to go about the house, especially when she comes to a staircase, and that she is never happier or more at ease than when, by closing her eyelids, she relapses into her former state of total blindness." A fifteen-year-old boy, who was also in love with a girl at the asylum for the blind, finally blurted out, "No, really, I can't stand it any more; I want to be sent back to the asylum again. If things aren't altered, I'll tear my eyes out."

Some do learn to see, especially the young ones. But it changes their lives. One doctor comments on "the rapid and complete loss of that striking and wonderful serenity which is characteristic only of those who have never yet seen." A blind man who learns to see is ashamed of his old habits. He dresses up, grooms himself, and tries to make a good impression. While he was blind he was indifferent to objects unless they were edible; now, "a sifting of values sets in . . . his thoughts and wishes are mightily stirred and some few of the patients are thereby led into dissimulation, envy, theft and fraud."

On the other hand, many newly sighted people speak well of the world, and teach us how dull is our own vision. To one patient, a human hand, unrecognized, is "something bright and then holes." Shown a bunch of grapes, a boy calls out, "It is dark, blue and shiny. . . . It isn't smooth, it has bumps and hollows." A little girl visits a garden. "She is greatly astonished, and can scarcely be persuaded to answer, stands speechless in front of the tree, which she only names on taking hold of it, and then as 'the tree with the lights in it.'" Some delight in their sight and give themselves over to the visual world. Of a patient just after her bandages were removed, her doctor writes, "The first things to attract her attention were her own hands; she looked at them very closely, moved them repeatedly to and fro, bent and stretched the fingers, and seemed greatly astonished at the sight." One girl was eager to tell her blind friend that "men do not really look like trees at all," and astounded to discover that her every visitor had an utterly different face. Finally, a twenty-two-year-old girl was dazzled by the world's brightness and kept her eyes shut for two

26

27

28

weeks. When at the end of that time she opened her eyes again, she did not recognize any objects, but, "the more she now directed her gaze upon every-thing about her, the more it could be seen how an expression of gratification and astonishment overspread her features; she repeatedly exclaimed: 'Oh God! How beautiful!'"

I saw color-patches for weeks after I read this wonderful book. It was summer; the peaches were ripe in the valley orchards. When I woke in the morning, color-patches wrapped round my eyes, intricately, leaving not one unfilled spot. All day long I walked among shifting color-patches that parted before me like the Red Sea and closed again in silence, transfigured, wherever I looked back. Some patches swelled and loomed, while others vanished ut-terly, and dark marks flitted at random over the whole dazzling sweep. But I couldn't sustain the illusion of flatness. I've been around for too long. Form is condemned to an eternal danse macabre with meaning: I couldn't unpeach the peaches. Nor can I remember ever having seen without understanding; the color-patches of infancy are lost. My brain then must have been smooth as any balloon. I'm told I reached for the moon; many babies do. But the color-patches of infancy swelled as meaning filled them; they arrayed them-selves in solemn ranks down distance which unrolled and stretched before me like a plain. The moon rocketed away. I live now in a world of shadows that shape and distance color, a world where space makes a kind of terrible sense. What gnosticism is this, and what physics? The fluttering patch I saw in my nursery window—silver and green and shape-shifting blue—is gone; a row of Lombardy poplars takes its place, mute, across the distant lawn. That humming oblong creature pale as light that stole along the walls of my room at night, stretching exhilaratingly around the corners, is gone, too, gone the night I ate of the bittersweet fruit, put two and two together and puckered forever my brain. Martin Buber tells this tale: "Rabbi Mendel once boasted to his teacher Rabbi Elimelekh that evenings he saw the angel who rolls away the light before the darkness, and mornings the angel who rolls away the darkness before the light. 'Yes,' said Rabbi Elimelekh, 'in my youth I saw that too. Later on you don't see these things any more.'"

Why didn't someone hand those newly sighted people paints and brushes from the start, when they still didn't know what anything was? Then maybe we all could see color-patches too, the world unraveled from reason, Eden before Adam gave names. The scales would drop from my eyes; I'd see trees like men walking; I'd run down the road against all orders, hallooing and leaping.

Seeing is of course very much a matter of verbalization. Unless I call my attention to what passes before my eyes, I simply won't see it. It is, as Ruskin says, "not merely unnoticed, but in the full, clear sense of the word, unseen." My eyes alone can't solve analogy tests using figures, the ones which show, with increasing elaborations, a big square, then a small square in a big square, then a big triangle, and expect me to find a small triangle in a big triangle. I have to say the words, describe what I'm seeing. If Tinker Mountain erupted, I'd be likely to notice. But if I want to notice the lesser cataclysms of valley life, I have to maintain in my head a running description of the present. It's not that I'm observant; it's just that I talk too much. Otherwise, especially in a strange place, I'll never know what's happening. Like a blind man at the ball game, I need a radio.

When I see this way I analyze and pry. I hurl over logs and roll away   32
stones; I study the bank a square foot at a time, probing and tilting my head. Some days when a mist covers the mountains, when the muskrats won't show and the microscope's mirror shatters, I want to climb up the blank blue dome as a man would storm the inside of a circus tent, wildly, dangling, and with a steel knife claw a rent in the top, peep, and, if I must, fall.

But there is another kind of seeing that involves a letting go. When I   33
see this way I sway transfixed and emptied. The difference between the two ways of seeing is the difference between walking with and without a camera. When I walk with a camera I walk from shot to shot, reading the light on a calibrated meter. When I walk without a camera, my own shutter opens, and the moment's light prints on my own silver gut. When I see this second way I am above all an unscrupulous observer.

It was sunny one evening last summer at Tinker Creek; the sun was low   34
in the sky, upstream. I was sitting on the sycamore log bridge with the sunset at my back, watching the shiners the size of minnows who were feeding over the muddy sand in skittery schools. Again and again, one fish, then another, turned for a split second across the current and flash! the sun shot out from its silver side. I couldn't watch for it. It was always just happening somewhere else, and it drew my vision just as it disappeared: flash, like a sudden dazzle of the thinnest blade, a sparking over a dun and olive ground at chance intervals from every direction. Then I noticed white specks, some sort of pale petals, small, floating from under my feet on the creek's surface, very slow and steady. So I blurred my eyes and gazed towards the brim of my hat and saw a new world. I saw the pale white circles roll up, roll up, like the world's turning, mute and perfect, and I saw the linear flashes, gleaming silver, like stars being born at random down a rolling scroll of time. Something broke and something opened. I filled up like a new wineskin. I breathed an air like light; I saw a light like water. I was the lip of a fountain the creek filled forever; I was ether, the leaf in the zephyr; I was flesh-flake, feather, bone.

When I see this way I see truly. As Thoreau says, I return to my senses.   35
I am the man who watches the baseball game in silence in an empty stadium. I see the game purely; I'm abstracted and dazed. When it's all over and the white-suited players lope off the green field to their shadowed dugouts, I leap to my feet; I cheer and cheer.

But I can't go out and try to see this way. I'll fail, I'll go mad. All I can   36
do is try to gag the commentator, to hush the noise of useless interior babble
that keeps me from seeing just as surely as a newspaper dangled before my
eyes. The effort is really a discipline requiring a lifetime of dedicated struggle;
it marks the literature of saints and monks of every order East and West,
under every rule and no rule, discalced and shod. The world's spiritual geniuses
seem to discover universally that the mind's muddy river, this ceaseless flow of
trivia and trash, cannot be dammed, and that trying to dam it is a waste of
effort that might lead to madness. Instead you must allow the muddy river to
flow unheeded in the dim channels of consciousness; you raise your sights;
you look along it, mildly, acknowledging its presence without interest and
gazing beyond it into the realm of the real where subjects and objects act and
rest purely, without utterance. "Launch into the deep," says Jacques Ellul, "and
you shall see."

The secret of seeing is, then, the pearl of great price. If I thought he   37
could teach me to find it and keep it forever I would stagger barefoot across a
hundred deserts after any lunatic at all. But although the pearl may be found,
it may not be sought. The literature of illumination reveals this above all:
although it comes to those who wait for it, it is always, even to the most
practiced and adept, a gift and a total surprise. I return from one walk knowing
where the killdeer nests in the field by the creek and the hour the laurel
blooms. I return from the same walk a day later scarcely knowing my own
name. Litanies hum in my ears; my tongue flaps in my mouth Ailinon, alleluia!
I cannot cause light; the most I can do is try to put myself in the path of its
beam. It is possible, in deep space, to sail on solar wind. Light, be it particle
or wave, has force: you rig a giant sail and go. The secret of seeing is to sail
on solar wind. Hone and spread your spirit till you yourself are a sail, whetted,
translucent, broadside to the merest puff.

When her doctor took her bandages off and led her into the garden, the   38
girl who was no longer blind saw "the tree with the lights in it." It was for
this tree I searched through the peach orchards of summer, in the forests of
fall and down winter and spring for years. Then one day I was walking along
Tinker Creek thinking of nothing at all and I saw the tree with the lights in
it. I saw the backyard cedar where the mourning doves roost charged and
transfigured, each cell buzzing with flame. I stood on the grass with the lights
in it, grass that was wholly fire, utterly focused and utterly dreamed. It was less
like seeing than like being for the first time seen, knocked breathless by a
powerful glance. The flood of fire abated, but I'm still spending the power.
Gradually the lights went out in the cedar, the colors died, the cells unflamed
and disappeared. I was still ringing. I had been my whole life a bell, and never
knew it until at that moment I was lifted and struck. I have since only very
rarely seen the tree with the lights in it. The vision comes and goes, mostly
goes, but I live for it, for the moment when the mountains open and a new
light roars in spate through the crack, and the mountains slam.

Topics for Discussion and Writing

1. What does the following mean? "I just don't know what the lover knows; I just can't see the artificial obvious that those in the know construct."
2. How does Dillard use words to make you see? Construct a list of examples with your class.
3. Dillard's work is as much a description of personal reaction and self-discovery as it is a discovery of natural phenomena. Comment on this statement.
4. Review the definition of the word *see* that you constructed before reading Dillard's essay. Revise this definition based on "sparks" from Dillard's intense reflection.

ALDO LEOPOLD

from *A Sand County Almanac*

"There are two spiritual dangers in not owning a farm. One is the danger of supposing that breakfast comes from the grocery, and the other that heat comes from the furnace."

Aldo Leopold was known as the father of wildlife conservation in America. He graduated with a master's degree from the Yale Forestry School, the first graduate school of forestry in the United States, and in 1909 joined the U.S. Forestry Service. In 1933 he was appointed to the newly created chair in game management at the University of Wisconsin. While there he wrote the text, Game Management, *which is still in use today. He also wrote over 350 articles and served as an advisor on conservation to the United Nations.*

A Sand County Almanac *traces the evolution over several decades of Leopold's thinking on environmental issues. The name derives from Sand County, Wisconsin, where he lived the last years of his life trying to recreate a 19th-century rural existence in an America quickly losing its wilderness. He died of a heart attack on April 21, 1948, while helping to fight a fire on a neighbor's farm.*

Before and as You Read

1. One way to describe an object is by recounting its history. Focus on a favorite object that you've had for a long time—perhaps a toy or a piece of driftwood picked up on a beach vacation long ago—and write about it in order to recall particularly memorable moments. What was going on in your family, in the outside world, at those times? At any point in this history can you perceive a relationship, if only a symbolic one, between the object and what was going on around it?
2. As you are reading, think about the way Leopold lives. Does his type of life appeal to you? Do you think it possible to be a sincere champion of the wilderness and not to undertake sacrifices of physical comfort? Explain.
3. In this selection, note how Leopold feels about the tree he is cutting down. Cite phrases that illustrate his feelings.

FEBRUARY

Good Oak

THERE ARE two spiritual dangers in not owning a farm. One is the danger of supposing that breakfast comes from the grocery, and the other that heat comes from the furnace.   *1*

To avoid the first danger, one should plant a garden, preferably where   *2*
there is no grocer to confuse the issue.

To avoid the second, he should lay a split of good oak on the andirons,   *3*
preferably where there is no furnace, and let it warm his shins while a February
blizzard tosses the trees outside. If one has cut, split, hauled, and piled his own
good oak, and let his mind work the while, he will remember much about
where the heat comes from, and with a wealth of detail denied to those who
spend the week end in town astride a radiator.

The particular oak now aglow on my andirons grew on the bank of the   *4*
old emigrant road where it climbs the sandhill. The stump, which I measured
upon felling the tree, has a diameter of 30 inches. It shows 80 growth rings,
hence the seedling from which it originated must have laid its first ring of
wood in 1865, at the end of the Civil War. But I know from the history of
present seedlings that no oak grows above the reach of rabbits without a
decade or more of getting girdled each winter, and resprouting during the
following summer. Indeed, it is all too clear that every surviving oak is the
product either of rabbit negligence or of rabbit scarcity. Some day some
patient botanist will draw a frequency curve of oak birth-years, and show that
the curve humps every ten years, each hump originating from a low in the
ten-year rabbit cycle. (A fauna and flora, by this very process of perpetual
battle within and among species, achieve collective immortality.)

It is likely, then, that a low in rabbits occurred in the middle 'sixties,   *5*
when my oak began to lay on annual rings, but that the acorn that produced
it fell during the preceding decade, when the covered wagons were still passing
over my road into the Great Northwest. It may have been the wash and wear
of the emigrant traffic that bared this roadbank, and thus enabled this particular acorn to spread its first leaves to the sun. Only one acorn in a thousand
ever grew large enough to fight rabbits; the rest were drowned at birth in the
prairie sea.

It is a warming thought that this one wasn't, and thus lived to garner   *6*
80 years of June sun. It is this sunlight that is now being released, through the
intervention of my axe and saw, to warm my shack and my spirit through
80 gusts of blizzard. And with each gust a wisp of smoke from my chimney
bears witness, to whomsoever it may concern, that the sun did not shine in vain.

My dog does not care where heat comes from, but he cares ardently that   *7*
it come, and soon. Indeed he considers my ability to make it come as something magical, for when I rise in the cold black pre-dawn and kneel shivering
by the hearth making a fire, he pushes himself blandly between me and the
kindling splits I have laid on the ashes, and I must touch a match to them by
poking it between his legs. Such faith, I suppose, is the kind that moves
mountains.

It was a bolt of lightning that put an end to wood-making by this   *8*
particular oak. We were all awakened, one night in July, by the thunderous
crash; we realized that the bolt must have hit near by, but, since it had not hit

us, we all went back to sleep. Man brings all things to the test of himself, and this is notably true of lightning.

Next morning, as we strolled over the sandhill rejoicing with the cone-   9
flowers and the prairie clovers over their fresh accession of rain, we came upon a great slab of bark freshly torn from the trunk of the roadside oak. The trunk showed a long spiral scar of barkless sapwood, a foot wide and not yet yellowed by the sun. By the next day the leaves had wilted, and we knew that the lightning had bequeathed to us three cords of prospective fuel wood.

We mourned the loss of the old tree, but knew that a dozen of its   10
progeny standing straight and stalwart on the sands had already taken over its job of wood-making.

We let the dead veteran season for a year in the sun it could no longer   11
use, and then on a crisp winter's day we laid a newly filed saw to its bastioned base. Fragrant little chips of history spewed from the saw cut, and accumulated on the snow before each kneeling sawyer. We sensed that these two piles of sawdust were something more than wood: that they were the integrated transect of a century; that our saw was biting its way, stroke by stroke, decade by decade, into the chronology of a lifetime, written in concentric annual rings of good oak.

It took only a dozen pulls of the saw to transect the few years of our   12
ownership, during which we had learned to love and cherish this farm. Abruptly we began to cut the years of our predecessor the bootlegger, who hated this farm, skinned it of residual fertility, burned its farmhouse, threw it back into the lap of the County (with delinquent taxes to boot), and then disappeared among the landless anonymities of the Great Depression. Yet the oak had laid down good wood for him; his sawdust was as fragrant, as sound, and as pink as our own. An oak is no respecter of persons.

The reign of the bootlegger ended sometime during the dust-bowl   13
drouths of 1936, 1934, 1933, and 1930. Oak smoke from his still and peat from burning marshlands must have clouded the sun in those years, and alphabetical conservation was abroad in the land, but the sawdust shows no change.

Rest! cries the chief sawyer, and we pause for breath.   14

Now our saw bites into the 1920s, the Babbittian decade when every-   15
thing grew bigger and better in heedlessness and arrogance—until 1929, when stock markets crumpled. If the oak heard them fall, its wood gives no sign. Nor did it heed the Legislature's several protestations of love for trees: a National Forest and a forest-crop law in 1927, a great refuge on the Upper Mississippi bottomlands in 1924, and a new forest policy in 1921. Neither did it notice the demise of the state's last marten in 1925, nor the arrival of its first starling in 1923.

In March 1922, the Big Sleet tore the neighboring elms limb from limb,   16
but there is no sign of damage to our tree. What is a ton of ice, more or less, to a good oak?

Rest! cries the chief sawyer, and we pause for breath.   17

Now the saw bites into 1910–20, the decade of the drainage dream,   18
when steam shovels sucked dry the marshes of central Wisconsin to make
farms, and made ash-heaps instead. Our marsh escaped, not because of any
caution or forbearance among engineers, but because the river floods it each
April, and did so with a vengeance—perhaps a defensive vengeance—in the
years 1913–16. The oak laid on wood just the same, even in 1915, when the
Supreme Court abolished the state forests and Governor Phillip pontificated
that 'state forestry is not a good business proposition.' (It did not occur to the
Governor that there might be more than one definition of what is good, and
even of what is business. It did not occur to him that while the courts were
writing one definition of goodness in the law books, fires were writing quite
another one on the face of the land. Perhaps, to be a governor, one must be
free from doubt on such matters.)

While forestry receded during this decade, game conservation advanced.   19
In 1916 pheasants became successfully established in Waukesha County; in
1915 a federal law prohibited spring shooting; in 1913 a state game farm was
started; in 1912 a 'buck law' protected female deer; in 1911 an epidemic of
refuges spread over the state. *Refuge* became a holy word, but the oak took
no heed.

Rest! cries the chief sawyer, and we pause for breath.   20

Now we cut 1910, when a great university president published a book   21
on conservation, a great sawfly epidemic killed millions of tamaracks, a great
drouth burned the pineries, and a great dredge drained Horicon Marsh.

We cut 1909, when smelt were first planted in the Great Lakes, and   22
when a wet summer induced the Legislature to cut the forest-fire appropriations.

We cut 1908, a dry year when the forests burned fiercely, and Wisconsin   23
parted with its last cougar.

We cut 1907, when a wandering lynx, looking in the wrong direction   24
for the promised land, ended his career among the farms of Dane County.

We cut 1906, when the first state forester took office, and fires burned   25
17,000 acres in these sand counties; we cut 1905 when a great flight of gos-
hawks came out of the North and ate up the local grouse (they no doubt
perched in this tree to eat some of mine). We cut 1902–3, a winter of bitter
cold; 1901, which brought the most intense drouth of record (rainfall only
17 inches); 1900, a centennial year of hope, of prayer, and the usual annual
ring of oak.

Rest! cries the chief sawyer, and we pause for breath.   26

Now our saw bites into the 1890s, called gay by those whose eyes turn   27
cityward rather than landward. We cut 1899, when the last passenger pigeon
collided with a charge of shot near Babcock, two counties to the north; we

cut 1898 when a dry fall, followed by a snowless winter, froze the soil seven feet deep and killed the apple trees; 1897, another drouth year, when another forestry commission came into being; 1896, when 25,000 prairie chickens were shipped to market from the village of Spooner alone; 1895, another year of fires; 1894, another drouth year; and 1893, the year of 'The Bluebird Storm,' when a March blizzard reduced the migrating bluebirds to near-zero. (The first bluebirds always alighted in this oak, but in the middle nineties it must have gone without.) We cut 1892, another year of fires; 1891, a low in the grouse cycle; and 1890, the year of the Babcock Milk Tester, which enabled Governor Heil to boast, half a century later, that Wisconsin is America's Dairyland. The motor licenses which now parade that boast were then not foreseen, even by Professor Babcock.

It was likewise in 1890 that the largest pine rafts in history slipped down   28
the Wisconsin River in full view of my oak, to build an empire of red barns for the cows of the prairie states. Thus it is that good pine now stands between the cow and the blizzard, just as good oak stands between the blizzard and me.

Rest! cries the chief sawyer, and we pause for breath.   29

Now our saw bites into the 1880s; into 1889, a drouth year in which   30
Arbor Day was first proclaimed; into 1887, when Wisconsin appointed its first game wardens; into 1886, when the College of Agriculture held its first short course for farmers; into 1885, preceded by a winter 'of unprecedented length and severity'; into 1883, when Dean W. H. Henry reported that the spring flowers at Madison bloomed 13 days later than average; into 1882, the year Lake Mendota opened a month late following the historic 'Big Snow' and bitter cold of 1881–2.

It was likewise in 1881 that the Wisconsin Agricultural Society debated   31
the question, 'How do you account for the second growth of black oak timber that has sprung up all over the country in the last thirty years?' My oak was one of these. One debater claimed spontaneous generation, another claimed regurgitation of acorns by southbound pigeons.

Rest! cries the chief sawyer, and we pause for breath.   32

Now our saw bites the 1870s, the decade of Wisconsin's carousal in   33
wheat. Monday morning came in 1879, when chinch bugs, grubs, rust, and soil exhaustion finally convinced Wisconsin farmers that they could not compete with the virgin prairies further west in the game of wheating land to death. I suspect that this farm played its share in the game, and that the sand blow just north of my oak had its origin in over-wheating.

This same year of 1879 saw the first planting of carp in Wisconsin, and   34
also the first arrival of quack-grass as a stowaway from Europe. On 27 October 1879, six migrating prairie chickens perched on the rooftree of the German Methodist Church in Madison, and took a look at the growing city. On 8 November the markets at Madison were reported to be glutted with ducks at 10 cents each.

In 1878 a deer hunter from Sauk Rapids remarked prophetically, 'The *35*
hunters promise to outnumber the deer.'

On 10 September 1877, two brothers, shooting Muskego Lake, bagged *36*
210 blue-winged teal in one day.

In 1876 came the wettest year of record; the rainfall piled up 50 inches. *37*
Prairie chickens declined, perhaps owing to hard rains.

In 1875 four hunters killed 153 prairie chickens at York Prairie, one *38*
county to the eastward. In the same year the U.S. Fish Commission planted
Atlantic salmon in Devil's Lake, 10 miles south of my oak.

In 1874 the first factory-made barbed wire was stapled to oak trees; I *39*
hope no such artifacts are buried in the oak now under saw!

In 1873 one Chicago firm received and marketed 25,000 prairie chick- *40*
ens. The Chicago trade collectively bought 600,000 at $3.25 per dozen.

In 1872 the last wild Wisconsin turkey was killed, two counties to the *41*
southwest.

It is appropriate that the decade ending the pioneer carousal in wheat *42*
should likewise have ended the pioneer carousal in pigeon blood. In 1871,
within a 50-mile triangle spreading northwestward from my oak, 136 million
pigeons are estimated to have nested, and some may have nested in it, for it
was then a thrifty sapling 20 feet tall. Pigeon hunters by scores plied their trade
with net and gun, club and salt lick, and trainloads of prospective pigeon pie
moved southward and eastward toward the cities. It was the last big nesting in
Wisconsin, and nearly the last in any state.

This same year 1871 brought other evidence of the march of empire: *43*
the Peshtigo Fire, which cleared a couple of counties of trees and soil, and
the Chicago Fire, said to have started from the protesting kick of a cow.

In 1870 the meadow mice had already staged their march of empire; *44*
they ate up the young orchards of the young state, and then died. They did
not eat my oak, whose bark was already too tough and thick for mice.

It was likewise in 1870 that a market gunner boasted in the *American* *45*
Sportsman of killing 6000 ducks in one season near Chicago.

Rest! cries the chief sawyer, and we pause for breath. *46*

Our saw now cuts the 1860s, when thousands died to settle the question: *47*
Is the man-man community lightly to be dismembered? They settled it, but
they did not see, nor do we yet see, that the same question applies to the man-
land community.

This decade was not without its gropings toward the larger issue. In 1867 *48*
Increase A. Lapham induced the State Horticultural Society to offer prizes for
forest plantations. In 1866 the last native Wisconsin elk was killed. The saw
now severs 1865, the pith-year of our oak. In that year John Muir offered to
buy from his brother, who then owned the home farm 30 miles east of my
oak, a sanctuary for the wildflowers that had gladdened his youth. His brother
declined to part with the land, but he could not suppress the idea: 1865 still

stands in Wisconsin history as the birth-year of mercy for things natural, wild, and free.

We have cut the core. Our saw now reverses its orientation in history;   *49*
we cut backward across the years, and outward toward the far side of the stump. At last there is a tremor in the great trunk; the saw-kerf suddenly widens; the saw is quickly pulled as the sawyers spring backward to safety; all hands cry 'Timber!'; my oak leans, groans, and crashes with earth-shaking thunder, to lie prostrate across the emigrant road that gave it birth.

Now comes the job of making wood. The maul rings on steel wedges   *50*
as the sections of trunk are up-ended one by one, only to fall apart in fragrant slabs to be corded by the roadside.

There is an allegory for historians in the diverse functions of saw, wedge,   *51*
and axe.

The saw works only across the years, which it must deal with one by   *52*
one, in sequence. From each year the raker teeth pull little chips of fact, which accumulate in little piles, called sawdust by woodsmen and archives by historians; both judge the character of what lies within by the character of the samples thus made visible without. It is not until the transect is completed that the tree falls, and the stump yields a collective view of a century. By its fall the tree attests the unity of the hodge-podge called history.

The wedge, on the other hand, works only in radial splits; such a split   *53*
yields a collective view of all the years at once, or no view at all, depending on the skill with which the plane of the split is chosen. (If in doubt, let the section season for a year until a crack develops. Many a hastily driven wedge lies rusting in the woods, embedded in unsplittable cross-grain.)

The axe functions only at an angle diagonal to the years, and this only   *54*
for the peripheral rings of the recent past. Its special function is to lop limbs, for which both saw and wedge are useless.

The three tools are requisite to good oak, and to good history.   *55*

Thinking Like a Mountain

A deep chesty bawl echoes from rimrock to rimrock, rolls down the   *56*
mountain, and fades into the far blackness of the night. It is an outburst of wild defiant sorrow, and of contempt for all the adversities of the world.

Every living thing (and perhaps many a dead one as well) pays heed to   *57*
that call. To the deer it is a reminder of the way of all flesh, to the pine a forecast of midnight scuffles and of blood upon the snow, to the coyote a promise of gleanings to come, to the cowman a threat of red ink at the bank, to the hunter a challenge of fang against bullet. Yet behind these obvious and immediate hopes and fears there lies a deeper meaning, known only to the mountain itself. Only the mountain has lived long enough to listen objectively to the howl of a wolf.

Those unable to decipher the hidden meaning know nevertheless that it   *58*
is there, for it is felt in all wolf country, and distinguishes that country from
all other land. It tingles in the spine of all who hear wolves by night, or who
scan their tracks by day. Even without sight or sound of wolf, it is implicit in
a hundred small events: the midnight whinny of a pack horse, the rattle of
rolling rocks, the bound of a fleeing deer, the way shadows lie under the
spruces. Only the ineducable tyro can fail to sense the presence or absence of
wolves, or the fact that mountains have a secret opinion about them.

My own conviction on this score dates from the day I saw a wolf die.   *59*
We were eating lunch on a high rimrock, at the foot of which a turbulent
river elbowed its way. We saw what we thought was a doe fording the torrent,
her breast awash in white water. When she climbed the bank toward us and
shook out her tail, we realized our error: it was a wolf. A half-dozen others,
evidently grown pups, sprang from the willows and all joined in a welcoming
mêlée of wagging tails and playful maulings. What was literally a pile of
wolves writhed and tumbled in the center of an open flat at the foot of our
rimrock.

In those days we had never heard of passing up a chance to kill a wolf.   *60*
In a second we were pumping lead into the pack, but with more excitement
than accuracy: how to aim a steep downhill shot is always confusing. When
our rifles were empty, the old wolf was down, and a pup was dragging a leg
into impassable slide-rocks.

We reached the old wolf in time to watch a fierce green fire dying in   *61*
her eyes. I realized then, and have known ever since, that there was something
new to me in those eyes—something known only to her and to the mountain.
I was young then, and full of trigger-itch; I thought that because fewer wolves
meant more deer, that no wolves would mean hunters' paradise. But after
seeing the green fire die, I sensed that neither the wolf nor the mountain
agreed with such a view.

Since then I have lived to see state after state extirpate its wolves. I have   *62*
watched the face of many a newly wolfless mountain, and seen the south-
facing slopes wrinkle with a maze of new deer trails. I have seen every edible
bush and seedling browsed, first to anaemic desuetude, and then to death. I
have seen every edible tree defoliated to the height of a saddlehorn. Such a
mountain looks as if someone had given God a new pruning shears, and
forbidden Him all other exercise. In the end the starved bones of the hoped-
for deer herd, dead of its own too-much, bleach with the bones of the dead
sage, or molder under the high-lined junipers.

I now suspect that just as a deer herd lives in mortal fear of its wolves,   *63*
so does a mountain live in mortal fear of its deer. And perhaps with better
cause, for while a buck pulled down by wolves can be replaced in two or three
years, a range pulled down by too many deer may fail of replacement in as
many decades.

So also with cows. The cowman who cleans his range of wolves does 64
not realize that he is taking over the wolf's job of trimming the herd to fit the
range. He has not learned to think like a mountain. Hence we have dustbowls,
and rivers washing the future into the sea.

We all strive for safety, prosperity, comfort, long life, and dullness. The 65
deer strives with his supple legs, the cowman with trap and poison, the states-
man with pen, the most of us with machines, votes, and dollars, but it all
comes to the same thing: peace in our time. A measure of success in this is all
well enough, and perhaps is a requisite to objective thinking, but too much
safety seems to yield only danger in the long run. Perhaps this is behind
Thoreau's dictum: In wildness is the salvation of the world. Perhaps this is the
hidden meaning in the howl of the wolf, long known among mountains, but
seldom perceived among men.

Topics for Discussion and Writing

1. Why do you think that Leopold wrote about the cutting of the tree in
   terms of human history? Does this make you value the tree more? Why is
   the sentence, "Rest! cries the chief sawyer, and we pause for breath," used
   throughout?
2. Observe how personification—writing about a nonhuman entity as if it
   were human—is used by Leopold. As you read other selections in this
   chapter, observe how these writers personify the creatures about which
   they write. How does this convention illustrate the values held by the
   authors?
3. Comment on the following sentence used by Leopold: "Perhaps this is
   behind Thoreau's dictum: In wildness is the salvation of the world. Perhaps
   this is the hidden meaning in the howl of the wolf, long known among
   mountains, but seldom perceived among men."
4. Compare Leopold's farm to Annie Dillard's Tinker Creek. How are these
   actual places used in the essays by each author? How would the essays
   change in content and in their impact on you as a reader, if the writers
   wrote about these issues without reference to these special places?

DIANE ACKERMAN

from *The Moon by Whale Light*

"I chose to write about bats, crocodilians, whales, penguins, and such because each would teach me something special about nature and about the human condition: about our terror of things that live by night, or the advantages of cold-bloodedness; about intelligence, and music, or our need to withstand most any ordeal to behold a nearly extinct life form before it vanishes."

Diane Ackerman shows us the world of the nature writer in The Moon by Whale Light *(1991). She grew up in the Chicago suburb of Waukegan and traces her love of nature back to her forbidden walks through a "dark and deep woods," as a six-year-old on her way to school. Her interest in writing both prose and poetry were nurtured in college at Penn State, and in the M.F.A. and Ph.D. programs at Cornell.*

Her works of nonfiction include On Extended Wings *(1985) and* A Natural History of the Senses *(1990). She has published poetry in five books, including* Jaguar of Sweet Laughter: New and Selected Poems.

Before and as You Read

1. Write about an animal that has visited your nightmares. Are you afraid of snakes? Rats? Spiders? Bats? In your writing, try to account for the sources of your fear, such as actual events in your life, movies, TV shows, or stories. Do you recall times when you've specifically avoided a place where you thought these animals might lurk? If you have seen these animals, what have you done in reaction? Have you tried to overcome this fear?

2. Find a book that describes in unemotional terms the habits and character-istics of the creature you fear. How does this book address your fears, either directly or indirectly? What questions remain for you?

3. List the images that Ackerman uses to describe the bat cave. What senses does she call on to illustrate the scene for her audience? Why are multi-sensual images the most powerful?

INTRODUCTION

FOR A month in 1989 I sailed around Antarctica, a landscape as sensuous as it is remote, whose crystal desert I had wanted to see for a long time. Some months earlier I helped raise baby penguins in quarantine at Sea World in San Diego. One fluffy brown yeti-shaped chick, which I became particularly fond of, I named Apsley, after Apsley Cherry-Garrard, who in 1911 trekked across Antarctica, and wrote a vivid and poignant book

1

about it, *The Worst Journey in the World*. For two years, I had been writing natural-history essays for *The New Yorker*, the magazine that sent me to see and write about penguins in the wild. To be haunted by the ghostly beauty of pastel icebergs and astonished by the Antarctic's vast herds of animals is an experience few people have ever known or will ever know, and I felt privileged—and still do. Not so long ago—in the days of Sir Richard Burton, T. E. Lawrence, D. H. Lawrence, Lady Hester Stanhope, Beryl Markham, Herman Melville, Washington Irving, and others—there was a crossroads where physical and literary adventure converged. There is also a long history of the bards called nature poets, and this brimming category includes writers as different as Lucretius and Marvell. But my prose now seems to locate me among a small tribe often referred to as nature writers. How curious that label is, suggesting as it does that nature is somehow separate from our doings, that nature does not contain us, that it's possible to step *outside* nature, not merely as one of its more promising denizens but objectively, as a sort of extraterrestrial voyeur. Still, the label is a dignified one, and implies a pastoral ethic that we share, a devotion to the keenly observed detail, and a sense of sacredness. There is a way of beholding nature that is itself a form of prayer.

In my Antarctic journal I wrote: "Tonight the moon is invisible, darkness itself has nearly vanished, and the known world, which we map with families, routines, and newspapers, floats somewhere beyond the horizon. Traveling to a strange new landscape is a kind of romance. You become intensely aware of the world where you are, but also oblivious to the rest of the world at the same time. Like love, travel makes you innocent again. The only news I've heard for days has been the news of nature. Tomorrow, when we drift through the iceberg gardens of Gerlache Strait, I will be working—that is, writing prose. My mind will become a cyclone of intense alertness, in which details present themselves slowly, thoroughly, one at a time. I don't know how to describe what happens to me when I'm out in 'nature' and 'working'—it's a kind of rapture—but it's happened often enough that I know to expect it." 2

I had been wondering then about the little penguin Apsley. Soon he would have fledged, replacing his thick brown down with black and white feathers, and would look very different. My plan was to gather pebbles from the rookery at Salisbury Plain, on South Georgia (where the egg he hatched from was collected), and take them back to him as a souvenir. Apsley was not the sort of penguin that builds nests from stones, but he might recognize the rich amalgam of smells. 3

Because I write at length about little-known animals in curious landscapes, people often ask, for example, Do you prefer whales to bats? I prefer life. Each of the animals I write about I find beguiling in and of itself; but in all honesty there is no animal that isn't fascinating if viewed up close and in detail. I chose to write about bats, crocodilians, whales, penguins, and such because each would teach me something special about nature and about the human condition: about our terror of things that live by night, or the advantages of cold-bloodedness; about intelligence and music, or our need to 4 withstand most any ordeal to behold a nearly extinct life-form before it vanishes. Before beginning each expedition, I knew some of my motives, but I always returned nourished by unexpected experiences. What is necessarily missing from the essays is all the fun, turmoil, stress, and welcome obsessiveness that went into setting them up. The emotional marginalia sometimes included acts of great generosity of spirit, and at other times revealed less becoming sides of human nature.

Much of a nature writer's life is spent living by seasonal time, not mere chronicity, as you wait for nature to go about its normal ways. There are long pastures of quiet, broken suddenly by the indelible thrill of seeing a whale or an alligator, and then the long hours afterward, as the excitement mellows. Of course, we also live by the clock. Shifting one's allegiance between those two perceptions of time is one of the most curious and uncanny things that naturalists do. On the way out into the field, and on the return, there comes a point when the two notions of time meet, as if they were nothing more than high mountain roads converging in the wilderness, and you must leap from one to the other and quickly get your footing. I found this especially true when writing *The Moon by Whale Light,* which required trips to both Hawaii and Argentina. Half the time I fretted about airplane schedules, boat rentals, getting permits and permissions, or fixing my tape recorder in the middle of lengthy interviews. But the other half I spent on the desolate, fossil-strewn beaches of Patagonia, watching the hypnotic movements of mother and baby whales. Falling asleep to their snoring and snuffling sounds, attuned only to their lives, I lived on whale time.

Entering an alternate reality that has its own social customs, time zones, routines, hierarchies, and values is not easy. You leave all the guideposts, the friends and relatives you rely on, and become part of a social group whose laws are rarely explained but include you, rule you. You have no bank account of esteem. You are judged by everyone. You are admired for your affiliations rather than your character or qualities. You meet people who wish in one way or another to exploit you. You can become distracted from yourself and enter a cone of ambiguity where you move as if you were an interloper or an outlaw. It is like waking up in a sci-fi story where people travel along a different time-line and you slide among them. In one sense, that freedom feels exhilarating, but in another it fills you with unsurpassable loneliness. It is difficult to explain the exact appeal of this paradox. Most field naturalists I know relish being new, anonymous, at their own disposal, untrackable, freed from their past, able (even required) to reinvent themselves; and yet they also tend to phone and write home often when they're in port, many times a day blazing a link to their loved ones.

Some people think I court danger. After all, I straddle alligators and swim up to a whale's mouth and climb down cliffs and stand in the midst of millions of bats and risk frostbite at the ends of the earth. Although there have been many times when I was truly frightened and a sentence such as *Why the hell do you get into situations like this?* would run through my mind, such moments passed quickly. I don't take unreasonable chances. I'm always accompanied by experts who have spent many years working with the animal we are studying and who have been close to that animal countless times, often enough to know what may be dangerous.

"How could you walk across a lagoon when there were alligators under 8 the water and not know where the alligators were?" one woman asked, clearly horrified. Simple: I followed the invisible footsteps of Kent Vliet, who was a yard in front of me. Kent and his colleagues had been working with alligators in St. Augustine for some time, and he knew where it was probably safe to walk and also what to do if attacked. But frightened? My heart was pounding.

"How could you let a big bat tangle in your hair?" That was a different 9 situation—bats aren't dangerous, just misunderstood. So I felt no fear at all, or, rather, was fearful for the bat, which I didn't wish to hurt in any way.

I often find things renewing about *ordeal*. When I went out into the 10 Texas desert with Merlin Tuttle and his friends, to net wild bats and photograph them, we didn't get even two hours of sleep. By day we looked for likely batting spots and set up our nets. By night we patroled the nets or photographed bats. One night I spent hours aiming photographic lights for Merlin in an abandoned barn while startled bats peed on me nonstop. On the wall in my study I have one of the photographs of pallid bats that Merlin took that night, and it makes me smile, remembering just what the event looked, smelled, and felt like.

There were times handling alligators that I got banged up pretty hard. I 11 didn't jump back fast enough when climbing off an alligator, and it swung its head around and clobbered me on the shin. Alligators have exceedingly powerful heads, and this was like being slammed with a baseball bat made of pure bone. My shin bruised savagely, but the bone didn't break. And that was a trivial price to pay for the privilege of being able to study an alligator intimately, to touch its mouth and eyes and the folds of its neck and the claws on its back feet and really get to know the look and feel of it up close.

At a later time, on an expedition to Japan to see certain rare albatrosses, 12 I managed to break three ribs. Once I was sure that I would live through the injury, it became strictly a matter of pain. The pain was torrential. The top half of my body was paralyzed by pain. Every movement sent lightning forks through my chest and back. Standing absolutely still hurt badly, sitting hurt badly, lying down hurt badly, and trying to keep my balance on a small, rolling ship was agony. Once lying down, I could not get up. My muscles were too inflamed to work. On shipboard, leaving the island, the crew settled me into one of the tiny capsule bunks, which are small open cubicles recessed into the wall. I will never forget waking in pain some hours later and discovering that I was trapped in my low-ceilinged, coffinlike bunk. For two hours, I tried everything I could think of to get out. I have never known such helplessness. Because I couldn't expand my chest, I was unable to call for help, hard as I tried. Finally, a Japanese passenger across the room woke up and crawled sleepily from his bunk. I pantomimed that I needed help, that my ribs were broken, and would he drag me carefully out of my narrow bunk. Sliding his arms under my shoulders, he pulled me out like a war casualty, as pain twisted its ragged knives. Then, holding on to the ceiling, I crawled up to the middle deck and sat against a wall. But this was just pain. I know now that I can withstand great pain. I was much more concerned by how *inconvenient* the injury was for everyone. I also learned about the generosity and concern of strangers—my journey out of Japan was a trail strewn with kindness. The animal adventures recounted in this book cost me no pain as violent as broken ribs (now my benchmark for a tough trip), just the occasional allergy, bruise, parasite, or heartache.

Outside the train station in Washington, D.C., these words are inscribed: 13 "He that would bring home the wealth of the Indies must carry the wealth of the Indies with him. So it is with travelling. A man must carry knowledge with him if he would bring home knowledge." That maxim is particularly true for a nature writer. I never mind abandoning habits, preferences, tastes, plans. I prefer to become part of the new landscape, fully available to the moment, able to revise or ad lib a perspective without warning, open to the revelations of nature. But you also need to know what you're looking at. So I read everything I can—science, folklore, novels, whatever—and then plague my scientist companions with questions. This all adds to the creative feeding frenzy that each essay sets in motion.

In writing about rock-climber Mo Anthoine, A. Alvarez cites a phrase 14 from an unlikely source—Jeremy Bentham. The father of utilitarianism dismisses as "deep play" any activity in which "the stakes are so high," as Alvarez puts it, "that it is irrational for anyone to engage in it at all, since the marginal utility of what you stand to win is grossly outweighed by the disutility of what you stand to lose." Alvarez is wise to see that Bentham despises deep play for some of the very same reasons Mo Anthoine cherishes it. Anthoine confesses that a couple of times a year he has to "feed his rat," by which he means that wonderful mad rodent inside him that demands a challenge or a trip that will combine adventure, fun, wonder, risk, and ordeal. Although I'm not a rock-climber, I know how the rat gnaws, and I must admit there is nothing like deep play. In *On Extended Wings,* a memoir about learning to fly, I wrote:

> It isn't that I find danger ennobling, or that I require cheap excitation to cure the dullness of routine; but I do like the moment central to danger and to some sports, when you become so thoroughly concerned with acting deftly, in order to be safe, that only reaction is possible, not analysis. You shed the centuries and feel creatural. Of course, you do have to scan, assess, and make constant minute decisions. But there is nothing like *thinking* in the usual, methodical way. What takes its place is more akin to an informed instinct. For a pensive person, to be fully alert but free of thought is a form of ecstasy.

Being ecstatic means being flung out of your usual self. When you're enraptured, your senses are upright and saluting. But there is also a state when perception doesn't work, consciousness vanishes like the gorgeous fever it is, and you feel free of all mind-body constraints, suddenly so free of them you don't perceive yourself as being free, but vigilant, a seeing eye without judgment, history, or emotion. It's that shudder out of time, the central moment in so many sports, that one often feels, and perhaps becomes addicted to, while doing something dangerous.

Although I never take unnecessary chances, a tidy amount of risk, discomfort, pain, or physical challenge does not deter me. At some point in the research for each of these essays, my rat found sustenance, and there were above all wonderful moments of deep play.

Why this form of play should include wild animals is no mystery. In many ways we're totemic creatures who wear the hides of animals on our bodies and, in affectionate cuteness, at times even address one another by animal names—"pussycat," "honey-bunny," "my little minx," and so forth. Animals share our world, accompany us through life, and frequently figure as symbols of one sort or another. Everyone has a bat story fluttering around in the half-lit mansion of memory. In my case, bats are inextricably linked to the first hint that I might be an artist. 15

In the small Chicago suburb of Waukegan, Illinois, which for some reason has driven over 80 of its onetime residents to become writers of some kind, my family lived in a bay-windowed house on the outskirts of town, where paved streets gave way to vast flat housing tracts and the tallest objects for miles were the orange bulldozers standing like mastodons in the dirt. Right across the street from us there was a small field and beyond it a plum orchard through which I sometimes walked on the way to Greenwood Elementary School. This was not the route preferred by my parents. The woods were overgrown and, as Frost wrote, dark and deep, and I was just a six-year-old with a Roy Rogers writing tablet and a mop of unruly hair my mother had temporarily tamed in a ponytail. 16

The route I was supposed to take went around the block, on sidewalks all the way, past the vacant lot on the corner, past the little blue frame house of Mrs. Griffith, who once phoned my mother to report: "Your daughter is talking to herself again! Lord knows what she talks about. I just thought I'd better tell you, Marcia." Then on past the bookmobile stop across from the drugstore where I sometimes bought plastic horses and riders. I loved playing with the horses, whether they were ridden by cavalrymen or cowboys, and most of all I liked it when they came with small red rubber saddles and reins that fit into the groove in the horse's mouth and even stirrups you could slide onto the foot of the rider. But the figures themselves were always frozen in a state of alarm or rest: the horses were always galloping, trotting, or standing stock-still at some invisible hitching post, the riders were always waving their arms or hunkering 17 low in the saddle or sitting up stiffly on parade march. Though I tried to make them move, by bending or heating or twisting, I soon learned as I would later about real soldiers and cowboys, that they could break beyond repair and disappear from my life. I never really thought of them as frozen; I thought of them as always frightened, always angry, always sad, always silently yelling.

Around the corner from the drugstore stood Victor's house. I called my cousin Tic-Toc, and he was my best friend until his mother came between us. Once she shrieked to find me talking her son into tying a towel around his shoulders and leaping from the back roof onto the brick barbecue to see if people really could fly. On another occasion we concocted a gruesome brew of unmentionable fluids to give to Normy Wolf, a nerd who lived across the street. I wanted to see if it would kill him, and we would have found out if Victor's mother hadn't caught us crossing the street with the disgusting, full mayonnaise jar. On another day I drafted Victor into a bolder experiment. Was it possible to navigate an entire house without touching the ground? His mother walked in from shopping just as I was jumping from a bannister onto a doorknob, swinging into the living room, and then leaping from couch to chair to chair as if they were ice floes. I was not a hyperkinetic child, just curious. I wanted to see if it was possible—and would have, if she hadn't banished me at once. Victor was told to play with boys from then on. It was clear girls were too dangerous.

But I didn't know I was different, truly, irrevocably different, different in what I saw when looking out of the window each day, until one morning when I was going through the orchard with three first-grade schoolmates. We were late, and there were silhouette drawings, which none of us wanted to miss, so we cut through the orchard. I can still remember the sheen of the green-and-red plaid dress that Susan Green wore. She had a matching ribbon in her hair and a petticoat that made her skirt rustle as she moved. Above us, the trees were thick with dark plums huddled like bats. Susan dragged at my arm and pulled me along because I was dawdling, staring up at the fruit—or bats—and when she demanded to know what I was looking at, I told her. She let go of my arm and all three girls recoiled. The possibility of bats didn't frighten them. *I* frightened them: the elaborate fantasies I wove when we played store, telephone operator, or house; my perverse insistence on drawing trees in colors other than green; my doing *boy* things like raising turtles and wearing six-shooters to tap-dance lessons; my thinking that the toy cowboys we played with had emotions. And now this: plums that looked like bats. All these years later, the memory of the look on their faces is indelible. But most of all I remember flushing with wonder at the sight of my first metaphor—the living plums: the bats.

IN PRAISE OF BATS

One winter evening, I took a seat in a natural amphitheater of limestone boulders, at the bottom of which was the wide, dark mouth of Bracken Cave. Nothing stirred yet in its depths. But I had been promised one of the wonders of our age. Deep inside the cavern, Mexican free-tailed bats were hanging up by their toes, 20 million of them. They were the largest concentration of warm-blooded animals in the world. At dusk, all 20 million would fly out to feed, in a living volcano scientists call an emergence. They would flow into the sky with their leathery wings and ultrasonic cries, and people 50 miles away, in cities like San Antonio and Austin, would, without realizing it, rarely be more than 70 feet from a feeding bat.

"I've sat here for three hours and still seen them pouring out," the man   21
next to me said, radiant with anticipation. If anyone should have known their habits, it was this man, Merlin D. Tuttle, the world's authority on bats, founder and science director of Bat Conservation International, and an explorer whose cliff-hanging exploits put Indiana Jones to shame. On the ground beside us lay some of the tools of his trade: an infrared nightscope of the kind much used in Vietnam; a miners' headlamp powered by a large heavy battery that he carried in a khaki ammunition belt around his waist; a mini–bat-detector, which picked up the ultrasonic echolocating calls of many species of bats. Noticeably absent were gloves, sticks, or other protective gear.

"Bats are among the gentlest of animals," he said. "They're really shy   22
and winsome creatures who have just had bad press." *Winsome* is not a term often used by scientists. On a list of "winning" creatures, bats would not rank very high.

A blond man in his mid-forties, with gray sideburns, a mustache, and   23
gold-wire-rimmed glasses, he had a thin, muscular build, an emphatic mouth, and wisps of hair falling across a large forehead. Before I could say anything, his eyes darted to the cave mouth, a smile drifted over his face along with the fading rays of sunlight, and I followed his gaze. Hundreds of small bats had appeared suddenly, darting and climbing, swirling and looping. Then they spiraled up and scrolled off to the east. It was an odd, small spectacle.

"Just wait," Tuttle said, reading my mind. An acrid tinge of ammonia   24
mixed with the other night scents. "What you're smelling is the ammonia from guano—bat dung—in the cave. Two hundred and forty tons of bats roost in there and they heat the air with their body temperature. If it's a cold night, the body heat in there creates a chimney effect."

Down by the cave mouth, something slithered in the dusk, but I couldn't   25
be sure if it was a shadow or a snake. Coachwhip snakes prowled there some-times, hoping to eat fallen bats. The floor of the cave itself was alive with insects, small invertebrates, and other predators eager to devour any bat that lost its toehold. Because this was a nursery cave—full of mother and baby bats—the boiling cushion of hungry jaws on the cave floor was rarely disap-pointed. Tuttle told me that a local university had once brought out a small whale carcass on a flatbed and left it in the cave briefly for the dermestid bugs to strip clean. It took about two days. Normally, outside the cave, the bugs would be feeding on carrion. Though they were beetles as adults, their half-inch larvae were fuzzy eating machines. The cave itself sprawled 1,000 feet long, 130 feet deep, and an average of 60 feet in diameter, so there were countless crevices for bats with plenty of floor room for bugs.

Researchers who ventured into the cave wore respirators and tightly   26
fitting clothes. Not only could they be showered with droppings from the bats
overhead (1,800 adults per square yard in some places, and in the crèche, where
the bald pink babies are, a squealing hungry mass of 5,000 pups per square
yard), there would be the thick layers of powdery guano, the crawling beetle
larvae, the infernal heat, and the intense vapor of ammonia. To the bats, it's
bliss: a toasty incubator. For them, hell would be trying to live where we do,
in refrigerated boxes without fresh air or sunlight, which we litter with obstacles and perfume with such irritating essences as peppermint, lemon, and
chlorine bleach. Perhaps they would find it strange, as I do, that we feed on
dismembered animals no longer resembling what they are; and yet, paradoxi-
cally, we insist on cooking them to the warmth of fresh prey.

Small clouds began to swell, spinning like an open funnel, as the bats   27
orbited until they were high enough to depart. Like airplanes in a mountain
valley, they must circle to climb, so they whisk around one another, wing to
wing, in tight echelons. As they revolve, they pick up speed. Over open
country, free-tailed bats can cruise at 35 miles an hour.

"They're spiraling counterclockwise. Do they always turn in the same   28
direction?"

"No," Tuttle said. "In the mornings, when they return, they tend to go   29
straight in. They come in real high, peel off, and then dive in fast with their
wings half folded."

Shadows marched through the trees as the whirlpooling bats set off on   30
a night's cross-country journey, to forage for food. A natural pesticide, they
eat 150 tons of insects every night. Born in June, then weaned when they
were about five weeks old, the new babies were strong enough to fly with
their mothers, who had taught them some of the arcane arts of bathood: how
to leave a cave waltzing and veer off into twilight; how to be guided by the
land and feed in midair; how to swoop down to a pond with their small pink
tongues out and drink on the wing; how to find the warmth they crave among
the huddled masses; how to rely on the mob-law of the colony. Did they fly
nonstop all night long, or did they pause somewhere to put their feet up for a
spell? Did the mothers demonstrate for their own offspring, the way bird
mothers do, or did the babies learn from studying the habits of the whole
colony? "Probably, they break off into recognizable groups that understand
where they're headed," he said. "But we just don't know. So little is known
about bats."

A hawk appeared, swooped, grabbed a bat straight out of the sky, and   31
disappeared with it. In a moment, the hawk returned, but hearing his wings
coming, the bats all shifted sideways to confuse him, and he missed. As wave
upon wave of bats poured out of the cave, their collective wings began to
sound like drizzle on autumn leaves. Gushing out and swirling fast in this
living Mixmaster, newly risen bats started in close and then veered out almost
to the rim of the bowl, climbing until they were high enough to clear the
ridge. Already, a long black column of bats looked like a tornado spinning out

far across the Texas sky. A second column formed, undulating and dancing through the air like a Chinese dragon, stretching for miles, headed for some unknown feeding ground. The night was silent except for the serene beating of their wings. But when Tuttle switched on his mini–bat-detector, we heard a frenzy of clicks. Beyond human hearing, the air was loud with shouts as the teeming bats fluttered wing to wing, echolocating furiously so as not to collide. Like a Geiger counter gone berserk, the bat-detector poured static, and Tuttle laughed. There was no way to hear individual voices in the ultrasonic mayhem of the emergence. Such a gush of bats flowed upward that two new columns formed, each thick and beating, making long pulsing ribbons, climbing two miles high to ride rapid air currents toward distant feeding sites. Some groups twisted into a bow shape, others into a tuning fork, then a claw, a wrench, a waving hand. Buffeted by uneven currents, they made the air visible, as it rarely is. In the rosy dusk, their wings beat so fast that a strobe light seemed to be playing over them.

"Some bats live to be more than 30 years old, you know," Tuttle explained. "If someone goes on a rampage and kills a bat, they may be killing an animal that's lived on this planet for 30 years. It's not like killing a roach. For their size, they're the longest-lived mammal on earth. But unfortunately, they're also the slowest-reproducing mammal for their size. Mother bats usually only rear one pup a year. If you took a pair of meadow mice and gave them everything they needed for survival, theoretically they and their progeny could leave a million meadow mice by the year's end. If you provided an average pair of bats with the same opportunity, in one year there would be a total of three bats—mother, father, and baby. And bats cluster in large colonies in the most vulnerable places. Here we have the world's largest concentration of warm-blooded animals, and it could be destroyed in five minutes. I personally know of caves where people have wiped out millions of bats in one day."

The four largest summer bat colonies in eastern North America would not exist if Tuttle hadn't recognized the peril they were in and waged a campaign to protect them. Born in Honolulu, Hawaii, Tuttle, the son of a biology teacher who traveled often, finally settling his family in Tennessee, grew up not far from a bat cave. By the time Tuttle was nine years old, he was studying bats. He made his first serious scientific contributions when he was in high school and went on to write a doctoral dissertation on population ecology and the behavior of gray bats at the University of Kansas. A mammologist by disposition, he found the decline and plight of bats especially poignant. One day, a few years after graduate school, he returned with friends to show them the extraordinary emergence of 250 thousand gray bats from Hambrick Cave, in Alabama.

"At almost the same time every evening," he said, "you could see this big, dark column of bats, 60 feet wide and 30 feet high, going all the way to the horizon. The sound was like a white-water river. As you can see here at Bracken, a bat emergence can be one of the most spectacular sights in nature.

We were all excited, with cameras ready, but the bats never came out. It was quite a shock when it dawned on us that the bats were gone. I had had a lot of emotional attachment to them. These bats had played a major role in my doctoral research and I had gotten to know them. We went into the cave and found sticks, stones, rifle cartridges, and fireworks wrappers beneath the former bat roost. I knew they had been killed. Many were banded, but they no longer showed up at their traditional hibernating caves. There were so many ways they could have died. Even a single blast from a cherry bomb could have severely damaged their sensitive hearing, making it impossible for them to use their sonar. Hambrick Cave was five miles from the nearest human habitation, not a threat to anyone, and you could get there only by boat. It was one of the last places in the world where I expected bats to be destroyed." Tuttle shook his head.

"Follow that albino one!" he said suddenly, pointing to the cave entrance, where a white ball had just appeared among what looked like a swarm of black peppercorns. Once, twice, three circuits of the bowl. It drifted far out to the rim toward us, its mouth open, then floated over the ridge and joined one of the columns. Gesturing with one hand, as if to press down a stack of invisible myths, Tuttle said, "Their mouths are open when they fly because they need them that way to echolocate. They're not snarling or mean; they're just trying not to bump into anything. We associate that look—open mouth and bared teeth—with menace, but they're not being aggressive. That's how their sonar works. Look, I'll show you." With that, he led me down into the center of the bowl, toward the cave, right into the thick of the swarming, fluttering bats, which flew around our shoulders, over our heads, beside my chin. Too amazed to flinch, I felt them graze my head with their flutters, but they did not touch me with their wings. The breeze they made blew my long hair back. We were standing in the middle of 20 million wild bats. Tuttle swung both arms above his head, then did it again. On the third time, he grabbed a bat right out of the air. 35

After we filed back up to our original spot, I sat down on a boulder beside him, to see what he had captured. Its wings held closed by Tuttle's grip, its small furry brown head sticking out, a little bat looked up at us, frightened and fragile. It used its chin as a pry bar, trying to escape, but made no attempt to bite. 36

"See how ferocious he is?" Tuttle said. 37

The face was gnomic, the wet eyes black as Sen-Sen, and the body covered with a thick, fluffy brown fur. What must it have made of us—large, powerful animals, with big eyes and big teeth? It opened its mouth to echolocate, but did not snap or nip, and in any case its teeth were very small. Tuttle loosened his grip a little. Still holding the wings closed with one hand, he stroked its back with the other, following the grain of the fur, and the little bat quieted down. I knew better than to pick up a bat I might see lying on 38 the ground—or any wild animal acting abnormally, for that matter. But a veteran bat-handler snatching a healthy bat out of the air was different.

"Want to touch?" he asked. 39

I ran a finger over the tiny back, felt the slender bones and the fur soft 40 as chinchilla. Then we opened out the wings and I stroked their thin rubbery membrane, traced the elongated fingers that held up the wings, and looked at the tail from which the free-tailed bat got its name. The scientific name for all bats is *Chiroptera,* "hand wing," and even on a small version like this one the hand wings were clear.

"Isn't he a winsome little fellow?" Tuttle asked. "Here, you can let him 41 go." When he placed the bat on my open palm, I felt a swift scuttle as it crept, wing over wing, to my fingertips, then launched itself into the air to rejoin its colony, which now had filled the sky with black magic. . . .

Topics for Discussion and Writing

1. What does Ackerman mean by, "Like love, travel makes you innocent again"? Can you relate to Ackerman's feelings here? What does she mean by *innocent?* Write about this empathy by recalling a similar experience in your life.

2. Ackerman describes the process by which she writes: "Tomorrow, when we drift through the iceberg gardens of Gerlach Strait, I will be working— that is, writing prose. My mind will become a cyclone of intense alertness, in which details present themselves slowly, thoroughly, one at a time. I don't know how to describe what happens to me when I'm out in 'nature' and 'working'—it's a kind of rapture—but it's happened often enough that I know to expect it." Notice the positive, concrete description she uses. Describe the process by which you write. Use positive images.

3. What role does Tuttle play in the story? Why is he important?

4. How would you compare Ackerman's view of nature with Anne Dillard's in the selection from *Pilgrim at Tinker Creek* (the first reading in this chapter). What similarities and differences do you see in the ways that Ackerman and Dillard relate to the natural phenomena they write about? With which writer do you more closely identify?

MARY ANN GWINN

"A Deathly Call of the Wild"

"Its beaches are broad and slope gently, in contrast to the rocky, vertical shores of many of the other islands in the sound. For that reason, Green Island is favored by wildlife. Now the oil has turned the gentle beach into a death trap."

Before becoming a reporter for the Columbia, Missouri, Daily Tribune *in 1979, Mary Ann Gwinn (born 1951) taught public school in Decatur, Georgia, for three years. She'd prepared for teaching by completing a master's degree in special education at Georgia State University, to complement her B.A. in psychology from Hendrix College.*

Gwinn joined the staff of the Seattle Times *in 1983. Her article, "A Deathly Call of the Wild," reprinted here, won the Pulitzer Prize for National Reporting in 1990.*

Before and as You Read

1. The oil spill from the tanker *Exxon Valdez* has been one of the most publicized environmental disasters of recent years. Think–write for several minutes to recall as much as you know or have heard about this incident. List questions about the incident and its environmental impact that come to you as you write.

2. Draw from memory a map of Alaska. Try to pinpoint Prince William Sound; try to trace the route of the Alaska Pipeline. Now consult a map of Alaska with these features marked. Write briefly about the discrepancies between your map and the one you consulted. As you read Gwinn's story, consider how her writing helps you fill in your mental map of Alaska. Consider also how your knowledge—and gaps in your knowledge—of geography affect your awareness of environmental dangers.

I HAD TRIED to prepare myself for Green Island, but nothing 1 can prepare you for the havoc wreaked on the creatures of Prince William Sound.

From the helicopter that took me there, the 987-foot tanker *Exxon* 2 *Valdez,* stuck like a toy boat on Bligh Reef, was dwarfed by the immensity of the sound. It was hard to believe that we could fly 60 miles, land, and walk right into the ruination of a landscape, so far from that broken boat.

The helicopter landed on the beach of Green Island. Its beaches are 3 broad and slope gently, in contrast to the rocky, vertical shores of many of the other islands in the sound. For that reason, Green Island is favored by wildlife. Now the oil has turned the gentle beach into a death trap.

No sooner had the Alaska National Guard helicopter roared away than   *4*
a black lump detached itself from three or four others bobbing in the oil-streaked water. It was an old squaw, a sea bird normally recognizable by its stark black-and-white plumage. The tuxedo plumage had turned a muddy brown and orange.

It staggered up the beach, its head compulsively jerking back and forth,   *5*
as if trying to escape the thing that was strangling it. Tony Dawson, a photographer for *Audubon* magazine, and I watched it climb a snowbank and flap into the still center of the woods. "They move up into the grass, along the creek beds and into the woods, where they die," Dawson said. "It's like they're fleeing an invisible enemy."

Dawson used to be a veterinarian. He said documenting the oil spill   *6*
makes him feel like a photographer in Vietnam: "Every day, a new body count." As in that war, helicopters drone across the sky, boats beach on shore, men land, size up the situation and depart.

Eleven days into the spill, scientists are trying to decide which beaches   *7*
to clean and which to leave alone, reasoning that disruption would hurt some more than it would help. Very little actual beach cleanup is taking place. Most of the animals are going to die, a few dozen or hundred every day, by degrees.

I walked along the beach, which in some places was glutted with oil like   *8*
brown pudding; in others, streaked and puddled with oil the consistency of chocolate syrup. The only sounds came from a few gulls and the old squaw's mate, which drifted down the polluted channel toward its fate. Far away, a cormorant spread its wings and stretched in a vain attempt to fluff its oil-soaked feathers. A bald eagle passed overhead.

It was then that I heard a sound so strange, for a brief moment all my   *9*
20th century rationality dropped away.

Something was crying in the vicinity of the woods, a sound not quite   *10*
human. I looked into the trees.

Whooooooh. Whooooh. Whoooh. Up and down a mournful scale.   *11*
Something is coming out of those woods, I thought, and is going to take vengeance for this horror on the first human being it sees.

Then I saw a movement in the grass at the end of the beach. It was   *12*
a loon.

Loons have become something of a cause célèbre to bird lovers. They   *13*
are beautiful birds, almost as large as geese, with long, sharp beaks, striking black-and-white striped wings and a graceful, streamlined head. They are a threatened species in the United States because they need large bodies of water to fish in and undeveloped, marshy shorelines to nest on, and most shoreline in this country has been landscaped and pruned.

The most compelling thing about the loon is its call—something be-   *14*
tween a cry, a whistle and a sob, a sound so mournful and chilling it provoked the word "loony," a term for someone wild with sorrow, out of their head.

This was an artic loon in its winter plumage, brown instead of the   *15*
striking black and white of summer. It had ruby-red eyes, which blinked in
terror because it could barely move. It was lightly oiled all over—breast, feet,
wings, head—destroying its power of flight. Its sinuous head darted here and
there as we approached. It flapped and stumbled trying to avoid us, and then
it came to rest between two large rocks.

As Dawson photographed it, it intermittently called its mournful call. Its   *16*
mate swam back and forth, calling back, a few yards offshore.

I could see it tremble, a sign that the bird was freezing. Most oiled birds   *17*
die because the oil destroys their insulation.

"It's like someone with a down coat falling into a lake," Dawson ex-   *18*
plained. The breeze ruffled its stiffening feathers. As Dawson moved closer
with the camera, it uttered a low quivering cry.

After 10 minutes or so, I just couldn't watch anymore. It was so beautiful,   *19*
and so helpless and so doomed. We had nothing like a bag, sack or cloth to
hold it in. I walked around the point.

Then I heard Dawson calling. He walked into view holding the furious,   *20*
flapping loon by its upper wings, set it down on the grass and said, "Come
here and help me. He won't hurt you."

I was stunned by the rough handling of such a wild thing, but it devel-   *21*
oped that Dawson, the former veterinarian, knew his birds. He had grasped
the loon exactly in the place where his wings would not break. He would tell
me later that most bird rescuers are too tender-hearted or frightened of birds
to contain them, and let a lot of salvageable birds get away.

We had to wait for the helicopter, and Dawson had to take more pic-   *22*
tures, so I grasped the loon behind the upper wings, pinning them together,
and took up the loon watch. The bird rose, struggled and fell back to earth,
then was still.

I was as afraid of the loon as it was of me in a way that touching a   *23*
totally wild thing can provoke. But I began to feel its strength. It was warm, it
had energy, and it could still struggle. I could hear it breathing, and could feel
its pulse. It turned its red eye steadily on me. We breathed, and waited, together.

Dawson returned, took a black cord from a lens case and neatly looped   *24*
it around the bird's wings. The helicopter dropped out of the sky and settled
on the beach. I held the string as the loon, unblinking, faced the terrific wind
kicked up by the machine. Then Dawson neatly scooped up the bird and
settled into the helicopter. The loon lashed out with its needle beak until
David Grimes, a fisherman working with the state on the spill, enveloped it
in a wool knit bag he carried with him. The bird stilled.

Dawson and I were both streaked with oil and blood from the loon's   *25*
feet, lacerated by barnacles on the beach. He gave me a small black and white
feather that had fallen from the bird's wing.

We took the loon to the bird-rescue center in Valdez. I don't know if it   *26*
will live. Dawson thought it had a good chance. I thought of the mate we
had left behind in the water.

Afterward, we talked about whom bird rescues help more, the rescued   27
or the rescuer. Most rescued birds don't make it. And tens of thousands more
from the Valdez spill will die before they even get a chance.

I know only that the loon told me something that no one other thing   28
about this tragedy could. If only we could learn to value such stubborn,
determined life. If only we could hold safe in our hands the heart of the loon.

Topics for Discussion and Writing

1. List words or phrases that Gwinn uses to describe the scene. What terms "jar the senses"; that is, help you feel the sensations of destruction?
2. How does Gwinn's presentation differ from other news reports of the Valdez oil spill? Consult several from your library newspaper files. How does the impact of Gwinn's personal narrative differ from that of the news reports?
3. Why do you think "A Deathly Call of the Wild" was chosen as the title of this piece?
4. What do you think Gwinn is implying when she states, upon hearing the call of the loon, "for a brief moment all my 20th century rationality dropped away"?
5. What does Gwinn imply by the sentence, "Afterward, we talked about whom bird rescues help more, the rescued or the rescuer"? Think about a "rescue mission" in your own life, and how that sentence relates to your feelings during and after the event.
6. From reading Gwinn's essay, try to characterize her views of wildlife. Compare them with what the excerpt from Dillard's *Pilgrim at Tinker Creek*, earlier in this chapter, suggests about that writer's values regarding wild creatures. Compare them with the values of Ackerman and Tuttle in Ackerman's *The Moon by Whale Light.*

JOEL GARREAU

"Earthmover"

> *"Each piece of the new world we build caters to our dreams of freedom. But right now, the totality does not make us feel like individuals. It makes us feel like strangers in our own land."*
>
> *A native of Pawtucket, Rhode Island, Joel Garreau (born 1948) began his newspaper career while still in high school, as a special assignment reporter and photographer with the Pawtucket* Times. *While in college at Notre Dame, Garreau was a founding editor of* Focus/Michiana. *He joined the staff of the* Washington Post *in 1970, just after graduation. He has been assistant editor of* Outlook, *the* Post's *Sunday editorial section, since 1980. Garreau is the author of* The Nine Nations of North America *(1981), which divides the continent into nine regional cultures or "power clusters," each with unique views, values, and traditions.*
>
> *"Earthmover" is an excerpt from Garreau's most recent book,* Edge City: Life on the New Frontier *(1992).*

Before and as You Read

1. If you have lived in a community long enough to have seen it undergo great change or growth in the numbers of buildings, roads, and population, write about the community now and how it used to be. What good things, from your perspective, have been lost? What good things have been gained?
2. Write definitions of two terms: *progress* and *ownership of land*. Besides consulting dictionaries or law books, write about what these terms mean in your own life. Interview at least two other people about their definitions and compare them with yours.
3. Go to your local government offices and find out the local process by which land is zoned for particular kinds of use, such as high-rise office buildings, private homes, and factories. Find out where in the zoning process citizens' opinions about zoning can be heard.
4. Imagine that a developer is proposing to have part of your community rezoned for commercial use. Your property will be affected; in fact, you might even lose some of it. How much control do you believe individuals should have over their private property? Share your views with others doing this exercise.

THIRTY MILES west of the U.S. capitol, out Interstate 66, there is   *1*
a small Virginia stream, name of Bull Run. More than a century and a quarter ago, in the brutally hot summers of 1861 and 1862, great armies

clashed in the swale of this brook, testing no less than whether a nation conceived in liberty could long endure.

In the Second Battle of Manassas, in 1862, Robert E. Lee had his head-   *2*
quarters on Stuart's Hill, overlooking this field of blood. In 1988, 542 acres of this land, including that hill, came into the hands of an organization headed by John T. "Til" Hazel, by far the most prominent developer in these parts. Hazel had started his law career in the '50s by condemning the land for the road that would come to be known as the Capitol Beltway. And for 30 years he had been a key player in the economic and social revolution that had culminated in the late '80s with eight Edge Cities blooming in Northern Virginia.

These places we were building were cities like we had never seen before.   *3*
They were Information Age workplaces like those along the Dulles Access Road in Fairfax County or Rosslyn/Ballston in Arlington County, not to mention the Interstate 270 corridor in Montgomery County. Although they looked nothing at all like our old cities, and rarely had a mayor or a city council, each was bigger, by any functional urban measure, than downtown Memphis. One of them, Tysons Corner, drew astounded observers from all over the world to its high-rises and intersections, for it was twice the size of downtown Miami.

Til Hazel, who was born and raised Southern, took no little satisfaction   *4*
in watching his native land of Northern Virginia approach and then eclipse the economic energy of that Yankee bastion across the Potomac, the District of Columbia. Lee's personal command, after all, was not called the Army of Northern Virginia for nothing.

Thus it was, with a firm faith in the inevitability of progress, that Hazel   *5*
in the late 1980s turned his attention to the land he had acquired near the exit to I-66 labeled "Manassas." For right there next to the Manassas National Battlefield Park—Bull Run to Northerners—was a prime place for a new Edge City. It could contain as much as 4.3 million square feet of nonresidential space—the size of downtown Fort Lauderdale—plus 560 homes. It would do the local economy a lot of good.

The last thing he expected was a fight.   *6*

In the dust and the swirl of the 1988 battle in which Americans debated   *7*
the moral worth of Til Hazel's land, it was difficult, as always in war, to pinpoint exactly when the turn of fortune came.

It may have been the ad with the photo of the churning bulldozer and   *8*
the words: "Without Your Support, the Soldiers Who Died at Manassas Will Be Turning Over in Their Graves."

The work of volunteer copywriters from an obscure Richmond agency,   *9*
the advertisement was prepared for a ragtag collection of preservationists and history buffs called the Save the Battlefield Coalition. That ad hit people's hot buttons. The idea of bones of the Civil War dead rising up before the racking blades of bulldozers as they pushed dirt for a mall—that really, *really* got to people.

The ad continued: "As you read this plea, bulldozers are razing a sacred   10
place in American history. A place where the blood of over 28,000 men was
spilled in two valiant struggles which would determine the fate of the American republic . . .

"Indeed, the slaughter was so great that the bodies were piled into mass   11
graves. Many who died here were not men at all. They were little more than
boys doing what they thought was right.

"If developer John T. Hazel has his way, the tranquil 542-acre tract at   12
Manassas Battlefield will be transformed overnight into a snarling traffic jam
adjacent to a huge office park and shopping mall . . . This national historical
site will no longer pay tribute to the men who paid the ultimate price for
their country. Instead, it will pay tribute to plastic watches, fastfood, movie
theatres and video stores . . . If Manassas Battlefield can be turned into a
parking lot, then is any part of our heritage safe from developers? Help us
stop the 'progress.'"

Then again, maybe the turning point was the testimony of Princeton's   13
James M. McPherson before a panel of the U.S. Senate.

McPherson's book, *Battle Cry of Freedom,* having been widely reviewed   14
as the best one-volume history of the War Between the States, had just rocketed up the national best-seller lists on its way to winning the Pulitzer Prize.
The book helped create the greatest wave of interest in that conflict since the
bloodshed actually stopped, a wave that would culminate in Ken Burns's
hugely popular PBS television series "The Civil War."

McPherson called Stuart's Hill—the site that Hazel had bought and re-   15
christened "William Center"—"one of the most significant Civil War mon-
uments I've ever seen . . . equally important in historical significance to
Seminary Ridge at Gettysburg, where Longstreet and Lee had their headquarters, from which Pickett's Charge was launched . . .

"What was at stake in the Civil War and at Second Manassas and in the   16
William Center tract," the historian told the senators, "was the very fate of
the nation. Whether it would be one country or two, would be a nation with
slavery or without slavery. That part of our heritage can best be understood
by studying it. And Civil War battles can best be studied by going to the
battlefields. Walking them as I've done to this one several times. Bicycling over
them as I've tried to do in the midst of the traffic that we've heard about
today.

"I would have liked to go to the William Center tract—to go on Stuart's   17
Hill—so that I could see from that height the large part of the battlefield, to
go where Longstreet's troops were, and to try to understand why Fitz-John
Porter would not attack across there. That has not been my opportunity in the
past, but I hope that as a result of congressional action it will be my opportunity in the future."

Maybe the shift was the cumulative work of the world media. Every   18
outfit with a Washington bureau from *Time* to the Japanese newspapers saw
the larger implications of this battle. Their reports, day after day, had their

impact, congressional mailbags showed. Especially powerful was the piece on "CBS News Sunday Morning." That was the one with the chopper shots showing the land laid open like a raw red wound beneath the frenzied earth-movers. Even more wrenching were the clear young voices, backed by two acoustic guitars, singing the battle hymn of the resistance:

> Rolled out to Manassas,
> Stood alone and watched the sunset,
> I imagined I could see grandfather fall.
> Behind the place where he was standing
> Just before the bullet took him
> Is where they're gonna build a shopping mall.

When all was said and done, however, the pivotal moment probably came when Annie Snyder cried.   19

Annie Snyder was not the kind of woman you ever expected to see cry.   20
Snyder, the spark plug and ringleader of the Save the Battlefield Coalition, had a curious face. Its lower half was that of a man. She had a powerful jaw, a broad nose and cheeks flat as plates. Nonetheless, from the bridge of her nose up, she really was quite a vamp, her eyes flashing vivaciously beneath the fashionably short cut of her auburn hair. In fact, she was more sensitive about her good looks than might be thought common in a woman of 67, even if she did appear 15 years younger. When a builders' magazine referred to her as a little old lady she went so crazy as to send the publication a rather fetching photo of herself doing aerobics in tights, which of course the magazine proceeded to print. As she discussed the work of various reporters who had reported sympathetically on "her" battlefield, it was as if she were reminiscing about old flames.

The contradictions were not all in her face. The more innocent and   21
exposed Snyder seemed—as when she discussed her diabetes complicated by coronary artery disease, for example—the more her incongruities had the capacity to startle. They might include her casual references to her professional prowess as a long-gun marksman. Or her cattle operation, which routinely required her, at 135 pounds, to pick up calves that weighed 90 pounds. Or her devout belief in conservative Republicanism. Or the way she chose to adorn her lima-bean-size earlobes with large, flat earrings, the crimson color of which matched exactly the red of the U.S. Marine Corps emblem on her polo shirt.

Her history was as illuminative of the strains on America at mid-century   22
as was Til Hazel's. Anne D. Snyder, née Annie Delp, was born nine years before him, in 1921. The daughter of a prosperous Pittsburgh attorney, she was as intellectually gifted as Hazel, accelerating through high school to enter college at 16. She was also just as bull-headed.

"I'll tell you how I got liberated," she recalls. "I grew up in a neighbor-   23
hood of boys. There were no girls. We lived next to a farm, and we were allowed to play baseball and football in their pasture. So I grew up with all

these boys. I could play football as well as the rest of them. But when I started developing bosoms they decided I was an embarrassment to them and they kicked me off the football team. I've been a women's libber ever since. That made me so *mad.* Yeah! So it was perfectly normal for me to join the Marine Corps."

Which she did. The outbreak of World War II found her enrolled in   24 law school at the University of Pittsburgh—hardly routine or even welcome at the time. But as the war progressed, she espied a far greater challenge. "I'm a flag-waver. Yeah, really. My brother was a Marine," she says simply, to explain what she did next.

Annie left law school to join the first class of women to graduate from   25 Marine Officer Candidate School. Then she became a recruiter, attracting other young women to the world of leathernecks.

The men hated all of it. The Marine Corps was absolutely the last   26 service to accept women. It capitulated only because of the exigencies of war. "'Free a man to fight' was our motto," Snyder recalls. Her father was beyond shocked. "The men had the idea all women in uniform were prostitutes." She had to constantly conquer men's worlds, proving her mettle not only to other Marines but to her own family, as well as the fathers and brothers of the women she was trying to recruit.

"When I graduated from OCS I was a recruiter in New Orleans, and   27 the first day I arrived there—my first plane trip—the commanding officer met me and said, 'Come on, lieutenant, you have to give a speech at the St. Charles Hotel in 20 minutes.' I'll never forget it. The St. Charles had these gorgeous, gorgeous staircases, ceilings 40 feet high. Very impressive to a 21-year-old. We go careening up these steps and over to this room and I looked in and there were 150 men sitting there. I was just stunned. I backed up; I thought we were in the wrong place. What the hell was I doing talking to men? Well, you didn't have to talk the women into joining. You had to talk their fathers, husbands, sons. My job was to convince them they wouldn't be selling their daughters into prostitution. Of all the Western civilizations that participated in that war, we had the worst representation of women. I think it was the male chauvinist pigs in this country. To somebody living in your era, that might just seem incredible, I know."

When she mustered out of the Marines after the war, it was with some   28 magnificent stories to tell, as well as a marriage to Pete Snyder, one of the Marines' earliest Pacific theater aviators. Pete would soon join that new elite— airline pilots. But most important, Annie Snyder came away with a foundation that was singular for young women of that day and time: There were not many challenges she would ever view as daunting. Not compared with what she'd already done.

Of *course* she helped dig the foundation footings by hand when she and   29 Pete built their first house after the war. Of course she raised six kids; of course one of the girls is now a lawyer. Of course she and Pete ended up buying a 180-acre farm in Prince William County, where she ran her own registered Angus cattle operation for 28 years while he was flying airliners. "I think I'm the only woman in the world who annually asked for something for Christmas that I never got," she says. "And that was a hay-bale elevator." Over the years, she and the kids threw hundreds of tons of hay into the loft by hand.

Of course her farm would turn out to have a stream running through it called Little Bull Run. That accident of geography ended up changing her life, as she fought fight after fight for the battlefield next door that she came to love.   30

All those fights. And of course it would end up with Snyder squaring off against the most powerful force in the region, Til Hazel. It's curious, but Til Hazel's most persistent and successful opponents in life have always been women. In fact, throughout America, from California to Texas to Florida, it is striking how often, when the partisans in the battle over "progress" collide, the builders are men, and the preservationists, women. It is by no means a hard and fast divide—there are always crossovers—but it is a notable pattern.   31

The media would enjoy describing the collision between the forces marshaled by Annie Snyder and those of Til Hazel as the Third Battle of Bull Run. But that clever label was misleading. The intense struggles over the use of this land really began almost before the rebel yells—heard for the first time at Manassas—had died away. The land was bought by a real estate speculator only two days after that first battle in 1861. He thought it would make a good tourist attraction.   32

New battles, in fact, always seemed to swirl around this haunt of ghosts where—only three months after Fort Sumter fell—it became clear that there would be no cheap victory. Annie counted the 1988 struggle as her sixth "Third Battle of Manassas." And she only got started in the second half of the 20th century. One reporter checking the newspaper clips back to 1890 counted it as at least the 10th.   33

The first battle Snyder was involved in came in the 1950s, over the interstate. That was an awesome fight. Deflecting the intentions of highway engineers in those days was unheard of—even if they did see the shortest distance between two points as straight through the middle of a battlefield. In the end, however, deflected they were. That battle is marked on the maps of Virginia to this day: Just west of Fairfax, for no apparent reason, the highway dips to the south.   34

Another of Snyder's several "battles of Manassas" involved Marriott's plan in 1973 to put a Great America theme park on the land. That plan too was brought to its knees. And it too served to burnish Annie's legend.   35

But by the late 1980s, it seemed the battles might finally have come to an end. For decades, the Prince William County government had desperately tried to encourage more commercial development. A broader tax base was urgently needed to ease the crushing burden of providing schools and services for all the residential subdivisions popping up around one of the fastest growing jurisdictions in the nation. The county had earmarked nearly 600 acres   36 adjacent to the interstate—and thus, incidentally, next to the National Battle-field Park—as among the most promising sites. In the late 70s, the county had fought desperately to prevent those woods and fields from being included in the national park. It wanted jobs there. So in 1986, the Hazel/Peterson Cos. came up with a plan. Its centerpiece, the county believed, would be a wooded Edge City corporate park of glass and steel and trees for highly educated, high-tech, white-collar workers. The buildings would be screened from the battlefield, and the traffic impact was promised to be minimal.

It seemed that the outline of a decent compromise was at hand. Those   37
like Snyder who had fought so much for the battlefield were hardly happy with the idea of having mid-rise offices where Longstreet swept forward to close the vise on the Federals. But if development was inevitable, a relatively classy planned mixed-use development such as the one the Hazel/Peterson Cos. was proposing, with 560 new homes and 2.9 million square feet of commercial space—half the size of downtown San Antonio—might be about as good a deal as they were going to get.

Hazel/Peterson ran tours of its office park eight miles down the inter-   38
state, at Fair Lakes. It did indeed have trees and lakes and geese. The shopping area was small-scale. Politics, after all, is the art of the possible. A special PMD zoning ordinance was passed for the proposed development, and that seemed to be about the end of that. Snyder even announced her retirement as an activist. The doctors had read her the riot act. If she didn't slow down, they told her, a combination of ills threatened her life.

In the *Washington Post* article intending to bid her farewell and recap her   39
long history of struggle, however, up cropped another one of those Annie Snyder incongruities. She was photographed out in one of her lovely fields, attractively dressed. But what she was leaning on was her shotgun. Almost as if she knew.

When the final battle resumed in Manassas on January 28, 1988, it   40
started with a shock like that of a thunderclap on a sunny day. Without warning, Hazel/Peterson announced a change in plans. Its future corporate campus at William Center needed a shot in the arm, it announced. So it was going to switch some uses in its planned mixed-use development. Almost half the 2.9 million square feet of nonresidential use to which it was entitled was not going to be corporate campus after all. The Page One headline in the *Washington Post* the next day said it all:

Huge Mall
Planned at
Manassas
600-Acre Project
To Be Located
Near Battlefield

"It excites me in the sense that we're no longer going to stand in the   41 shadow of Fairfax County," said the Prince William supervisor representing the district. "This is going to be nicer than Fair Oaks," he said, referring to the mall of astounding size only eight miles away with 1.4 million square feet and 213 stores.

Once again, the earth had moved. But this time the shudder produced an emotional and political Richter reading above anything Manassas had seen in a century. 42

In the torrent of abuse directed at Til Hazel in the ensuing weeks, "double-crossed," "defrauded," "cheated" and "deceived" were among the more printable words. Hazel swore that when the Edward J. DeBartolo Corp.—the largest shopping center developer in the United States—approached him with the idea of putting one of its five-anchor 1.2 million-square-foot behemoths next to the battlefield, it was a bolt out of the blue. A mall was the furthest thing from his mind at the time. Although, truth to tell, he'd always felt a little uncomfortable about whether the market was really ready for office parks this far out into the countryside. Thus, when the idea came up, he said, he decided that the mall was needed as a "catalytic agent" to attract corporate offices on the remaining acreage at William Center. "That's been the history of malls all over the country," he said. "They bring along offices." 43

Besides, his spokesman pointed out, it was a done deal. There would be no chance to challenge the decision, no public hearings. No additional action by the county supervisors would be required. The head of the National Park Service could write as many letters as he wished saying that the new plan "does not even resemble the good faith agreements we thought had been made." They would be beside the point. The language of the rezoning that the county had gratefully accepted two years before had been very carefully crafted by Hazel's preeminent legal arm. There was nothing in there about "corporate parks" or "malls." All it had been written to say was that permission was hereby granted to develop 2.9 million square feet of nonresidential space. 44

Hazel thought that said it all. Little did he know. He had rumbled a deep sleeping fault in the American psyche, a revolt against everything about growth that Americans had come to despise. If there was any one piece of paper that summed it up, it was probably not the boilerplate in the legal documents. The mark that something different was afoot was the brand new sticker on the bumper of Charlie Graham's truck. It read: 45

"Have a Nice Day. Shoot a Developer."

This was no small deal. Charlie Graham made his living as a *carpenter*. 46

As it turned out, there were historic dimensions to that tension between Graham's chosen profession as a builder and his bumper sticker. Graham was the kind of independent cuss who carried a Civil War-replica .58-caliber black-powder Minie-ball Springfield rifle into battle reenactments. Although he was a Fauquier County Virginian, he wore the Union uniform of the 116th Pennsylvania. Harvard historian William R. Taylor described such romantics at the end of his 1957 work *Cavalier & Yankee. The Old South and* 47

American National Character. The Charlie Grahams of the 1980s were those young, mustachioed, skilled small-business entrepreneurs who made so much of America tick. As Taylor described them, they were the direct psychological descendants of the Southern yeomen whom Thomas Jefferson revered as the foundation of the republic. They were "ardent and impassioned," "strongly partisan to liberty," possessing "a great natural intelligence" and a "chivalric sense of honor." At the same time, they were just plumb ornery—and of precious little comfort to those in positions of authority. In this way, said Taylor, they were the reincarnation of the original Virginia Cavaliers. Those Cavaliers, of course, were the men who, when they arrived in America 13 years ahead of the Pilgrims, saw the land as Paradise, as the Garden.

Poor Hazel. In hindsight there is a kind of awful inevitability to it all. *48* The women who saw themselves guarding the flame of Western civilization would take this man of the Machine high. They would succeed largely by not playing the game of dollars and numbers he played, by the rules he knew. They would appeal to the truths recognized by the heart, a practice he viewed as underhanded and dastardly, if not immoral. Meanwhile the swashbucklers, the Cavaliers—of whom there were more than a few feisty enough to have become U.S. senators—would take him, if not low, then any way they could get him.

Hazel, the Pilgrim lawyer, had it all correct, legally. But he had it all *49* wrong in the terms that turned out to matter—those of human emotion and the American *Zeitgeist.* He made the same two errors as the Union at Bull Run a century and a quarter before. First, he gravely underestimated what he was up against. Second, he was blindsided by the counterattack.

But that is only hindsight. In the early days of the struggle, there seemed *50* to be no possibility that he could lose. When the battle cry of freedom rose once again it seemed as forlorn as ever in its time. The first day the plan for the mall was announced, the sound of the opposition seemed quite hollow. "It would destroy the battlefield," The Post quoted one lonely "civic activist"—one Annie D. Snyder—as saying. "We'll fight it with everything we've got."

Long after the battle for William Center was over, Robert C. Kelly, Til *51* Hazel's spokesman, was still groping to explain how he managed to run himself into a buzz saw. Kelly, being a thoughtful man who took considerable pride in his ability to get along with people, finally explained it to himself this way: Developers, he said, are agents of change. That is what they do. That is what they are for. That is their social and economic role. They look for ways to convert land profitably from one use to another.

And, Kelly concluded, that is what the American people finally began *52* to rebel against. The Change.

Fair enough. Kelly was onto something. But perhaps he did not push his *53* logic far enough. He didn't take the next step. What, then, was the problem with the Change?

Maybe it was the way the Change was so impersonal, driven only by the   *54*
relentless logic of the marketplace—which is wildly efficient, but incapable of
quantifying the human ecology of a place, its sense of home, those intangibles
of our culture. Maybe that's why when we see the bulldozers, we cringe.
Maybe deep down we see the problem as the Change denying—even attacking—the specialness of our lives. We see it as attacking the very individuality
and individualism that we had been building this stuff to achieve in the first
place. Each piece of the new world we build caters to our dreams of freedom.
But right now, the totality does not make us feel like individuals. It makes us
feel like strangers in our own land. We look around and recognize nothing. It
is all changing so fast we cannot find our own place in the universe. Not even
our old house or favorite hangout. Sometimes we barely recognize ourselves.

Now *that* would be a core contradiction in our souls. *That* would explain   *55*
a lot about our reaction to Manassas. It would also explain why our hearts sink
when we see other landscapes that we love threatened.

We see those places as distinct. As one-of-a-kind. Just like each of us.   *56*
And to the extent that they are removed from the face of the Earth, especially
to be replaced by a symbol of homogeneity—like a mall!—well. It would be
the symbol of the mass, of the ubiquitous, of the ordinary, destroying the
singular, the irreplaceable. And just to that extent would we see the singular
and the irreplaceable in our own lives, in our very selves, diminished.

Maybe that is why we cling so tenaciously to whatever history we can.   *57*
Maybe that is why we are rallying to save sad art deco movie houses and Main
streets with old Kresges. This is us, we say; this is our time. Time is the only
thing we have; it is the measure of our lives. These places are our memories
of a time when our identities were clear. And you're taking that away.

Perhaps that is why the idea of violating Manassas—the symbol of a   *58*
place in which our forefathers died to define our identities as Americans—
made something snap.

The first mass meeting in opposition to the William Center mall on   *59*
Friday, February 5, 1988, did not make strong men quake. Yes, an American
flag hung upside down in distress from the Groveton Road overpass, and, yes,
227 people gathered at the visitors center of the National Battlefield Park,
and, yes, they reached deeply into their wallets to finance the impending legal
battles. But the take? Fifty-six hundred dollars. Heartwarming, but beside the
point. There were not many ways to challenge the legalities of the mall. And
with the news full of budget deficits and spending cuts, the idea of the federal
government stepping in to buy the land at a projected cost of $50 million or
more seemed ludicrous.

Hazel's machines were soon grinding the earth at breakneck speed.   *60*
Quartz lights turned the night to death-pallor day as crews worked round the
clock, double shift, blasting dynamite as late as 1:30 a.m. to tunnel a sewer
under I-66. Legions of belly-dumping earthmovers wheeled at speeds akin to
tanks on flank attack. An antebellum-style house disappeared one night; all

that was left were the surrounding trees. Dust clouds as if from brigades on maneuver rose to the sky. Wetlands were banked. Chain saws roared. If Hazel thought the land was not "particularly pretty" in its original state, when it was planed of all its green it made people sick. Hazel chastely claimed that the delirious attack of the heavy equipment was normal—just meeting contract schedules. Could he help it if that drove the cost of condemning the land to unthinkable heights?

The frenzied destruction backfired. The national and international media   *61* knew a great story when they saw one. The red raw ground, the bulldozers running roughshod, probably over Confederate bones—it was agonizing. And galvanizing. The Park Service likened it to "booking a roller derby in the Sistine Chapel." The idea that in a matter of weeks a portion of the battlefield would be completely gone drew high-powered action. Some of the country's leading preservation groups, including the National Trust for Historic Preservation and the National Parks and Conservation Association, took Manassas on as a cause celebre. Tersh Boasberg, a nationally recognized preservation attorney, was retained. Most visibly, Jody Powell, the savvy former presidential press secretary with the politically useful Southern drawl, came on board as a tactician and spokesperson.

It was Powell who sat by Annie Snyder in the congressional hearing   *62* room and delivered the impassioned speech that made the big fat tears run down Snyder's cheeks.

"On that little hill, Mr. Chairman, history is palpable. Today you can see   *63* it and feel it . . ." As Powell orated, the network cameras were zooming in tight, filling screens nationwide with Snyder's face. Her blue eyes filled to overflowing. Her face scrunched up as she fought unsuccessfully to control her lower lip. "You can see it and feel it, a blood-soaked piece of Virginia countryside." In countless living rooms around the country, viewers discovered that they too seemed to have something in their eyes.

Those who knew Annie Snyder well knew that she could get emotional   *64* about the way her husband dealt with dirty dishes. But that was beside the point. What mattered was a woman like Snyder puddling up before the U.S. Senate, on national television, over a battlefield and a landscape that she deeply loved. It was not something the citizens of the republic saw every day. The signatures on petitions from around the country rolled in by the tens of thousands.

In some ways, the war for Manassas and the future of our lives will never   *65* end. But Friday, October 7, 1988, will probably be marked by future historians as the decisive battle, even if it didn't seem that way at the time. That is when Sen. Dale Bumpers of Arkansas—the kind of Cavalier *The Almanac of American Politics* described as "challenging" and "the town iconoclast"—got up in the well of the Senate to argue for a "legislative taking" of Hazel's land.

Bumpers, the respected chairman of the national parks and forests sub-   *66* committee, gave a long, impassioned and very Southern version of history that night. It was late. The sense of the Senate was that everybody desperately wished to be someplace else—especially home campaigning in the election season that marked the end of the Reagan years. Nonetheless, an astounding number of senators remained on the floor to listen to history.

"[Longstreet] sent out a couple of brigades to see what the strength of 67 the Union was right here," Bumpers intoned emotionally, pointing to the Civil War maps behind him. "And this occurred on the William Center tract, bear in mind. He found out that the Union was there in strength. He pulled those brigades back and deployed all 30,000 of his men in woods. Those woods are *still there.* You go down there *right now* and you will see where Longstreet had his men deployed behind all those trees down there . . .

"Sixteen thousand men in about 48 hours either lost their lives or were 68 wounded in this battle. It was perhaps the third bloodiest battle of the war. Lee, after he won this, thought France and England would recognize the Confederate states. But they were not quite ready. They said you have not won a battle on Northern soil. So Lee took his troops to Antietam . . .

"I told you about these hospitals. They are our Confederate troops bur- 69 ied on this property around the hospitals . . . I believe strongly in our heritage and think our children ought to know where these battlefields are and what was involved in them. I do not want to go out there 10 years from now with my grandson and tell him about the Second Battle of Manassas. He says, 'Well, Grandpa, wasn't General Lee in control of this war here? Didn't he command the Confederate troops?'

"'Yes, he did.' 70

"'Well, where was he?' 71

"'He was up there where that shopping mall is.' 72

"I can see a big granite monument inside that mall's hallway right now: 73 General Lee stood on this spot.

"If you really cherish our heritage as I do, and you believe that history 74 is very important for our children, you will vote for my amendment. I yield the floor."

James A. McClure, the serious and reserved Idaho Republican who has 75 one of the most conservative voting records in the Senate, got up in opposition to the Bumpers amendment. But he actually added great fuel to the greater argument over the land. Said he:

"There is not a single battlefield free from development pressures. We 76 are not just talking about Manassas; we are talking about what is going to happen to every one of the other elements of the National Park System where battlefields are involved . . . A cable franchise in Frederick, Maryland, proposes construction of a 160-foot microwave reception and transmission tower on Red Hill, less than one mile from Bloody Lane, the center of the Antietam Battlefield.

"Does it sound familiar in the context of this debate? 77

"A 100-foot microwave tower threatens the Bolivar Heights Battlefield 78 associated with Major General T.J. 'Stonewall' Jackson's siege and capture of Harpers Ferry, the site of the largest surrender of U.S.-led troops. Such a structure, within five feet—I repeat, five feet—of the park boundary will impair not only the battlefield but also much of the skyline about historic Harpers Ferry.

"Sound familiar in the context of this debate?   *79*

"Fredericksburg and Spotsylvania National Military Park's greatest need   *80* is to establish a legislated boundary, as land immediately adjacent to the park is scheduled for development."

He went on and on. Cold Harbor, threatened by development from   *81* an expanding Richmond. Kennesaw Mountain National Battlefield Park in Georgia. Vicksburg, Chickamauga-Chattanooga and Stones River. "The list," he acknowledged, "is overwhelming." Where will this all end?

In context, he was asking a budgetary question. "This will not be an   *82* acquisition for spare change. By this action we are signaling other landowners at other sites that the way to obtain federal funds is to destroy, or threaten to destroy, resources which the federal government has authorized for acquisition but which have not filtered to the top of the annual appropriations process; or, as in the case of Manassas, resources which are not even within the boundaries of an established park."

Of course in the context of our futures, he was asking a more profound   *83* question—perhaps more profound than he knew. Where, indeed, will this battle over the land all end?

Then again, maybe McClure did have an inkling. In what was meant to   *84* be his clinching argument, he said, "Perhaps the most significant battle of the entire Manassas Battlefield with respect to the William Center tract is that being fought now, not the ones that were fought there 125 years ago."

With that, he sat down, and the Senate came to a roll-call vote.   *85*

Adams . . .

Armstrong . . .

Baucus . . .

Boschwitz . . .

At the start, it was not clear what the result would be.   *86*

. . . Thurmond.

. . . Trible.

. . . Warner.

. . . Wirth.

When the votes were tallied, the vote was 50 to 25 to save the battlefield. *87*

Sen. John Warner of Virginia, the Republican who had tried to find   *88* some wiggle room between the two absolute positions of this battle, who had tried to write legislation that amounted to a compromise on the cheap, voted against the amendment. But the instant the vote was tallied, he got up to save his soul.

WARNER: Mr. President, I ask unanimous consent to vitiate [cancel]   *89* the roll-call vote.

THE ACTING PRESIDENT PRO TEMPORE: Is there objection?   *90* Hearing none, it is so ordered.

That was the passing of the Bumpers amendment. And you could say *91* that at that moment on October 7, 1988, the people of the United States of America redeemed their heritage.

Not that this would be the end. On October 12, the Senate passed the *92* tax bill to which the amendment was a rider. A Reagan veto, however, seemed likely. Two days later, the battlefield measure survived conference with the House.

On Friday, October 14, George Bush, in a speech in La Jolla, Calif., *93* tried to cast himself as a modern-day Teddy Roosevelt, distancing himself from the years of controversy over Ronald Reagan's environmental policies.

"In George Bush you will have a president committed to conservation," *94* he said. Bush promised to "strengthen and preserve our parks" under a new program called "America the Beautiful" and to seek new clean air legislation. He vowed to pursue reductions in acid rain pollutants, stop ocean dumping of sludge and medical wastes, enforce the Superfund restrictions, convene an international conference on the environment, back new parkland acquisition in the California locale in which he spoke, "take a very close look" at his earlier opposition to restrictions on offshore drilling in the area, back urban "greenways," propose using oil and gas tax revenue funds to finance new park acquisitions and create a new National Endowment for the Environment. (Three years later, the verdict on Bush as environmentalist is mixed: better than Reagan, but not as good as his campaign hype.)

The fate of the Manassas bill, meanwhile, was still uncertain. Negotia- *95* tions between key House and Senate conferees over the tax bill in which it was embedded broke off. It appeared almost certain that a tax compromise could not be worked out before the 100th Congress passed into history. By October 21, the headlines read "Bill to Buy Mall Site Nears Failure."

Nonetheless, at 1 a.m. on the 22nd, with the legislative equivalent of *96* seconds left to play, the bill did pass. On Wednesday, November 2, it reached the White House. And on Friday, November 11, without fanfare or even comment, Ronald Reagan signed it.

"The moment the ink from the president's pen was dry," reported John *97* F. Harris in that Saturday's Washington Post, "ownership of the property transferred from the developer, Northern Virginia's Hazel/Peterson Cos., to the federal government as an addition to the adjacent 3,800-acre Manassas National Battlefield Park.

"'We're done,' said Robert Kelly, a spokesman for Hazel/Peterson Cos. *98* 'My understanding is we're supposed to leave the property in an orderly fashion . . . and we'll be doing that.'"

Harris noted that Hazel would make a fortune on the taking. The federal *99* government ultimately paid $81 million for the William Center property. Hazel had bought it for $11 million two years before.

But it was a wonder nonetheless, and the next morning Annie Snyder *100* led 50 of her resistance fighters into the promised land. They marched for the first time onto Stuart's Hill, the land on which the frenzied workings of the machines had just been stilled. Soon, signs around the perimeter of the once but not now future William Center were posted by park rangers. They encircled three model homes, a stretch of four-lane divided road, water and sewer work, and bulldozed land throughout most of the eastern section of the 542-acre place. The sledgehammers drove the message home. "U.S. Property," the signs read.

In the summer of 1991, the safest thing that can be said about Til Hazel is that he is no Donald Trump. In the face of an economic downturn, a developer can do one of two things: He can believe his press releases and think he's immortal—an almost sure-fire way to ensure that he won't see tomorrow—or he can fire his press spokesman and batten down the hatches. As early as 1988, Hazel/Peterson started doing the latter, winding down speculative office construction, wooing tenants well before their leases were up, concentrating on managing existing assets. In 1990, that half of the company's senior management in charge of office development was let go, for the sensible reason that there was not going to be any new development by much of anybody any time soon.   *101*

By 1991, Hazel said, all the $81 million from the federal government had already been spent. A lot of it went to solidifying positions in previous deals, lowering the costs of carrying property through the downturn. But even if he was relatively secure himself, it was frustrating to watch friends and colleagues suffer—sometimes teetering on the edge of collapse—and be asked to help, and have to grapple with the limits of what he could do. "It's not a fun time," he said ruefully.   *102*

Still, it never occurred to Hazel that he should thank Annie Snyder for the cash windfall she had made possible. To him that would have been an utterly repulsive idea.   *103*

As for the stalwarts of the Save the Battlefield Coalition: Back in those first dark months of the winter of 1988, they had promised one another that if they ever won this battle, on the first Saturday afterward, they would have a ceremony of thanksgiving. If the bulldozers were ever stilled, to thank the Lord for the miracle—which at times had seemed as improbable as the parting of the Red Sea—they would gather one more time to honor the spirit of the place.   *104*

That Saturday, November 19, dawned foul. As they gathered near the site of one of the houses that had been used as a field hospital during the war, the air was dank and chill. Rain fell in a steady drizzle.   *105*

But that did not dampen the spirits of the coalition. They had survived 104-degree heat the previous July when they had held a massive rally at the battlefield. It had featured a March of the Ghosts, in which specters with astonishing resemblances to Abraham Lincoln, Robert E. Lee, James Longstreet, Stonewall Jackson and J.E.B. Stuart had prowled the land as drums rolled and bagpipes keened. A little rain and cold would not disturb them.   *106*

And, they joked, they finally had no tactical considerations. It was not as if they had to worry anymore about the television cameras shorting out. This was for the faithful.

That is why, as the crowd of 140 began their hymns and their prayers, they wondered exactly how it happened: When the engine roar came from the north, they murmured to each other, Where in the name of God will this all end?   *107*

If they'd thought the war was over, they were wrong.   *108*

The roar came from a small, single-engine Cessna. It passed above them again and again, across the lowering skies, its low-altitude buzz a never-ending pain. It would not go away. It seemed it would always be there. As indeed it would resonate into the future.   *109*

The Cessna pulled a banner behind its tail, through the cold mists, over the battlefield of centuries. Once again it proclaimed defiance. Endless defiance. It promised that the war was not over among the Americans. The battle would be fought again that had been fought this year, for it was the same battle we've been fighting since we landed on these shores.   *110*

It comes down to who we are, how we got that way, where we're headed and what we value. Whether we will ever resolve the difference between what we can do, and what we should. Whether the land belongs to us, or we belong to the land.   *111*

Behind the tail of the little buzzing plane was this reminder: THE TAK-ING OF PRIVATE LAND IS UNAMERICAN.   *112*

Topics for Discussion and Writing

1. In another article about Til Hazel (the *Washington Post Magazine,* July 21, 1991), Garreau reported that "Hazel saw (the land) as no different from coal or oil; it was a natural resource. That is why the most fervent swear word in his vocabulary was 'waste'. . . . When he looked out over the land, he saw it as starkly vacant until the brilliance of the human mind was brought to it, to find its most ingenious use." How do you define the word *waste* as it pertains to land? Write a dialogue between Til Hazel and Aldo Leopold, whose *Sand County Almanac* is excerpted in this chapter. Clearly state the differing points of view as each argues how a piece of land should be treated.

2. This selection is very different from the others in this chapter, not only in the values of the person featured in the essay, but also in that the writer does not write about himself or speak in the first person. Does Garreau's viewpoint come through in his writing? What would you judge this author's value system to be?

3. In the article cited in question 1, Garreau wrote, "MIT cultural historian Leo Marx, author of *The Machine in the Garden,* points out that nowhere in the American national character is there as deep a divide as that between

our reverence for 'unspoiled' nature and our enduring devotion to 'progress.'" Write about this statement in terms of your own community, and share your writing with your class.

4. How did Garreau describe Annie Snyder? How is she different from Hazel? How is she like him? Write a dialogue between these two personalities, highlighting their differing viewpoints.

STEPHEN GETLEIN

"Three Generations of Environmental Concern"

> *"She doesn't see a dramatic swing over to environmental protection by the public, but rather a slow shift. 'You won't see dramatic changes in values. I used to feel, during the war on poverty, for example, we could help everyone. We can't help everyone; we're going to lose people in the cracks.'"*
>
> *Stephen Getlein, a biology major, wrote this report for an anthropology course called "Culture and Ecology." About his writing process for the essay, he wrote:*

> *I often write introductions very quickly, assuming that the real first paragraph may be the second, third, or fourth paragraph for the first draft. The eventual first paragraph, "Aldo Leopold's* Sand County Almanac. . . ," *was in fact the third paragraph of my first attempt. Writing through beginnings just to get started seems to work well for me, once my attachment to the first few sentences weakens enough that they can be discarded.*
>
> *. . . Reading aloud exposes overly long sentences, awkward phrases, and abrupt endings. It also pops up pontificating for the hot air it is. By this time, I was on a fourth draft. I let it sit for a few days before polishing and buffing, which involved only minor changes.*
>
> *The audience for this paper was, beyond the class instructor, several people who were interested in environmental work, but who were unsure how to get started. I wanted them to realize other people had feelings of despair and that it was possible to work toward a goal even when you're personally unsure about whether that goal will be reached.*

Before and as You Read

1. One of the persons interviewed in the following essay quotes Aldo Leopold (see the excerpt of his work earlier in this chapter): "Much of the damage to the land is invisible to the layman." Write about the implications you see in that statement. Write about an environmental problem that was "invisible" to you before it was brought to your attention by environmental science. Why are many such problems invisible? Who benefits when these problems remain invisible?

2. Find out who in your locality is responsible for determining the environmental impact of proposed construction. Are public hearings held at which citizens can raise environmental objections to building projects? Write a journal entry about the procedures you discover, about the attitudes you encounter in your questioning, and about the availability of information to the public about citizens' roles in approving construction.

3. As you read "Three Generations of Environmental Concern," observe how Stephen Getlein uses his three subjects to achieve the objective he sets forth

in his comments, printed above, about his essay. Observe the usefulness of employing three subjects who represent different age groups. Note how he establishes each of his subjects as a reliable authority.

ALDO LEOPOLD'S *Sand County Almanac* is a powerful, succinct 1 statement of where we have to go as a society to survive. As he put it, "The land ethic simply enlarges the boundaries of the community to include soils, waters, plants, and animals, or collectively, the land." Enlarging that boundary has proven difficult in a place like Fairfax County, which is expected to grow from a 1960 population of 249,000 to an estimated population of almost a million in the year 2000.

There wasn't room for everything. As people settled on the county's 2 dairy farms and crossroads turned into shopping malls, the county's forests declined. Fairfax grew from 554,500 people in 1976 to almost 684,000 in 1986, a gain of 23.3 percent. The county lost about 24,000 acres of forest during the same time, a fifth of its woods.

An older, slower Fairfax County was lost with those woods. Many of 3 the people who watched them go gave up. Some didn't, and they've been joined by other people who refuse to accept a future of endless sprawl and ever-larger but still-clogged roads and a county whose values rest on the bottom line. This paper is about three of those people, three people from three different generations. These three Fairfax County residents are tied to the larger environmental problems facing society by those problems' manifestation at Huntley Meadows Park in southern Fairfax County.

Huntley Meadows Park holds more than 1,200 acres of upland woods 4 and meadows, forested wetlands, brush, streams and ponds. For 15 years, Fairfax County citizens and their elected and appointed officials have argued over the park: about how preventable development impacts are; and about the need for a road that would have cut across the park, destroying its esthetic wholeness and possibly disrupting the hydrology that kept it a wetland. Huntley was a workshop in real-world environmental education for the 600-plus members of Citizens Allied to Save Huntley (CASH), and the focal point for the three people who found environmentalism on the boardwalks, paths, and meadows of Huntley.

Charles Lepple

Charles Lepple is 12 years old. He's a seventh-grader at Carl Sandburg 5 Intermediate School, where he's studying "speech arts," English, United States history, math and science ("It's supposed to be environmental science, but it's more ecology," Lepple complained.) Charles is what used to be called a whiz kid; he won the last Math Meet he went to at Fairfax County's

Thomas Jefferson High School for Science and Technology. Strongly backed by parents with advanced degrees, he'll probably flourish in a society hungry for competence.

Charles, however, has reservations and worries about the society he's a few years from entering fully as a wage-earner, taxpayer and citizen. He's afraid environmental degradation will sneak up on us, without the kind of catastrophes that get people's attention: "Unless something really drastic happens, there will probably be a slow decline: a little land taken away here, a little there. At Huntley, for example, runoff from development all around it has hurt it. Safeguards don't necessarily work. One company went bankrupt and couldn't pay for the erosion protection they'd promised to do." He hasn't noticed "obvious" pollution at the park, but has noticed that water in the park's central wetland rises faster and farther after a rain.

Charles started working at Huntley a few years ago. He used to work the desk with his mother. Now he runs the mailing list on the park's computer. He expects to volunteer at Huntley as long as he lives in the area and also expects to be involved in environmental defense: "As long as there's development in this area there will probably be reasons to fight for something." The pleasures of volunteering and the idea of endless conflict may turn into a career for Charles. He'd like to "have a job where I had some power over what happened: runoff, pollution emissions or something like that."

Charles sees the "grown-up" world he's on the edge of entering as a place where hope duels with despair, where popular concern about the environment still needs to be converted into action: "With everyone so informed about environmental problems, there's hope for parks like Huntley. For things like global warming, it could be just sort of a cycle. Some problems can't be solved. Others like holes in the ozone layer, you might be able to solve by campaigns convincing people that restrictions on ozone-depleting chemicals are not just more regulations to get around, but something that could help them.

"There are other things, like stream pollution. There's just so much development around here, but things could be cleaned up a lot more if they just realized what impact things had. It's one thing to pass a law to tell people not to do something, but if people don't understand why they shouldn't do something, then you can't have an impact."

Does Charles try to live in keeping with his ideals? "I try not to throw things away and not buy things I don't need, but it's kind of hard. If things are complicated or people have to go out of their way and make big changes, it's going to be hard."

Technical quick fixes, like colonizing the oceans or space, don't have too much appeal for Charles, who understands how much effort would be needed and the possible adverse effects. "It may get to a point where people leave this area. In the 1800s, people went West because of overcrowding; I don't know if people should go out to the oceans and maybe ruin the oceans. The universe doesn't have air or water or earth. It's a lot of effort to fuse hydrogen to get water. People are still going to have to depend on the earth for some things. It would more likely be little space colonies."

So how does a population rapidly exhausting its resources get back in balance? The answer isn't one you'd expect from a kid whose quick grin still flashes through braces: "In the future, there might just be a population cutback somehow, since nature does work like that. For example, the Black Death. It could be disease or it could be the environment." 12

Susan Becker

Susan Becker, 39, is a scientist. She has a B.A. and M.S. in geology, and before she got distracted by computers, she earned a living traveling the East Coast, tapping and mapping igneous outcroppings, following strikes and dips down into the past, looking into hard rock and ridgelines for clues to the ground we stand on today. She and her economist husband have one child, with another on the way. 13

President of Friends of Huntley Meadows, she's a new Fairfax Audubon Society board member, and wonders how she'll balance the baby's demands with the computer consulting she loves, her family and the environmental activism that has allowed her organizational and speaking abilities to flower. She also wonders where we're going as a society, whether we could be near the end of a long road of human progress. 14

The philosophical foundation of her environmentalism is surprisingly simple for a woman comfortable with the mind-wrenching theories of modern geology: "I'm not a Christian, but if there is spirituality in the world, it's in nature. I'm also motivated by a sense of justice. Mankind is destroying the natural order. 15

"Why do I do what I do? Maybe the last spring meeting at Huntley is part of the picture. We went out on a bird walk, and I saw the spring migrants. We saw a red-headed woodpecker in its nest hole. There's a beauty in the natural order. The natural environment was there first, it's self-sustaining, and will be there after us, I hope. Nature works: it's a tremendously complicated system, but it works. 16

"If we continue, life as we know it for people will end, and I could see it ending in my daughter's generation. I could see people not going outside because of ozone depletion. We could be looking at rapidly rising sea levels. Bush is dragging his feet on greenhouse emissions: you have to act globally sometimes; slogans aren't always enough." 17

Sue's work as president of Friends of Huntley Meadows involves backing up the park staff and organizing volunteers. She also set up a park species data base. She doesn't chain herself to trees or pour sugar in bulldozer fuel tanks, and she worries about people who do: "It's important that ecologists not alienate people. We're going to be asking people to make major changes over the next 20 years. If we piss people off like Greenpeace does, they won't listen." 18

What future does she see, for herself and for the country? "In some ways   *19*
I'd like to be like [George Mason University biology professor] Fran Heliotis,
maybe merge avocation with vocation. The next 10 years are a critical juncture. We're either going to stay with one-car, one-driver, huge parking lots—
or someone will be brave enough to commit real money to mass transit and
brave enough to change zoning to cluster zoning, like Reston.

"Can you change culture? It's going to take a generation or more. The   *20*
changes that need to be made are going to hurt people, but it's always been
like that. We'll lose jobs, but we need to, a lot of those jobs are destroying
what we have."

Asked about her place in the natural order, Sue's answer mixes the hu-   *21*
mility of the devout with the scientist's cybernetic ideal: "I'm a speck, a piece
of dust in the universe. We owe it to the other living creatures to get back in
balance. The optimal good is a perfectly functioning system.

"Geology gives me a long-term perspective. Things have gotten very   *22*
bad in a hurry. It's going to come down to some kind of major crisis, probably
groundwater contamination or a general increase in cancer. Until there's a real
scare in the population I don't think things will change. I like to think people
like us and younger are oriented more toward the environment. My parents,
the big event in their life was World War II. They just don't think the environment is important."

Norma Hoffman

Norma Hoffman is closing in on 70, but she's doing it with the grace of   *23*
the dancer she was a long, long time ago back in Boston. She moved to
Washington in 1945, and worked at two jobs that were perfect preparation for
her fight for Huntley Meadows Park. She ran the office at the Potomac Appalachian Trail Club (PATC) and later worked for the Alexandria Democratic
Committee. Her husband is a semi-retired journalist and her only child, a
daughter, is also a journalist.

Her first environmental mentor was PATC President Benton MacKaye.   *24*
MacKaye taught her the value of a simple goal that can seize and hold people's
imagination. MacKaye's was the Appalachian Trail, a footpath from Maine to
Georgia that he worked for all his life. Norma's was the protection of Huntley
Meadows Park, and she's fought roads, developments, shopping centers, new-
car malls, and everything else that threatened her park.

Aldo Leopold was a more indirect inspiration. She digested his writings   *25*
and still returns to them when things look bleak: "Whenever I get discouraged, I refer to something from Aldo Leopold: 'Education is the learning to
see one thing by going blind to another. One thing we've all lost is the ability
to see the value of marshes. One of the penalties of ecological education is
that one lives alone in a world of wounds. Much of the damage to the land
is invisible to the layman. An ecologist must either harden his shell and make
believe that the consequences of science are none of his business or he must

be the doctor who sees the marks of death in a community that believes itself well and does not want to be told otherwise.'" Norma chose to take up the healing arts.

Her Boston background left her no illusions that keeping the Lockheed Connector, a proposed six-lane highway, out of Huntley would be a short fight: "I grew up hearing again and again, you can't fight city hall. Except for the four people I worked with in the beginning, no one thought we could stop the road." 26

She's "more encouraged now. There's a new land ethic and a new sense of responsibility." Can you have a land ethic in a county where the land may be worth more than the homes that sit on it? "There has to be a marriage of economy and ecology. Public officials have always put the balance on the side of economy." 27

Environmental education is often cited as the way out of our environmental ills. Skeptics, however, say that environmental education will take at least a generation to work, and so carefully avoids controversy that it leaves students with little to do other than take their empty pop bottles to a recycling center. Norma has worked at Fairfax County Schools for 30 years. Is education the answer? "Workshops are vital: teaching children about nature is the answer. They won't all get it, but some will." 28

She doesn't see a dramatic swing over to environmental protection by the public, but rather a slow shift. "You won't see dramatic changes in values. I used to feel, during the war on poverty, for example, we could help everyone. We can't help everyone; we're going to lose people in the cracks." 29

Some environmentalists assume that conflict is outmoded, that the good guys have won. Norma Hoffman, who fought almost alone for so many years, agrees, with reservations. "We have their respect now. There was a brick wall that they put up: They played extremely hard ball. If there's evidence of respect for our opinions, we can work with them. What I see is a balance achieved between growth and environmental needs. Environmental groups have achieved a voting-bloc status, on the local, state, and federal levels. Environmental priorities are moving to the top, but they're not there yet." 30

When—if—the fights over Huntley ever end, what would Norma do in peacetime? "One of my personal secret ambitions has been to teach. I take enormous pride in inspiring even one youngster to work for environmental goals." 31

Late last year, the National Park Service played its hole card on Huntley Meadows Park. If Fairfax County tried to build a road across the park, the Park Service would exercise its option as landowner (it still holds the deed to the park, although Fairfax County operates it), and take the park back. Fairfax County jumped the gun on the Park Service's press release, with a bland announcement that because of its zealous environmental consciousness, it was abandoning its 15-year attempt to pave a big piece of the park. Norma's victory announcement was typically low-key and self-effacing, thanking her 32 many helpers and supporters and ending with a quote from Margaret Mead: "Never doubt that a small group of thoughtful, committed citizens can change the world. Indeed, it's the only thing that ever has."

Topics for Discussion and Writing

1. This essay contains two criticisms of "environmental education" in public schools. Find these. What are the shortcomings identified? Analyze why such education would likely be superficial. Write about what you have learned in school about the environment. Did you find it valuable? Did it change your views or behavior in any way? Based on what you have since learned, how would you improve the way that environmental issues are taught in schools? Discuss your ideas in class.

2. Identify an environmental issue that has aroused controversy in your locale. Study press reports. Who are the principal spokespersons? What groups do they represent? How are these persons spoken about in the press and by their opponents? Which arguments are most compelling to you? Why? What would it take to change your view?

3. Focus on 12-year-old Charles Lepple. How does Getlein account for this young person's environmental consciousness? As an observer of the influences on young people today, assess the likelihood of a young person's sharing Lepple's views. Describe in detail the influences on young people's attitudes to such concepts as "wetlands" and "deforestation."

4. In what ways do the three subjects reinforce your views of environmental activists? In what ways do they differ from any prior generalizations you might have made?

5. Identify a group of people, like CASH, dedicated to an environmental objective. Interview several of them, much as Stephen Getlein did. Brainstorm a list of questions that will allow you to probe their motives and their knowledge about the issues they confront. Write an analysis, based on what your questions help you discover, of the group's work and its chances for success.

For Further Thought

1. Reread the description of your environment that you wrote before reading these selections. Rewrite this description to reflect ideas and perspectives you have acquired from the readings. If possible, compare your rewritten description with those of others.

2. Review the list of technologies you wrote earlier. Are there other technologies of which the readings have made you aware? If so, write an essay in

which you describe the change that has occurred in your thinking. Cite in your essay passages from the readings that have influenced you.

3. Choose any two of the authors represented in this chapter. Imagine each of these persons writing about some aspect of the environment in which you live; imagine each writing in the same style and form that he or she used in the work included in this chapter. Try writing these two pieces. After making these attempts, write briefly about the features of style you've tried to capture and how successful you feel you were.

CHAPTER FOUR

Seeking Justice through Political Action

In chapter 3 we stated the belief that the most compelling environmental factor is not earthquakes, hurricanes, floods, or draughts, but humanity. Our action upon the environment—or our inaction—may well be its undoing.

The defect of character that created the climate for all of humanity's ills, including slavery, greed, cruelty, violence, and poverty, is undoubtedly present in us all. But it is also true that individual human beings create justice. And by this creation we help to save ourselves. But where does one begin?

This section provides some answers to that question. The people represented here march to the proverbial different drummer. Few may have a calling as distinct as the one that Mother Teresa relates to us. But all, be they lawyer, social advocate, or ordinary citizen, have shared the vision that citizenship in the human race is accompanied by responsibility.

Thinking about the Issues

1. Define what is meant by the phrase "person of vision." What attributes or characteristics would such a person possess? Think of a relative, friend, teacher, or acquaintance whom you believe fits your definition. Write a short personality sketch of this person to share with your class.

2. Interview the person you sketched in response to question 1. Is she or he aware of your admiration? How does this person describe him or herself? Ask the person to tell you about an event from the past that influenced his or her vision of life.

3. Write about a time when you got involved in a project or a cause. Why did you choose to become involved? Will you continue to volunteer in the future? Why do you suppose that more people do not get involved in their communities?

4. It is easy to see how the activist or the volunteer creates a better world by virtue of concern, time, and energy given. But what personal benefits does that activist or volunteer gain? Discuss this question with your class. Is giving of oneself mainly a one-way street? Try to come up with as many benefits for those who give as you can find for those who receive.

MOTHER TERESA
from *My Life for the Poor*

> *"Some time ago, in Bombay, our sisters picked up a man from the street. In lifting him up, the whole of his back remained on the street."*
>
> *Mother Teresa, born in Albania on August 27, 1910, is well known for her work in India with the homeless and dying. She had taught in a Catholic girls' high school in Calcutta for 20 years when she felt a calling from God to change her vocation. She founded the Missionaries of Charity in 1948 and continues to work with those forgotten by society. She won a Nobel Prize in 1979.*
>
> *The following excerpt is from Mother Teresa's autobiography,* My Life for the Poor, *edited by José Luis Gonzales-Balado and Janet N. Playfoot. The book is a transcription of interviews with Mother Teresa about her life with the Missionaries of Charity. This selection focuses on the founding of the order and its philosophy.*

Before and as You Read

1. The Indian culture operates under a caste system. Briefly describe how each social group is determined. With whom do you think the Missionaries of Charity primarily work?
2. Notice the simplicity of this selection. Rather than a written account of Mother Teresa's life, you will be reading a verbal recollection written down by close friends. Why do you suppose it takes this form?
3. As you read, picture the place where Mother Teresa works and lives. How does she use language to describe her work? List some of the phrases that make her story come to life for you.
4. Many have called Mother Teresa a saint. What are your feelings about such a claim? Do you believe in such people? If so, could they be among us, like Mother Teresa? Discuss your ideas in class.

IN 1948, twenty years after I came to India, I actually decided upon this close contact with the poorest of the poor. It was for me a special vocation to give all to belong to Jesus. . . .   1

In quiet, intimate prayer with our Lord, I heard distinctly, a call within a call.   2

The message was quite clear: I was to leave the convent and help the poor whilst living among them. It was an order. I knew where I belonged, but I did not know how to get there.   3

I felt intensely that Jesus wanted me to serve him among the poorest of the poor, the uncared for, the slum dwellers, the abandoned, the homeless.   4

Jesus invited me to serve him and follow him in actual poverty, to practice a kind of life that would make me similar to the needy in whom he was present, suffered and loved. . . .

Soon after leaving Loreto, I was on the street, with no shelter, no company, no helper, no money, no employment, no promise, no guarantee, no security.   5

Then I prayed, "My God, you, only you. I trust in your call, your inspiration. You will not let me down."   6

I needed a roof to shelter the abandoned, so I started to search.   7

I walked and walked all the time, until I couldn't walk any more.   8

Then, I understood better the exhaustion of the really poor, always in search of a little food, of medicines, of everything.   9

The memory of the material security that I enjoyed in the convent of Loreto came then to me as a temptation and I prayed like this: 10

"O God, through free choice and through your love, I want to stay here and do your will. No, I cannot go back. My community are the poor. Their security is mine. Their health is my health. My home is the home of the poor: not just of the poor, but of those who are the poorest of the poor. Of those to whom one tries not to get too close for fear of catching something, for fear of the dirt, or because they are covered in germs and disease. Of those that do not go to pray because they can't leave their houses naked. Of those that no longer eat because they haven't the strength. Of those that fall in the streets, knowing that they are going to die, while the living walk by their sides ignoring them. Of those who no longer cry, because they have no tears left. Of the untouchables."   11

I was sure that the Lord wanted me to be where I was.   12

I was sure he would offer me a solution.   13

In March 1949, on the feast of St. Joseph, there was a knock at my door.   14

I opened it and stood motionless. My heart beat faster as I looked at the frail figure facing me and heard her say, "Mother, I have come to join you." 15

"It will be a hard life. Are you prepared for it?" I asked the girl.   16

"I know it will be hard; I am prepared for it," said the girl. And she stepped in.   17

Then I turned to our Lord, and thanked him: "Dear Jesus, how good you are. So you are sending them! You keep the promise you made me. Lord Jesus, thank you for your goodness."   18

The first sisters to join were students that I had taught in Loreto.   19

One by one, I saw young girls arrive after 1949.   20

They were my students. They wanted to give everything to God, and they were in a hurry to do it.   21

They took off their expensive saris with great satisfaction in order to put on our humble cotton ones.   22

They came fully aware of the difficulties.   23

When a girl who belongs to a very old caste comes to place herself at   24 the service of the outcasts, we are talking about a revolution, the biggest one, the hardest of all: the revolution of love! . . .

We have high-, middle- and ordinary-class girls, and that's the most *25* beautiful thing about these young girls, so fully dedicated and determined to give their all to Christ. They are all very anxious to live a life of poverty. (For us, this is very important: *if we really want to know the poor, we must know what poverty is. It is why in our society, poverty is our freedom and our strength.*)

The Missionaries of Charity do firmly believe that they are touching *26* the body of Christ in his distressing disguise whenever they are helping and touching the poor.

We cannot do this with a long face. *27*

We cannot do it just anyhow, because it is to Jesus that we are doing it. *28*

The whole of our society is engaged in doing just that: feeding the *29* hungry Christ, clothing the naked Christ, taking care of the sick Christ, and giving a home to the homeless Christ.

It is very beautiful to see our young people so fully devoted, so full of *30* love for God's poor!

The generous surrender of our young sisters is a most wonderful gift of *31* God to our society and to the whole church.

It is not the excitement of the work that is drawing them. It is some- *32* thing much deeper and more wonderful.

Many of our sisters come from well-to-do families. To see them just *33* leave their life behind is something wonderful.

To be able to understand the poor, to be able to understand the poverty *34* of Christ, we choose to be poor. Many times we just choose not to have things that we could easily have, but we freely choose not to have them.

We joyfully accept to spend 24 hours with the kind of people with *35* whom sometimes we cannot even converse properly.

They are the poorest of the poor, covered with dirt and with maggots. *36*

They are the lepers, the abandoned destitute, the homeless, the sick, the *37* dying.

It is wonderful to see the joy and the greatness of love in these young *38* sisters.

It is a living miracle that impresses hundreds of people, even non- *39* Christians, who come close to them.

All our sisters are full of joy. They are the most striking example of *40* living faith with joy.

We try to teach them, from the very beginning, to pray while working, *41* doing it for Jesus and doing it to Jesus.

This brings a tremendous closeness with him. *42*

This helps us to be in love with Jesus and to find him in the distressing *43* disguise of the poorest of the poor as we find him in the appearance of bread in the Eucharist.

A young girl wishing to join our society must meet the four conditions *44* that are required to be a Missionary of Charity. She must be healthy of mind and body. She must have ability to learn. She must have plenty of common sense and a cheerful disposition.

If she meets these four conditions, then she comes and sees the work (like in the gospel, when our Lord said, "Come and see"). 45

She goes to one of our houses and comes into close contact with the poor, with the people, with the sisters. She works with them, prays with them, stays with them. 46

Then, she decides if this is what God wants from her. 47

If she joins, then she spends six months as an aspirant, six months as a postulant and two years as a novice. 48

After this, there are six years of temporary vows. Then, one year before final vows, she comes back again to the noviciate to deepen her spiritual life, because we are not social workers: we are trying to live a contemplative life by spreading the love and compassion of Jesus in the world by doing the work of salvation. 49

As a rule, the age of seventeen is the youngest we accept girls applying to join our society. 50

As I said before, we have six months for a girl to "come and see." (We call it this, but it is what used to be called aspirancy.) 51

We try to put the gospel's words into life. 52

Then we have six months of postulancy and two years of noviciate. And then, six years of temporary vows. 53

One year before temporary vows end, the girls come back to the noviciate for a third year with more intense spiritual life and deeper oneness with Christ. Before they come for the tertianship, as we call it, they go home for a fortnight to decide, "Is this what I want to have for life?" 54

They go back to their parents for a fortnight. Then they decide if they really want to take the final vows. 55

We have very few girls who leave: only those girls who don't meet the four conditions listed above. (Some of them become ill before they are professed.) 56

They don't leave because our life is hard. Not at all. Up to now, only a few have stayed back, and most of them for family reasons. Otherwise, God has been very good to us. 57

Ours is a mission of love. 58

We are there to bring Christ to the people and to bring the people to Christ. 59

A Missionary of Charity is a person who is sent. Being Missionaries of Charity, we are sent to bring God's love, to prove God's love: that God loves the world, that God loves the poor. He shows his love through us for them. . . . 60

It is an exchange between God and us. God uses us to show his love for the poor through our dedication and consecration to him. 61

We use his love to prove to the people our love for God in ac- 62
tion through our service to the poorest of the poor—be they the lepers
or the dying, the crippled, the unloved, or the uncared for. Whoever they
may be, for us they are Christ in the distressing disguise of the poorest of
the poor.

I remember one of our sisters who had just come from the university. 63
She came from a well-to-do family.

As we have in our rules, the very next day after the girls have joined the 64
society, they go to the Home for the Dying.

Before they went, I told them, "You saw the priest during Mass: with 65
what love, with what delicate care he touched the body of Christ! Make sure
you do the same thing when you go to the Home, for Jesus is there in the
distressing disguise."

And they went. 66

After three hours, they came back and one of them, the girl who had 67
come from the university, who had seen so much, so many things, came to
my room with such a beautiful smile on her face. She said, "For three hours I
have been touching the body of Christ."

And I said, "What did you do, what happened?" 68

She said, "They brought a man from the street, covered with maggots. 69
And I knew, though I found it very difficult, I knew that I was touching the
body of Christ."

Some time ago, in Bombay, our sisters picked up a man from the street. 70
In lifting him up, the whole of his back remained on the street.

They brought him home: cleaned him, washed him, but the man never 71
said a word.

After a few hours, after giving him a bath, there was nothing you could 72
see, apart from all the bones on his back.

Then I asked the sisters, "What did you feel when you were touch- 73
ing him?"

One of the sisters answered my question in the name of the others, "I 74
have never felt the presence of Christ so real, Mother, as when I was touching him."

Topics for Discussion and Writing

1. The Catholic Church today is having increasing difficulty attracting men
   and women to work as priests and nuns. Yet the Missionaries of Charity
   order seems to flourish with those who want to serve. Speculate why this
   might be so. What kind of leadership does Mother Teresa appear to offer
   those who work with her?

2. Why was it necessary, in Mother Teresa's view, to give up all earthly comforts to serve the poor? Why did she choose, for example, not to live with
   even the simplest amenities? Could such comforts change the care that she
   and her coworkers give? If so, in what way?

3. When Mother Teresa says, "I heard distinctly a call within a call," what do you suppose she means?
4. This selection is structurally different from other pieces you've read because of the manner by which it was obtained. Point out ways that the spoken narrative here differs from the written narratives elsewhere in this text. Give specific examples.

WALT HARRINGTON

"The Mystery of Goodness—What Makes Bryan Stevenson Different from the Rest of Us?"

"You know a college friend of Bryan's once asked me quite seriously, '[Mrs. Stevenson] could Bryan be an angel?'"

Walt Harrington, a journalist for more than 20 years, has described himself as a "specialist in in-depth human profiles," of which "The Mystery of Goodness" is a superb example. A staff writer for the Washington Post Magazine, *Harrington is also the author of* Crossings: A White Man's Journey into Black America *(1993).*

"The Mystery of Goodness" originally appeared in the Washington Post Magazine, *January 6, 1991.*

Before and as You Read

1. How would you define *goodness*? In your journal detail how you would rate yourself with regard to your definition. In what ways do you hope to improve?
2. Lawyers have been stereotyped for centuries and are often the butt of jokes and cartoons. Share with your class any personal or secondhand experience you've had with lawyers. Do you believe that the profession is a victim of bad press?
3. The mood or prevalent atmosphere created by an author establishes the tone of a piece. What is the tone of this selection? What is Harrington trying to make you feel? Does he succeed? How well does Harrington understand his subject? Is thorough understanding of a subject a prerequisite for a writer? Explain your answer.
4. Stevenson confounds his peers by giving up a lifestyle that should "rightfully" be his. But he also vexes the majority of society by defending the forgotten. As you read, discover what you think moves this man. Do you believe that he could be in personal danger doing this work?

On the threshing-floor, in the center of the crying, singing saints, John lay astonished beneath the power of the Lord.
　　　　　—*From* Go Tell It on The Mountain *by James Baldwin*

I AM NOT an expert on religion, far from it. But somewhere along the   *1*
way, I learned that in ancient Jewish legend there is told the story of
the *lamedvovniks,* the 36 Righteous Men who were sent by God to live and

work among us, always poor, unnoticed and without glory, unaware of their own perfection. If a Righteous Man was ever discovered, various versions of the legend went, he would deny his identity, disappear and reappear, unknown and unknowing, in a distant place. I do not believe in *lamedvovniks*. I do not even believe in God. But over the years, I've sometimes puzzled at the *idea* of these Righteous Men living secretly among us, been reminded that what it means to be truly good was as mysterious to those who lived a thousand years ago as it is to us, with all our modern sophistication.

Lately, after meeting Bryan Stevenson, I've found myself puzzling over these questions once again. But then, that often happens to people after they meet Bryan Stevenson.

This morning, Bryan—31, a lawyer and a black man—is on the road out of Montgomery, Ala., where he lives, headed for Phenix City, a tiny Alabama town where Bryan's black client George Daniel has been locked in the Russell County jail awaiting his execution for murdering a white policeman. Just yesterday, a federal court overturned his conviction and ordered that he be given a new trial.

That is what Bryan Stevenson does. He files appeals. He is one of those much-maligned lawyers who supposedly clog the courts with frivolous petitions meant only to postpone deserving men's dates with the electric chair, gas chamber or needle. He is one of the reasons Chief Justice William H. Rehnquist and countless politicians, including President Bush, have called for limits on the number of court reviews for those sentenced to death. He is one of the reasons that, with nearly 2,400 people on death row, only 143 have been executed since the Supreme Court declared the death penalty constitutional in 1976. Today, about 75 percent of Americans favor capital punishment, compared with 42 percent in 1966. For the first time, even a majority of blacks favor capital punishment. So far, this new public thirst for final vengeance has gone largely unquenched.

Bryan Stevenson is one of the reasons.

At the Russell County jail, Bryan is ushered into a small room where George Daniel is waiting. As Bryan tells him that he'll have a new trial— which might literally save George's life—the thin, 34-year-old man smiles blankly, squeezes his nose tightly, rocks his body gently and bounces his legs to some rapid, internal rhythm. He wears a white jail uniform that is filthy at the crotch. The last time Bryan visited George, his cell was dirty with his own urine. Court records show that at least once during his incarceration George Daniel ate his own feces and that he is mildly retarded. "I need cigarettes," he says finally. Bryan promises to get cigarettes, and George is led away. As Bryan leaves, a guard stops him at the jailhouse gate and says of George Daniel, "I think he's crazy. I really do. That's just my opinion. We have to make him take a shower and change clothes. I think he's crazy. Some people are playin'. I don't think he is."

Outside, past the electric door and the tall wire fence, Bryan says, "George is one of the men America believes is so evil he must be strapped into an electric chair and killed." He doesn't say this harshly or self-righteously.

He says it gently, with eerie understatement. "You know, people always ask me how I can defend these 'animals.' I never understand how they can ask that. The criminal justice system is so corrupt, so racist. I wouldn't want George Daniel out fending for himself. He can't. He's ill. But a civilized society does not execute people like him. Rehnquist can restrict legal options for the convicted, because he can't imagine himself or anyone he loves ever being in George Daniel's situation. But how would Rehnquist feel if his son were in George's place?

"In the end, we are too frail to make these decisions." 8

I met Bryan Stevenson by chance while traveling through the South, 9 which boasts more than half of America's death-row inmates and about 85 percent of its executions since 1977. Right off, Bryan fascinated me. A graduate of Harvard's law school and John F. Kennedy School of Government, he's the director of the Alabama Capital Representation Resource Center, which is involved in some way with most of the 119 death-row inmates in Alabama. He was offered $50,000 to $60,000 a year to take the director's job, one of the center's board members told me, but Bryan said it was too much money. He settled on $18,000—now up to $24,000. In corporate law, he could make five to ten times that.

Bryan worked seven days a week, still does, often from 8:30 in the 10 morning to 11:30 at night. On Saturdays and Sundays, he knocks off early to do his laundry and maybe catch a movie. These days, he has little time to play his electric piano, compose music, play basketball or attend church, all of which he once did regularly. He hasn't had a vacation in years. Once a voracious reader, Bryan has read three books for pleasure in the last year. He sometimes worries that he doesn't laugh enough anymore.

Simply put, the man was hard to figure. A person didn't need to believe 11 Bryan's cause was noble, or even correct, to be touched and fascinated by his passion. All through the '80s, while most of his Harvard classmates got rich, he defended penniless murderers. His parents—working people from Milton, Del., near Rehobeth Beach—certainly didn't understand what their son was doing. "Take the money," Bryan's father said, more than once. With all his degrees, Bryan still drove a beat-up Honda Civic. His mother drove a jet-black BMW 325i. She couldn't figure her son either. What had made him so different—from his folks, his classmates, from America, really?

"I've asked him how he does this day in, day out," said William New- 12 man, a Massachusetts lawyer in Alabama to work with Bryan on a death-row appeal. "It's Bryan. It's who Bryan is. I'm telling you, Bryan is a prince. I bet you won't find one person who *doesn't* say that. I'm telling you, he's a saint. You can't say that, I know, but he is. That's exactly what he is." Another Massachusetts lawyer, Stewart Eisenberg, also in Alabama working on an appeal, said, "I am extraordinarily impressed with Bryan, but I'm curious about why a black Harvard Law School graduate who could write his own ticket spends his time earning next to nothing in Klan country on the back roads of the South."

His curiosity was my curiosity. Bryan Stevenson had rejected America's   *13*
reigning view of success and money, even justice. Perhaps understanding
him—America's reverse image—would tell us something about ourselves. So,
not yet having the legend of the *lamedvovniks* in mind, I set about trying to
discover what had made Bryan Stevenson so unlike the rest of us.

The road is home to Bryan. He spends more time driving than he does   *14*
in his apartment, which is furnished with a single folding director's chair, a
stool, two end tables, two small ceramic lamps, a television and a mattress and
box spring on the floor. At the office, the phone rings incessantly. Bryan
advises about 60 private lawyers who work on Alabama death-row cases pro
bono. He handles an additional 24 death-row cases himself. He supervises a
staff of five young lawyers who deal with about 30 cases. At the same time,
he must raise about $200,000 a year in private or foundation grants to go with
the $300,000 the federal government gives to the center. So it is only in his
car, now a gray Toyota Corolla, on the back roads of the South, that Bryan
has time to himself. He thinks, meditates, sometimes prays.

He is a thin, athletic man, just shy of six feet, a soccer star in high school   *15*
and college. He wears short, natural hair and a short beard. He wears unstylish
clothes and clunky sunglasses. He talks so softly that I must sometimes strain
to hear him. He has no discernible accent, strictly Middle American. In phone
conversations, prosecutors and defense attorneys who don't know him usually
assume he's white. Once, when Bryan suggested that a defense lawyer try to
plead his client down from a death sentence charge to life without parole, the
lawyer said, "Didn't I tell you? He's a nigger. Can't get a life plea for a nigger
in this county."

"I have always felt," Bryan says, as he drives toward Atlanta to visit   *16*
another death-row client, "that I could just as easily have ended up as one of
the men I am defending. I've had friends, cousins who fell into trouble. It
could have been me." Bryan says this quietly and deliberately, with little emotion. When he talks about the death penalty, he talks mostly facts and fairness.
He talks like a lawyer. Unless asked again and again, he rarely speaks about
himself, not even in the little asides through which most people reveal so
much. When I later read his words, I will see that he was, more or less, on a
soapbox, plunging point by point through his list of horrors about the death
penalty. But as I sit next to him, listening, a gentle intimacy in his manner
masks his single-minded agenda.

"I could go through the South's prisons and put together five death rows   *17*
of men not condemned whose crimes were far more vicious," Bryan says.
"The people who end up on death row are always poor, often black. And
almost always they had bad lawyers—real estate lawyers who never handled a
capital case and who had to be dragged screaming into the courtroom. In one
case, the judge actually sent the defense lawyer out to sleep off a drunk.

"Appointed lawyers, paid a maximum of $1,000 in Alabama and several   *18*
other Southern states, often do almost no work on their cases. It takes 800

hours to do a capital case. The Supreme Court declared it unconstitutional, but prosecutors in the South still keep blacks off capital juries by giving bogus reasons to strike them. In one rural Alabama county we found potential jurors labeled by the prosecutor as 'strong,' 'medium,' 'weak' and 'black.'

"Maybe it would help the congressmen who are so hot for the death   19
penalty if they thought of it this way: Imagine a senator is accused of stealing campaign funds and he is told that he gets a lawyer who's a drunk, who's being paid $1,000. Then the senator is told, if he's a Democrat, that only Republicans will sit on his jury—just as blacks are still tried by all-white juries. That's our system of justice today.

"Why do I do what I do? How can anyone do anything else?"

Bryan Stevenson was always different. In rural southern Delaware, he   20
was the only black child in his first-grade class in 1965. His mother, who migrated from Philadelphia through marriage to Bryan's father, had volunteered to put Bryan and his older brother in the white school even before formal integration was in place. She had only to look at the ramshackle schoolhouse black children attended to know where her kids were going. Years later, when Bryan was put in a slow-learner class with the black children who had arrived with integration, it was Bryan's mother who went to the school and raised hell until he was bumped to the top class.

Alice Stevenson was a firebrand by the yardstick of southern Delaware.   21
"Don't be a fool, don't be silly and grin," she'd tell her two sons and daughter. "You are here to make a mark. Otherwise you will be the mark." Appalled at the docility she perceived in southern Delaware's blacks, she admonished her children never to show false deference to whites. She insisted on perfect grammar, diction and pronunciation. And there was one absolute rule: "I never want to hear that you can't do something because you're black. You can do anything you want."

Bryan's father, Howard, a native of southern Delaware, gave less assertive   22
advice. The child of a prominent black mechanic in nearby Georgetown, he had grown up playing with the children of the town's prominent whites. He recalls few incidents in which he was mistreated by whites. In fact, because he dressed nattily—refusing to wear the jeans and overalls then worn by most of the blacks he knew—it was more often blacks who insulted him with the charge that he was highfalutin. Howard's advice to his children—born of his own unusual experience—was that most white people will treat you well if you treat them well.

Between the two of them, Howard and Alice Stevenson sent a singular   23
message: Whites were not to be feared.

Both had good jobs. She was an accounting clerk at the Air Force base   24
in Dover, and he was a lab technician at the General Foods plant. They bought three acres on County Route 319 and built a little ranch house that was elegant by local black standards of the day. Up the road, their neighbors lived with dirt floors and no running water. In a sense, the Stevensons were local black gentry.

Alice worried about her children being in school all day with whites,   *25*
worried they'd be picked on, worried they'd forget they were black. In high
school, where Bryan was popular, she worried about the white girls who kept
calling the house. "Please don't marry a white girl just to do it," Bryan's
mother pleaded. Today, she says, "I didn't order him, but I did beg." On the
other hand, Alice worried too about her children hanging around with too
many black kids who said "mens" for "men" or who said "I be fixin' to go
home now."

But most importantly, she worried about a more profound influence.   *26*
Howard was a deeply religious man with a Pentecostal bent to his faith. Alice
had realized this near the time of their wedding while they were attending a
service at her white-gloved black Baptist church in Philadelphia. Out of the
blue, Howard was struck by the power of the Holy Spirit. In the words of
the Pentecostals, he "got happy"—and he stood and danced wildly in unconscious, joyful exultation. The ushers came to restrain him. The fiercely proud,
urbane and proper Alice was mortified. And back in Delaware at Howard's
Prospect AME Church, it was more of the same. To Alice, the congregation's
emotionalism was ignorant and hickish. It did not fit with her plans for her
children.

The Stevenson kids all did well, went to college and graduate school.   *27*
But Bryan was always the family's darling. Howard Jr., the oldest, came to
resent his father's strict discipline. Christy, the youngest, used to sneak off to
listen to rock music. But Bryan—as far as anyone knows—did none of these
things. Not to say he was perfect: He picked on his sister sometimes, fought
with his brother, bent a few of his father's strict rules. But all in all he was
about as good as kids come. A self-taught musician, he played organ and piano
at the Prospect AME Church and learned to shift his tempo to the spontaneous outbursts of congregants as they, like his father, "got happy." He showed
no interest in being a minister, but he could preach up a storm.

In his overwhelmingly white high school, Bryan was president of the   *28*
student council. He was a star athlete. He was a straight-A student who would
eventually graduate No. 1 in his class. He would be pursued by Ivy League
schools but take a soccer scholarship to Eastern College, a small Baptist school
in Pennsylvania, where he would lead the gospel choir and a Christian fellowship. In high school, he was a champion public speaker, and he played the lead
in "A Raisin in the Sun." After 30 years of teaching drama, Harriett Jeglum
still remembers it as the play of which she is the proudest. At Cape Henlopen
High, Bryan held an odd status. He was one of only a handful of blacks in
the advanced classes, and it was common for black kids in that situation to be
teased, even harassed by other black kids—accused of "trying to be white."
Bryan's sister, Christy, got some of that grief, but she and her brother and
other old acquaintances of Bryan's say he never did.

"He was just so kind and decent," says Kevin Hopkins, a childhood   *29*
neighbor of Bryan's. "Nobody would ever have thought of saying anything
like that about Bryan, black or white."

Bryan's mother tells this story: When the kids were young, she always   *30*
told them they could make requests for their favorite meals and she'd do what
she could to fix them. Christy and Howard made requests, but Bryan never
did. "He just ate whatever I cooked and said it was the best food he'd ever
eaten," she says, still sounding a bit puzzled. "That's just the way he was about
everything. If I was in a bad mood, he was always the first to notice it. He'd
say, 'You all right, Mom?'"

Back on the road to Georgia's death row: "I had the happiest childhood,"   *31*
says Bryan, finally loosened up and talking about himself for a change. "I was
at church two, three nights a week, all day on Sundays," he says. "At school, I
knew everybody—the white kids from class, the black kids from sports. But
we lived in the country, and I didn't hang with any clique. My parents cared
about me and I wanted to do things to make them care about me more. Years
later, at Harvard, so many kids I met felt that if they hadn't gone to Andover
and Harvard, their lives would be over." He smiles. "But I always figured that
people with even zillions of dollars couldn't be happier than me.

"I had fights with the white kids on the bus. They'd call me 'nigger.' In   *32*
first grade, I remember holding my hand up and never being called on. In
second grade, a teacher's aide made me get off the monkey bars while the
white kids were on it. When they did integrate the schools, all the black kids
were in 3-C. I was the only black kid in section A until junior high. Year after
year, the counselors tried to get me to take vo-tech: 'Everybody needs to
know how to make bricks,' they said." Finally, as Bryan talks, it becomes clear
that the racism he has experienced, mild by the standards of the generation
before him, is still tightly woven into his work against the death penalty.

"The reason I always say I've never met a client whose life isn't worth   *33*
saving," he says, "is because they are like me—except they didn't get in 3-A.
They were in 3-C. A few breaks the other way, and I could be on the other
side of the table. You know, as a kid, I spent my summers at my aunt's in
Philly. You couldn't get police to come to her neighborhood. You had to call
and say a police officer had been shot. My grandfather was murdered, stabbed
dozens of times, in his own home. The killers pleaded to a low charge. I had
a black friend raped on campus, but the case was never pursued. She was
leaving town, had no family there to pressure the prosecutor. That's our justice: We over-prosecute crimes against whites and under-prosecute crimes
against blacks, because whites have political power and blacks don't. I saw it
in my own life long before I studied the death penalty.

"But when I did, and discovered that a man who murders a white has a   *34*
4.3 times greater chance of getting the death penalty in Georgia, I saw it as a
symbol of all the race and poverty bias in our society. We're not yet capable
of valuing the life of a black mother of four in the projects the same way we
value the life of, say, the ex-president of Chevron. We're just not capable.

"Do you know that in Montgomery, Alabama, there's a paper called the   *35*
Bulletin Board that still runs ads seeking white renters? I spent weeks looking

for an apartment. On the phone, a man said, 'You don't sound black, but I ask everyone.' I lost all humility. I told one woman I was a lawyer with a Harvard degree. She said the apartment was $250. I put on a suit, but when she saw me her whole body sagged. She said the rent was $450. It's very demoralizing and debilitating. None of my Harvard degrees, my suits, meant anything next to my little black face.

"All these things are of the same cloth."   36

At the Georgia Diagnostic and Classification Center, which houses that   37
state's death row, Bryan's client, Roger Collins, is waiting in the visitors' room, a deep narrow place with a wall of screened bars and a long row of empty stools. After four years of handling his case, Bryan has come to think of Roger as a friend. Roger stands to greet him, takes away his sunglasses and puts them on, hams it up. He is a black man and Bryan's age exactly, 31, handsome, with short hair and a close-cut beard. He is on death row for brutally murdering a black woman 13 years ago. Roger was 18. His accomplice was 25. They had separate trials. Roger got death. His accomplice got life. Roger could get an execution date any day.

Bryan tells him about his appeal and about how Congress might pass a   38
law that would help his case. (As it turned out, Congress did not.) "I understood right from wrong," Roger says. "I did, yeah. It just started out one thing and ended up another. I've done some hellful things in my past." When he was 13, Roger says, he and his father and brother would go to Florida from Georgia and rob places every weekend. In ninth grade, he still couldn't read. He thinks, but isn't sure, that his mother and brother are in prison. His father, who eventually went to prison for murder, is out now, and he visited a few weeks ago. "He said they went for the death sentence," Roger says, "and missed."

"It looks real good," Bryan says. "Don't get down."   39

Roger says, almost to himself, "Ain't set no date."   40

Outside, on the road again, Bryan says, "I meet people like Roger every   41
day. Their lives are a mess. Half of my clients have had somebody in their families murdered. They are always getting their electric turned off, or their telephone. Or they mention that their daughter has been in jail for six months, and, by the way, what should they do about it? They live at the margins of society, with no sense of control over their lives. We've given up trying to help them. To mention it is to be ridiculed as naive and weak. You know, as a boy George Daniel was hung in a sheet from a tree when he wet the bed, and beaten with a bat." Bryan is quiet for a long time.

Then he says, "I'm afraid they're going to kill Roger."   42

Something happens to idealistic young people at Harvard Law School.   43
On the first day, Bryan recalls, his entering class was asked how many planned to practice public interest law after graduation, and probably 70 percent of the hands went up. But very few entered the field. Last year, only about 3 percent of Harvard Law's graduates went directly into legal or public service organi-

zations. In Bryan's class, the overwhelming majority of graduates took prestigious clerkships or cut to the chase and took $70,000-plus jobs with big law firms. "Everybody came into law school wanting to help the poor," Bryan says. "But when the big law firms offered $1,500 a week, they all went."

It was a seduction. On that first day, students were told to look around at their 500 classmates. "They tell you that you're sitting with future congressmen, leading partners of important law firms. You are pushed to compete, get to 'the top.' Only nobody ever stops to define 'the top.' There's no value orientation about finding meaning in what you do." Students are encouraged to feel special, he says, as if they are better than everyone else and therefore deserving of wealth, power and privilege. It can be a very appealing pitch, especially to youngsters from the bottom, who yearn to be accepted by the elite and who are willing to pay the price of distancing themselves from their roots. Bryan didn't bite. It sounds hokey, but Bryan seems instead to have cut a swath of goodness through his years at Harvard. In the remarks of his former classmates, there is an unmistakable tone of testimony. 44

"He is just this incredibly exceptional person," says Jeffrey Nussbaum, a lawyer in San Francisco and a former Harvard Law classmate. "Bryan radiated a sense of goodness and kindness, which sounds so mushy. But he definitely radiated it. He has some kind of inner peace." Nussbaum says Bryan was once harassed by a gang of whites in Cambridge. "He wasn't angry. That was the thing. How can I put it? He felt sorry for the people who had attacked him." 45

Another Harvard classmate, Jerry Salama, now an assistant to one of New York's deputy mayors, even remembers Bryan once talking about his opposition to the death penalty. "What about the guy who cuts people in 50 pieces?" Salama asked pointedly. First, Bryan mentioned that his grandfather had been savagely murdered. Then he said something Salama has never forgotten: "It's not right to kill them back." Says Salama, "He just couldn't fathom the idea of wanting to 'kill them back.'" 46

Again and again, old Harvard classmates mention that Bryan, who clearly didn't share the law school's dominant values, never criticized anyone for wanting to get rich and powerful by serving the already rich and powerful. "A lot of us were talkin', talkin' all the time about helping the poor, but very few of us did anything about it," says Kimberle Crenshaw, a former Harvard Law classmate and now a UCLA law professor. "Bryan never talked about it. He just did it. He didn't do it to win other people's approval. He did it for himself. He was one of the few people not tainted by Harvard. He's got something else that gives him energy. I don't know what it is. I don't know anybody like him. I think Bryan is religious. I don't know how religious." 47

Bryan's old classmates mention repeatedly that they "think" Bryan is religious, but they say he never talked about that either. They knew he went to church, but nobody knew where. In fact, Bryan went to church in a poor black Cambridge neighborhood, where as a volunteer he helped people fight their way through the city's housing and welfare bureaucracies and gave kids free piano lessons. 48

"Bryan is the kind of person who, even though I don't see much any-   *49*
more, I will always consider a close friend," says Frederick Smith, a lawyer in
New Jersey and a former Harvard Law classmate. "The word for Bryan is
seminal. It's hard to be close to him and not be profoundly influenced and
deeply changed. I very quickly fell under his wing. Bryan was from a little
country town, and I had gone to prep school, Harvard College and spent two
years at Oxford, but I had to run to keep up with Bryan, literally." He laughs.
"It sounds like I'm talking about someone who is older, but I'm five years
older than he is.

"I always assumed that what happened to me would happen to Bryan.   *50*
'Well, now's the time to grow up. We have bills to pay.' Everybody else in the
class, like lemmings, hopped off the cliff and went to large law firms. But not
Bryan. I have another friend from Harvard, and he and I still talk about the
phenomenon of Bryan Stevenson. What makes him what he is? We talk about
how much we hate what we're doing. Why did we fall so short and Bryan is
out there as a beacon? I hate to admit to character flaws, but maybe Bryan is
the clearest example of what true character is all about."

Bryan Stevenson doesn't like to hear this kind of talk about himself. It   *51*
is, he believes, another kind of trap, not unlike the one Harvard lays for its
"special" young students. "I know they are trying to be nice," he says, as he
drives off to yet another rural Alabama town, this time Monroeville, to talk
to the family of his death-row client Walter McMillian. "I hear it when I go
to a reunion or I run into an old classmate who's doing something he hates.
These people act like I'm a priest, making such sacrifices. I'm not. It's easy for
me to do what I do. What people don't understand when they say I could be
making all this money is that I *couldn't* be making all this money. I could *not*
do it. I could not get up in the morning and go to work. If the death penalty
were abolished tomorrow, I wouldn't be a corporate lawyer. I'd probably be a
musician. When people say I'm great, what I'm doing is great, they aren't
talking about me. They're talking about themselves, about what's missing in
their lives."

Bryan has struggled with the idea that he is special, denied it, all his life.   *52*
"Whites have always treated Bryan like he walked on water," says his brother,
Howard Jr., a psychologist and visiting professor at the University of Pennsylvania. "But the label of specialness is impossible to swallow, because to be
black and special to whites means you aren't really black, which puts a distance
between you and your people, who are to whites very unspecial. To accept
the label of special is to absolve people of their responsibility to be good. It's
a different kind of control. It's the desire to take what you have and make it
their own."

As Bryan cruises toward Monroeville, past cotton and cane and giant   *53*
pecan trees, past Alabama's Holman Prison and its death row, I recall for the
first time the legend of the *lamedvovniks,* the Righteous Men, who forever
deny their own virtue. Bryan would understand why ancient legend required

good men to deny their goodness: To believe you are good, special, better than the rest, is to be neither good nor special.

Finally, I ask, "How important is your faith?" *54*

"It's very important," Bryan says. He explains that in the 1970s he was *55* involved in the charismatic Christian movement. It was a modern version of the backwoods Pentecostalism—with its emotional and sublime encounters with the Holy Spirit—that Bryan's father had practiced all his life. In the 1960s, the faith burst forth and profoundly changed America's stodgy and ritualized mainline denominations. Yet, traditionally, Pentecostalism was a faith of the dispossessed—the poor and the uprooted, from white Appalachia to black Los Angeles. And Bryan knows this.

"Church is not so important to me today," he says, "but I still glory in *56* the charisma and spontaneity of the black church, still love to play the piano for a person who stands and dances to the Spirit. It is restorative. A grandmother who stands up and says, 'I've lost my son and daughter in the fire, all my belongings, but I'm here with my grandson and we're gonna make it'—it is more restorative than praying with people who are thankful for their wealth. I must return to that well. If there's an afterlife, that's who it's for—those whose lives have been hellish and who've struggled to be better. That's who Christianity is for—the rejected, despised and broken. And those are my clients."

It's dark when Bryan arrives in Monroeville and meets Walter Mc- *57* Millian's sister, niece and nephew in the cold wind outside the IGA food market at Ollie's Corner. He tells them an appeals court has ordered the local court to consider whether the county prosecutor had secret deals with the two main witnesses against McMillian, a 49-year-old black man who was convicted of killing an 18-year-old white woman in cold blood during a robbery. One witness against McMillian was his alleged accomplice, who pleaded guilty to the murder and got a life sentence. In many of Bryan's cases, it's clear that his clients actually did murder someone. But the evidence against McMillian is strictly circumstantial. If Bryan can prove the secret deals, Walter McMillian gets a new trial.

"Is everything else going all right?" Bryan asks. *58*

"Did my daughter call you?" McMillian's sister asks. *59*

"From Mobile, yes. I haven't had a chance to call back." *60*

"They got her son for capital murder." *61*

"Is that right?" Bryan says, masking his shock with studied calmness. *62* "Have her call me. Make sure she tells him not to say anything to the police. Does he have an attorney?"

"No." *63*

"Make sure she calls tonight." *64*

"How late?" *65*

"Anytime, anytime." *66*

Back on the road, Bryan says, "It's probably too late." *67*

As always, Bryan worries first about the man accused, but right now I *68* can't help thinking about the victim, for whom it is already too late. And I ask the question that is unavoidable, the one so many people believe challenges Bryan's entire work: "But what about the victims, the people your men kill? What about their husbands and wives, their kids? Don't these murderers deserve to die?"

Bryan is silent for a long moment. He has, of course, heard the question *69* many times before. "I feel worse for the families than I do my clients. It's the hardest thing." He is silent again. "But I tell them, 'I don't care what you did, how awful it was. I'm here to get you off. I don't believe you should be killed.'"

"It's not right to kill them back?" I ask. *70*

"It's not right to kill them back," he answers. *71*

By now it's late, nearly 11, and on the drive back to Montgomery I close *72* my eyes, very tired. But Bryan is wide awake, ready to go back to the office tonight to work on several briefs and to meet with Amnesty International representatives who are in town visiting his center. The schedule is grueling, and Bryan does sometimes yearn for regular hours, a wife, kids. But he finds working with his clients so absorbing that he doesn't think much about what he's missing. Besides, he figures he's still young, with plenty of time for a family later. After a while, when we are nearly back to Montgomery, I ask, "Your parents have never understood why you do this, have they? They think you could be earning gobs of money."

Bryan laughs. "They've come to understand me recently. *73*

The next week, on a beautiful autumn day, I leave Washington and drive *74* to Milton, Del., where Bryan grew up. I find his home, the little white ranch house on County Route 319, and his father, Howard Sr., a short, trim man with dark gray hair and black plastic glasses. He takes me to the Prospect AME Church on Railroad Avenue, past the road signs riddled with bullet holes, past Vern's Used Furniture.

It's a small, not so sturdy, white clapboard church about the size of some *75* living rooms I've seen. The sanctuary is adorned with bright flowers, a cloth rendering of the Last Supper and a piano and an organ, much like the ones Bryan once played here on two, three nights a week and all day on Sundays. The church, with its vaguely musty aroma, is the very image of the tiny churches that dot rural America, particularly in the South, the very image of the backwoods church that embarrassed Bryan's mother when she first moved to Milton decades ago.

It's a long way from Prospect AME to Harvard Law School, but some- *76* how Bryan made the distance look short and easy. I am marveling at this when I notice that Bryan's father is standing before the little altar, framed by the bright flowers and the cloth rendering of the Last Supper, lost in thought. He shakes his head, looks around at the empty sanctuary and says wistfully, "Bryan used to set me on fire when he prayed out loud." And once again I am reminded of how often Bryan's behavior—in childhood, in law school, still today—evokes inspiration in those around him, even his own father.

Back at the house, I see that Bryan's old room is filled with storage boxes   77
now, but that the walls are still papered with dozens of his awards from childhood: the Golden Scroll for the Promise of Greatness, the Thespian Society
Award, awards for music, sports, student council—you name it, the guy won
it. His parents' pride is not disguised, and the dark-paneled walls of the house
are covered with photographs of Bryan, Howard Jr. and Christy.

"Bryan said you only recently came to understand him," I say. "What   78
did he mean by that?"

Without hesitation, Howard jumps up from the couch and dashes to the   79
television. He roots around in a cabinet full of videotapes and pops one in the
VCR. "This was last April," he says. "Bryan spoke to the national youth
conference of the AME Church." In a few moments Bryan, all grainy, comes
on the screen. And for half an hour, he speaks, starting slowly and then,
moved by the power of his own emotions, quickly, like rapids. He says we
execute the retarded, the young and the mentally ill. He says we execute men
for killing whites far more often than we do for killing blacks. He talks of the
defense lawyer who was drunk and of the blacks who are so often struck from
murder juries. He talks of the judge who said of a convicted man's parents,
"Since the niggers are here, maybe we can go ahead with the sentencing
phase."

Then Bryan says, "It's not enough to see and deal with these things from   80
a humanistic perspective. You've got to have a spiritual commitment. So many
talk that talk, but they don't walk that walk. We've got to be prepared to pay
the cost of what it means to save our souls." Then he quotes the Bible—
Matthew 25:34–45: "Then the King will say to those at his right hand, 'Come,
O blessed of my Father, inherit the kingdom prepared for you from the
foundation of the world, for I was hungry and you gave me food; I was thirsty
and you gave me drink; I was a stranger and you welcomed me; I was naked
and you clothed me; I was sick and you visited me; I was in prison and you
came to me . . . Truly, I say to you, as you did it to one of the least of these
my brethren, you did it to me.'"

The place is bedlam. "I wouldn't exchange what I'm doing for any-   81
thing," Bryan says, voice rising. "I feel the pleasure of God."

Bryan's father gets up quietly, rewinds the tape. Tears are in his eyes. "I   82
didn't understand his faith until this talk," he says. "He never talked about
himself, ever."

Sadly, Bryan's mother, Alice, is in the hospital being treated for a life-   83
threatening illness, and his father and I go to visit. Her lean, elegant body and
handsome face are the image of her son, as are her slow, deliberate mannerisms, perfect diction and clear, accentless voice. She sits in a robe in a chair
next to her bed, illuminated by a single lamp. Seeming tired, she closes her
eyes as she speaks. "I told him he was not going to live in the sticks all his life.
Please do not be satisfied." She opens her eyes and laughs. "Sometimes I think
he listened too well. He is so far away. I miss him so. Did Howard tell you we
didn't understand him until April of this year when we heard him speak? He

never talked about himself. Me, I've been a money-grubber all my life. But now that I've been sick, I see that Bryan is right. Really, what are we here for? We're here to help one another. That's it." After a pause, she says, "You know, a college friend of Bryan's once asked me, quite seriously, *'Could Bryan be an angel?'* "

Alice and Howard Stevenson talk into the evening, and just as I'm about to leave, Howard says, "The Lord touched him." And Alice tells this story: When Bryan was 13, in a hot little Pentecostal church in Camden, Del., where she'd taken the Prospect youth choir to sing, "Bryan went off in the Spirit. He got happy. He danced." I ask what that means, and Alice and Howard chuckle at my naivete. "It is to be in a realm of complete and absolute joy," Alice says, although that day she did not feel joy. "I cried because I never wanted that to happen to Bryan. I didn't want him to be a backwoods cultist Christian. He broke out in a sweat, completely physically immersed, and the Spirit took him over. I held him, hugged him and cried." Because for all the years Alice—proud, urbane Alice from her white-gloved Philadelphia Baptist church—had gone to Prospect AME, she'd never been a true Pentecostal believer. 84

"But this was my child, my darling, my flesh. I knew there was no falseness in him. So I knew this was a real gift from God. I stopped turning my nose up at it as something only ignorant people did." And looking out the window one morning soon afterward, watching the rising sun, Alice was suddenly overwhelmed with the presence of God. Simply put, Bryan had saved his mother. 85

"That feeling," she says, "can't be put into words." 86

Perhaps not, but I remember that James Baldwin seems to have come very close in the final pages of *Go Tell It on the Mountain.* And rereading his words at my home late that night, I try to imagine Bryan as Baldwin's character John, try to imagine how transforming must have been Bryan's experience— whether spiritual or psychological. 87

Baldwin wrote: "And something moved in John's body which was not John. He was invaded, set at naught, possessed. This power had struck John, in the head or in the heart . . . The center of the whole earth shifted, making of space a sheer void and a mockery of order, and balance, and time. Nothing remained: all was swallowed up in chaos . . . His Aunt Florence came and took him in her arms . . . 88

"'You fight the good fight,' she said, 'you hear? Don't you get weary, and don't you get scared. Because I *know* the Lord's done laid His hands on you.' 89

"'Yes,' he said, weeping, 'yes. I'm going to serve the Lord.'" 90

I put down the book, and I think again of the 36 Righteous Men: The ancient legend, I now realize, isn't the answer to what it means to be truly good; it is only one more way of asking the question. With or without religion, maybe that's all good people can ever really do: live their lives as a 91 question posed to others. I think of a priest I once knew. He told me that Christians would have no need to evangelize if only they lived their lives as mirrors of goodness in which others could glimpse the goodness of Christ— and thus the goodness in themselves. And I think of Bryan: His deepest mission, I now see, is not to save the lives of convicted men, but to live in such a way that his own life is a question posed to others.

"I want to be a witness for hope and decency and commitment," Bryan *92* had said, before I understood what he meant. "I want to show in myself the qualities I want to see in others." Bryan's own motive is to "feel the pleasure of God." Yet whether graced with the power of God, the power of a strong, decent family or the power of some buried psychological zeal, Bryan's life is like the priest's mirror: Looking into him, people see their failings and possibilities. Like the *lamedvovniks,* Bryan must deny this power—not because he will disappear in a flash of God's will, but because if others can call him "special," they can excuse their failings and avoid struggling to find the goodness in themselves.

Finally, I think of Frederick Smith, Bryan's friend from Harvard Law, *93* the man who said he was forever changed by meeting Bryan: "If religion created Bryan Stevenson," he had said, "we all need a lot more religion."

Pray it were only that easy. *94*

Topics for Discussion and Writing

1. Draw a parallel between Mother Teresa and Bryan Stevenson. These two people come from very different backgrounds, yet they may be the people most alike in this chapter. Comment.
2. List reasons why people discriminate against others. Go back over the text and find ways that Stevenson has witnessed racial discrimination, either personally or on behalf of his clients.
3. You may have read *To Kill a Mockingbird* by Harper Lee. How are Bryan Stevenson and Atticus Finch alike? Compare the racial climate in which they both live and work. Both of these lawyers are defending black men. How might their experiences as Southern lawyers be different based on the fact that Atticus Finch is white while Bryan Stevenson is black?
4. "Simply put, the man is hard to figure." What does Harrington mean by this statement? Why is Harrington perplexed? Cite examples in the selection that seem paradoxical regarding the life Stevenson has chosen.

KEN ADELMAN AND RALPH NADER

"There Ought to Be a Law"

"I had a thirst to give voice to voiceless people."

The following is taken from the interview series What I've Learned, *which Kenneth Adelman conducts on the Learning Channel on cable television. The interview with Ralph Nader was reprinted in the* Washingtonian *magazine, June 1990.*

Before and as You Read

1. Research a consumer concern such as auto safety, food additives, or environmental pollution. Study the background of the issue, including the government agency, if any, by which it is regulated. In what ways can consumers turn their concerns into action for change? Make a list of consumer groups that have made a difference in our country.

2. Both Ralph Nader and Bryan Stevenson went to Harvard Law School. As you read, make note of how these two men are alike. What differences do you perceive? What character traits do these two men share that empower them to strive for distant and, in some cases, impossible goals?

3. Ralph Nader deals with the federal government on behalf of the people he serves. Do you see his goals changing as he works within the changes of presidential administrations, for example from Bush to Clinton? How might his goals change?

4. If you were going to interview Ralph Nader, what questions would you ask? Brainstorm a list of questions with your class and rank them in terms of their importance to you. As you read Adelman's interview with Nader, compare your list with the questions Adelman asks here. Note follow-up questions that you would ask Nader in response to his answers.

FEW CITIZENS have had a bigger impact on day-to-day life than   1
Ralph Nader. Starting in the mid-1960s, he inspired the consumer movement, and since then has generated wave after wave of citizen activism over highway safety, public health, food additives, industrial pollution, congressional reform, federal pay, and other issues. He has trained a generation or two of activists.

One of four children of Lebanese immigrants, Nader is from Winsted,   2
Connecticut, near Hartford, where he grew up rooting for the New York Yankees and reading the *Congressional Record*.

After graduating with a combined major in economics and Far Eastern   3
affairs from Princeton University, he went to Harvard Law School, where he

took up the research that would make him famous. He made himself an expert on automobile engineering and design.

Nader joined a Hartford law firm, but in 1963, at the age of 29, he quit, hitchhiked to Washington, and a few months later signed on as an employ-ment-safety consultant to Daniel Patrick Moynihan, then assistant secretary of labor. He also advised a Senate subcommittee exploring the federal role in auto safety. 4

Two years later he published *Unsafe at Any Speed: The Designed-In Dan-gers of the American Automobile.* One section described the tendency of General Motors' Corvair model to swing out of control on turns. After GM admitted hiring private detectives to trail and discredit him, the book became a best-seller, and Ralph Nader a household name. 5

He recruited teams of idealists who, like himself, would do prodigious homework on an issue and then doggedly press for reform. In 1968, the first group of "Nader's Raiders" investigated the Federal Trade Commission's rela-tionship with the businesses it was regulating. The following year, Nader founded the Center for Study of Responsive Law, from which his campaigns are still conducted. It publishes several books each year on issues as varied as the environment, multinational corporations, trucking and railroad regulation, food standards, and land development. 6

Nader, 56, helps keep the movement alive with dedication and asceti-cism; he has never married, and he lives modestly in Northwest DC. 7

During a typically hectic day in his disheveled, paper-filled offices on 17th Street, we discussed what he's learned. 8

Q: While you were at Harvard Law looking into automobile design, your friends were eager to join Wall Street firms. What made you different? 9

A: It was growing up believing that the pursuit of happiness involved the pursuit of justice. When I was 12 years old I started reading the early muckrakers—Upton Sinclair, Lincoln Steffens—and I was shaking with excitement. 10

At Princeton I noticed that the grounds-keeper would spray the trees with DDT in the spring. It was so thick that students walking to class had to wipe it off their faces. In the dawn I'd see birds dead on the sidewalk. So I went down to the college paper. The editor sat back in his chair, put his feet up, and said, "Well, we've got the best chemistry and biology professors in the country. If there's anything wrong, they would have blown the whistle." 11

That's when I learned an important lesson—most experts aren't willing to go into controversial arenas. Princeton didn't do anything about the spray-ing for at least fifteen years. 12

I had a thirst to give voice to voiceless people. I got an intellectual and al-most an aesthetic pleasure from it. Never was it a chore; it didn't feel like a duty. 13

Q: And you're still happy with it? 14

A: Oh, yes. What could be better than trying to improve the quality of democracy? 15

Q: What led you to focus on cars? 16

A: I was a champion hitchhiker, going back and forth to school and 17
around the country. I would happen upon accidents—sometimes we were the
first ones there—and I saw some pretty grisly sights. I could see that people
were hurt because of what they'd hit *inside* the car. Like a pop-open glove
compartment door with a sharp edge, like a guillotine. Or "cookie cutters" on
the dashboard, the little hoods around the dials on the panel.

Q: Was this when your activism began? 18

A: I entered the consumer area by writing a paper at Harvard Law 19
School on the liability of automakers for unsafe design. The seminar dealt
with medical factors that can end up in court—things like trauma, death, and
injury. And the principal source of those things is on the highways of
America.

This was the jukebox era of automotive design—gas guzzlers, rust-prone 20
and unsafe. I dug into engineering and medical literature and learned how
little work was done in traffic safety. The entire policy was just to exhort the
driver to drive better.

I went over to MIT and asked for their Department of Automotive 21
Engineering. They didn't have one. I asked for professors who specialized in
that field. They didn't have any. I asked for a graduate student—usually there's
a grad student on every subject—but they didn't have one.

Here was the largest operating engineering system in the US, the high- 22
way-vehicle system, which costs billions of dollars in accidents, results in
thousands of deaths and hundreds of thousands of injuries, and there was no
scholarship on it.

Q: Why'd you go after General Motors? 23

A: Nobody could dismiss it as a small auto company misbehaving. GM 24
was a standard-setter. When it put things on cars, the other companies put
those things on cars. And there were so many obvious hazards on their cars,
like the sharp edges, which harmed thousands of pedestrians hit at slow
speeds.

Q: At first you were not well received. People thought you were weird. 25
When did it turn around?

A: When Senate hearings on the issue started in 1966, with the Govern- 26
ment Operations Committee and the Commerce Committee. Before that, I'd
go into the *Washington Post* and say, "I've got a great story," and they'd think I
was fronting for some car inventor.

There was a lot of skepticism then, and, unlike today, the auto industry 27
was not regulated at the national level and hardly regulated at the state level.
Auto companies had no lobbyists or law firms here. The credibility of us critics
rose when senators Abe Ribicoff and Warren Magnuson began digging into it.

Q: People were suspicious, since there had never been a Ralph Nader 28
before.

A: Now it seems bizarre, but then people couldn't believe anybody 29
pushing for auto-safety legislation. That now happens all the time—parents
who lose children from unsafe toys start a group to lobby for safer toys. It's

amazing how far we've come. Back then, official-source journalism was the norm. The government was covered, trade associations, and sometimes unions. That was it—citizens didn't make news.

Q: Isn't that one of the things you're proudest of, sparking this phenomenon of public awareness and public organizations for greater consumer protection? *30*

A: By all means. It shows people across the country that they can make a difference. If they learn how to be more skilled citizens, they can have major impact. And it'll be fun. *31*

Q: You've taken on big government, written a book castigating the Congress, and spent a lifetime on failings in the executive branch. Yet you want to regulate almost everything. That means bigger government. How do you sort this out? *32*

A: I use judgment, not ideology. I look for the best approach to any problem. If you're walking down the street breathing polluted air, you're coerced. You can't refuse to inhale. There's nothing you can do about it as an individual except band together with other individuals to move a government agency to require more stringent standards. *33*

In some areas, we've got to focus on private and public institutions. For example, we and other groups pressure the tobacco industry to admit that tobacco causes cancer and to scale down its promotion to hook the young. We also need a massive education program to help people who have smoked for years. *34*

So some things require national standards. Others are better suited for state and local standards. In Washington, you're supposed to be either this way or that way. That's why our work leads to such puzzlement. *35*

Q: You began your career on GM's Corvair. If you've publicized its dangers, I don't have to buy one. It doesn't mean the government has to regulate whether I buy a Corvair. Why must the government regulate if consumers understand the dangers? *36*

A: First, until *Unsafe at Any Speed* came out in 1965, you never would have heard about the problems. The media never talked critically about a car by brand name. When I first criticized the Corvair, the television announcers referred to it as a "medium-sized, rear-engine American car." *37*

Second, this message will be countered by massive GM advertising telling how it's safe. Third, what about children or passengers in that car? And the people it injures? They don't have a choice. *38*

That's why we advocated a national vehicle handling standard, which, sadly, still hasn't come from the Transportation Department. That's why we advocated preserving the right of injured people to file suit—not only to receive compensation for injuries, but to signal GM that it's more efficient to build a properly handling car than to build one with a rear-end swing-away potential. *39*

Q: Isn't the danger of your approach that people think we have a right to a risk-free society? That everyone ends up suing everyone else? Since your *40* movement, we've got lawyers by the bushelful. We've become among the most litigious societies ever.

A: Anything can be driven to extremes. Still, only a fraction of those 41 injured by negligence or worse ever get a lawyer, much less a settlement, much less a verdict, much less get it upheld on appeal. The few that do break through show companies that they'd better be more careful.

Actually, we're not a very litigious society. Studies show that in civil cases 42 per capita, we compare with Denmark, Australia, and New Zealand. Business litigation here is what's increasing faster than the population.

Q: But the class-action suits you encourage lead to more litigation. 43

A: Some 50,000 private liability suits are filed each year in federal and 44 state courts; that's a minuscule number, given all the products, pharmaceuticals, fabrics, construction failures, cars defective in design or construction, et cetera.

And why do you think it's bad to channel conflicts through the courts 45 of law? Otherwise they're suppressed, as they were in Eastern Europe, or they come out in vigilante ways.

I don't see what's wrong, in a society that's growth-oriented, about 46 growth in lawsuits, particularly since they're not growing faster than the population. They're also not giving verdicts mandating payments higher than the rate of inflation for the bulk of routine cases, according to the Rand Institute for Civil Justice.

Q: Isn't there a danger of presuming we deserve a risk-free society? 47

A: No. We should start at the margins and nibble toward a risk-free 48 society, but we'll never achieve one. Let's deal with infant mortality, with instances of asbestos-caused cancer, with contaminated drinking water or preventable trauma on the highways. Let's deal with malpractice. We're far from a risk-free society.

Q: Do you see solving all these problems through government action? 49

A: No. Some solutions can be through government. On malpractice, 50 for example, the government should establish more stringent standards, especially for hospitals that Medicare taxes help to support. We also need more citizens banding together to buy insurance, banking services, fuel oil, whatever. Then people can negotiate better deals with oil companies or banks.

We've started one co-op, Buyers Up—it's in the phone book—to which 51 13,000 households belong in the Washington-Baltimore area. They average a 20-cent discount per gallon on their heating oil. The staff holds news conferences and testifies on energy matters, to balance those from the oil industry. It's been fairly successful. . . .

Q: Let's talk about the young and the old. You've been trying to boost 52 empowerment of the elderly. What does that mean?

A: That they have the knowledge, the opportunity to participate in 53 government, to organize themselves.

Why are the generations ruptured from one another? Why are young 54 people spending less time with adults, including their parents, than any generation in history? Why, for 2,000 years, were the elderly respected for their wisdom and experience, and thus kept in a leadership role, but now cast aside to play shuffleboard in Sun City, Arizona, out of sight, out of mind?

Q: Don't the elderly already have political power? I read about "gray power" all the time.   55

A: They have political power. They can defend Social Security and Medicare. But they're still subjected to an awful cultural deprivation—they're viewed as unnecessary. They're not wanted enough, not needed enough.   56

Why can't they become the civic leaders in our society? They're free to speak out; they don't have to worry about what the boss might think. They've got the experience. They're living longer and are more active physically. Why can't they connect with the younger generation? They might teach crafts, tell them about history, have fun.   57

Q: Don't you find that already, with foster-grandparent programs and such?   58

A: That's what needs to be expanded. There are millions of older people who sit bored, depressed—   59

Q: So what are you doing about it?   60

A: We've started a movement called "ageless living," and put out a book, *Spices of Life,* to address older adults' concerns about shelter, transportation, financial planning, Social Security, nutrition, recreation, and learning, and to create a more resourceful way of life.   61

Q: To change what?   62

A: The kinds of discomforts and anguish they face when they try to get value for their dollar, to get a telephone call answered by some government agency, try to get decent shelter or transportation to stores.   63

Professor Edgar Cahn, who teaches at the DC School of Law—he and his wife, Jean, conceived of the Legal Services Corporation and helped get it through Congress in the '60s—recently took barter, the oldest concept of exchange, and connected it to the computer. If you give, say, 50 hours to help somebody in your community, you can draw 50 hours of someone else's time to help you. Older people can tutor teenagers, who can cut grass for a middle-aged couple, who can transport elderly people to the shopping stores.   64

It can become even more flexible. It's not bureaucratic. It's inflation-proof. It's egalitarian—a lawyer's hour is worth as much as a teenager's hour, and it binds a community together. People discover who lives down the street. Strangers become neighbors. Neighbors become friends.   65

Already 9,000 hours a month are being generated in time dollars in one place in Miami, where it started. It's now in nine states and the District, and it's working marvelously. In Brooklyn, people work as a volunteer for an HMO, which cuts their premium by 25 percent. Boredom disappears. Elderly people feel like they're needed.   66

Q: They find meaning in life.   67

A: It's wonderful to see the joy of people. An electrical inspector I met on a plane in California said he had recently retired. He visited his daughter, who gave him poetry books. He read them and said he could do better than that. She said, "Dad, you've never written poetry before." He said, "Wait and 68 see." He's now got a poetry circle of 60 elderly people and has written poems on all kinds of subjects.

Q: It makes them feel fulfilled. 69

A: And it makes them better citizens. When they are not absorbed in anguish and depression, they become better citizens. I've learned that people tend to give up on themselves if the society doesn't want or need them. That's true for teenagers and for elderly people. 70

Q: You think we've given up on teenagers today? 71

A: We have, mostly. We don't spend enough time with them. We let their peer group be their tyranny. Companies have massive advertising that bolsters the peer group. That's thrown at parents who try to discipline or even advise a teenager. 72

Look at teenagers today. Where is their purpose? Do they have a purpose? Some do, and they're going to be the leaders. But too many don't have what old-timers used to call useful pursuits. 73

Q: Come on! I remember hearing that when my father was the age I am now. 74

A: There are certain verities that persist and grow through history. 75

Q: But older folks always think teenagers are wayward. Certainly my parents did with me. Do we know that teenagers are more adrift today? 76

A: Most definitely. They're spending more time with goods and services produced by corporations. They're induced to eat food that's bad for them. Their music is more like noise that's designed to blow their minds. 77

Q: I remember my grandfather talking about Elvis that way. 78

A: That's right, but it keeps getting worse. You didn't walk down the street with a Walkman, oblivious to cars crossing near you. 79

Companies are more and more adept at raising our children. Kindercare raises the kids, McDonald's feeds them, Disney and Time Warner entertain them. The food they eat is a reflection of goading on Saturday-morning TV. There's massive over-medication, over-the-counter drugs handed out to kids. 80

Many parents are so seldom at home that they feel guilty and then spoil their children worse—"Sure, you can have a car at age 16." Already we have lower literacy, lower academic achievement. Kids don't know where India is. They can't name ten states. They can't write. 81

How do we answer someone who says, "Oh, well, MTV, junk food, over-medication, tobacco addiction, alcohol, drugs, so what?" *That's* what! The real issue coming up is a collision between parents who want to raise their kids and corporations who'd rather raise the kids to spend the almighty buck. 82

Q: Do we know things are worse? 83

A: We do. We've got 40 percent dropout rates in some major cities in our country. Almost 25 percent of children don't finish high school. 84

Look at the addiction level. It's much greater. Sure, teenagers and college students would get drunk in the old days, would smoke cigarettes. But now we have a drug epidemic. 85

Look at this junk food—high salt, high sugar, high fat content. Kids   86
have the highest level of obesity and flabbiness since records were kept.

Consider the discipline factor. In the 1940s, the bad student activities a   87
school superintendent would report were talking out of turn, throwing gum
wrappers in the corridor, tickling another student. That same list today would
include bringing weapons to school, arson, rape, vandalism, drugs—

Q: With such problems, isn't the consumer movement left in the dust?   88
It's not pressing to most Americans anymore.

A: That depends on how you define it. If it includes work on health or   89
auto insurance, it's up there on the front burner. If you define it in terms of
pollution, it's up there. If you define it to tackle bad services by government,
it's up there. What about utility rates? Lemon cars? Housing? Fuel? The list
goes on and on.

Your image of consumerism is an old-fashioned one, involving a little   90
deceptive advertising or being cheated a bit in the supermarket. Today, tobacco
is a big consumer issue.

Q: Tobacco consumption is going down. That's been a success.   91

A: Very much so. And it illustrates something. Government could never   92
ban tobacco, since it's hard to regulate an addiction. But the government did
pour out information about the link between smoking and cancer, heart disease, and other ailments. Then talk shows and consumer groups relayed this
information. Then groups began to help people stop smoking. And guess
what—now about 30 percent of the male adults in the US smoke, where it
used to be 50 percent.

So we've had an ocean change against a marauding form of addiction.   93
It was a shift based on millions of incremental individual perceptions, fueled
by responsible information.

Q: That's how American government is supposed to work.   94

A: Yes, but it didn't for a long while. It wasn't until 1964 that the   95
government had the guts to issue the first *Surgeon General's Report*. Look how
long it took before someone like Surgeon General Everett Koop really told it
the way it was. Even today we don't tax the tobacco industry enough.

Q: We still subsidize it, don't we?   96

A: Yes. And we don't offer enough stop-smoking clinics. Worst of all,   97
we don't crack down on the tobacco industry's absolutely malicious attempt
to hook our youngsters. The industry loses 5,000 customers a day—about
1,000 die from tobacco-connected diseases, and 4,000 stop smoking. That's
why they try to hook the younger generation. . . .

Q: When you look back at all your causes since the Harvard Law   98
School days, what lessons have you learned?

A: To have patience mixed with impatience. If you have too much   99
patience, years go by and nothing gets done. If you have too much impatience,
you'll get so discouraged that you'll lose in the first round.

Second, realize that you'll never reach paradise, but you have to keep   100 striving for it. Some people are so idealistic and set such impossible short-term goals that they get burnt out after two or three years.

Third, the most important feeling people need to have is that they can make a difference in terms of power. This notion that you can't fight city hall, or Exxon, becomes morbid apathy, which runs counter to the human personality. *101*

Last, we have to hold officials in power more accountable. We just cannot delegate the future to a handful of people. If you don't have self-government, you're not going to have good government. *102*

Q: When will your job be through? *103*

A: Never. We must keep grappling with problems, so that instead of a calamity we may have a minor tragedy; instead of a minor tragedy, we may have an inconvenience; instead of massive famine, we'll have problems of people eating too much junk food. Then entice people to eat more nutritious food. Always reduce the anguish. That's what I want to achieve in this world. *104*

Q: Has it been rewarding to you personally? *105*

A: Nothing could be more rewarding. I get letters all the time saying— *106*

Q: Not just letters. Do you feel good inside about this? *107*

A: Even more so. There's nothing more rewarding than contributing to a just outcome and being able to see it all around you. *108*

Topics for Discussion

1. Explain the barter concept of the Legal Services Corporation. Give an example of how it might work in your community. Why do you suppose there are not more such organizations? What do you think it would take to establish such a system in the remaining 41 states? In a pool (or bank) of hours, what help do you think you could contribute, and what kind of help would you want to withdraw?
2. Ralph Nader said, "Always reduce the anguish. That's what I want to achieve in this world." How does Ralph Nader live by these words?
3. This selection is an interview. How does it differ from the autobiographical selection of Mother Teresa? The biographical selection about Bryan Stevenson?

   In your journal discuss in some detail and defend your choices regarding which selection of the three you found easiest to read and which selection made the greatest impact on you. Share your thoughts with your class.
4. For 30 years, Ralph Nader has been one of the most outspoken consumer advocates in our country. Some in government and industry argue that consumer advocacy has damaged U.S. economic competitiveness with other nations because the threat of lawsuits has made U.S. manufacturers

afraid to sell new products that may or may not be dangerous. As a consumer—and as part of the U.S. economy—where do you stand on this issue? What safety measures in the manufacture of cars, toys, food, drugs, and so on have you benefitted from? What examples can you cite of consumer advocates perhaps having gone too far? Share your examples in a class discussion.

DAVID FLORY
"One Day, South Africa"

> "*He passed along the fence poking a knobkerrie in the sod to steady himself. He walked along alert and strong, surrounded by a quiet dignity that the insults of white ten-year-olds who in town ordered him as 'boy'— 'Come boy,'— 'Do this, boy'—had not been able to reach.*"
>
> David Flory wrote the following while studying advanced composition at George Mason University in 1992. His teacher was Professor Terry Zawacki.

Before and as You Read

1. Write to summarize what you know or feel you know about conditions in South Africa under the *apartheid* system. What questions arise for you as you write? Study a variety of recent books and articles about South African politics and history to try to answer your questions. What important changes in the political system have recently occurred?

2. Have you protested in any way against the *apartheid* system or against U.S. economic dealings with the government of South Africa? If so, what was the substance of your protest? If not, read newspaper articles about protests that have occurred in the U.S. over the past five years. What were the protesters criticizing? How are the U.S. and South African economies related in ways that might affect the average American consumer?

3. Imagine yourself as a visitor in South Africa. Based on what you have heard, seen, or read, what would you expect to find? What difficulties would you expect to encounter in trying to understand the cultures and the issues?

4. As you read "One Day, South Africa," note how David Flory uses narrative, dialogue, and description to convey implicitly a point of view that he does not openly express. Do you think it appropriate to call this piece an essay, or does it belong to a different genre? What kind of work would you call it? Why? What features might make it more essaylike? (Refer, if you wish, to the definitions of personal and reading-based essays in chapter 2.)

FOR THREE days I waited for us to leave the town, drive up out of the valley, and go over the brown hills into the bush. But instead the family with whom I was staying passed the days with an unhurried contentment, and with each one I felt a sense of urgency grow within me as if time irreplaceable were drifting slowly away. *1*

On that first day, Don Collins and I had gone down to the bank in the city square and had withdrawn fifty rand for the week; the second was a *2* holiday; on the third I was taken down to the farmers' supply where I bought a pair of black rubber boots and stiff green overalls. And on this, the fourth morning, we were starting later than I thought we should.

Through the rolled-up window, the dashboard clock read 9:15. Behind the truck, Don bent down, grasped the last bag of ninety-pound concrete and swung it smoothly into the bed. I threw two shovels and a hoe in on top of it and slammed up the tailgate.   *3*

"Alright. Let's go," I said.   *4*

Don walked around to the driver's side and stuck the key into the lock while I impatiently flipped the handle. He looked up at me and rested both of his long arms on the roof of the truck. He was smiling.   *5*

"David," he said. "Don't you know that in Africa there will be time for everything?"   *6*

I was still too fresh and naive to understand, for Africa was too large. For close to a month, I had been traveling through the country and staying with friends and friends of theirs. It was half for the pure adventure of the continent, and half to know, because I saw them, the beauty and injustices of the country. Little of what I had found out until then was more than what I could see at the surface. Its deeper secrets, the ones that feed the hearts of its people, were still hidden deeply in the earth.   *7*

Don was a lanky Canadian who had left a thriving wheat farm in Saskatchewan and had brought his family to South Africa to work among the villagers. He was a devout man, and deeply moved by the suffering of the blacks in the highlands north of Pietermaritzburg. I had been given his address while in Cape Town, and had made the trip up to visit him and his family, and to experience something of his work and the people for whom he did it.   *8*

We drove out of the white city of Pietermaritzburg in his small pickup, slung low with the load of concrete and tools in the bed. Outside of town, we picked up the modern highway that snaked up out of the valley on terraces cut into hillsides, and rose above the urban black area of Edendale that lay in the adjoining valley and above the pall of smoke from cooking fires that covered it. Further up into the countryside, we turned onto a two lane road stretching past the well-tended pasture land and irrigated crops of white farmers. At the sign for Impendle that signaled we were well into the bush and the rural black areas, we turned onto a bone-jarring, one track, dirt road.   *9*

Outside, the air was cool like a northern autumn day and the sky was that rare shade of cobalt blue that has a strange kind of depth to it. It seemed both very close and very far. I opened the window enough to let a breeze in because the direct sun had made us both hot, and the refreshing currents of warm air and wind swirled around me.   *10*

Don turned to me.   *11*

"Today you'll see one of our most successful projects," he said grinning. He was missing two molars from the left side of his smile and seemed hardly able to contain the warmth and enthusiasm he felt at being part of something to help the villagers.   *12*

"We've got a two stage chicken run going up here that the village has   *13*
really taken on. Most all the outside walls are up and so are a few of the inside
ones as well. The idea is that soon there'll be one room for the chicks and one
room for the broilers and one room resting. That way we'll get a cycle going.
And that'll be somethin'."

"Somethin, huh," I said.   *14*

"Yep," he said. "Something to write home about."   *15*

From the high rolling hills near Impendle one can see very nearly into   *16*
the heart of South Africa. It was after we had bounced for a half an hour over
the rutted road that we gained enough altitude to catch a glimpse of the peaks
that guard it.

The brown hills continue to roll and pitch and gently rise, each valley   *17*
higher than the last, until finally they empty themselves up onto a vast escarp-
ment that stretches around the feet of the Drakensburgs; they tower almost
vertically in walls several thousand feet high. In English, the Afrikaans word
for the mountain range means dragon's back and I could see the sleeping
monster wrapped around the heartland of the country very clearly thirty miles
away near Impendle.

The road made a gentle sweep around to the left and suddenly Don put   *18*
on the brakes.

"We're here," he said.   *19*

"Where?"   *20*

I looked around and saw nothing but tall grasses. Don wrenched the   *21*
wheel around and drove off the road onto a narrow trail.

"You should get this fixed."   *22*

"Don't need to," he said.   *23*

The surrounding hill country of Impendle that during the spring and   *24*
summer after the rainy season would be a carpet of green grasses and wild
flowers is dry and barren. Though it is July, these are winter months and the
long grasses that cover the hills have stored their goodness in their roots to be
protected from the cool winter nights and occasional snow. There are few trees
on the hills. They grow in small stands and never seem to be more than ten
or fifteen feet high. An African woman with a panga can strip the branches
off of most every low tree and carry them all home in a long bundle balanced
on her head.

We came around a small rise, and there before us stretched a wide and   *25*
shallow, beautiful valley—and a low, roofless building. A new barbed wire
fence, seventy feet wide, six feet high, and a hundred and fifty-odd feet long
enclosed it from the rest of the valley. Fifteen village men were already working up on the walls of the chicken run and women and children were scurrying about on the ground.

Don looked pleased. "That's my baby," he said.   *26*

The area around the village of Impendle and the chicken run is Zulu,   *27*
and it has been since the days of Shaka in the early 1800s when he unified
the various tribes of the area into one, highly disciplined, conquering nation.

Their short spears and cattle hide shields proved powerless, however, against the continuing expansion of British and Afrikaner influence. On December 7, 1838, the Day of the Covenant, the most sacred day of Afrikaner nationalism, five hundred Afrikaner pioneers killed over three thousand Zulu warriors in a fierce battle. The nearby river ran thick red with Zulu blood. The Afrikaners lost not a single man.[1] Today the South African government occasionally buys up pockets of white-owned farm land and cedes it to the homeland of KwaZulu. What good that actually does these villagers is difficult to say. And then there are white men like Don Collins trying to teach them how to use it.

Don was once the most successful ag-consultant in western Canada—in demand by everyone until he left it for a people he loves. Now he lives on donations arranged through a foundation in the States. In 1983, he left Canada with his wife and five of his six daughters, and watched as four of them grew up and moved back to Canada. He hasn't been home in three years, since his third daughter was married.   28

"What I really'd like to do one day," he told me once, "is get out of the house in 'maritzburg and have a small place in one of the villages up here."   29

"You've got to be kidding," I said. "Leave Canada for good? And, live way up here?"   30

"Why not?" he said. "It's where we'd like to be."   31

I slipped out of the truck and Don headed over to the men to check on their work. They put down their tools and sat on the top of the walls as he talked with them. The air was busy with the constant clank and churning of an ancient cement mixer sitting off to the side between two piles of sand. A Zulu man, middle-aged and dressed in green overalls just like mine, stood beside it, leaning on a shovel. He had a gray band that wrapped around a Panama hat.   32

"Hello," I called out.   33

He raised his hat and smiled.   34

The Zulu men were at first reluctant to let me work with them. Eight children and several women had formed a chain from the cement mixer to one of the rising walls. From one to the other they passed milking pails, wash buckets, and large wide bowls full of cement one way, and dirty, dripping, empty ones the other. I got in the end of the line near the wall where the last link was having trouble lifting the mix up to the men above. A bowl was passed and I lifted it up.   35

"No no no no!" One of the men above me was wildly flapping his arms. He looked angrily at the one who had passed the cement to me. She looked to the ground.   36

"No no no. No, inkosan.[2] You mustn't. You will get soiled."   37

1. Richard Neuhaus. *Dispensations: The Future of South Africa as South Africans See It*. William B. Erdmans Publishing Co., 1986. p. 16. Other estimates of the casualties range up to 10,000.
2. *Inkosan* literally means "the chief's son" and is a term of deference older blacks will often use. They'll often call older white men *baas* from the Afrikaans word for master.

I looked up at him in shocked amazement, wondering what wrong I   *38*
might have done. Suddenly I understood what he had meant: this work was
beneath a white man like me; it was too menial, too dirty. The heavy buckets
were piling up in the arms of the children. I reached over for one and hoisted
it up and looked the man in the eyes.

"Doesn't matter. That's why I'm here."   *39*

He thought for a moment then reached over and grabbed the bucket.   *40*
He emptied and shoved it back at me. I grabbed it back and lifted up another
one. Some of the concrete slopped over the side and landed on my shoulder
and ran down my arm. The village man was watching me out the corner of
his eye. He was smiling. We understood one another.

For part of the day I worked with the man with the Panama hat mixing   *41*
mud for the walls. He had a system. One boy stood by a pile of coarse sand
which was brought up from the stream. When the mixer started, he was to
throw in twelve heaping shovelfulls. Another boy stood next to split open bags
of concrete. He was to add three more. And a frail barefooted girl, no more
than nine or ten, carried buckets of water from the spring at the corner of
the run, balanced on her head. She worked quietly. Streams of water ran
through her hair and down her face. They soaked into the front of her cotton
dress. Drops of gleaming water hung fleetingly at the tips of her eyelashes,
and fell to the ground like rain whenever she walked.

The man with the Panama hat had gathered up a pile of stones that he   *42*
kept on the cement mixer. I noticed that when the children didn't work
quickly enough for him, he threw them—hard and intending not to miss. He
made the girl afraid. He threw them at her as well. When I started working
with him, working in the sand pile, he stopped throwing the stones. But when
he thought I wasn't looking, he made little pretending motions. The children's
eyes would get big and their bodies would flinch.

Perhaps it is true of everyone who finds that someone is interested in   *43*
their life and their language, but two Zulu boys in particular delighted in
taking special pains to teach me to speak a few words of isiZulu. In between
mixings, they would come and stand behind me.

"Hello. How are you?" They would say. They pronounced the words   *44*
very carefully.

"I am fine," I said, "Kunjani?"[1]   *45*

And they would laugh because I spoke one of their words and they   *46*
knew that was probably all I could say. They were almost right. They aimed
to change it.

Once they each took hold of my hands and ceremoniously led me up   *47*
to the spring and the pool of water beside it. They knelt down beside the
clear, shallow water. One of the boys dipped in his hand, made it into a cup,
and spilled the water back into the pool.

---

1. For asking informally: how are you, you'd say: *Kunjani?* To say it formally, you would say: *U sapila na?*.

"Amanzi," he said. 48

"Amanzi," his friend echoed. 49

I looked at my little teachers. "Amanzi," I repeated. 50

"Zulu: Amanzi. In English?" 51

"In English: water." 52

"Water," they said very seriously. They nodded their heads slowly, yes. 53
"Water."

A swallow flew overhead diving through the air with erratic beatings of 54
its wings. One of the boys pointed up.

"I-nyoni." 55

"I-nyoni," I said. "In English: bird." 56

For the rest of the afternoon, when we had the time, we taught each 57
other words. They would take me to different parts of the yard, and soon
they taught me the Zulu words for leg, goat, sky, mountain, nail, and snake,
and many others which I forgot. I learned also to say: it is hot today, and:
you are working very hard. When we went back to mixing, in the middle
of work I would look up and say to one of the boys: You are working very
hard. And the boy would smile and say to me: Yes, it is hot today. And
though they were the only sentences we could say, they meant much more
than that.

Along one side of the fence ran a trail that came from the dirt road and 58
ended out of sight to the west. Years of padded feet had worn out its narrow
bottom so that it was concave and trough-like as it meandered through the
high grass. Along the path came those from the Kombi drop a hundred yards
away,[1] or those from the chief's kraal[2] across the stream and to the left, or
those simply traveling to the huts of the more western villages. Often I saw
them look with concerned wonder at the villagers working inside the fence
with the tall white man, building the concrete building—for what?—they
probably didn't know. Except for one very old man.

He passed along the fence poking a knobkerrie[3] in the sod to steady 59
himself. He walked along alert and strong, surrounded by a quiet dignity that
the insults of white ten-year-olds who in town ordered him as "boy"—
"Come, boy," "Do this, boy,"—had not been able to reach. I stretched up from
my shovel work in the sand pile and watched him come nearer. His eyes were
focused in the middle distance beyond both me and the building. But when
he came nearer—ten feet, no more—a smile both aware and mysteriously
aloof spread through his wrinkled cheeks, his heavy, gnarled hand with pink,

1. Many African taxi services drive mini-buses which South Africans call Kombies. They are
built to carry about ten passengers. They are often crowded with many more. A Kombi drop is
a popular stopping-off point.
2. A kraal is an African living compound made up of several rondovels. Rondovels are circular
and are usually made of mud bricks and have thatched roofs. Each rondovel in the kraal functions
like a separate room in a house; there is usually one for cooking, living, sleeping, etc.
3. A knobkerrie is club about the length of a cane with a thin shaft and a heavy wooden knot at
one end. They are perfect for walking and for killing black mambas surprised in the tall grass.

moonless nails rose to his brow, and his eyes closed slowly. With the faintest curve of his neck, he nodded as he passed.

"Sabonna, Baba," I said.[1]   60

His head tilted back as if to laugh. I imagined white teeth flashing   61
against the sun.

I turned to the two young boys.   62

"Where's this trail go?"   63

It was beyond their pidgin English. Puzzled, they turned to one another. 64

"Don, where's that old man going?" I called.   65

"Who knows. The nearest village is three miles away."   66

The trail cut a thin line around the shoulder of the hill and where it 67
met the sky it caused a brief interruption in its smooth slope. With musical
steps the old man was shuffling along it—with distance, growing smaller,
blending into the countryside. Right foot. Left foot. Stab the earth. Again,
and over, and again.

For miles into the distance and probably for each aged day of his past 68
there were these three miles and always walking. Now the sighs of the wind
through the grasses were breath for his wheezing lungs. Only the hill had
remained ageless silhouetted against the changing sky. Left foot. Right foot.
Stab the earth. The world seemed very quiet as this man of profound grace
moved along the trail. I stood in the middle of an African valley, with the
blue sky coming down around me and the warm, brown earth tenderly holding it up. I watched until he was out of sight.

Topics for Discussion and Writing

1. In what ways does this selection exemplify the principles of political action displayed in other writings in this chapter? How is the work of Don
   Collins, David Flory, the Zulu workers, and others in the narrative political? List as many "political moments" in this essay as you can. What
   features make them so? Do you feel that the participants are in any danger?
   Explain.

2. In what ways does David Flory seem to you to be an authoritative commentator on what he sees and hears? In what ways does he lack credibility
   as a commentator? Note occasions when he proclaims his ignorance. Note
   occasions when he seems certain of his interpretation of an event. When
   is he most authoritative and believable? Compare your perceptions with
   those of other readers.

3. Use Flory's narrative/essay (see "Before and as You Read" topic 4 on the
   question of the genre of this piece) as a model for your own writing about
   a "small" event in your life that might be seen as politically significant.
   Describe the event in detail, but avoid telling the reader how or why it

---

1. *Sabonna* is the Zulu equivalent of "hello." Literally it means: I see you. *Baba* means "father"
and can generally apply to respected elders.

might be significant. How can you indicate significance without proclaiming it?

4. Write a different version of Flory's day from the perspective of one of the other people present (for example, the "man with the Panama hat," Don Collins, one of the children, the old walker). How does this person describe and interpret the events? How does this person assess the significance and the possible danger? Share your version with others who have also done this exercise.

STUDS TERKEL

from *The Great Divide*

> *"Maybe I'm not always at home, not as much as I should be, as much as some parents are, but I'm giving [my children] a vision. I'm an example to them that as individuals, we can make a difference in life."—Maria Elena Rodriguez-Montes.*

> *Studs Terkel (born Louis Terkel in 1912 in New York) has forged a brilliant writing career by presenting the lives of a wide spectrum of "average" Americans of all ages, professions, skills, ethnic heritages, and beliefs. After gaining early recognition as a Chicago radio and TV broadcaster in the 1940s and 1950s, Terkel turned seriously to oral history. His collections include* Division Street: America *(1967), about an ethnically diverse Chicago neighborhood;* Hard Times: An Oral History of the Great Depression *(1970);* Working: People Talk about What They Do All Day and How They Feel about What They Do *(1974), which won the Pulitzer Prize;* American Dreams: Lost and Found *(1980);* The "Good War": An Oral History of World War II *(1984); and* The Great Divide: Second Thoughts on the American Dream *(1988), from which we have reprinted one of the oral histories.*

Before and as You Read

1. In this short selection, Maria Elena Rodriguez-Montes tells her story about how she organized a citizens' group to fight big business in their Chicago neighborhood. Studs Terkel relates her words but maintains a presence as the author of the piece. How is his presence felt? Why do you suppose that he intrudes on the narrative, rather than just relating what Rodriguez-Montes said?

2. American history is filled with the deeds of ordinary citizens who see a community need or an injustice and produce extraordinary efforts that make a difference. Recall an example of someone who has impressed you by his or her work, and write an essay about what she or he accomplished.

3. As you read, notice how the ingenuity of the group led by Rodriguez-Montes obtained swift results. List the tactics that they used to deal with the Chicago officials. Were they proper, in your view? Why did they work? Discuss these ideas with others.

4. Compare Maria Elena Rodriguez-Montes to Mother Teresa. Do you think that they see themselves as extraordinary in any way? If so, how have they expressed this feeling?

MARIA ELENA RODRIGUEZ-MONTES

"I was born with an excessive amount of energy. My daily schedule is very   *1*
busy. People ask me, How do you do it? I don't know. God gave me
something."

   To say she is active in her community and city is to say Babe Ruth was   *2*
a baseball player. She serves on a dozen or so committees, among them:
Board of Trustees of the City Colleges of Chicago; chairman, UNO, *
Southeast Branch; director of Illinois Fiesta Advocativa . . .

   She is petite, delicate-featured, offering the impression of a china doll.   *3*
She is twenty-nine, a mother of three children, twelve, eight, and six. "I
was seventeen when I got married, a senior in high school. I don't have a
formal education. I think of going back to school. My parents were migrant
workers. There were seven of us. I'm the pickle in the middle.

   "I'm a person who was born and raised on the Southeast Side of Chi-   *4*
cago, two blocks from where I now live."

F IVE YEARS ago, August 1982, an organizer from UNO knocked on   5
  my door. He was knocking on a lot of doors, trying to get people
to fight the proposed landfill for the neighborhood—289 acres, for toxic waste.
Waste Management, the company, is the largest in the world.

   Two hundred and eighty-nine acres, in comparison to sixteen acres in   6
Love Canal. Two, three blocks away from the school our kids go to. It scared me.

   Would you be willing to host a small meeting at your house? Sure. Four   7
people showed. We called others. A couple of weeks later, there were thirty,
meeting in the basement. We had expected twenty at most. There was an
interest. People who had just bought homes in the area were afraid the property values would go down. Senior citizens were scared. The smell was bad
already, and it was going to get worse with this.

   We identified IEPA† as responsible. At the first meeting with them, they   8
said talk to the alderman, talk to the mayor, talk to USEPA.‡ Passing the buck.
It was somebody else's problem, not ours.

   About thirty of us went to the governor's office downtown. How can   9
we get these guys to respond? Our strategy was: We'll take our kids down,
with taffy apples. The kids were grabbing things, getting all the furniture
sticky. The secretaries and staff were getting real upset—(laughs)—how else
would we get their attention, unless we disrupted formal office procedure?

   This was our first action.§ It was kinda scary. I had never been so assertive   10
before. I was the spokesperson. I said to this guy, the state director of EPA,

*United Neighborhood Organization, a citywide community action group.
†Illinois Environmental Protection Agency.
‡United States EPA.
§A phrase coined by Saul Alinsky in *Reveille for Radicals,* an early guide to community organizing.

we're not leaving. Of course, our kids are running around with their sticky taffy apples.

He got the governor on the telephone and wanted me to go in the next room to talk to him. I said, "I'll talk to him over the phone with these people present." So every time the governor said something to me over the phone, I would turn to my people and ask them, "What do you think?" The governor agreed to come to our meeting. It was our first victory, our first sense of power.

He didn't show, but sent the IEPA director. There were about two hundred people. We demanded a study of contamination in our soil, water, air. And no permit issued to Waste Management until the results were in. They agreed. Again, we felt it was a tremendous victory. People by this time were feeling good.

It wasn't a great study. Yes, we have cancers higher than in other parts of the city. Yes, we have a lot of lead around. Yes, we have a lot of toxins in the air. "But you're not really at that much of a risk."

Congressman Washington was running for mayor and needed the His-panic vote. When he was elected, we had a big meeting at St. Kevin's Church. Six hundred people showed up. I was chairing the meeting. It was my debut as a community leader.

The mayor came out with the kind of speech you expect from a politi-cian, okay? It was many, many words. He talked wonderfully and the people applauded. They thought he had said something, but I knew he hadn't. He was shaking people's hands as he was walking away.

As she recreates the moment, she walks around the room, ignoring the micro-phone, hilariously simulating the mayor's departure. Often, during the conversation, she demonstrated, tape recorder be damned.

I remember feeling angry. Did he really think he was fooling us? I called out, "Mayor, will you please come back here? We're not done with you yet, buddy." (Laughs.) I said, "You spoke a long time, but you haven't answered any of my questions. I'm going through them, one by one, and I want an answer to each one." You don't normally speak to a mayor like that, but I wanted somebody to be accountable. Why not the mayor?

"Will you look at that zoning permit, and if possible revoke it? Yes or no?" He'd look at me: "Yes, Mrs. Montes." (Laughs.) "Will you, as soon as you get back to City Hall, look at those contracts?" We went through them all. "Final question—let me make this clear—will you keep this company out of our neighborhood? Yes or no?" He said yes.

I remember I grabbed him, hugged him, and kissed him on the cheek. The whole crowd was standing and applauding. It was the best thing ever happened to us. It was great. We got a real commitment that day. The mayor did put a moratorium in effect.

It does not allow any new landfills in the city of Chicago. Waste Man- 20
agement is still out. Waste Management is still thinking of coming in the
neighborhood. I personally will not allow it.

We took two hundred people and jammed the annual stockholders' 21
meeting of Waste Management. Sisters of Mercy, who own some stock, gave
us their proxies. They stopped us at the door, but we created such a ruckus
that their stock went down three, four points the next day.

We knew we had to aggravate them. So we formed a human chain that 22
didn't allow the garbage trucks into the landfill. We had a big sign: THE MUCK
STOPS HERE. We're talking about the Dan Ryan Expressway, okay? Trucks
were backed up for miles. A week later, we brought double amount of people
and our kids, too. Again, we backed the trucks up for miles.

They brought in the paddy wagons. It was scary because none of us had 23
ever been arrested before, okay? We had people there who weren't willing to
be arrested and certain ones who were willing to go all the way. The police
got very confused and arrested the wrong people. They arrested one little girl
of four or five. I was the last one they took away.

We were singing all the time: "All we're asking is give South Deering a 24
chance." I remember saying, 'If we don't get to see the president, we'll be
back. I don't care if we have to go to his house, his church, or the school
where his kids go." These things made us all the tighter.

I may have got some of this energy from my mother. She was active in 25
bringing in bilingual education. She was PTA president. She worked hard
forming youth groups in the community. She was in everything.

Two years ago, when my daughter was ten, she organized an action. My 26
children go to a magnet school, so they're bused. The driver was drinking.
He'd stop, go to a bar, and leave all the children in the bus. My daughter and
another leader decided they weren't going to allow this to continue. They
organized thirty, forty kids on the bus and decided to go see the principal.
The person at the top. They all marched into the principal's office and requested a meeting then and there. She came out, they explained the situation
and made demands. The principal was impressed. They made a difference: the
driver was fired.

Maybe I'm not always at home, not as much as I should be, as much as 27
some parents are, but I'm giving them a vision. I'm an example to them that
as individuals, we can make a difference in life.

There's a young lady that I just recently met. She reminds me of myself 28
when I was younger. Her mother said, "I want you to be her mentor." I want
this young lady to feel the way I feel now, okay?

Topics for Discussion and Writing

1. This selection might have been called, "The Birth of a Community
   Leader." Outline Rodriguez-Montes' evolution from citizen to chairwoman
   for the meeting of 600 attended by the mayor.

2. What do you suppose gave this Hispanic woman with only a high school education the courage to stand up to state and big city politicians? Where do you think her courage came from? How common do you believe her leadership talents are?

3. Identify a problem in your college community that you and your classmates would like to solve. Have a brainstorming session listing different actions you could take. Elect a spokesperson and draw up a proposal for change. If possible, engage the support of other students in the school and present your proposal to the administration. Write an article about this experience for the college or local community newspaper.

4. Define oral history. What are some of the differences between oral history and the reporting of history from the third-person perspective? How are the roles of the writer different in these two methods of writing history?

Try writing Rodriguez-Montes' story as if it were a third-person report in a group of brief biographies of American community activists. Compare your report with that of others doing this assignment. Note how the reports differ in their selection of details and in the statements made about her work. What do these differences tell you about the responsibilities of the historian?

MARILYN DAVIS

from *Mexican Voices/American Dreams*

> *"Really, I never think about this being illegal. I know it is, but I don't have time to stop and think about that."*

For nearly 20 years Marilyn Davis has studied the culture and lives of the people of western Mexico. Her research resulted in Mexican Voices/ American Dreams *(1990), about the plight of Mexican citizens working illegally in the United States. She has lived with and made many friends among the people she writes about. She has taught their children in one of the village schools and has become godmother to 25 Mexican children over the years.*

Davis's book is primarily a collection of the oral histories of 90 people she has met and worked with over two decades. The histories are connected by Davis's summaries of political events that have shaped the experiences of her informants. Lidia Sanchez, who is quoted above, is one of those who speaks.

Before and as You Read

1. Use your library's periodical index to find articles on the Underground Railroad before the Civil War. How did this operation get started? How did it work? Who were the people who risked their lives so that others could be free?

2. Explore your feelings about illegal immigrants. What do you think the U.S. government should do with those who seek economic refuge here? What should the government do with those who help them? Would you ever offer your home and hospitality to those seeking illegal entry to the United States? Why or why not?

   Note that U.S. immigration law distinguishes between those who emigrate from their countries for political reasons and those who emigrate for economic reasons; immigration policy gives priority to those who are labeled "political refugees." Imagine instances when it would be difficult to distinguish a political reason from an economic one. Discuss this issue in class.

3. As you read this selection, try to get a sense of why Lidia Sanchez does this work. In what ways does she appear fearless? Compare her leadership with Maria Elena Rodriguez-Monte's leadership in her Chicago community (see the previous selection).

4. The United States used to be called a "melting pot" in which people of all nations and languages were assimilated into one society. Most social scientists today question this theory. Based on your readings and on your observation of diverse people in the United States today, what do you feel would be a more realistic metaphor for the relationship of the many cultures that exist in the United States today? If you were a new arrival who intended to stay in the United States, what difficulties do you think you might encounter in beginning your life in this country?

LIDIA SANCHEZ: SAFE HOUSE OWNER, CHULA VISTA, CALIFORNIA

It's an insignificant little stucco house, beige with white trim, in the middle of an older neighborhood. A well-maintained square patch of green lawn, roses lining the driveway, and a bicycle and scooter on the front porch; an "average American family" must live here. Inside it's the same. The living room–dining room combination is neat and orderly, furnished with the standard couch, easy chair, rocking chair, TV, coffee table, dining table, and six chairs, all in an early American style. From the books and games on the shelf and pictures on the wall children obviously live here, but at ten in the morning they are in school and Lidia's day is well underway. She has already been to the grocery store and has a load of wash in the machine. 1

So where are all the illegal aliens? Four who stayed last night left with rides early this morning. A pretty young woman in an old-fashioned print dress with pink roses and a white collar is washing dishes. The conversation is about children: getting them to eat, high fevers and ear infections. Obviously comfortable in Lidia's kitchen, she must be a friend or relative, certainly not the skulking fugitive from the Border Patrol—but she is. Her husband, who has resident papers, and her baby boy, who was born in the United States, passed yesterday. But with only four years here, she always has to pass with a coyote. Her sister-in-law will pick her up this afternoon. She is one of Lidia's clients. 2

Lidia has coffee and is putting groceries away. Her warm and easygoing manner makes people comfortable. 3

WHEN I graduated from high school I got a job in food service at Mercy Hospital. I was thinking I'd like to be a nurse, but I met my husband there and we got married. When my son was born I left my job, and before you know I had three children. I really never had time to go back to school. At that time I was busy with the children, and my husband supported us, so I didn't think about working. 4

Then in 1979 he left us. He left me with a five-year-old, a two-year-old, and the baby was just six months. That's when I moved here with my mom. This was her house. At first I thought my husband would come back, but I'm sure he's got another family in Mexico by now. I get aid for dependent children, and for the first few years I babysat my neighbor's children. She has three too, so I was taking care of six little kids. 5

But the thing is, my oldest son, from the time he was a baby he was sick. He learned to walk and all, but by the time he was eight he couldn't walk anymore, and I had to spend every day going to the hospital, or to the doctor, or therapy, so I couldn't babysit anymore. But by that time all the kids were in school, except my daughter. 6

Of course I would like to go out and work, but what would I do with   7
my son? He's in eighth grade and goes to a special school. The bus picks him
up at nine o'clock, but they bring him home at one and I have to help him
do everything. That's why I can't just go out and get a job. They pay his
medical bills and that, but to feed and clothe three kids, it isn't enough. We
can't get by on what I get from welfare.

My mom, she died in 1985, but she always helped people coming across.   8
So she always had someone here. Then when I wasn't babysitting, I would
help her. Around that time more people started coming, so I've just kept it up.

It's quiet today, but it gets hectic around here sometimes. I don't mind.   9
Really, it's the only thing I can do and stay home with my son. My other boy
is in sixth grade and my daughter is in fourth grade, so they still need me too.
I think of it as a job, but it's not bad. Most of the people are real nice, and it's
good for my son. There's always different people to talk to. He likes that. He's
in a wheelchair now.

The men begin bringing people from ten o'clock at night on. Oh,   10
sometimes we have someone come during the day, but most people cross at
night. But they have the key, so I don't have to get up for them. I have couches
and cots set up back there in the garage so they can sleep. As it is, most of
them leave early in the morning between five and six, so I get coffee for them.
Some people have to stay. They have other arrangements, or they have to fly
to other places, or relatives have to come pick them up. But they can stay here
and I let them bathe or wash their clothes. They eat their meals with us. They
can sit here and watch TV, whatever they want.

I get to know the people who stay over. I've had people stay for a week   11
or more. Sometimes they're waiting for their money to arrive. They mostly
come from Mexico. I've never been there myself, except to Tijuana. But we
always spoke Spanish at home, so I can speak with them. Some of them are
from other places in South America. When you talk to them it makes you
realize how much we have here, because they come from areas that are very
poor. I'll often have to show them how to use the shower or washing machine
because they have never seen one. Some of them don't even have toilets and
indoor plumbing where they come from.

When they get to where they are going they will call and thank us, or   12
they'll recommend us to a relative. You'd be surprised, we often hear from
them again. You get some that go back and forth so you see them. One lady,
who went to Chicago a couple of weeks ago, sent a postcard to my son. They
come here with hardly anything, but they always want to leave us something.

They pay me $10 for each person. If they stay and eat meals and all, it's   13
$20 a day. It's not like a fancy hotel, but I always have a pot of beans and
tortillas. They can have eggs, fruit, bread, milk, whatever they want. For
dinner I make some meat or fish. Whatever we eat is what I serve. When I
have women here they always help me. I don't ask them to, but they're nervous
and always want to clean, wash, or do dishes.

I've had up to forty people here in one night. But that doesn't happen   14 very often. Usually there are three or four, and I almost always have someone eating with us. Every once in a while I'll get a day off with no one here.

I always try to treat the people who come here fair. I think about the hard times they're going through and all. I always think, we're the first family they meet in the United States. I feel sorry for those poor people. Sometimes they're left off at a motel. You know they don't come here with that kind of money. Then the *coyote* tells them someone will pick them up and no one comes. There are *coyotes* that leave people in the back of trucks, for days, without food. You wouldn't believe the stories. I feel sorry for them. I only deal with a couple of people I know. They were friends of my mother's, so I know them pretty well.

You know these people just went to a lot of trouble to get here, so they're not going to do something stupid now. No, really they never cause me any problems: drugs, fights, nothing. Oh, sometimes you have someone who is very nervous, or upset, maybe crying and like that, but I just talk to them.

Really, I never think about this being illegal. I know it is, but I don't have time to stop and think about that. In my mind, this is my house, and I'm not endangering anyone. I think I'm helping people and doing what I have to, to make a life for my kids. At the same time, I am careful. I have rules. They always bring people around the back alley, and they are picked up out in back. The people have to be quiet. My neighbors know what I do, they understand, but I don't have a lot of noise and people back there bothering them. I know they would never report me. I grew up in this house and I've known them since I was a little girl.

Topics for Discussion and Writing

1. In your journal assume the character of a Mexican national coming to spend a night in Lidia Sanchez's home. What are your feelings, hopes, dreams? How does Sanchez help you deal with your fears? Describe her hospitality to you and the other people she serves.

2. Sanchez speaks of the *coyote*. From reading the text, what do you think this term means? In what ways is it appropriate to the people performing this task? (Do not hesitate to seek outside information, such as Davis's *Mexican Voices/American Dreams,* to help you with these questions.)

3. Lidia Sanchez states that her neighbors all know what she is doing and that "I know they would never report me." What do you suppose makes her believe that? Is she being too trusting perhaps? What kind of a community do you envision her neighborhood in Chula Vista, California, to be?

4. In Davis's preface, she speaks of being "at great physical risk." How is she at risk? What factors minimize her risk? Can you imagine yourself in a similar effort to get to the people behind the headlines and discover a deeper reality? Write about your curiosity and your fears in this regard.

For Further Thought

1. Consider the work and service that those represented here have given. Imagine trying to hire people to take over the work that these people do. What would a fair starting salary be? (Think about the salaries commanded by football or baseball players, rock musicians, and movie actors when considering the financial worth of work.)

2. One element that all those represented in this chapter have in common is the courage (though some would call it the irresponsibility, foolishness, or even criminality) to confront those in power. To what extent do you believe that "seeking justice" requires such confrontation? In what circumstances do you feel it is justified to break laws, as some represented here have? Write an essay, using the stories told here as evidence, that explains and argues your point of view.

3. Now that you have read at least several of the selections in this chapter, think again about yourself as a seeker of justice. Write about ways in which your life promotes justice. (Don't underestimate yourself!) At the same time, use the examples from this chapter to explore ways in which you feel you would have to change your way of life to fulfill the terms of your definition of justice. Write about these issues, perhaps setting for yourself a small first step in this direction. Share your work with others.

4. Choose a community organization in which you can seek justice for others by volunteering your time. You might organize your class or another group of students to join you. In your journal write about your goals and what you anticipate you will learn and accomplish. Continue to write in your journal after each day you work. What surprises did this experience reveal?

CHAPTER FIVE

Striving for Equality

"All men are created equal. . . ."
Declaration of Independence

Does any other sentence so well capture the essence of the democratic ideal envisioned by the signers of the declaration? The United States was founded on the bold idea that "all men" should be free from imposed hierarchies of birth and from the tyranny of kings and nobles who demanded to rule because of inheritance and what some called "divine right." This idea of equality—so radical in 18th-century Europe—has become woven into American myth and proverb: "Anyone can grow up to be president," "with liberty and justice for all," "You can be anything you want to, if you just work hard enough."

Succeeding generations of Americans, our numbers grown into the hundreds of millions by wave upon wave of immigrants inspired by the same ideal, have taken the idea of equality far beyond what the signers of the Declaration imagined. To the representatives in Philadelphia in 1776, "all men" did not mean men and women, or even all men. The U.S. Constitution, written 11 years later, counted the African-American slave as only three-fifths of a man (for the purpose of "fairly" assigning Congressional representatives to the new states) and surely did not intend this three-fifths person to vote. (American Indians were not counted as people at all.)

But the ideal of equality, spurring people to endure humiliation, physical and mental torture, and even death, proved stronger than the constitutional limitations on it. The 13th, 14th, and 15th Amendments, ratified between 1865 and 1870 in the aftermath of the Civil War, granted freedom, full citizenship, and the right to vote to all men, regardless of race. The 19th Amendment (1920) gave women the right to vote. The 24th Amendment (1964) took away from states the right to impose the fees called poll taxes on those wishing to vote, thus promoting equality. The 26th Amendment (1971) extended the right to vote to citizens 18 years of age, in acceptance of the theory that those mature enough to fight in a war were mature enough to vote. A further proposition, popularly called the "Equal Rights Amendment," first introduced to Congress in 1923, was finally passed by Congress in 1972 and endorsed (as of 1978) by 35 of the minimum 38 state legislatures which must ratify an amendment. The "ERA," like all amendments simply worded:

> Men and women shall have equal rights throughout the United States
> and every place subject to its jurisdiction,

would prevent Congress, states, and localities from making or keeping any law which upheld different treatment for women and men. Though the "ERA" itself has not been ratified by three-fourths of the legislatures, some of the objectives of its millions of proponents have been subsequently realized in Supreme Court decisions that have interpreted the earlier equality amendments as applying to women, despite their explicit references only to men.

Because the ideal of equality is so deeply ingrained in Americans, regardless of their sides in a dispute, equality battles almost always include charges and countercharges that opponents are really anti-equality while "we" are for it. The many-years battle over the legality of abortion (see the essays by Ferraro and Hussey and by Francke in chapter 7) is fought on the grounds of equality: those who call themselves "pro-life" argue for "equal protection of the laws" for the unborn child, and those who call themselves "pro-choice" argue for "equal protection of the laws" for pregnant women. Each side charges the other with the attempt to limit equality and thus deny freedom. Even more enduring have been the battles for equality—equal employment opportunity, equal educational opportunity, equal justice—waged by African-Americans. Every step in this struggle has been met by a counterstep from those who argue that what they call "preferential treatment" for blacks serves to deprive whites of equal opportunity (see the essay by Williams in this chapter) because it deliberately reduces the former domination of educational and job opportunities enjoyed by whites. Claims of "discrimination" by African-Americans, by women, by Hispanics, by American indians, by gay men and lesbians, and by other traditionally disenfranchised groups are met by claims of "reverse discrimination" from those who feel their freedom reduced by laws or proposed laws meant to reduce the inequality of the disenfranchised.

We include a chapter on "Striving for Equality" in *A Sense of Value* because the ideal of equality is so central to democratic thought. So many of the decisions we are asked to make as voting citizens—and as neighbors in an increasingly diverse community—force us to consider carefully all arguments made on the basis of equality. Because each disputant seems to argue for equality and accuse opponents of being against it, we need to be able to read beneath the claims and carefully weigh the evidence advanced. Just as important, we need to examine our own motives, predispositions, and prejudices. Why do we hold the views we do on the critical issues of our time? What experiences have shaped our views? Have we seriously tried out opposing views, read divergent opinions, worked to explain our positions to those who don't agree with us? Have we really tried to keep an open mind, or is that something we just say to comfort ourselves amid the confusion of conflicting voices?

In choosing essays for this chapter we have felt it most important to represent the conscientious struggle to develop values and viewpoints not based on prejudice but on careful study of one's past and the words and deeds of others. The essays we've chosen are not polemics or position papers but conscientious personal explorations that proceed through questioning and doubt and do not necessarily answer all the writer's questions. We have also felt it important to represent several of the more enduring struggles for equality in our society. We recognize that we cannot do more than suggest the complexity of these struggles, and we trust our readers to use the selections, the questions, and the exercises (both in this chapter and in many of the others) to go beyond what these materials provide.

Thinking about the Issues

1. Define *equality*. How important is this idea to you as you contemplate your past, your family's past, and your future? Do you feel that you tend to take equality for granted? Or do you easily recall experiences (or family stories) that help you appreciate this ideal?

2. Compare *equality* and *freedom*. Think of an event in your life, or in your family history, when your or another person's freedom to speak or act came about only because society upheld the ideal of equal treatment. Conversely, can you think of an event in your life or in your family's history when equal treatment of another might have in some way limited your or a family member's freedom?

3. Find a political statement (such as an excerpt of a speech or a campaign brochure) in which a candidate or an official cites equality, fairness, or nondiscrimination as a reason to favor some proposed action. Now find a statement by an opponent of this proposed action. How does this person use the same terms to argue on behalf of her or his view? Note how the meanings of the terms change depending on their use. How do you decide which speaker has a better claim to use these terms? Write about how you make this decision.

4. Identify an equality issue, such as abortion rights, affirmative action in the hiring of women and minorities, or the rights of gay men and lesbians to serve in the military, on which you have changed your views. On what did you base your earlier views? What caused you to change? Are you still undecided to some extent? Write in response to these questions, then discuss your writings with others who have also considered these questions.

FREDERICK DOUGLASS

from *My Bondage and My Freedom*

> *"This tray was set down, either on the floor of the kitchen, or out of doors on the ground; and the children were called, like so many pigs; and like so many pigs they would come, and literally devour the mush—some with oyster shells, some with pieces of shingles, and none with spoons."*

> *Born on a plantation in Maryland in 1817, Frederick Douglass fled slavery at age 21, was befriended by white abolitionists who helped him fulfill his great desire for learning, and by age 30 had become the preeminent African-American spokesperson on behalf of the abolition of slavery in the United States. His* Narrative of the Life of Frederick Douglass, *published in 1845, became a best-seller. A revised and expanded version of his autobiography, entitled* My Bondage and My Freedom, *was published in 1855. Scholars have shown how this autobiographical work established a model for other writers of what have come to be called "slave narratives," though Douglass's story of his life as a slave is just a small part of what is in essence a profoundly philosophical work about slavery, freedom, and social relations.*

> *As an orator, editor, organizer, and diplomat, Douglass was a leader of the abolitionist struggle until the passage of the 13th, 14th, and 15th Amendments, and a continuing critic of discrimination until his death in 1895. The portion of* My Bondage and My Freedom *that follows summarizes his life as a plantation slave and details his early—frequently disillusioning—education in the city of Baltimore.*

Before and as You Read

1. Write as much as you know about slavery in the United States before the Civil War. As you review what you've written, think about the sources of your information (for example, histories, novels, textbooks, television shows, movies, and family stories). What are the most powerful images that have influenced you?

2. Use writing as a tool to help you imagine yourself a slave. Assuming that *slavery* means "no freedom," describe plausible details of your daily life and how you as a slave might think about those events. How do you feel that you would have to behave and think in order to survive?

3. Now imagine yourself as an owner of slaves. To tolerate your life in this role, how would you have to think about yourself and about the slaves? What beliefs would you cultivate to justify your way of life? How would you regard those who disagreed with your beliefs?

4. As you read, observe how Douglass uses stories (narratives) as part of his larger argument about slavery and freedom. Note places in the work where the story precedes a point that Douglass wishes to make; note other places where Douglass uses a story to illustrate a point that he has already expressed.

As I have before intimated, I was seldom whipped—and never severely—by my old master. I suffered little from the treatment I received, except from hunger and cold. These were my two great physical troubles. I could neither get a sufficiency of food nor of clothing; but I suffered less from hunger than from cold. In hottest summer and coldest winter, I was kept almost in a state of nudity; no shoes, no stockings, no jacket, no trowsers; nothing but coarse sackcloth or tow-linen, made into a sort of shirt, reaching down to my knees. This I wore night and day, changing it once a week. In the day time I could protect myself pretty well, by keeping on the sunny side of the house; and in bad weather, in the corner of the kitchen chimney. The great difficulty was, to keep warm during the night. I had no bed. The pigs in the pen had leaves, and the horses in the stable had straw, but the children had no beds. They lodged anywhere in the ample kitchen. I slept, generally, in a little closet, without even a blanket to cover me. In very cold weather, I sometimes got down the bag in which corn-meal was usually carried to the mill, and crawled into that. Sleeping there, with my head in and feet out, I was partly protected, though not comfortable. My feet have been so cracked with the frost, that the pen with which I am writing might be laid in the gashes. The manner of taking our meals at old master's, indicated but little refinement. Our corn-meal mush, when sufficiently cooled, was placed in a large wooden tray, or trough, like those used in making maple sugar here in the north. This tray was set down, either on the floor of the kitchen, or out of doors on the ground; and the children were called, like so many pigs; and like so many pigs they would come, and literally devour the mush—some with oyster shells, some with pieces of shingles, and none with spoons. He that eat fastest got most, and he that was strongest got the best place; and few left the trough really satisfied. I was the most unlucky of any, for Aunt Katy had no good feeling for me; and if I pushed any of the other children, or if they told her anything unfavorable of me, she always believed the worst, and was sure to whip me.

As I grew older and more thoughtful, I was more and more filled with a sense of my wretchedness. The cruelty of Aunt Katy, the hunger and cold I suffered, and the terrible reports of wrong and outrage which came to my ear, together with what I almost daily witnessed, led me, when yet but eight or nine years old, to wish I had never been born. I used to contrast my condition with the black-birds, in whose wild and sweet songs I fancied them so happy! Their apparent joy only deepened the shades of my sorrow. There are thoughtful days in the lives of children—at least there were in mine—when they grapple with all the great, primary subjects of knowledge, and reach, in a moment, conclusions which no subsequent experience can shake. I was just as well aware of the unjust, unnatural and murderous character of slavery, when nine years old, as I am now. Without any appeal to books, to laws, or to authorities of any kind, it was enough to accept God as a father, to regard slavery as a crime.

I was not ten years old when I left Col. Lloyd's plantation for Baltimore.

I left that plantation with inexpressible joy. I never shall forget the ecstacy with which I received the intelligence from my friend, Miss Lucretia, that my old master had determined to let me go to Baltimore to live with Mr. Hugh Auld, a brother to Mr. Thomas Auld, my old master's son-in-law. I received this information about three days before my departure. They were three of the happiest days of my childhood. I spent the largest part of these three days in the creek, washing off the plantation scurf, and preparing for my new home. Mrs. Lucretia took a lively interest in getting me ready. She told me I must get all the dead skin off my feet and knees, before I could go to Baltimore, for the people there were very cleanly, and would laugh at me if I looked dirty; and, besides, she was intending to give me a pair of trowsers, which I should not put on unless I got all the dirt off. This was a warning to which I was bound to take heed; for the thought of owning a pair of trowsers, was great, indeed. It was almost a sufficient motive, not only to induce me to scrub off the *mange,* (as pig drovers would call it,) but the skin as well. So I went at it in good earnest, working for the first time in the hope of reward. I was greatly excited, and could hardly consent to sleep, lest I should be left. The ties that, ordinarily, bind children to their homes, were all severed, or they never had any existence in my case, at least so far as the home plantation of Col. L. was concerned. I therefore found no severe trial at the moment of my departure, such as I had experienced when separated from my home in Tuckahoe. My home at my old master's was charmless to me; it was not home, but a prison to me; on parting from it, I could not feel that I was leaving anything which I could have enjoyed by staying. My mother was now long dead; my grandmother was far away, so that I seldom saw her; Aunt Katy was my unrelenting tormentor; and my two sisters and brothers, owing to our early separation in life, and the family-destroying power of slavery, were, comparatively, strangers to me. The fact of our relationship was almost blotted out. I looked for *home* elsewhere, and was confident of finding none which I should relish less than the one I was leaving. If, however, I found in my new home—to which I was going with such blissful anticipations—hardship, whipping and nakedness, I had the questionable consolation that I should not have escaped any one of these evils by remaining under the management of Aunt Katy. Then, too, I thought, since I had endured much in this line on Lloyd's plantation, I could endure as much elsewhere, and especially at Baltimore; for I had something of the feeling about that city which is expressed in the saying, that being "hanged in England, is better than dying a natural death in Ireland." I had the strongest desire to see Baltimore. My cousin Tom—a boy two or three years older than I—had been there, and though not fluent (he stuttered immoderately,) in speech, he had inspired me with that desire, by his eloquent description of the place. Tom was, sometimes, Capt. Auld's cabin boy; and when he came from Baltimore, he was always a sort of hero amongst us, at least till his Baltimore trip was forgotten. I could never tell him of anything, or point out anything that struck me as beautiful or powerful, but that he had seen something in Baltimore far surpassing it. Even the great house itself, with all its pictures within, and pillars without, he had the hardihood to say "was nothing to Baltimore." He bought a trumpet, (worth six pence,) and brought it home; told what he had seen in the windows of stores; that he had heard shooting crackers, and seen soldiers; that he had seen a steamboat; that there were ships in Baltimore that could carry four such sloops as the "Sally Lloyd." He said a great deal about the market-house; he spoke of the bells ringing; and of many other things which roused my curiosity very much; and, indeed, which heightened my hopes of happiness in my new home.

We sailed out of Miles river for Baltimore early on a Saturday morning. *4* I remember only the day of the week; for, at that time, I had no knowledge of the days of the month, nor, indeed, of the months of the year. On setting sail, I walked aft, and gave to Col. Lloyd's plantation what I hoped would be the last look I should ever give to it, or to any place like it. My strong aversion to the great house farm, was not owing to my own personal suffering, but the daily suffering of others, and to the certainty, that I must, sooner or later, be placed under the barbarous rule of an overseer, such as the accomplished Gore, or the brutal and drunken Plummer. After taking this last view, I quitted the quarter deck, made my way to the bow of the sloop, and spent the remainder of the day in looking ahead; interesting myself in what was in the distance, rather than what was near by or behind. The vessels, sweeping along the bay, were very interesting objects. The broad bay opened like a shoreless ocean on my boyish vision, filling me with wonder and admiration.

Late in the afternoon, we reached Annapolis, the capital of the state, *5* stopping there not long enough to admit of my going ashore. It was the first large town I had ever seen; and though it was inferior to many a factory village in New England, my feelings, on seeing it, were excited to a pitch very little below that reached by travelers at the first view of Rome. The dome of the state house was especially imposing, and surpassed in grandeur the appearance of the great house. The great world was opening upon me very rapidly, and I was eagerly acquainting myself with its multifarious lessons.

We arrived in Baltimore on Sunday morning, and landed at Smith's *6* wharf, not far from Bowly's wharf. We had on board the sloop a large flock of sheep, for the Baltimore market; and, after assisting in driving them to the slaughter house of Mr. Curtis, on Loudon Slater's Hill, I was speedily conducted by Rich—one of the hands belonging to the sloop—to my new home in Alliciana street, near Gardiner's ship-yard on Fell's Point. Mr. and Mrs. Hugh Auld, my new mistress and master, were both at home, and met me at the door with their rosy cheeked little son, Thomas, to take care of whom was to constitute my future occupation. In fact, it was to "little Tommy," rather than to his parents, that old master made a present of me; and though there was no *legal* form or arrangement entered into, I have no doubt that Mr. and Mrs. Auld felt that, in due time, I should be the legal property of their bright-eyed and beloved boy, Tommy. I was struck with the appearance, especially, of my new mistress. Her face was lighted with the kindliest emotions; and the reflex influence of her countenance, as well as the tenderness with which she seemed to regard me, while asking me sundry little questions, greatly delighted me, and lit up, to my fancy, the pathway of my future. Miss Lucretia was kind; but my new mistress, "Miss Sophy," surpassed her in kindness of manner. Little Thomas was affectionately told by his mother, that "*there was his Freddy,*" and that "Freddy would take care of him;" and I was told to "be kind to little Tommy"—an injunction I scarcely needed, for I had already fallen in love with the dear boy; and with these little ceremonies I was initiated into my new home, and entered upon my peculiar duties, with not a cloud above the horizon.

I may say here, that I regard my removal from Col. Lloyd's plantation as one of the most interesting and fortunate events of my life. Viewing it in the light of human likelihoods, it is quite probable that, but for the mere circumstance of being thus removed before the rigors of slavery had fastened upon me; before my young spirit had been crushed under the iron control of the slave-driver, instead of being, today, a FREEMAN, I might have been wearing the galling chains of slavery. I have sometimes felt, however, that there was something more intelligent than *chance,* and something more certain than *luck,* to be seen in the circumstance. If I have made any progress in knowledge; if I have cherished any honorable aspirations, or have, in any manner, worthily discharged the duties of a member of an oppressed people; this little circumstance must be allowed its due weight in giving my life that direction. I have ever regarded it as the first plain manifestation of that

> Divinity that shapes our ends,
> Rough hew them as we will.

I was not the only boy on the plantation that might have been sent to live in Baltimore. There was a wide margin from which to select. There were boys younger, boys older, and boys of the same age, belonging to my old master—some at his own house, and some at his farm—but the high privilege fell to my lot.

I may be deemed superstitious and egotistical, in regarding this event as a special interposition of Divine Providence in my favor; but the thought is a part of my history, and I should be false to the earliest and most cherished sentiments of my soul, if I suppressed, or hesitated to avow that opinion, although it may be characterized as irrational by the wise, and ridiculous by the scoffer. From my earliest recollections of serious matters, I date the entertainment of something like an ineffaceable conviction, that slavery would not always be able to hold me within its foul embrace; and this conviction, like a word of living faith, strengthened me through the darkest trials of my lot. This good spirit was from God; and to him I offer thanksgiving and praise.

Once in Baltimore, with hard brick pavements under my feet, which almost raised blisters, by their very heat, for it was in the height of summer; walled in on all sides by towering brick buildings; with troops of hostile boys ready to pounce upon me at every street corner; with new and strange objects glaring upon me at every step, and with startling sounds reaching my ears from all directions, I for a time thought that, after all, the home plantation was a more desirable place of residence than my home on Alliciana street, in Baltimore. My country eyes and ears were confused and bewildered here; but the boys were my chief trouble. They chased me, and called me "*Eastern Shore man,*" till really I almost wished myself back on the Eastern Shore. I had to undergo a sort of moral acclimation, and when that was over, I did much better. My new mistress happily proved to be all she *seemed* to be, when, with her husband, she met me at the door, with a most beaming, benignant countenance. She was, naturally, of an excellent disposition, kind, gentle and cheerful. The supercilious contempt for the rights and feelings of the slave, and the petulance and bad humor which generally characterize slaveholding ladies, were all quite absent from kind "Miss" Sophia's manner and bearing toward me. She had, in truth, never been a slaveholder, but had—a thing quite unusual in the south—depended almost entirely upon her own industry for a living. To this fact the dear lady, no doubt, owed the excellent preservation of her natural goodness of heart, for slavery can change a saint into a sinner, and an angel into a demon. I hardly knew how to behave toward "Miss Sopha," as I used to call Mrs. Hugh Auld. I had been treated as a *pig* on the plantation; I was treated as a *child* now. I could not even approach her as I had formerly approached Mrs. Thomas Auld. How could I hang down my head, and speak with bated breath, when there was no pride to scorn me, no coldness to repel me, and no hatred to inspire me with fear? I therefore soon learned to regard her as something more akin to a mother, than a slaveholding mistress. The crouching servility of a slave, usually so acceptable a quality to the haughty slaveholder, was not understood nor desired by this gentle woman. So far from deeming it impudent in a slave to look her straight in the face, as some slaveholding ladies do, she seemed ever to say, "look up, child; don't be afraid; see, I am full of kindness and good will toward you." The hands belonging to Col. Lloyd's sloop, esteemed it a great privilege to be the bearers of parcels or messages to my new mistress; for whenever they came, they were sure of a most kind and pleasant reception. If little Thomas was her son, and her most dearly beloved child, she, for a time, at least, made me something like his half-brother in her affections. If dear Tommy was exalted to a place on his mother's knee, "Feddy" was honored by a place at his mother's side. Nor did he lack the caressing strokes of her gentle hand, to convince him that, though *motherless,* he was not *friendless.* Mrs. Auld was not only a kind-hearted woman, but she was remarkably pious; frequent in her attendance of public worship, much given to reading the bible, and to chanting hymns of praise, when alone. Mr. Hugh Auld was altogether a different character. He cared very little about religion, knew more of the world, and was more of the world, than his wife. He set out, doubtless, to be—as the world goes—a respectable man, and to get on by becoming a successful ship builder, in that city of ship building. This was his ambition, and it fully occupied him. I was, of course, of very little consequence to him, compared with what I was to good Mrs. Auld; and, when he smiled upon me, as he sometimes did, the smile was borrowed from his lovely wife, and, like all borrowed light, was transient, and vanished with the source whence it was derived. While I must characterize Master Hugh as being a very sour man, and of forbidding appearance, it is due to him to acknowledge, that he was never very cruel to me, according to the notion of cruelty in Maryland. The first year or two which I spent in his house, he left me almost exclusively to the management of his wife. She was my law-giver. In hands so tender as hers, and in the absence of the cruelties of the plantation, I became, both physically and mentally, much more sensitive to good and ill treatment; and, perhaps, suffered more from a frown from my mistress, than I formerly did from a cuff at the hands of Aunt Katy. Instead of the cold, damp floor of my old master's kitchen, I found myself on carpets; for the corn bag in winter, I now had a good straw bed, well furnished with covers; for the coarse corn-meal in the morning, I now had good bread, and mush occasionally; for my poor tow-linen shirt, reaching to my knees, I had good, clean clothes. I was really well off. My employment was to run of errands, and to take care of Tommy; to prevent his getting in the way of carriages, and to keep him out of harm's way generally. Tommy, and I, and his mother, got on swimmingly together, for a time. I say *for a time,* because the fatal poison of irresponsible power, and the natural influence of slavery customs, were not long in making a suitable impression on the gentle and loving disposition of my excellent mistress. At first, Mrs. Auld evidently regarded me simply as a child, like any other child; she had not come to regard me as *property.* This latter thought was a thing of conventional growth. The first was natural and spontaneous. A noble nature, like hers, could not, instantly, be wholly perverted; and it took several years to change the natural sweetness of her temper into fretful bitterness. In her worst estate, however, there were, during the first seven years I lived with her, occasional returns of her former kindly disposition.

The frequent hearing of my mistress reading the bible—for she often   11 read aloud when her husband was absent—soon awakened my curiosity in respect to this *mystery* of reading, and roused in me the desire to learn. Having no fear of my kind mistress before my eyes, (she had then given me no reason to fear,) I frankly asked her to teach me to read; and, without hesitation, the dear woman began the task, and very soon, by her assistance, I was master of the alphabet, and could spell words of three or four letters. My mistress seemed almost as proud of my progress, as if I had been her own child; and, supposing that her husband would be as well pleased, she made no secret of what she was doing for me. Indeed, she exultingly told him of the aptness of her pupil, of her intention to persevere in teaching me, and of the duty which she felt it to teach me, at least to read *the bible.* Here arose the first cloud over my Baltimore prospects, the precursor of drenching rains and chilling blasts.

Master Hugh was amazed at the simplicity of his spouse, and, probably   12 for the first time, he unfolded to her the true philosophy of slavery, and the peculiar rules necessary to be observed by masters and mistresses, in the management of their human chattels. Mr. Auld promptly forbade the continuance of her instruction; telling her, in the first place, that the thing itself was unlawful; that it was also unsafe, and could only lead to mischief. To use his own words, further, he said, "if you give a nigger an inch, he will take an ell;" "he should know nothing but the will of his master, and learn to obey it." "Learning would spoil the best nigger in the world;" "if you teach that nigger—speaking of myself—how to read the bible, there will be no keeping him;" "it would forever unfit him for the duties of a slave;" and "as to himself, learning would do him no good, but probably, a great deal of harm—making him disconsolate and unhappy." "If you learn him now to read, he'll want to know how to write; and, this accomplished, he'll be running away with himself." Such was the tenor of Master Hugh's oracular exposition of the true philosophy of training a human chattel; and it must be confessed that he very clearly comprehended the nature and the requirements of the relation of master and slave. His discourse was the first decidedly antislavery lecture to which it had been my lot to listen. Mrs. Auld evidently felt the force of his remarks; and, like an obedient wife, began to shape her course in the direction indicated by her husband. The effect of his words, *on me,* was neither slight nor transitory. His iron sentences—cold and harsh—sunk deep into my heart, and stirred up not only my feelings into a sort of rebellion, but awakened within me a slumbering train of vital thought. It was a new and special revelation, dispelling a painful mystery, against which my youthful understanding had struggled, and struggled in vain, to wit: the *white* man's power to perpetuate the enslavement of the *black* man. "Very well," thought I; "knowledge unfits a child to be a slave." I instinctively assented to the proposition; and from that moment I understood the direct pathway from slavery to freedom. This was just what I needed; and I got it at a time, and from a source, whence I least expected it. I was saddened at the thought of losing the assistance of my kind mistress; but the information, so instantly derived, to some extent compensated me for the loss I had sustained in this direction. Wise as Mr. Auld was, he evidently underrated my comprehension, and had little idea of the use to which I was capable of putting the impressive lesson he was giving to his wife. *He* wanted me to be *a slave;* I had already voted against that on the home plantation of Col. Lloyd. That which he most loved I most hated; and the very determination which he expressed to keep me in ignorance, only rendered me the more resolute in seeking intelligence. In learning to read, therefore, I am not sure that I do not owe quite as much to the opposition of my master, as to the kindly assistance of my amiable mistress. I acknowledge the benefit rendered me by the one, and by the other; believing, that but for my mistress, I might have grown up in ignorance.

I had resided but a short time in Baltimore, before I observed a marked   *13* difference in the manner of treating slaves, generally, from that which I had witnessed in that isolated and out-of-the-way part of the country where I began life. A city slave is almost a free citizen, in Baltimore, compared with a slave on Col. Lloyd's plantation. He is much better fed and clothed, is less dejected in his appearance, and enjoys privileges altogether unknown to the whip-driven slave on the plantation. Slavery dislikes a dense population, in which there is a majority of non-slaveholders. The general sense of decency that must pervade such a population, does much to check and prevent those outbreaks of atrocious cruelty, and those dark crimes without a name, almost openly perpetrated on the plantation. He is a desperate slaveholder who will shock the humanity of his non-slaveholding neighbors, by the cries of the lacerated slaves; and very few in the city are willing to incur the odium of being cruel masters. I found, in Baltimore, that no man was more odious to the white, as well as to the colored people, than he, who had the reputation of starving his slaves. Work them, flog them, if need be, but don't starve them. There are, however, some painful exceptions to this rule. While it is quite true that most of the slaveholders in Baltimore feed and clothe their slaves well, there are others who keep up their country cruelties in the city.

An instance of this sort is furnished in the case of a family who lived   14
directly opposite to our house, and were named Hamilton. Mrs. Hamilton owned two slaves. Their names were Henrietta and Mary. They had always been house slaves. One was aged about twenty-two, and the other about fourteen. They were a fragile couple by nature, and the treatment they received was enough to break down the constitution of a horse. Of all the dejected, emaciated, mangled and excoriated creatures I ever saw, those two girls—in the refined, church going and Christian city of Baltimore—were the most deplorable. Of stone must that heart be made, that could look upon Henrietta and Mary, without being sickened to the core with sadness. Especially was Mary a heart-sickening object. Her head, neck and shoulders, were literally cut to pieces. I have frequently felt her head, and found it nearly covered over with festering sores, caused by the lash of her cruel mistress. I do not know that her master ever whipped her, but I have often been an eye witness of the revolting and brutal inflictions by Mrs. Hamilton; and what lends a deeper shade to this woman's conduct, is the fact, that, almost in the very moments of her shocking outrages of humanity and decency, she would charm you by the sweetness of her voice and her seeming piety. She used to sit in a large rocking chair, near the middle of the room, with a heavy cow-skin, such as I have elsewhere described; and I speak within the truth when I say, that those girls seldom passed that chair, during the day, without a blow from that cowskin, either upon their bare arms, or upon their shoulders. As they passed her, she would draw her cowskin and give them a blow, saying, "*move faster, you black jip!*" and, again, "*take that, you black jip!*" continuing, "*if you don't move faster, I will give you more.*" Then the lady would go on, singing her sweet hymns, as though her *righteous* soul were sighing for the holy realms of paradise.

Added to the cruel lashings to which these poor slave-girls were sub-   15
jected—enough in themselves to crush the spirit of men—they were, really, kept nearly half starved; they seldom knew what it was to eat a full meal, except when they got it in the kitchens of neighbors, less mean and stingy

than the psalm-singing Mrs. Hamilton. I have seen poor Mary contending for the offal, with the pigs in the street. So much was the poor girl pinched, kicked, cut and pecked to pieces, that the boys in the street knew her only by the name of *"pecked,"* a name derived from the scars and blotches on her neck, head and shoulders.

It is some relief to this picture of slavery in Baltimore, to say—what is but the simple truth—that Mrs. Hamilton's treatment of her slaves was generally condemned, as disgraceful and shocking; but while I say this, it must also be remembered, that the very parties who censured the cruelty of Mrs. Hamilton, would have condemned and promptly punished any attempt to interfere with Mrs. Hamilton's *right* to cut and slash her slaves to pieces. There must be no force between the slave and the slaveholder, to restrain the power of the one, and protect the weakness of the other; and the cruelty of Mrs. Hamilton is as justly chargeable to the upholders of the slave system, as drunkenness is chargeable on those who, by precept and example, or by indifference, uphold the drinking system. 16

I lived in the family of Master Hugh, at Baltimore, seven years, during which time—as the almanac makers say of the weather—my condition was variable. The most interesting feature of my history here, was my learning to read and write, under somewhat marked disadvantages. In attaining this knowledge, I was compelled to resort to indirections by no means congenial to my nature, and which were really humiliating to me. My mistress—who, as the reader has already seen, had begun to teach me—was suddenly checked in her benevolent design, by the strong advice of her husband. In faithful compliance with this advice, the good lady had not only ceased to instruct me, herself, but had set her face as a flint against my learning to read by any means. It is due, however, to my mistress to say, that she did not adopt this course in all its stringency at the first. She either thought it unnecessary, or she lacked the depravity indispensable to shutting me up in mental darkness. It was, at least, necessary for her to have some training, and some hardening, in the exercise of the slaveholder's prerogative, to make her equal to forgetting my human nature and character, and to treating me as a thing destitute of a moral or an intellectual nature. Mrs. Auld—my mistress—was, as I have said, a most kind and tender-hearted woman; and, in the humanity of her heart, and the simplicity of her mind, she set out, when I first went to live with her, to treat me as she supposed one human being ought to treat another. 17

It is easy to see, that, in entering upon the duties of a slaveholder, some little experience is needed. Nature has done almost nothing to prepare men and women to be either slaves or slaveholders. Nothing but rigid training, long persisted in, can perfect the character of the one or the other. One cannot easily forget to love freedom; and it is as hard to cease to respect that natural love in our fellow creatures. On entering upon the career of a slave-holding mistress, Mrs. Auld was singularly deficient; nature, which fits nobody for such an office, had done less for her than any lady I had known. It was no 18 easy matter to induce her to think and to feel that the curly-headed boy, who stood by her side, and even leaned on her lap; who was loved by little Tommy, and who loved little Tommy in turn; sustained to her only the relation of a chattel. I was *more* than that, and she felt me to be more than that. I could talk and sing; I could laugh and weep; I could reason and remember; I could love and hate. I was human, and she, dear lady, knew and felt me to be so. How could she, then, treat me as a brute, without a mighty struggle with all the noble powers of her own soul. That struggle came, and the will and power of the husband was victorious. Her noble soul was overthrown; but, he that overthrew it did not, himself, escape the consequences. He, not less than the other parties, was injured in his domestic peace by the fall.

When I went into their family, it was the abode of happiness and con- *19* tentment. The mistress of the house was a model of affection and tenderness. Her fervent piety and watchful uprightness made it impossible to see her without thinking and feeling—*"that woman is a christian."* There was no sorrow nor suffering for which she had not a tear, and there was no innocent joy for which she had not a smile. She had bread for the hungry, clothes for the naked, and comfort for every mourner that came within her reach. Slavery soon proved its ability to divest her of these excellent qualities, and her home of its early happiness. Conscience cannot stand much violence. Once thoroughly broken down, *who* is he that can repair the damage? It may be broken toward the slave, on Sunday, and toward the master on Monday. It cannot endure such shocks. It must stand entire, or it does not stand at all. If my condition waxed bad, that of the family waxed not better. The first step, in the wrong direction, was the violence done to nature and to conscience, in arresting the benevolence that would have enlightened my young mind. In ceasing to instruct me, she must begin to justify herself *to* herself; and, once consenting to take sides in such a debate, she was riveted to her position. One needs very little knowledge of moral philosophy, to see *where* my mistress now landed. She finally became even more violent in her opposition to my learning to read, than was her husband himself. She was not satisfied with simply doing as *well* as her husband had commanded her, but seemed resolved to better his instruction. Nothing appeared to make my poor mistress—after her turning toward the downward path—more angry, than seeing me, seated in some nook or corner, quietly reading a book or a newspaper. I have had her rush at me, with the utmost fury, and snatch from my hand such newspaper or book, with something of the wrath and consternation which a traitor might be supposed to feel on being discovered in a plot by some dangerous spy.

Mrs. Auld was an apt woman, and the advice of her husband, and her *20* own experience, soon demonstrated, to her entire satisfaction, that education and slavery are incompatible with each other. When this conviction was thoroughly established, I was most narrowly watched in all my movements. If I remained in a separate room from the family for any considerable length of time, I was sure to be suspected of having a book, and was at once called upon to give an account of myself. All this, however, was entirely *too late*. The first, and never to be retraced, step had been taken. In teaching me the alphabet, in the days of her simplicity and kindness, my mistress had given me the *"inch,"* and now, no ordinary precaution could prevent me from taking the *"ell."*

Seized with a determination to learn to read, at any cost, I hit upon   *21* many expedients to accomplish the desired end. The plea which I mainly adopted, and the one by which I was most successful, was that of using my young white playmates, with whom I met in the street, as teachers. I used to carry, almost constantly, a copy of Webster's spelling book in my pocket; and, when sent of errands, or when play time was allowed me, I would step, with my young friends, aside, and take a lesson in spelling. I generally paid my *tuition fee* to the boys, with bread, which I also carried in my pocket. For a single biscuit, any of my hungry little comrades would give me a lesson more valuable to me than bread. Not every one, however, demanded this consideration, for there were those who took pleasure in teaching me, whenever I had a chance to be taught by them. I am strongly tempted to give the names of two or three of those little boys, as a slight testimonial of the gratitude and affection I bear them, but prudence forbids; not that it would injure me, but it might, possibly, embarrass them; for it is almost an unpardonable offense to do any thing, directly or indirectly, to promote a slave's freedom, in a slave state. It is enough to say, of my warm-hearted little play fellows, that they lived on Philpot street, very near Durgin & Bailey's shipyard.

Although slavery was a delicate subject, and very cautiously talked about   *22* among grown up people in Maryland, I frequently talked about it—and that very freely—with the white boys. I would, sometimes, say to them, while seated on a curb stone or a cellar door, "I wish I could be free, as you will be when you get to be men." "You will be free, you know, as soon as you are twenty-one, and can go where you like, but I am a slave for life. Have I not as good a right to be free as you have?" Words like these, I observed, always troubled them; and I had no small satisfaction in wringing from the boys, occasionally, that fresh and bitter condemnation of slavery, that springs from nature, unseared and unperverted. Of all consciences, let me have those to deal with which have not been bewildered by the cares of life. I do not remember ever to have met with a *boy,* while I was in slavery, who defended the slave system; but I have often had boys to console me, with the hope that something would yet occur, by which I might be made free. Over and over again, they have told me, that "they believed *I* had as good a right to be free as *they* had;" and that "they did not believe God ever made any one to be a slave." The reader will easily see, that such little conversations with my play fellows, had no tendency to weaken my love of liberty, nor to render me contented with my condition as a slave.

When I was about thirteen years old, and had succeeded in learning to   *23* read, every increase of knowledge, especially respecting the FREE STATES, added something to the almost intolerable burden of the thought—"I AM A SLAVE FOR LIFE." To my bondage I saw no end. It was a terrible reality, and I shall never be able to tell how sadly that thought chafed my young spirit. Fortunately, or unfortunately, about this time in my life, I had made enough money to buy what was then a very popular school book, viz: the "Columbian Orator." I bought this addition to my library, of Mr. Knight, on Thames street, Fell's Point, Baltimore, and paid him fifty cents for it. I was first led to buy this book, by hearing some little boys say that they were going to learn some little pieces out of it for the Exhibition. This volume was, indeed, a rich treasure, and every opportunity afforded me, for a time, was spent in diligently perusing it. Among much other interesting matter, that which I had perused and reperused with unflagging satisfaction, was a short dialogue between a master and his slave. The slave is represented as having been recaptured, in a second attempt to run away; and the master opens the dialogue with an up-braiding speech, charging the slave with ingratitude, and demanding to know what he has to say in his own defense. Thus upbraided, and thus called upon to reply, the slave rejoins, that he knows how little anything that he can say will avail, seeing that he is completely in the hands of his owner; and with noble resolution, calmly says, "I submit to my fate." Touched by the slave's answer, the master insists upon his further speaking, and recapitulates the many acts of kindness which he has performed toward the slave, and tells him he is permitted to speak for himself. Thus invited to the debate, the quondam slave made a spirited defense of himself, and thereafter the whole argument, for and against slavery, was brought out. The master was vanquished at every turn in the argument; and seeing himself to be thus vanquished, he generously and meekly emancipates the slave, with his best wishes for his prosperity. It is scarcely necessary to say, that a dialogue, with such an origin, and such an ending—read when the fact of my being a slave was a constant burden of grief—powerfully affected me; and I could not help feeling that the day might come, when the well-directed answers made by the slave to the master, in this instance, would find their counterpart in myself.

This, however, was not all the fanaticism which I found in this Colum- *24* bian Orator. I met there one of Sheridan's mighty speeches, on the subject of Catholic Emancipation, Lord Chatham's speech on the American war, and speeches by the great William Pitt and by Fox: These were all choice documents to me, and I read them, over and over again, with an interest that was ever increasing, because it was ever gaining in intelligence; for the more I read them, the better I understood them. The reading of these speeches added much to my limited stock of language, and enabled me to give tongue to many interesting thoughts, which had frequently flashed through my soul, and died away for want of utterance. The mighty power and heart-searching directness of truth, penetrating even the heart of a slaveholder, compelling him to yield up his earthly interests to the claims of eternal justice, were finely illustrated in the dialogue, just referred to; and from the speeches of Sheridan, I got a bold and powerful denunciation of oppression, and a most brilliant vindication of the rights of man. Here was, indeed, a noble acquisition. If I ever wavered under the consideration, that the Almighty, in some way, ordained slavery, and willed my enslavement for his own glory, I wavered no longer. I had now penetrated the secret of all slavery and oppression, and had ascertained their true foundation to be in the pride, the power and the avarice of man. The dialogue and the speeches were all redolent of the principles of liberty, and poured floods of light on the nature and character of slavery. With a book of this kind in my hand, my own human nature, and the facts of my experience, to help me, I was equal to a contest with the religious advocates of slavery, whether among the whites or among the colored people, for blindness, in this matter, is not confined to the former. I have met many religious colored people, at the south, who are under the delusion that God requires them to submit to slavery, and to wear their chains with meekness and humility. I could entertain no such nonsense as this; and I almost lost my patience when I found any colored man weak enough to believe such stuff. Nevertheless, the increase of knowledge was attended with bitter, as well as sweet results. The more I read, the more I was led to abhor and detest slavery, and my enslavers. "Slaveholders," thought I, "are only a band of successful robbers, who left their homes and went into Africa for the purpose of stealing and reducing my people to slavery." I loathed them as the meanest and the most wicked of men. As I read, behold! the very discontent so graphically predicted by Master Hugh, had already come upon me. I was no longer the light-hearted, gleesome boy, full of mirth and play, as when I landed first at Baltimore. Knowledge had come; light had penetrated the moral dungeon where I dwelt; and, behold! there lay the bloody whip, for my back, and here was the iron chain; and my good, *kind master,* he was the author of my situation. The revelation haunted me, stung me, and made me gloomy and miserable. As I writhed under the sting and torment of this knowledge, I almost envied my fellow slaves their stupid contentment. This knowledge opened my eyes to the horrible pit, and revealed the teeth of the frightful dragon that was ready to pounce upon me, but it opened no way for my escape. I have often wished myself a beast, or a bird—anything, rather than a slave. I was wretched and gloomy, beyond my ability to describe. I was too thoughtful to be happy. It was this everlasting thinking which distressed and tormented me; and yet there was no getting rid of the subject of my thoughts. All nature was redolent of it. Once awakened by the silver trump of knowledge, my spirit was roused to eternal wakefulness. Liberty! the inestimable birthright of every man, had, for me, converted every object into an asserter of this great right. It was heard in every sound, and beheld in every object. It was ever present, to torment me with a sense of my wretched condition. The more beautiful and charming were the smiles of nature, the more horrible and desolate was my condition. I saw nothing without seeing it, and I heard nothing without hearing it. I do not exaggerate, when I say, that it looked from every star, smiled in every calm, breathed in every wind, and moved in every storm.

I have no doubt that my state of mind had something to do with the change in the treatment adopted, by my once kind mistress toward me. I can easily believe, that my leaden, downcast, and discontented look, was very offensive to her. Poor lady! She did not know my trouble, and I dared not tell her. Could I have freely made her acquainted with the real state of my mind, and given her the reasons therefor, it might have been well for both of us. Her abuse of me fell upon me like the blows of the false prophet upon his ass; she did not know that an *angel* stood in the way; and—such is the relation of master and slave—I could not tell her. Nature had made us *friends;* slavery made us *enemies.* My interests were in a direction opposite to hers, and we both had our private thoughts and plans. She aimed to keep me ignorant; and I resolved to know, although knowledge only increased my discontent. My feelings were not the result of any marked cruelty in the treatment I received; they sprung from the consideration of my being a slave at all. It was *slavery*—not its mere *incidents*—that I hated. I had been cheated. I saw through the attempt to keep me in ignorance; I saw that slaveholders would have gladly made me believe that they were merely acting under the authority of God, in making a slave of me, and in making slaves of others; and I treated them as robbers and deceivers. The feeding and clothing me well, could not atone for taking my liberty from me. The smiles of my mistress could not remove the deep sorrow that dwelt in my young bosom. Indeed, these, in time, came only to deepen my sorrow. She had changed; and the reader will see that I had changed, too. We were both victims to the same overshadowing evil—*she,* as mistress, *I,* as slave. I will not censure her harshly; she cannot censure me, for she knows I speak but the truth, and have acted in my opposition to slavery, just as she herself would have acted, in a reverse of circumstances.

Topics for Discussion and Writing

1. List what for you are the most striking events and ideas in this essay. Compare this list with your earlier writing on your knowledge about slavery. What powerful images of Douglass's contrast with the images that had earlier influenced you?

2. Write about the relationship of the slave "Freddy," Mrs. Auld, and Mr. Auld. Reread and comment on Douglass's analysis of how he was initially treated and of how his treatment by the Aulds, especially Mrs. Auld, changed. What would you add to his analysis, from your vantage point a century and a half later?

3. Review Douglass's argument about the effect of the city (versus the country) on the institution of slavery. What conditions does he imply are necessary in order for slavery to flourish? What conditions hinder slavery? Translating Douglass's discussion from his time to ours, what contemporary factors do you feel are the most effective hindrance to the master/slave mentality? What contemporary factors do you feel might encourage a society with a few masters and many slaves? How would you define these masters and these slaves?

4. Note how Douglass refers to *nature* throughout this excerpt. How does he characterize what it is "natural" for humans to believe and do? How might a slaveholder, such as Mr. Auld, try to counter his arguments with his own assessment of natural behavior? Imagine yourself as a third party in this debate. How would you argue?

PATRICIA J. WILLIAMS
from *The Alchemy of Race and Rights*

> *"It seems to me that the stigma of 'Dr. Martin Luther King Boulevard' or 'Roxbury' is reflective of deep personal discomfort among blacks, a wordless and tabooed sense of self that is identical to the discomfort shared by both blacks and whites in even mentioning words like 'black' and 'race' in mixed company."*

> *A popular speaker and an author of articles in leading law journals, Patricia J. Williams (born in 1951 in the Roxbury section of Boston) is an associate professor of law at the University of Wisconsin. "The Obliging Shell (an informal essay on formal equal opportunity)" is taken from her book* The Alchemy of Race and Rights: Diary of a Law Professor *(1991).*

Before and as You Read

1. Find a copy of the U.S. Constitution and read the texts of the 14th, 15th, and 24th Amendments. You'll note that these amendments are simply stated and avoid citing particular cases to which the laws might apply. Write your own interpretation of one of the amendments: what, to you, does the law mean and what, do you feel, does it not mean? How might others disagree with you on this interpretation? Cite an example of a dispute over which people might argue about the applicability of this law.

2. Take part in a discussion among those who have done the previous exercise. As each person presents her or his interpretation, take notes on (1) the meanings each applies to the laws, (2) the evidence or reasons each gives for the interpretation, and (3) the cases each mentions. Look for ways in which the writers are consistent with one another, and ways in which they differ.

3. Write as honestly as you can in your journal about your views and experiences of racism. Have you been the object of racist behavior? If so, describe one such experience. Have you been guilty of racist behavior? If so, describe one such experience and reflect on your feelings and questions about it.

4. As you read Patricia Williams's closely argued essay, keep track of how she focuses on the meanings that people give to key terms. Note how she analyzes the language of statements and court decisions to show the subtle force of deeply ingrained beliefs.

THE OBLIGING SHELL (AN INFORMAL ESSAY ON FORMAL EQUAL OPPORTUNITY)

I HAVE DECIDED to attend a Continuing Education of the Bar course on equal-employment opportunity. Bar-style questions are handed out for general discussion. The first question reads:

Question One: X and Y apply for the same job with firm Z. X and
Y are equally qualified. Which one should get the job?

I panic. What exactly is meant by Question One? But apparently this is supposed to be a throwaway question. On the blackboard the instructor writes:

Right Answer: Whichever one you like better.

As usual I have missed the point and am busy complicating things. In my
notebook I write:

> Wrong Answer: What a clear, graspable comparison this is; it is   *2*
> like choosing between smooth pebbles. X, the simple crossing of two
> lines, the intersection of sticks; Y, the cleaned bones of a flesh-and-
> blood referent. There is something seductive about this stone-cool
> algebra of rich life stories. There is something soothing about its static
> neutrality, its emotionless purity. It is a choice luxuriantly free of
> consequence.
>
> At any rate, much of this answer probably depends on what is   *3*
> meant by "equal qualifications." Rarely are two people absolutely
> equally qualified (they both went to Harvard, they graduated in the
> same class, they tied for number one, they took all the same classes,
> etc.) so the judgment of equality is usually pretty subjective to begin
> with (a degree from Yale is as good as one from Harvard, a degree in
> philosophy is as useful as a degree in political science, an editor of
> the school paper is as good as the class president) and usually over-
> looks or fills in a lot of information that may in fact distinguish the
> candidates significantly (is it the same to be number one in a small
> class as in a huge class; is the grading done by some absolute standard,
> or on a strictly enforced bell curve; did X succeed by taking only
> standardized tests in large lecture courses; does Y owe his success to
> the individualized attention received in small seminars where he could
> write papers on subjects no one else knew or cared about?). All such
> differentiations are matters of subjective preference, since all such
> "equality" is nothing more than assumption, the subjective willing-
> ness not to look past a certain point, or to accept the judgments of
> others (the admissions director of Harvard, the accuracy of the LSAT
> computer-grader).
>
> The mind funnels of Harvard and Yale are called standards. Stan-   *4*
> dards are concrete monuments to socially accepted subjective prefer-
> ence. Standards are like paths picked through fields of equanimity,
> worn into hard wide roads over time, used always because of collec-
> tive habit, expectation, and convenience. The pleasures and perils of
> picking one's own path through the field are soon forgotten; the logic
> or illogic of the course of the road is soon rationalized by the mere
> fact of the road.
>
> But let's assume that we do find two candidates who are as alike as   *5*

can be. They are identical twins. They've had exactly the same training from the same teachers in a field that emphasizes mastery of technique or skill in a way that can be more easily calibrated than, say, writing a novel. Let's say it's a hypothetical school of ultraclassical ballet—the rules are clear, the vocabulary is rigid, artistry is judged in probably far too great a measure by mastery of specific placements and technical renderings of kinetic combinations. (The formal requirements of the New York City Rockettes, for example, are that a dancer must be between 5 feet 5½ inches and 5 feet 8 inches tall precisely and be able to do twenty eye-level kicks with a straight back.) I could probably hire either one, but I am left with the nagging wonder as to my own hypothetical about whether I want either one of these goody-two-shoed automatons. I wonder, indeed, if the fact that the "standard" road is good may obscure the fact that it is not the only good road. I begin to wonder, in other words, not about my two candidates, but about the tortoise-shell nature of a community of employees that has managed to successfully suppress or ignore the distinguishing variegation of being human. (Even if we were talking about an assembly line, where the standard were some monotonous minimal rather than a rarefied maximum, my concern holds that certain human characteristics are being dishonored as irrelevant—such as creativity, humor, and amiability.)

I wonder if this simple but complete suppression of the sterling   6
quirks and idiosyncrasies of what it is that makes a person an individual is not related to the experience of oppression. I wonder if the failure to be held accountable for the degree to which such so-called neutral choices are decided on highly subjective, articulable, but mostly unarticulated factors (the twin on the left has a higher voice and I like high voices) is not related to the perpetuation of bias.

By the time I finish writing this, the teacher is well along into discussion   7
of the next question, this time a real one:

Question Two: X and Y apply for the same job with firm Z. X and Y are equally qualified. X is black and Y is white; Z is presently an all-white firm. Which one should get the job?

It feels almost blasphemous to complicate things like this. I feel the anger in the challenge to the calm neatness of the previous comparison; it seems to me that this is a trick question, full of labyrinthian twists and illusion. Will I be strong enough to cut my way through the suggestions and shadows, the mirror tricks of dimensionality? I hold my breath as the teacher writes on the blackboard:

Right Answer: Whichever one you like better, because race is irrelevant. Our society will impose no rules grounded in preference according to race.

In my notebook I write: *8*

> Left Answer: The black person should get the job. If the modern white man, innocently or not, is the inheritor of another's due, then it must be returned. I read a rule somewhere that said if a thief steals so that his children may live in luxury and the law returns his ill-gotten gain to its rightful owner, the children cannot complain that they have been deprived of what they did not own. Blacks have earned a place in this society; they have earned a share of its enormous wealth, with physical labor and intellectual sacrifice, as wages and as royalties. Blacks deserve their inheritance as much as family wealth passed from parent to child over the generations is a "deserved" inheritance. It is deserved as child support and alimony. It is ours because we gave birth to it and we raised it up and we fed it. It is ours because our legal system has always idealized structuring present benefit for those who forbore in the past.
>
> But, then, I'm doing what I always seem to do—mistaking the rules of fraud and contract for constitutional principles. How's this: It's important to hire the black person because the presence of blacks within, as opposed to without, the bell jar of a given community changes the dynamic forever.

As I write, a discussion has been raging in the room. One of the course participants growls: "How can you force equality down the throats of people who don't want it? You just end up depriving people of their freedom, and creating new categories of oppressed, such as white men."

I think: the great paradox of democratic freedom is that it involves some   *9*
measure of enforced equality for all. The worst dictatorships in history have always given some freedom: freedom for a privileged some at the expense of the rest is usually what makes oppression so attractively cost-effective to begin with. Is freedom really such a narrowly pluralistic concept that, so long as we can find some slaves to say they're happy with the status quo, things are fine and free? Are they or the rest of the slaves less enslaved by calling enslavement freedom?

The tension voiced by the growler seems to be between notions of   *10*
associative autonomy, on the one hand, and socialized valuations of worth—equality and inequality notions—whose foundations are not in view and go unquestioned. Categorizing is not the sin; the problem is the lack of desire to examine the categorizations that are made. The problem is not recognizing the ethical worth in attempting to categorize with not only individual but social goals in mind as well. The problem is in the failure to assume responsibility for examining how or where we set our boundaries.

Privatized terms so dominate the public discourse that it is difficult to   *11*
see or appreciate social evil, communal wrong, states of affairs that implicate us whether we will it or not. Affirmative action challenges many people who believe in the truism that this is a free country. For people who don't believe

that there is such a thing as institutional racism, statements alleging oppression sound like personal attacks, declarations of war. They seem to scrape deep from the cultural unconscious some childish feelings of wanting to belong by forever having others as extensions of oneself, of never being told of difference, of not being rent apart by the singularity of others, of the privilege of having the innocence of one's most whimsical likes respected. It is a feeling that many equate with the quintessence of freedom; this powerful fancy, the unconditionality of self-will alone. It is as if no others exist and no consequences redound; it is as if the world were like a mirror, silent and infinitely flat, rather than finite and rippled like a pool of water.

The "it's a free country" attack on affirmative action is also an argument, *12* however, that is profoundly inconsistent with the supposed rationale for the imposition of "standards," however frequently the arguments are paired. The fundamental isolationism of individual preference as an arbiter is quite different from the "neutrality," the "blindness," and the "impersonality" used to justify the collectivized convenience of standardized preference. I wonder what a world "without preference" would look like anyway. Standards are nothing more than structured preferences. Preferential treatment isn't inherently dirty; seeing its ubiquity, within and without racial politics, is the key to the underground vaults of freedom locked up in the idea of whom one likes. The whole historical object of equal opportunity, formal or informal, is to structure preferences for rather than against—to like rather than dislike—the participation of black people. Thus affirmative action is very different from numerical quotas that actively structure society so that certain classes of people remain unpreferred. "Quotas," "preference," "reverse discrimination," "experienced," and "qualified" are con words, shiny mirror words that work to dazzle the eye with their analogic evocation of other times, other contexts, multiple histories. As a society, we have yet to look carefully beneath them to see where the seeds of prejudice are truly hidden.

If, moreover, racism is artificially relegated to a time when it was written *13* into code, the continuing black experience of prejudice becomes a temporal shell game manipulated by whites. Such a refusal to talk about the past disguises a refusal to talk about the present. If prejudice is what's going on in the present, then aren't we, the makers and interpreters of laws, engaged in the purest form of denial? Or, if prejudice is a word that signified only what existed "back" in the past, don't we need a new word to signify what is going on in the present? Amnesia, perhaps?

We live in an era in which women and people of color compose and *14* literally define both this society's underclass and its most underserved population. A recent study by the Urban League reports:

> The difference in the percentage of blacks and whites holding managerial and professional jobs is unlikely to narrow significantly before the year 2039. Currently, white men are twice as likely as black men to hold sales, managerial or professional positions.

With the wages of white men averaging $450 a week in 1987 as against $326 a week for black men, income parity between the two groups will not be achieved before 2058.

Black children are completing high school at a slower rate than whites. But the paper said that the percentage of blacks finishing high school rose from 55 percent of the white graduation rate in 1967 to 79 percent in 1985, and it estimated that equal percentages of blacks and whites will graduate in 2001.

This last statistic is complicated by the fact that "between 1976 and 1985, the college-going rate of black high school graduates fell from 34 to 26 percent, despite the fact that the percentage of black high school graduates rose from 67 to 75 percent." This decrease was largely due to the Reagan Administration's cuts in federal financial aid to students.

Remedying this, therefore, must be society's most pressing area of rep-   15 resentational responsibility; not only in terms of fairly privatized issues such as "more pro bono" or more lawyers taking on more cases of particular sorts, but in closely examining the ways in which the law operates to omit women and people of color at all levels including the most subtle—to omit them from the literature of the law, from the ranks of lawyers, and from the numbers of those served by its interests.

One week after the end of the equal-opportunity course, the Supreme   16 Court came down with its opinion in *City of Richmond v. J. A. Croson Co.* That case presented a challenge, as well as its own model of resistance, to the pursuit of "proper findings . . . necessary to define both the scope of the injury [in race and gender cases] and the extent of the remedy."

Croson involved a minority set-aside program in the awarding of munic-   17 ipal contracts. Richmond, Virginia, with a black population of just over 50 percent had set a 30 percent goal in the awarding of city construction contracts, based on its findings that local, state, and national patterns of discrimination had resulted in all but complete lack of access for minority-owned businesses. The Supreme Court stated:

> We, therefore, hold that the city has failed to demonstrate a *compelling* interest in apportioning public contracting opportunities on the basis of race. To accept Richmond's claim that past societal discrimination alone can serve as the basis for rigid racial preferences would be to open the door to competing claims for "remedial relief" for *every* disadvantaged group. The dream of a Nation of equal citizens in a society where race is irrelevant to personal opportunity and achievement would be lost in a mosaic of shifting preferences based on *inherently unmeasurable* claims of past wrongs. [Citing *Bakke:*] Courts would be asked to evaluate the extent of the prejudice and consequent harm suffered by various minority groups. Those whose societal injury *is thought* to exceed some *arbitrary* level of tolerability then

would be entitled to preferential classification. We think such a result would be contrary to both the letter and the spirit of a constitutional provision whose central command is equality.

What strikes me most about this holding are the rhetorical devices the court employs to justify its outcome:

(a) It sets up a "slippery slope" at the bottom of which lie hordes-in-waiting of warring barbarians: an "open door" through which would flood the "competing claims" of "every disadvantaged group." It problematizes by conjuring mythic dangers.

(b) It describes situations for which there are clear, hard statistical data as "inherently unmeasurable." It puts in the diminutive that which is not; it makes infinite what in fact is limited.

(c) It puts itself in passive relation to the purported "arbitrariness" of others' perceptions of the intolerability of their circumstances ("those whose societal injury is thought to . . .").

These themes are reiterated throughout the opinion: Societal discrimi- *18* nation is "too amorphous"; racial goals are labeled "unyielding"; goals are labeled "quotas"; statistics are rendered "generalizations"; testimony becomes mere "recitation"; legislative purpose and action become "mere legislative assurances of good intention"; and lower-court opinion is just "blind judicial deference." This adjectival dismissiveness alone is sufficient to hypnotize the reader into believing that the "assumption that white prime contractors simply will not hire minority persons is completely unsupported."

And as I think about the *Croson* opinion, I cannot but marvel at how, *19* against a backdrop of richly textured facts and proof on both local and national scales, in a city where more than half the population is black and in which fewer than 1 percent of contracts are awarded to minorities or minority-owned businesses, interpretative artifice alone allowed this narrow vision not just that 30 percent was too great a set-aside, but that there was no proof of discrimination. Moreover, the rhetorical devices that accomplished this astonishing holding are comprehensible less from the perspective of traditionally conceived constitutional standards—whether rational relation or strict scrutiny—than by turning to interpretive standards found in private law. The process by which the court consistently diminished the importance of real facts and figures is paralleled only by the process of rendering "extrinsic" otherwise probative evidence under the parol evidence rule. In particular, I am struck by the court's use of the word "equality" in the last line of its holding. It seems an extraordinarily narrow use of equality, when it excludes from consideration so much clear inequality. Again it resembles the process by which the parol evidence rule limits the meaning of documents or words by placing beyond the bounds of reference anything that is inconsistent with or even supplementary to the written agreement.

A few months after the *Croson* decision, the Supreme Court followed up *20* with a string of famous cases that effectively gutted enforcement of the whole Civil Rights Act, to say nothing of affirmative action. After the first of these, *Martin v. Wilks,* in which consent decrees setting goals for the hiring of black firefighters in Birmingham, Alabama, were permitted to be challenged collaterally by white firefighters, Reagan's Assistant Attorney General Charles J. Cooper was reported in the *Washington Post* as having said that the case was "a home run for white men." Two days later the *Post* printed a clarification saying that Cooper's remarks had been "incorrectly characterized": "Cooper felt that the ruling was a 'home run' for the proposition that people injured by affirmative action plans should be allowed to challenge them." In the *New York Times* David Watkins, a lawyer for the city of Birmingham, hailed reverse discrimination cases as "the wave of the future": "I think whites have correctly perceived the new attitude of the U.S. Supreme Court, which seems to be giving encouragement to white citizens to challenge black gains in virtually every aspect of social and economic life."

. . . Affirmative-action programs, of which minority set-asides are but 21 one example, were designed to remedy a segregationist view of equality in which positivistic categories of race reigned supreme. "White" had an ironclad definition that was the equivalent of "good" or "deserving". "Black" had an ironclad definition that was the equivalent of "bad" or unworthy of inclusion.

Although the most virulent examples of such narrow human and lin- 22 guistic interpretations have been removed from the code books, much of this unconsciously filtered vision remains with us in subtler form. An example may be found in the so-called Ujaama House incidents that took place on Stanford University's campus in the fall of 1988. (Ujaama House is one of several "theme" houses set up with the idea of exposing students to a variety of live-in cultural and racial exchanges. There is a Hispanic theme house, a Japanese theme house; Ujaama is the African-American theme house.)

On the night of September 29, 1988, a white student identified only as 23 "Fred" and a black student called "Q.C." had an argument about whether the composer Beethoven had black blood. Q.C. insisted that he did; Fred thought the very idea "preposterous."

> The following night, the white students said that they got drunk and decided to color a poster of Beethoven to represent a black stereotype. They posted it outside the room of Q.C., the black student who had originally made the claim about Beethoven's race.
>
> Later, on October 14, after the defacing but before the culprits had been identified, a black fraternity's poster hanging in the dorm was emblazoned with the word "niggers." No one has admitted to that act, which prompted an emergency house staff meeting that eventually led to the identification [of Fred as one] of the students who had defaced the Beethoven poster.

In subsequent months there was an exhaustive study conducted by the 24 university, which issued a report of its findings on January 18, 1989. There were three things about Fred's explanation that I found particularly interesting in the report:

(1) Fred said he was upset by "all this emphasis on race, on blackness. Why can't we just all be human—I think it denies one's humanity to be 'racial.'" I was struck by the word boxes in which "race," "blackness," and "humanity" were structured as inconsistent concepts.

(2) Fred is a descendant of German Jews and was schooled in England. He described incidents that he called "teasing"—I would call them humiliation, even torture—by his schoolmates about his being Jewish. They called him miserly, and his being a Jew was referred to as a weakness. Fred said that he learned not to mind it and indicated that the poster defacement at Ujaama House had been in the spirit of this teaching. He wondered why the black students couldn't respond to it in the spirit in which it was meant: "nothing serious," just "humor as a release." It was a little message, he said, to stop all this divisive black stuff and be human. Fred appeared to me to be someone who was humiliated into conformity and then, in the spirit of the callousness and displaced pain that humiliation ultimately engenders, was passing it on.

(3) Fred found the assertion that Beethoven was black not just annoying but "preposterous." In the wake of the defacement, he was assigned to do some reading on the subject and found that indeed Beethoven was a mulatto. This discovery upset him, so deeply in fact that his entire relation to the music changed: he said he heard it differently.

Ultimately, Stanford's disciplinary board found no injury to Q.C. and recommended no disciplining of Fred because they felt that would victimize him, depriving him of his first-amendment rights. As to this remedy, I was struck by the following issues:

(1) The privatization of remedy to Q.C. alone.
(2) The invisibility of any injury to anyone, whether to Q.C. or to the Stanford community, whether to whites or to blacks.
(3) The paradoxical pitting of the first amendment against speaking about other forms of injury—so that the specter of legal censorship actually blocks further discussion of moral censure. This is always a hard point to make: I am not arguing against the first amendment; what I am insisting upon is some appreciation for the power of words—and for the other forms of power abuses that may lurk behind the "defense" of free speech.

As in *Croson*'s definition of equality, I think that the resolution of the Ujaama House incident rested on a definition of harm that was so circumscribed in scope as to conceal from any consideration—legal or otherwise—a range of serious but "extrinsic" harms felt by the decisionmakers to be either inconsistent with the first amendment or beside the point ("additional to," according to the parol evidence rule). In limiting the investigation and remedy to Fred and Q.C. exclusively, the group harm (to the collective of the dorm, to the Stanford community generally, to the group identity of blacks) was avoided. To illustrate this point, I will try to recount my own sense of the Beethoven injury.

Even though the remark was not made to me or even in my presence, I 27 respond to it personally and also as a member of the group derogated; I respond personally but as part of an intergenerational collective. I am the "first black female" in many circumstances. I am a first black pioneer just for speaking my mind. The only problem is that every generation of my family has been a first black something or other, an experimental black, a "different" black—a hope, a candle, a credit to our race. Most of my black friends' families are full of generations of pioneers and exceptions to the rule. (How else would we have grown up to such rarefied heights of professionalism? Nothing is ever really done in one generation, or done alone.) It is not that we are all that rare in time—it is that over time our accomplishments have been coopted and have disappeared; the issue is when we can stop being perceived as "firsts." I wonder when I and the millions of other people of color who have done great and noble things or small and courageous things or creative and scientific things—when our achievements will become generalizations about our race and seen as contributions to the larger culture, rather than exceptions to the rule, isolated abnormalities. ("If only there were more of you!" I hear a lot. The truth is, there are lots more of me, and better of me, and always have been.)

The most deeply offending part of the Beethoven injury is its message 28 that if I ever manage to create something as monumental as Beethoven's music, or the literature of the mulatto Alexandre Dumas or the mulatto Alexander Pushkin, then the best reward to which I can aspire is that I will be remembered as white. Perhaps my tribe will hold a candle in honor of my black heart over the generations—for blacks have been teaching white people that Beethoven was a mulatto for over a hundred years now—and they will be mocked when they try to make some claim to me. If they do press their point, the best they can hope for is that their tormenters will be absolved because it was a reasonable mistake to assume I was white: they just didn't know. But the issue is precisely the appropriation of knowledge, the authority of creating a canon, revising memory, declaring a boundary beyond which lies the "extrinsic" and beyond which ignorance is reasonably suffered. It is not only the individual and isolating fact of that ignorance; it is the violence of claiming in a way that denies theories of group rights and empowerment, of creating property that fragments collectivity and dehumanizes.

This should not be understood as a claim that Beethoven's music is 29 exclusively black music or that white people have no claim to its history or enjoyment; it is not really about Beethoven at all. It is about the ability of black and brown and red and yellow people to name their rightful contributions to the universe of music or any other field. It is the right to claim that we are, after all, part of Western Civilization.

The determination that Beethoven was not black is an unspoken determination that he was German and therefore could not be black. To acknowledge the possibility of his mulatto ancestry is to undo the supposed purity of the Germanic empire. It challenges the sanctification of cultural symbols rooted in notions of racial purity. One of the most difficult parts of the idea that Beethoven was not pure white has to do with the implication this has for the purity of all western civilization: if Beethoven, that most western musical warlord, is not really white, if the word "German" also means "mulatto," then some of the most powerfully uplifting, inspiring, and unifying of what we call "western" moments come crashing down to the aesthetic of vaudevillian blackface. The student who defaced the poster said that before he "knew Beethoven was black he had a certain image of Beethoven and hearing he was black changed his perception of Beethoven and made him see Beethoven as the person he drew in the picture."

All of this is precisely the reasoning that leads so many to assume that the introduction of African-American or South American or feminist literature into Stanford's curriculum is a threat to the very concepts of what is meant by "western" or "civilization." It is indeed a threat. The most frightening discovery of all will be the eventual realization of the degree to which people of color have always been part of western civilization.

When Fred's whole relationship to the music changed once he discovered that Beethoven was black, it made me think of how much my students' relationship to me is engineered by my being black; how much I am marginalized based on a hierarchy of perception, by my relation to definitional canons that exercise superhuman power in my life. When Beethoven is no longer übermensch, but real and really black, he falls to a place beneath contempt, for there is no racial midpoint between the polarities of adoration and aversion. When some first-year law students walk in and see that I am their contracts teacher, I have been told, their whole perception of law school changes. The failure of Stanford to acknowledge this level of harm in the Ujaama House incident allows students to deface me. In the margins of their notebooks, or unconsciously perhaps, they deface me; to them, I "look like a stereotype of a black person" (as Fred described it), not an academic. They see my brown face and they draw lines enlarging the lips and coloring in "black frizzy hair." They add "red eyes, to give . . . a demonic look." In the margins of their notebooks, I am obliterated.

The Beethoven controversy is an example of an analytic paradigm in which "white equals good, and black equals bad." Although that paradigm operated for many years as a construct in United States law, it cannot be said to exist as a formal legal matter today. Rather, an interpretative shift has occurred, as if our collective social reference has been enlarged somewhat, by slipping from what I described above as the first level of sausage analysis to the second: by going from a totally segregated system to a partially integrated one. In this brave new world, "white" still retains its ironclad (or paradigmatic) definition of "good," but a bit of word stretching is allowed to include a few additional others: blacks, whom we all now know can be good too, must therefore be "white." Blacks who refuse the protective shell of white goodness and insist that they are black are inconsistent with the paradigm of goodness, and therefore they are bad. As silly as this sounds as a bare-bones schematic, I think it is powerfully hypostatized in our present laws and in Supreme Court holdings: this absurd type of twisted thinking, racism in drag, is propounded not just as a theory of "equality" but as a standard of "neutrality." (This schematic is also why equality and neutrality have become such constant and necessary companions, two sides of the same coin: "equal . . ." has as its unspoken referent ". . . to whites"; "neutral . . ." has as it hidden subtext ". . . to concerns of color.")

Consider, for example, the case of the Rockettes. In October 1987 the Radio City Music Hall Rockettes hired the first black dancer in the history of that troupe. Her position was "to be on call for vacancies." (Who could have thought of a more quintessentially postmodern paradox of omission within the discourse of omission?) As of December 16, 1987, she had not yet performed but, it was hoped, "she may soon do so." Failure to include blacks before this was attributed not to racism but to the desire to maintain an aesthetic of uniformity and precision. As recently as five years ago, the director of the Rockettes, Violet Holmes, defended the all-white line on artistic grounds. She said that the dancers were supposed to be "mirror images" of one another and added: "One or two black girls in the line would definitely distract. You would lose the whole look of precision, which is the hallmark of the Rockettes." I read this and saw allegory—all of society pictured in that one statement.

Mere symmetry, of course, could be achieved by hiring all black dancers. It could be achieved by hiring light-skinned black dancers, in the tradition of the Cotton Club's grand heyday of condescension. It could be achieved by hiring an even number of black dancers and then placing them like little black anchors at either end or like hubcaps at the center, or by speckling them throughout the lineup at even intervals, for a nice checkerboard, melting-pot effect. It could be achieved by letting all the white dancers brown themselves in the sun a bit, to match the black dancers—something they were forbidden to do for many years, because the owner of the Rockettes didn't want them to look "like colored girls."

There are many ways to get a racially mixed lineup to look like a mirror image of itself. Hiring one black, however, is not the way to do it. Hiring one and placing her third to the left is a sure way to make her stick out, like a large freckle, and the imprecision of the whole line will devolve upon her. Hiring one black dancer and pretending that her color is invisible is the physical embodiment of the sort of emptiness and failure of imagination that more abstract forms of so-called neutral or colorblind remedies represent. As a spokeswoman for the company said: "[Race] is not an issue for the Rock-ettes—we're an equal opportunity employer."

An issue that is far more difficult to deal with than the simple omission   37
of those words that signify racism in law and society is the underlying yet
dominant emotion of racism—the very perception that introducing blacks to
a lineup will make it ugly ("unaesthetic"), imbalanced ("nonuniform"), and
sloppy ("imprecise"). The ghostly power of this perception will limit everything the sole black dancer does—it will not matter how precise she is in feet
and fact, since her presence alone will be construed as imprecise; it is her
inherency that is unpleasant, conspicuous, unbalancing.

The example of the Rockettes is a lesson in why the limitation of   38
original intent as a standard of constitutional review is problematic, particularly where the social text is an "aesthetic of uniformity"—as it appears to be
in a formalized, strictly scrutinized but colorblind liberal society. Uniformity
nullifies or at best penalizes the individual. Noninterpretive devices, extrinsic
sources, and intuitive means of reading may be the only ways to include the
reality of the unwritten, unnamed, nontext of race.

In *Croson* the Supreme Court responded to a version of this last point   39
by proclaiming that the social text, no matter how uniform and exclusive,
could not be called exclusionary in the absence of proof that people of color
even *want* to be recipients of municipal contracts, or aspire to be Rockettes,
or desire to work in this or that profession. But the nature of desire and
aspiration as well as the intent to discriminate are far more complicated than
that, regulated as they are by the hidden and perpetuated injuries of racist
words. The black-power movement notwithstanding, I think many people of
color still find it extremely difficult to admit, much less prove, our desire to be
included in alien and hostile organizations and institutions, even where those
institutions also represent economic opportunity. I think, moreover, that even
where the desire to be included is acknowledged, the schematic leads to a
simultaneous act of race abdication and self-denial.

In January 1988, for example, on the day after Martin Luther King's   40
birthday, the *New York Times* featured a story that illustrates as well as anything
the paradoxical, self-perpetuating logic of this form of subordination and so-
called neutrality. In Hackensack, New Jersey, African-American residents resisted efforts to rename their street after King because it would signal to
"anyone who read the phone book" that it was a black neighborhood. It was
feared that no white person would ever want to live there and property values
would drop: "It stigmatizes an area."

The Hackensack story struck a familiar chord. I grew up amidst a clutter   41
of such opinions, just such uprisings of voices, riotous, enraged, middle-class,
picky, testy, and brash. Our house was in Boston on the border of the predominantly black section of Roxbury. For years the people on my street argued
about whether they were really in Roxbury or whether they were close
enough to be considered part of the (then) predominantly white neighborhood of Jamaica Plain.

An even more complicated example occurred in North Baltimore. Two 42
white men, one of them legally blind, heaved a six-pound brick and a two-
pound stone through the front window of a black couple's house. They did
so, according to the U.S. attorney, "because they felt blacks should not be
living in their neighborhood and wanted to harrass the couple because of their
race." The two men pleaded guilty to interfering with the couple's housing
rights. The couple, on the other hand, criticized the prosecutor's office for
bringing the indictment at all. "Describing himself as Moorish-American, [the
husband] said he does not consider himself black and does not believe in civil
rights. 'I'm tired of civil rights, I hate civil rights,' Mr. Boyce-Bey, a carpenter's
apprentice, said. Moorish-Americans associate civil rights with racism and
slavery."[18] Subsequently, the couple moved out of the house.

It seems to me that the stigma of "Dr. Martin Luther King Boulevard" 43
or "Roxbury" is reflective of a deep personal discomfort among blacks, a
wordless and tabooed sense of self that is identical to the discomfort shared
by both blacks and whites in even mentioning words like "black" and "race"
in mixed company. Neutrality is from this perspective a suppression, an insti-
tutionalization of psychic taboos as much as segregation was the institutional-
ization of physical boundaries. What the middle-class, propertied, upwardly
mobile black striver must do, to accommodate a race-neutral world view, is to
become an invisible black, a phantom black, by avoiding the label "black" (it's
all right to be black in this reconfigured world if you keep quiet about it).
The words of race are like windows into the most private vulnerable parts of
the self; the world looks in and the world will know, by the awesome, horrific
revelation of a name.

I remember with great clarity the moment I discovered that I was "col- 44
ored." I was three and already knew that I was a "Negro"; my parents had told
me to be proud of that. But "colored" was something else; it was the totemic
evil I had heard my little white friends talking about for several weeks before
I finally realized that I was one of *them*. I still remember the crash of that
devastating moment of union, the union of my joyful body and the terrible
power of that devouring symbol of negritude. I have spent the rest of my life
recovering from the degradation of being divided against myself; I am still
trying to overcome the polarity of my own vulnerability.

Into this breach of the division-within-ourselves falls the helplessness of 45
our fragile humanity. Unfortunately, the degree to which it is easier in the
short run to climb out of the pit by denying the mountain labeled "colored"
than it is to tackle the sheer cliff that is our scorned mortality is the degree to
which blacks internalize the mountain labeled colored. It is the degree to
which blacks remain divided along all sorts of categories of blackness, including class, and turn the speech of helplessness upon ourselves like a firehose.
We should do something with ourselves, say the mothers to the daughters and
the sons to the fathers, we should do something. So we rub ointments on our
skin and pull at our hair and wrap our bodies in silk and gold. We remake and
redo and we sing and pray that the ugliness will be hidden and our beauty will

shine through and be accepted. And we work and we work and we work at ourselves. Against ourselves, in spite of ourselves, and in subordination of ourselves.

We resent those of us who do not do the same. We resent those who are not well-groomed and well-masked and have not reined in the grubbiness of their anger, who have not sought the shelter of the most decorous assimilation possible. So confusing are the "colored" labels, so easily do they masquerade as real people, that we frequently mistake the words for ourselves. 46

My dispute is perhaps not with formal equal opportunity. So-called formal equal opportunity has done a lot but misses the heart of the problem: it put the vampire back in its coffin, but it was no silver stake. The rules may be colorblind, but people are not. The question remains, therefore, whether the law can truly exist apart from the color-conscious society in which it exists, as a skeleton devoid of flesh; or whether law is the embodiment of society, the reflection of a particular citizenry's arranged complexity of relations. 47

All this is to say that I strongly believe not just in programs like affirmative action, but in affirmative action as a socially and professionally pervasive concept. This should not be understood as an attempt to replace an ideology controlled by "white men" with one controlled by "black women"—or whomever. The real issue is precisely the canonized status of any one group's control. Black individuality is subsumed in a social circumstance—an idea, a stereotype—that pins us to the underside of this society and keeps us there, out of sight/out of mind, out of the knowledge of mind which is law. Blacks and women are the objects of a constitutional omission that has been incorporated into a theory of neutrality. It is thus that omission becomes a form of expression, as oxymoronic as that sounds: racial omission is a literal part of original intent; it is the fixed, reiterated prophesy of the Founding Fathers. It is thus that affirmative action is an affirmation; the affirmative act of hiring—or hearing—blacks is a recognition of individuality that includes blacks as a social presence, that is profoundly linked to the fate of blacks and whites and women and men either as subgroups or as one group. Justice is a continual balancing of competing visions, plural viewpoints, shifting histories, interests, and allegiances. To acknowledge that level of complexity is to require, to seek, and to value a multiplicity of knowledge systems, in pursuit of a more complete sense of the world in which we all live. Affirmative action in this sense is as mystical and beyond-the-self as an initiation ceremony. It is an act of verification and vision, an act of social as well as professional responsibility. . . . 48

Topics for Discussion and Writing

1. Choose one of the incidents Williams examines in the essay. Write your thoughtful reaction to the incident she describes and your reaction to her interpretation of the incident. Try to be as careful in your thinking as she is in hers.

2. Focus on Williams's use of the first person in this essay. Elsewhere in the book she relates her students' criticism of her telling personal stories in her law classes, the students complaining that telling stories isn't teaching "real law." How do you react to her personal style of writing? Do you feel that it helps or hinders your understanding of the legal issues? In their asking for "real law," what do you think the students were expecting?

3. Use your reflections on Williams's essay as a basis for revising your writing of "Before and as You Read" topic 3. Do you see in your own writing on that topic evidence of the deeply ingrained beliefs about race that Williams identifies? Write a response to what you observe in the rereading.

4. Affirmative action is one of the key concepts that Williams deals with in this essay. What is your understanding of this concept? What have you heard or read in its favor or in opposition? Using the Library of Congress subject headings or an on-line service in your school or public library, identify books and articles on this concept. Use several sources to add to your understanding.

CAROL MULLEN

"Bus 94 to Anacostia"

"Then I was the only white person, as usual. I wanted to appear at ease, like this was an everyday thing for me; which it was."
    Carol Mullen wrote "Bus 94 to Anacostia" for a class in advanced nonfiction writing at George Mason University.

Before and as You Read

1. Write about the separation, or integration, of people by race or ethnicity in the place where you live, work, or go to school. Are there neighborhoods or sections that are characterized as "all black," "all white," "Hispanic," and so on? When you go into, or through, these neighborhoods, if you do, how do you feel? What, if anything, do you fear? What do you imagine about the people? How do you change your behavior depending on the neighborhood you are in? Are there neighborhoods you avoid? Why?

2. As you read "Bus 94 to Anacostia," observe how the writer uses her daily journey to organize her investigation of her feelings. If you have read the previous essay, by Patricia Williams, use what you have learned there as you note how Mullen uses such "loaded" terms as *black* and *white*.

3. How does increasing one's knowledge of other cultures and places increase or decrease one's freedom?

4. As you read the essay, pay attention to what the speaker says about her fears. Mark statements that seem to you to be based on actual knowledge and others that you feel are based on perhaps mistaken speculation. Mark statements that puzzle you as to their basis in fact. Compare your notations with those of others who have done this exercise.

I STEPPED ONTO the crowded 94 bus near the Eastern Market Metro   *1*
Station in SE Washington, DC, more people pushing on behind me. I only had a second or two to decide where to sit, but it was always a conscious decision. All my movements during this part of my daily commute were conscious decisions. Three open seats: one up front, one mid-way back next to a child, one in the far back among some tough looking males in their twenties.

Damn, why don't these buses run more often, I thought to myself as I   *2*
moved down the aisle. But I already knew the answer. They don't run on time, and they are the most run down buses—with bad shocks and windows that won't open and air-conditioners that won't work—because they are going

over to the ghetto. No one complains, or if they do, nothing is ever done about it. Waiting 20 minutes on bus 94 made me feel dependent and frustrated, I thought as I settled down in the middle seat, next to a small black girl with her school books.

I'd been riding this same bus for over a year. It's the second bus I take to get to work. The first bus leaves South Arlington and goes to the Pentagon, where I catch the subway. The buses there run every 3–10 minutes during rush hour, and are brand new. I see the same people everyday: blacks and whites, all conservatively dressed, in their military uniforms and business suits that look like uniforms, too. Because I leave my Park Ranger clothes at work, I am dressed in blue jeans, but no one seems to notice me. 3

It's a different story on bus 94. I never see the same commuters, though I look. The only uniforms I see are security guards' or white nurse's aides outfits. Most people are dressed like me, in jeans, t-shirts, tennies. I'm usually the only white person on bus 94, but that day I saw another white woman sitting up front. 4

The driver pulled out into traffic and the people standing grabbed on to the nearest pole or seat railing to keep from falling. I opened my book and pretended to read. Late for work again, I thought, as I looked at my watch and then casually around me. The white woman up front was cooing over a small black baby and I felt a strange embarrassment. I stared out the window and tried to find Frederick Douglass's house, high up on the hill where I worked everyday. I couldn't see it for the trees. 5

I glanced at the black child next to me, with her grade school books and pencils and colorful ribbons in her hair. She could have been one of the children I talked to at the Douglass Home, but on the bus we said nothing to each other. I saw the white woman get off at the Navy Yard, and more people piled on. Then I was the only white person, as usual. I wanted to appear at ease, like this was an everyday thing for me; which it was. 6

And I wasn't really afraid. People rarely talked to me, though one wild-eyed man once started telling me about how I reminded him of his white third grade teacher who used to beat his hands with a ruler. I didn't tell him I had a nun in third grade who used to do the same thing. It's never safe to talk with a crazy person. Usually people left me alone. But I was always uncomfortable. Every morning I felt eyes on me. What is she doing on this bus, where is she going? I could almost hear people think. I could never blend into the crowd. As the only white person on a full bus of black people, there was no way I could not be white. 7

As I sat there during my 15-minute ride across the river, I thought about race, and what it meant to be sitting among strangers where the most obvious fact was that they were black and I was white. We all had so many stereotypes driven into our heads about each other. I thought I understood something of what the word minority meant. I was thankful for this insight, but it didn't make me feel any more at ease. I never talked to anyone on bus 94, so I don't really know what they thought of me. But I sensed resentment. Why wasn't I 8 driving, what was I doing on their bus? I didn't have a car, or I would have driven. I was just as poor as they were (wasn't I?), new in town and struggling on my Park Service salary to make it in this very expensive area.

I just wanted to get to work, where I could put on my ranger hat and *9* badge and talk to the school children (always black, whites rarely visit the site) about Frederick Douglass. There I was still the only white person, but people accepted me, or had to, because I had the information they had come to hear. Because I chose to work there, the visitors must realize I wasn't racist. But until I got to my job, everyday on that bus I was just a white woman, alone, riding into the inner city for an unknown reason; I was suspect and vulnerable.

We crossed over the Anacostia River and I thought about Douglass *10* walking everyday to his job on Capitol Hill. He had a horse and buggy and driver but walked the five miles for the exercise. Douglass had taken his share of public transit in his life—sometimes traveling hundreds of miles in winter, speaking out against slavery, and later for women's rights. He was once told to get off a whites-only car on a train and had refused to leave his seat, so they threw him off, seat included.

By the time Douglass moved to the then all-white Anacostia, he was a *11* national figure, and a wealthy man. I tried to picture him walking through the streets, with his bowler hat and cane. It was after Reconstruction and racism was on the rise. Did he get insulted as he walked to his job as U.S. marshall? Did people recognize him from his many lectures? Once at his office, he was Mr. Douglass, or Honorable Douglass. But while he was walking, he was just a black man on his way somewhere, in a neighborhood many people felt he didn't belong in.

I spied the landmark for my stop—the incongruous Big Chair, a symbol *12* for a furniture store long since gone. I pulled the bell, and waited at the back door of the bus for the green light to go on, feeling people stare at me as I stood there. About 30 people were waiting for various buses at this stop, and school children were walking by, on their way to Ketcham Elementary, Anacostia High School. I elbowed my way through the crowd, the only white person. I told myself we're all just people, people, not black and white; but it didn't work. I felt very out of place.

Before crossing Martin Luther King Blvd., I had to decide which side *13* of the street to walk on. One side was quicker because I could cross at the light, but it meant I'd have to walk past another bus stop with many black teenagers waiting for a bus. Teenagers of any color are always more bold when they are in groups, and I could sometimes feel hatred in their stares. Everyday busloads of black teenagers came from all over the country to the Douglass Home and most of them seemed to respect me, ask me questions, answer the questions I asked them. Their teacher or leader was with them and I was in my Ranger uniform. On the street, in an economically depressed, all black neighborhood, we were on different grounds. I didn't feel up to the pressure that day, and chose the longer route.

The streets became more residential, and I slowed down and enjoyed the   14
morning air. I walked past a church and admired the flowers. I walked through
a small park, kicking a broken quart beer bottle. I peered into the yards as I
passed some of the well-kept homes, hoping to see a face I could become
familiar with and greet, but saw none. I nodded to the Korean man who ran
the corner grocery store as he unlocked the iron gate. I noticed the "Clean it
or Lien it" sign was still in the empty lot, the yard full of rubbish.

Finally I came up to the familiar brown National Park Service sign at   15
the corner of Douglass's lot and climbed the steep drive up to the house.
Douglass's eight acres—with its old magnolia trees, litter free lawns and white
Victorian house sitting high on a hill—were a wonderful oasis in this historic
but poor section of town. I knew I was late, but I sat down on one of the
rocking chairs on the porch, tired from my climb up the hill and the long
stressful commute on public transit. I looked across the river at Capitol Hill
and the city of Washington, and marvelled at the incredible view Frederick
Douglass had had.

Topics for Discussion and Writing

1. Write a reaction to Mullen's essay. Do you identify with her feelings in any
   way? Using, as she does, a narrative to organize your reflections, write
   about an event in your life during which you felt at least somewhat as
   she does.
2. Mullen's essay employs powerful images that tend to inspire strong reactions
   in U.S. citizens. Reread the essay and mark terms that for you qualify as
   strong U.S. symbols. Focusing on two of these symbolic terms, write about
   how you feel Mullen is using them to move her reader's emotions.
3. Review your answers to "Before and as You Read" topic 1. Use your
   reflective reading of Mullen's essay as a basis for revising your response to
   that topic. Does her writing in any way inspire you to change your views
   of—and perhaps learn more about—a neighborhood that you had previously avoided?
4. Compare Mullen's essay with the "Mascot" excerpt from *The Autobiography
   of Malcolm X* reprinted in chapter 9. Are there similarities in tone and idea
   between her position on the bus and his position in the school? What
   differences do you observe, particularly in the relative power or powerlessness of the two key figures?

JANE O'REILLY
from *The Girl I Left Behind*

> " 'Oh, yes, you are the housework lady,' welcomed a talk-show host. Hearty laughter from the audience. A weak smile from me. A strong urge to bite him. Equality for women seemed to be a far more complicated issue than I had thought."

> Jane O'Reilly (born 1936), a native of St. Louis, grew up in a home she describes as "comfortable," attended Catholic schools, graduated from Radcliffe College, married, and started a family before coming to the realizations that she describes in her book The Girl I left Behind: The Housewife's Moment of Truth and Other Feminist Ravings (1980). As a freelance writer O'Reilly has written articles for such magazines as The Atlantic, House and Garden, Ms., and The New Republic. She wrote a syndicated weekly column, "Jane O'Reilly," from 1976 through 1979. Since 1979 she has been a contributing editor for Time.

> Of The Girl I Left Behind, O'Reilly has said that men should read the book "from back to front"—from the essay on issues back to the personal experiences that begin the book, because "that's how men move, from being distant, objective, and intellectual to the world of their emotions. Women, on the other hand, should read it from front to back because we are moving from our emotions and inner experiences to try to grasp the general experience and apply it to our lives."

Before and as You Read

1. What does the term *feminism* mean to you? Do you regard yourself as a feminist? In what ways do you share the objectives of the women's movement?
2. Write about the family in which you grew up. Would you regard your mother as a feminist? Why or why not? Describe an event that illustrates your answer to these questions.
3. Generalize about the roles of women and men in the culture or cultures in which you grew up. What distinctions in these roles are generally accepted in that culture or cultures? Do you feel that your experience and that of your family are typical in this regard?
4. As you read the Introduction to *The Girl I Left Behind*, observe how O'Reilly shows her awareness of points of view that differ from hers. Mark passages that either imply or state explicitly the assumptions or arguments that she is contending against. Note how she responds to these opposing ideas.

THIS BOOK is a collection of responses to an idea, to my own dis-   *1*
covery that, as Elizabeth Hardwick best put it, "There are cultural, social and economic boundaries for women which are immoral and unnecessary and which should be resisted publicly and privately."

It seems to have taken me quite a while to realize that the idea applied   *2*
to me. Ten years, at least. Perhaps forty-four. Probably the rest of my life. At any rate, longer than I imagined when, sometime in the late 1960s, my attention was drawn to the possibility that what I accepted as normal was in fact an arbitrary distinction. Gloria Steinem was the person who first insisted I pay attention. I used to call her at two or three in the morning, whenever I lost track of whatever I was trying to write, and as she patiently eased me into the next paragraph, she also eased me into feminism's first premise: women are not equal members of the human society, and we are not equal simply because we are women. I remember thinking Gloria was becoming too preoccupied with the subject of women.

After all, why was it necessary to go on and on about it? The principle,   *3*
once noticed, seemed so obvious. Women were not equal. Women should be equal. There had been some strange oversight which, once explained—"Hey guys, something seems to be unfair here"—would be remedied. I began to explain, often at the top of my lungs, pointing out that the women's movement would require us to question all our most basic assumptions. In my enthusiasm I forgot that, historically, revision of those assumptions had not usually occurred through the application of a sense of fair play (a concept that itself evades consensus).

In 1970, I spent a green summer afternoon in Vermont interviewing   *4*
John Kenneth Galbraith. After a long discussion of such matters as inflation, war, unemployment, and Richard Nixon, he said: "I think we should have talked more about women's liberation. This will have a more permanent, a more lasting effect than any of the things we have been talking about." I was not surprised that he thought so. His instincts for justice, compassion, and generosity are as complete as any man's living. But I think I also really expected that women would be liberated by the next summer—certainly by the summer after that.

Confidently, I awaited equality. (Did I think it would come by United   *5*
Parcel, gift wrapped? Or that there would be a sign—perhaps a tongue of flame over our heads?) Then for the first issue of *Ms.* magazine I was asked to write a light piece on housework—the only subject in the movement inventory I felt qualified to address. Housework turned out to involve the most basic of basic assumptions. I began to grasp that *waiting* for equality might not be the most effective political tool. It took me three months to write "Click! The Housewife's Moment of Truth" and when I finished, I had become a wild-eyed radical libber—a woman people edged away from at social gatherings. Writing "Click!" was my own moment of truth, my consciousness raising, my astonished realization that Gloria's "preoccupation" might be only the most rational and disciplined of possible responses.

And yet, I cannot tell you how silly I felt raving on about something so 6
unimportant as housework.

I felt even sillier when *Ms.* dispatched me to various cities on a promo- 7
tional tour. "Of course women are afraid of speaking out in public. So was
I," said Gloria. "The only thing I've learned in all these years is you don't
actually die." She did not add that I would wish I could. It is one thing to
write about one's newly articulated principles. It is quite another to make a
spectacle of oneself. "Oh, yes, you are the housework lady," welcomed a talk-
show host. Hearty laughter from the audience. A weak smile from me. A
strong urge to bite him. Equality for women seemed to be a far more complicated issue than I had thought. I was, after all, only talking about housework.
Why, then, was a man from Vandalia, Illinois, calling in to a late-night radio
show in St. Louis to accuse me of contravening natural law? I had no prepared
answer for that accusation, was in fact woefully innocent of the implications
of what I was saying, prattling on about sweet reason to an audience that
would have more enthusiastically welcomed inside information about the end
of the world. This seemed to see me as a symptom of an onrushing day of
judgment. What manic impulse, what misdirected perception, had brought me
into this dark midnight studio overlooking the Mississippi River? I wished,
very much, to be back home.

Another voice came over the sound system, a woman from the Ozarks. 8
"Honey," she said, "I've lifted bales of hay and calves and children all my life,
and all the time they fed us a lot of nonsense about being the weaker sex. You
just keep right at it." The next caller was a woman named Marcy, who made
a statement I have found useful ever since. "Natural law," she observed, "is
only whatever happens in your lifetime within fifty miles of you."

Very late that night I called Gloria to announce that sisterhood was 9
powerful. She was not surprised. Several evenings later I turned on the television set in my Atlanta hotel room. A woman on the evening news was talking
about the women's movement. She seemed to make a good deal of sense.
Several long seconds passed before I realized she was me.

If, on that trip, I began to learn that They were really We, I had still not 10
quite connected me—not connected the personal and the political. Matters
such as wage disparities, role expectations, family breakups, working mothers,
systemic sexual discrimination, could—if discussed at arm's length—be reasonably described as issues. If described in personal terms they could—and
were—dismissed as the selfish whining of spoiled crybabies who placed
self-fulfillment above responsibility. Besides, my situation was different. I
blamed the oddities of my life on my own choices: I chose to be divorced
(had so chosen, in fact, twice), chose to live in New York City, chose to
support myself and my son by working as a freelance writer. I considered
myself excluded, by reason of eccentricity, from the general experience.

I blamed myself and missed the point: mine *was* the general experi- 11
ence—including the blaming myself. (Nowadays I divide the blame more

equitably: half for me and half for societal arrangements.) Marriage had been, for me, a brief, destructive clash of irreconcilable expectations, our mistaken choices as much the fault of role modeling as of our own delusions. Divorced, as a Single Female Head of Household, I lived below the poverty line. My situation had much to do with responsibility and very little to do with self-fulfillment, and I still earned less than men. I cannot say what determined my choice of profession: a rather specialized skill perhaps, a fairly severe inability to cooperate (despite a solid childhood grounding in team sports). It could have been simply an impulse to remove myself from hierarchies after being told in 1962 that the Washington bureau of a national newsmagazine did not hire women reporters, not even a woman with a Radcliffe degree, a small file of clippings, and a strong urge to be a foreign correspondent. I never questioned the policy, never sought out advice from women who were already reporters for other publications. I simply withdrew from the field, remarried, took jobs as a researcher, wrote freelance articles at home, got divorced, moved to New York, plodded on, until something clicked.

What happened to me then is not very different from the experiences   *12* of many women over the last several years. For this book, I tried to arrange the articles and newspaper columns I wrote about those experiences according to the expansion, from the private to the public, of my own—our own—responses to the women's movement. I have added many new thoughts, and some second thoughts, and decided to include the contradictions because I have not, in fact, yet discovered how to resolve them.

The arrangement has turned out to be more like a kaleidoscope or a   *13* seismograph than the chronology we had hoped and expected to be tidy. The private and the public do not (cannot) conveniently separate. Issues are not settled, but only enlarged. We are nearer to seeing a woman on the Supreme Court than we are to solving the problems of housework and love and families, but at least we know now that the questions asked apply to both. Our resolve veers and ebbs; we are in turn exhilarated, exhausted, reasonable, enraged, full of hope, freshly surprised, newly incredulous. Without the reality of daily life—of family, friends, responsibilities, the pleasures of a summer's day—we would go mad.

I go mad quite regularly. Particularly when I realize I am still only begin-   *14* ning to identify the problem. Recently a man, a relative by marriage, arrived in New York and insisted on staying in my apartment. It was not a convenient time: a sick child, no baby-sitter, an essential trip to take, a deadline to meet. He promised: "You won't even know I'm here." He practiced invisibility by complaining, with wit and charm, that there was nothing to eat in the house and no one to talk to. One evening he proudly brought home a steak. Instead of offering the thanks he expected, I calculated the time necessary to cook, eat, and clean up after the steak. I do not know and cannot explain why, after all these years, I asked him how he would like it cooked instead of directing him to the stove. He said: "With a little béarnaise sauce?"

No, I did not make the béarnaise sauce. But three hours later, after the   *15* cooking, eating, and cleaning up, I sat down and began to write words I had never used before: images, explanations, accusations I had dismissed when they were used by earlier, quicker feminist writers as too extreme, strident, bewildering. (Even they did not know, then, how far back those unheard voices echoed. I certainly did not know when I "discovered" housework that Charlotte Perkins Gilman had said in 1903, "The home is a human institution. All human institutions are open to improvement.") My anger is still in front of me, written in blue ink on a page from a yellow pad: "Blood, death, suffocation, ruined lives wasted by oppression. Only now do I understand what I have written." The truth is, I am only beginning to understand what I have written.

"Don't you write about anything but *women*?" asks a crestfallen voice. 16 Sure. This book is a kind of scrapbook, but it does not tell the whole story, not of my life, still less of the women's movement. I could offer, with some satisfaction, published records of trips to Scotland, Italy, New Orleans. Book reviews, restaurant reviews, observations on the meaning of romance. Events recorded at political conventions, complaints about America's transportation system. Advice—written to pay the rent—on getting through a bad year and how to fight with your mate. Thoughts on buying children's shoes, methods of choosing schools and country houses and avoiding suicide. A lot of words, a lot of work, a certain amount of gaiety and excitement and achievement— a thought that somehow reminds me that there is something I have forgotten to mention. The effort was not easy, and it became much, much harder after I began to write about women.

There was a time, from about the middle of 1972 to the end of 1975, 17 when I stopped speaking to old friends, provoked scenes in editorial offices, became irrationally attached to inexplicable love affairs. I could barely write, and finally I could barely speak. Yet not once did it ever occur to me that my terror, my outraged sense of betrayal, my insistence on romance as a solution, had anything at all to do with the phrases I was reading, and even writing. "The courage to change," "fear of success," "the risk of autonomy," did not seem to describe my feelings, which were, roughly: scared as a wet cat stuck out on a limb with no fireman in sight; sulky as a princess whose frog-kissing skills have been declared obsolete due to a shortage of bewitched princes; mad as a child who insists "I'll do it myself" and can't. I described this amazing disarray as "being depressed," ascribed it to a variety of irrelevant causes, and (I see now, peering at the spectacle with the wisdom of hindsight) thrashed bitterly against the discovery that the only way out was forward. There was no going back.

As an alternative to going forward, I chose to go limp. I decided (secretly, 18 to myself) that I was bored with women's issues. It was boring to take so seriously what others took so lightly, to feel foolish, to have developed a reflexive index finger that pointed, hectoring and admonishing, at the most inopportune moments. (And, after all, hadn't women, in the last hundred years, been equally sure that the vote, or purity, or temperance, or a ban on contraceptives, would change the world?)

Then someone asked me to review Susan Brownmiller's book on rape, *Against Our Will,* a powerful, brilliant, enlightening work that wiped away all doubt. I was no longer bored by women's issues. Scared, but not bored. Jim Bellows, then editor of the *Washington Star,* invited me to be a guest columnist and suggested as a topic women in Washington. As it happened, in the fall of 1975 there were many, many women in Washington who had already figured out that the question of who is presumed to be responsible for the housework has something to do with the presumptions of public policy, and they seemed to have no qualms at all about hectoring and admonishing. They gave me facts, examples, phone numbers, observations, determination, and hope. I had a wonderful time.

Two years later thousands of women representing millions of women from all over the United States traveled to Houston, Texas, for the National Women's Conference. They, too, had a wonderful time, exchanging facts, experiences, phone numbers, hope, and determination, discovering they were not alone and had not imagined a women's movement. Again, They were revealed to be We.

Being able to take a joke is, perhaps, the first sign that you are taking yourself seriously, a rather necessary preliminary toward making anyone else take you seriously. One day in Washington a genial male colleague greeted me in the city room by shouting: "Here she comes, hormones raging." I laughed.

Washington is (muted roll of drums, flutter of flags) a contradictory city. Organized by and for the established power, it is still the place (and one bows toward the notion of Democracy) where people without power go to march for their civil rights, for the end of poverty, to stop a war. And they do not march entirely in vain. In the years that I wrote stories on those marches and those movements, I do not remember my male colleagues making jokes. They were part of those movements, took them seriously. But they, like most men, failed to take seriously women as a part of those movements—as indeed they did not take seriously the changing realities of women's lives, our contributions to the economy, even our part in civilization—and that reflexive omission resulted in the rebirth of the women's movement. Women marched again to Washington, this time demanding our own equal rights.

The usual justifications were invoked against us, and great was the confusion when we refused to agree that God's will, or natural law, or human nature, or the wishes of constituents, consign certain races, some nations, and one sex to inferiority. Instead we insisted on affirmative action, an Equal Rights Amendment, the right to choose abortion—and the more we insisted (which was not enough, but still far more than we achieved), the clearer the true meaning of those justifications became: "I've got mine and you can't have any because I want more."

Men—bureaucrats, elected representatives, newspaper editors, husbands—

19

20

21

22

23

24

determined whether women's causes would be understood, and even the most sympathetic professed themselves to be baffled. "My wife doesn't feel oppressed" they assured themselves. That a large number of such men now find themselves referring to "my former wife" suggests that they were misinformed. As an argument, "my wife doesn't feel oppressed" was irrelevant. But as a response, it was at least an honest expression of surprise at the idea that men and women no longer shared the same basic assumptions about the arrangements that governed their lives.

Maybe their wives felt oppressed, and maybe they didn't. But the 25 assumption that their wives did not, and that therefore all women did not (except for a few radicals in New York City), explains why the women's movement, because of its particular necessity to transform both the personal and the political, is a revolution like no other, one that, as Adrienne Rich has said, will transform thinking itself. Women are not the first group to find that our analysis of our condition can be dismissed *because* of our condition. But we are the only group that loves, marries, and raises children with the people who must change—as we must change—if our condition is to improve. And that is why there will be no liberation by next summer, or even the summer after that.

Where are we now, in this reborn revolution? Not very far, if all the 26 numbers are added up: the number of women holding public office, the number of women with influence, the number of women and children who still make up three quarters of the poor in the United States. ("The movement is really over, accomplished, for middle-class women, isn't it?" asserts a well-meaning, white, male corporate lawyer. And I, now resigned to the fact that I will always, for the rest of my life, be the person who shouts at dinner parties, shout: "No! Without a man and his income, a woman is not yet even in the middle class." He smiles, and his elegant, graceful, talented wife avoids my eyes.)

But we no longer feel foolish. We have learned to take ourselves seri- 27 ously, and that is very far to have come. We rejoice that we are struggling together, but the question remains: how goes the struggle? It goes slowly. We mark our progress in grains of sand heaped against the tide: a senator here, an executive there, a center for displaced homemakers, a sympathetic newspaper editorial, a construction job. We can take courage (whistling in the backlash darkness) from the opposition, because they have taken us more seriously than we have ourselves. They knew before we did that such apparently simple ideas as equal pay, equal rights, and equal parenting mean in fact redistribution of wealth, reallocation of power, and redefinition of roles.

Every woman who believes that becoming an executive is enough, every 28 daughter who thinks she was accepted to medical school simply because she was smart (and forgets the women who fought a hundred years for her admission), every woman who accepts her own opportunity within the system and does not open a way for other women (and thus, inevitably, change the system), stands with the tide. The point of feminism is not that the world should be the same, but that it should be different.

We must remember the past, define the future, and challenge the present—wherever and however we can. It will take the rest of our lives even to begin.   *29*

But then, what else have we to do?   *30*

Topics for Discussion and Writing

1. Reread the excerpt from *The Girl I Left Behind* and note the changes that O'Reilly says she went through in her thinking. Mark what you regard as turning points. In particular, note how she distinguishes between her sense of herself and her sense of the people and topics about which she wrote.

2. In the second paragraph of the excerpt, O'Reilly writes: "It seems to have taken me quite a while to realize that the idea applied to me. Ten years, at least. Perhaps forty-four. Probably the rest of my life." What is O'Reilly saying about her process of change? How might a similar statement apply to you? Write about an idea, not necessarily the idea O'Reilly describes, toward which you feel that you have a similar relationship.

3. Throughout the selection, O'Reilly explores diverse fears and doubts. Note the people, the readings, and so on that sustain her and give her confidence. Write about these influences and their effect on her. Focus on one such sustaining friend or resource. Speculate how her life might have changed, or not changed, without this influence.

4. Refer back to your writing in response to "Before and as You Read" topic 1 or topic 2. Now write on this topic again. Have your views about yourself or your family changed in any way? Explain.

RUTH SIDEL
from *On Her Own*

> *"We must have the courage and the wisdom as a society to recognize that we need a new vision of America for the twenty-first century, perhaps even a new American Dream. We need a vision that recognizes that we cannot survive without one another, that families must have supports in order to thrive, that women cannot make it alone any more than men ever have."*

> *So Ruth Sidel, a sociologist who teaches at Hunter College, speaks in the final chapter of* On Her Own: Growing Up in the Shadow of the American Dream *(1990). To compile this book, her latest in a productive writing career, Sidel conducted, transcribed, and analyzed interviews with more than 150 American women from 12 to 25 in every region of the country. Sidel's earlier books include* Women and Child Care in China: A First Hand Report, Families of Fengsheng: Urban Life in China, Urban Survival: The World of Working Class Women, *and* Women and Children Last: The Plight of Poor Women in Affluent America.

> *We have reprinted most of the third chapter, "The Outsiders," from* On Her Own.

Before and as You Read

1. Part of the research for the second chapter (entitled "The Neotraditionalists") of *On Her Own* was done via a questionnaire given to students at Hunter College. The survey asked "what they thought their lives would be like when they were ages twenty-five, thirty, and thirty-five." Write your vision of your future 5, 10, and 15 years hence.

2. What is your "American Dream?" While topic 1 asks you to envision your future as you think it will be, this topic asks you to envision your ideal future. Go ahead, fantasize.

3. If you have responded to topics 1 and 2, think about why you answered as you did. Where do the images in your "American Dream" come from? How do you account for the differences between your "dream" and your vision of what your future will be? If the differences are great, do they make you unhappy? To limit your dissatisfaction, how do you deal with this difference between the ideal and the likely?

4. As you read "The Outsiders," observe how Sidel quotes her sources and uses their words to underscore her ideas. Note that Sidel does not present to us her "raw data"—the transcribed interviews—but weaves quotations and personal anecdotes into her essay. As you read, keep in mind the social scientist's dual mission to (1) report accurately and (2) interpret the data in a coherent, organized way.

FOR MANY adolescents, being an Outsider is a transitional stage,   *1*
. . . one that may pass in time and in the meanwhile can be offset—
as the interviews we have just discussed illustrate—by belonging to specific
friendship or interest groups. But there is another group of adolescent Outsiders, those for whom being an Outsider permeates their existence and may last
a lifetime. While some young women feel entitled to "have it all," others
clearly have great difficulty thinking about the future. When asked what they
hope for, what they plan for, how they would like their lives to be, they say
with a dismissive wave of the hand, "I can't think about that" or "I just have
to get through tomorrow." If the New American Dreamers and many of the
Neotraditionalists dream of work, family, success, and material rewards—in
short, "the good life"—many Outsiders are unable to dream at all. They are
either so burdened by day-to-day living or feel so hopeless about their lives
that they can barely envision a future for themselves.

There are many ways of not belonging. Amanda Chapman, a young   *2*
woman from New Jersey, describes herself as "a circle within a square"; she
just never quite fit in. "I might appear to be part of things," she said, "but I
don't quite get along with my peers. I never really fit in. Right now I have
four friends, and that's not too many." When I spoke with her, she was five
months pregnant. She had dropped out of college and was living at home.
She never quite fit in there, either. Her mother often told her when they got
into a fight, "You're not worthy of anything." Most recently, because she is
pregnant and home almost constantly, her parents are insisting that she do all
the household chores—the cleaning, the shopping, the dishes. She even must
drive her sixteen-year-old sister everywhere she wants to go. "I don't want to
feel like the black sheep," she says, "but I've got no choice." It is almost an
updated Cinderella story—but Prince Charming is not likely to come along
with a glass slipper.

Dorothy Kovak is nineteen and lives in central New Jersey. Dorothy's   *3*
mother, a computer programmer, and her father, a truck driver, are divorced.
She talks about being an Outsider in her small town: "My crowd? We all wore
makeup, tight jeans and thought we had to be cool. We hung out, we par-
tied—there was nothing else to do. Movies weren't cool; bowling is totally
impossible. So we hung out at the roller rink.

"There were basically three groups: the jocks, the brains, and the burn-   *4*
outs. You had to fit in somewhere, so we were the burn-outs; we were in with
the outcasts."

Dorothy thinks back and tries to explain how she got to be one of the   *5*
"outcasts": "I was always an outcast in school—at least until the seventh grade.
My home was all screwed up. My mother and father were either drinking or
fighting, so I couldn't bring people home. I didn't talk to people, and they
didn't talk to me. If you're not *in* in kindergarten, you're not in.

"And I wanted friends. I wanted someone to be my friend. The only   *6*
way I found I could have friends was to be part of this group."

Dorothy described her group as being heavily into drugs and alcohol   *7* since they were eleven, twelve, and thirteen. They drank daily and used "a lot of pot, speed, and cocaine. We would party till we dropped." She says she used speed every day for two years; she didn't use downers because "I was already depressed and certainly didn't need downers." Dorothy talks about the summer when she was sixteen: "I just wanted to die. I had contemplated suicide for some time. It was a major part of my thought process during the day. I felt like shit. I hated myself.

"The train tracks in Manville [New Jersey] are famous for suicide. Trains   8 go through at about sixty miles an hour. A kid I went to school with com- mitted suicide on the tracks, and it hit me real hard. I just didn't want to deal with life anymore. I felt I had a choice: commit suicide or get high. I would come out of blackouts on the tracks."

Dorothy is describing an all-too-frequent phenomenon in contemporary   9 American society. Every 1.1 seconds a teenager makes an attempt at suicide; every 80 minutes one succeeds. According to the Federal Center for Disease Control, since 1950 the suicide rate has tripled among young people ages fifteen to nineteen. In 1977 the rate peaked at 13.3 deaths per 100,000; in 1984 a total of 5,026 young people aged fifteen to twenty-four took their own lives. Females are more likely to attempt suicide; males are more likely to succeed. The suicide rate for men between the ages of fifteen and twenty- four rose 50 percent between 1970 and 1980. Comparable rates for young women rose 2 percent.

National attention focused on teen suicide in 1987 when four young   10 people from Bergenfield, New Jersey—two boys and two girls, aged sixteen and nineteen—killed themselves in a suicide pact. Within six days four more young people were dead in the Chicago suburbs, and other "suicide clusters," as they are called, were reported in Westchester County, New York; Plano, Texas; and Omaha, Nebraska. Some estimates suggest that four hundred thou- sand teenagers attempt suicide each year. Why are so many of our young people contemplating suicide, attempting to kill themselves, and all too often succeeding?

Explanations of this phenomenon vary. Some experts point to the easy   11 access of instruments of death such as drugs and guns, teenagers' favorite methods of killing themselves. Others attribute teenage suicide to a variety of contemporary social problems: "faster-paced lives, the decline of organized religion, competitiveness at school, the tightening of the job market and, in less affluent families, bleaker prospects for the future." Some mental-health professionals link teenage suicide to "the drugging of America," the availability and widespread use of both legal prescription drugs and illegal drugs. Others suggest that young people are victims of intolerable levels of anxiety and alienation. Parents and other adults are less available to give support and reas- surance. According to one psychiatrist who specializes in the treatment of adolescents, "From the point of view of most adolescents there's not much that looks secure or desirable. They're faced with anxieties I was not exposed to at that age and they're able to experiment with drugs or sex before they're ready to deal with the emotional consequences of those things." Yet another theory is that the pressure for them to succeed—academically, economically, socially—is so great that they often perceive personal failure as a sign of worthlessness.

Adolescent suicide is, of course, part of a larger pattern of risk taking   12
on the part of young people. From the enormous use and abuse of alcohol among all classes and among children as young as twelve and thirteen, the continued although somewhat diminished use of illegal drugs other than crack, which is increasingly used, dangerous driving (automobile accidents are the leading cause of death for people up to age thirty-nine), and sexual inter-course without appropriate protection against both pregnancy and sexually transmitted diseases, young people are risking their well-being and indeed their lives with astonishing frequency. Of particular concern to many experts is the rise in problem drinking among young women, particularly among single, well-educated young women. According to one expert on alcoholism, "What we are seeing is the first generation of women who drink like men." Studies indicate that women under thirty are starting to drink earlier and more heavily than did previous generations, often "consuming five or six drinks at one sitting." According to Dr. Sheila Blume, a psychiatrist who works with alco-holics, "Young women, seeking to ease some of their social pressures, are turning to alcohol at an alarming rate. But because of their greater sensitivity to alcohol, they are going to have bigger problems, and sooner, than men." A recent survey of eleven thousand teenagers found that 26 percent of the eighth graders and 38 percent of the tenth graders studied said they had had five or more drinks on one occasion in the two weeks preceding the survey; one in ten said they had smoked marijuana, and one in fifteen said they had used cocaine, in the past month. Forty-two percent of the females and 25 per-cent of the males said they had "seriously thought" about committing suicide; nearly one in five girls and one in ten boys said they had attempted it.

These data help to explain Dorothy's rather offhand response when I   13
asked her what had happened to the other members of the group. She re-sponded casually, "Oh, the usual—some are dead, some have been put away, some are out there getting worse."

Today Dorothy is seven months pregnant and about to be married. She   14
started college at Fairleigh Dickinson but after two weeks found out she was pregnant. She seriously considered having an abortion but couldn't bring her-self to do it. Her future husband is a floor waxer and carpet cleaner; she is currently working at a job doing data entry. "It's boring," she says in a flat tone of voice.

What kind of future does she envision? "It's going to be hard. There are   15
going to be rough times. But we can make it. We've survived everything else. We'll just have to take one day at a time."

Taking one day at a time is something Linda Smith, a seventeen-year-   16
old high-school dropout who lives in North Carolina, feels she needs to learn. After her parents divorced and her mother made it clear that she did not really

want her around, Linda went to live with her grandmother. During her senior year she discovered that she was pregnant by her boyfriend. She decided to have an abortion, arranged and paid for it herself. "I wanted to get it over with," she said. "I didn't even get scared until I was on the operating table."

Linda currently works in a fast-food restaurant and plans to take courses for her high-school equivalency diploma. In thinking about the future Linda has a clearer picture of what she does not want than what she does want. "I don't want to stay in one place. I don't want to have kids until I'm thirty. I don't like to depend on a man." While she says she likes to travel, likes to communicate with different people, and might like to be an airline stewardess, when asked about plans for the future she responds, "I don't plan. I don't look to the future. I can't plan, 'cause my plans never work out. They never go through." 17

Norma Merino, a slight, pale, worn-looking mother of two who lives in Arizona, is two and a half months pregnant with her third child. She has been with the father of her children for seven years, since she was twelve and he was eighteen. Their first child was born when she was fourteen. "Thank God he never left me when I was younger," she says. "I know a lot of girls whose guys left when they got pregnant." Norma has thought about going back to school. She is currently receiving AFDC (Aid to Families with Dependent Children) but knows she needs to be able to take care of herself, because "I can't count on John and I don't run to Mom and Dad." 18

How does she see her future? "I don't even think about it. What if I die tomorrow or today? I just hope God gives me lots of days until the children are of age." What she does want is for her children to "grow up and finish school, not be out there in the streets, and to have a better life than mine." 19

Sex or gender is not the only minefield that females must face as they are growing up; there are also the minefields of class and race. The poor and the near-poor are surely Outsiders in this affluent, commercial society in which we are all relentlessly driven to consume. The working class is at best marginal, holding on as long as nothing goes wrong, as long as the factory has not been closed and the paycheck keeps coming in, as long as everyone remains healthy. But if any disaster strikes, a working-class family can become Outsiders in a flash—outside the workplace, outside the health-care system, outside the feel-good system of consuming, even literally outside on the streets. 20

Are the ultimate Outsiders nonwhite as well as poor? For while the rest of us can try to "pass" as insiders even when we know we are really living beyond the pale, nonwhites cannot. Gary Hart, like millions of Americans from immigrant families, can change his name to escape being identified as coming from ethnic stock; but blacks, Asians, Native Americans, and other nonwhites in our society have no such option. The identification is there every minute of the day. Black men are surely Outsiders within American society, but if adolescents by virtue of their developmental stage are Outsiders, if female adolescents by virtue of their gender are also outside the system, if the 21 poor are outside the American Dream, then, if we think in terms of concentric circles, those who are poor, nonwhite, and female must be farthest from the center, farthest from our image of what is good, what is shining, what it means to be an American. Can these young women on that periphery even see the center? Can they touch it? Can they imagine it? Or is it just too far—too far even to dream?

Toni Morrison has written perhaps the most compelling description of   22
what it is like to be the true Outsider:

> Outdoors, we know, was the real terror of life . . .
> There is a difference between being put *out* and being put outdoors. If you are put out, you go somewhere else; if you are outdoors, there is no place to go. The distinction was subtle but final. Outdoors was the end of something, an irrevocable, physical fact, defining and complementing our metaphysical condition.

Ellen Simpson, a college student in her mid-twenties, talks about what   23
it was like growing up as a Japanese-American girl: "My mother was Japanese and my father was American. When I was growing up, I was taught to be a servant. Women were supposed to serve others. My mother would have tea parties; I never interacted, I never participated—I just served.

"We came here from Japan when I was five. When I entered school I   24
remember speaking Japanese and the whole class laughed. There were always insults about Pearl Harbor, but I bore them and kept them inside. I had Japanese mannerisms like bowing to people, and I felt ostracized.

"I didn't even look right. Growing up in California everyone was sup-   25
posed to be tall, blond, very thin. I was five-feet-two, dark, mild, soft-spoken, and I had been taught that if I seemed too intelligent it would be threatening to others. I wanted to be attractive but was scared of drawing attention to myself. Instead, I had hair down to my knees—I parted it in the middle and hid behind it."

Ellen talks about W.E.B. Dubois's theory of "double consciousness." In   26
1903, DuBois wrote in *The Souls of Black Folk*:

> The Negro is a sort of seventh son, born with a veil, and gifted with second-sight in this American world,—a world which yields him no true self-consciousness, but only lets him see himself through the revelation of the other world. It is a peculiar sensation, this double-consciousness, this sense of always looking at one's self through the eyes of others, of measuring one's soul by the tape of a world that looks on in amused contempt and pity. One ever feels his twoness,—an American, a Negro; two souls, two thoughts, two unreconciled strivings, two warring ideals in one dark body, whose dogged strength alone keeps it from being torn asunder.

Ellen feels DuBois is saying that the Negro in him needed to love himself while the American in him needed to hate himself. Ellen says she felt the same way. "I finally stopped bowing," she says somewhat wistfully.

Three young Chicanas discuss growing up as Mexican-Americans while 27
trying to cope with the phenomenon of "double consciousness." Cecilia Mar-
tinez, a lively, bright, articulate twenty-one-year-old college student who
hopes to become a city planner, was bused to an integrated school not far
from her neighborhood. She feels that the "Anglos" were not accepting of
Mexican-American kids and that she "had to learn white ways." She describes
how discrimination persists in her life today, how "guys come on in a very
cheap way" when she and her friends go to a club in the evening. They
"assume we are there for sex." Their view is "Oh, she's a dumb Mexican
bitch!" Even at school, where she is a member of the finance committee, she's
always aware that she's "the Mexican member of the committee."

Tory Hostos describes growing up in an all-white area in southern Cal- 28
ifornia and attending nearly all-white schools: "When I was a little kid I had
secondhand clothes, and while I was the prettiest, I was also the poorest. Then
my family acquired some money, and the kids in school started to hate me.
They used to say Mexicans were dirty, and I hated that. I hated being Mexican.
I used to say 'Don't call me that,' and I tried to be white.

"Once in high school I got a perm and it came out looking like an Afro. 29
Then they spray-painted my clothes, ruined all my stuff, and called me
'nigger.'

"I constantly switched schools and learned to play white people's games. 30
I hated Mexicans. I dated white guys—Italians, Jewish guys—and even forgot
that I was Mexican. Once I drove with this guy into Mexico (he came from a
very white family), and he's saying all these terrible things about Mexicans and
treating me as though I'm white. I suddenly thought, 'I must be a disgrace to
Mexicans. I'll just have to start acting like I'm Mexican.' But really I felt that
I'd rather be dead."

Jacqueline Gonzalez has had a somewhat different experience. She grew 31
up in a working-class Mexican-American family in the barrio but was one of
the students who were bused from her neighborhood to a very affluent neighborhood. She feels that the students at her new school always felt they were
superior, always looked down on the Mexican-Americans. As a result, she says,
she became "really shy, afraid to express myself; I never felt like one of them."
She continues: "I didn't want to be Hispanic, but I had to be; I couldn't be
Anglo. I was caught between the two groups."

Jacqueline feels that she will most likely marry someone who is Hispanic; 32
but she hopes that later, when she's a successful lawyer, she can live in the
same area to which she was bused all those years. Those "Anglos" might have
treated her badly, but Jacqueline wants to live an upper-middle-class life among
them. Tory feels she will almost certainly "marry someone who is white" and
says that the worst part is that "every day I wake up and have to deal with it
all over again."

Pamela Vincent is a dynamic, articulate, outgoing black woman in her 33
mid-twenties. Like Tory she grew up in an affluent neighborhood in southern
California; her family was the only black family in the area. Even though they
were middle-class, she says, "I always felt different—like an outsider. The other

girls were little, with blond hair; I always felt I wasn't any good. People talked to me using terms they thought black people use; I was always fighting against the stereotype."

A turning point in her life came during the summer between her junior   *34* and senior years in high school. Through a program run by the American Field Service she went to Brazil, lived with a family there, and fell in love with the culture. "I loved it there!" she says. "I loved the energy! I loved the jazz and the dancing! I loved their focus on the family." Pam has been trying ever since to integrate Brazilian music and dance into her life and into this culture. One of her dreams is to develop a multilingual, multicultural program for children in the schools, combining movement, music, and other aspects of culture to help Americans become more sensitive to the differences between groups in our society. Pam is trying to use her experience of feeling like an Outsider to bring people a bit closer together.

These Asian-American, Mexican-American, and African-American   *35* women feel like Outsiders primarily because of their racial and ethnic backgrounds. What does it feel like to grow up both black and poor? Four young black high school students describe the town in which they live—interrupting each other as people do when they know one another well and are involved in the topic. "It's like a circle." "No, it's like a Q—one road in, around in a circle, and the same road out." They are describing a small city in northern California, a black ghetto nestled in the lush, green hills of affluent Marin County, where chardonnay and Brie are staples of life.

This city was developed in the early 1940s to house the thousands of   *36* workers employed in the shipyards of Sausalito. During the Second World War the community was integrated and thriving. At the end of the war most of the shipyard workers left, and virtually all business within the area disappeared. Black residents remained, and by 1980, according to the U.S. Bureau of the Census, the city was 75 percent black, 23 percent white, and 2 percent "other." This composition contrasts dramatically with that of Marin County, which in 1980 was 88.6 percent white, 2.5 percent black, and 8.9 percent "other."

In addition to being a predominantly black community, Marin City is   *37* also a poor community. In 1980 its median family income was $8,676; Marin County's was $29,721. In the same year 29 percent of Marin City's residents lived below the poverty line, and in 1984 the unemployment rate was 23 percent.

What are the key issues facing young women in this black ghetto today?   *38* The answer is immediate: "Drugs. Pregnancy. Having kids." Candida Dixon, an articulate seventeen-year-old senior who quickly becomes the spokesperson for the group, says, "Ninety percent of the people here are doing drugs. And maybe 50 percent of kids our age. They're doing cocaine, some weed." And, they all agree, more girls than guys are doing drugs. And alcohol—more girls than guys are drinking. Why? They all say at once that there is nothing else to do. What are the guys doing? They are out driving around in their cars, if they have one, and selling dope—"Every guy is selling dope." Candida continues, "If you don't have a car, you hang around out on the street. You get drunk or high just to have fun. Otherwise, everyone is bored, just standing around doing nothing."

"And lots of kids are pregnant," says a quiet sixteen-year-old. "And lots *39* of abortions," chimes in another. "And at twelve and thirteen—seventh and eight graders!" states a third, as though speaking disapprovingly about the younger generation. "And they're doing it with guys twenty and older!" "And," says another, "everyone is related—everyone has sex with everyone. Sexual diseases—chlamydia, AIDS—are a big problem."

I ask them why they think all this is going on. The theories come all at *40* once: "'Cause the mothers are on dope." "The parents don't care; some let their kids run wild." "The mothers don't have time to teach them." "They are trying to be grown up; the girls feel important going with dope dealers."

These young women go to an integrated regional high school in a *41* nearby upper-middle-class community, home of California yuppies, BMWs, and kids taking swimming lessons at the nearby swim club after school. These high-school students recognize that most of the people they are describing are so outside the system that they'll never get back in. They describe a desolate scene and vow that they themselves will get out. Lerae Andrade, a seventeen-year-old high-school senior, says she hopes to go to a local community college, transfer to UCLA, and become an X-ray technician. June Bennett, also seventeen, wants a fancy car and maybe to marry "someone rich." Candida, by far the liveliest of the four, plans to go to law school, marry, have kids, be "well off," with a "nice home" and "some travel." Three of the four are New American Dreamers; the fourth cannot imagine life beyond tomorrow. When I tell a friend who has worked and taught in the area that three of the four plan to leave the ghetto, she shakes her head in disbelief and says, "No one ever gets out of there."

The next morning at the San Francisco airport the magnitude of the *42* effort necessary to fulfill their dreams struck me with incredible force and sadness. A little girl in a pink-and-white flowered dress trimmed with eyelet and lace, with puffed sleeves and a sash that ties in the back, was waiting patiently at the American Airlines gate; she was wearing white tights, white shoes, and pink barrettes to hold back her light-brown curls—Shirley Temple, Goldilocks, a young Daisy Buchanan come to life! She was five years old and going to Mexico on a holiday with her grandmother. Her name is Alison, but people call her "Muffin." A golden girl already! Seeing her after just talking with the young women from the black ghetto spotlighted the enormous gap in life chances between those who are born Insiders and those who are born Outsiders. What a long way these women have to go! Can they possibly have sufficient strength and stamina to make it out of the ghetto, one with economic, social, and psychological walls at least as high as the stone walls that separated the Jews from mainstream Italian life in sixteenth-century Venice and that gave us the word "ghetto"?

A recurring image among nonwhite girls and young women is that 43 "everyone else," or at least everyone who counts, has blond hair and blue eyes. The United States is, of course, made up of many people who have neither blond hair nor blue eyes; but this is the image of beauty—and, more than beauty, of goodness and perhaps power—that has been transmitted throughout the decades. Still, today, in this heterogeneous society of ours, when designers want to place the ultimate stamp of authority on their clothes, furnishings, or other artifacts, a model or group of models with an upper-class, WASP image is often used. It is no accident that Ralph Lauren uses all those generations of models from children to supposed grandparents, all looking like Boston Brahmins out for a sail in Chatham Harbor on Cape Cod. The hegemony of the upper-class WASP image is still very much a part of our symbol of success and belonging and legitimate authority in this society.

Toni Morrison describes what it meant to small black girls in the 1940s 44 to be growing up in a culture that idolized Betty Grable, Ginger Rogers, and, above all, Shirley Temple. When Claudia, the young narrator of *The Bluest Eye,* is given a Shirley Temple doll for Christmas, she describes her reaction: "I had only one desire: to dismember it. To see of what it was made, to discover the dearness, to find the beauty, the desirability that had escaped me, but apparently only me . . . All the world had agreed that a blue-eyed, yellow-haired, pink-skinned doll was what every girl child treasured." But while Claudia readily admits that at first she "destroyed white baby dolls" and, moreover, wanted to do the same to "little white girls" in order to discover the "secret of the magic they weaved on others," in time she, too, learned to "worship" Shirley Temple ("knowing, even as I learned, that the change was adjustment without improvement"). Today, when people are haunted by being "different," they need only to go to the nearest optician, where they can purchase contact lenses that will instantly alter the color of their eyes. We should not be surprised to learn that blue eyes are by far the most popular.

Sociologist Patricia Hill Collins discusses the importance of "Black 45 women's insistence on self-definition, self-valuation and the necessity for a Black female-centered analysis":

> The status of being the "other" implies being "other than" or different from the assumed norm of white male behavior. In this model, powerful white males define themselves as subjects, the true actors, and classify people of color and women in terms of their position vis-a-vis this white male hub. Since Black women have been denied the authority to challenge these definitions, this model consists of images that define Black women as a negative other; the virtual antithesis of positive male images.

This analysis is, of course, equally applicable to Native Americans, per- 46 haps the quintessential Outsiders in American society. The Papago Indians live in the Sonoran Desert in Arizona and Mexico. It is a land of dust and cactus, thorns, century plants and prickly pear. It is a land of 115-degree summer heat, of dry reservoirs, and of jackrabbits, blackbirds, desert cottontails, and gophers. And yet when ethnobiologist Gary Paul Nabhan asked a Papago child what the desert smelled like, he responded with little hesitation, "The desert smells like rain." Ironically, it is that which is rare and treasured that gives the desert its scent. Nabhan points out that the Papago are fascinated by the unpredictability of the rain and that this fascination with unpredictability has led to a society that is "a dynamic, lively world, responsive to stormy forces that may come at any time."

One group of Papago Indians lives on a reservation in Arizona. The land, flat with mountains in the distance, is covered with sandy dirt and dotted with low brush and delicate trees. Shades of beige, brown, and taupe set off the yellowish green of the trees and provide a quiet, arid background for the houses, made of brown or sand-colored cement blocks. In the distance is a mountain covered with cactus, behind which, it is said, is a secret burial ground. — 47

According to a physician who works at the local health clinic, the main problems of the local residents are alcohol consumption, obesity, diabetes, and unemployment. While unemployment is not as severe as it is among other groups of Native Americans, primarily because the reservation is so close to the city, most people on the reservation are nevertheless unemployed. According to one health worker, "There is nothing to do here and no transportation to get to work in the city." — 48

Girls become pregnant at fourteen or fifteen. A health worker reported that they used to be given IUDs but that these are no longer approved. Many of the women "don't use the pill successfully"; health workers give out foam and condoms "like water." Do the men use the condoms? "No. We do it to ease our consciences." — 49

Alberta Montoya is a thirty-two-year-old licensed public nurse who looks more like forty-two. She has five children, who range from fourteen years to nineteen months. She was eighteen at the birth of her first child and gave birth to a second child two years later. Somehow she was able to overcome the enormous disadvantage of being a single mother, finished high school, then trained to be an LPN. She feels that some of the girls on the reservation don't understand the connection between sex and pregnancy and that virtually none of them understand what they are getting themselves into when they have a baby. Some young women have had such difficult and painful childhoods, she says, that it's a wonder they survive at all. — 50

Lucy Barrow and I stand outside of the house where she lives with her two children, a two-year-old and a baby of just four weeks, and with their father, his parents, and other family members. Ten people live in what looks to be a very small house. Lucy prefers to talk standing in the sun, leaning against a car. Beer cans are everywhere, and in the next yard is a junk heap with assorted pieces of machinery. — 51

Lucy is eighteen. Perhaps her story illustrates the need for Papago Indians to be "responsive to stormy forces that may come at any time." Lucy seems — 52 hesitant at first about talking but gets involved in her story as she goes along.

She starts by describing how the tribal council took her older daughter   *53*
from her when she was three days old: "They took her from me. She was sick,
and they said I wasn't taking care of her because there was no adult living
with us. They gave her to another family living far from here, but finally her
father helped me to get her back.

"Now everything is okay. We live with his family, and everything seems   *54*
easy. He works but keeps getting laid off. He's twenty-four. No, we're not on
welfare—he gathers wood and his parents help us out."

Until now Lucy has been talking slowly, hesitantly, as though she's not   *55*
sure what to say. I then ask her about her childhood, and she starts to speak
with no prompting from me, picking up speed until my note taking can barely
keep up with her story.

"My mother died when I was just a baby. I lived with an aunt and then   *56*
was switched back and forth between my aunt and my grandma until I ran
away. Then I stayed with a cousin and was going to school. They [the tribal
council] took me from my cousin's and placed me in a children's home, but I
ran away. I ended up in juvenile court, and they sent me to a foster home far
away. I was there one year, but I didn't like it. I found out who my sister was
and stayed with her for a while but was picked up and sent back to the
children's home.

"Then they sent me to boarding school, and then I stayed with a lady   *57*
here for two years. I quit running away and stayed there. She understood
everything.

"But then I started messing up. I started meeting girls, not staying home.   *58*
I would stay at their houses. So I had to go back to the children's home, but I
didn't like to be there so I ran away. I didn't want to do what they wanted me
to do—I didn't want to stay with other people—so I ran away. I stayed with
friends. Then the police picked me up and took me to detention and they
sent me back to the children's home. I didn't like to be there, but I stayed until
I was released.

"I then lived with another lady. One day I went to the clinic. I said I   *59*
wasn't pregnant; I didn't think I was pregnant, but they told me I was. The
first lady I stayed with told me she would help me out if I would stay with
her. But I didn't want to give her more trouble, so I went back to juvenile
detention; but I finally went back and stayed with her while I was pregnant.

"Now I'm eighteen and I'm glad, because now I don't have to worry   *60*
about where they'll send me."

When I asked Lucy what she thought her life would be like in the future,   *61*
she said, "I don't know. I think about that. I need to go to school; I need to
get a job so I can take care of myself and the children. I know I'm not going
to be with him [the father of her children]. When's he's drinking, he gets
violent. But he's nice. It's only when he's drunk. He says he's going to quit
drinking. I tried to get help for him, for his drinking, but he doesn't want
help. He has a terrible temper. He used to hit me a lot, but now he watches

himself. Now when he's drinking he goes off to be by himself and comes back when he's sober. When I want to go for help at the clinic, he says we can solve our problems ourselves.

"I don't know what to do when he's drunk—I don't know how to treat   62
him. He gets mad and yells at us. When he's sober, he does lots of things for us. It's just when he drinks. My only problem is the drinking part."

Among the young women I interviewed, there were clearly levels of   63
Outsider-ness. There are those young women who are transient Outsiders. Many adolescents fall into this category: after a few years, they will find their group, their goals, their dreams. Some who are more fundamentally outside the culture because of race, religion, class, or family structure will succeed in spite of their Outsider status. These are the lucky ones, the talented, the superbright, the ones who are able to develop, in the words of W.E.B. DuBois, a "true self-consciousness" and separate their image of themselves from society's image of them. Some will succeed in some sense because of the strength and insight they have gained by coping with being outside of the system. But many young women, as American society is at present constructed, are permanent Outsiders. They have no dreams for themselves. The most they can hope for is a future for their children. They themselves may never feel part of the culture; they may never feel entitled to a future.

While Americans are often held to a middle-class or upper-middle-class   64
standard of behavior and achievement under the prevailing myth that everyone has an equal chance at achieving success, the reality is that the opportunities are far from equal. Young people who grow up in a technologically advanced society but do not even learn to read and write know that they will always be outside the system; Americans who do not have enough to eat while the government pays farmers millions not to grow crops are being told they are expendable; and children who spend months, perhaps years, in roach-infested welfare hotels are being sent a clear message about their value to society. The ideology of the American Dream may be based on the notion that we Americans control our own destiny; but in reality, our destiny is often based on myriad factors over which we have little or no control.

Perhaps in no other area is our ideology as remote from our practice as   65
in the area of education. We communicate to our young people every day our hopes and expectations for them by the condition of the schools they attend, the quality of the teaching, the attitude of administrators. But while we believe that democracy should "begin at the schoolhouse door" and that every child should have an equal chance in the race toward success, we know that in reality, life chances vary enormously by class, race, ethnic group, gender, and even geography, and that these differing life chances are mirrored in the educational system.

According to sociologists Peter W. Cookson, Jr., and Caroline Hodges   66
Persall, authors of *Preparing for Power: America's Elite Boarding Schools,* certain schools train select young people for a life of power and privilege and enable elite families to maintain their social class. The young women and men in

these schools learn how to exercise power over others, how to have the "habit of command," how to acquire "taste," how to use money and yet conceal it, how to be elite and yet "disguise their eliteness," and learn, above all, that they are worthy of power and privilege. Cookson and Persall describe how even the physical atmosphere creates a sense of individual worth:

> Wood-paneled rooms are graced with antique furniture, oil paintings, and china bowls brimming with fresh-cut flowers . . .
>
> In one sense the beauty of prep school campuses is an exterior validation of the student's sense that "Yes, I am special," or perhaps even, "Yes, I am beautiful." A headmaster articulated his belief that architecture affects a student's psyche when he reported that a student said, "This school requires quality in what I do, because I have leaded glass windows in my bedroom."

If paneled rooms and leaded glass windows signify the expectation of quality work, what are the messages of schools with "insufficient heat," "perennially clogged toilets," and "inadequate lighting"? What are schools such as one in the South Bronx, "a 66-year-old dull, brick building down in a landscape of vacant lots, dead cars, stray dogs and troubled men," telling the students about society's commitment to their future? When suburban schools look like affluent community colleges and inner-city schools look like London after the blitz, what are we telling our young people? If some schools are preparing students for power, can we not postulate that other schools, those in our poorest neighborhoods, are all too often training many of their young people for a life of failure and despair? Many of our young people do not come out of school with the skills or the credentials to work in the regular economy. Why, then, are we surprised at the rate of teen pregnancy, crack addiction, gang membership, or at the flourishing of the underground economy?

The messages are clear—that nothing is too good for the children of the *67* elite and that not even the bare minimum will be provided to the children of the poor and near-poor. As a 1988 report issued by the Carnegie Foundation for the Advancement of Teaching stated, urban schools are "little more than human storehouses to keep young people off the streets." The report continues, "No other crisis—a flood, a health epidemic, a garbage strike or even snow removal—would be as calmly accepted without full-scale emergency intervention."

If young people who receive an inferior education are often outside the *68* system, what about the growing number of homeless people in the United States? Are they the ultimate outsiders? Estimates of the number of the homeless in the U.S. vary widely, from the Reagan administration estimate of 250,000 to the estimate of the National Coalition for the Homeless of as many as three million people.

According to a survey conducted in forty-seven cities by the Partnership *69* for the Homeless, during the winter of 1987 families with children became the largest segment of the homeless population. From November 1986 to mid-March 1987 the number of homeless families rose by 25 percent; this increase meant that by March 1987 families with children made up 35 percent of the homeless—the largest group within the homeless population. What messages are we sending these Americans? What does it mean to grow up homeless in America?

The effects of homelessness, particularly among mothers and children, can be devastating. The homeless receive grossly inadequate medical care and frequently have a far higher rate of health problems than do other comparable groups. A recent study indicated that one out of every six homeless children suffers from chronic health problems. Homeless children frequently are unable to attend school because schools are reluctant to accept students on a "temporary" basis. Conditions are incredibly crowded, often several people to a room, with a lack of cooking facilities and grossly inadequate sanitation. Often families housed in emergency shelters eat only one hot meal a day. Moreover, these shelters are often places of violence and exploitation. Drugs are sold freely, alcoholism is rampant, teenage girls are recruited into prostitution, and fights and child abuse become everyday occurrences.

Not far from the Presbyterian church in Westchester—symbolic of all that seems safe and secure in American society—nearly seventy homeless adults and children are housed in a motel. The rooms have neither hot plates nor refrigerators. The only way to keep milk is if you are lucky enough to have a cooler.

Most of the adults in this motel are young black single mothers. Lisa, twenty-one years old, is the mother of three children, ages three, two, and ten months. She and her children were evicted from their apartment; prior to that, she had worked driving a van for the disabled. She says that the worst thing about living in the motel is the stigma. Even when she crosses the street to go to the supermarket, "people follow you like you might steal something." Lisa dreams of a job and a two-bedroom apartment.

It is clear that there are many levels of Outsider-ness among young women in American society—from those who feel temporarily outside their family/community/society to those who because of a complex convergence of factors become virtual pariahs. While we must recognize that young women of any class, race, and family background may at some time feel like Outsiders, that an unhappy childhood, an unintended pregnancy, abuse of alcohol or drugs may precipitate hopelessness and alienation, we must also recognize that the structure of American society and American social policy often combine to thrust millions of young women into either temporary or permanent Outsider status. Growing up with little sense of community or connection to others, growing up poor in an affluent society with little hope of moving into the working or middle class, growing up nonwhite in a profoundly racist society, growing up illiterate in a complex technological society, growing up homeless in a society that largely ignores and disdains the homeless, and growing up female and feeling passive and powerless to determine one's future leads all too many young women to feel disconnected, irrelevant, and often despairing. While the New American Dreamers hope to take control of their lives and capture some of the power and wealth American society promises, and the Neotraditionalists hope to connect and combine their worlds of work and home, to these young women, the Outsiders, the American Dream seems not only remote and unattainable but often unimaginable as well.

Topics for Discussion and Writing

1. Compare your responses to any of the first three "Before and as You Read" topics with the visions of the future that Sidel reports in this essay. How are your visions similar to and different from those of the Outsiders? If you responded to "Before and as You Read" topic 3, compare your estimate of the sources of your images with what Sidel writes about where the Outsiders' dreams come from.

2. Reread the essay to note how Sidel evaluates each subject's chances to realize her dreams. Do you agree with her assessments? Explain. Whether you agree or disagree with Sidel, what do you feel are the key factors that determine a person's chances of reaching her dreams in the United States? What does Sidel say about this?

3. With several others, design a survey that seeks similar information as Sidel's. Through interviews and/or written questionnaires, gather this information from as broad a cross-sample of young people as you can. Using this selection as a model, analyze and report your data. (*Note:* It would be helpful to use the full text of Sidel's book as your model. The first and second chapters of her book report responses from populations quite different from that used for this selection; the respondents used in those two chapters include a high proportion of college students from much more affluent backgrounds.)

4. Compare Sidel's brief portraits of one or two of the Outsiders with Jane O'Reilly's self-portrait of her youth and of her consciousness-raising as a woman. What events and influences in O'Reilly's life brought about her "click" of awareness? Imagine a pattern of events and influences that would make such a realization possible for an Outsider.

KATSI COOK

from *New Voices from the Longhouse*

"*Delfina Cuero, a Diegueno born in 1900, came of age in an area of California (San Diego) where the missionaries had done much to destroy traditional 'pagan' ceremonies. In doing so, they also destroyed the moral, educational, and ethical systems by which the Diegueno lived their lives.*"

Katsi Cook was one of the founders of Akwesasne Notes, *a publication of writing in many forms by members of the Haudenosaunee (Iroquois) peoples. Her articles have been published in* Mothering, Ms., *and* Northeast Indian Quarterly, *among other periodicals. Since 1978, she has been a practicing midwife. She lectures on women's health practices and organizes programs on health and toxicity issues with the Akwesasne Environment Project.*

We have taken "The Women's Dance" from New Voices from the Longhouse: An Anthology of Contemporary Iroquois Writing *(1989), edited by Joseph Bruchac.*

Before and as You Read

1. The term *equality* implies to many an equal desire by all to share in that American Dream defined by advertisers on television. But *equality* has also meant an equal chance for all to respond to very different ideals or to maintain traditions far older than those imposed by industrial technology. Try thinking about equality in this way. Does your vision of the ideal future in any way differ from those images broadcast most loudly in popular culture?

2. Write as much as you feel you know in response to these terms: *Native American, Iroquois, Mother Earth.* What immediate images come to you when you hear these terms? What questions come to you as you write these responses?

3. As you read the selection, note how Cook uses information from different peoples in making her generalizations. What kinds of information and sources does she cite? Note also how she uses her childhood and adolescence in contrast with the "traditional" puberty experiences she has learned about.

4. As you read, observe how Cook speaks about the roles of women in Haudenosaunee and other Indian cultures. If anything she describes or if any of her comments surprises you, mark those surprises. Why are you surprised?

THE WOMEN'S DANCE: RECLAIMING OUR POWERS

Traditional Values

IT IS important to begin at the beginning. In everything the People 1
do, they start at the beginning. When I asked, "How do we teach the
young about birth?" I was told, "Begin with the story of the first birth." So,
we turn to our origins to understand women's ways. The Creation stories, the
cosmologies, contain the world view and values of Indigenous Peoples. They
are the spiritual foundation of traditional communities, and an important place
to start when we need to understand how to deal with the problems we face
here and now today.

In Iroquois cosmology, a pregnant woman in the sky world wanted some 2
bark from the roots of the Great Tree that stood at the center of the universe.
In digging up the roots for her, her husband made a hole in the floor of the
sky world, and the pregnant woman curiously peeked through the hole. As
she bent and looked through the empty space and ocean far below, she fell.
She grabbed at the edges of the hole, but she slipped through. In her hands
were bits of things that grow in the sky-world. She landed on the back of
a great turtle, and was aided by the animals to found a new firmament. As
the woman walked in a circle around the clod of dirt supplied by a muskrat
from the bottom of the ocean, the earth began to grow. She planted the
things she carried in her hands from the sky-world. She continued to circle the earth, moving as the sun goes. Her time came and she delivered a
daughter. They both continued to walk in a circle around the earth, and lived
on the plants that were growing there. A man appeared; some say it was the
West Wind. The daughter of Sky Woman was soon pregnant with twins,
and these twins argued within their mother's body. They argued about their
birth. The right-handed twin was born in the normal way, and the left-handed
twin was born through his mother's armpit. This killed her. In the world
outside their mother's body, they continued to quarrel. They buried their
mother and from her grave grew corn, beans and squash, the "three sisters"
which still sustain us, and Indian tobacco, which is used in ceremonies. The
twins continued to quarrel and with their creative powers contested one another. From their contests they created the world, which was balanced and
orderly.

In the way these things are told to us, these intricate stories which take 3
many days to relate, there is room which motivates the individual to seek their
own perception about life. This is why there are so many different versions of
the Creation story. Different versions follow different threads of perception.
And they all teach something about life, and the world. We learn about op-
posites, and a world that is neither all good nor all bad. We learn that the
entire universe is a family, and we learn that the greatest good is harmony. We
learn the responsibilities and original instructions that all Creation has in maintaining this harmony.

Moon Cycles, Earth Cycles

In the Native American consciousness, health is a matter of balance and 4
harmony. Our old people maintained this balance by a sophisticated system of
ceremonies and knowledge based on an awareness based on our relationship
to everything in the universe and a respect for all life. Everything in Creation
was expressed in dualities, such as male and female. Everything in Creation is
paired and in balance with each other. The winds, the rains, rocks and rivers,
all have their male and female. In between these two poles is the life force
which comes to rest on Mother Earth.

A powerful force in our universe is the Sun. "Brothers and Sisters," 5
Sitting Bull said, "the spring has come. The Earth has received the embraces
of the Sun and we shall soon see the results of that love. Every seed is
awakened and so has all animal life. It is through this mysterious power that
we too have our being."

Some people say the energy from the Sun is too strong, however, for the 6
Earth to contain. Therefore, it reflects itself to the Moon. The Moon, the
mother of the Universe, absorbs this excess energy. In this action she then
reflects the Sun back to himself so that he will not overwhelm her, and she
can make full use of his lifegiving power. The duality of male and female is
basic in life. This concept finds its way even into the political systems of some
Native communities, as with the Iroquois Confederacy where male and female
sit in council together.

> I'll tell you, the women—they had the power. If you wanted to get 7
> anything done you had to go to your grandmother. If she agreed,
> you could take it to the clan mothers, and they would decide if they
> would take it to the Chiefs and put it through Council.
>
> *Ernie Mohawk, Seneca Elder*

The Women's Community

In a traditional world, Native American women understood their bodies 8
in terms of the Earth and the Moon. In the universal community of women,
the Earth was perceived as our Mother from whom all Life comes. A Dene
origin myth tells of the menstrual flow of the Earth by which vegetation and
reproduction are possible. This flow, which we know as dew, was created from
the maple dew of the horizontal skyblue and the female dew of darkness.
Reproduction originated from this menstruation of the Earth. The Moon,
our Grandmother, is the leader of all female life. She controls all things female
or procreative. She causes movement of the great waters of reproduction, of
birth itself, and the oceans. That the Grandmother Moon controls the forces
of reproduction is basic to the health, or balance, of female life. The time of
the menses is referred to as "my grandmother is visiting me."

The old women tell us, "A woman is like the Moon. When she is young 9
and just becoming a woman, she is like the New Moon. She will usually

menstruate on the New Moon. As she walks further into life, she reaches her peak and becomes like the full moon. She, too, is full and fertile. As she ages, she wanes with the Moon. Throughout life, as with every monthly cycle of fertility and purification, she wanes with the Moon. It is as if she were holding hands with her grandmother."

In *Kwakiutl Ethnography,* Franz Boaz says: "Pregnancy lasts ten moons   10
after the last period. At the first appearance of the new Moon, in the last month of her pregnancy, she goes outside and prays to the moon for an easy delivery. This is done four times. The child is generally born at full moon of that month."

Grandma Moon's effect on the procreative waters was also known by the   11
Wichita People: "The Spirit of the water, Woman Forever in the Water, is closely associated with the Moon Spirit, yet their functions differ: one creates life, the other makes possible its growth and continuation. As an illustration a woman desiring a child would not pray to the water spirit, but would address her supplication to the Spirit of the Moon, then when the child was born the mother implored the beneficence of the Water Spirit, the Moon Spirit, and included the Supreme Spirit." (Man Not Known On Earth. Curtis, Volume 19, *The North American Indian*).

Woman's Ways: Changing Women

In many Native American origin stories, puberty ceremonies were a gift   12
to women from the Moon or other primal being. The ritual passage into womanhood was fundamental to the development and growth of a healthy woman. With much variation from nation to nation, this was generally a time of elaborate and joyful recognition of the appearance of the first menstrual flow which marked the change from girlhood to womanhood. "On the occasion of her first menses a Cahuilla girl was laid recumbent on a bed of brush and herbs heated in a trench. Covered with a blanket she remained there throughout three nights, while men and women danced and sang songs alluding to the institution of this custom by Moon and to the proper conduct of menstruating girls."

The puberty ceremony was perhaps the most important ceremony in the   13
life of the Native American woman. At this time, she was isolated from the general community and, attended by her female relatives, was instructed in the skills and character essential for her survival in the community. There is a great wealth of anthropological and autobiographical information on Native women's experience at puberty.

Of the many remarkable stories told by and about Indian women con-   14
cerning their passage into womanhood, all have common characteristics, although the ceremony itself was incidental to cultural variances. In *The Sacred,* Beck and Walters state that: "The patterns of behavior prescribed for menstru-

ating women and pubescent girls were similar in their reasoning and objectives. Menstruation was equated with power which could be utilized for healing or curing. The power had to be recognized by a woman and others around her. When she adhered to the prescribed rules of behavior, this power was acknowledged."

Delfina Cuero, a Diegueno born in 1900, came of age in an area of   15
California (San Diego) where the missionaries had done much to destroy traditional "pagan" ceremonies. In doing so, they also destroyed the moral, educational, and ethical systems by which the Diegueno lived their lives. "My grandmother told me about what they did to girls as they were about to become women. They had already stopped doing it when I became a woman.

"Grandmothers taught these things about life at the time of a girl's   16
initiation ceremony. Nobody just talked about these things ever. It was all in the songs and myths that belonged to the ceremony. All that a girl needed to know to be a good wife, and how to have babies and to take care of them was learned at the ceremony, at the time when a girl became a woman. We were taught about food and herbs and how to make things by our mothers and grandmothers all the time. But only at the ceremony for girls was the proper time to teach the special things women had to know. Nobody just talked about those things, it was all in the songs. But I'm not old, they had already stopped having the ceremonies before I became a woman, so I didn't know these things until later. Some of the other girls had the same trouble I did after I was married. No one told me anything. I knew something was wrong with me but I didn't know what. One day I was a long way from home looking for greens. I had terrible pain. I started walking back home but I had to stop and rest when the pain was too much. Then the baby came, I couldn't walk anymore, and I didn't know what to do. Finally an uncle came out looking for me when I didn't return. My grandmother had not realized my time was so close or she would not have let me go so far alone. They carried me back but I lost the baby. My grandmother took care of me so I recovered. Then she taught me all these things about what to do and how to take care of babies." (Delfina Cuero: *The Autobiography of Delfina Cuero,* as told to Florence Shipek pp 42–43)

The Sovereignty of Women

Control over production and the reproduction of human beings and all   17
our relations is integral to sovereignty. It is this area of sovereignty which falls primarily in the domain of the female universe and encompasses the balances and forces which promote the harmony and well-being of the People. Women are the base of the generations. They are carriers of the culture. In many traditional societies, the children "belong" to the woman's lineage. Among the

Iroquois, the Haudenosaunee, the women "owned" the gardens, and thereby controlled a major portion of the food supply. Supported by the Clan, the healers, and a community in harmony with the Creation, women had more to do with health than doctors are able to in today's fragmented world.

The concept of a universal "women's community" gives us the founda-   18
tion with which to comprehend our physical and spiritual powers as women. What threatens the sovereignty of the women: of the women's community? What threatens the self-sufficiency of women in matters of production and reproduction, not just of human beings, but of all our relations upon which we depend for a healthy life? With the development of new and dangerous technologies affecting the control of women's cycles and female mechanical means of reproduction, it is more important now than ever to perceive what meanings lie in our existence as human beings and as Native women.

Everywhere we look, the measure of suffering for female life is the same.   19
Reproduction for human beings and many of our relations is hardly a natural process. Chemicals, instruments, machines and distorted values sap the foun-dations of women's ways. Sterilization abuse, which has decimated the gene pool of less than a million Indians now in existence in the U.S., is a violation of Native women. Chemical contamination of our bodies and our environ-ments is known to be the leading cause of high rates of cancer, genetic mutation and disease. On Pine Ridge reservation in South Dakota, 38% of the pregnant women suffered from miscarriages in one month in 1979. The miscarriage rate there is close to seven times greater than the U.S. national average.

In the not-too-long ago days and even still in some Indian communities,   20
women were taught at puberty the things they needed to know to survive, physically and spiritually. These things were reflected in the songs, dances, various ceremonies, the everyday culture, in the stories the old ones told. For example, within the Iroquois social dances, the Woman's Dance is done to remind the women of their connection to the Mother Earth. We are an extension of Her. You look at the Earth and the old people will tell you that everything we need for a good life is provided for us by our common mother. Our laws, our education, our medicines, our religion, our food, shelter and clothing: everything came from the Earth, our Mother.

What are we doing as mothers to provide these things for our children?   21
You look around in the Indian communities on the reservations and in the cities and you see how Indian women are losing their power on the female side of life. We have become more and more dependent on a way of life that does not belong to us. So dependent that breastfeeding, home births, parent-ing, and control over our own health and reproduction have become unfamil-iar skills to us.

The consciousness of the Women's Dance, the awareness of our spiritual   22
quality as women, and the concept of personal sovereignty, has to be the consciousness of our survival as women. We need to reclaim our powers on the female side of life.

Woman's Thread

I was born at home in 1952 in my grandmother's bedroom. I was the   23
fourth child of a woman who had been told by doctors to not even have
children because her heart suffered the damage of childhood rheumatic fever.
Grandma delivered me and many of the children in my generation on the
reservation at Akwesasne. I have been told that after I was born, I was placed
in a basket next to my mother. Soon my grandmother walked by me and she
noticed that my blanket was bloody. When she pulled it back, she saw that I
was bleeding from the cord stump. Having raised 13 children of her own and
having cared for so many others in the time of the Depression, Grandma was
an excellent seamstress. So she took a needle and thread, sterilized it, and
sewed up my navel. My brothers and sisters would always tease me as I was
growing up, "You'd better not make Grandma mad or she's going to take her
thread back!"

Grandma's large farm house sheltered her extended family through many   24
passages in life. She delivered babies, held wedding receptions and funerals,
and cared for family invalids. She was a one-woman institution. Her Mohawk
name, Kanatires, means "she leads the village." Her beautiful quilts were sewn
from the cast off clothing of her many children and grandchildren. In the way
of old women, Grandma could not tolerate waste and she found a use for
everything.

Grandma would rest in the evening, reading while she sat in her rocking   25
chair. "Oh, Baby," she would sigh, and then she would go to her big iron bed
that was separated only by a chintz curtain from where I slept. I remember
thinking what a strange exclamation "Oh, Baby" was for such an old woman
whose only romance (although my sister and I would tease her about her
occasional visits from Captain DeHollander) had died with my grandfather
many years before. I carry the memory still of one such evening when my
grandmother went to her bed to undress and put on her long flannel nightgown. I walked into her room and I saw her, sitting on the edge of the bed,
naked to the waist, undressing. Her brown, wrinkled breasts sagged clear down
to her waist. I was a young girl and I had never seen an old woman's breasts
before. Grandma had felt my child's eyes upon her and she made no effort to
hide herself, nor did she show any embarrassment, only an acknowledgment
of my presence. At that moment I felt only a tremendous respect for this
woman.

I spent a great deal of my childhood in my grandmother's care because   26
of my mother's heart condition. I remember when my mother's exhausted
heart had failed her for the final time, she was *waked* in the sitting room, next
to my grandmother's bedroom where she had given birth so selflessly to me. I
lay in my small bed and in the next room I could hear the old men sing
Mohawk songs for my mother all night before they buried her. I was twelve
then. That same spring, I had become a woman, or as they say in Mohawk,
"her grandmother is visiting her." My mother's wish to live long enough to

see her youngest child become a woman had been fulfilled. "Keep yourself clean here," she would say when she bathed me. "Someday a baby is going to come out of there." It had been strange how it happened when the blood came from between my legs for the first time. Ista (mother) was talking on the phone to an auntie about her upcoming open heart surgery, and as I passed by her on the way to the bathroom I could hear her say, "if only I could live long enough to see my baby become a woman." That is how it happened.

These are the women I come from and the spirit of their ways speaks to me still. My mother's heart, indestructible heart—she had survived long beyond her expected years out of pure love of a mother for her children—came to me last in a dream, bringing my daughter, Wahiahawi, to me three months before she would be born. I knew I would bear a girl and today I tell my daughter when I bathe her, "Keep yourself clean here, someday a baby is going to come out of there." My own mother's love is a source of strength to me as a mother.   27

Grandma delivered her last baby in 1953, her grandson Donald Louis. But she always kept her black bag of supplies on hand until she died in 1968. I remember how, after a series of strokes, death had claimed her slowly. Laboring to breathe, she was lying in a hospital bed inside an oxygen tent connected to a web of tubes. She was surrounded by the faces of her children and grandchildren. I touched her weathered hands that had worked so hard for so many all through her 83 years.   28

Grandma was drifting in and out of semiconsciousness. Suddenly she called for her husband who had died many years before. "Where's Louie?" she wanted to know. "The baby is almost here."   29

"My God, she thinks she's having a baby . . . we're here mother," my Uncle Noah comforted her.   30

In her final moments, as her family helped birth her into another world, Grandma's thoughts were of new life.   31

Grandma's nurturing breasts, withered melons whose roots did not die, gave new growth to me, her granddaughter (the Moon, after all, is our grandmother; she controls the cycles of all female life). When now, as a midwife myself, I see a woman's body yield to the emerging infant at childbirth, I too sometimes sigh, "Oh, Baby," and it is in these many small ways that I still carry my grandma's thread—the spirit that fuels the courage of my work.   32

Topics for Discussion and Writing

1. Recall in writing your own experience of puberty. Compare that experience with that described by Cook. Who guided you? From whom (or what) did you seek counsel during this time of change?
2. In what ways is this selection about equality? With others, discuss this question; list your responses. If you responded to "Before and as You Read" topic 1, use this discussion as the basis for a revision.

3. Compare Cook's essay with others in this book that concern either traditional learning (for example, N. Scott Momaday's in chapter 9); equality of women (the O'Reilly and Sidel selections in this chapter); or sexuality, pregnancy, and childbirth (chapter 7). What ideas are reinforced? What seems different to you about Cook's article?

4. Using Cook's and Ruth Sidel's essays as sources, write about the difficulty in the United States today of sustaining traditions and rituals like those described by Cook. Have you faced a similar challenge? Use that experience in writing on this topic.

MARI SANDOZ

from *Cheyenne Autumn*

> "The winter was the worst Little Wolf had seen, with the coughing sickness in the hungry lodges and nothing for the idle hands. So the Cheyennes took on the white man's quarreling ways. Some even whipped their women and children, a shocking, paleface thing to do."

"The Sioux Indians came into my life before I had any preconceived notions about them, or about anyone else," wrote Mari Sandoz in the foreword to her 1961 book These Were the Sioux. *Sandoz, born to German-Swiss home-steaders in northwest Nebraska, grew up as a neighbor to the Sioux people and developed a strong hatred for the destruction of Indian cultures by the U.S. government and other whites. Sandoz became one of America's most prolific and powerful writers of Native American history. By the time of her death in 1966, Sandoz had written many essays and stories for such periodicals as* Prairie Schooner, The Atlantic, *and* The Saturday Evening Post; *and many books, including the autobiographical* Old Jules; *the histories* Crazy Horse *(1942),* Cheyenne Autumn *(1953),* The Buffalo Hunters *(1954),* These Were the Sioux *(1961), and* The Beaver Men *(1964); and several novels and collections of short stories.*

We have selected two chapters from Cheyenne Autumn, *which Sandoz titled "Gone Before" and "Evening Song."*

Before and as You Read

1. If you are unfamiliar with the Great Plains region of the United States, particularly western Nebraska and South Dakota, use a map of the region to locate the places mentioned in this excerpt from *Cheyenne Autumn*. Maps from an historical atlas would be best for this purpose, but even a current road map will suffice, if you can concentrate on the physical features of the land rather than the network of highways.
2. Summarize what you know or have heard about the western migration of whites. What people and events stand out for you? How was this migration presented to you in school? How were Native Americans pictured in history lessons? How were the killings and forced resettlings of Indians explained?
3. As you read the excerpt from *Cheyenne Autumn*, notice Sandoz's narrative style, which makes the history seem more like a novel than a report. How does she heighten the drama of the events? How does she make the events seem to be happening in the present rather than over a century ago?
4. Write what you know or have heard about contemporary life on Indian reservations. What sources do you rely on? Try to explain in writing any connection you see between current conditions and what you know or speculate about the 19th-century history of European-American westward expansion.

GONE BEFORE

EARLY IN the spring of 1877 nearly a thousand hungry and half- 1
naked Northern Cheyennes came in from the Yellowstone country
to Red Cloud Agency in northwest Nebraska. They surrendered to the promise of food and shelter and an agency in their hunting region. But almost
before the children were warmed on both sides, they were told they must go
to Indian Territory,* the far south country many already knew and hated. The
two Old Man Chiefs, as the tribal heads were called, listened to this command
in silent refusal, but some lesser men shouted the "*Hou!*" of agreement almost
before the white men got their mouths open. These Indians were given horses
and fine blue blankets, and the meat and coffee and tobacco for a big feast that
would build their power and following in the tribe.

"It is a trick of the spider," the chiefs protested. "The *veho*† has long 2
spun his web for the feet of those who have wings but are too foolish to
fly. . . ."

Yet even after the feasting there were barely as many as one has fingers 3
who wanted to go south, so the Indian agent announced that he would issue
no more rations to the Cheyennes here. While the Sioux women moved in
their long line, holding their blankets out to receive their goods, the Cheyennes were kept off on a little knoll, their ragged blankets flapping empty in
the wind, the children silent and big-eyed, watching.

Then Little Wolf and Dull Knife were told by the coaxing interpreters 4
that the officials had said, "Just go down to see. If you don't like it you can
come back. . . ." Finally they agreed, for meat for the kettles, and so, with
blue-coated troopers riding ahead and behind, they pointed their moccasins
down through Nebraska and Kansas toward their southern relatives who were
already hungry.

The chiefs rode ahead, old Dull Knife on his yellow and white spotted 5
horse, Little Wolf beside him on a strong, shaggy black with patches white as
winter snow. At the ridge south of the agency the Indians stopped, in spite of
all the urging against it, looking back toward the country that had fed and
sheltered them long before one white man's track shadowed the buffalo grass.
The women keened as for death, and water ran down the dark, stony faces of
old Dull Knife and the rest.

It wasn't that these Cheyennes had not seen years ago that their hunting 6
life must pass as certainly as summer died. Back in 1846, Little Wolf heard his
cousin Yellow Wolf say that the buffalo was angered by the chasing with gun
and bullet and by his carcasses left to rot on the prairie, and so was turning
back to the place of his coming, leaving the Indian to die. Yellow Wolf spoke
of this before an army officer at Bent's Fort, earnestly offering to hire a man
to build the Indians a fort too, and teach them to plow the earth and grow

*Now the state of Oklahoma.
†Cheyenne word for spider, and after the white man's coming, for him also.

cattle to eat. The soldier chief listened, but the wind of laughter from Bent and many of the Indians blew the words away, and when Yellow Wolf, the prophet and man of peace, was shot down at Sand Creek almost twenty years later, nothing had been done.

Through Little Wolf's boyhood the Cheyennes had been very friendly   7
to all the whites except those of the whisky wagons that carried the brown water of violence and death. In those days these Indians ranged as far south-west as the Staked Plains of Texas, but mostly they still returned to the traders of the Platte River and up toward the Black Hills. Then, by 1832, William Bent established a trading post on the upper Arkansas River and married a Cheyenne woman. After that her relatives and their adherents no longer made the long journey by pony drag to the northern traders.

All this time more and more blue-coated troopers came riding, and the   8
emigrants began to run on the trails like dark strings of ants hurrying before the winter, bringing strange sicknesses, eating up the grass of the pony herds, killing the buffalo until the wind stank and the bleaching bones lay white as morning frost on the valleys of the Platte and the Arkansas.

The leaders of those who still traded around the Overland Trail, like   9
Dull Knife, had held the angry young men from attack, but the pockmarked face of Little Wolf grew dark as any in the hooding blanket of the warriors as they watched the white man come. The Cheyennes were famous for their reckless war charges, their pony herds like clouds over the hills, their painted villages, and their regalia and trappings that were as handsome as their country under the October sun. They had been a rather small tribe even before the new diseases scattered their dead over the prairie, but while no one owned the earth and the buffalo herds, any people who fought well and worked to keep the parfleches full of meat could live.

As more hungry Indians were pushed westward and the encroaching   10
whites grabbed the earth in their hands, the Cheyennes of the north began to move closer to the powerful Sioux. With bold warriors and handsome straight-walking women among both peoples, there was considerable inter-marriage. Warrior societies like the Dog Soldiers set up lodges in both tribes and often fought their red enemies together. Then, in 1851, the whites called a great conference at Fort Laramie to bring peace forever to the land west of the Missouri, with wagon trains of goods to pay for the emigrant trails and for giving up the glories of the warpath. More goods would keep coming, and government agencies would be established, with an agent, a Little Father, perhaps to live there much of the year to enforce the treaty on the Indians and to distribute the annuities. The agency for the Southern Cheyennes, as the whites called them now, was at Bent's fort, but the Northern Cheyennes had to go to the Sioux agency far up the Platte.

The first big break in the peace came three years later from the whites   11
themselves. A few whisky-smelling soldiers under Grattan killed the leading chief of the Sioux with a cannon. It was after this that the Cheyenne chiefs showed their first real anger in the government council. They wanted no more

drunken soldiers shooting into peaceful camps, or emigrants scaring their buffalo. It was then that one spoke of something new, so quietly that his soft Cheyenne was barely to be heard. "We want a thousand white women as wives," he said, "to teach us and our children the new life that must be lived when the buffalo is gone. . . ."

The chiefs saw the bearded dignity of the white men break into anger   12
at this. Plainly they did not understand that the children of Cheyennes belong to the mother's people and that this was a desperate measure to assure the food and the survival of their descendants, although in a few generations there might be not one left to be called Cheyenne anywhere under the blue kettle of the sky.

The white women did not come, and the Indians received little or   13
nothing of the treaty goods for the lands and privileges they had sold. In 1856, some restless young men went to beg a little tobacco at the Oregon trail and got bullets instead. They fired arrows back, hit a man in the arm, and troops came shooting. For months General Sumner chased them around their south country. Angry that they got away, he went to Bent's fort, where Yellow Wolf was waiting peacefully for his treaty goods stored in the fort. Sumner took what he wanted for his troops and gave the rest to the Arapahos while the Wolf's young men had to look on, their empty fingers creeping toward the trigger. But their women and children were surrounded by troops like those who had killed Little Thunder's peaceful Sioux on the Platte last summer, so the chiefs fled with their people up beyond the North Platte, where their relatives lived in peace.

Little Wolf had watched them come, and a spark of anger to smolder a   14
lifetime was lit in his breast. He had never heard of Cheyennes running from anybody, but he lived to see it again, for this was only the first of many times.

Perhaps because the tribe seemed too few to make much trouble, they   15
got very little of their treaty goods, and never an agency of their own. The chiefs had even been to Washington, where Little Wolf smelled the hated whisky on the general who was the Great Father, and yet they had to beg him to pity their hungry children. But his promises were like the others—no more than the shimmering mirage lakes on the summer horizon.

For most of the twenty years since that first flight north, the Cheyennes   16
had tried to keep peaceful, but repeatedly starvation drove them out to the shrinking buffalo herds, up north to the roving Sioux, in the south to the Kiowas and the Comanches. Everywhere their strong warriors were welcomed. Yet when the Army was sent to punish Indians for making trouble, there seemed always a camp of peaceful Cheyennes near, where some agent had told them was a safe place to go. So Chivington had found them at Sand Creek in 1864, Custer on the Washita in 1868, and who could say how many times more?

By 1876, Little Wolf, long a peace man, and Dull Knife, who had   17
worked for peace half his life, were starved off the hungry Sioux agency of Red Cloud once more. They slipped away north for their treaty-given summer

hunt. Most of them were too late for the Custer battle but not for the soldiers who came chasing the Crazy Horse Sioux afterward, driving the Indians indiscriminately over their snow-covered treaty grounds with cavalry and cannon. In one of the fights Dull Knife lost three warriors from his family and Little Wolf got six wounds. Constantly fleeing, they could not hunt the few buffaloes left, and so to save their people, they surrendered while some of the strong young men still lived, and the fine young women like the daughters of Dull Knife and the Pretty Walker of Little Wolf. They came in on the good promise of friendship and peace, of plenty of food, warm clothing, and a reservation in their own country, with wagons and plows, and the cattle they had wanted so long. But instead they were dismounted and disarmed, except for a few guns they managed to hide, and now, with blankets drawn in sorrow to the eyes, they had to start far south, the 980 Indians going quietly, morosely, mostly afoot. Seventy days later 937 arrived at the Cheyenne and Arapahoe Agency in the Territory, and no one mentioned the missing who had slipped back northward along the road, some perhaps left dead by the pursuing soldiers.

There had been a little trouble on the way. It was after they saw that the buffalo trails through their old hunting grounds were edged with sunflowers. Bleaching bones lay all around, the ribs standing naked as the wagon bows of the settlers who drove their shining plows where the great dark herds had grazed even two years ago. Then one day a leader among the women was found hanging from a cottonwood, a noose made of her long braids. [18]

Lieutenant Lawton came to see about the women keening as for a warrior dead. "Our sister had three husbands, all famous chiefs," the wife of Little Wolf told him. "One after the other was lost to the soldiers, the last in the Custer fighting. Now the same bluecoats are riding around us here, and just ahead is the place where many of her relatives died from their guns." [19]

When the long string of Indians reached the Sappa Creek where the Cheyennes were killed under a white flag of surrender two years ago, the warriors stopped, their faces covered with the blankets of sorrow and anger. Men who were crippled here or compelled to leave their dead harangued for a fight, and when the lieutenant galloped back to see, he was surrounded by stripped and painted warriors, singing, ready to die empty-handed. They jerked away his pistol and were knocking him off his horse when the angry Little Wolf charged in, striking to both sides with his fork-tailed pony whip. [20]

"Will you have all the helpless people here killed?" he roared out. "Your hearts are as empty as your hands. This is not the time!" [21]

The warriors broke before the chief's fury, the officer escaped, and the ringleaders were put into irons and thrown on the supply wagons. But their followers slipped away in the night. [22]

On the North Fork of the Canadian the chiefs were led to the wide agency bottoms, the earth already worn bare by too many Indians. The soldiers set up their tents close by to watch. That night the Southern Cheyennes [23]

made the customary feast for the newcomers, with a small circle for the head-
men, and for others farther out—such a thin feast as Little Wolf had never
seen before. Plainly the people here were very poor with no horses or guns
allowed them.

"Ahh-h, game is very scarce for the bow," the agency chief Little Robe   24
said meaningfully. "But hungry men have good eyes and the fast moccasin, is
it not true, my friends?"

Dull Knife and Little Wolf and the rest looked down into the water soup   25
of their bowls, as their warrior sons and wives did in other circles. It was an
embarrassment to eat from the kettles of the hungry, and hard to pretend the
great appetite that was good manners. But the northerners would not stay to
divide the little of this poor country. They would go back immediately, where
there was game, good water, tolerable heat, and clean air. They said this over
their moving eagle-wing fans, sitting in grass smoke that burned the eyes but
kept some of the swarming mosquitoes away.

Later Little Robe carried these words to the agency, and a light bloomed   26
in a window there until morning. Then Standing Elk was sent for, the Elk
who had said "*Hou!*" to coming south. As Little Wolf watched him go, he
pressed his arm against the sacred bundle of chieftainship under his shirt,
the bundle that made him keeper of the people. Trouble had already begun,
and so with Dull Knife he went to tell the agent that they did not like anything here and were starting home right away, before the snows fell on the
Yellowstone

But the Quaker agent said they could not go. He was a man of peace,   27
but if the Indians left, the soldiers would whip them back.

Soon a cold wind blew up between the younger Indians too. The new-   28
comers were full of stories of the fighting up north only a few moons ago,
some from the killing of Custer, the man who had left the southern chiefs
dead down here on the Washita in 1868. They showed a few Custer trophies,
even a carbine that had been hidden under a woman's skirts all the way
through the disarming and the road here.

The southern chiefs moved their turkey-wing fans. Killing the Long   29
Hair Custer was a strong thing, they said, even though he was a relative to
some here, the man who took their Monahsetah as wife and became the father
of her son, the Yellow Swallow.

Many listening ones drew in their breath and wished to ask more about   30
this Custer son, but the southern faces seemed turned away, and soon the
tauntings against them as agency sitters came out bold as spring snakes when
the rocks grow warm. So Little Wolf and the others tried to talk of the old-
time victories against Pawnee and Kiowa and Comanche, where no south-
erner need look bad-faced. But his younger men talked of the soldier victories
over these tame southern relatives, victories which ended with the survivors
always running north for refuge. Finally an agency sitter matched their rude-
ness. Was it not, he asked, the wise and wily old Dull Knife himself who let
his village be destroyed last winter?

"Ahh-h, yes, but the soldiers were led by Cheyenne scouts, our own 31
relatives," one of the northern warriors defended.

"Relatives of the Sioux led soldiers against them the same way, but 32
Crazy Horse was never caught!"

So it went, Dull Knife sitting, a silent gray rock in his blanket, the angry 33
words washing over him as he remembered all those left with their faces turned
up to the cold winter light that morning on the fork of the Powder.* It was
Old Bear and the blunt, outspoken Hog who finally answered the southerners.
Everybody knew soldiers were close that time. The horses were saddled for
flight, the lodges coming down fast under the direction of Little Wolf's Elks.
But some Fox soldiers brought in two Crow scalps and demanded that a dance
be made. Last Bull, their warrior society little chief, had the cinches of the
saddles cut, the goods scattered—a small, stubborn man feeling big that he
could do this because none must shed Cheyenne blood, even to stop him. So
Last Bull held the people for a late dancing, and at dawn the soldiers struck.
That could not have happened when the Cheyennes were a larger people.
"But now we must make the war leader too big a man, bigger than our oath-
bound Old Man Chiefs or our wise and holy men. And still they have not
saved us. Today we are only a crumbling sand bar in the spring Platte, with
the flood waters rising all around. . . ."

In two months the newcomers were even fewer. Seventy had died of 34
the measles and of the starvation that was everywhere except in the lodges of
the agency yes-sayers like Standing Elk, whose women walked proud and
plump in their new dresses. General Pope wrote to Washington, asking that
the Cheyenne issues be increased to cover the new people from the north. It
was important, "both in view of the safety of this new frontier and in the
interest of humanity and fair dealing that all these Indians be far better fed
than they are now or have been."

Nothing was done except that the agent complained against rising beef 35
prices, cuts in appropriations, and grafting contractors. The winter was the
worst Little Wolf had ever seen, with the coughing sickness in the hungry
lodges and nothing for the idle hands. So the Cheyennes took on the white
man's quarreling ways. Some even whipped their women and children, a
shocking, paleface thing to do. Families were broken, men threw away the
mothers of their children, wives slipped out the side of the lodge at night,
daughters hung up their chastity ropes and became the pay women of the
soldiers, a thing never seen before among these people, whose women General
Crook called the most chaste he had known. And always the soldier guns were
there, long shadows across the moccasin toe. Yet many young southerners were
drawn to the camp of the visitors.

Then Little Wolf heard that Crazy Horse was killed up at Fort Robin- 36
son. He carried the news like gall in the mouth to Dull Knife's lodge. Their
friend had led the roaming Sioux of the Powder and Yellowstone country

---

*Mackenzie attack on Dull Knife village, November 25, 1876.

since Red Cloud moved to the agency eight years ago. A fiercely brave man with the simple ways of his fathers, who were holy men, many Cheyennes had gladly fought beside him. Later some joined him against the whites too, the time Fetterman was destroyed, in 1866, and when he whipped General Crook on the Rosebud and the next week cut off the retreat of Custer on the Little Big Horn. But with the buffalo going he came to the agency under the same promise given the Cheyennes: food, safety, and an agency for his people. Now he was dead, killed by a soldier in an attempt to take him away to a Florida prison because some agency Indians were jealous and lied about him.

Dull Knife sat bleak-faced. Here, too, the agency chief was jealous be- 37
cause his young warriors strayed, and men like Standing Elk were hot to be Old Man Chiefs. But for that Little Wolf and the Knife would have to be sent away or, like Crazy Horse, die.

So the chiefs went to the agent. "You are a good man," the Wolf said. 38
"You can see that in this small hungry place we must stand on the moccasins of our brothers. Let us go before something bad happens."

First the agent tried to content the Wolf with a pretty southern girl for 39
his bed. The chief refused, but the girl was sent anyway, and turned out to be his fifteen-year-old granddaughter through the wife of his youth who had died of cholera. Next the agent tried making policemen of some Southern Cheyennes just back from prison for causing trouble in 1874. Fifteen of them were given soldier coats and guns and set to walk the angry village. But no Cheyenne could take the life of a fellow tribesman, even in self-defense, so the agent gave the jobs to the Arapahos, old-time allies of the Cheyennes, who, like the whites, could kill anybody.

Summer brought Indian trouble all through the West. The Northern 40
Cheyennes were shaking with malaria, and there was none of the bitter white powder the agent had promised. There was dysentery too, and very little food, but they were not allowed to go on their authorized summer hunt. They must remain quiet, foment no trouble, husband the issues carefully, and till the earth, the Quaker man told them.

"Make the issues last, when there was too little even before we were 41
brought here? Till the earth with plows that never come—make no trouble, while our people die?" Dull Knife demanded, with the warriors so noisy and threatening against the whites that Little Wolf had to rise in his shaking chill to roar out his anger against them. It was too late for anything now, the Wolf said. The people were too sick, with someone carried to the burial rocks every day. They longed for their mountain and pine country, where there was no sickness and few died. If the agent would not let them go, he could telegraph the Great Father or let a few see him again.

Now the agent roared too. He wanted the young men who had already 42
started north. Little Wolf said he knew of no one gone except to hunt stolen horses or try to get a deer or some rabbits for the sick. But still the agent demanded ten young men as hostages until everybody was back.

Hostages—for prison, for the irons on hands and feet—this was some-   *43*
thing the chiefs could not decide. They must go ask the people.

Anger broke out that night against Standing Elk, riding in with a fine   *44*
new blanket and another new horse. Yes, he had talked for coming down here
and was now talking strong for staying. Otherwise they would all be killed.
Any man who advocated leaving now should be broken, even if it was the
bundle-bearing chief, Little Wolf. For his bad counsel the Wolf should be
thrown from his high place.

Ahh-h, now it was out—Standing Elk wanting to be head chief! There   *45*
was a roaring as of battle, red shots cut through the air, and the women ran
toward the dark hills with the children. But the peace pipe was hurried in and
before it the silence came back. Then Standing Elk folded his new blanket and
moved from the camp, his followers along, never to return.

Afterward Little Wolf went across the night to the north ridge, to sit   *46*
alone as in other times of hard decision. As the chief began to sing his old-
time medicine song, there were moccasin steps in the dry darkness. He did
not stop the song or move, for if his place was to be emptied by death, that
too he must accept by his oath.

It was the Keeper of the Sacred Buffalo Hat, old, and sick too. Little   *47*
Wolf must not think of giving himself up as hostage for the young men.
Several chiefs had done that here and had been killed. "You cannot let yourself
be turned from what seems right, not by gun or knife or the wounded pride
and weakness of doubt. We made you the bearer of our Medicine Bundle,
our leader."

"But if I have lost the vision of the good way?"   *48*

"No Cheyenne can be compelled to do anything, nobody except our   *49*
Selected Man. You must lead even if not one man follows, not even a village
dog—if any had escaped the hungry pot," the Keeper added ruefully.

Afterward they went back down to the camp, silent, with no drumming,   *50*
no singing from the young people. The hot, still air was thick with mosquitoes
and the stink of a village too long unmoved, one full of the running sickness.
And now there was the stench of dissension too.

In the morning they went a day's pony drag up the river for wood and   *51*
grass and air. The agent called for soldiers. Two companies of cavalry with a
howitzer took up the trail, and troops were readied northward to the Yellowstone, the telegraph wires humming with the demand for extermination. Then
the Indians were discovered just above the fort inside a little horseshoe of
reservation hills, the men trying to snare rabbits and gophers, the women
digging roots. Still the howitzer was set to look down into the camp, and the
red-faced captain galloped into the lodge circle, his double line of troopers
close behind, their guns shining. The women and children fled but were
ordered back, to hear the officer announce that, until they all returned to the
agency and sent the children to school, there would be no rations—not just a
little as before, but nothing, not even the moldy flour.

The women trembled in their rags as they shielded the sick and the   *52* young, remembering the guns that had killed so many helpless ones before. The soldiers stayed and the howitzer too. Finally, on the eighth of September the agency doctor came. With the chiefs silent beside him he walked among the lodges, past all the sick ones, the women turning the kettles upside down in the symbol of emptiness as he came, or holding out bowls of roots and grass for his eyes.

"This is a pest camp, a graveyard!" the doctor exclaimed. 53

But he had no medicine, no food, and besides, everything was already 54 settled. The chiefs had gone to the last conference at the agency with their few guns hidden on their warrior guard, for surely now the protesting ones would be killed. It was a tumultuous meeting, and one of the young warriors forgot himself enough to speak out in the council. "We are sickly and dying men," the slender young Finger Nail told the agent there in his soft Cheyenne. "If we die here and go to the burial rocks, no one will speak our names. So now we go north, and if we die in battle on the way, our names will be remembered by all the people. They will tell the story and say, 'This is the place.'"

There had been a roaring of *"Hous!"* from many of the young south- 55 erners too, and to the agent's angry order to draw the troops closer Dull Knife rose with a hand lifted for silence. He spoke of the many Indian complaints: peaceful people shot by soldiers, the buffalo destroyed, the lands taken, with too little of the pay promised in the white papers, and now nothing at all. No food, no houses, no cattle or wagons or plows. So they were going back north while some were still alive.

This too brought a roaring of approval from many of Little Robe's 56 warriors. The agency chief had once been dragged back wounded from a Pawnee war charge by Dull Knife, but that was long ago, and now he rose and knocked the old chief into the dust with the butt of his leaded sad- dle whip.

In that moment every warrior was up, scarred breast against breast, 57 knives and pistols against panting bellies, the white men pale as old paper in the silence that waited for the one thrust, the one shot to start the massacre, the soldier guns up, ready.

But almost at once Dull Knife was on his feet and the warriors were 58 ordered back, all going except one who gashed himself and held up his bloody knife, shouting, "Kill! Kill the white-man lovers!" As Little Wolf had him dragged away, Dull Knife shook the dust from his blanket and, with it folded about himself, looked down at the agent, his lips curling proud.

"My friend," he said, "I am going." 59

Slowly, majestically, the man feared by Crow and Shoshoni and Pawnee 60 for forty years walked from the council, his warrior son and his band chiefs around him. Afterward Little Wolf talked very earnestly for peace, for permis- sion to go home in peace as they had been promised. He could not give the young men as hostages never to be returned, and if the agent loved their food too much to give them any, he must keep it all. "I have long been a friend of the whites. The Great Father told us that he wished no more blood spilled, that we ought to be friends and fight no more. So I do not want any of the ground of the agency made bloody. Only soldiers do that. If you are going to send them after me, I wish you would first let me get a little distance away. Then if you want to fight, I will fight you and we can make the ground bloody on that far place."

Evening Song

From several versions of a song by one of the Southern Cheyenne 61 chiefs, winter 1876–77, while imprisoned in old Fort Marion, Florida, for resisting white encroachments on their treaty land. It was sung each evening from the highest wall, the Indian in chains facing the west.

Sun-Going-Down! 62
Sun-Going-Down!
From our prison we call you, O Sun,
Look in pity upon our barred faces,
    see our chained feet, our ironed hearts.

Sun-Going-Down, 63
Sun-Going-Down,
Soon you will shine
Into the winter faces of our deserted Ones.
Light them, comfort them, warm them
    with the love you see in my face,
    the water standing red upon my face.

Sun-Going-Down, 64
Tell them of this—but
    not of the irons trapped on my hands,
    the ball hard as the blacksmith's
    iron rock upon which he hammers,
    rooting my feet.

Sun-Going-Down, 65
Speak to them of the eternal earth,
Shine on them as they place my young son
    upon his first pony, teaching him to ride,
    selecting well the second father to guide him.

The time is long and we must learn a new road. 66

Sun-Going-Down, 67
Sun-Going-Down,
Touch the cheeks in that far country,
Touch the cheek of my wife,
    the brown cheek of my unknown son.

Topics for Discussion and Writing

1. What events and ideas surprise you in this account? Note passages that perhaps call you to question anything you wrote in response to "Before and as You Read" topic 2. Discuss these passages with others who have read the selection.

2. Try writing two or more brief point-of-view narratives of one of the events Sandoz relates. First write from the point of view of one of the Cheyenne participants (Name the person; note that Sandoz does not characterize all the Cheyennes as possessing the same perspective); then write from the point of view of one of the white soldiers (again, note that Sandoz makes some distinction among attitudes). Try in each writing to empathize with the person from whose perspective you are writing.

3. If you have responded to "Before and as You Read" topic 4, use your reading of the selection to revise your explanation of contemporary life on reservations.

4. For further information on Native American history and on contemporary reservation life, read among the following (to mention just a few of many sources):

> Paula Gunn Allen, ed., *Spider Woman's Granddaughter* (Boston: Beacon, 1989)
>
> Dee Brown, *Bury My Heart at Wounded Knee* (New York: Holt, 1972)
>
> Joseph Bruchac, ed., *New Voices from the Longhouse* (Greenfield Center, NY: Greenfield Review, 1989)
>
> Vine Deloria, Jr., *Custer Died for Your Sins.* (Norman: U of Oklahoma, 1987)
>
> Michael Dorris and Louise Erdrich, *Crown of Columbus* (New York: HarperCollins, 1991)
>
> Louise Erdrich, *Love Medicine: A Novel* (New York: Holt, 1984)
>
> Mari Sandoz, *Old Jules Country: A Selection from the Works of Mari Sandoz* (New York: Hastings, 1965)
>
> Leslie Marmon Silko, *Storyteller* (New York: Seaver, 1981)

LUIS VALDEZ

from *Aztlan*

"Man has been in the Americas for more than 38,000 years. White men have been around for less than five hundred."

Essayist, dramatist, theatrical producer, filmmaker, and political activist, Luis Valdez was born in Delano, California, in 1940 to a farm-working family. He is best known as founder of El Teatro Campesino, the dramatic company that helped raise the nation's consciousness about the conditions of migrant farm workers during the 1960s. Valdez's work has received the Los Angeles Theatre Critics award and an Obie (off Broadway) award for "demonstrating the politics of survival." As a filmmaker, Valdez is best known for his 1987 work, La Bamba, about the Chicano rock star Richie Valens.

Valdez's essays have appeared in such periodicals as Arte Nuevo, Latin American Theatre Review, Performing Arts, and Ramparts. His "Tale of La Raza" and "El Teatro Campesino, Its Beginnings" (both 1966) describe projects of the United Farm Workers, the union of campesinos founded by Cesar Chavez, and place this work within the context of the many centuries of Mexican revolutionary efforts against European domination. Valdez has also edited two collections: Aztlan: An Anthology of Mexican American Literature (with Stan Steiner, 1971) and Zoot Suit and Other Plays (1992).

We have reprinted "La Plebe," the introductory essay to Aztlan.

Before and as You Read

1. Write something of what you feel you know about the history of the Mexican people. What images dominate your thinking? What questions arise as you write? Where have you learned this history?

2. How do you regard yourself as a speaker of Spanish? Do you feel that American students should be required or at least strongly encouraged to study Spanish as well as English? Write a response. As you read the selection, mark words (both English and Spanish) that you do not understand. Note how Valdez defines Spanish terms within the essay.

3. How do you define the term *American*? Who are Americans, according to your definition? Who are not Americans? What issues arise in your thinking as you contemplate these questions? Discuss your responses with others.

4. As you read the selection, note how Valdez uses history to shape his argument about the present and future. What key events does he use? How does his interpretation of these events differ from other interpretations you've heard or read?

Introduction: La Plebe

Aun cuando el "pelado" mexicano sea completamente desgraciado, se con-
suela con gritar a todo el mundo que tiene "muchos huevos" (asi llama a los
testiculos). Lo importante es advertir que en este organo no hace residir
solamente una especie de potencia, la sexual, sino toda clase de potencia
humana.

—*Samuel Ramos*

IT IS the task of all literature to present illuminating images of man-   *1*
kind. This, as most writers are surely aware, is not easy to do. It takes
the clearest, most unassuming effort on the part of the poet to speak for Man.
This effort is very often confused and frustrated when the writer is a victim
of racism and colonization. His birthright to speak as Man has been forcibly
taken from him. To his conqueror he is patently subhuman, uncivilized, backward, or culturally deprived. The poet in him flounders in a morass of lies
and distortions about his conquered people. He loses his identity with mankind, and self-consciously struggles to regain his one-to-one relationship with
human existence. It is a long way back.

Such is the condition of the Chicano. Our people are a colonized race,   *2*
and the root of their uniqueness as Man lies buried in the dust of conquest.
In order to regain our corazon, our soul, we must reach deep into our people,
into the tenderest memory of their beginning.

Alurista, a Chicano poet, writes: *3*

   . . . razgos indigenas
the scars of history on my face
   and the veins of my body
that aches
   vomito sangre
y lloro libertad
   I do not ask for freedom
I AM freedom . . .

Man has been in the Americas for more than 38,000 years. White men   *4*
have been around for less than five hundred. It is presumptuous, even dangerous, for anyone to pretend that the Chicano, the "Mexican-American," is only
one more in the long line of hyphenated-immigrants to the New World. *We*
are the New World.

Our insistence on calling ourselves Chicanos stems from a realization   *5*
that we are not just one more minority group in the United States. We reject
the semantic games of sociologists and whitewashed Mexicans who frantically identify us as Mexican-Americans, Spanish-Americans, Latin-Americans,
Spanish-speaking, Spanish-surname, Americans of Mexican descent, etc. We
further reject efforts to make us disappear into the white melting pot, only to

be hauled out again when it is convenient or profitable for *gabacho* (*gringo*) politicans. Some of us are as dark as *zapote,* but we are casually labeled Caucasian.

We are, to begin with, *Mestizos*—a powerful blend of Indigenous America with European-Arabian Spain, usually recognizable for the natural bronze tone it lends to human skin. Having no specific race of our own, we used poetry and labeled ourselves centuries ago as La Raza, the Race, albeit a race of half-breeds, misfits, and mongrels. Centuries of interbreeding further obfuscated our lineage, and La Raza gave itself other labels—*la plebe, el vulgo, la palomía.* Such is the natural poetry of our people. One thing, however, was never obscured: that the Raza was basically Indio, for that was borne out by our acts rather than mere words, beginning with the act of birth.   6

During the three hundred years of Nueva España, only 300,000 gachupines settled in the New World. And most of these were men. There were so few white people at first, that ten years after the Conquest in 1531, there were more black men in Mexico than white. Negroes were brought in as slaves, but they soon intermarried and "disappeared." Intermarriage resulted in an incredible *mestizaje,* a true melting pot. Whites with Indios produced *mestizos.* Indios with blacks produced *zambos.* Blacks with whites produced mulattoes. *Pardos, cambujos, tercernones, salta atrases,* and other types were born out of mestizos with zambos and mulattoes with Indios, and vice versa. Miscegenation went joyously wild, creating the many shapes, sizes, and hues of La Raza. But the predominant strain of the mestizaje remained Indio. By the turn of the nineteenth century, most of the people in Mexico were mestizos with a great deal of Indian blood.   7

The presence of the Indio in La Raza is as real as the barrio. Tortillas, tamales, chile, marijuana, la curandera, el empacho, el molcajete, atole, La Virgen de Guadalupe—these are hard-core realities for our people. These and thousands of other little human customs and traditions are interwoven into the fiber of our daily life. América Indigena is not ancient history. It exists today in the barrio, having survived even the subversive onslaught of the twentieth-century neon gabacho commercialism that passes for American culture.   8

Yet the barrio is a colony of the white man's world. Our life there is second hand, full of chingaderas imitating the way of the patrón. The used cars, rented houses, old radio and TV sets, stale grocery stores, plastic flowers—all the trash of the white man's world mixes with the bits and pieces of that other life, the Indio life, to create the barrio. Frijoles and tortillas remain, but the totality of the Indio's vision is gone. Curanderas make use of plants and herbs as popular cures, without knowing that their knowledge is what remains of a great medical science. Devout Catholics pray to the Virgen de Guadalupe, without realizing that they are worshipping an Aztec goddess, Tonatzin.   9

The barrio came into being with the birth of the first mestizo. Before we imitated the gringo, we imitated the hacendado; before the hacendado, the   10 gachupin. Before we lived in the Westside, Chinatown, the Flats, Dogtown, Sal Si Puedes, and El Hoyo, we lived in Camargo, Reynosa, Guamuchil, Cuautla, Tepoztlán. Before the Southwest, there was México; before México, Nueva España. The barrio goes all the way back to 1521, and the Conquest.

> We are Indian, blood and soul; the language and civilization are Spanish.
>
> —Jose Vasconcelos

Imagine the Conquistadores looking upon this continent for the first time. Imagine Pedro de Alvarado, Hernando Cortes! Fifty-foot caballeros with golden huevos, bringing the greed of little Europe to our jungle-ridden, god-haunted world. They saw the land and with a sweep of an arm and a solemn prayer claimed this earth for the Spanish crown, pronouncing it with Catholic inflection and Ciglo de Oro majesty, Nueva España. *New* Spain. Imagine now a fine white Spanish veil falling over the cactus mountains, volcanoes, valleys, deserts, and jungles; over the chirimoya, quetzal, ocelotl, nopal. Imagine, finally, white men marching into the light and darkness of a very old world and calling it new.

This was not a new world at all. It was an ancient world civilization based on a distinct concept of the universe. Tula, Teotihuacan, Monte Alban, Uxmal, Chichen Itzá, México-Tenochtitlan were all great centers of learning, having shared the wisdom of thousands of generations of pre-Columbian man. The Mayans had discovered the concept of zero a thousand years before the Hebrews, and so could calculate to infinity, a profound basis of their religious concepts. They had operated on the human brain, and had evolved a mathematical system which allowed them to chart the stars. That system was vigesimal, meaning it was based on a root of twenty rather than ten, because they had started by counting on their fingers and toes instead of just their fingers as in the decimal system.

It was the Mayans who created the countless stone stellae, studded with numerical symbols utilizing the human skull as number ten. Did this imply a link between mathematics and the cycle of life and death? There is no telling. Much about the Mayans is mysterious, but it is clear they had more going for them than frijoles and tortillas.

Then there were the Toltecs, Mixtecs, Totonacs, Zapotecs, Aztecs, and hundreds of other tribes. They too were creators of this very old new world. The Aztecs practiced a form of "plastic" surgery, among other great achievements in medicine. If a warrior, an Eagle or Ocelot Knight, had his nose destroyed in battle, Aztec surgeons could replace it with an artificial one. They also operated on other parts of the body and stitched up the cut with human hair. All cures, of course, were not surgical, for the Aztec had a profound knowledge of botany, not to speak of zoology, astronomy, hieroglyphics, architecture, irrigation, mining, and city planning. The design of entire cities was an ancient art in the Americas when Madrid, London, and Paris were suffocating in their own crowded stench.

As a matter of fact, it came as a shock to the Spaniards to discover that   *15*
the inhabitants of Tenochtitlan bathed daily; and that Moctezuma Xocoyotzin
II, the Uei Tlatoani, Chief Speaker, bathed twice a day. Any European would
have been just as shocked, for bathing was less than encouraged in Europe at
that time. Perfume, of course, was already used in France.

The sight and smell of human blood on the altars and stone steps of the   *16*
temples shocked the Conquistadores more than anything else. In the teocalli,
the great central square of Tenochtitlan, stood a gigantic rack with a hundred
thousand human skulls. It was a monument to another aspect of América
Indigena, human sacrifice. How terrifying yet fascinating it must have seemed
to the Conquistador. How alien yet familiar. Astonished by the ritualistic
cannibalism of Aztec priests, the Spaniard went to mass and ate the ritualistic
body and blood of Jesus Christ in Holy Communion.

América Indigena was obsessed with death. Or was it life? Man was a   *17*
flower. A mortal, subject to the fugacity of all natural things. Nezahualcoyotl,
Chief of Texcoco (1402–72), was a philosopher king and one of the greatest
poets América has ever produced. His poem "Fugacidad Universal" pondered
the philosophical question of temporal existence. *An nochipa tlaltipac: zan achica
ye nican.* His words lose much in a double translation from the Nahuatl to
Spanish, then English:

> It is true we exist on this earth?
> Not forever on this earth: only a brief moment here
> even jade shatters
> even gold tears
> even the plumage of quetzal falls apart
> not forever on this earth: only a brief moment here.

Man was born, blossomed, then deteriorated unto death. He was an   *18*
intrinsic part of the cosmic cycle of life and death, of being becoming non-
being, then back again. Coatlicue, Aztec goddess of fertility, was sculpted as a
poet's vision in stone: with a death's head, scales like a serpent, and a belt of
human hands and hearts. She was the embodiment of the nature of existence.
Death becoming life; life becoming death. Fertility.

Life on earth was ephemeral, but impossible without the sacrifice of   *19*
other living things. Did man not survive by devouring death, the dead bodies
of animals and plants? Was he not in turn devoured and disintegrated by the
earth? Even Tonatiuh, the Sun God, must eat, so man offered Him human
hearts as sustenance, and thus became deified.

The religion of Ancient America abounds in natural symbols of the flux   *20*
of life. Feathers and scales, birds and snakes, symbols of heaven and earth, of
the spiritual and the material. The blue of the waters and the green of jungles
combined to make turquoise and jade more precious to the Indio than gold.
Yet the yellow brilliance of gold reminded him of the sun, so he valued it and
learned to work with it, to mold it into the symbols of his belief. So too with
feathers, especially the green feathers of the sacred Quetzal bird, which only

the Uei Tlatoani, the Chief, could wear in his headdress. So too with crystal, a symbol of water and therefore of life. The most outstanding achievement of Aztec sculpture is a beautiful crystal cut with incomparable skill into the shape of a human skull. The duality of life and death again.

The *Popol Vuh,* sacred book of the Ancient Quiche Maya, describes 21
Creation as American man saw it thousands of generations ago:

> . . . There was only immobility and silence in the darkness, in the night. Only the Creator, the Maker, Tepeu, Cucumatz, the Fore-fathers, were in the water surrounded with light. They were hidden under green and blue feathers, and were therefore called Cucumatz.

How natural, how fitting, how deep is this Indio vision of genesis! Where else 22
could life have begun but in the water? And with the Creator hidden under *blue and green feathers!* The sophisticated use of natural life symbols is so pro-found that the Catholic Conquistador, confident in his ignorance, must have thought it naïve.

None of the achievements of Indigenous America meant very much to 23
the Conquistador. Nor was he content to merely exploit its physical strength. He sought to possess its mind, heart, and soul. He stuck his bloody fingers into the Indian brain, and at the point of the sword, gun, and cross ripped away a vision of human existence. He forced the Indio to accept his world, his reality, his scheme of things, in which the Indio and his descendants would forever be something less than men in Nueva España's hierarchy of living things. Murder and Christianity worked hand in hand to destroy the ancient cities, temples, clothes, music, language, poetry. The women were raped, and the universe, el Quinto Sol, the world of the Earthquake Sun, was shattered.

> Desgraciada raza mexicana, obedecer no quieres, gobernar no puedes.
> —Amado Nervo

In the twilight of the Conquest, the Mestizo was born into colonization. 24
Rejected as a bastard by his Spanish father, he clung to his Indian mother and shared the misery of her people, the overwhelming sense of loss:

> Nothing but flowers and songs of sorrow are left in Mexico and Tlaltelolco, where once we saw warriors and wise men.

Soon there was not even that. Death overtook all who remembered what it had been like, and colonization set in for three hundred years.

Our dark people looked into one another's eyes. The image reflected 25
there was one the white man had given us. We were savage, Indio, Mestizo, half-breed: always something less than simple men. Men, after all, have a tendency to create God in their own image. No, men we could never be, because only the patrón could be a god. We were born to be his instrument, his peon, his child, his whore—this he told us again and again through his religion, literature, science, politics, economics. He taught us that his approach to the world, his logical disciplines of human knowledge, was truth itself.

That everything else was barbaric superstition. Even our belief in God. In time there was nothing left in our hearts but an empty desire, a longing for something we could no longer define.

Still, for all the ferocity of the Conquest, the Mestizo cannot totally condemn the Spaniard. He might as well condemn his own blood. Anglos particularly are very fond of alluding to the black legend of the Conquistador in Mexico, perhaps to mask the even more inhuman treatment of the Indian in the United States. The gachupin offered the Indio colonization; the Anglo, annihilation. There is no question that Nueva España was more human to América Indigena than New England. *26*

Some white men, such as Fray Bartolomé de las Casas, saw the evils of New Spain and denounced them: *27*

> All the wars called conquests were and are most unjust and truly tyrannical. We have usurped all the kingdoms and lordships of the Indies.

Others, like Sahagun and Motolinia, saved what they could of ancient chronicles, *los codices de la tinta negra y roja,* the life thought of a dispossessed world civilization.

It is doubtful, however, that any white man in colonial Mexico or New England was aware of the ultimate importance of the Mestizo. As the real new man of the Americas, he was the least likely candidate to be called an American. The reason may be that the name *America* was an imported European title, and reserved therefore only for European types. By right of discovery, the honor afforded to Amerigo Vespucci should have gone to Christopher Columbus. Yet *Columbia* would have been just as alien to the native people of this land as *America*. The naming of the continent had nothing to do with the Indios or their Mestizo children. It was strictly an amusement of white, western European man. *28*

Once America was named, Europe yawned and went on with the dull but profitable business of exploitation and colonization. Wherever possible, North and South America were built or rebuilt in the image of Europe. Spain gorged itself on the gold of New Spain; and England did a brisk trade on the tobacco of New England. Aside from mercantile ventures, the Old World was so uninterested in the New that even white colonists felt neglected. *29*

It took a revolution in the thirteen colonies of New England to again raise the issue of America. Once again the Indios and Mestizos were forgotten. In 1776 the United States of America usurped the name of a continental people for a basically white, English-speaking, middle-class minority. It revealed, perhaps, the continental ambitions of that minority. But an American was henceforth defined as a white citizen of the U.S.A. The numerous brown Quiche, Nahuatl, and Spanish-speaking peoples to the south were given secondary status as Latin Americans, Spanish Americans, and South Americans. It was a historical snow job. The descendants of América Indigena were now foreigners in the continent of their birth. *30*

Gabacho America, however, was not to touch the Mestizo for at least   *31*
another half century. While the Monroe Doctrine and Manifest Destiny were
being hatched in Washington, D.C., the Mestizo was still living in Nueva
España. During the colonial period, he easily achieved numerical superiority
over the white man. But the dominant culture remained Spanish. So the
Mestizo stood at a cultural crossroads, not unlike the one he later encountered
in the United States: choose the way of Mexico Indio and share degradation;
or go the way of the white man and become Hispanicized.

The choice was given as early as 1598, when Don Juan de Oñate arrived   *32*
in the Southwest to settle and claim New Mexico, "from the edge of the
mountains to the stones and sand in the rivers, and the leaves of trees." With
him came four hundred Mestizos and Indios as soldiers. Many of the Hispa-
nos, or Spanish Americans living in New Mexico today, are descended directly
from those first settlers. Their regional name reveals the cultural choice their
ancestors made; but it also reveals a reluctance to choose, for Hispano to some
New Mexicans also means Indiohispano. In 1598 there was not, of course,
national status for Mestizos as Mexicanos. Even so, after Independence, His-
panos refused to identify with the racial, cultural, and political confusions of
Mexico.

The internal conflicts of nineteenth-century Mexico resulted from a   *33*
clash of races as well as classes. Conservative Criollos and the clergy usurped
the War of Independence against Spain; after 1810, the bronze mass of Indios
and Mestizos continued to be exploited by a white minority. Avarice and
individual ambition superseded the importance of national unity. Coups and
pronunciamentos became commonplace, and further weakened the new nation.
Mexico did not belong to her people.

Watching the internal struggles south of the border, the United States   *34*
circled around Texas and hovered above California like a buzzard. Mexico was
ill-equipped to defend either state. When rebels struck at the Alamo, President
Antonio López de Santa Ana unfortunately decided to rout them out personally. Leaving General don José Maria Tornel in charge of the government, he
drafted an army of six thousand. Through forced loans from businessmen, he
equipped them poorly, and with promises of land in Texas won their allegiance. The long march to Texas was painful and costly. Supplies, animals,
ammunition, and hundreds of soldiers were lost due to the rigors of winter.
Inept as a general, Santa Ana despotically ordered the worst routes for his
convoys. He almost accomplished the failure of the expedition before even
reaching Texas.

The rest is "American" history. The rebels lost the Alamo, but regrouped   *35*
under Samuel Houston to finally defeat Santa Ana at San Jacinto. Some important historical facts, however, are never mentioned in U.S. classrooms. After
the fall of the Alamo and San Antonio Bejar, the rebels resorted to guerrilla
warfare. They destroyed crops and burned towns, so that the Mexican troops
would have no place to get supplies. They in turn received weapons, food,
and men from the United States. The South particularly was interested in

Texas as a future slave state. Mexico had outlawed slavery in 1824, but some of the defenders of freedom at the Alamo died for the freedom of holding black slaves.

Slavery was foremost in the minds of the Mexican signers of the Treaty   36
of Guadalupe Hidalgo in 1848. Ceding fully half of the national territory of Mexico to the United States, they were concerned about the 75,000 Mexican citizens about to be absorbed into an alien country. They feared that the dark Mexican Mestizo would share the fate of the black man in America. They asked for guarantees that Mexican families would not lose their ancestral lands, that civil and cultural rights would be respected. But the United States, still hot from its first major imperialistic venture, was not ready to guarantee anything.

Witness the memoirs of Ulysses S. Grant, who was with General Zach-   37
ary Taylor at the Rio Grande, which admit that the United States had goaded Mexico into "attacking first." No stretch of the imagination can explain why Mexico, bleeding from internal conflict, would want to provoke war with the U.S. Known as *la invasion norte-americana* in Mexico, the Mexican War polluted the moral climate of America. Abraham Lincoln debated with Stephen Douglas over the ultimate wisdom and morality of the war. It was an early-day version of Vietnam. Manifest Destiny won the day, however, and the U.S. acquired the Southwest. When the Treaty of Guadalupe Hidalgo came before Congress for ratification, Article Nine was replaced and Article Ten was stricken out. The two Articles dealt, respectively, with civil rights and land guarantees.

The no-nonsense attitude of American politics merged with white rac-   38
ism to create the stereotype of the Mexican greaser. Carrying the added stigma of defeat in battle, the Mestizo was considered cowardly, lazy, and treacherous. Anglo America was barely willing to recognize his basic humanity, much less the nobility of his pre-Columbian origins. He was a Mexican, and that was it. But contrary to the myth of the Sleeping Giant, the Mexican in the Southwest did not suffer the abuses of the gringo by remaining inert.

In 1859 Juan N. Cortina declared war on the gringos in Texas. On   39
November 23 from his camp in the Rancho del Carmen, County of Cameron, he released a proclamation:

> Mexicans! When the State of Texas began to receive the new organization which its sovereignty required as an integrant part of the Union, flocks of vampires, in the guise of men, came and scattered themselves in the settlements . . . many of you have been robbed of your property, incarcerated, chased, murdered, and hunted like wild beasts, because your labor was fruitful, and because your industry excited the vile avarice which led them. A voice infernal said, from the bottom of their soul, "kill them; the greater will be our gain!"

The document was intense but despairing for a real solution to the problem of gringo domination. Cortina proposed to fight to the death if need be, and offered La Raza in Texas the protection of a secret society sworn to defend them. He addressed his people as Mexicanos, but the fact remains that they were no longer citizens of Mexico. They were Mestizos cast adrift in the hellish limbo of Anglo America. Cortina got his war, and lost.

There were others, before and after Cortina, who waged guerrilla war- 40
fare from the mountains of the Southwest. In California, from 1850 to 1875, Joaquín Murieta and Tiburcio Vásquez span a period of unmitigated struggle. History dismissed them as bandits; asinine romanticized accounts of their "exploits" have totally distorted the underlying political significance of their rebellion.

Bandits in Mexico, meanwhile, were on the verge of creating the first 41
major revolution of the twentieth century. The Revolution of 1910. The revolution of Emiliano Zapata and Pancho Villa. *El indio y el mestizo.* At Independence, only one fifth of Mexico's population had been white. A century later, it was less than one thirteenth. In the hundred years between Independence and the Revolution, the number of Mestizos had *quadrupled.* In 1910 they numbered fifty-three percent of the total population, while the Indios had remained fairly stable at close to forty percent. Yet white men ruled, while the blood and flesh of Mexico went hungry.

A new motivating force was behind the Revolution of 1910, and that 42
force was La Raza, la plebe, los de abajo. Indigenous Mexico discovered itself and so arose with all the fury that four hundred years of oppression can create. The bloodroot of la patria exploded, and Mestizos and Indios fought to the death to make Mexico what it had not been since Cuauhtemoc: a unique creation of native will. La plebe burst into the private halls and dining rooms of the rich; it broke down the great walls of the haciendas and smashed the giant doors of holy cathedrals, shouting obscenities and laughing, crying, yelling, sweating, loving, killing, and singing:

> La Cucaracha, La Cucaracha
> Ya no puede caminar
> Porque le falta, porque no tiene
> Marijuana que fumar!

It was a revolution with few restraints, and La Raza expressed itself as 43
never before. A half-breed cultural maelstrom swept across Mexico in the form of corridos, bad language, vulgar topics, disrespectful gestures, *pleberías.* It was all a glorious affront to the aristocracy, which, wrapped in their crucifixes and fine Spanish laces, had been licking the boots of American and British speculators for a lifetime. In 1916, when Woodrow Wilson sent Pershing into Mexican territory on a "punitive" expedition, looking for Pancho Villa, U.S. intervention had already seriously crippled the Revolution. Pershing failed to find Villa, but la plebe launched a corrido against the gringo:

> Que pensarían esos gringos tan patones que nuestro suelo pretenden conquistar. Si ellos tienen cañones de amontones aquí tenemos lo mero principal!

Three years later Emiliano Zapata was dead in Chinameca, and the ter- 44
rible reality of a dying Revolution began to settle on the people. In 1923

Pancho Villa was assassinated by a savage hail of bullets in the dusty streets of Parral, Chihuahua. That same year, almost 64,000 Mexicans crossed the fictitious border into the United States. During the following years 89,000 poured across, and the U.S., alarmed by the sudden influx, organized the border patrol. This was the first time the boundary between Mexico and the Southwest had ever been drawn, but now it was set, firmly and unequivocably. Even so, ten percent of Mexico's population made it across, *pa' este lado.* La plebe crossed the border, and their remembrance of the patria was forever stained by memories of bloody violence, festering poverty, and hopeless misery. For all their hopes of material gain, their migration (and it was only a short migration into the Southwest) meant a spiritual regression, for them and for their sons—a legacy of shame for being of Mexican descent in the land of the gringo.

Yet the *Revolución* would persist, in memory, in song, in cuentos. It would reach into the barrio, through two generations of Mexicanos, to create the Chicano. *45*

The Chicano is the grandson, or perhaps even the son, of the Mexican *pelado.* Who is the *pelado*? He is the Mestizo, the colonized man of Mexico, literally, the "stripped one." La Raza is the *pelado en masse.* He is almost inevitably dirt poor, cynical about politics, and barely manages to live. He earns his immediate survival day by day, through any number of ingenious schemes, or *movidas.* During the last thirty years or so, he has been epitomized in the cine mexicano by the genius of Mario Moreno's Cantinflas. Yet he is hardly a mere comic figure. The humor in his life is born of such deep misfortune that the comedy takes on cosmic proportions and so becomes tragedy. *46*

The pelado is the creator of the corrido and the eternal patron of mariachi. His music, in turn, inspires him to express all his joy and sorrow in a single cry. So he lets out a grito that tells you he feels life and death in the same breath. *"Viva la Raza, hijos de la chingada!"* *47*

In Mexican history, the pelado undoubtedly gave voice to the "Grito de Dolores" in 1810, and then went off with Miguel Hidalgo y Costilla to fight the War of Independence against Spain. In other generations, the pelado took orders from Santa Ana at the Alamo, and probably finished off Davy Crockett. He also fought with Don Benito Juárez during *La Reforma,* and most certainly rode with Pancho Villa. It was the pelado who crossed the border into the United States, only to be viciously stereotyped as the sleeping Mexican, leaning against a cactus. *48*

There is no understanding of the pelado in the literature of the United States. None, that is, except for the embryonic works of Chicano literature. Comadres, compadres, pachucos, and campesinos begin to emerge from the pen of the Chicano poet: people of the rural and urban barrios of the Southwest, with names like Nacho, la Chata, Tito, Little Man, Pete Fonesca, and "el Louie Rodriquez, carnal del Candi y el Ponchi." Some are sketched, some are fully drawn, but they are all intimately real—a far cry from the racist stereotypes of the John Steinbeck past. *49*

Yet they are all drawn against the background of the barrio, replete with 50
the spiritual and material chingaderas of colonization. Beset by all the pain
and confusion of life in los estados unidos, the pelados in Chicano literature
take drugs, fight, drink, despair, go hungry, and kill each other. Some resist
the racism of the gringo, and become pachucos. Some acculturate and sell out
as Mexican Americans. Some are drawn from a distant twenty-year-old memory, and some are as real as today. But they are not to be confused with the
writers that created them, for they are Chicanos.

The Chicano is not a pelado. His very effort to cut through nearly five 51
centuries of colonization defines him as a new man. This effort is so total, in
fact, that it is characteristic of Chicano writers to also be teachers, community
organizers, and political leaders. In one sense, *being Chicano* means the utiliza-
tion of one's total potentialities in the liberation of our people. In another
sense, it means that Indio mysticism is merging with modern technology to
create *un nuevo hombre*. A new man. A new reality, rooted in the origins of
civilization in this half of the world.

Neither a pelado nor a Mexican American, the Chicano can no longer 52
totally accept as reality the white, western European concept of the universe.
Reason and logic are not enough to explain the modern world; why should it
suffice to explain the ancient world of our ancestors? The sciences of arche-
ology and anthropology may unearth the buried ruins of América Indigena,
but they will never comprehend, through logic alone, its most basic truth: that
man *is* a flower. For there is poetry in reality itself.

In an effort to recapture the soul-giving myth of La Raza, the Chicano 53
is forced to re-examine the facts of history, and suffuse them with his own
blood—to make them tell his reality. The truth of historical documents can
sometimes approach poetic truth. So the Chicano poet becomes historian,
digging up lost documents and proclamations other men saw fit to ignore. Yet
he will inevitably write his own gestalt vision of history, his own *mitos*. And
he will do it bilingually, for that is the mundane and cosmic reality of his life.

Anglo America, no doubt, will resent the bilingualism of the Chicano. 54
The average educated gabacho will probably interpret bilingual Chicano literature as reflecting the temporary bicultural confusion of the "Mexican
American." He will be reluctant to accept in the Chicano poet what he
proudly accepts in a T. S. Eliot. Both are bilingual, or even multilingual poets;
but the former intersperses his English with mere Spanish, while the latter
alludes in the "highly sophisticated" Latin or French.

If the Anglo cannot accept the coming reality of America, *que se lo lleve* 55
la jodida. Otherwise, he can learn Spanish, which is the language of most of
the people in América.

The time has come to redefine all things American. If our bilingualism 56
has prompted gabachos to wonder if we are "talking about them," in the street,
in school, at work, this time, the Chicano literature, we certainly are discussing
them. If Anglos insist on calling us Mexican Americans, then we must insist on
asking: What is an American? Nobody pursues the title with such vehemence

as the white man in the United States. He does on occasion recognize the existence of "Latin" America, and so calls himself a *norteamericano*. Still, North American does not define him clearly enough. After all, North America is not only the United States. It is also Mexico, Jamaica, Haiti, Puerto Rico, Canada, and Cuba. Fidel Castro is a *norteamericano*.

Who then is this resident of the United States known by the Chicano   57
as an Anglo, gringo, yanqui, bolillo, or gabacho? Who is this person whose immediate ancestors were so incapable of living with Indigenous America that they tried to annihilate it?

He is the eternal foreigner, suffering from the immigrant complex. He   58
is a transplanted European, with pretensions of native origins. His culture, like his name for this continent, is imported. For generations, despite furious assertions of his originality, the "American" has aped the ways of the Old Country, while exploiting the real native peoples of the New. His most patriotic cry is basically the retort of one immigrant to another. Feeling truly American only when he is no longer the latest foreigner, he brandishes his Americanism by threatening the new arrival: "America, love or leave it!" Or, "If you don't like it here, go back where you came from!"

Now the gringo is trying to impose the immigrant complex on the   59
Chicano, pretending that we "Mexican Americans" are the most recent arrivals. It will not work. His melting pot concept is a sham: it is a crucible that scientifically disintegrates the human spirit, melting down entire cultures into a thin white residue the average gabacho can harmlessly absorb. That is why the Anglo cannot conceive of the Chicano, the Mexican Mestizo, in all his ancient human fullness. He recognizes him as a Mexican, but only to the extent that he is "American"; and he accepts Mexican culture only to the extent that it has been Americanized, sanitized, sterilized, and made safe for democracy, as with taco bars, chile con carne, the Mexican hat dance, Cantinflas in *Pepe,* the Frito Bandito, and grammar school renditions of *Ay Chiapanecas Ay, Ay* (Clap, clap, children).

But we will not be deceived. In the final analysis, frijoles, tortillas, y   60
chile are more American than the hamburger; and the pelado a more profound founding father of America than the pilgrim. No, we do not suffer from the immigrant complex. We suffered from it as its victims, but history does not record the same desperation among our people that twisted and distorted the European foreigner, that made the white immigrant the gringo.

We left no teeming shore in Europe, hungry and eager to reach the New   61
World. We crossed no ocean in an overcrowded boat, impatient and eager to arrive at Ellis Island in New York. No Statue of Liberty ever greeted our arrival in this country, and left us with the notion that the land was free, even though Mexicans and Indians already lived on it. We did not kill, rape, and steal under the pretext of Manifest Destiny and Western Expansion. We did not, in fact, come to the United States at all. The United States came to us.

We have been in América a long time. Somewhere in the twelfth cen   62
tury, our Aztec ancestors left their homeland of Aztlán, and migrated south to

Anáhuac, "the place by the waters," where they built their great city of México-Tenochtitlan. It was a long journey, for as their guiding deity Huitzi-lopochtli had prophesied, the elders of the tribe died en route and their children grew old. Aztlán was left far behind, somewhere "in the north," but it was never forgotten.

Aztlán is now the name of our Mestizo nation, existing to the north of 63 Mexico, within the borders of the United States. Chicano poets sing of it, and their *flor y canto* points toward a new yet very ancient way of life and social order, toward new yet very ancient gods. The natural revolutionary turn of things is overthrowing outmoded concepts in the life of man, even as it does in nature; churning them around in the great spin of Creation, merging the very ancient with the very new to create new forms.

The rise of the Chicano is part of the irrevocable birth of América, 64 born of the blood, flesh, and life spirit of this ancient continent. Beyond the two-thousand-mile border between Mexico and the U.S.A. we see our uni-versal race extending to the very tip of South America. We see millions upon millions of bronze people, living in Mestizo nations, some free, some yet to be freed, but existing: Mexicanos, Guatemaltecos, Peruanos, Chilenos, Cuba-nos, Bolivianos, Puertoriqueños. A new world race born of the racial and cultural blending of centuries. La Raza Cosmica, the true American people.

Topics for Discussion and Writing

1. Note five terms, Spanish or English, that are either new to you from this essay or that Valdez interprets in an unfamiliar way. Paraphrase his definition or interpretation of each, then write how his use of these terms might influence your view of history or of Mexican people. Has your view of yourself changed?
2. Valdez's essay was written in 1971. Do you feel that the conditions and assumptions he describes have substantially changed, or do you feel that they have remained largely the same? Defend your point of view by citing particular examples of change or lack of change.
3. Review your response to "Before and as You Read" topic 3. Based on your reading of the selection, revise your answers to these questions.
4. Compare this essay with Victor Villanueva's essay from chapter 9. Note similarities and differences. Compare their assessments of history. Use these readings to revise your responses to "Before and as You Read" topic 2.

RUDOLFO ANAYA
"The Censorship of Neglect"

> *"We have not been free to teach. We have accepted the literature which is presented to us by publishers, those producers of books who have a direct link and a vested interest in the status quo."*

Thus speaks Rudolfo Anaya in "The Censorship of Neglect," the essay we have reprinted from The English Journal *of September 1992.*

Anaya is a teacher and a writer. Born in 1937 in Pastura, New Mexico, he taught seven years in the public schools of Albuquerque while earning graduate degrees in English and in counseling. In 1974 Anaya joined the faculty of the University of New Mexico and continues to teach there.

His first novel, Bless Me, Ultima *(1972), has won wide acclaim and continues to attract a wide audience. Three novels, including* Tortuga *(1979); two screenplays; and a collection of short stories followed, plus histories and book-length personal essays (*A Chicano in China, *1986, and* Lord of the Dawn: The Legend of Quetzalcoatl, *1987). His short stories, articles, essays, and reviews have appeared in such journals as* La Luz, New Mexico Magazine, *and* Bilingual Review—Revista Bilingue.

Before and as You Read

1. List as many as you can of the books you have been assigned to read or have chosen to read in the past six years. How representative have these books been of the diverse ethnic and racial groups, and of the diverse histories, that make up America? Compare your list with those of others. Which are the most frequently read titles and authors?

2. How do you define *censorship?* Can you think of a time when your freedom to read a book of your choice was hindered (for whatever reason)? Describe the event in writing. What reasons were you given for the restriction? How did you react? How do you feel now about the incident?

3. Do you believe in the idea of a "canon" of literary works that should be required or recommended reading for high school and college students? If so, why? If so, what works would you like to see on the list? If you do not accept this idea, how would you argue against it? What alternatives to a "canon" would you propose (or have you experienced)?

4. As you read "The Censorship of Neglect," observe how Anaya develops his concept of censorship. Note how he answers, either explicitly or implicitly, the tough questions that he says teachers must ask themselves.

THE THEME of the 1991 NCTE convention in Seattle was the freedom to teach and to learn. In a country which is finally acknowledging its multicultural nature, the idea proved engaging. I want to examine this theme from my point of view as a Mexican American educator and writer.

I have taught English language and literature for twenty-five years in this country, and I know that we have not been free to teach. The literary history of this country has been shaped by forces far beyond the control of the classroom teacher. Our curriculum has been controlled by groups with a parochial view of what the curriculum should and should not include. These groups include teachers who hold narrow views of what literature should be, publishers who control what is printed, and politicians who defend their particular social and political interests. These groups represent the status quo and call themselves "universalists." For a long time these groups have told us they know what is universal in literature, and this has translated into a course of action which has kept the ethnic literatures of this country out of the curriculum.

The time for that narrow view to be exposed is now, and the time for us to take charge and implement into the curriculum the many literatures of this country is today.

For generations, freedom to learn has meant reading only the very narrow spectrum of literature proposed to us by the universalists. Most of us know there is no literature with a capital L. There are many literatures, and our country is rich with them. And yet most of us have succumbed to the pressures brought to bear by those in power.

Folk wisdom says, you can lead a horse to water, but you can't make it drink. You can lead students to books, but if the content doesn't engage them, they lose interest and soon become dropouts. My experience, and the experience of many teachers I know, has taught me that part of the cause for our alarming dropout statistics is this narrow, circumscribed curriculum in language and literature. To reverse these deplorable dropout statistics and to help create a positive self-image in our students, I firmly believe we need to present the literatures which reflect our true diversity.

The literature of the barrio, of the neighborhood, of the region, of the ethnic group can be a useful tool of engagement, a way to put students in touch with their social reality. What is pertinent to our personal background is pertinent to our process of learning. And so, if students are going to be truly free to learn, they must be exposed to stories that portray their history and image in a positive manner. They must be given the opportunity to read the literatures of the many different cultures of our own country.

That we are free to teach is a myth. We know every nation has a vested interest in perpetuating the myth of national unity and coherence. We know there is a social and political intent behind the concept of national unity. Those who hold political power in this country have used it to try to create a homogenous, monolithic curriculum. That intent betrays the many communities which compose this country because it denies their histories.

This country cannot continue on this limited path and serve its people. Those in power can no longer be allowed to believe they are the sole possessors of the truth. I believe I represent, as a Chicano writer, part of that truth. Every educator represents part of that truth. We are tired of being told that we do not understand the needs of our youth because we belong to a particular ethnic group. We are told that because we are Mexican, Native, Black, or Asian American—or women—that somebody else has the right literature and language to describe our reality. Each of our communities has much to teach this country. Each barrio, each neighborhood, each region, men and women, all have a vested interest in education, and it's time we made that interest known.

We have not been free to teach. We have accepted the literature which   9 is presented to us by publishers, those producers of books who have a direct link and a vested interest in the status quo. Big publishers have neglected or refused to publish the literature of minority communities of our country; their lack of social responsibility has created a narrow and paternalistic perspective of our society. The true picture of this country is not narrow: it is multidimensional; it reflects many communities, attitudes, languages, beliefs, and needs. Our fault, as teachers, is that we have accepted the view of those in charge: teacher-training programs, publishers, politicians, and sectarian interests.

And yet we know better. We know one approach is not best for all;   10 we know we have to incorporate the many voices of literature into the curriculum.

It is time to ask ourselves some tough questions. Exactly what literature   11 are we teaching in classrooms? Who writes it? What social reality does it portray? Who packaged it for us? How much choice do we really have as teachers to step outside this mainstream packaging and choose books? Who provides the budget? Who calls the shots?

I raise this issue and try to analyze and understand it from my experience.   12 I am a native son of the Mexican American community of New Mexico, a member of the broader Hispanic population of the country. When I published my first novel in the early seventies, I was part of the Chicano literary movement. We asked ourselves then the same questions we are still asking today.

We knew then that the desire to form a monolithic social reality which   13 served those in power was very costly in human terms. We knew the oral and written literature of Native Americans had been neglected. It was never in the curriculum I studied. Even the better known African American writings have not been a consistent part of our undergraduate education. Chicano literature, in a country that has over fifteen-million Mexican Americans, is still virtually unknown in the classroom.

Our community stretches from California to Texas, and into the North-   14 west and Midwest. But not one iota of our social reality, much less our aesthetic reality, is represented in the literature read in the schools.

Where is our freedom to teach? Who trained us, or brainwashed us, to   15 the point that we cannot see fifteen-million people? The teachers of this country cannot see, I mean that literally, the children of fifteen-million people.

That is how strong the censorship of neglect has been. That is why I say we have not been free to teach.

Living within the confines of a mainstream culture has caused me to look at this idea of cultural and self-identity. You have to ask yourselves the same question: how do your students create their self-image? Specifically, what role does the school and the curriculum play in the formation of identity? Literature is one of the most humanistic endeavors which has been used to reflect back to readers their own images. And yet until very recently the image, and therefore the history, of the Mexican American was missing from the spectrum of literature. Most teacher-training programs and departments of English still refuse to admit the presence of the ethnic literatures of this country. Much of that training never teaches the diverse stories of the country, and so the teachers who go into the classroom are never really "free to teach." 16

Reading is the key to a liberated life. We must take action to wrest our freedom to teach from those forces that still don't acknowledge the existence of the multidimensional and multicultural realities of our country. We must infuse into the study of language and literature the stories of the many communities that compose our country. 17

The cost of having denied these many voices their rightful role in the study of language and literature has been enormous. The ethnic communities of this country have suffered the loss in human terms for many generations. We see the loss each day, and it hurts us. Now the loss is being felt in monetary terms by business and government agencies, and perhaps this is what will wake up this country. Our children who go into the world unprepared to deal with real-life experiences, our children lost to dope and prisons and those who suffer from poor images of themselves, are all a costly burden. Our ideal to be free to teach is based on our desire to enlighten humanity, our desire to contribute to a better world. Now, belatedly, those in power are waking up and seeing the devastation their universalist, colonialist approach has caused. Now they awaken and produce token changes in education, not because they are interested in freedom for the individual but because they understand that an uneducated populace is not good for the business of the country. 18

Our diverse communities are rightfully demanding to be included in the curriculum of language and literature courses. This is perceived as a threat to those who want to keep the status quo, those who want to stay in power. There is a very strong element among writers and educators who insist that the ethnic writers of this country are not writing according to universalist guidelines that have been established. We, the people of the multiple communities of this country, no longer trust, nor do we believe, those who hold that view. We will no longer be demeaned and lose our students to that view. Our challenge is to incorporate into the curriculum all the voices of our country. Old world views have been crumbling since the advent of the twentieth century. Change and new views of reality must be acknowledged. And yet educators have resisted the formation of the new multidimensional world. Why? 19

Have we become the problem itself? Have we become the defenders of   20
the status quo? Is it really we who have refused to see the reality of the African
American experience, the Chicano world, the Asian American struggle, the
woman's search for her own self-representation? Are we free to teach when
we fear the social and aesthetic reality of other groups?

If you are teaching in a Mexican American community, it is your social   21
responsibility to refuse to use the textbook which doesn't contain stories by
Mexican American authors. If you teach Asian American children, refuse the
textbook which doesn't portray their history and social reality. This kind of
activism will free you to teach. If you don't refuse, you are part of the problem. But you don't have to be teaching in a Mexican American barrio to insist
that the stories and social reality of that group be represented in your textbook. You shortchange your students and you misrepresent the true nature of
their country if you don't introduce them to all the communities who have
composed the history of this country. To deny your students a view into these
different worlds is to deny them tools for the future.

The future is only going to get more complex. We need better and more   22
educated answers to a plethora of issues which face us. The old, one-dimen-
sional, narrow view of the world hasn't worked and will not work. It was kept
in place by power that sacrificed human potential. We cannot applaud the
liberation the eastern European countries have recently achieved and still es-
pouse a colonial mentality when it comes to teaching in this country. We
cannot applaud the democratization of the Soviet Union if we still believe a
monolithic, iron fist must rule our curriculum. Wake up, America. We are a
diverse country, let us be free to teach that diversity.

Topics for Discussion and Writing

1. Based on your reading of the essay, revise one of your "Before and as You
   Read" responses. Note the ideas and passages that have particularly influenced you.
2. Based on Anaya's objectives and his method of argument, how do you
   think he would define the *purpose* of requiring students to read literary
   works throughout their schooling? Write about your purposes for reading
   fiction, poetry, drama, history, and so on. Do your purposes jibe with what
   you believe are Anaya's reasons for wanting children to read?
3. Explore the holdings of your local public library or of the libraries in local
   public or private schools, from the elementary level to high school. How
   easy is it for students to find works by the types of authors Anaya identifies?
   Note displays of books, lists of magazines, and other features. With others,
   design ways for the library to improve, if necessary, its access to works by a
   greater diversity of authors.
4. Extend Anaya's censorship argument from books to broadcasting. Study for
   a time a sample of network (noncable) television and radio programs. Pay
   particular attention to advertising. Describe the America you see and hear

through advertising on TV and radio. How diverse or narrow is this vision of America? What and who are the ideals that corporate sponsors want the audience to emulate?

For Further Thought

1. If you have written on any of the topics in the "Thinking about the Issues" section that began this chapter, review that writing. Using information and insights from two or more of the selections in this chapter, write a second essay on one of the topics. Share your writing with others. Use your reading of their insights and interpretations to compose a third version of your work on the topic.

2. Ruth Sidel's selection in this chapter is from a chapter entitled "The Outsiders," but indeed all the selections are written from the perspective of people who regard themselves as being outside the power structure of U.S. society. Do two kinds of analysis. First, review four of the essays and identify in each the insiders to whom the outsiders are being compared. Be precise in this analysis because the distinctions from piece to piece may not be sharp. Second, place yourself in terms of the outside-inside distinction. Do you feel yourself attacked as an insider in some of the pieces and supported as a fellow outsider in others? Write about these conflicting feelings: As an attacked insider, how do you respond? As a fellow outsider, how do you regard the author's support and your own desires for equality?

3. In the introduction to this chapter, we stated our intention to include works representing "several of the more enduring struggles for equality in our society." Comment on our choices and on our omissions. If you were creating an anthology of works on the theme of equality—and if you were faced with the typical editor's concerns about lack of space and high printing costs versus the huge diversity of good material—how would you go about it? Are there certain "must reads" that you would include? Are there certain issues or causes that you would feature? Are there certain points of view that you would be sure to represent? Design one or more lists of works (no more than ten) and compare these with similar lists drawn by others.

4. Focus on your "regular routine" activities. Contemplate your most frequent interactions with people. How has your reading (and your associated writing and discussion) of selections from this chapter increased your awareness of the concerns of the people you work and talk with? Can you identify a few specific ways in which what you say or do might change as a result of this study?

CHAPTER SIX

Athletics:
Driving to Excel

"Let's have fun!" yells the coach to the young players on the field. But the coach doesn't act as if the game is fun, because she (or he) rarely smiles; most often the expression is of worry, sometimes panic, as the opposition threatens to score. The parents in the stands and along the sidelines don't smile either, but watch with grim intensity as their children play. And the kids don't seem to be having fun. Their little faces mirror the anxiety of parents and coaches; their voices echo the critical, intense tones of the adults.

As we compiled this chapter of *A Sense of Value,* we admitted our complicity in the American culture of athletics: Years of playing organized sports and more years of watching (and coaching) as our children have played have given us empathy for the people we present here. We certainly cannot step outside "sports mania" to pass judgment on its excesses, but we can, and do, try to learn from the experiences of others to broaden our perspective and clarify our decision making as parents.

It becomes harder and harder to separate athletics from the serious business of living. The fitness craze that began in the 1960s and has escalated since has spawned mammoth industries in food, clothing, equipment, and training services and facilities. To be fit and stay fit has become an important value for many Americans; it influences what we eat, where we want to live, and how we strive to look and dress and feel. TV and magazine images of sleek, taut women and thickly-muscled men who train religiously have become our idols. The multimillions paid to top professionals—and even to some athletes just turning pro—have intensified the competitiveness in most sports. There is no longer an off season for athletes who now feel they must train year-round to maintain their "edge." People laugh at the parents of 4-year-olds who are already buying the best equipment and looking for the best coaches, but when 13-year-olds are winning Olympic gold medals on worldwide TV and 20-year-olds are considered "over the hill" in some sports, the concern of those parents seems logical.

We've included this section in the book because the athlete's values have to a significant degree become everyone's values. What are the consequences for society? What have we gained and lost in this pursuit of excellence?

Thinking about the Issues

1. Brainstorm a short list of the best-known athletes. Select two from the list who strike you as different from each other in significant ways and write about the qualities that each represents, as these have been portrayed in the media. What do the two have in common? How are they different? Are there qualities that neither possesses that you feel are important for any individual?

2. How does the term *athlete* apply to you? Write about yourself as an athletic competitor and/or as a person who works to stay in shape. How are athletic values part of your personal value system? Conversely, have there been ways in which you have deliberately rejected certain qualities that you attribute to athletes?

3. How have your behavior, dreams, and ambitions been influenced by athletes or their portrayal in the popular media? If you've ever looked upon a particular athlete as a role model or hero, write about the qualities you've admired in that person and how you've tried to emulate him or her.

4. Some people are called natural athletes or are said to possess a gift for particular sports. But all athletes seem to spend endless hours practicing, honing their talents. What part of athletic success do you feel is attributable to natural talent and what part to dedicated, regular work? Support your ideas with examples. Do you know of people whose athletic careers defy your generalization?

ATHLETES AND DRUGS

> ". . . I think that there are a lot of athletes in danger. . . . Almost everyone I know. They are so intent on being successful that they're not concerned with anything else."

> Lyle Alzado, a former pro football star, died of brain cancer in 1992. In July 1991, months after the cancer was diagnosed, he gave an interview to Sports Illustrated *writer-reporter Shelley Smith, who revised it as a personal essay by Alzado.*

> *Reprinted here, the interview is followed by a "sidebar" interview with Robert Huizenga, M.D., former team physician of the Los Angeles Raiders, one of the teams for which Alzado played. Because of the controversial nature of Alzado's claims in the interview, we have also reprinted a related article from the* Washington Post, July 14, 1991, *by staff writer Mike Freeman.*

Before and as You Read

1. If you are a fan of professional football, you might know about the career of Lyle Alzado. If so, write what you recall about him as a player, including his reputation and accomplishments.

2. The use of so-called performance-enhancing drugs, such as various anabolic steroids, has become one of the most hotly debated topics in sports. If you have ever considered using such substances, or know others who have, write about the experience. On what evidence did you or others base your decision to use or not use performance-enhancing drugs?

3. As you read the three pieces included in this selection, observe how the writers establish their authority on the topic. Be particularly aware of the writer's responsibility to report, as closely as possible, the truth. Do you feel that the Alzado interview is responsibly reported? Compare the levels of responsibility in the three pieces.

4. Write about the reporter's relationship with a person she or he interviews. To what degree should a reporter seek the approval of a subject for what is published? Does a reporter owe greater loyalty to the subject of the interview or to the readers who are to be informed? How can a reporter balance these responsibilities?

LYLE ALZADO AND SHELLEY SMITH

"I'm Sick and I'm Scared"

I LIED. I lied to you. I lied to my family. I lied to a lot of people for a lot of years when I said I didn't use steroids. I started taking anabolic steroids in 1969, and I never stopped. Not when I retired from the NFL in 1985. Not ever. I couldn't, and then I made things worse by using human growth hormone, too. I had my mind set, and I did what I wanted to do. So many people tried to talk me out of what I was doing, and I wouldn't listen. And now I'm sick. I've got cancer—a brain lymphoma—and I'm in the fight of my life.

Everyone knows me as a tough, tough guy. And I've never been afraid of anything. Not any human, not anything. Then I woke up in the hospital last March and they told me, "You have cancer." Cancer. I couldn't understand it. All I knew was that I was just so weak. I went through all those wars on the football field. I was so muscular. I was a giant. Now I'm sick. And I'm scared.

It wasn't worth it. Sure, I played 15 years as a defensive end with the Denver Broncos, Cleveland Browns and Los Angeles Raiders and twice made All-Pro. But look at me now. I wobble when I walk and sometimes have to hold on to somebody. You have to give me time to answer questions, because I have trouble remembering things. I'm down to 215 pounds, 60 pounds less than I weighed just a few months ago, and I've got to grow back into my pants, they're so baggy. I've been in chemotherapy at the UCLA Medical Center and have done pretty well. I haven't thrown up or anything yet, but I don't have any hair and I wear a scarf on my head. The other day my wife, Kathy, and I drove into a gas station, and a guy there started making fun of my scarf. My "hat," he called it. I wanted to beat him up, but Kathy reminded me I wasn't strong enough. She said I'd have to wait until I get better.

I'm 42 years old. I have a nine-year-old son, Justin, who lives with his   4
mother, Cindy, in New York. Kathy, who's a fashion model, and I were married last March, and we live in West Los Angeles. I got sick and went into the hospital two days after the wedding. And it was a few days later I found out I had cancer.

I know there's no written, documented proof that steroids and human   5
growth hormone caused this cancer. But it's one of the reasons you have to look at. You have to. And I think that there are a lot of athletes in danger. So many of them have taken this same human growth hormone, and so many of them are on steroids. Almost everyone I know. They are so intent on being successful that they're not concerned with anything else. No matter what an athlete tells you, I don't care who, don't believe them if they tell you these substances aren't widely used. Ninety percent of the athletes I know are on the stuff. We're not born to be 280 or 300 pounds or jump 30 feet. Some people are born that way, but not many, and there are some 1,400 guys in the NFL.

When I was playing high school football in Cedarhurst, N.Y., I hadn't   6
heard about steroid use by anybody. It wasn't until I got to college when I realized that, even though I'd been high school All-America, that wasn't enough to make it as a football player. I didn't have the size. I had the speed but not the size. I went to Kilgore College, a J.C. in Texas, and my speed enhanced my progress, but my size didn't. Then I went to Yankton College in South Dakota, the only school that would accept me. I realized I wasn't even big enough for a small school like that, so I started taking steroids. I don't remember now where I got them or how I even heard about them, but I know I started on Dianabol, about 50 milligrams a day.

The Dianabol was very easy to get, even in those days. Most athletes go   7
to a gym for their steroids, and I think that's what I did. I remember a couple of weeks later someone mentioned how my biceps seemed to look bigger. I was so proud. I was lifting weights so much that the results were pretty immediate and dramatic. I went from 190 pounds to 220 by eating a lot, and then I went up to about 300 pounds from the steroids. People say that steroids can make you mean and moody, and my mood swings were incredible. That's what made me a football player, my moods on the field.

As I progressed, I changed steroids whenever I felt my body building a   8
tolerance to what I was taking. It's hard to remember all the names now. I

studied them a little. And I mixed combinations like a chemist. You had to take them both orally and inject them, mostly into your butt so no one would see the marks. I always gave myself injections at home in my bedroom. I got pretty good at it. I kept the steroids in my dresser.

My first year with the Broncos was 1971. I was like a maniac. I outran, outhit, outanythinged everybody, and I made the team after Pete Duranko got hurt in a preseason game against the Chicago Bears. I took his place. All along I was taking steroids, and I saw that they made me play better and better. I kept on because I knew I had to keep getting more size. I became very violent on the field. Off it, too. I did things only crazy people do. Once in 1979 in Denver a guy sideswiped my car, and I chased him up and down hills through the neighborhoods. I did that a lot. I'd chase a guy, pull him out of his car, beat the hell out of him. *9*

We had such a defense in Denver, especially that Super Bowl year, 1977. I can't say if anybody else on the Broncos was on the stuff, but because I was, I have to think some of the others were. But I wasn't liked on the team, so I really didn't know what was going on. *10*

I was so wild about winning. It's all I cared about, winning, winning. All I thought about. I never talked about anything else. I spent three years with the Browns, 1979 through '81. I had brought the steroids with me to Cleveland from Los Angeles, where I spent the off-seasons. It's easier to get them in L.A. than anywhere else. Guys on the Browns came to me and asked about steroids, and I'd tell them who to call or I'd give them what I had. They'd take them in the privacy of their own homes, and it wasn't talked about much—not in the locker room. If you were in the gym, you might say something, but you had to be very quiet because there were detectives around. I wasn't a dealer, but if I was asked, I'd help other guys get steroids. Because they were doing for me what I wanted them to do, I hoped they would do the same for the other players. *11*

When I went to the Raiders in 1982, I took more and more doses and different combinations. Orally and injecting. I felt I had to keep up. I didn't sleep much, maybe three or four hours a night. My system would run so fast. I was taking the whole spectrum now. I'd feel my body close up on one drug, and I'd switch to another until my body would open up to the first one again. *12*

I'm convinced that my biggest mistake was never going off cycle. According to the guys around the gym, if you go on steroids for six to eight weeks, then you're supposed to stop for the same number of weeks. Me, I'd be on the stuff for 10 or 12 weeks, and then I'd go off for only two, maybe three weeks, and I'd feel that was enough. It was addicting, mentally addicting. I just didn't feel strong unless I was taking something. *13*

A lot of the guys on the Raiders asked me about steroids, and I'd help them get what they needed. A lot had their own sources. But I was the guy to get them if they needed something. I kept progressing into stronger things, the last stuff I remember taking was something called Bolasterone and Quinolone—very dangerous. Steroids can raise your cholesterol level, and at one *14* point late in my career my cholesterol was over 400. I was warned, but I wouldn't listen.

I had injected so much that a few years ago a plastic surgeon operated 15 on my butt. I had these lumps under my skin from where the needles went in. He went in and removed one baseball-sized mass of tissue and then found a bigger one underneath.

I got moodier and moodier, too. I had a couple of divorces. I yelled all 16 the time. Anytime I'd walk into a restaurant or a bar, I always felt like I had to check everything out to make sure no one was going to mess with me. I was so high-strung that I needed to play a game every day. That is what was so hard when I decided to retire. I'd had an Achilles injury, which I'm sure was a result of all the steroid use. I've heard that steroids can lead to weakened tendons. I tore my biceps clear in half, everything on the left side of my body tore, and I think it was because of the long usage of some of that stuff.

All along, even after I retired, I was getting stuff from a gentleman who 17 works out of one of the L.A. gyms. He was making a ton of money. In fact, most of the dealers don't have to do any other work. I went up to northern California a couple of times and bought stuff from a guy in San Jose, Steve Coons. He sold me the Bolasterone. [Coons is in custody awaiting trial after being indicted in a drug-related conspiracy and mail fraud case in the U.S. district court in San Jose.]

As I said, I kept taking the stuff after retiring from the Raiders in 1985. 18 I couldn't stand the thought of being weak. I tried to taper down. Mostly I was taking lower dosages of Anavar and Equipoise. I thought it was stuff that would help me. But I know now I should have gone off it. I stayed too big, too mean. And that's probably why the idea came into my head to try to make a comeback last year. Everyone kept asking me why the Raiders weren't tough anymore, and I just decided to prove to everyone that I could come back. But that's what got me into real trouble. That's when things got really crazy.

I decided to take human growth hormone. They used to get it from 19 glands in cadavers, but they started making genetically engineered HGH in 1985. I was 41 last year, and I decided that in order for me to make that comeback, for my body to remain intact, I had to use the growth hormone. I started taking it in mid-June and used it right up until this March along with testosterone cypionate, an anabolic steroid.

The cypionate gives you the size. And the growth hormone, well, it 20 gives you muscle mass. I'd take two vials—one a fluid and one a white substance—and mix them together, and I'd have growth hormone. Then I'd inject it. It cost me a lot of money, $4,000 for 16 weeks just for the growth hormone. At times in my career I probably spent $20,000 to $30,000 a year on different stuff. But the HGH was still a big added expense. I got it from the guy at the gym. It wasn't the stuff from cadavers; it was the other kind.

I was working out so hard. Every day, long hours, long days. I remember 21 every workout. I was tested for drugs along with everyone else in camp. I lined up, signed up and took the test, with everyone from the Raiders watching. And I passed. My teammates all were saying, "How did you pass that test?" I had been told to stop the cypionate a month before the test, that this would be enough time for me to pass. And human growth hormone can't be detected by testing, so I kept taking that. I passed with flying colors.

Did the Raider coaches know I was taking stuff no matter what the test said? It was just like it was when I was playing with the Broncos and Browns. I think the coaches knew guys were built certain ways, and they knew those guys couldn't look the way they did without taking stuff. But the coaches just coached and looked the other way. 22

My comeback hit a snag when I injured my knee. I had arthroscopic surgery, which went well. A month later I played in an exhibition game against Chicago. I came off the ball so fast, so hard. Oh, god, it felt great. I was working so hard. They cut me anyway. I think the only reason they didn't keep me was because they figured I was too old. I could have made it. I know I could have. 23

So I was out of football again, this time for good. I kept taking human growth hormone, and I was still doing the steroids. One day last fall I was on Melrose Avenue in Los Angeles in a yogurt shop with Justin. I felt a big cough coming on so I went outside so I wouldn't spread any germs. I fainted. The next thing I knew I was getting up off the sidewalk with all this blood pouring from my face. I had fallen right on my face, on my nose. I broke the nose so bad they had to use plastic surgery to put it back together. 24

I stayed in the hospital four days while they fixed me up and ran a bunch of tests. They couldn't find anything. But I think that was the start. I think the tumors were beginning to fester in my head. In February I started to get a little dizzy. At first the doctor told me it was an inner ear infection and gave me some medication. For a while it helped. 25

Kathy was getting on me pretty good about the steroids I was taking, and I promised her I wouldn't take anything more after our wedding. I started tapering down even before the wedding. I think I was so excited about marrying Kathy that I didn't allow myself to notice that I was starting to get sicker. When I watch the video of the wedding, I see that, when I'm walking back down the aisle with her, I'm almost limping, listing to the right. 26

Two days later, in the apartment in Marina del Rey where we were living at the time, I started feeling dizzy. I couldn't talk. And I was seeing double. They put me in the hospital and took all kinds of tests and they told me I had some sort of virus. I went home and got worse and worse. I didn't eat for four days. 27

Finally, Kathy insisted to the doctors that I go back in, and they did a brain biopsy. I woke up the morning after, and they told me I had cancer. I couldn't believe it. I was just so weak. They started me on the radiation treatments, and I went home. Then I got an infection. But Kathy's dad was there. He saved my life. I wasn't breathing. I was purple. Kathy called 911, and her dad gave me CPR. 28

They took me to the hospital, and I kept having brain seizures every 20 minutes. It was so bad they put me in intensive care for two weeks, and I 29 don't remember it at all. I keep trying, but I don't remember anything. They said I looked like I was just fading away.

On top of everything else, I'm told that my name has come up in *30* various steroid cases. And, oh yes, my medical bills are enormous. But there are plans to have a benefit for me in the next few months.

This is the hardest thing I've ever done, to admit that I've done some- *31* thing wrong. If I had known that I would be this sick now, I would have tried to make it in football on my own—naturally. Whoever is doing this stuff, if you stay on it too long or maybe if you get on it at all, you're going to get something bad from it. I don't mean you'll definitely get brain cancer, but you'll get something. It is a wrong thing to do.

I'm sorry I lied. I'm sorry success meant so much to me. I just got *32* married to a beautiful, beautiful woman. And I can't take her dancing. I can't take her to dinner. Justin understands that I'm very sick. I try to be real strong on the phone when I talk to him. I hope he'll read this article.

When I first got out of the hospital I felt inferior. Going from being *33* built like I was to being built like this is very hard. But I don't feel inferior any longer. My strength isn't my strength anymore. My strength is my heart. If you're on steroids or human growth hormone, stop. I should have.

DR. ROBERT HUIZENGA

"A Doctor's Warning Ignored"

WAS LYLE Alzado's cancer caused by the performance-enhancing *1* drugs he took—anabolic steroids and human growth hormone? Alzado thinks so, and Dr. Robert Huizenga, one of the physicians treating him, believes Alzado may be right. Huizenga, an internist practicing in Beverly Hills, was one of the Los Angeles Raiders' team doctors from 1983 until last fall. Sources close to the doctor say that Huizenga quit because the Raiders refused to tell a player that the player had a heart condition. Huizenga says that he resigned because of a "misunderstanding about the care the players were receiving." The Raiders deny the sources' claim and say they released Huizenga. With Alzado's permission, Huizenga discussed Alzado's case with SI's Shelley Smith.

SI: Did you know Lyle was taking steroids at the time he was playing *2* for the Raiders?

R.H.: Yes. A difficult thing about medicine is what to do when some- *3* body is doing things you might not agree with. Lyle and I battled since the early 1980s about his ingestion of certain things. I tried to be there and not be judgmental.

SI: What steroids did he take in those days? *4*

R.H.: To my knowledge he took everything—injectable, oral, he cy- *5* cled. When he played, we talked about it because his blood tests suggested he was taking massive amounts of steroids, but he never really discussed doses. He said in generalities what he was taking. Despite my admonitions that this was a major health risk, he kept doing it. He said it was a risk he wanted to take.

SI: When did you learn of his illness? 6

R.H.: He came to me at the end of February with symptoms of dizziness, loss of coordination of the right side of his body, double vision and slurred speech. Through a series of tests we were finally able to diagnose that he has a form of brain cancer that is very, very rare. He has T-cell lymphoma. That isn't to be confused with B-cell lymphoma, which is the lymphoma most commonly linked with AIDS. 7

SI: What kind of human growth hormone (HGH) was he taking? 8

R.H.: There are two types of human growth hormone. One is taken from cadaver pituitary glands and is homogenized and purified as much as possible. And then there is the genetically engineered hormone. He injected the genetically engineered hormone. 9

SI: We've had reports that Lyle may have taken cadaver-type human growth hormone before last year. Do you have any knowledge of this? 10

R.H.: Lyle told me he didn't take any HGH before his comeback attempt. 11

SI: Could Lyle's cancer have been caused by what he took? 12

R.H.: I think there's no question. We know anabolic steroids have cancer-forming ability. We know that growth hormones have cancer-growing ability. 13

SI: What other explanation could there be? 14

R.H.: Either bad luck or some kind of genetic quirk. 15

SI: Did Lyle undergo surgery after his illness was detected? 16

R.H.: He had a brain biopsy in early April and had some complications that required a second surgery to eradicate a brain abscess that had formed and become infected. 17

SI: And he's had chemotherapy? 18

R.H.: He's getting an unusual form of chemotherapy for lymphoma. It gives us a measure of hope, but you always have to be realistic. 19

SI: How does this chemotherapy work? 20

R.H.: The drug is called cisplatin. It gets a lot more of the cancer-fighting agent to the brain and less to the rest of the body. 21

SI: What is Lyle's prognosis? 22

R.H.: It's a tough, tough cancer. We have not had tremendous success with it. On the other hand, he's getting very good therapy, and he's responding well. 23

SI: Lyle says that he now wants to come out and help. . . . 24

R.H.: That's the new Lyle. 25

SI: Is there really a new Lyle? 26

R.H.: Lyle is a great, great guy, but steroids can change a person. You can be talking to two different people. 27

SI: Are there other NFL players who could be at risk? 28

R.H.: A number of players on a number of teams who were heavy   *29*
users in the past are at risk. We are very worried about those players.

SI: Why don't we know more about steroid usage by athletes and its   *30*
effects?

R.H.: There are very few studies, and, frankly, the best group that could   *31*
be studied and give useful information is NFL players. We—all the doctors of
the clubs—agreed to back a study. We have not been embraced by the players'
union or the league. Olympic athletes won't let us go back and study them
because they're afraid they'll have their records taken away. We want to follow
former players, and I believe we can get very honest answers from them
because they have nothing to lose. From my contact, they're apprehensive
about their past use, especially those who used heavy amounts.

SI: Does the steroid danger go beyond the NFL?   *32*

R.H.: Conservative estimates say a million people in the U.S. use ana-   *33*
bolic steroids, not just for sports but for appearance. Most are young people. I
think we have a real time bomb on our hands.

MIKE FREEMAN

"In NFL's Fight against Steroids, New Technology Is Half the Battle"

A s NATIONAL Football League training camps open, an unknown   *1*
percentage of the players is using some sort of steroid or other
performance-enhancing drug. It is a fact, and it is also illegal. John A. Lombardo, in charge of the league's steroid testing program, insists that most steroid
users will be caught. But not all of them.

"What we've tried to build is a deterrent program," Lombardo said.   *2*
"We're not going to catch everybody, but we'll certainly try to stop people
from using steroids. We don't want this to be a witch hunt, but the NFL isn't
going to make it easy for players to use these things.

"Are there going to be people who beat these tests? Probably. But we're   *3*
in for the long haul. When you're not testing at all there is a green light to
take whatever you want. Testing at least closes some windows. And when the
windows begin to close, soon no windows will be open at all."

Lombardo was appointed NFL drug adviser for anabolic steroids in April   *4*
1990, a position created by Commissioner Paul Tagliabue. Lombardo is one
of the country's leading specialists in the field of sports medicine and anabolic
steroids and has been given a difficult task: He must eradicate steroid use in an
age when anyone who really wants to take steroids can usually beat the system.
Lombardo is limited to the technology available. He explained that there is a
never-ending battle between the athlete attempting to find a new substance
that can't be detected and the ability of the laboratory to detect the substance.
Picture a race with steroids in the lead, and just as technology and people such
as Lombardo learn to detect a particular steroid (or to discover how it's

masked), they see another steroid up ahead (or another masking technique), and the race starts all over again.

"We need to get sophisticated enough technology," Lombardo said. "We need to surpass . . . not catch up. I'm not big on ties." 5

Some think that steroid use in the NFL is a major problem. Bob Ward, who was the conditioning coach for the Dallas Cowboys from 1976 to 1990, said steroids were used by some players throughout his tenure with the team. He would not say who used steroids or how widespread was their use. 6

"I'd be a fool to say steroids weren't being used by the Cowboys when I was there," said Ward, now out of football. "That's all I want to really say about it. But I think basically we still have a major problem around the league." 7

That's what Lyle Alzado—a former defensive end with the Denver Broncos, Cleveland Browns, and Raiders when they were in Oakland—also maintains. Alzado told Sports Illustrated this month that he had been taking anabolic steroids since 1969 and later began injecting human growth hormone. Alzado believes the performance-enhancing drugs led to his brain lymphoma. Most doctors, however, maintain that steroids probably cannot cause that type of cancer. 8

Alzado says he is fighting for his life. He has lost 60 pounds in several months and, because of chemotherapy, he has lost his hair. 9

He told Sports Illustrated: "I think there are a lot of athletes in danger. So many of them have taken this same human growth hormone, and so many of them are on steroids. Almost everyone I know. They are so intent on being successful that they're not concerned with anything else. No matter what an athlete tells you, I don't care who, don't believe them if they tell you these substances aren't widely used. 10

"Ninety percent of the athletes I know are on the stuff. We're not born to be 280 or 300 pounds or jump 30 feet. Some people are born that way, but not many, and there are some 1,400 guys in the NFL." 11

Lombardo said that Alzado "overstated the situation. When people start saying 90 percent . . . just think of 90 percent of 1,400 people. Ninety percent? That can't be right. 12

"Start putting names to these things. Does that mean [former Raiders quarterback] Jim Plunkett took steroids? Or [Raiders defensive end] Howie Long? Take an NFL roster and look at it. I have a problem with people making blanket statements like that. It's not fair to the individuals who are genetically special people." 13

Lombardo, who feels steroid use is decreasing, would not estimate how many people in the NFL he feels take performance-enhancing drugs. "I don't like to guess," he said. "It's not fair." 14

Several medical experts and former sports officials believe Lombardo *and* Alzado. It is probably true that the steroid use among NFL players is on the decline. It probably also is true, as Alzado says, that a large percentage of players, perhaps as much as 75 percent, was using steroids and other chemical enhancers when Alzado retired from professional football in 1985. 15

At that time, the NFL had officially banned the use of steroids since the early 1980s. But until the teams decided to start enforcing the policy by testing, the ban was widely ignored, said former NFL drug adviser Forest S. Tennant, a physician and director of a drug treatment clinic in West Covina, Calif. Tennant—who as NFL adviser was embroiled in a far-reaching drug testing controversy—resigned in February 1990 after his program was criticized for being inconsistent, slipshod and racist in its selection of athletes for testing. *16*

In 1987 the NFL announced that it would test players for steroid use, but there would be no penalties for positive results. Of those tested, starting with preseason physical, nearly one-third were found to be using steroids, Tennant said. *17*

The NFL got tougher on steroid use in 1989 when it announced that players would be suspended for four games the first time they were caught and suspended for the season the second time. Thirteen players tested positive. *18*

Last year, with the expanded testing program including unannounced, randomized sampling, three more players were caught using steroids and Carl Bax of the Tampa Bay Buccaneers was caught importing steroids for sale. All were suspended for four games. *19*

If the NFL really has suspended all the players it caught, then there is some indication that steroid use among professional football players is on the decline. *20*

"We live in a society where the end justifies the means," Lombardo said. "That is at the root of the problem with steroids." *21*

Staff writer Larry Thompson contributed to this report.

NFL STEROID TESTING PHASES
NFL players are tested in four phases. John A. Lombardo, NFL drug adviser for anabolic steroids, explained the stages.
■ *PRESEASON: Everyone on the team is tested and the date is announced.*
■ *IN-SEASON AND POSTSEASON: There is weekly, random testing, with Lombardo's computer selecting at random who is tested. The number of players chosen is also random.*
■ *OFFSEASON: The testing is set at irregular intervals determined by Lombardo. The selection of players is strictly random but the player is notified in advance (Lombardo would not specify how far in advance). "Most of these things [steroids] stay in the system for a long time," he said.*
■ *REASONABLE CAUSE: This is for players who have tested positive in the past. The test date is unannounced.*
—Mike Freeman

Topics for Discussion and Writing

1. The three articles present varying speculations about the percentage of pro football players who take, or have taken, performance-enhancing drugs. From your reading, what estimate seems reasonable to you? Why? Compare your viewpoint and your reasoning with those of others.

2. Based on your reading and thinking, what do you feel would be the most appropriate policy for the National Football League regarding the use of steroids, human growth hormone, and other such substances? Should testing of athletes be mandatory? Collaborate with a few others to write a report on this topic.

3. Use the articles and whatever other evidence you have to draw conclusions about the factors that push athletes to "cheat." In particular, think about all the people, including fans, who are implicated in the football player's drive to excel, even to the point of breaking laws.

4. Watch a telecast of a pro football game, including the advertisements. What kinds of things are said about the athletes? What is implied, even if not stated, about them? Do you feel that the telecasts, including the ads, subtly encourage drug-taking by athletes?

ELISABETH BUMILLER

"Junko Tabei: At the Peak of Her Profession"

> *"Today, Tabei is convinced she never could have climbed Everest if a man had been leading the group. . . . 'A woman is unsentimental about another woman's endurance. A man could never drive a woman to her limits.'"*

> *Elisabeth Bumiller (born 1956), a native of Aalborg, Denmark, grew up in Cincinnati, Ohio, and attended college and graduate school in journalism in Illinois and New York. She became a staff writer for the* Washington Post *in 1979.*

> *"I always wanted to report from overseas," she says in the introduction to her 1990 book,* May You Be the Mother of a Hundred Sons: A Journey Among the Women of India; *since 1985 she has lived her wish, first working in New Delhi and now reporting from Tokyo, where she met and interviewed Junko Tabei, the subject of the essay that follows.*

Before and as You Read

1. Do a cluster, mindmap, or list in response to the term *mountainclimbing*. (See Part One, chapter 2, for brief descriptions of these writing techniques, if necessary.) Write quickly; try to capture the images and feelings that come to you in response to the word. Use your responses as the basis of a reflective writing.

2. As you begin "At the Peak of Her Profession," observe how Bumiller's first paragraph presents issues that will be important in the rest of the article. Before you read on, mark terms that you feel Bumiller is using for shock value. Write down two or three questions that you would expect the article to answer for you, based on the first paragraph.

3. "At the Peak of her Profession" appeared in the "Style" section of the *Washington Post*. Among other features, "Style" typically includes book and movie reviews, interviews with celebrities, and profiles of people that *Post* readers are presumed to find interesting. As you read the article, consider how Bumiller tailors the portrait of Tabei for such a publication. From the way in which the article is written, what would you imagine to be some of the interests of "Style" readers?

4. Write about an adventure in which you engaged that required definite physical risk. Be sure to choose something that you did only because you wanted to, not something that you and others agreed needed to be done (for reasons of justice, for example) or something that occurred by accident. Why did you do it? (Be honest!) What happened? How did others react to what you'd done? Did you at any time regret your decision?

THE HOUSEWIFE from the suburbs of Tokyo was camped 22,000   *1*
feet up the slope of Mount Everest when the avalanche struck,
burying her in her sleeping bag under a jagged block of ice. "I couldn't move
at all in the snow," she remembers. "Suddenly, the image of my 3-year-old
daughter appeared before my eyes. For a short time I thought, 'If I die, what
will happen to her?' But then I thought, 'I have to stay alive—for my daughter,
for myself, for everybody.'"

She says she lost consciousness for six minutes, but was saved by the   *2*
Sherpas who dug her out. Some two months later, on May 16, 1975, at 12:35
p.m., Junko Tabei made history as the first woman in the world to reach the
top of Mount Everest. She was 35 years old, 4 feet 11 inches tall, and had
helped raise the $300,000 her women's expedition needed by giving piano
lessons in her home after school. When she reached the summit, she remembers, "there was no enjoyment—just relief. I was very, very happy that I didn't
have to climb any more." The first American woman to reach the top of
Everest, Stacy Allison, would not get there until 13 years later.

Since her triumph, Junko Tabei has climbed Mount Blanc in Europe,   *3*
Mount Kilimanjaro in Africa, Mount Aconcagua in Argentina and Mount
McKinley in Alaska. She also briefly interrupted her climbing schedule to
have another child. This winter, after scaling Vinson Massif in Antarctica, she
set a new world record as the first woman to climb the highest mountains on
six of the Earth's seven continents. To make it an even seven, a feat accomplished by perhaps a half-dozen men, she will have to conquer Australasia's
Mount Jaya in Indonesia, a mountain surrounded by jungle that is inhabited
by what H. Adams Carter, the editor of the *American Alpine Journal,* calls
"very primitive and sometimes very hostile people. It's not something you'd
do on the weekend."

But Junko Tabei would like to try, and is just waiting for Indonesia to   *4*
give her permission. Meanwhile, her biggest conquest may not have been
Everest as much as it was prevailing over one of the more sexist of the indus-
trialized nations. Once, when Tabei went to a Japanese corporate executive to
ask for funding, she was politely told it was impossible for a woman to climb
Mount Everest. "He told me to stay home and take care of my baby," she says.
Some of the neighbors have clucked that she is neglecting her children; Tabei's
husband, a supervisor at the Honda Motor Co. and an apparently saintlike
person who fully supports his wife's mountaineering, is at the end of the day
still a Japanese man who leaves his dishes in the sink.

Tabei's lifetime goal is to climb the highest mountain in each of the   *5*
169 countries in the world. Even in the Netherlands, where much of the
country is under water? "Even if it's small and even if it's flat, I don't care,"
she says. So far, her score is 21 countries down, 148 to go. She estimates
she'll be finished in 2020, when she's 80. If this seems a somewhat extreme
manifestation of the Japanese love of statistical achievement, Tabei is un-
daunted.

"Life is not forever," she says. "I don't think people should leave behind 6
a fortune, or things. When I die, I want to look back and know that my life
was interesting. I want to leave behind a personal history."

Moved by a Mountain

Monday morning, 10 a.m. Junko Tabei is at home in Kawagoe, a bed- 7
room town an hour and a half from Tokyo, and by all appearances she should
be losing her mind. Ever since her ascent of Everest she has been a celebrity
in Japan, and now, just back from Antarctica, there is a new rush of Japanese
press clamoring for attention. The phone rings every three minutes and the
fax machine hums. Tabei has no secretary, press agent or handler. Incredibly,
she answers every call herself, imploring each supplicant to phone back in
15 minutes. This goes on from morning until night. At the end of the day,
60 faxes will have piled up. "Receiving faxes makes me more tired than climbing mountains," she says.

Tabei looks like a librarian who took a wrong turn in Katmandu. She 8
has big glasses and bangs, and is dressed in a sweater made from a bright blue
and orange swatch of fabric she bought in Bhutan. Her house, a modest split-
level, is filled with the booty of her adventures: Tibetan rugs, a Bhutanese
wood carving on the front door, an Indian hanging from Kashmir, pictures of
her atop Annapurna and Everest, big bouquets of flowers from friends con-
gratulating her on her ascent of Vinson Massif. The ringing phone gives the
morning a certain frantic quality, but Tabei seems only moderately distracted.
She manages to steer some Darjeeling tea to the table and sit still long enough
to say that she grew up in rural Japan as the daughter of a small-time printer,
and was never interested in sports until she climbed a small mountain one day.
She was 10 years old, on a school class trip, and it changed her life.

"I began to understand there were so many places I knew nothing 9
about," she says.

She went to college in Tokyo, worked as an editor for a medical journal, 10
then married—all the while climbing Japanese mountains every time she got
the chance. In 1969 she organized a group of friends into the Ladies Climbing
Club, and the next year climbed Annapurna in Nepal. Buoyed by the trip,
Tabei set her sights on Everest.

"She can be a very hesitant and cautious person," says one of Tabei's 11
longtime climbing friends, Setsuko Kitamura. "But she knows how to set her
priorities. If she decides to do something, she'll do it."

Long Climb to the Top

Mount Everest looms 29,002 feet over the border of Nepal and Tibet, 12
a lethal slab of ice and rock that has tantalized climbers since it was first
opened to mountaineering in 1920. In 1924, the British climbers George

Leigh-Mallory and Andrew Irvine were last seen at about 28,000 feet; no one knows how far beyond that they got. In all, seven major expeditions tried and failed to conquer Everest until May 1953, when Sir Edmund Hillary and Tenzing Norgay of the British Everest Expedition at last reached the summit. (Hillary looked, but found no trace of Mallory and Irvine at the top.) "Nothing above us, a world below," Hillary later told the National Geographic in a play-by-play of the final ascent. "I feel no great elation at first, just relief and a sense of wonder. [Tenzing] throws his arms around my shoulders, and we thump each other, and there is very little we can say or need to say." Their feat caught the imagination of the world. Dwight Eisenhower honored the expedition members at the White House, and the next day, more than 7,000 people jammed two sessions of the "Everest lecture" that Hillary and his colleagues delivered at Constitution Hall.

Since then, there have been 349 successful ascents of Everest by 313   13 climbers. About 60 have been Sherpas, the local mountain guides. About 40 have been Americans and 14 have been women. Of those, Stacy Allison, the first American, was the seventh woman to reach the top; U.S. climbers say the relative slowness of American women in scaling Everest is more the result of bad weather and bad luck than of inability. At least 96 people have died climbing Everest. Today, there are about 12 Everest expeditions a year, and a years-long waiting list. The government of Nepal charges a "peak fee" of $4,000, which is among the least of an expedition's expenses.

Among elite Himalayan climbers, Everest does not have the cachet of   14 K2 in Pakistan or of Makalu in Nepal, the second and fourth highest mountains in the world, both of them far more technically difficult. But Everest's altitude is unforgiving.

"Above 26,000 feet, it's 90 percent mental and 10 percent physical," says   15 Barry Bishop, who was one of the first Americans to climb Everest, and whose 10 toes had to be amputated afterward because of frostbite. "Who gets to the summit and who doesn't is a question of whose mindset is ready for it. It's a never-never land up there. You're down to a third of the oxygen you receive at sea level. The human body can't stay alive up there indefinitely. Everything seems to be going in slow motion."

"Tenacity is the most important skill," agrees Glenn Porzak, the president   16 of the American Alpine Club, who has also climbed Everest. "At 28,000 feet, you're going on autopilot. Your senses are dulled, and you're feeling like hell. You haven't eaten well, and you haven't slept well. After a month, a lot of people can't stand it."

If Junko Tabei is anything, it's tenacious—a quality that would serve her   17 well in the long, frustrating years of planning leading up to Everest. After Annapurna, many of the women in the original Ladies Climbing Club got married, had children or lost interest, shrinking the Everest expedition to five. But Tabei knew she needed at least 15 members, given the expenses that had to be shared and the virtual certainty that half would drop out during the climb from sickness, altitude problems or exhaustion. So Tabei went recruiting, heading for the big Ueno and Shinjuku train stations in Tokyo where she knew Japanese climbers gathered before their weekend expeditions.

She found 15, and then the group set to work raising money. "Five of the expedition members washed windows after their regular jobs," she says. It soon became clear they needed major help. Pressed, Tabei allowed Nippon Television, one of the country's major networks, and the Yomiuri Shimbun, Japan's largest newspaper, to serve as sponsors—a deal that would later cause problems.   18

Tabei left Tokyo for Katmandu in mid-December 1974, leaving her daughter and husband in the care of her sister. She spent the next two months overseeing the transport of 15 tons of food and equipment from Katmandu to the trekking center of Lukla. From there, she hired 600 porters to carry it through forests of blue pine and rhododendron to the Everest Base Camp. By mid-March, all members of the expedition were in place, ready at the Base Camp at the foot of the Khumbu ice fall. For the next two months, the expedition slowly made its way to the top, from Camp I to Camp VI; Tabei's group, like all Everest expeditions, did not climb in a straight, steady line. Instead, it was a case of one step forward and two steps back—climbing up to establish Camp III one day, for example, then descending to Camp II to spend the night and the next day at rest. The gradual pace is essential for acclimatization at altitudes that provide the body with so little oxygen.   19

Although Tabei's expedition was made up of only women, Nippon TV and the Yomiuri had insisted on sending eight male climbers as photographers and cameramen, giving them complete access to the story they had bought. "It would have been much easier without them," Tabei says. "If you climb with men, there are so many troubles. The other women tended to listen to the men, even though I was the expedition leader. After the avalanche, I thought we could continue to climb. But one of the journalists said we shouldn't go on. I had to say, 'I am the leader, and I determine that—even if you are the sponsor.' I wanted to concentrate on climbing, and here I had to worry about these other issues. Since then, I haven't had sponsors. I'm much happier."   20

Tabei's final ascent of the summit took six hours; she was climbing with Ang Tsering, a Sherpa. "It was very steep and very sharp," she says. "The snow was very deep. I was carrying 20 kilos on my back—oxygen, camera, water, food." Climbers like to say that Everest saves the best for last when they come face to face with the last "knife's edge" ridge, with a vertical drop of 10,000 feet to the right, 8,000 to the left. "It was very difficult for me," Tabei says. "Each step required such a difficult technique." Ang Tsering reached the summit just three steps ahead of her. The two spent 50 minutes on top, took pictures, then descended.   21

When Tabei got back to Base Camp, there was a telegram from the prime minister of Japan. The King of Nepal gave her a medal and a parade   22 in Katmandu. In New Delhi, Indian Prime Minister Indira Gandhi, herself the mother of two, asked Tabei how she managed to climb mountains with a small child at home. "I told her I got a lot of cooperation from my husband," Tabei says. Back in Tokyo, a crowd of thousands welcomed her at the airport. Tabei, reunited after six months with her daughter, refused to feel guilty.

"I didn't want to have to tell her someday that because of her I couldn't   23
climb Mount Everest," she says. "My husband told me I'd never have such an opportunity again in my life, and not to worry about the family."

Today, Tabei is convinced she never could have climbed Everest if a man   24
had been leading the group. "If you go with only women, the physical conditions are the same—it's much more equal," she says. Or, as she told a reporter in 1984: "A woman is unsentimental about another woman's endurance. A man could never drive a woman to her limits. It was the other women members of the team who drove me on."

Typical Japanese Wife

Monday, two weeks later. Junko Tabei has been up since 5:30 a.m. She   25
gave her kids breakfast at 6:30, had two press interviews, then left home at 10 to catch a bullet train to the city of Sendai, north of Tokyo, for a lecture. These days, lecture fees—and bank loans—are her main method of paying for expeditions.

Back from Sendai, she stops for dinner in Tokyo, where, mercifully, there   26
is no phone to ring off the hook. From there she'll move on to a television station for an appearance on a midnight interview show. She won't be home until 2 a.m. Nonetheless, this morning she fixed a salad, soup and a meat sauce—with instructions to her husband to boil the pasta—so her family would have a nice dinner while she's gone.

"Working women are much better at using their time than full-time   27
housewives," she says. "My husband says I don't have to do this, but while I'm in Japan, I want to do my best."

Topics for Discussion and Writing

1. Elisabeth Bumiller gives Junko Tabei center stage in this story. As a third-person reporter, Bumiller doesn't write explicitly about herself; nevertheless, she sets the agenda for the story and she makes Tabei appear as she wants her to. What do you feel is Bumiller's point about Tabei? If there were a moral to this story, what do you think it should be? Compare your moral with that of others writing about the article.

2. What gives Junko Tabei her drive to conquer mountains? What does the article suggest about her motivation? What questions remain for you? If you were to interview her about her drive, what would you ask?

3. Review the article for generalizations or stereotypes about Japanese culture. What so-called Japanese values are noted in the article? Does Bumiller

assume that her readers already hold certain views of Japanese people? If so, where are these implied in the article?

4. Compare Junko Tabei with other athletes featured in this section of the book. How is she like them? How is she unique? How, in your view, is she admirable? How, to you, is she not to be admired? To place her in a very different context, compare her with people portrayed in other chapters, such as chapter 5.

BO JACKSON AND DICK SCHAAP

from *Bo Knows Bo*

"We never had enough food. But at least I could beat up other kids and steal their lunch money and buy myself something to eat. I could steal candy bars, too. But I couldn't steal a father."

Vincent "Bo" Jackson (born 1962) grew up in Bessemer, Alabama, as one of ten children raised by a mother whom Jackson described as "the only person who is stronger than I am—and more stubborn." A multisport star in high school, Jackson turned down a lucrative contract from the New York Yankees in favor of a scholarship from Auburn University, where he lettered in three sports and won college football's highest award, the Heisman Trophy, in his senior year. Because of his prodigious talent in both football and baseball, Jackson accepted pro offers in both sports and for three seasons performed at stellar levels in both, becoming during the late 1980s perhaps the most publicized athlete in the world. In 1990, however, not long after the publication of his autobiography, Bo Knows Bo, which we excerpt here, Jackson suffered a crippling hip injury in football that led to his leaving pro athletics for a time to devote himself to physical rehabilitation. Jackson, fabled in the media for his confidence and determination, has since returned to baseball as an outfielder with the Chicago White Sox.

Dick Schaap (born 1934) is best known as a sports columnist in newspapers, magazines, and on television, but he has written on a wide range of topics, including crime and politics, and has held prestigious editorial positions with The New York Herald Tribune, Sport *magazine, and* Newsweek. *He has coauthored numerous autobiographies of sports and entertainment celebrities.*

Before and as You Read

1. Write as much as you know or have heard about Bo Jackson, including, if possible, information about his childhood, his college athletic performance, and his work as a professional, including his persona on TV commercials. As you read the excerpt from *Bo Knows Bo*, note discrepancies between your portrait and his self-portrait. How do you account for the errors in your recollection?

2. Write about what you perceive to be the ethical pressures faced by the contemporary star athlete. What are the sources of pressure? What ethical decisions must be made? What factors make such decision-making difficult?

3. As you read "Set Your Goals High—And Don't Stop," mark all references to the various media and to jet travel and other elements of high technology. In what ways has Bo Jackson's career, particularly the decisions he has had to make, been shaped by modern technology? Consider both the benefits and drawbacks of these technological influences.

4. As of 1993, Bo Jackson has returned as a professional baseball player with the Chicago White Sox. Read recent newspaper and magazine articles

about Jackson and his team that help you create the present context into which to place your reading of this essay about Jackson's past.

I Couldn't Steal a Father

REMEMBER "THE Brady Bunch" from television? They were the perfect family. Everybody loved them. I hated them. I hated them because they had a mother *and* a father and enough food on the table for all of them.

We never had enough food. But at least I could beat on other kids and steal their lunch money and buy myself something to eat. I could steal candy bars, too. But I couldn't steal a father. I couldn't steal a father's hug when I needed one. I couldn't steal a father's ass-whipping when I needed one. I didn't have a man to look up to, or to listen to.

Biologically, I did have a father, of course. His name was—and is—A. D. Adams, and he used to work in the steel mills, like most of the men in Bessemer. He was my father and the father of two of my sisters. He was married, but not to my mother. He had his own family on the other side of town. He'd come by sometimes and give me a little money, but then I wouldn't see him again for months.

I lived with my mother and my brothers and sisters in a three-room house on a dirt road on the outskirts of town, in a rural neighborhood called Raimond. When I was born, we had all eight children living in the house. After my sister Millicent was born, we had nine living at home. That was the most. My oldest sister, Jennifer, moved to Chicago before my baby brother, Clarence, was born.

Nobody had a bed all for himself. We had two beds in the bedroom, and usually we'd sleep two to a bed, one at the top and one at the bottom. The rest of us would sleep on the floor. In the winter, we had a coal stove for the bedroom and a gas heater for the living room, and most of the time I tried to sleep right in front of the heater. Sometimes I'd wake up with burn marks on my butt where I bumped against the heater during the night.

The gas heater would warm the kitchen, too. There was no door between the living room and the kitchen, where my mom slept.

We didn't have indoor plumbing. Nobody did out in the country where we lived. We had an outhouse. When we got a new outhouse, we thought that was heaven. Kids came to see it: tarpaper roof, concrete floor, painted green, the same as our house.

Sometimes we didn't have anything to eat but grits and margarine. Sometimes we didn't have anything at all. I'd be home and not have anything to eat and then I'd go over to a friend's house and they'd have a nice dinner on the table, and they'd ask me do I want anything, and I had so much pride I'd say no, and my stomach would be singing a tune.

When I asked my mom why we didn't have a refrigerator full of food, why my Aunt Bea used to have to bring us leftovers from the school where she was a janitor, my mom used to say, "Well, I provide for all of you the best that I can, and you have to accept what you got, and be thankful for it." 9

I knew how hard my mom worked, but I wasn't thankful. I was angry. I was a hoodlum and a bully. I was the bad little Jackson kid—and foolish enough to be proud of it. When I watched "Sesame Street," my favorite character was Oscar, the grouch who lived in the garbage can. 10

I fired rocks through the windows of passing cars and I ran when they swerved off the road. I threw rocks at the heads of other kids, too—and I had a strong arm and good aim. I once beat on one of my cousins with a softball bat—one of my *girl* cousins. Twice I raised a loaded gun and aimed it at kids who had crossed me, and twice I came close to squeezing the trigger, to shooting them and probably destroying me. 11

My mom used to whip me with a cherry switch and warn me I was going to end up in the penitentiary, but I didn't mind the switch and I didn't hear the words. I knew I didn't have a father to answer to. 12

I used to take money from my mom. Most of the time, I just took pocket change, but once, when I was five years old, I found a gold envelope with a big word on it: INSURANCE. I opened it up and saw a bunch of bills and took it and went next door, to an old gutted-out house, and hid the envelope there. A few days later, I was playing with some of my friends, and I started bragging, "I got some money," and we went and got it—I think they gypped me out of most of it—and we walked about five miles to Burger King and stuffed ourselves. I don't know how my mom got the money to make her insurance payment, but she did. 13

She used to leave her purse lying on the floor next to her bed in the kitchen. Early in the morning, I'd crawl in, open her purse, grab a quarter or fifty cents, then crawl back to the living room and go to sleep. One morning, about six o'clock, she caught me. She just flipped over and said, "Don't you move. You keep your hands right there." 14

She lay back down till about seven-thirty and then she got up and tied me to the bedpost and wore my ass out. She whipped me good. She used the extension cord. When she was really angry, she used the extension cord instead of the cherry switch. The extension cord didn't break. It gave you welts that looked like somebody played tic-tac-toe on your back. 15

Some of my friends and I had a passion for stealing bicycles. We called ourselves The Bicycle Bandits. I could steal a bike, take it home and, within an hour and a half, strip the bike, throw it in a fire, burn the paint off, spray-paint it a different color and then ride it down the street, doing wheelies past the house I stole it from. I only got caught one time, and a couple of kids saw me get caught and laughed at me. I kicked their asses. 16

Kids wanted to be my friends just so I wouldn't beat them up. I was   17
hard on everybody who wasn't my friend. Keith Mack was my best friend. I
was envious of him—and not just because he had a father. His father was a
scoutmaster, and Keith and his brothers were the first kids in our neighborhood to have footballs and bikes and then go-carts and motorbikes.

I wanted to live the way the Macks did, and if I had, I probably never   18
would have gotten out of Bessemer. I'd probably still be there, like Keith is.
But I *had to* get out; he didn't. . . .

I used to talk at the Pepperell Elementary School in Opelika, tell the   19
kids that people who use drugs are crazy and people who use alcohol are crazy,
and I used to speak at the Helen Keller School for the Blind and Deaf in
Talladega, tell them about what I went through as a child. I also visited the
Girls' and Boys' Ranch in Auburn, a home for children who had been sexually
abused. The kids needed someone to teach them right from wrong, but more
important they needed someone who cared. I don't know how much I accomplished, but I cared. . . .

SET YOUR GOALS HIGH—AND DON'T STOP

. . . The day after I saw Jon Greenwood, I ran for more than 200 yards   20
against Southern Miss and scored two touchdowns. In our first six games, I
averaged more than 200 yards rushing a game, averaged two touchdowns a
game and had a pair of 76-yard runs. The only game in which I failed to
score, the only game in which I didn't gain even 100 yards, was the Tennessee
game, which was our only defeat in the first six games.

I strained my knee in the third quarter against Tennessee, and I remem-   21
bered the Texas game from the year before, when I kept playing after I banged
up my shoulder. If you play hurt, you get hurt worse. I took myself out of
the game. I let the coaches know my knee was hurting. I was healthy for our
next game.

Then, in our seventh game of the season, against Florida, I bruised my   22
thigh in the second quarter, bruised it bad enough to cause internal bleeding.
I sat out almost all the rest of the game. I tried to carry the ball once in the
fourth quarter, but I was just hurting the team and hurting myself.

The following week, the thigh was still bothering me, so after we built   23
a good lead in the first half against East Carolina, I sat out the second half. I
took a lot of crap for going out of three games.

The most ignorant comments were in *Sports Illustrated,* the kind of cheap   24
shots you'd get kicked out of the game for—if you were a player. Just to get
a few laughs, the writer made it sound like I was a coward who couldn't stand
pain and didn't care about winning. He was the worst asshole, but he wasn't

the only one. There were other writers and some fans, too, who questioned my courage, though I don't recall any of them who stood up and did it to my face.

Ninety percent of the people who attacked me never played football themselves, wouldn't even know how to hold a football. They were just showing their stupidity. I'll play banged up, I'll play in pain, but I'm not going to play to the point where I get permanently damaged—no way. *25*

When it's all said and done, when I'm sitting home, and limping, my knee torn up at the age of twenty-three, these sportswriters and these fans are still going to be up in the stands, ripping someone else. I know what my body can do and what my body can't do—I know better than anyone else—and I'm not going to go out and force my body to do some superhuman thing just to please a sportswriter. . . . *26*

A few days after my final Alabama game, the Auburn sports information office arranged for me to meet with the media, to talk about the Heisman Trophy. The winner was going to be announced in New York that Saturday. The Heisman is the most prestigious individual award in college football. *27*

The same day I faced the press, a group called Gifts, Inc., arranged for me to meet an eleven-year-old boy named Rusty. Gifts, Inc., granted wishes to children who were chronically or terminally ill or were the victims of child abuse. Rusty had leukemia. He was hoping to go to Seattle to have a bone marrow transplant. *28*

Rusty's wish was to meet me. He told me he also wished that I would win the Heisman Trophy. I wished I could have taken him hunting or fishing or swimming. I wished I could have shown him how to get in trouble, doing the things kids are supposed to do. It's so sad that kids like Rusty don't get a chance to see what the world is really like. Hospitals and needles and chemotherapy and doctors and nurses—that's all they know. *29*

Rusty helped me keep the Heisman in perspective. I wanted to win it, I wanted to win it very much, but if I didn't, I still had my health, I still had my family. There are so many things more important than honors and awards. *30*

I guess I'd been the favorite for the Heisman, the front-runner, until my last four games, until my stats fell off. I was one of four candidates who were brought to New York to be present for the announcement of the winner. It was being done on television—live. *31*

Two of the four finalists were quarterbacks—Chuck Long of Iowa and Vinny Testaverde of Miami. Two were tailbacks—me and Lorenzo White of Michigan State. Long and I were both seniors, and I was pretty sure that one of us was going to be the winner. *32*

We sat together, the four finalists, waiting to hear who'd won. The president of the Downtown Athletic Club, which presents the Heisman Trophy, stood up and said, "It's a pleasure to announce the winner of this year's Heisman Memorial Trophy. In the closest vote in the history of this trophy . . ." *33*

He paused. For about three days. I wasn't nervous—until then. It seemed *34* like an eternity. My heart started pounding so hard I thought everyone in the room could hear it.

". . . Bo Jackson of Auburn." *35*

I stood up, shook hands with the other players and accepted the trophy. *36* Then I called my mom. Everybody in the neighborhood was at her house, all my family, all my friends. They were having a party. I could hear the caps coming off the beer bottles. The party lasted through the night.

I stayed over in New York till Monday, and then when I flew back to *37* Auburn, I couldn't believe the crowd that was waiting for me outside Sewell Hall, the band playing, thousands of people cheering, standing on cars, waving banners, demanding that I give a speech. It was the most exciting moment of my four years at Auburn. "It's nice to get away from New York," I told the crowd. "It's too fast for me."

Linda sent me roses, and like a dumb ass, instead of going to celebrate *38* with her, I went out with my buddies. You name it, and I drank it that night. I'm glad all the kids I used to give talks to didn't see me. I was so drunk I passed out on the floor of a buddy's place. When I woke up in the morning, I was sick as a dog. That was the last time in my life I was drunk.

I recovered in time to go back to New York a few days later for the *39* Heisman dinner. I aimed my acceptance speech at young people. "Set your goals high," I told them, "and don't stop till you get there." I was wearing a tuxedo for the first time in my life, and I was in a room full of people wearing tuxedos, and I was scared. But I took my time and, even if I stuttered a little, I said what I wanted to say.

A few weeks later, we lost to Texas A&M in the Cotton Bowl, the only *40* bowl game we lost during my four college years. Then I played in the Japan Bowl, had a ball in Tokyo, my first and, so far, only trip overseas. The next week was the Senior Bowl, another all-star game, and they wanted me to fly from Japan to Los Angeles to Atlanta to Mobile and go right to practice.

"No, I'm going home," I said. "If I can't take a day or two to get over *41* this jet lag, I won't play."

I went home, then drove to Mobile. In the game, I broke away and *42* somebody ran me down and caught me from behind, I was so tired.

Everywhere I went, people wanted to know whether I was going to play *43* professional football or professional baseball. I told them the truth. I told them I didn't know. I told them I wasn't going to make up my mind until June, until I had finished my senior year at Auburn. "Money isn't the main thing," I kept saying. "Money can't buy happiness, and Bo Jackson wants to be happy." I told them the truth, and nobody believed me.

In February, I started getting ready for my senior baseball season. I was *44* really looking forward to it. We had a strong team, a powerful lineup. I got off to a slow start—I was batting only .246 through twenty games—but I was leading the team with seven home runs.

Then I got in trouble. *45*

The trouble started with a friend—I *thought* he was a friend—who was   46
acting as sort of an adviser to me. Not an agent, a family adviser. When I was
a teenager, I used to cut his lawn, and he used to pay me and give me little
gifts: a pair of cowboy boots, a stereo, a shotgun. He didn't ask for anything
in return. Then later, when I was in college, he said, "You ought to think
about letting me act as your agent." I didn't want to hurt him, I didn't want
to say no, so I just said, "I'll think about it."

All he was thinking about was him. He was just out for one thing: to   47
make money for himself. He tried to make a fool out of me.

There are plenty of vultures who are looking to take advantage of   48
athletes. Some of them are white, and some are black. Most of the athletes
who get taken advantage of are black. Maybe 95 percent of us grew up with
nothing, and so, when somebody says to us, "Hey, here's five hundred, here's
a thousand to hold you over, let me know if you need more and, oh yeah,
when you're ready to turn pro, I'll get you the best deal," we get sucked in,
too many of us. They con you and they fool you, and they get you locked in.

It's bad enough when it's white guys taking advantage of black athletes,   49
but to me, it's even worse when black guys do it:

"You should let a brother handle your business."   50

"Where'd you go to school, brother?"   51

"Well, I didn't exactly finish."   52

"You think I'm gonna allow somebody who didn't finish college to   53
handle my money? Man, get a real life! Stop mooching off people."

I had that conversation more than once.   54

The guy I thought was my friend told a lot of people that he was my   55
agent. He told the Tampa Bay Buccaneers that he was my agent. The Bucs
had the first choice in the National Football League draft. They had the first
pick because they won two games and lost fourteen in 1985, the worst record
in the NFL. Tampa Bay was thinking about making me their first choice.

The NFL draft was scheduled for the end of April. In March, my so-   56
called friend got together with the owner of the Bucs, Hugh Culverhouse,
and they arranged for me to fly to Tampa Bay in Culverhouse's private jet for
a physical examination. I was a little worried. I didn't want to violate any
NCAA or Southeastern Conference rules. I didn't want to lose my eligibility
in baseball.

My "friend" assured me that he and the Bucs had checked with the   57
NCAA and the SEC and there was no problem. "You're just going for a
physical," he said. "You're not signing anything. You're not getting any money.
It's perfectly okay. Trust me."

I trusted him. I trusted the Bucs. I took the ride in Culverhouse's jet,   58
took the physical and flew back to Auburn. A couple of days later, my baseball
coach, Hal Baird, asked me about the trip. "Did you go to Tampa Bay for a
physical?" he said.

"Yes, I did," I told him.   59

"I think they've declared you ineligible to play baseball," Coach Baird said. 60

That was it. My college baseball career—my college athletic career—was 61
over. I went behind the dugout and cried.

I think I know what happened. I don't know for sure, but I suspect my 62
"friend" made a deal with the Bucs—a you-get-Bo-to-come-down-to-
Tampa-and-here's-what's-in-it-for-you deal. Then, after I made the trip,
somebody—it could've been my "friend" or somebody associated with the
Bucs—called the SEC and told them about it. Somebody knew it was against
SEC rules. Somebody knew I'd be declared ineligible. Somebody *wanted* me
to be declared ineligible. Somebody thought I'd forget about baseball—I'd *have*
to forget about baseball—and Culverhouse would have me.

After I was declared ineligible, my "adviser" came to my room. "I don't 63
want to talk to you," I told him. "I don't want to see you."

"Well, if that's the case," he said, "you have to pay me back for all the 64
stuff I've given you."

I exploded. "Here's the boots, here's this, here's that, take it, take every- 65
thing, I don't want anything that reminds me of you," I said. "Just get the hell
out of here, and good riddance."

I hope I never see him again.   66

I was miserable not playing baseball. In April, not long before the NFL 67
draft, I accepted an invitation to visit a baseball team, the California Angels.
The Angels no longer had the right to sign me—that right automatically
expired when I returned to Auburn for my senior year—but they were still
interested in me. They wanted me to see a ball game—I had never been to a
major league baseball game, or to a regular season NFL game, for that matter—
and meet some of their people. They especially wanted me to meet Reggie
Jackson.

I never was much at following professional sports, and when I was 68
young, when Reggie was at his peak, I didn't know him from Adam, I just
knew he was a black guy who played for the Yankees and his last name was
Jackson. Because of his last name, I used to tell kids that he was my cousin.

Reggie wasn't my hero. I only had two heroes in my life: my mom and 69
Chuck Yeager. If I had gone into the military, instead of going into profes-
sional sports, I would've become a test pilot. I would've become a black Chuck
Yeager.

When I met Reggie Jackson in the spring of 1986, he told me that I 70
was in a great position. "You can play football and be the next Jim Brown,"
he said, "or you can play baseball and be the next Reggie Jackson."

I thought maybe he was trying to be funny. He wasn't. A few years later, 71
when I was with the Royals and he was in the last season of his career, he
said to me, "Baseball's been good to me, but I've been *great* to baseball."

He was serious. I just walked away. I was kind of sorry we had the same last name.

Everyone kept pressing me—football or baseball? Tampa Bay or the 72 minor leagues?—and I told everyone I didn't like buses, didn't like buses since I had to ride one to junior high, and I knew that you had to ride buses in baseball's minor leagues. But I also told everyone that I loved baseball, and I loved football, each in its own season, and I wasn't going to make my decision before June. When I say something, believe it.

I knew I needed someone to represent me. I wanted someone who was 73 smart and honest, someone I could trust. I went to the Auburn trustee who was the president of the Colonial Bank in Birmingham and I asked him for his advice. I respected his experience and his judgment. He recommended a law firm in Mobile. Richard Woods and Tommy Zieman worked for that firm. By the middle of April 1986, they were my lawyers.

I was lucky. With the right help, I picked the right people. Tommy 74 Zieman represented me just in the spring of 1986, but Richard Woods is still my lawyer. He went to Wesleyan University and to Alabama Law School. I respect his intelligence, and his opinions, and he respects mine. Susann McKee works for Richard. I've known her since I was a freshman at Auburn; her daughter was a friend of mine. Richard does all the legal work; Susann does a lot of the legwork. If I shoot a commercial, she's usually there; if I appear on a TV show, she's usually there. She's always reminding me of what I have to do, and where I have to be, and when. She stays in touch with Linda and with my mom, too. Susann cares about me, and so does Richard. They care about my kids, too.

My lawyers immediately made it clear to Tampa Bay—to Hugh Culver- 75 house—that I was seriously considering baseball as a career. Culverhouse didn't believe it. He said he'd talked with people in baseball and they'd told him I didn't have the talent. I don't know who he talked to. Maybe George Stein- brenner. Steinbrenner lives in Tampa. Maybe they're neighbors. (I'm thinking of building my permanent home in Florida, but I don't think I'll live in *that* neighborhood.)

Several NFL teams tried to persuade Tampa Bay to trade their number 76 one choice. The San Francisco 49ers were one of them. Before the NFL draft, I flew out to California, talked to a few baseball teams and talked to Bill Walsh, who was then the coach and general manager of the 49ers. I liked Walsh. "I'd love to play for you," I told him. Walsh tried to make a deal with Culverhouse—I heard he offered a package of players and draft choices, a good package—but Culverhouse said no.

If the 49ers had made the trade, if they had been able to draft me, I 77 probably would've gone right into football. I probably wouldn't have been able to resist. San Francisco is a special organization—they treat their players with respect—and by now, I'd have at least two Super Bowl rings, and maybe more.

Culverhouse turned everybody down. He had made up his mind. He was going to choose first, and he was going to choose me. 78

I wasn't happy about it. I didn't want to play for him. I didn't like what the Bucs had done to me, costing me my senior baseball season, and I didn't like Culverhouse's attitude toward me. And I really didn't want to play for a team as bad as Tampa Bay. I'd seen their offensive line. I didn't want to get beat up every week. 79

My lawyers started talking money, and Tampa Bay's first offer was insulting. "Tell Culverhouse I'm going to be the first player picked in the first round of the draft," I said to Richard, "and I think I should name my own price." 80

The Bucs came back with another offer, which wasn't much better than the first. "If you don't take this by Monday," they said, "we're going to cut it in half." 81

I told Richard and Tommy to tell them to go fuck themselves. "I won't play for Culverhouse," I said. "Unless he trades me, I'm not going to play football, not as long as Tampa Bay has the rights to me. When my name goes back in the draft, then I'll think about football again." 82

I suppose Tampa Bay could've made me an offer that I couldn't turn down, but I was still hoping they'd trade me. (I never *demanded* that they trade me; I didn't think that would do me any good.) The Bucs acted as if they still thought I'd come running to them. They figured the USFL was dead, and they were the only game in town. The only football game. 83

My lawyers kept looking into baseball. They checked, directly or indirectly, with guys like Kirk Gibson and Rick Leach and Steve Bartkowski, guys who'd had a choice of football or baseball, and almost to a man they said they were glad they chose baseball or wish they had. But of course none of them had won the Heisman Trophy. 84

Richard Woods talked to a lot of baseball teams, and I went to meet some of them, Kansas City and Toronto, for instance. The hard part was convincing people that I really was thinking about playing baseball. Everyone knew I could make more money right away by playing football, but if quick money was all I cared about, I would've signed with the Yankees in high school. I knew—and my advisers knew—that baseball, with a much higher pay scale and longer careers, could be more profitable in the long run. *If*—if I had big league talent. There never was any *if* in my mind. 85

When I went to visit Toronto, one of the Blue Jays' outfielders, Lloyd Moseby, saw me in the clubhouse and said, "I hear you're supposed to be pretty fast." 86

I kind of looked at him and nodded, and he reached into his locker and pulled out a stack of money, a thick stack—I don't know how much—and said, "I'll bet you I can beat you." 87

I didn't have any money, but no way I was going to back down. "Okay," I said. "You wear your cleats, and I'll wear my street shoes." 88

Moseby looked at me like I was crazy, then put his money back in his   *89*
locker. He shook his head. "I'm not running against nobody that cocky,"
he said.

A few baseball teams said that if I would commit myself to baseball,   *90*
they would pick me in the first round of the draft. They said they really
couldn't talk money up front, but one general manager said he'd pay me
$4 million for four years if I gave him my word I'd choose baseball.

I told him what I told everyone, that the size of the offer wouldn't be   *91*
the determining factor. What was important was what was going to make Bo
Jackson happy. I don't think anybody really believed me.

At the end of May, a month after the football draft and a few days before   *92*
the baseball draft, I went off to the Caribbean to do some scuba diving. I
had no phone, no television, nothing to do but dive down more than a hundred feet and stare at sharks and barracudas. It was a lot like negotiating with
Tampa Bay.

A few days after I returned to Auburn, the Kansas City Royals selected   *93*
me in the fourth round of the baseball draft. I was glad it was Kansas City. Of
the baseball teams I'd visited, I'd been most impressed by the Royals. The
world champion Royals.

Richard and I went to Memphis, the hometown of the new co-owner   *94*
of the Royals, Avron Fogelman. Like most people in baseball, Mr. Fogelman
thought I was probably going to play football. I was a known quantity in
football; I was a question mark to some people in baseball. I told Mr. Fogelman I really hadn't made up my mind, I wanted to hear his best offer. Then
I'd decide what was right for Bo Jackson.

Kansas City made its proposal, Tampa Bay made its proposal—and the   *95*
offers came down to this:

> If I chose Tampa Bay and football, I would be guaranteed $2 million—
> and I would probably earn more than $4 million in the next five
> years.
> If I chose Kansas City and baseball, I would be guaranteed $200,000—
> and I would probably earn no more than $1 million in the next
> three years.
> In addition, Nike wanted to sign me to an endorsement contract, and
> they offered to pay me several times more if I chose football than if
> I chose baseball.

On the basis of dollars and cents, I had to pick football.   *96*
Anyone would pick football.   *97*
I picked baseball.   *98*
Why? For a variety of simple reasons. I liked batting practice. I hated   *99*
football practice. I liked the idea of a long career. I hated the idea of a knee
injury. I liked Avron Fogelman. I hated Hugh Culverhouse.

And, of course, I loved to surprise people.   *100*

"Now it's time for what I love to do," I announced on June 21, 1986. *101*
"It's the first day of summer. Let's play ball!"

I never said I didn't love football, too. *102*

Topics for Discussion and Writing

1. *Bo Knows Bo* was written before Jackson's crippling injury, which he suffered in a pro football game. Does this injury make any aspects of the
   excerpt we've reprinted appear ironic to you? Explain. Conversely, are there
   aspects of the excerpt that indicate Jackson's awareness of, and preparation
   for, such a possibility?

2. One reason we read autobiography is to seek some identification between
   the subject and ourselves. Do you identify with Bo Jackson in certain ways?
   Explore these in writing. Do you feel that Jackson and Schaap, at least in
   this small excerpt, have crafted the book more to emphasize the subject's
   closeness to or distance from the reader? Explain.

3. Consider the effect of the writers' use of the first person (as is the nature
   of autobiography) instead of the use of the third person (typical of biography). Does it make you feel differently about Bo Jackson that he seems
   to be speaking rather than being spoken about? Choose a page of the
   excerpt and rewrite it as a third-person description of what Jackson does
   and thinks. Compare your rewrite with those of others. How does Bo
   Jackson appear differently in the different rewrites? How is the Bo Jackson
   of all the rewrites different from the Jackson of the autobiography?

4. Write about Jackson, as portrayed in this excerpt, as a possible role model
   for children. Do you feel that the first part of the excerpt, about Jackson's
   childhood, enhances his exemplary stature or detracts from it? In particular,
   how do you react to the violence shown both by the young Bo and by his
   mother? How would you explain this to a child who would like to "be
   like" Bo?

JAMES WASLEY

"Going Home a Winner"

> *"It was not a national title, we were not paid athletes, and we were not going to Disneyworld for our great triumph. No, we were just a bunch of guys who wanted to win, and also wanted to stay together, if only for one more week."*
>
> *James Wasley was a junior at George Mason University when he wrote this essay for Professor Terry Zawacki's course in advanced nonfiction writing.*

Before and as You Read

1. Write about the experience of winning. Describe an experience in which you as an individual or as a member of a team, not necessarily in athletics, won a competition. Recall your complex of emotions during and after the competition. How did winning itself compare with the anticipation or hope of winning?

2. Write about the team experience in athletics, either from your own background or through interviewing one or two members of teams. How can one remain an individual while also subordinating one's ego in the interests of team unity? Write about a time when you felt truly part of a collective effort, not necessarily in sports.

3. During athletic contests or other competitions, what happens to a person's concept of the opposition, those one competes against? Write about at least one relationship you have had with a person whom you competed against and whom you also regard as a friend. How did the competition affect your relationship?

4. As context for James Wasley's writing, research the typical lives of college athletes while in school. How much time do they devote to their sports during the school year? How many of the athletes on a team have athletic scholarships and how many do not? How do athletes balance their sports and their academic and other responsibilities?

WINNING. ON May 16 of this past spring, our baseball team from   1
George Mason University won the CAA championship. We had done all that winning stands for. We had to overcome our opponent, the University of Richmond, to win, 6 to 3. We had achieved something, proving we were the best baseball team out of the seven schools in the Colonial Athletic Association. I was even a part of the title, contributing throughout the season to help us along. Sure, it was only a conference championship. It was not a national title, we were not paid athletes, and we were not going to

Disneyworld for our great triumph. No, we were just a bunch of guys who wanted to win, and also wanted to stay together, if only for one more week.

The first game of our season was on February 23, but our practices 2 began in late August. This was where the first step towards winning, and the bonding of teammates, began. Every afternoon we spent hours on the field, working at baseball like it was our job. Built to win. The hitters took countless rounds of batting practice, swing after swing, enduring through blistered fingers and sore palms to improve their contact with the baseball. When they weren't inside the frayed nets of the batting cage, they were at their positions taking ground balls, hundreds a day. Keeping their bodies in front of them, taking balls off their chests and off their "cups." The pitchers threw in the bullpens and to hitters, trying to locate their fastballs in the strike zone, while also snapping off side-winding curveballs. As if a full afternoon of practice in the August humidity were not enough, the end of each day signaled our conditioning time. Running, sprinting until our jerseys were saturated with whatever our bodies had left in them.

This ritual was no different from any other fall season, but this year it 3 was done with a purpose. Our coaches, Skip, D-Man, and Wally, knew this was our year to win. We were a loaded gun, but they had to show us how to shoot straight. Our team had veteran and experienced starters at every position. Our catcher, Widge, was an All-American and received an invitation to the Olympic try outs. Besides Widge, we had Burr-Man, Puddin', T-Bone, Hammer, and Moony. All of them sparkled at the plate and in the field. We had some guys who could pitch too, like Scramble, Bubba, Eddie, Stump, and myself. To us, we were the best team ever assembled here. None of the other teams' coaches thought we would win though. They had all picked Old Dominion, East Carolina, and Richmond to be the best teams in the conference. We were the only one who expected us to win, which was fine.

When the spring semester began in January, so did our preseason prac- 4 tices. Everyone on the team knew each other by now. The veterans and rookies were no longer strangers in the same uniform. New friendships had been made, which is easy to do when you eat, live, and practice together daily. Each passing practice meant we were one day closer to the season, which was the only reason we practiced: to play. This year, we were playing to win.

We began sluggishly, opening the season 1 and 3. No one hit the panic 5 button because pretty soon we were 18 and 4. We had gone 4 and 1 on our Spring break trip, something we had never done before. The conference regular opened up and we found ourselves on top of that, another milestone we had never accomplished. We were in control now. Widge, Hammer, and Burr-Man were our offensive catalysts, hitting home runs, driving guys in, and stealing bases. We were unstoppable. Bring on the conference tournament, 'cause we're ready.

The regular season ended, with us the first place team. We had beaten 6 every team in the conference soundly, but anything could happen in the tournament. In previous years we would come off a see-saw season and explode in the tournament, pounding the opposition in the early rounds, only to fall in the end. That would all change this year, because now we knew how to win. Winning takes desire and heart. Talent isn't necessary, although we had plenty of it. It can sometimes be a burden. The team which is expected to win may start off slowly, not playing to its full potential. The team will press, try to make too much happen to atone for its earlier failures. It may hit a rhythm and showcase its full capabilities for a time, clicking and playing together fluidly, everyone pitching in to the winning effort. Once it has seen how good it can be, it gets big eyed, expecting to play its best the rest of the way. It can't. Winning can't be turned on like a switch. Winning comes from learning; learning to hate losing and failure and the miserable feelings that come along with them; learning to stand your ground when your opponent is fired up; learning to fight and claw your way back when it looked like the game was over once it began; learning to keep a lead against a team that is throwing its best hitters at you late in the game; learning to pick each other up, picking up the slack for a teammate who's having a rough game. We knew how to win by now. The only thing left was to do it.

In a double elimination tournament, the first game is the most impor- 7 tant. Winning keeps you out of the losers' bracket, where you have to win more games to get to the finals. We were ready for JMU, not overlooking them as if the game would be a cakewalk. We prevailed 6 to 4. Our beloved Richmond Spiders were next up in the semifinals. We hated them and our bats showed it with an 18 to 5 romping. One last piece was needed for the puzzle. We now had a day off before the finals, the day we had been waiting nine months for.

Richmond stayed alive in the losers bracket to play us for the champi- 8 onship. They needed to beat us twice to swipe the title out from under us. We laid back in the opener, forgetting how far we had come and how much we had sweated for this day to come. The Spiders took game one, 5 to 1. They had the momentum now. They no longer feared our hitters, like they had forgotten the beatings we had dished out to them. They wanted it.

Our season had come down to one game. We had a great year so far, 9 but now, one game would determine if our season was a great success or a great failure. One game. It didn't matter we had already set a school record for wins. It didn't matter we had beaten nationally ranked teams. Nothing would matter except the next nine innings. The seniors sat in the dugout, eyes wide open and lips closed tight, pondering the fact that a loss would mean their last college game ever. Going out on a loss while the other team paraded the field victoriously.

We jumped out to a 1 to 0 lead early, as if the electric paddles brought 10 us back to life. Our dugout was screaming. Those of us on the bench believed and our shouts were making the others believe too. I had no voice by the second inning, and didn't care. There was no tomorrow. The Spiders tied it up, but just as quickly we went up 3 to 1. We were gaining on it. They tied it at three, and now their dugout was emitting some vocal charges too. "Boys, this here is a Texas death match," Wally calmly said, with no worry or doubt in his tone.

The game was still tied in the eighth. Widge came up with two out and Hammer on second base. We all knew we had to score now, before Richmond could take control and steal our dream. Our dugout was muffled; Widge was our best hope of scoring. He launched a fly ball into left field. It carried. The outfielder ran back to the fence to catch it. We all sprinted from our benches to urge the ball on. Go, go. The fielder jumped up at the fence, leaping to keep the ball in the park. The ball went out inches above the outstretched leather of the fielder, a homerun. Yeah!

Their jugular had been cut and we knew it. All we needed now were outs. We tacked another run on in the ninth to go up 6 to 3. Three more outs. "Waz, go warm up." Eddie-T had been tying the Spiders in knots. I went to the pen in case he needed help. Ground ball, one out. I knew he wouldn't come up for air now. Pop fly, two outs. He's home free now, I thought. "One more out for the championship," Hammer yelled from second base, reminding all of the fielders we still had work left. Fly ball, Evvy is under it, AH!

When the last out was made, a pile of humanity formed on the infield of Harrington Field at East Carolina University. Our whole team was yelling, shouting loud enough to let every person in Greenville, North Carolina, know we had won. Smiling faces were seen in all directions. Guys hugged whoever they could grab, arms engulfing torsos, wrapping around, not wanting to let go of the smiling teammate in their arms, but wanting to move onto others whom they haven't yet embraced. A few tears fell to the grass too, the only perspiration our bodies had left. Even the coaches, who were trying their damnedest to look professional and under control, had to whoop it up and let some emotions out of their system.

"We did it!" was the most commonly heard scream of joy from people's mouths. "We're going on the bird baby!" was another common shout heard within the infield. We had never done that before either. Nobody on the team had made it past the conference tournament in their years here. I was hugging everyone within my reach. Nassty, one of the freshmen I had become good friends with, put his arms around me. "We did it. It's because of us we won it." I appreciated the thought, but also knew it was the effort of the whole team that made us succeed, not just us two pitchers.

Scramble was in sight and he jumped into my arms, lifting him up and laughing the whole time. Burkie jumped in and the three of us yelled and hollered about getting on a plane to an NCAA regional. We were already planning how we would celebrate together, and we hadn't left the field.

I had grabbed almost everyone when I saw Hammer. His eyes were raining but his face was smiling. We had been here through all the losing streaks. Each of us also had to overcome injuries to be here. By the time

Hammer and I hugged we were so exhausted from letting all of our steam out we just leaned against each other, happy to see our dream come true.

The pile was breaking up. Guys were walking to the gate to see parents and girlfriends still cheering for our victory. The cameras were unleashed on us all. Flashes went off all over the field. Guys were lining up in front of the lens and some were even focused through the watchful eye of a video camera. This was definitely a moment each of us would be reliving.   17

By the time we made it onto the bus, each of us looked like an unmade bed. We sat in our seats with the unremovable smiles still there. The bus smelled like our locker room and we loved it. Each of us knew this win was more than just a trophy and a ticket to a regional. We were champions for the first time, and for the first time we were not going to say goodbye to each other on a loss. Baseball is a cruel game to those who pour their hearts into it. When the season ends, we get in the bus and go home so tomorrow everyone can leave. You now have 24 hours before the team is broken up. Twenty-four hours to spend with the guys you've sweated on the practice field with, sat in smelly vans with and told jokes with, played card games on 12-hour bus trips with, gone to parties with, sat around and watched tv with, done everything on and off the field with for the past nine months. They'd be gone in one day because of a loss. Goodbyes are short. "Nice playing with you, man," will be said to someone you've known for 4 years and who will now be a memory.   18

That wasn't happening this year because we did not allow it to. This win was keeping us together to celebrate and drink in victory, and not the end of college careers and friendships. The seniors were going out in style, while the rookies knew how lucky they were to be here for this season. It no longer mattered what lay ahead for we were champions now, and always would be. As the bus pulled out of Harrington Field, a silence came over us. Everyone was thinking about how good this felt and how they were never going to forget winning, or each other.   19

Topics for Discussion and Writing

1. Describe the dominant tone of Wasley's writing. Mark terms or passages that convey this feeling to you. Where in his essay does he vary tone or change the mood? Mark places where this occurs and note how he moves from mood to mood.
2. Why does James Wasley want to go out a winner? Study the essay to determine your perspective on his motives. Compare Wasley's motives with those of Bo Jackson, as expressed in the previous selection. How do you account for the similarities and differences?
3. Study Wasley's comments about the demands of team play. Note that he frames the essay on team play with a narrative of his team's varying success during the season. Do you agree with his views on the role of team attitudes in bringing about success? Why? Use your response to these questions to revise your response to "Before and as You Read" topic 2.

4. Imagine that you are a player on the opposing team in this work. Write a brief essay, also entitled "Going Home a Winner," that describes the key game and your emotions as it unfolds. How crucial is the final score of the game in determining your attitude? (Note that Wasley's team lost in the first round of the ensuing regional playoffs, but that he chooses to end the piece with the conference championship game.)

JUDY OPPENHEIMER

from *Dreams of Glory*

> *"Only by writing, I knew, could I come to any real understanding."*
>
> *The sentence above comes from the Preface to* Dreams of Glory: A Mother's Season with Her Son's High School Football Team *(1991), Judy Oppenheimer's second book. Primarily a reporter and feature writer for newspapers and magazines, Oppenheimer's first book (1987) had been a literary biography of short story writer Shirley Jackson.*
>
> *We have reprinted here the Preface and part of Chapter Two of* Dreams of Glory.

Before and as You Read

1. If you have been an athlete, write about your parents' views of your participation in sports. How did you react to them when you were taking part in sports? How do you feel about their views now? If you are a parent, write about how you view your children's participation in athletics. What are your goals for your children as athletes? What seem to be their goals?

2. If applicable to your experience, write about coaches you have played for. If you have been a coach, write about your experience. What characteristics are needed by a good coach? What should be the coach's goals? In particular, how important is winning in comparison with other possible coaching goals?

3. In team sports, teamwork is obviously a prime value. Write about the benefits of teamwork not only in sports but also in other areas of life. For yourself, what has it meant to be a team player? Focus on an experience during which you felt conflict between your loyalty to a group and your sense of self.

4. If you like to read about sports, think about your favorite sportswriters. Identify two, and find some of their writing to analyze. List characteristics of the writing of each. How are they similar? How are they different? As you read this excerpt, note features of Oppenheimer's style. With which of your two favorites does she seem to have more in common?

PREFACE

I N THE fall of 1987, I had just completed my first book and was *1*
waiting anxiously for critical response. Walking along a suburban street on a warm Saturday afternoon, I fell rather easily into one of those pact-with-the-devil interior dialogues familiar, I imagine, to many first-time authors.

Let's see, said a voice from inside my brain craftily. You've finished the book. You want it to do well. In fact—why lie?—you would prefer that everyone who reads it loves it wildly, that it be received with a blast of critical acclaim, that it bring you fame—not just ordinary fame, but the sort that causes every person in the world who ever bought you a soda in the past to realize, with terrible poignancy, what a jewel they lost. That kind of fame. You want it. The question is, how much? 2

Would you (the voice pursued) prefer that the book do wonderfully, or that everyone you love has a happy, healthy life? Choose. 3

Happiness all around, of course, came the prompt response. Much too easy; a ridiculous choice. 4

Fine, we'll narrow it down, then. The book does well—or everyone in your immediate family has a good year? 5

Again, reaction was swift—the year, naturally. One good year for everyone was too much to give up. 6

Okay, the voice persisted, a bit testily. The book does well, or your oldest son, away at college for the first time, has an enjoyable first semester. Just that. 7

Another strikeout. Not even tempting. Hey, I'd spent eighteen years on him; naturally his welfare was going to be more important than my book, right? 8

By this time my husband and I were walking down the narrow path that led to the high school football stadium. We had gotten close enough to hear the band. ALL RIGHT, said the voice inside, now thoroughly disgusted. We'll make it real easy, okay? The book does well—or they win this game? 9

And to my amazement—to the complete shock of my entire system—the answer came roaring back, unmistakable. I WANT US TO WIN THIS GAME! 10

The force of that realization was almost physical; there was no underestimating its validity. What was going on here? Somehow, in some unknown way, a team of high school football players had become so important to me that I was willing to throw away my own success, at least figuratively, to ensure theirs. Not just willing—eager! There was no way to minimize that reaction. 11

I was not being swept away by the moment. We had not even reached the stadium yet; the band was barely audible. Nor was it mother ego. My own son, a first-year player, would be on the sidelines for the whole game, I knew. No, it was something else that had me in its grip, as fiercely powerful as it was mysterious. What the hell could it be? 12

And I knew then that I would have to find out. 13

There are those who grow up in homes where serious attention is given to lobbing, spiking, swinging, and dunking. I wasn't one of them. I had almost nothing to do with the world of sports as a kid; I was insulated by gender, by a largely female family—two sisters, six aunts, a mass of girl cousins—by the bookish atmosphere of my own home, and by the times themselves—the fifties. My mother had fond memories of basketball and tennis games she had 14 played in the thirties; by the late seventies, girls would once again start showing up on the fields. My age group fell between the cracks. Then, too, there was my own physiology: a case of scoliosis that kicked in at age twelve, a sudden awkward growth spurt at fourteen, that left me with even less grace than before. Which had not been much.

But there was something more subterranean at work, too, an attitude I   15
had somehow incorporated, a very real sense that such matters were not serious, not for real minds, not worthy of true attention. Or was it just that they were truly foreign, and so not for me, in the way junior cotillions were not? A lingering mind set, legacy of my Eastern European immigrant grandparents? For there were older members of the family, my grandmother, for instance, who still divvied up the world sharply into Jewish and non-Jewish sectors, and sports definitely fell in the latter category.

Whatever the reason, no baseball or football games ever poured out of   16
the console radio in our living room, or later, out of the small black and white TV. No RBIs or ERAs were discussed at our table. As long as I lived at home I never once attended a professional game of any kind. This was a world we did not move in, which therefore, in the inherent logic of childhood, did not exist.

Right away I think of an exception. My aunt and uncle in Queens had   17
allowed, even encouraged, their children to catch the baseball fever rampant in their city. Perhaps surer of their place, Jews who had not settled in the diaspora of suburban Northern Virginia, as we had, and perhaps, also, because they had finally produced a son, they did attend to scores and sports announcers, and one summer day I even went with my cousin Ellen to the Polo Grounds to watch the New York Giants. The experience elated me: I was entranced by the green turf, the bat's crack, the soaring ball, even while feeling like an imposter. My knowledge of the game was slight, but the scene itself charged me with emotion, an excitement similar to the one I would later feel watching Elvis appear on television. There was a danger, a freedom, a force at work here, and yes, it did have a sexual—or at any rate, highly male—component. For a time I even attempted, self-consciously, to attend to scores and ratings, but this interest withered quickly back home.

Other than that one small frisson, though, the door seemed permanently   18
closed to a world I never thought I wanted or missed. I attended a few high school games, rarely even glancing at the field—for me these were social events only. In college my post-Beat pre-hippie circle viewed all sports and sportsmen with contempt, and if any whiff of sour grapes emanated from the intense young men I knew, I was not the one to recognize it. Eventually I did begin to notice that most men seemed to like to watch football games, but this I took as one of those inexplicable quirks of the sex. Actually I did not believe for a minute they really enjoyed them; I was cynically sure this was something they felt they had to do, for peculiar Freudian reasons best left unexplored. Sports remained a mystery—not one I had any interest in piercing, not one I ever expected I would. By the time I reached adulthood, my own opinions

were solidly in place: athletes were fools, nonintellectuals, macho jerks. Sports were ridiculous. Parents who cheered themselves hoarse at games, getting vicarious thrills, were especially repulsive.

Then life, as it often does, threw me a curve. I gave birth to boys, not girls. Yes, I raised them in that supremely feminist-conscious decade the seventies, doing my best to introduce them to dolls and peace toys and artistic pursuits. And no, it didn't make any difference. I gave birth to boys; inevitably, sports began to seep into my life. I found myself at hockey arenas, basketball courts, baseball stadiums. It wasn't my idea, of course; it was theirs. Left to my own devices, I would have continued wheeling them through art galleries, as I had when they were tiny and compliant—but what parent is ever left to her own devices? *19*

So we went to games. And the realization began to grow—slowly, slowly—that there might be something to this stuff after all. Standing at one arena or another, the roars of the crowd washing over me, I found myself responding almost despite myself to the pure drama of the thing, the way each event followed a familiar pattern, yet was fraught with endless possibilities—for heroics, for tragedy—like the best theater. Of course, none of this was personal—yet. But that was coming. *20*

Both my boys were active youngsters, but Toby, the younger, seemed to have an especial zest for the physical right from the start. At four months he wore out the springs on his baby jumper; at nine months he was climbing up the table, to the stove, to the top of the refrigerator, regularly and relentlessly. Jesse, my older, loved to listen to me read books aloud. With Toby, I was literally forced to act them out with him strenuously, if I wanted to keep his attention. Both boys enjoyed the tire swing in our backyard, but only Toby spent an entire summer on it—he was three at the time, and accuracy forces me to add, stark naked. *21*

There was no question of hyperactivity—amazingly, since those were the years they were pinning that label on everyone. No, the kid just liked to keep moving. What was most striking though was the amount of control he seemed to have over his body. Even as our hearts jumped to our throats, several times a day, watching or grabbing for him, it finally began to dawn on us that he almost never got hurt. He seemed to go at nearly every physical endeavor with a kind of inherent grace. Not quite two, he grabbed a Frisbee for the first time and, ignoring our instructions, sent it flying in a perfect arc. When, a few months later, he picked up a whiffle-ball bat, we stared at each other in shock. Feet apart, knees bent, he had automatically assumed a perfect batter's stance. *22*

What was going on here? Unlikely as it seemed, impossible as it seemed, had we produced some kind of . . . athlete? *23*

With that realization, my entire prejudice against sports began to crumble. Within a few short years I was standing on a soccer field making an utter fool of myself, screaming my head off in the best tradition. What had happened? It was obvious even to me. Toby had thrown open the door to a world *24*

I had never known I missed. All along, it seemed, I had been missing it like crazy.

My husband, it is important to mention, did not react like this, not at all. A sedentary man, he enjoyed throwing an occasional ball to his sons, he watched sports on television with them, he could now and then be persuaded to attend a baseball game. But he regarded my enthusiasm for Toby's personal athletic involvement with distaste—his wife, who had passed herself off for years as a serious, thoughtful person, had apparently been harboring a secret all this time. What she'd really wanted, it turned out, was to be a cheerleader.

Yet this reaction bothered me not at all. For I knew my enthusiasm to be oddly impersonal, in a way. I enjoyed, tremendously, discovering this energetic new world and was grateful to Toby for opening the gate. After all, I had begun to realize by now that this was a major perk of parenthood: children took you places you had never been before. You were a fool, I figured, not to enjoy the ride.

At the same time, though, I knew I had no deep urge to see Toby on the cover of *Sports Illustrated*. I had seen too many parents taken over by their kids' talents to a dangerous degree. A boy down the street was being groomed to be a tennis champion, daily and arduously. Sports were fun in their place, that was enough. Toby was a warm, open, delightful kid; sports were a part of his joy, and I enjoyed sharing it. But serious?

Over the years I cheered his soccer, basketball, and baseball endeavors. Yet I knew he was a team animal, quintessentially—practically the only physical activities he avoided were running, biking, and swimming, activities generally done alone. So perhaps it was not a complete surprise that he finally gravitated, quite late, at age sixteen, to the king of all team sports: football.

Football, however, was another matter. Football terrified me. Everything I had ever felt about sports, pre-motherhood, went triple for football. My revulsion, my distaste, my horror, all ran deeper. I had never taken the kids to football games; I didn't even like to be around when my husband and sons occasionally watched them on TV, venting the horribly coarse, macho noises the game seemed to demand. Football was not an arena for casual enjoyment, for joy. Football was a sport for killers. I had always been glad we lived in a suburb, Chevy Chase, Maryland, where most families steered their kids firmly toward soccer when they were growing up; far fewer played Peewee football, which was viewed by many with suspicion, if not contempt, a sport with a brutish, even blue-collar, cast to it. A person could get hurt doing that. As my *bubbe* would have put it, what does a Jewish person need with football?

Soccer and baseball were fun; football had always struck me as a grim and joyless business. All that bulky equipment, all those tense bodies smashing into each other with such lethal purpose. What would playing such a game do to my child? What would happen to that warm and joyous spirit out there on that killing field?

But at sixteen, already six feet two inches tall, Toby was no longer a child—that was obvious. When he announced his intention to try out for the team at Bethesda-Chevy Chase High School, urged on by one of his closest friends, Billy Stone, a veteran player, we were faced, yet again, with one of parenthood's most difficult and constant balancing acts: the eternal seesaw between protective urges (we'd always had more than our share) and the desire to see one's child emerge as an independent being. In the end, teeth clenched, we voted for independence.

Nervous, edgy, I showed up each week that first season to see the games, getting my first close look at the sport I'd despised for forty-five years. And in the process, of course—human perversity being what it is—discovered what I really felt. No way to dodge it—I was insane about football. More than soccer, more than basketball, more than any sport I had ever come in contact with, I purely adored the entire wild, maddened, electric, power-pumping totality of this game. Football unleashed something primitive buried deep inside me, something that had obviously always been there, waiting to spring to life. A coach would later tell me at length about the need to unearth the buried animal when training players, the animal that lies dormant in our soul. Well, football released my animal, too. Even that epiphany should have come as no surprise, really—I had known from the start that this game exerted a powerful pull on my heart. *32*

I had no illusions that this was the same force that had fueled my pleasure standing on soccer sidelines for so many years. No, there was something darker and infinitely more powerful about this enthusiasm; it swept you up, took you over completely. And yet my reaction did not come as a total surprise. More than midway through the journey of our life, years into the humbling thicket of parenthood, I suppose I had finally come to acknowledge the terrible truism: while what you despise may not *always* be what you secretly love, it is invariably a big mistake not to cover the bet. *33*

And the truth was, Toby's first year on the team made it easy on us. Yes, us, because to my amazement, my husband too seemed suddenly interested; no one had to beg him to go to games anymore. As a first-year player, our son was rarely on the field; his safety seemed insured. I could yell and scream for harder hits, rougher play, to my heart's content—hey, it wasn't my kid out there. *34*

But all the time, throughout the 1987 season and the rest of the school year, I could hear the muffled drums drawing closer. His time, I knew, was coming. The next season, my son, too, would be on the line. *35*

And I wanted him there! That was the most shocking part. I wanted to see him big, looming, triumphant—the warrior. What scared me was that God was going to punish me for taking pleasure in his risks, but what chilled me even more was something else. If this was how I was about football, how would it be if one of my sons were marching into combat? Along with the icy horror, would I also feel a heart-leaping thrill? Good God, would it turn out after all this time that I loved war too? The famous scene from *Patton* swam in my head—the one where the general kisses a fallen soldier on the battlefield, saying huskily, "I love it more than life." Repulsive, I had thought *36* at the time—or at least, had *thought* I thought. Was Patton, of all people, going to turn out to be *mon semblable, mon frère?* If so, I was in real trouble.

My embrace of sports, but particularly football, and most particularly this coming season, had led me finally to this pass . . . murky waters, indeed. I found myself feeling deeply jealous of other parents of team players—both those who were frankly opposed to their sons' playing and those who were frankly, unapologetically, excited and happy. Only I, it seemed, was caught up in the barbed wire of ambivalence, twisting slowly in the wind. 37

I needed to examine more closely both my own feelings about the game and its effect on all involved—coaches, parents, and boys. 38

Particularly the boys. For over the years I had been raising my own sons, I had come to realize something—that sports, in some bone-deep, almost mythic, way, has much to do with what forms a man. True, only a handful of boys play football, basketball, or baseball, even in high school—but this does not matter. The sports ethic is in the language they speak, the air they breathe, the business and professional arenas they enter. Aware or not, players or not, their views of themselves and the world are formed by sports. 39

And I wanted to know how that worked, to know more about this process, and the ways it changed and affected men. For it had, I had come to realize, affected them all. 40

Shortly before the football season began, my father told me a story. As a young teenager in the late twenties, he had lived with his older sister in the Bronx for a year, attending Yeshiva classes. The schedule was grueling, with a school day that ended at nightfall, too late for play. But every morning, my father and a few of his friends gathered early, before six o'clock, to play baseball in a neighborhood sandlot. Once and only once, up at bat, he hit the ball with the pure, total impact of a perfect slice. It rose high in the air, cleared the fence, and dropped to the gray dawn streets far below. 41

That was over sixty years ago. Yet sometimes still even now, when he is drifting off to sleep, he has a sharp vision. He sees the ball coming toward him again, he swings, he hears the crack of that connection, sees the ball arc high in the air, out of sight. Peace falls over him. He sleeps. 42

My father has never in his adult life participated in a sport. He has rarely attended a professional game. He is a learned man who nurtured learning in his daughters, imprinting each of us with a deep respect for the life of the mind, in part because we knew this was his world, and we loved him. It was his world, true enough. But it was not, as it turns out, the whole story. 43

Yet my father never told me about that one moment until I was middle-aged—and the mother of a football player. Maybe he thought that would help me understand certain things—why he never missed one of his grandson's games, why he took such pleasure watching him play. Or maybe not. He simply handed me the story without comment; another piece of the puzzle. A piece I had not known was missing. 44

For it had never been just sports that was a mystery to me growing up . . . it was men as well. And in an odd way, I had always been loath to 45 pierce that veil, too. Mystery can fuel romance, even passion; mystery lends itself to endless Heathcliff-Cathy scenarios, and I had certainly done my share of howling on the moors. But the time had come. My sons had been babies, then little boys, but the years had passed, their bodies had lengthened and hardened, childhood had ebbed. They were landing on another shore now, one I still, after all the years of marriage and motherhood, knew little about. They were becoming men. It was time, past time, to learn something about that world.

I was determined to start. I would spend the next season, the season of 1988, with my son's team, the B-CC Barons, watching carefully, a visitor to a foreign land, talking to coaches, parents, but most of all to the boys. Attending, noting, recording the changes they went through on the way to becoming football players—and the changes I went through myself. I would listen, learn, and then write about all of it. Only by writing, I knew, could I come to any real understanding.   46

Once the idea had seized me, I became obsessed, talking about it to everyone. There was only one negative reaction, but unfortunately, it came from Toby. "Mom, the locker room? You'll be in the locker room?" he groaned. He had a point, and I knew it; how could I do that to him? Liberation or no, freedom of the press or not, what seventeen-year-old wants his mother hanging around a locker room? Years ago his brother, then ten, saw a piece I had written in *The Village Voice,* liberally sprinkled with his quotes; he was enraged. "You do that again and you pay me—that's me in there, not you," he said with icy dignity. And I knew he was right. Using your kids in your writing could be a form of betrayal . . . could be, well, using your kids. No writer can completely avoid using the people she knows and loves in her work, but it's a fine line, always. When does use become abuse? If Toby felt that strongly, I would respect his wishes.   47

Months went by; the season got under way, with myself in close attendance, working for the Booster Club, getting to know the parents, coaches, and boys, hanging around the field with elaborate casualness, even—I couldn't help it—taking notes, a little furtively. I was, I had to admit, consumed by this idea still, despite Toby's opposition. Who knew? Perhaps when he was forty, he would change his mind.   48

It happened long before that, however. "If you're still interested in doing that book, it's okay now," he said casually one day. Still interested? It was, in fact, the only thing I wanted to do.   49

Certainly it was a challenge—one that made me feel anxious, fearful, and thrilled. I was going to chart the progress of a season, of boys becoming players. I had a quick vision of myself being lowered, in a Jacques Cousteau sort of bubble, to the bottom of the sea. It was unknown territory I was descending into, without question. But it was a voyage I had been moving toward for years.   50

It was not until I was well on my way that I realized that the boys themselves had a name for this process I was trying to learn about so avidly, a   51 name for the entire alchemy involved in becoming a football player—and more. A name so fitting there was no way I could ever have improved on it. They call it "being the man."

CHAPTER ONE

. . . Standing in the small gym—the large gym was for everyone else— forced inside by the rain, viewing the players lined up in front of him, Bob Plante grimaced, his lip curling upward automatically. If these were the prospective offensive linemen, he had his work cut out for him. 52

The first three days of two-a-days had been a chaotic, bureaucratic blur—making sure everyone's medical forms were in, issuing uniforms and helmets, taking the kids through conditioning drills. No hitting—that was the rule, in the county. You had to spend a few days getting the guys in shape before you let them loose. Didn't want any of the little babies passing out on you in the heat. Of course, a few of them had started sneaking in an occasional solid whack or two by the second day—when they were supposed to be just walking through plays—and by the third day, nearly all of them had smashed into someone at least once. Couldn't stop kids from hitting completely. But still, that was the rule. 53

Today was the first day they could legally go all-out, and none too soon, either. It was also the first time Bob had had a chance to isolate the offensive linemen and take a good, hard look at them. It wasn't exactly a cause for joy. Most of them weren't even that big, and the ones who were—Erik Karlson, only a junior, barely out of nursery school; Alex Burgess, center, the only veteran, huge, but so badly out of shape he could hardly squat—Christ, the kid must be carrying 320 pounds! And then there were the lightweights, like Tae Uk Kim. Good God, how were these kids supposed to do anything on a line? Toby Oppenheimer—the kid was big enough, but Jesus, he looked so knocked out he could barely stand straight; it was obvious, too, that he knew absolutely nothing about the game. 54

They were a sorry bunch, that was for sure. Bob had spent the last forty-five minutes stalking up and down, observing them, as they struggled to stay in one of three football stances—two point, three point, four point—knees bent, helmet UP—five minutes at a time. It was a good way to see who was in shape and who wasn't, and he had his answer—no one. Christ, Burgess had barely lasted thirty minutes before he stumbled out of the room, retching, his overstuffed buddy Dimarlo Duvall, a black kid, following close behind. 55

The thing about the offensive line—Bob knew this well—it wasn't a glory position. Important, yes; as the old saw had it, the game was won in the trenches; or, as Pete put it, the horses pull the plow. Glorious, no. The glory went to the skill men, the quarterbacks, running backs, wide receivers. 56

Defense was another matter—that was where you had your fucking lu- *57*
natics, guys who ripped heads off. A player could really let it all out in defense.
Most football players who wanted to be real men wanted to play defense, and
Bob could hardly blame them. Hell, he loved defense himself.

For the offensive line, you needed more control—it was the one place *58*
on the team, the way Bob saw it, where a dorky, slow-moving guy could
do well. Your lesser athlete. Linemen were clumsy, they lacked that special
grace that made a quarterback or a wide receiver; these were your meat-and-
potatoes guys. Quieter, too—you could be in a room with one and not know
it. Not your best-looking guys, either, usually; more the back-of-the-rack
type. "Take a look around you, men," he would tell them in a few days.
"These are all the guys who won't be going to homecoming this year."

He knew what he wanted in a lineman, what he looked for. "I'd prefer *59*
him to be ugly, spend a lot of time in the weight room, be quiet, shy, and just
have murderous tendencies. That's what makes a great offensive lineman. The
kind of guy who's quiet, doesn't say much, but if you really got him mad he
might pull an M-60 on you." Once you got one, of course, it was up to the
coach to motivate him.

And how did you motivate an offensive lineman? Ah, that was where it *60*
got interesting—at least to Bob Plante, who was a keen student of management techniques. The offensive lineman wasn't going to hear the crowd roaring for one of his blocks; he wasn't going to get his name announced over the
loudspeaker; he wasn't going to have his picture in the local newspaper, the
Montgomery County Journal. So what did you do?

What you did first was isolate them. The offensive line was a team within *61*
a team, operating on its own, pretty much independent from everybody else.
Anything you could do to underscore that was a boost. That's why he had
them back here, in the small gym, even though it was at least 20 degrees hotter
than the main gym, which was no picnic either. It was also why he'd urge
them in the coming days to stay together as much as possible. "I want you
guys to hang out together, eat together, drink together." "If he'd had his
choice, I think we would have slept together," said one kid. The idea was to
forge a unit—strong, tight, impenetrable. More than a unit: an identity.

It boiled down to one thing, basically—the lineman was going to have *62*
to do it for the line itself, for pride, for his sense of himself as a man, and for
his coach. Especially for his coach. So it was extremely important to be the
right kind of coach.

The way Bob saw it, there were three different types. There was the *63*
camp counselor, the buddy-buddy, let-me-help-you, I-want-you-to-love-me
coach—a coach like Pete White, to tell the truth. Then there were the nuts-
and-bolts guys—the eggheads, all numbers and chalk talk, Tom Landry types,
the kind players never really loved.

Then there was the third kind, his kind—the romantics, the warrior *64*
types, the Pattons. Guys were scared to death of them, but they respected
them, too. Like the coach he'd had in high school, Tom George. The guy was

incredible; Bob still remembered the greatest speech he'd ever made. It had been two words long.

"We were in a 7-7 tie. And he didn't come in the locker room at half time. We were waiting and waiting. What's going on, where is he? Finally the ref came in and said, 'Let's go, boys, you got to get out on the field.' And just before we all left he walked in and just said, 'We *will*.' That was it: 'We *will*.' And he walked out. 65

"We charged out. We were so pumped, we ended up winning, 21-7." 66

A true romantic, Tom George. All football players were romantics at heart, and so were the best coaches, Bob thought. "I guarantee you, if we went back to Renaissance days, the Knights of the Round Table, those knights would be the best football players ... in the arena, with the women in the stand waving handkerchiefs, the men on the field with their gear going into combat." 67

That was the kind of coach he wanted to be. Of course, you had to keep a certain distance from the kids in order to pull it off, but that was okay. Bob believed there should be clear lines between coaches and players; that was how you got true leadership. "I'm Mr. Enigma, I don't want you to know me," he would tell his troops in the coming days. You let the lines down, you left the gate open for mutiny, and Bob wanted none of that. "A player does it my way or highway. When Coach Plante says jump, all he wants to hear is how high?" 68

Drama, theatrics, control, that was the ticket. Well, it was up to him now to assume the mantle. 69

Bob stalked down the length of the room one more time while the boys sat on the floor, recovering. He was ready to start the process. "Gentlemen," he said in clear, cold tones, "I want to talk to you about something important for each of you to know—what makes a pussy. Are you a pussy? Are all of you pussies? Do you want to be a pussy? That's what we gotta know right now. 70

"A man is born a fucking pussy. You either are a pussy or you're not; there's no other way. Now, we saw that in wartime. In Nam. In wartime the pussies came out—they showed themselves. Nonpussies kicked ass; they killed some gooks. They were men. Pussies were pussies. 71

"In football, gentlemen, you're either a fucking pussy or you're not. It's as simple as that. You think about that right now. Any of you want to be pussies? Do you?" 72

His eyes moved up and down the group; they were listening, all right. Burgess, Oppenheimer, all of them. Motivation—that was the key. And he was going to make it work. 73

Alex Burgess was listening intently. The way Bob Plante was stalking up and down the line—arrogant, assured, totally in control—reminded him of his favorite scene from his favorite movie, *Patton*. Taking charge—leadership— a man who could lead other men, that was what fascinated Alex about football; about the line—and about the military, too. He had been reading books 74 on military strategy since he was a kid; he wanted to be a career military officer. His father had been a career officer in the Navy. The funny thing was, his father had almost no use for football, though he came to the games. He thought sports were silly; men acting macho. Alex guessed that maybe when you'd seen the real thing—watched enough of your friends get blown to bits—you lost patience with games. It was his mother who loved it—she'd come to the games and scream like a banshee. You could always hear her, too, since she had such a powerful voice, she was a singer. Even before he'd played, she used to watch football on TV. His father would drive her nuts by asking her what inning it was. Different types, all right; divorced now, several years.

What his father couldn't see was that football could be a good training ground for someone like himself, who was interested in leadership. He wasn't one of those guys who had always had a burning need to play the game, like Geoff, who lived for it. Actually, he'd gotten into it for one reason only: to lose weight. But it wasn't long before he'd realized that football was a damn good leadership-training arena. And this year, when he'd be the head guy on the line, should be very interesting indeed. | 75

Alex listened carefully, taking mental notes. The guy was good; he was going at it the right way. Alex approved. He might be able to use some of this speech himself sometime. | 76

Toby was listening too. He had already been the target of Bob's scorn. It was sad but true, as Coach White said, that if you're bigger, more is expected of you. And Toby was big, nearly six-three. But so far he hadn't shown much strength. | 77

On the inside, he'd made a decision that day to take an enormous risk, but nobody knew about that. | 78

He'd gone to school all summer long, straight through: two sessions, advanced algebra and chemistry, six full weeks. There wasn't any choice, not if he wanted to play football. He had to bring up his grades. He had done the crime, spent the spring quarter having fun and letting his grades go to hell, so he would do the time, even if it meant missing any vacation at all, sticking around when his family cleared out to go to the beach. Not that he'd been happy about it—when he first learned he'd have to go, he'd grabbed an old guitar, gone outside, and swung it against the brick wall until it exploded in a thousand chips. When his mom yelled at him to stop, he'd been firm. "I just need to smash something, then I'll be okay." And of course, he was, as he had known he'd be—once he'd gotten out his anger, he was ready to do what he had to do. | 79

Last year had been his first season ever; his friends had talked him into going out. Then, on the night before two-a-days started he had broken his toe in a pickup softball game. He had spent almost the entire season on the sidelines; it wasn't until a late-season scrimmage that they saw he might be able to do them some good. Coach White had said it at the football banquet, when he announced his name to the audience: "We think this big guy might be able to help us out next season." | 80

So he'd pushed himself with summer school, getting more and more   81
exhausted, until he found out about the mono. Even after that, he'd kept
pushing, getting up, going to school, barely conscious. You had to—one day's
absence from summer school meant an automatic fail. Then a few weeks
before two-a-days started, he'd gone to the doctor he'd known all his life, a
doctor who had played football himself, someone he'd thought would understand. The guy wouldn't budge an inch. No playing for another five weeks.
Even his mom had felt bad about that, tried to intervene. She knew the kind
of summer he'd spent.

"He has an enlarged spleen; it could burst," the doctor told me when I   82
called, seeking leniency for my son. His voice rose. "I am not performing an
emergency splenectomy on this kid! No way—five weeks is the absolute
minimum."

"At least you'll be able to play during the season. It's just training you'll   83
miss," I told Toby comfortingly, I thought.

Just training—the proving ground, the make-your-bones arena. Just   84
training, with hungry juniors eyeing any free position, straining for a chance
to jump into the breach. Some comfort. What did I know?

The doctor's warning ringing in his ears ("He didn't just tell me, he gave   85
me a half-hour lecture"), Toby went to practice and sat out. For two days. It
felt awful. "I was getting glimpses of the previous year, with my toe, and
watching people run around and hit, sitting there like an asshole again—I had
heard rumors I was up for a position on the defense or offense line, and now
I was watching eleventh-graders trying to take my spot. . . ."

And so he made his decision. "I just said to myself, it's my spleen—it's   86
my spleen. It's not my mother's spleen, it's not the doctor's spleen, it's my
spleen and I'll do what I want with it."

With cold purpose, he strapped on his shoulder pads, strapped on his leg   87
pads, and entered the fray. He had made his choice (one I would not know
about until most of the season was over). Good or bad, crazy or sane, it was
his; he was taking responsibility for his own body. In a way, it felt like he was
taking over the reins of his own life for the first time.

But barely recovered mono victims make lousy football players, so Toby   88
was not impressing anyone right now. "Bag of pus," Bob Plante had snarled at
him outside earlier, the first time he saw him try to block. Along with pussies,
it was his favorite expression, the boys would learn, soon to be abbreviated to
"bopper."

"We thought we'd seen signs of goodness in Toby, back there at the end   89
of last season, but Bob wasn't around then," Pete said. Well, he was now, and
what he was seeing wasn't exactly the sort of thing that made him jump up
and down. Alex, Dimarlo, Toby—all of them looked ready to croak any
minute. But they were listening, all right.

"Gentlemen, it's as simple as this—there ain't no place in football for a   90
fucking pussy." He glared at them all. Yeah, he had 'em; he was going to take

this sorry bunch and turn them into his own little hit squad, sure enough. "Now tell me, all of you—are you pussies?" he roared. . . .

Topics for Discussion and Writing

1. React to Oppenheimer's growing realization of her feelings about football. How does she explain the change she experienced? How do you feel about it? Do you in any way identify with her experience? Are you in any way repelled by her new outlook? Explore these ideas in writing.

2. React to the section about Alex Burgess and his parents. What do you feel is the connection, if any, between football (or a sport with which you are more familiar) and leadership skill outside athletics? With which of the three—Alex, his mother, or his father—do you tend to agree most? Why?

3. React to the pep talk by Bob Plante. Do you react differently as a reader of this book than if you had been a player in that locker room? Try to imagine yourself present as a parent in that setting, as Judy Oppenheimer was. How would you have felt? What might you have said to Plante, or thought about saying? Do you feel that his reasons justify what he says?

4. Think about what Judy Oppenheimer tries to achieve in this book. Could you imagine yourself doing something similar (for example, openly investigating an environment usually off limits to a member of your gender)? What do you think of her ambition? What do you think of the results, at least as excerpted here?

ATHLETES AND AIDS

> *"They're out there [people with AIDS]. Ten years, 12 years, 14 years. They come up to me all the time and introduce themselves."*

On November 7, 1991, pro basketball superstar Earvin "Magic" Johnson revealed in a press conference that he had contracted the AIDS virus, and that he was therefore retiring from the Los Angeles Lakers, for whom he had played a dozen years. His announcement occasioned more public concern about the spread of the AIDS epidemic than any previous revelation by a celebrity because of Johnson's international reputation as a role model for athletes and for the young. Public-spirited, committed to racial harmony, generous to fans and colleagues, prudent and far-sighted in business dealings, he had earned an esteem from all strata of society that is granted to few athletes.

Since his announcement, Johnson has honored a demanding schedule of public hearings and appearances at schools and other community forums to argue for increased funding for AIDS research and treatment, as well as to lecture young people on how the disease is transmitted and to warn them against sexual promiscuity (to which he himself has admitted). He has remained in the headlines because of his decision to come out of retirement to play on the U.S. Olympic basketball team, which captured the gold medal, and to consider returning to the Lakers. (After a brief return to the Lakers, Johnson retired again in fall 1992 in response to other players' fears about the remote chance of their contracting the disease through contact during games.)

We've reprinted Johnson's post-Olympics interview with Sports Illustrated's *Jack McCallum, as well as two interpretive reports by* Washington Post *sportswriters Allison Muscatine and Michael Wilbon that appeared at the time of Johnson's announcement that he had contracted AIDS.*

Before and as You Read

1. Use your library's newspaper and periodical files to find articles and editorials about Magic Johnson's November 7, 1991, announcement. On what features of his press conference did individual articles concentrate? What generalizations, if any, did articles make about athletes? Do these generalizations seem fair to you? Why or why not?

2. If you are familiar to any extent with Magic Johnson's career and his reputation through the press and TV, write your feelings about him. Do you recall your feelings changing about him after his announcement? Write about its effect on you. Consider also the meaning for you of his attempt to make a professional comeback. As you read the Muscatine article, reflect on your own feelings about Johnson as you consider her thesis about the impact of athletes' illnesses.

3. An old song says: "You've got to be a football hero / To get along with the beautiful girls." As we've explored the athlete's "drive to excel," we've not to this point emphasized sexual motivation, though it could be argued that

such motivation is implicit in every story we've included. Before you read Michael Wilbon's essay, write about both your experience of this motivation in your own athletic endeavors and about the sexual attractiveness of athletes. What factors contribute to this allure?

4. As you read the three articles, compare the "voices" of McCallum, Muscatine, and Wilbon. Which of the three do you feel you learn the most about from how they construct their articles? Why?

EARVIN JOHNSON AND JACK McCALLUM

"I'm Still Strong"

SPORTS ILLUSTRATED: Let's cut to the chase. What's your time-table for making a decision to return to the NBA? And has the Dream Team experience been substantial enough for you to judge your ability to return to pro basketball? *1*

Magic Johnson: I'll make a decision probably about a month or three weeks after I get back home. The practices, workouts and games have been enough to tell me that, yes, basketballwise, everything is fine. So it will come down to a medical decision. I will meet with my doctors, get my physical, listen to what they have to say and talk it over with my wife. *2*

SI: Is owning a team still in your thinking? *3*

MJ: By all means. I'm meeting with [NBA commissioner] David Stern in September to talk about that. *4*

SI: You can't be a player-owner, is that correct? *5*

MJ: David Stern has told me that it's not allowed. It would have been nice to be the first man to be a player-owner, but it's not something I had counted on much. *6*

SI: On the court, have you performed better, worse or about the way you thought you would? *7*

MJ: I've performed the way I expected. All the while I was away from the NBA I kept myself in shape and I kept my timing, and I'm still strong. *8*

SI: In any way are you any better as a player for having missed last season? *9*

MJ: Yes. I'm healthier and stronger. During an NBA season, when you might play all the way to June, your body doesn't have a chance to recover. You might get one thing fixed, but then something else is still a problem. But this year I obviously didn't have to deal with that. And I started on a serious weight-training program, and I feel anywhere from 70 to 100 percent better. *10*

SI: Could you explain the state of your health right now, specifically regarding the HIV virus? *11*

MJ: My T-cell count is up; that is, it's higher and better than before I   12
found out I had the virus. T cells help you fight off colds, flu, different things
you come down with. What the virus does is beat up those T cells, and that
causes you to get AIDS, because you don't have a healthy immune system. As
long as your T-cell count is good, you are beating the disease.

SI: Your fight against the virus essentially consists of daily doses of   13
AZT, healthy diet. . . .

MJ: I take my medication. I watch my diet—which has not been quite   14
as easy over here as it is at home—I rest, I work out.

SI: I notice you always say "medication" rather than "AZT." Why is   15
that?

MJ: Everybody knows about the AZT, but I don't like to get specific   16
about it because then, with some people, I get bogged down in talking about
the way I'm fighting off AIDS. See, everybody's got a cure.

SI: Do people try to give you offbeat cures?   17

MJ: Oh, all the time, all the time. Things you wouldn't believe, a hun-   18
dred cures, a thousand cures. They send them to me, they give them to me,
they send them to my office. Somebody not long ago sent a jar of what looked
like milk that was two or three months old and said, "If you drink this, you'll
get better." Can you imagine actually trying that from somebody you don't
know? Somebody else suggested that I drink all my blood and replace it with
warm blood. I have a whole pile of these "cures" in my office back home.

SI: During All-Star weekend last February you talked about how many   19
people have been living with either the virus or the disease for a long time.
Do you still meet them?

MJ: They're out there. Ten years, 12 years, 14 years. They come up to   20
me all the time and introduce themselves.

SI: People with the virus or with full-blown AIDS?   21

MJ: Both. Look at Elizabeth Glaser [the wife of actor-director Paul   22
Michael Glaser; she contracted the disease after a blood transfusion]. She's had
[the virus] for 11 years, but she won't give in. She keeps going and going and
going. She is a model for me and should be for anyone with any disease. And
that type of I'm-going-to-fight-it attitude is the most important thing. That's
my Number One weapon, too.

SI: One of your goals was to make people forget that an HIV-positive   23
player is on the court when you are competing. Do you think you've
succeeded?

MJ: I know I have. Nobody has said anything about it since I've been   24
over here.

SI: Is anyone on the U.S. team curious about the disease, and are you   25
asked questions about it?

MJ: John Stockton asked me about it early, when we were in La Jolla   26
[the California site of the Dream Team's pre-Olympic training]. He was curious about what it took to fight it off, and we talked a long time about it. I
had already talked to Michael [Jordan] about it and a couple of the others I

know well, like Clyde Drexler. But by this time I think everybody on the team is pretty educated, and we don't have to talk about it. I had a long conversation with Karl Malone a few nights ago, but it was about other things.

SI: I would guess that such conversations must be enjoyable, because *27* you don't have a chance to do them with these guys during the regular season, right?

MJ: It's been the best thing about this Olympic experience. I didn't *28* know, for example, how much Karl was into business and that he had used me, the way I've done things, as his model. David [Robinson] and I talk about religion, and he's told me things I didn't know about the Bible. Patrick Ewing's sense of humor is something I never noticed before. And there's not a day goes by that Michael and I don't do something together, or at least talk for a long time.

SI: Before you came over here, I think most people would have thought *29* that Jordan was, on a world scale, a more popular athlete than you. But it hasn't developed that way. During your stay in Monte Carlo before the Olympics and here in Spain, you clearly have been the more popular. Have you been able to analyze the phenomenon and does it go beyond fans recognizing your fight against AIDS?

MJ: [Shakes his head for a long time.] I agree that, yes, Michael was *30* more popular and well known. It's strange, it really is. I think, first of all, a lot of people didn't think I was going to be here. That's what was being written, mostly in Europe. So when they saw me, they were really happy, for me and for themselves. What happened is that people missed seeing my style, the passes, the fakes and all that. Michael and these guys played for a whole season, but I'm getting welcomed back in a way. And then, you know what else it is? Everybody wants me to smile. Everybody. I'll hear that in my sleep. "Ma-jeek! Ma-jeek! Please smile for me. Smile for the camera." And as you know, I've always been able to smile.

SI: Has the attention made you feel good? *31*

MJ: Real good. Real, real good. Marching in the opening ceremonies *32* was one of the wildest, most incredible things that ever happened to me. Everybody running over, breaking lines to get an autograph, a picture or to just shake my hand, I never thought that would happen. Never. We're used to attention, but I just couldn't believe that that many athletes from that many countries would want to meet me.

SI: You seemed to earn a lot of points by marching. Michael and the *33* two other players from the 1984 team, Ewing and Chris Mullin, did not. You said that you understood their decision, but I'm wondering if you would march if you came to the Olympics again.

MJ: Being me, yes, I probably would. But everybody's different. Mi- *34* chael wants to play golf, and I like to go to events. Going to sporting events, you've got to understand, is a big part of my life. You know what I'm looking forward to? The start of the football season. I'll be going to all the Los Angeles Raider games and other games. I like being out, and Michael doesn't. You can't put a guy down for having a different opinion on it. And we don't talk about that at all. That's the best part of our relationship. We can enjoy each other's success and not worry about the fact that we handle it differently. I understand that he makes more money than I do, and that's great. He understands that I get something out of being in public and things like that. There is no jealousy, absolutely none.

SI: You've always been a leader, and from the beginning, you seized the reins of this team. That isn't surprising, but what is a little surprising is that everyone seems to have accepted it, Michael included, Larry Bird included, Karl Malone included. Why has it developed like that? *35*

MJ: I just feel comfortable in that role, even on a team of superstars like this one, and I'm not sure that anyone else does. Larry could certainly be a leader, but he just doesn't want it that much. And I think the players have confidence that I won't steer them wrong, that I'll bring them the right information. *36*

SI: What's an example of something you've had to decide as a team? *37*

MJ: We've been invited by everybody to everything, 10 things a day, every day. A millionaire wanted us to come to dinner, so I got the guys together for a vote. *38*

SI: Did you go? *39*

MJ: No. They wanted suit and tie. [Laughs.] Anybody who wants us in suit and tie can forget it. I just come up with things for us to do. Going as a group to the women's game, for example. I got it organized, talked about the times, saw who wanted to go. *40*

SI: Does the criticism you guys have received about staying in a plush hotel, some of it from USOC president-elect LeRoy Walker, hurt? *41*

MJ: It hurts a lot. And what makes me mad is that these guys haven't come to see what the facts are, they haven't done their homework. They should have gone someplace with us or just walked around and seen the people outside the hotel that we talk to and sign autographs for. When we leave the hotel, it's like the pope is leaving. It surprises me every time I see it. That's what we're dealing with all the time, every minute of the day. So don't just make accusations about us without getting to know the situation. *42*

SI: The circumstances that led to the attention the Dream Team is getting this year—do you think they'll be present again in 1996 or 2000? *43*

MJ: No. We have grabbed the world in a way that won't happen again. The excitement of the fans, the excitement of the other players who don't care how bad you beat them as long as they get a picture. And I don't think you'll have 12 guys together like this, either, 12 guys with big egos who have put them aside. *44*

SI: Was the ego thing a worry for you coming in here? And when did you know that everything was going to be O.K.? *45*

MJ: It was my biggest worry. And I'll tell you exactly when we came together—after the young guys [the college development team selected to scrimmage the Olympic team in La Jolla] crushed us in that practice scrim- *46* mage. The next day, instead of anyone blaming anyone, we all just came together and said, "Let's go, let's show them what the NBA is all about." And we did. After that it was easy.

SI: Returning once more to next season, you made an offhand comment in Monte Carlo about the possibility of playing for another team. Just to make things clear, there is no scenario, except a trade, by which you could be playing for any other team than the Lakers, correct? *47*

MJ: If they want to go in a different direction—young, building for the future—then maybe that's not the team for me. I have been with the Lakers when they always wanted to win the championship, always tried to get the pieces they needed to do that. It would be hard to play for them if they didn't want to go after the championship. *48*

SI: Do I detect a lot of concern on your part that the Lakers have decided to become a "team of the future" rather than a championship contender? *49*

MJ: I don't know that. I haven't talked to [general manager] Jerry West in any great detail. I did talk to [team owner] Dr. Buss when the story came out that made it sound like I was looking to play somewhere else. [Laughs.] He made sure he called me. I hope that if I play it's with the Lakers. *50*

SI: Another thing to clear up: There was some discussion recently that if you came back, you would limit yourself to, say, only 65 games or 68 games. Is that part of your thinking? *51*

MJ: Naturally, I wouldn't like it. But I've got to listen to what my doctor says. He just got back from a big AIDS summit and has all kinds of new information. We will sit down sometime in September and discuss all of it. *52*

SI: In essence, you're a study group of one six-foot-nine-inch world-class athlete with the AIDS virus who is trying to come back and play a grueling sport. *53*

MJ: Well, I guess I am. But there's got to be a first, right? *54*

ALLISON MUSCATINE

"Magic's Revelation Transcends Sports"

BEFORE HE died of a rare form of paralysis in 1941, baseball player Lou Gehrig was known as "the Iron Horse." His death at age 37 so moved the entire nation that the disease that killed him was named for him. *1*

Roberto Clemente, the great Pittsburgh Pirates outfielder, died on New Year's Eve in 1972 in a plane crash while on a humanitarian mission to help earthquake victims in Nicaragua. Only 38 when he died, Clemente's tragedy cast a pall far beyond his native Puerto Rico. *2*

And then there was the shocking death of University of Maryland basketball player Len Bias, who died in June 1986 of a cocaine overdose two days *3* after the Boston Celtics picked him second overall in the NBA draft. Overnight, his mother, Lonise, was transformed into a national spokeswoman about drug abuse. Her son's death at age 22 helped awaken a slumbering public about the problems of drugs and young people.

Now we are stunned again, this time by news that one of the world's 4 most popular and most visible athletes, basketball superstar Magic Johnson, has contracted the AIDS virus. Is there anyone in America who isn't talking about it?

Tragedies that befall athletes seem to penetrate the American consciousness 5 more than any others, unleashing a wave of emotion and shock that crosses class, race, gender and generational lines. Most people, it seems, know and love Magic. Now, it seems, most people are worried about him.

"It's their youth, those astonishingly powerful bodies, the sense of youth 6 and immortality that because of television is ever more fixed in our minds," said David Halberstam, a Pulitzer Prize-winning journalist and author of numerous books, including ones about basketball, baseball and rowing. "It's someone who makes his or her living by dint of physical activity and achievement, and then we see them struck down in their prime."

Todd Gitlin, a sociologist at the University of California at Berkeley, 7 said Johnson's case has captured the public's imagination because athletes are among the few celebrities universally loved by the public. "There are very few figures in modern society who are famous and don't have enemies," Gitlin said. "And who, at the same time, embody some virtue, some talent, some charm, some larger-than-life humanity which many people feel embody their best selves."

Celebrities from various walks of life have reminded us over the years 8 that no one, however rich or famous, is immune to tragedy. Former First Lady Betty Ford's candid disclosure of her problems with alcoholism provided comfort and solace to millions of families who had experienced similar pain and shame. And movie star Rock Hudson's death from AIDS signaled that a disease often associated with those out of the mainstream—gays, minorities, drug users—could also strike down a Hollywood legend.

But despite their celebrity status in American society, neither Betty Ford 9 nor Rock Hudson ever touched our collective psyche the way Magic Johnson did when he appeared at a news conference in Inglewood, Calif. on Thursday and in typical good humor announced that he had tested positive for HIV, which causes AIDS.

"Even with what we know about athletes and the stories we've read 10 about them, they are still heroes," said Jim Frey, a sports sociologist at the University of Nevada-Las Vegas. "When one falls off the pedestal, it devastates us."

The affection reserved for athletes is part of a national folklore that 11 distinguishes them from other celebrities and makes sports a more binding activity in our culture than any other. We only know actors and actresses through the characters they play, and musicians through the music they create.

CAREERS SHORTENED BY ILLNESS
AUTO RACING
- *Tim Richmond, NASCAR driver (AIDS)*

BASEBALL
- *Ernie Bonham, Pitt. Pirates (appendectomy complications)*
- *Harry Agganis, Boston Red Sox (pneumonia)*
- *Dave Dravecky, San Francisco Giants (cancer)*
- *Lou Gehrig, N.Y. Yankees (amyotrophic lateral sclerosis)*
- *Dick Howser, manager, Kansas City Royals (cancer)*
- *Fred Hutchinson, manager, Cincinnati Reds (cancer)*
- *J.R. Richard, Houston Astros (stroke)*

BASKETBALL
- *Magic Johnson, L.A. Lakers (HIV)*
- *Johnny Moore, San Antonio Spurs (desert fever)*

FOOTBALL
- *Sal Aunese, University of Colorado (cancer)*
- *Ernie Davis, Syracuse University (leukemia)*
- *Dick Jorgensen, NFL referee (cancer)*
- *Doug Kotar, N.Y. Giants (cancer)*
- *Dan Lloyd, N.Y. Giants (cancer)*
- *Vince Lombardi, coach, Green Bay-Washington (cancer)*
- *Karl Nelson, N.Y. Giants (cancer)*
- *Brian Piccolo, Chicago Bears (cancer)*
- *Joe Roth, California (cancer)*
- *John Tuggle, N.Y. Giants (cancer)*
- *Bob Waters, coach, Western Carolina (Lou Gehrig's disease)*

VOLLEYBALL
- *Flo Hyman, U.S. Olympic team (Marfan syndrome)*

We may envy politicians for their power, but we don't necessarily like or trust them. We often admire businessmen for their wealth and success, but we don't see them on television and probably wouldn't recognize their faces on the street.

12 Athletes, by contrast, are right there in front of us, performing feats that most Americans—young and old—wish they could do too.

13 "I don't know a person yet who wouldn't change places with some athlete at sometime in their life, whether it's Chris Evert or Michael Jordan," said former tennis star Arthur Ashe. "They're the objects of fantasy and fantasizing, so when something happens to them, something happens to us too. It makes us more aware of our own mortality."

14 This is not to say that every athlete who succumbs to tragedy captures

our hearts. Football player Don Rogers died of a cocaine overdose a few days after Bias, but his death caused only a ripple by comparison. Several athletes, including former Washington Redskins tight end Jerry Smith and race car driver Tim Richmond, died with AIDS and there was little public commotion over their deaths. New York Yankees catcher Thurman Munson lost his life in a plane crash, a sad event that nonetheless lacked the resonance of Clemente's tragedy.

Johnson's experience seems likely to eclipse them all. With the initial reports of Johnson's illness, many found themselves recalling the impact of the news that John F. Kennedy and Martin Luther King Jr. had been killed.   15

"I don't even think the hostages in Iran brought out this sort of senti-   16
ment," Gitlin said, adding that the nation has been "obsessed" with news about Johnson. As in the case of Gehrig, whose emotional farewell in Yankee Stadium in 1939 has been replayed on television over the decades, Johnson's experience is of "iconic enormity," Gitlin said. "There is the same sort of resonance, the curtailment of the apparent immortality of someone great."

The reason is that, while athletes in general are symbols of energy and   17
vitality, Johnson is even more so. Everything about him is alive. His smile. His zest for the game. His fascination with business. His countless good deeds for those less fortunate. And his nearly unprecedented acceptance across racial lines. Now, in the face of a frightening and mysterious disease, he awaits an uncertain fate that underscores his vulnerability and shatters our notions.

"This is a tragedy that relates to the physical self," said Allen Guttmann,   18
a professor of American studies at Amherst College who has written several sports books. "Physical feats are what athletes do. That's why they're famous. Here is a 6-foot-9 athlete of tremendous physical ability who is doomed to disintegrate physically. And he's so young."

MICHAEL WILBON

"Available at Your Peril" (*Washington Post,* November 10, 1991)

EVERY AUTUMN in Dallas, the NBA convenes a mandatory orien-   1
tation seminar for rookies, during which the league's newest players are counseled on drugs, media relations and how to cope with the day-to-day rigors of a preposterous travel schedule. Mundane stuff, most of it, except the part where actresses are brought in to pose as groupies or hookers and play out the seduction of a jock.

Sex and sports are as inseparable as the pick and roll. If you're a profes-   2
sional male athlete, sex in any form is available in virtually any hotel or nightclub 24 hours a day, 365 days a year. Given that, until Earvin Johnson's revelation Thursday that he has the AIDS virus, many of us wondered aloud

how it was that high-profile athletes seem to have escaped the AIDS epidemic for so long.

If you've ever left an NBA arena late, real late, say an hour after the game is over, or followed a team back to the hotel and seen the literally dozens of women waiting outside both locker rooms, you understand that players don't have to go looking for sex; it's staring most of them in the face.

Whenever the athletes are not inside a stadium or arena, women (and sometimes men) of all ages, races and nationalities make it known they are available—maybe for a price, maybe not. And, as you might imagine, the phrase "Just Say No" usually isn't one of the first thoughts that crosses a guy's mind.

Twenty years ago, when Wilt Chamberlain was only at, say, 10,000 partners and counting, promiscuity, even on the all-pro level, was no more risky than reminding a team physician to pack some extra penicillin. That was before herpes and AIDS threw up a flashing yellow light that too many are running through without caution.

Sports reflects what's going on everywhere else in America, multiplied by 100. Magic Johnson might be the first, but he unfortunately won't be the last. HIV and AIDS have long incubation periods. A lot of rich, talented, well-conditioned athletes went to bed Thursday night scared to death. And with good reason for the many who have figured: "If a condom is available, fine. If not, well she [or he] doesn't look like she'd have it anyway."

I'm not suggesting for one millisecond that athletes are the only people who take potentially deadly risks. The percentage of athletes who do so probably isn't any higher than the percentage of construction workers, airline pilots, lawyers or sportswriters. But no group of men, with the possible exception of high-profile rock musicians, goes through life being sexually tempted as frequently as professional athletes.

Let's suppose Wilt is exaggerating. A lot. How about 90 percent? That still leaves 2,000 women with whom he's had sex. At a recent Super Bowl, I was out late with a famous player when a beautiful, married woman walked up to him, introduced herself and squeezed his hand. When the player opened his hand, her hotel room key was in his palm.

A year or so earlier, I was having a late snack with an NBA player in Philadelphia. A woman in a nearby booth had been playing kissy-face with, presumably, her boyfriend for about an hour. When the NBA player rose to leave the restaurant, the woman excused herself from her table and pursued the player into the parking lot. She proceeded to exchange phone numbers, hug and kiss him, apparently not knowing all of us—including the humiliated boyfriend—were watching through a picture window.

More than once, I've had a player ring my hotel room in the middle of the night, desperately seeking a condom or enlisting my help because there was more than one woman in the player's room. Somehow, I don't think failure to procure a condom has always stopped these guys.

Professional boxers either must be practicing the safest sex in the world or their time is coming too, because every big-time fight in Las Vegas or Atlantic City looks like a scene from the days of Caligula.

Not only is it not *easy* to say no, it's almost impossible. To abstain, we're *12* talking about a level of self-control that I, certainly, for one, would not have under similar circumstances.

The fact is, a large reason most men play sports, particularly at the start, *13* is to impress a girl. It's a fact. Becoming a professional athlete is the big pay-off, and I'm not talking about signing bonuses. And those athletes who are gay or bisexual, according to any reliable AIDS research, run a significantly greater risk.

This is where Magic's candor, again, becomes so helpful. Whether he is *14* heterosexual is totally insignificant to who he is or the challenge now facing him. He said he contracted HIV through a heterosexual encounter and I believe him.

It's only important in that most heterosexual men, this one included, *15* believed—to steal a line from *Playboy* magazine—that there weren't enough zeros on your pocket calculator to compute the chance that a heterosexual, non-drug using man could contract the AIDS virus from a woman. If Magic got the AIDS virus through a heterosexual encounter, then it's all the proof any athlete needs that he is as capable of becoming infected as anybody else who doesn't practice safe sex.

This is the wakeup call for those who thought HIV/AIDS was some- *16* body else's disease, but especially for the person who finds himself confronted with sexual opportunities so numerous and passing they can barely be remembered six months later. If Magic's plight doesn't make them go to whatever lengths to cut the risk, then perhaps nothing will. The alarm clock will never ring any louder than now. We close with the appropriate words from Spike Lee's "School Daze":

"WAKE UP!" *17*

Topics for Discussion and Writing

1. Use these three articles, the excerpt from Bo Jackson's autobiography (re-printed earlier in this chapter), and at least one other selection from this chapter as material for an essay on the physical power of athletes. An issue to consider would be athletes' hopes for, and our expectations of, their invulnerability versus the likelihood of illness or injury. Do you feel that the fan, and perhaps the athlete herself or himself, demands more than any body is capable of?

2. Imagine that you are facing the choice that Magic Johnson faced as he contemplated returning to competition in the National Basketball Association. What are the risks? What are the benefits? (Take into account that Johnson is married and has a baby son.) Write a monologue on this subject from Johnson's point of view. What questions about Johnson's illness come to you as you try to write this monologue?

3. Review the essay by Michael Wilbon. What values, including attitudes toward other people and principles of sexual behavior, are implied or stated in the essay? How might you take a different slant on the issues raised by Wilbon than the writer does? What advice would you give to aspiring professional athletes about sexual attitudes and practices? Use articles from chapter 7 for other perspectives on closely related issues.

4. Note that Allison Muscatine's list of athletes with "career-shortening" illnesses includes only one woman: Flo Hyman, the Olympic volleyball star. Certainly Muscatine's list is not exhaustive; many more women and men could be included. But the imbalance may suggest that the public is more likely to be dismayed when a male athlete succumbs to illness than when a female athlete does. Do you agree with this assessment? Explain your view. Do you think it possible someday for women to be accorded the same adulation for physical prowess as men?

JOAN BENOIT

from *Running Tide*

> *"'You shouldn't run when you're limping,' he said, shaking his head as he walked by. It was good advice, but from that day to this I have not heeded it."*
>
> *Joan Benoit Samuelson (born 1957), from a small town in Maine, became world famous in 1984 when she won the first official Olympic marathon for women. Her autobiography,* Running Tide *(1987), written with Sally Baker, details her childhood in an athletic and intellectual home, her earliest serious interest in running, her emergence as a world-class runner with her victory in the 1979 Boston Marathon, and her Olympic and post-Olympic successes, including her stunning victory in the 1984 Olympic trials, just 17 days after undergoing knee surgery.*
>
> *We have reprinted the Prologue and most of the first chapter of* Running Tide.

Before and as You Read

1. Perhaps no sport is as accessible to people as running. The present fitness craze has probably produced more runners than practitioners of any other sport, most people doing it not to compete but merely to keep in shape. Write about yourself as a runner, even if it's only something you wish you had time to do! What do you feel is the difference between you as runner and a champion marathoner like Joan Benoit?

2. Perhaps no Olympic event has the mystique of the marathon: It is far longer than any other footrace—so long that it occurs outside the pristine stadiums amid the everyday lives of the cities—and its history derives from the dramatic run of a messenger from Marathon to Athens to proclaim an Athenian victory in war. Write what you know or have heard about marathons and marathoners. If you have ever imagined yourself running a marathon, or if you have run marathons, write about the dream or the experience.

3. Write about an injury you have suffered that has limited your physical activity and may have ended your dreams of athletic success. How did you respond to the injury? What did others say about its effect on you? How did their attitudes affect your thinking? How important do you feel that injury has been in shaping your current attitude to adversity of any kind?

4. Write about the roles your family members played in regard to your participation and aspirations in athletics during your childhood and adolescence. As you read the excerpt from *Running Tide,* observe how Benoit speaks of the influence of her parents. Based on what she writes, what might Benoit list as the characteristics of good parenting in regard to athletics?

PROLOGUE

I WON'T FORGET that raw afternoon in 1973.   *1*
I stood at the top of the Main Slope at Pleasant Mountain in Maine.   *2*
I had been practicing for hours on this slalom course and wanted one last try
at a perfect run. I was a tired fifteen-year-old and the light on the mountain
was flat, but I pushed myself to ski.

I lost my concentration on the middle of the course and forgot which   *3*
way I was supposed to be turning into a gate. I rammed the gate and heard
my leg break. There was pain, but my scream was more out of surprise and
frustration.

People jumped off the T-bar lift and came running when they heard me   *4*
yell. Looking at them, I tried to take my mind away from my leg by imagining
they were dominoes falling in a neat line.

My brother Andy reached me first. He had been watching from the top   *5*
of the course. He tried to comfort me, saying that the leg might not be broken
after all. But I experienced a peculiar sense of knowledge lying in the snow.
The leg was broken for sure. I have felt that way only once since then: five
weeks before the 1984 Olympic Marathon trials my knee stopped moving and
I knew, certainly, that something serious had happened. In neither case was it
the pain that revealed the truth; it was a calm, persistent message from somewhere inside my head.

I was taken down the slope on a ski patrol toboggan. Thankfully, nobody   *6*
said what I was thinking: that it wouldn't have happened if I had only given
in to fatigue and quit for the day. My father met us at the bottom of the
mountain and took me to a local hospital. I was given a shot of morphine and
loaded into the backseat of our station wagon for the hour-long drive to the
Maine Medical Center in Portland.

I had gone to bed the night before planning to shower and wash my hair   *7*
in the morning, but an overnight snowfall meant we had to get going early.
So my hair was already dirty when I started out, and after a day of skiing it
was filthy. My sole concern at the Maine Medical Center was that no one
should see my hair. I tried to keep my ski hat on during the whole procedure,
but it was removed. I imagined the doctor and nurse at the emergency room
desk chuckling about the greasy-haired teenager.

I was fully sedated while my leg was set. I had expected some anesthesia,   *8*
but was surprised to find myself waking up in a strange room several hours
later. The doctor was leaning over me as I opened my eyes. He asked me
typical questions: how did I feel, what was my name, etc. I answered him by
saying "Thanks for fixing me!" and trying to jump out of bed. In the mist of
anesthesia my only thought was that he'd put my leg back into working order.
He convinced me otherwise and I settled back until the doctor let my father
take me home.

The broken leg was the last thing I needed. I had hoped to climb into   *9* the "A" ranks of ski racing and there were other things on my schedule that winter. I wanted to get an early start on preparations for the spring track season. Most of all, I wanted to get my driver's license: my exam was set for the following week.

I wondered if there wasn't some sort of compensation for my mishap. I had spent the whole weekend worrying over a paper I was supposed to write on Edith Hamilton's *Mythology*. I was thinking about that paper as I took my final run down the mountain. I didn't know where I would find the energy to write it after such a long day. Usually my schoolwork came first, but this was a rare occasion when I had put something off for too long. Now I had an excuse for an extension. I smiled for the first time since the accident.   *10*

I stayed away from school for a couple of days and did a good job on Edith Hamilton. If I had a favorite season in those days—and it is difficult to choose a favorite in Maine, since all four have something wonderful to offer—it was winter. So it was maddening, but I had to learn to live with the inactivity. I tacked a couple of cardboard signs to my bedroom door, reading "Stamp Out Summer" and "Half Fast Skier."   *11*

On my first day back at school I tried to sneak into biology class behind a crowd of students because I didn't want the teacher to ask what happened to my leg. Unfortunately, I was not yet graceful on my crutches, so I bumbled into the room and took my seat noisily. Nobody said anything as I pretended to be fully occupied in finding a pencil and my biology notebook.   *12*

The teacher, Keith Weatherbie, was also the coach of the boys' cross-country team, and I had run with them on one occasion the previous fall. He expected a great deal from his athletes and, to use his favorite metaphor, I already had one strike against me: I was a girl. That's what I thought, any way. I was sure he'd feel I was a hopeless nerd for breaking my leg. I was also certain he would be upset with me because I had not done my best as an athlete.   *13*

Keith introduced me to interval workouts when I was a junior, the season after I broke my leg. He'd picked up the nickname Catfish as a baseball pitcher, so the long workouts were called cat-killers; the shorter ones were mini-killers. Both were well named. A cat-killer consisted of a one-mile run, two half-mile repeats, four quarter-mile repeats, and eight 220-yard repeats. Even when I was a senior a cat-killer could make me drop to the ground, exhausted. Keith would stand over me and say, "Well, it must be time to go home and study," and that would bring me off the ground enraged at myself because I knew I could be doing better on his tests. The fact that I was always trying to impress him, in and out of class, was a great motivator. His style was similar to that of my current adviser, Bob Sevene, who has only to mention someone else's workouts or race results to get me out of a mental slump. Both Bob and Keith are also concerned with the academic preparation of athletes; while coaching at the college level, Bob made sure all of his athletes graduated.   *14*

My apprehension over Keith's reaction was wasted. He waited until my classmates had left before he asked about the accident, and he didn't chew me   *15* out or kid me. More than anything, I was upset with myself; my picture of a mocking Keith was a convenient vehicle for those feelings of inadequacy I was dragging around along with my cast.

The cast gave me fits until I got it changed for a smaller, lighter, walking   16
version. There were three flights of stairs at school and I had to climb each of them every day. All the hard work involved in just getting around probably kept me in shape for those months, and I had the solace of making high honors twice that year. I normally did my best schoolwork when I had to fit it in with a zillion other activities (excellent training for the life I am leading at the moment), so I was surprised when I found I could use leisure time so well.

There is a belief that I didn't start running until the spring after my   17
skiing accident, but actually I ran track as a freshman under the guidance of Paula Smith and Andrea Cayer. Andrea was the only Cape Elizabeth High School teacher who was shorter than I, and that in itself was an inspiration. But she was also a successful physical education teacher. She had a great rapport with her students as well as with her athletes, and she had been a good high school athlete herself. I felt her experience supported the advice she gave me. Some of my perseverance in athletics stems from the C that Andrea gave me in gymnastics. To get a C in any subject, much less phys ed, was devastating. I tried harder.

That spring I moped around the track after my cast came off. I wanted   18
so much to be involved with the team that I volunteered to rake the long-jump pit during practice and to drag the heavy foam high-jump landing pads from the field to the school building when the team was finished using them.

Running felt horrible at first. A couple of weeks after the cast was   19
removed I decided to take a strengthening run. I wasn't making much progress, but I kept it up for a while. A little boy crossed a nearby field and paused to watch me. He approached when I stopped to rest.

"You shouldn't run when you're limping," he said, shaking his head as   20
he walked by.

It was good advice, but from that day to this I have not heeded it.   21

The leg was not my first injury and it would not be my last. A cinder in   22
my hand reminds me of the time I dove for the finish line in a 50-yard dash. I carry bumps and scars from a lifetime of competition. My most celebrated injury was a knee that required arthroscopic surgery two weeks before the Olympic Trials. It would not have been so devastating (or so famous) without its poor timing. All athletes get hurt.

Injury, whether physical or emotional, is a personal ordeal. We learn   23
much about ourselves through injury and disappointment; the first time we fall down as children we learn that in order to overcome a force like gravity we must bend our wills to this peculiar harness that binds us.

My response to the lows and highs has been the making of me. My   24
worst races have been my best teachers. Every time I fail I assume I will be a stronger person for it. I keep on running, figuratively and literally, despite a

limp that gets more noticeable with each passing season, because for me there has always been a place to go and a terrible urgency to get there. For as long as I can remember I have been setting goals for myself and dealing with the consequences of either meeting or falling short of them. I have tried to accept my setbacks as the will of someone whose judgment I have no right to question. But I also believe that that someone—who, for me, is God—expects me to push against the obstacles with all my strength and to give up only when I am fairly and honestly defeated.

I guess I will eventually experience true success and true failure; I have not met with either yet. The only real failure is the failure to try. Perhaps one day I will find myself unwilling to try; I hope not. But should that day arrive, I will know what failure is. Similarly, it seems to me that real success comes when a person is able to say of one of her accomplishments, "That is a good job well done," and then leave that accomplishment behind. When I run a good race I think about how I might have done better and what I will do next time. True success eludes me, but I may be setting impossible standards for myself. Some day I may have to be satisfied with something less than the goals I set for myself: then and only then will I feel tested.

My skiing injury did lead me to run more, and because of my affection for running I was able to give up my dream of being a world-class skier. From the beginning of my development as an athlete I've been willing to learn the lessons injury can teach. I didn't surrender my dream lightly; but when I stood on a mountain the following winter and was scared, the realist in me took over. I could no longer hope to be a great skier if I was afraid. But because I ran and played other sports, I could give up competitive skiing; running was compensation.

The goal I can neither reach nor let go of is out there somewhere. I dread meeting it. So until it shows its face I will continue to do what I have always done: I will keep on doing my best.

ONE

. . . .There was no place for a shrinking violet around my house. My mother taught us the rules of etiquette—"ladies first," and so on—but neither my brothers nor I considered me a lady. If I couldn't beat them to the catcher's mitt, the best sandwich in the ski lunch, or the window seat in the car, too bad. If I had trouble carrying my skis off the mountain at the end of the day, that was cause for a merciless ribbing. They weren't being mean; they were treating me the way I expected to be treated: as an equal. In fact, the one thing they could do to get a rise out of me was try to relegate me to "girl" status. We all knew girls were wimpy.

I sometimes thought my parents treated me differently because I was a   *29*
girl. One thing I remember best about my early childhood is how much I
wanted to go skiing with my parents and the older boys. Every Saturday they
would head for a nearby mountain and leave John and me behind with our
grandmother. I was older than John and thought I should be taken along.

One Saturday I begged to go. I was three or four and probably about the   *30*
size of a throw pillow, but I could make a lot of noise. I pleaded and groaned
and carried on, but no one paid any attention to me. My parents said I was
too young and that was that. I asked if they were being so horrible to me
because I was a girl. They said no, very patiently. I was lucky they didn't settle
the whole argument with a spanking. No doubt Andy and Peter lorded it over
me, making me even more determined. I was sure I could do anything they
could do.

In the cellar I found some small skis, the official first pair for every kid   *31*
in the family. Dad gave them to each of us in turn as the older child outgrew
them; he would bring them out for Christmas and put a fresh coat of paint
on them. They still showed scars from Peter's use when I discovered them, but
even beaten up they were beautiful to me. I strapped them on and tried to ski
down our steep front lawn. The experiment was a failure—I fell down several
times and was deposited at Grandmother's house as usual. I sucked on black
jellybeans all afternoon to console myself.

The next year I went with my family to Sugarloaf Mountain in King-   *32*
field for the first time. There are things about Sugarloaf that I suppose I will
still remember if I live a hundred years. It was an imposing sight when I was
a child. With no condominiums and few roads at the base, the mountain was
a wild, thrilling place. Just driving toward it gave me goosebumps.

For a couple of winters the Benoits and four other families shared an   *33*
old house near the mountain. The place was small, but by sleeping dormitory-
style in the loft everyone could be accommodated. A wood stove was the only
source of heat; we burned dowels picked up at a nearby paper mill. The house
was always cold, but we children hardly noticed.

The skiing was terrific; I loved it from the beginning. The speed and   *34*
freedom it gave me were new, welcome sensations. Learning to make the
equipment respond to the movements of my legs and arms, learning to keep
my balance or fall safely, learning to relish the warmth and hot chocolate in
the lodge after a thorough chill: these were the great joys of my young life.

At first I stood between my father's legs—he on his skis and I on mine—   *35*
hugging his knees as he moved down a gentle slope, trying to feel the rhythm
in his movements. At times I almost felt his legs were mine; he made everything look easy. Skiing is bound up in grace and finesse, and my father had
both in abundance. After an hour or two with him I knew what I wanted
from my own skis.

Of course I expected to get right on and *ski*. I tried, but my skis   *36*
wouldn't do what Dad's had and I spent most days lying in the snow. Skiing

attire in the 1960s was not up to current standards—the damp and cold penetrated quickly despite careful dressing. Underneath my layers of clothing my skin was numb, then painful, from the frequent landings on the snow.

There were other unanticipated problems; for example, I had to learn to ride the T-bar. You are supposed to stand in front of the wooden bar and let it push you to the top of a slope, but since I was too small to hold it down that way, I had to sit on it. People thought I was hilarious. On those few occasions when I didn't fall, I hung on like a monkey, my skis dangling below me. *37*

The other feature of the T-bar I found daunting was that the lift attendants requested it be ridden by people in tandem, meaning that I had to ask strangers to ride with me. I would stand by the lift line for what seemed like an hour, trying to work up the courage to speak to someone. And when I finally did speak, I often got the jokers. "Are you single?" I'd ask, peeping like a bird. "No, I'm married," the joker would say. Very funny. *38*

I persisted despite the trials, fighting the T-bar until I had it beaten. After that it was fun to ride. The best fun of all was to ride alone, if you were coordinated enough to balance the bar without help. *39*

People ask how I can run with pain or keep working toward a goal that seems hopelessly distant. I think back on my early failures with the T-bar. I didn't want to look ridiculous, I didn't want people to laugh at me, and I didn't want to talk to strangers; but I knew if I was going to ski I would have to master the T-bar. If I want to run a marathon faster than I've run in the past, I have to cope with the discomfort that sometimes accompanies long-distance running. I know the end result will be worth the effort. It is too bad that very few T-bars are being installed at ski areas today. *40*

Skiing itself—along with the rituals that accompanied it in my family—was one of my best early teachers. It was a wonderful introduction to sports, but it also taught me about sacrifice, about picking myself up and going on in spite of adversity, and about striving. *41*

I didn't realize I was learning lessons. All I knew was, as long as there was snow on the ground we skied every weekend from November to April. There was more snow when I was a kid than there is now; during the past several winters my skiing has been limited by lack of snowfall. Once in a while I wonder if all the dire predictions some scientists have made about the destruction of our ozone layer are coming true. Perhaps the sun is melting our ice caps, or perhaps we are in the midst of a naturally produced warming trend. For whatever reason, we have less snow, which is frustrating for inveterate skiers like me. *42*

There were priorities ahead of skiing, of course. On Saturday mornings Dad would drop the four of us off for our instruction in C.C.D. (Christian Catholic Doctrine) on his way to work and Mom would pick us up from there and take us to the mountain. If we overslept and had to go to the nine o'clock, rather than the eight o'clock, class, it would be ten before we were *43* on the road and eleven thirty before we were on skis. And not only did we have to show up for class, we had to do the work once we got there.

On Sundays we got up for early mass. Easier said than done, since we were tired after skiing on Saturday. This was Dad's only free day, and he was anxious to get to the slopes. He would rouse us, moving from one child to another until he was reasonably sure we were all awake. 44

We went to mass in our ski clothes and tried to pay close attention, but the hour was early and the church was quiet; it was difficult not to doze. Recalling those times—and all the Easter Sundays when we felt like second-class citizens because we were in ski clothes and everyone else was decked out—I'm grateful for the institution of the Saturday evening mass in the 1960s. I was finally alert enough to listen to what was going on in church. I might have come to that point of my own accord once I got older, but I liked being able to sit up and take notice as a kid, too. Easter was still hard—you don't go to Easter mass on Saturday—but every year there was an Easter Classic race on the mountain, followed by an Easter egg hunt, so that made up for the feelings of inferiority I'd had in church. In any case, I was sorry for the little girls in their new bonnets. Those hats sported elastic chin bands that cut thin red lines into tender skin. And I was sure my ski boots were more comfortable than the tight patent leather shoes all the other girls wore. 45

Trying to budget time for skiing around religious obligations helped me form some of the priorities that would shape my later life. The clearest lesson was that there were some things in the universe that came before my interests and desires. God and my parents, for example. Prayer, too. There were times when I thought about skipping my prayers but didn't; they were important. 46

Skiing was also a physical challenge. Good skiers are somewhat ruthless in their training, forcing themselves to confront difficult trails over and over again until they are mastered. Good skiers ski in all weather. Any snowstorm short of a screeching blizzard found the four Benoit children on the mountain; wind and cold couldn't stop us. We were welcome to retreat to the lodge if we were cold, but there was pride involved in not being the one to leave the slopes first. I'm not sure about the source of that particular competition, but I do know why we were unwilling to complain: our father never groused about anything. Though he may have felt sympathy when we grumbled, he didn't show it in any obvious way. He must have figured we were smart enough to come in out of the cold without his urging. But every one of us hated to admit that anything as paltry as the weather could bring us down. So we shivered and got back on the T-bar for one last run even when we could hardly feel our feet and hands. I think I did some permanent damage to my fingers and toes by ignoring them back then; nowadays I feel the cold in them soon after my first trip down the mountain and I usually have to quit skiing long before I want to. Whatever my body suffered, however, was more than made up for by what I gained in tenacity. If it appears that running in pain doesn't bother me, it's because I learned to manage it when I was a young 47 skier. I found a part of myself which could go on in spite of it and I developed that part.

But I don't want to give the impression that I got up on weekend   48
mornings with the attitude of a stevedore about to spend a tough day on the docks. I loved skiing. Most days the weather was fine, especially in early spring. By March it would begin to get warm and we could ski in shirt sleeves. Then I would relish the feel of the wind dancing through the gaps in my clothes. I sometimes wore goggles, but on sunny days they weren't necessary—the warmth would cover my face like a mask. Skiers had the best, earliest tans in town.

Because I ski, I know why people enjoy driving race cars. Great speed is   49
an opiate, and speed that is under your control, open to your manipulation, is the best high of all. I don't race cars, but barring that, I have yet to find a sport which comes close to skiing for pure exhilaration.

I wasn't surprised, therefore, when I took it into my head to become a   50
world-class skier. I was young—eight or nine—but the goal wasn't set childishly. I didn't want to be a skier one day, a teacher the next, and a doctor the third. Underlying every other ambition I set for myself between those early skiing years and the time I broke my leg was the desire to ski in the Olympics. I knew I would have to train for a career to support myself, and there were many occasions when I faced reality and admitted that pinning my hopes on athletics was irresponsible, but the dream refused to be shunted aside.

I worked with it as well as I could. Fortunately, my ambition was entirely   51
in my own mind. Unlike many child athletes, I was under absolutely no pressure to train. In fact, when I was old enough to baby-sit I had to make money to pay for equipment and ski camp. During vacations from high school I waitressed at the Pleasant Mountain Inn so I would have a place to stay on the mountain. They didn't serve lunch; I could get on the slopes after breakfast and ski until the last bell. Regulars on Pleasant Mountain urged my father to send me away for coaching.

I had my heart set on attending a Vermont ski academy, but after much   52
thought my parents decided not to let me go. My hopes rose again when I learned that a similar academy was to be opened at Sugarloaf. Once again, my parents felt that education came before skiing.

I continued to train on weekends and during school vacations. In junior   53
high I joined an intensive training program at Pleasant Mountain and competed as much as I could. I had begun competition at age ten and always enjoyed it. I won as often as I lost, but .500 wasn't the average I was aiming for. I wanted to win every race: not because I took great pleasure in beating other people, but because I wanted to know I was getting better.

My parents wouldn't let me become as myopic toward life's other con-   54
cerns as you're supposed to be if you aspire to athletic prowess. Winning was neither everything nor the only thing; it was one of many things. My parents would have laughed uproariously if I'd come to them with fire in my eyes and

said, "Mom, Dad, from now on I'm going to train to be a skier and that's it!" They were never insensitive to my desires—I'm sure it hurt them to turn me down on going to ski academy—but there wasn't any room around our house for a Star, either. Mom and Dad were trying to rear four happy, intelligent, useful, loving kids. What we did with the grounding they gave us was our business. They had no intention of pointing us toward careers before we had grown into a sense of ourselves. We were exposed to the widest imaginable variety of pursuits from which to pick and choose. Andy and Peter both love to draw and paint; I took up stamp collecting and had piano lessons; John dabbled successfully in almost everything. None of us viewed life through a tunnel formed by a single, all-consuming passion.

I'll admit I was terribly serious about skiing. Once in a while my father   55
tried to slow me down. I suppose it's hard to see your child place enormous emphasis on any one pursuit, because with the disappointments you've suffered in your life, you know how far she can fall. Parents must walk a tightrope between protecting their children from heartache and encouraging them to develop their talents. Dad was always checking to make sure I thought skiing was worth all the time I was giving to it. When he was satisfied that I was happy, he placed few obstacles in my way.

We did argue over the type of bindings I should use. He wanted me to   56
be safe, so he made me wear a brand that had a guardian angel as its trademark. The slightest pressure on a turn released the binding—time and time again I zoomed into a turn in a race, only to feel my bindings let go. I carried on about it for years. Dad's standard, unbending reply was that safety was more important than winning races. That was easy for him to say, since I, not he, was the one piling up Did Not Finish results.

When I was finally permitted a pair of bindings that hung in there on   57
the turns, I broke my leg. To his credit, Dad didn't say, "I told you so." . . .

Topics for Discussion and Writing

1. Compare Benoit's description of her childhood with that of Bo Jackson. Note similarities and differences. Do you think it possible to generalize about the childhoods of successful athletes based on these two portraits? Expand on the research by reading more sports autobiographies and biographies. What patterns, if any, emerge? Consider doing this research with others.

2. Compare Benoit's drive to excel, as stated and implied in this excerpt, with those revealed in other selections in this chapter (for example, Bo Jackson's, Junko Tabei's, or James Wasley's). Do you admire some motives more than others? Explain in an exploratory essay.

3. If you have not already done so, read the Judy Oppenheimer selection from this chapter, especially coach Bob Plante's description of the three types of coaches. To which of the three types does Benoit's high school

coach, Keith Weatherbie, seem closest? Does he seem to represent a fourth type? If so, how would you describe him? Would you attribute to him, or to any coach, as much of the athlete's success as Benoit does to Weatherbie?

For Further Thought

1. Now that you have read selections in this chapter, return to pieces that you wrote in response to the "Thinking about the Issues" topics at the beginning of the chapter. Revise these writings in light of your experience as reader and writer as you worked through the chapter.

2. Use all or most of the selections from this chapter, and your writing about them, as source material for an essay on one of the following subjects:

    How to train for athletic success
    The influences of TV on the modern athlete
    The role of athletics in my life
    The ideal body
    Money as motive in sports
    or any other subject of your choice

    Use the essay to make a point about the subject: either to persuade a reader to feel a certain way toward athletes or to argue for a course of action. Use the suggestions in chapter 2 for getting constructive feedback on your essay from other writers. Revise accordingly.

3. Create in a genre of your choice (such as fictional story, lyric poem, narrative poem, dramatic dialogue, collage, painting, sculpture, dance, musical composition) a work that expresses an opinion that you now hold about athletes, this opinion based in part on your reading and writing in this chapter. Ask others to respond to your work in terms of the feelings that it inspires in them toward your subject.

4. Use your work in this chapter as context for writing a review of a new work related to athletics, such as an autobiography, a biography, a statistical summary, a collection of articles, a film or TV show (series or documentary), a TV or radio broadcast of a sporting event, or a magazine or TV ad campaign for sports-related merchandise. Remember that most reviewers try to place the work they are reviewing into a context of other works on the subject or at least to compare the ideas in the new work with their own related experience. These comparisons help the reader of the review to understand why the reviewer likes or dislikes certain parts of the new work.

CHAPTER SEVEN

Exploring Our Sexuality

"Every one of my dreams was shattered, blown away . . . Do you want to put your life in that other person's hands? Is that boy or girl worth dying for? I doubt it."
—*Amy Dolph, quoted in "Teenagers and AIDS,"* Newsweek *3 Aug. 1992:49.*

Sexuality today is more complicated than ever before. In the past, a teenager's worst fear was a loss of reputation or the birth of a baby. Today we know that the price for sexual curiosity, lust, or the expression of true love might be much higher for both partners—death from AIDS.

Despite this new danger, there is greater sexual freedom now, and society is beginning to accept a broader range of behavior.

At the same time, the definition of *family* has broadened: Step and single-parent families are the new norm, and more and more gay couples are raising children from previous relationships, as well as adopting hard-to-place children.

The controversy over sex education and abortion continues. Few deny the need to teach and guide young people who are developing their sexual values, but who should have that responsibility? What is the efficacy of making condoms available to students? What help should be available in communities for the pregnant teenager? Should abortion be available "on demand" or at all?

On the other side of the coin, reproductive science is developing more options. A few years ago, adoption was the only choice for infertile couples desiring a child. Now sperm banks, in vitro fertilization, and surrogate motherhood offer new possibilities to those who have the money and the desire for parenthood.

The care available for children and pregnant women is one barometer of our social values. In the United States obstetrics and its ancillary fields are among the fastest growing of medical specialties, and one might expect the conditions for childbirth in this country to be among the best in the world. But the United States has one of the highest infant mortality rates of all industrial nations. (According to the *Universal Almanac,* 1992 edition, Japan has the lowest mortality rate, while the United States ranks 24th from the top.)

Simple but life-saving prenatal care does not reach everyone. Hospital birth is frequently an impersonal matter made even more difficult by the dictates of insurance companies trying to control their costs. And there is no standardized system that assures adequate medical care and nutrition for the children of families in need. What do these facts say about how we regard our poor and how we value the health of women and children in general?

But this is not a chapter "for women only." Few topics affect us all more personally than those of sexuality, birth, and interpersonal relationships. The following selections present a number of these issues for you to study. You will have the opportunity to examine your own beliefs and consider new points of view in writing and discussion with others.

You will read about teenagers who paid too high a price for sexual expression and how some feel that it is now their mission to educate others. Two Catholic nuns who were forced to resign from their religious order so that they could continue to work for women's right to have abortions are here, as well as a father who deeply regrets the decision he and his wife made to exercise that right.

Women who call themselves "invisible" because they love other women share their emotional struggle and the satisfaction of having found who they really are. You will meet two mothers who relive their rite of passage into parenthood as unmarried high school students; you will witness the care given by one of this century's great doctor-writers as he relates the birth of one of his patient's babies on "A Night in June"; and you'll see how the rights of the surrogate mother are tested by the woman who gave birth to "Baby M" for another couple and then fought to keep her.

Thinking about the Issues

1. Study the men and women represented in the following selections. Think about how those captured here struggle within their circumstances. What part do social attitudes play in the choices that each person has? How are the conflicts of the men represented here different from those of the women? How are they alike? Which persons do you admire? Why?

2. Think about how society needs to develop new ethics to keep up with the advent of new diseases and the advances of science. How difficult is it to fashion values "on the heels" of the latest scientific discoveries? Name some issues in the recent news that present this challenge. Share your ideas with a group of classmates.

3. Some people might be of the opinion that having a baby is not much different from having your tonsils out: A woman should just lie there and rely on the experts. What are your thoughts about this idea? Consider, also, the dichotomy that only women give birth, but that the great majority of decision-making birth attendants in this country are men. Does our system of childbirth sometimes discriminate against women? How important do

you think it is that parents have some control in planning the birth of their children? Why?

4. Interview two mothers who are separated by at least a generation. What do these women remember about their children's births? What was their male partner's role during that time? As their children were growing up? Ask them to describe their family life. What would they change if they were to live it again?

   Interview two fathers, also separated by at least one generation. What do they remember of their children's births? What was their role as their children were growing up? Has the father's role changed in the last 20 years? In what way?

5. In your journal write down your feelings regarding a sexuality issue. Then play devil's advocate and make a case for the opposite viewpoint. How difficult is this for you? Does it help you gain a new perspective?

BARBARA FERRARO AND PATRICIA HUSSEY

from *No Turning Back*

> " 'It's not possible now,' said Cheryl. 'A baby isn't possible. We both have to finish school. And, well, we're not sure we want to be married. I'm going to have an abortion and I need your help.'

> "As Elizabeth spoke, I felt sick to my stomach. I hoped my face didn't reveal my disgust. I was surprised by the way that she told her story, in a kind of detached, flat narrative, as though she were watching a play unfold. At the time I didn't know that detachment was protection, but I would learn it during my last four years as a nun."

> Barbara Ferraro and Patricia Hussey spent a collective 47 years as nuns in the religious order Sisters of Notre Dame. In 1984 they joined with a group signing a New York Times advertisement that supported Geraldine Ferraro, a prochoice vice presidential candidate. Throughout two years of threats of dismissal from their order, the two women maintained their prochoice stand. Today they run a shelter for the homeless in Charleston, West Virginia. They are no longer nuns.

Before and as You Read

1. List the attributes that you believe define a "person of courage." Name at least three historical figures who meet your criteria. Write about someone in your personal life who fits that description.

2. Think about a time when you took an unpopular stand. Were you alone in your beliefs? How did this experience change you? When is it important to take the risks that certain values dictate?

3. Few subjects trigger more emotional debate than abortion. Write about how you arrived at your point of view. What role did your family values play? Those of your peers? Did your stand change at any time? If so, what was responsible for the change?

4. It is easy to hold a popular view. It is also easy to hold an unpopular view in the security of a crowd. As you read, describe the climate in which these two women revealed their beliefs. What did they have to gain by adhering to their values? What did they have to lose?

5. Should those who take a prolife stand focus on abortion as their only issue? Or is it important for them to work for social change and the financial, educational, career, and child-care needs of mothers who have few or no resources? When prolife proponents use "adoption is an option" as a slogan, do you believe they should also become active on a personal level, raising funds, and providing homes if need be, for the babies of women who decide against abortion?

Barbara Ferraro

W HEN CHERYL came to me I was pleased but not surprised. I had 1
visited her at home several times, and gotten to know her family.
Tony, one of the priests, and I had begun a young adult group in the parish,
and Cheryl was an active member, a very thoughtful young woman of twenty-
one. During our weekly meetings when we sat in a circle and shared problems,
Cheryl had seen me responding to all kinds of questions about boyfriends and
girlfriends, about parents and jobs and drugs. Apparently she decided she could
trust me.

Tony and I were sitting in the parish house office when Cheryl came in, 2
looking like Miss Western States in her blue jeans and cowgirl shirt. I remember I made some admiring remark about her boots. And then she said:

"Uh, is anyone else here?" 3

"No, just us. Did you want anyone else?" I said. 4

"No, no, I need to talk to you." She looked doubtfully at Tony, and then 5
she seemed to decide it was all right if he stayed.

"What's wrong?" Tony and I asked together. 6

"I'm pregnant," she said, flatly. 7

"UmmHmm," said Tony, with a sympathetic dip on the "umm" that was 8
perfect. An old-fashioned priest would have said, "I'll have to tell your parents," or "I won't give you absolution until you get married." Or worse things.
But Tony and I were trained to help resolve moral dilemmas and human
conflicts. Therefore, I was smart enough to know she had not come to tell us
she wanted to get married.

"Are you sure?" I asked. She had just been elected president of her 9
sorority. We had talked often about her plans for after college.

"I'm two months late, and I had the test. I'm pregnant." 10

"Weren't you using some sort of birth control?" I asked. It was an inane 11
question, but I suddenly wanted to know the answer. True, the church
preached against birth control, but the church also forbids sexual intercourse
outside of marriage. I hoped Cheryl hadn't decided to dilute the sin of sex
by avoiding the sin of birth control.

A new thought flashed into my head: The church's teachings on birth 12
control and sex are really out of date.

"I can't take the pill," said Cheryl. "It gives me violent headaches." 13

"Oh," I said. This was no time for me to display my ignorance about 14
birth control methods.

"Umm," said Tony, "have you thought about getting married?" 15

"It's not possible now," said Cheryl. "A baby isn't possible. We both have 16
to finish school. And, well, we're not sure we want to be married. I'm going
to have an abortion and I need your help."

At least she hadn't asked for our permission. She was a grown-up Cath- 17
olic, exercising her own freedom of conscience. Cheryl wanted us to cover
for her, to tell her parents, if they called looking for her, that she was away on

a retreat with some girlfriends. She was positive her father would kill her if he found out. He hadn't seemed brutal or uncaring when I met him, but Cheryl knew him better than I did. She wasn't a child. I couldn't think of any good purpose that would be served by telling her parents.

What could I do? I couldn't run away from her or refuse her. God would not walk away from someone who asked for help, whatever the help might be. I wasn't being asked to go to the clinic, but to "be with her" as her church, her spiritual support, during this most difficult time. Uneasily, I did tell her that I would not choose to have an abortion if I were pregnant.   *18*

During the day of the abortion, while Tony and I kept an anxious vigil by the telephone, I thought about what I had told Cheryl, and I realized it wasn't true.   *19*

Until then I had never asked myself what I would do, because I never thought I would face the problem. The only way I could get pregnant would be if I were raped. I sat there, watching a lizard skitter across the ceiling, and for the first time in my life I tried to imagine what it would be like to be raped, and then to discover I was pregnant.   *20*

In 1974, in Tucson, there were no rape crisis hot lines, and no rape victims had ever come to the parish for counseling. Women had not yet learned to speak out and fight back. All I had to work with were images: a man standing behind my bathroom door, grabbing me around the neck. Hurting me, humiliating me, threatening to come back. And then, weeks later, when I was still terrified and sickened, afraid to go out, afraid of the dark—to find myself pregnant.   *21*

The truth was that I couldn't imagine going through a pregnancy in that state of mind. My body would become so abhorrent to me that my mind would detach from my senses and I would never be whole again. As an adult Christian woman, I would be treating myself irresponsibly if I did not have an abortion. It would be the only moral choice.   *22*

Cheryl had made a moral decision, after much reflection and prayer. She was a faithful churchgoer, she believed God was alive in her life, and she believed she had to take responsibility for what happened in her life. It was not the right time for her to have a child. How could anyone else, *anyone* else, possibly claim the right to make that decision for her?   *23*

My thoughts ran on, following an inexorable logic. A "good" woman, making a conscious moral choice, is a sympathetic figure. What about the women who do not go to church, who live recklessly and care nothing about prayer and reflection? What about "bad" women? Should their choice be made for them? Obviously not. Who would dare make such a judgment for someone else?   *24*

I began to think that there was something arrogant and repressive and morally indefensible about the Catholic church's attitude toward abortion—*and toward women.*   *25*

Unfortunately, I only *began* to think that afternoon. And as soon as I got that far, my thoughts veered away from my conclusion. After all, if I had fully   *26* understood what I was saying to myself, I would have had to leave right then, that afternoon. And I had nowhere to go. The church was my life. So for years to come I would try to make myself believe that as more and more women played a greater and greater role in the life of the church, the hierarchy would comprehend the injustice done to us. And in 1975 I was still fairly confident that the church, filled with the wisdom of the Holy Spirit, rededicated to peace and justice by Pope John XXIII, would amend the injustice within itself.

Instead, I discovered that my own little parish in Tucson, Arizona, despite its brave new rhetoric of equality and shared ministry and lay leadership, was still ruled absolutely by the whim of the male, hierarchical pastor. . . .   27

Patricia Hussey

My world had been so small! The staff at Smith Cottage was like an   28
ecumenical council for me. They were old and young; single and married; black, Puerto Rican, and white; Jewish, Protestant, Catholic, and atheist; born of both the poor and the middle classes. They knew I was a nun, but I dressed in regular clothes, and I did not wear my Notre Dame cross to work. I'm sure everyone else would have thought it was just a pretty, modern cross, but for me the decision not to wear it signified something very important, something I myself didn't fully understand at the time. The cross was part of our habit, and eventually it became the only remnant of the habit, the prime symbol of our vocation.

It was bronze, with *Ah qu'il est bon le bon Dieu* engraved on it, and was   29
worn around the neck. My conscious reason for not wearing it was that I was working for a secular institution, and I did not feel I was working "as a nun." But unconsciously I think it was because I wanted to be myself, Patricia Hussey, not someone special and separate. I didn't want to be put in a category. And I was so happy when I felt included.

I was working with atheists! And foul-mouthed atheists at that. From   30
Laurie the social worker I first heard the "F" word. When I was growing up I never even heard the word "hell" at home. Now, every morning I was greeted in the most loving tone of voice with "Hey, motherfucker, how ya' doin' today?" The first time, I thought my ears would catch on fire, but since most of my kids seemed to have one-word vocabularies—their conversations sounded like a barnyard: "Uck, uck, uck, uck, uckooo"—after about two years I stopped noticing. And of course the terrible day came when I forgot myself and said something in the Long Lane vernacular when I was visiting my parents. The only way I could calm down my father was to tell him some of the stories I had heard.

On the average there were twenty girls in residence at Smith Cottage.   31
About half of them were white, and the rest were black and Puerto Rican. Each had her own bedroom and was responsible for keeping it clean. They each had a daily community chore to perform for which they were awarded points. (It was kind of like the convent, except that we never got any points.)

Twenty points for cleaning their rooms, twenty points for doing the morning chores. Points added up to the right to visit home or go to dances.

The point system was part of a program of behavioral modification, a way to make the children experience limits and discipline. For emergencies, we had a system of "time-outs." "Time-out!" we yelled if someone was about to smash someone else with a broom. Then the enraged person would have to go sit down in a chair in the corner of the room until she could cool down and get in some fragile touch with her more adult self. Behavioral modification worked pretty well, but I think its success depended on the reinforcement we gave through personal contact with the kids. Actually, each depended on the other. 32

Ida★ deeply believed in group therapy. Every day after school, the staff and the residents of Smith Cottage would gather in the living room on straight-back chairs arranged in a circle so that we would feel the energy and power of the group. We all talked about what made us feel good or bad, or about whatever had happened in our lives that the staff and the girls wanted to share. Ida usually was the leader, and she worked from whatever was happening that day. If the mood was angry, we talked about anger. The more trust grew, the more the youngsters felt they were in a warm and caring atmosphere, the more they shared their life histories. 33

I think in the beginning I must have imagined those children as coming from a place looking like my own mother's kitchen. I suppose my sympathy was organized around the assumption that something had gone tragically wrong *within* the children. Imagine how naive and confused and frightened I felt when I heard their stories. 34

"Well, like, you know, I'd been in ten or fifteen different foster homes by the time I was twelve. When the last old man started climbing into my bed, I split." 35

"My guy took real good care of me. He made real sure my tricks were okay, not weird or anything." This from a fourteen-year-old who had been so starved for anything that looked like love that she could be exploited beyond endurance by a pimp who "cared" for her. 36

At first I couldn't believe their stories; I couldn't quite process what they were saying. Then I could not believe the world still turned when such things happened. And finally, most horribly, I could not believe that the stories were *routine*, that I was hearing them again and again from different children. 37

Children spoke of abuse, both physical and sexual. They spoke of becoming pregnant by their fathers, pimps, or their mother's boyfriends. They whispered or cried about being tied up or tied down. They wept about their hands being held to flames or hot stoves so they would "learn their lessons." Over and over I heard children tell of trying to escape their parents' murderous rages. "He held my head under water until I couldn't breathe anymore." 38

One day Ida asked me to think about taking in a girl named Ruby. She 39

★A counselor at Smith Cottage

was from the Hartford inner city. Her mother was an alcoholic who had once tried to hang all three of her children from the shower curtain rod. She got them all up in the air, but luckily she wasn't very good with knots and they just hung there until the rod broke and they escaped. When Ruby was thirteen she had a child, which meant she had gotten pregnant at twelve. When she came to Long Lane she was fourteen, and she had killed her boyfriend with a knife. It was especially horrible to think of that knife, of the physical direct-ness of stabbing someone. She killed him because he had begun to strangle her by the gold chain around her neck. He was dragging her through the kitchen by the chain, and he shouted, "You better grab that knife because it's either going to be you or me." She did grab the knife and plunged it into his heart and he died. She was devastated to lose him. I remember the day she arrived. I expected someone about 250 pounds, maybe six feet tall. And she was just a girl, just a gawky adolescent girl.

Sitting in that circle, we tried to let the girl-children sweep away enough of their past so that they could touch the good part of themselves and try to nourish it. But sometimes I could not imagine how any hope had survived. I will never as long as I live forget the afternoon that a girl named Elizabeth finally spoke in the circle. From a small town in Connecticut, she was sixteen years old, tall, with long, dark hair. She had already been with us for a couple of months. Other kids gravitated toward her; she was a kind of leader, direct and articulate. But she had never spoken about herself. 40

I could not imagine what she held within her. She always spoke in a soft voice, but with an edge to it, as though her rage might come boiling out at any moment. With India Ink and a pin she had tattooed herself across her thighs: "EAT ME." 41

Ida must have sensed that Elizabeth was reaching a breaking point that day because she leaned forward in her chair and said, "You can only begin to be free if you possess your own reality, Elizabeth. Say it, and let it go." 42

"My father has dogs," she began, holding her head down. "He taught me to 'do it' with animals. He showed me by doing it himself with one of the dogs and then I had to do it." 43

There was not one snicker, no nervous laughter, only quiet. 44

"He made me do it a lot . . . and then one day he did it to me too. Over and over again, he did it. When I got old enough to take care of myself, I ran away." 45

Old enough? She had been committed to Long Lane by the state of Connecticut's juvenile judge for being a runaway at the age of fifteen. Her father had reported her as a runaway, and her school reported her as a truant. No one, as far as I ever knew, had asked her why she had run away. 46

As Elizabeth spoke, I felt sick to my stomach. I hoped my face didn't reveal my disgust. I was surprised by the way she told her story, in a kind of detached, flat narrative, as though she were watching a play unfold. At the time, I didn't know that detachment was protection, but I would learn it during my last four years as a nun. 47

My mind kept rushing to thoughts of my own father, the man who   *48*
came home to dinner every night when his children were young, who turned
down promotions because they would require too much travel. The man we
Hussey kids called "Sergeant" because he handed out lists of Saturday morning
chores. The man who had always been ready to listen to me, and who would
support me through all of my battles. Now it seemed so unfair and so confusing for me to have been so lucky. No wonder people look for the easiest
explanation and blame the child.

There was more to Elizabeth's story.   *49*

"My boyfriend was a biker," she said. "You know, motorcycles. To get   *50*
to be someone's old lady you have to make it with all the guys in the gang.
All at once. I mean, one after another, in front of everybody. It's kind of like
rape." She looked up at that point, and then she ducked her head again.

"I'm pregnant," she said. And she lifted her head. "I'm going to have an   *51*
abortion."

It's all right, I kept thinking. It's all right.   *52*

In time, I would learn, as Barbara also did, that people don't ask permis-   *53*
sion when they are going to have an abortion. They may share the information
with someone they trust in the hope of being supported in their decision, but
the decision itself is so uniquely and primarily personal that notions of "con-
sultation" and "approval" ultimately have no bearing.

For several months, I acted as the Long Lane social worker, and I re-   *54*
member Ida making it very clear that I could not let the fact that I was a
Catholic affect my response to the girls who asked to get an abortion. On
January 22, 1973, the Supreme Court had declared, in the case of *Roe* v.
Wade, that an American woman had a legal, constitutional right to choose an
abortion. It was not my job to stand in the way of the law. I didn't have a
problem with that, nor did I say "That is an area that someone else will have
to deal with." It was my job to support the girls as much as possible, whatever
their decision.

I saw children happily bearing children, hoping that they could provide   *55*
their babies with all the good life and family they themselves had never known.
I saw children bearing children in homes for unwed mothers, taking on one
more stigma in a society that jumps at any chance to label and then reject
people. I saw children bearing children and, knowing they could never care
for the babies, giving them up for adoption.

And I saw children deciding not to bear children because they could not   *56*
deal with the harsh reality I called "life" and they called "survival." They had
abortions. And I could no longer judge them or be so certain of God's will.
It wasn't so easy anymore to declare a woman right or wrong, moral or
immoral.

I probably should have left the Sisters of Notre Dame in 1976. It would   *57*
have saved them, and me, a lot of trouble if I had. I had discovered the

obvious but painful truth that it was not necessary to be a nun to be committed to humanity. The women I worked with at Long Lane were motivated out of all their different religious traditions, or no religious tradition at all. They treated the children with respect and reverence, and they challenged and sustained me. I had as whole new idea of community, and a vastly enlarged view of the world.

Very often, as I think back on those years, I wish that more nuns had 58 allowed their parochial world to be expanded. There was nothing to be afraid of. My experience enriched my life, and I believe it made me a better nun— at least according to my own understanding of what made a nun.

At home, at St. Justin's Convent, the question of what made a nun was 59 destroying my primary community.

St. Justin's was once the pride of the Irish community in Hartford. But 60 by 1973 it had become a poor black parish in a declining neighborhood. The school was financially poor, but the eight nuns I lived with who taught there were excellent, committed teachers.

We tried to develop a meaningful program for nuns too. Almost every 61 morning we attended mass in the convent chapel. We experimented with our morning and evening prayers, creating mixtures of readings drawn from secular work and biblical passages. I was very conscious of being on a spiritual quest.

"I don't like the term 'God the Father,'" I grumbled to my spiritual 62 director one afternoon. She was astonished.

"But why? Your father is a good father," she said. 63

"I know, but the idea of God as Father seems exclusive somehow. Exclusive of me, I guess." 64

Pretty soon I would start reading books about God as Mother—and that 65 was the most inclusive idea I had ever come across.

I began to discuss the matter with the spiritual director. A spiritual 66 director was a kind of post-Vatican II version of a novice director. We would meet once a month and she would ask some questions: "How do you see God moving in your life? In what direction do you see yourself moving? What are the different challenges in your life as far as work and community goes?"

The last was the most pressing question. We were a community of 67 young women, and I deeply valued their support when I came home with the confusion and despair I sometimes felt after a day at Long Lane. But only two of us had already taken our final vows. The rest had to face an annual period of evaluation we all went through before renewing our vows.

Our weekly community business meetings became more and more 68 strained. Sometimes I wished I could bring in Ida with her therapeutic skills, and sometimes I wished I could work the evening shift at Long Lane permanently so I would never have to attend another community supper at St. Justin's. Without the old narrow rules we developed friendships, and connections beyond the convent, and opinions, and we didn't seem to be able to solve the resulting problems in our own circle.

The real problem was that my sisters had also realized they could live   69
committed lives without being nuns. Some were disillusioned with community living, and some wanted to get married and have children. Toward the
end the only topic at our meetings was whether to leave or to stay. Donna and
Peggy left, and then Mary Anne, Laura, and Julie. I began to have conversations with myself as I drove to Long Lane.

"Do you want to stay?"   70

"Are you sure you want to be a nun?"   71

"What about these vows you are supposed to be taking soon?"   72

"Who's going to be left?"   73

Why did I stay? My best friends had left, taking some part of me with   74
them. But their arguments were not my answers. And I could not, for myself, assemble enough reasons to leave. I was still committed to my own spiritual path.

If I was not going to leave, I would have to go forward. And, of all   75
things, I would have to go forward by going back to school. I had tangled
with reality, and I needed to make sense of it theologically.

I applied to the Jesuit School of Theology in Chicago for a three-year   76
course that would make me a Master of Divinity.

Topics for Discussion and Writing

1. Whether you agree with the values of Barbara Ferraro and Patricia Hussey
   or not, was it important that these women spoke out as they did? Why or
   why not?
2. What audience do you think Ferraro and Hussey were trying to reach by
   writing? Do you think that they were writing for an audience that holds
   similar beliefs?
3. In another passage the authors state that they are pro life, but that their
   interpretation of *prolife* includes the life of the mother as well as that of
   the unborn baby. Write your feelings about this statement. Does it seem
   contradictory?
4. Why do you think that these women decided to remain in the Catholic
   Church after they left the sisterhood?

LINDA BIRD FRANCKE

from *The Ambivalence of Abortion*

"*I don't think she killed the baby. The life we were living at that time did. We mutually killed the baby. Because of our own selfish circumstances, we caused the child to die. A child, regardless of sex, who would have been a hell of a child. He or she would have been a fantastic kid, and if it had been a boy . . . The abortion killed a part of our life together. A terribly important part was our children and the ones we were going to have. And this killed the next fantastic one . . .*"

Linda Bird Francke graduated from Bradford Junior College in Bradford, Massachusetts. A widely published author of popular culture, she has written for McCall's, MS., Harper's Bazaar, the New York Times, *and* Institutional Investor. *She has also worked as a contributing editor to* New York *magazine and as an editor of* Newsweek.

The following essay, Francke's revised version of her interview with Robert French, is reprinted from her collection The Ambivalence of Abortion.

Before and as You Read

1. Remember a time when you made an important decision that you later regretted. In your journal write about the situation. Did you finally resolve the conflict of regret in your mind? How?

2. Visit a local office of Planned Parenthood, or visit the student health office on your campus. What information do these offices give now that the gag rule on abortion counseling has been lifted by President Clinton? What changes do they foresee in the future? How does the staff feel about their work? Is there an attempt to offer a balance of options to young women and couples?

3. Many parents (or prospective parents) desire a child of a specific sex. What are some of the reasons? What are some ways that children might react if they perceive that they are not the child that the parents wanted? Think of some of the long-term affects that such children could face later in life.

4. As you read this selection, determine the response that French might be trying to elicit from you, his reader. What do you believe is the response that editor Francke is trying to achieve? (Keep in mind that French's story is an oral narration. How does this affect the story?)

5. Picture a meeting among French, Barbara Ferraro, and Patricia Hussey. How might these two women counsel French regarding his feelings of guilt?

THOUGH THREE years have passed since Robert French's wife had   *1*
an abortion, he has never forgiven her or himself for letting it
happen. The father of two girls and the stepfather of a ten-year-old boy,
French, forty-three, deeply wants a son of his own, and the thought that the
fetus might have been a son haunts him. Though he supported his wife
throughout the abortion and appeared to agree with her, he never aired his
deep sense of loss. The hostility and lack of communication between the
couple has now led them to the brink of divorce. French, a stockbroker in
San Francisco, is a man caught between the old concept of woman as wife
and mother and the more difficult concept of woman as wife, mother, and
professional. He is hopeful they will get back together. Thoughtful and articulate, he is obviously still very upset and broke down twice during the
interview.

"I don't think my wife was using any birth control at the time, mainly   *2*
because we slept together so infrequently. She felt that (a) the pill had complications because of its chemical content, and (b) she had gone back to the
diaphragm, which she resented using. I think she resented it because when she
thought that we might make love she put it in, and when we didn't make love
she felt foolish. It soured her and disappointed her. Also, she felt that it was a
one-sided deal, that it was the woman who had to use birth control. I refuse
to wear rubbers. Rubbers are very insensitive, and putting them on is the
fastest two-handed game in town. That night I didn't know whether she had
a diaphragm on or not. I didn't think about the circumstances at all.

"We made love rarely because there were tensions in our marriage,   *3*
which were unresolved. There were a lot of things unsaid that inhibited sex.
A lot of the things she was doing disturbed and interrupted my life. Her job
filled her life substantially. There was no room left for me. I wanted attention
and wasn't getting it. I think I was punishing her by not sleeping with her. I
don't know whether she wanted to sleep with me or not. I never asked her.
We never talked about that kind of thing, and we should have.

"The night she got pregnant was the first time we'd made love in maybe   *4*
two months. We'd gone to one of her assignments, which was to promote a
string of discotheques. I was slightly surly and resentful I had to go. It wasn't
something I had conjured and wanted to do, but off we went.

"While we were there, she did her job and I sat and had my head   *5*
pounded by insensate noise. Finally, we went to the last one, and it was a zoo
of a place, a cellar someplace. There were people crawling all over each other
and a couple humping in a corner by the men's room. You could get stoned
in the men's room just by smelling the air. I felt a disgust at the degeneracy of
the place, but that wasn't important. It was two A.M. I had a job that required
my being on the top of my game, and I wanted to go home. We were in a
seedy part of town and the crowd was fairly rough, lurching around half
stoned, half undressed. I felt wrong leaving her alone there. She could have
gotten in a lot of trouble or at least have been scared. I didn't want to leave a
woman alone under those circumstances. It would have been very irresponsible.

"But she kept working, and I was alone. Finally I was really furious. I was half drunk and madder than hell. It was close to three when we got home. I went slamming up to bed and turned my face and body as far away as I possibly could from her. She got in and came creeping over and was being affectionate and sexy. I spun right around, and we made love fairly rapidly but quite passionately. It was as passionate as our lovemaking had been in some time. I had emotions working. It was a combination of anger and sex that stimulated me. I don't know how she felt.   6

"I wasn't paying particular attention to her feelings at the time. I don't recall if she had an orgasm. And I almost always knew when she did, and I tried very hard to make sure she was pleased.   7

"Six weeks later I came home one night, and she said immediately, 'Let's have a drink.' We sat in the living room and she said something to the effect that 'You'll be glad to know your pencil still has lead in it.' I didn't understand her. Then she said, 'I'm pregnant,' and that was when my emotions became deeply ambivalent.   8

"In one sense I was deeply proud she was pregnant. I was proud I'd made her pregnant, and the idea of having children was terribly important to me. We had two girls, and I'd always very, very deeply wanted to have a son. When we first approached our marriage six years before, we'd talked gaily about raising a baseball team of boys, and we had two girls, both of whom I loved passionately. I recalled that her gynecologist had told me that the chances of a third child being of the same sex were 66 percent to 33 percent. My immediate reaction, without any attempt to use conception methods to determine having one sex rather than the other, was that this child had been created arbitrarily and that the gynecologist's odds would prevail, and we'd have another girl.   9

"She said, 'What should I do about it?' And I said, 'The one thing we don't need in our life is another Mergatrude.' My feeling was that if there were any reasonable chance it would have been a boy, I desperately wanted it. But the oddsmakers had told me it wouldn't.   10

"I was cold and rational at the time. As our life was then, things were stretched pretty thin. We had three children in the house, and she was working hard. I was trying to balance in my head the pluses and minuses of another child. If it could have been a boy, I would have said I very much wanted the child. If she had insisted on an abortion anyway, I would have been very upset and fought to have the child. If she had needed my consent for the abortion, for example, I wouldn't have given it.   11

"She wanted an abortion. I don't know what was going on in her head, but I don't think she wanted another child at the time, be it boy or girl. I guess I was presuming she was listening to the same oddsmakers. She knew my feeling about having a boy, and I think she shared it absolutely. Had it occurred to her it might have been a boy, she might have had a different view.   12

"She said, 'Shall I have an abortion?' and I said, 'I guess so.' She made all the arrangements for a week later. The whole week I was extremely jumpy   13 and preoccupied. People at work kept asking me why I was so preoccupied. I kept twirling the decision over and over in my head. A lot had to do with the women's movement, of which my wife was a part and which presumed a woman's ability to go out and make a good living without being dragged down by familial obligations. I felt this child would hurt that. She was just beginning to ascend in a good and important job. Pregnancy and all the things that go with it would have knocked the shit out of her career, it just having taken off after the birth of our second child.

"The contradiction was that under any circumstance, I wanted the child. 14 Period. Regardless of sex. And I was swinging on a bridge that it might be a boy. I would do anything for that regardless of her career. I was forced rationally to believe the goddamned oddsmaker because that's the way I think. Emotionally I felt shitty. I felt just terrible. I've always wanted lots of children. I just wanted more. I feel a very deep commitment to each child.

"On Saturday morning we went off to the abortion clinic. There were 15 all kinds of people there, all seemingly sad, which might have been my own emotional transference. The men seemed very nervous. I was very nervous. It was the build-up of all the ambivalence I felt all week. And was the whole procedure safe? There were serious things about to happen to her insides. What was going to be the effect on her body? All these clinics are bullshit. They all have nice reception rooms, but behind them is the risk of permanent harm and death. It's a scary procedure.

"I was also nervous because it was not clear to me that this was what I 16 wanted to do. My wife and I were being very stiff upper lip about going in because we'd made up our minds and it was an 'I'll see you through anything' sort of thing.

"We sat there and waited. There were all sorts of boobs and incompe- 17 tents hanging around saying, 'Miss So-and-so, it's your turn.' You can't trust those people.

"And then she left me. The minute she went through those doors I had 18 the feeling, 'Oh, God, I don't want this to happen.' Besides the rational reasons, all the emotional reasons happened at the moment she went through those doors. All the reasons that I'd conjured up that this was a good idea were stripped away. I had committed myself and her to this course of action for all good reasons, but without thought to the emotions it was causing. My whole emotional makeup went *phutz*. I felt bare and had a gut anguish. I stared at those doors she had vanished through in the hands of an incompetent, and I felt that I desperately wanted to impel myself through them and grab her away, but I did none of that.

"Instead I drove home and scurried around our house doing things to 19 make it pleasant for her return. I set out a table in front of the fireplace in the bedroom and got the fire all ready to light. I made myself very busy for the two hours she was in the clinic. I got some soup or something for her lunch.

"I picked her up at the hospital and brought her back and tried to make 20 her happy. She was very weepy and weak. When I came into the clinic, I brought her a piece of jade she had always wanted from Gump's. I wanted to give her something to hold onto as a token of my affection and love for the terrible thing she'd been through. I tried to tend to her. I didn't need tending to. I hadn't had an abortion. She didn't need me at that point doing a boo-hoo-hoo act. She needed help for herself.

"In retrospect I think a lot of damage was done to our marriage. My 21 fault was in not articulating sooner that it was a child of mine I wanted born. Mostly I was responsive to her life. She wanted to go on working, and there was the women's movement. I was not assertive enough about what I wanted, which was the child. It's pretty hard to have children without a woman, which is something the women's movement tends to ignore.

"In a sense I blamed her for the abortion. Without her requirements for 22 a career, the pregnancy would never have been an issue. I would have said, 'Fuck it.' I love kids. But there was an intensity about the moment regarding women and careers. I paid too much attention to that and not to what I wanted. I don't know how she would have reacted if I'd said this was a child of mine and I wanted it. Instead, I lost control of my own will and didn't say how much it would affect me.

"I left it to the oddsmakers so it wouldn't hurt so much that it might 23 have been a boy. I've been tortured by that thought. I had a desperate need to know what that fetus was, could I have ever known it. Had it been a boy, it would have killed me. At the same time I couldn't have borne knowing. At the same time I wanted to look into the discharge pan, I far more desperately *didn't* want to look into that discharge pan.

"Two weeks later we went to Hawaii on vacation. We were walking 24 down a path at night, and she looked at the palm trees and the flowers and said something about how beautiful it was and how sad not being able to show it to another child and having denied that bit of beauty to a soul. I felt desperate. That was the first chance we'd had to get out of our preoccupied selves and to think about the consequences of what we'd done. It just about killed me, and her too, I think. She wrote a poem and left it in the room. I read it, and I cracked completely. I openly wept for half an hour while she wasn't there.

"I didn't start making love to her again for a long time, and since then 25 we've made love even less than before the abortion. I felt that this child had been sacrificed to her work, and I resented her work from then on. Her work and our emotional life were always at odds. I blamed her work for the sacrifice I felt I'd made.

"From then on our sex life was a real strain. We rarely made love, and 26 when we did, it was very hard. In the summer of 1974, we didn't make love once. From then to the next summer, I was impotent with occasional lapses. The next summer I pulled the twin beds together in our summer house, but we didn't make love but once. I don't know why.

"Other strains had developed. There was even greater attention to her 27 work, greater focus on her life and less on mine. There was no time for us. I had started having affairs outside our marriage where I was not impotent. Between the spring of 1974 and the fall of 1976, I made love to my wife maybe four or five times, and then just because I felt I had to.

"I don't think she killed the baby. The life we were living at that time 28 did. We mutually killed the baby. Because of our own selfish circumstances, we caused the child to die. A child, regardless of sex, who would have been a hell of a child. He or she would have been a fantastic kid, and if it had been a boy . . . The abortion killed a part of our life together. A terribly important part was our children and the ones we were going to have. And this killed the next fantastic one . . .

"She's switched jobs now, and her career doesn't suck the life out of 29 everyone else's time. Our relationship is pretty good. Were she to say, 'I'm content with my life and my soul, and would you like to have a child?' I would say, 'Immediately,' and hope like hell it was a boy. But she hasn't said that, and we haven't discussed it. Nor have we made love in six months.

"I go to a psychiatrist now, and she and I have gone to a psychologist 30 together and I've removed a lot of the wounds. But you never know when they're going to open up again. The eight-year-old son of a close friend was killed in a car accident recently. I went to pieces. Couldn't handle it at all. It took a while to realize that my despair was the grief of the loss of my child, whom I had never had a chance to grieve for and bury. Three years later, I wept openly for hours about the kid who had been killed, a kid I didn't know very well—but then I didn't know mine either. I'm still not sure I have buried that fetus.

"Two years after the abortion a lot of these tensions came to a head. 31 Since that time, despite acknowledged affairs by both of us, we've been trying to weave back a fabric for our continued life together, and I think there's hope for the future. But if she had another abortion, I couldn't hack it. I would go crazy.

"This new breed of women has got it all wrong when they decide not 32 to have children. What these intelligent women owe the world is not just what they do or are—they owe the world a legacy to pass on. To take all the genetic superiors out of the world is to leave a world of moribund morons behind. But they never even consider that, and it would be political suicide to say it.

"I'm not against abortion per se. Abortion depends on the parents. Some 33 people want children and some don't. I want kids. Sure I've got two of them. This was another one."

Topics for Discussion and Writing

1. French describes in some detail how much he regrets his inaction on the day of the abortion. There seems to be a contradiction between his feelings and his actions. Yet, in some ways, what he did makes a great deal of sense. Why?

2. French states, "The minute she went through those doors I had the feeling, 'Oh, God, I don't want this to happen.'" He is eloquent in the pain that describes. Describe his sense of powerlessness. How might he have been able to stop what he felt he would later regret?

3. How does French describe his wife? Based on what he says, write a character sketch of this woman. Do you understand her? Why or why not? Do the same for French. What kind of a man is he? What kind of a husband? What kind of a father?

4. French is raising his two daughters and the son of his wife by a previous marriage. Why do you suppose that this boy does not qualify in his mind as the son he desperately wants?

5. In your journal, write a "postscript" page to end this story. Tell us what eventually happens to this family. How are they leading their lives today? Does French deal with his depression constructively or destructively? Share your work with your class.

"Teenagers and AIDS"

> *"The first thing the kids ask about is her sex life. 'I don't have a sex life,' she tells them, 'but that's because I don't have any energy to have a sex life. . . . I have just so much energy and I have to decide, do I come out here and talk to you, or do I have sex? I pick what's important, and you won.'"*
> —Krista Blake

Before and as You Read

1. Critics of sex education and of free condom distribution in schools believe that these practices might encourage promiscuity. What are your views on the subject? Discuss this issue in small groups and present your opinions to the class.

2. Talk to your parents or grandparents about how sexual standards have changed since they were in school. What were the standards to which they were expected to adhere? Who set those guidelines? How easy was it to be a young adult when they were growing up?

3. One mother of a teenager said, "If he doesn't learn anything else in four years of high school, I hope that he learns the importance of practicing 'protected sex.'" But what about those parents (reflected in question 1) who would keep such school-based information not only from their own children, but also from this woman's son? Should society expose children to certain basic information to protect both the individual and the community at large?

4. In your journal write a private entry about your thoughts on AIDS. As you read the following selection, imagine yourself to be one of these people. What do you learn from their attitudes? Fears? Courage?

THE DIN inside the downtown Seattle video arcade is overpowering: guns blasting away, bells ringing wildly. None of the 50 or so teens inside notices the tall kid with a Falcons cap who walks in. He steps up to two boys engrossed in a shooting game. "Hey, brothers, you using condoms?" he asks. They nod, barely looking his way. "Need some?" he says, shoving a handful toward them. The boys grab the condoms and stuff them into their pockets. The intruder isn't finished with them. "Know much about AIDS and HIV?" he continues, with the patter of a door-to-door salesman. "Yeah," they answer, in unison. "Then you know you can get it from unprotected sex and sharing needles?" They nod. He quickly hands them a brochure: "This will answer any other questions you have."

The kid in the Falcons cap is Kevin Turner and at 19, he is already an experienced warrior on the front lines of the battle against AIDS. He carries his weapon of choice, condoms, in a black leather bag strapped around his chest. Turner works for POCAAN (People of Color Against AIDS Network). Officially, he's a peer educator; unofficially, he's "Mr. Condom," on call 24 hours a day. He gives out hundreds of condoms every week and has been known to burst into conversations when he hears someone talking about sex. "You're going to use condoms, aren't you?" he'll ask. "Here, have a few."

It's a tough sell, even though it's literally a matter of life and death. A 3
congressional report issued in April warned that HIV, the virus that causes AIDS, is "spreading unchecked among the nation's adolescents, regardless of where they live or their economic status." Since the beginning of the epidemic, more than 5,000 children and young adults have died of AIDS; it is now the sixth leading cause of death among 15- to 24-year-olds. No one knows exactly how many teens are HIV-positive, but during the past three years, the cumulative number of 13- to 24-year-olds diagnosed with AIDS increased 77 percent. By the end of last year, AIDS cases in that age group had been reported in almost every state and the District of Columbia. Nearly half of the afflicted teenagers come from just six places: New York, New Jersey, Texas, California, Florida and Puerto Rico.

No one has yet managed to screen a true cross-section of any commu- 4
nity's adolescents, but Dr. Lawrence D'Angelo has come close. Since late 1987, the Washington, D.C., pediatrician has tested virtually all the blood samples drawn from 13- to 20-year-olds at Children's National Medical Center, a large public hospital serving kids from all over the metropolitan area. Of the samples drawn between October 1987 and January 1989, one in 250 tested positive. During the next study period (through October 1991), the infection rate rose to one in 90. D'Angelo predicts that one sample in 50 will test positive this year.

Up to now, the majority of afflicted teens have been males, minorities 5
and older adolescents—who, given the long incubation period, probably got the virus in their early teens. But the future holds the frightening prospect of much more widespread illness. A 1990 study of blood samples drawn from college students on 19 campuses found that one student in 500 tested positive. In 1991, the rate among 137,000 Job Corps participants was closer to one in 300. According to U.S. Surgeon General Antonia Novello, the ratio of female to male AIDS patients has doubled in the last four years, with females going from 17 percent of adolescent cases in 1987 to 39 percent of cases last year.

The virus is spreading because adolescent sexual behavior is risky. Some 6
studies have suggested that up to a quarter of teenagers report engaging in rectal intercourse, sometimes to avoid pregnancy or to retain their virginity. But that practice is more likely to cause the cuts and tears that invite infection. Many adolescents also report having multiple partners, again increasing their chances of infection.

The most effective ammunition against AIDS for other high-risk 7
groups—gays, drug users, hemophiliacs—has been education: blunt talk, reinforced by peer support groups. But this approach isn't working for teens.

High-risk adults are free to seek any information they want. But teens are at the mercy of adults—parents, teachers, politicians—who often won't give young people the information they desperately need to make the right choices about their sexual behavior. Even in areas where AIDS is widely acknowledged as a serious problem, there's powerful resistance to frank discussion of teenage sexuality—as if avoiding the issue will make it go away. Many communities avoid the issue altogether, says Rep. Patricia Schroeder, because "they know they are going to raise a firestorm" about whether discussing sex and AIDS will "degenerate morals and values." Jerry Permenter, an AIDS educator in east Texas, has offered to teach in many schools in his area, but few have taken him up on his offer, and he is frustrated. "Some people don't want to talk about issues below the waistline," says Permenter. "That is the conservative mind-set that exists right now in east Texas and that is the mind-set that will bury the next generation."

Clearly, teenagers aren't getting the safe-sex message—either at home or in school. Although many adolescents say they use condoms, experts think most don't. According to the congressional study, only 47 percent of females and 55 percent of males used condoms the first time they had intercourse. Roger Bohman, who teaches a popular course on AIDS at the University of California, Los Angeles, takes surveys of students' condom use before and after the course. He found that students didn't really change their behavior—even when they knew all the dangers. Says Bohman: "They think it can't happen to them."   8

Teenagers' feelings of invulnerability make them even more difficult to reach than other at-risk groups. Emotionally, they are still children and they still think they are going to be "rescued" from disaster. "We have a hard time gaining compliance from teens," says Dr. E. Richard Stiehm of the Los Angeles Pediatric AIDS Consortium. "They don't watch out for their own health care. I don't think it's ignorance of the consequences so much as the fallacy that it can only happen to someone else." Wendy Arnold, director of the Peer Education Program in Los Angeles, says that a typical attitude is: "I'm practically a virgin. He couldn't have HIV. He drives a nice car and I just had lunch with him."   9

That attitude is deadly. Bridgett Pederson always made her boyfriends use condoms until she met Alberto Gonzalez, then a 24-year-old bartender in Portland, Ore. Pederson, then 17, didn't protest when Gonzalez refused; he told her he was "safe." He was a clean, good-looking guy, so she went along. They began living together when she was 19; a year later, she says, he lost his job and they went to a plasma center to sell their blood. The doctors there told Pederson and Gonzalez that they were both HIV-positive. There was worse news to come. Gonzalez's brother told Pederson that Alberto had known for years that he had the virus—and had already infected a previous girlfriend, Shawn Hop. Armed with that information, Pederson went to the authorities and last October, Gonzalez became the first person in the nation   10 to be convicted on assault charges for passing the virus. He's now in a detention center in Portland.

As for Pederson, she has a new mission: getting the word out. She has become an AIDS activist, appearing on television and speaking to school groups. Her message is simple: "Don't trust someone, even someone you love, to come clean. People aren't always honest about their past sex life or HIV status. I'm a white, middle-class female who is well educated. I didn't fall into any of the high-risk groups, and it happened to me." Pederson, now 23, doesn't have any symptoms yet, but she knows her good health won't last forever. Although she's comfortable talking frankly to groups of teens about the virus, it was painful to visit Shawn Hop, Gonzalez's previous girlfriend, who died June 15. In her last days, Shawn was pale, gaunt and bedridden. Seeing her scared Pederson: "I wonder if I'm looking into my future."

Pederson's story is shocking—and when the young people she talks to hear it, they can't ignore the message. But AIDS educators say that while first-person testimony is important, teens also need careful instruction in how to prevent the disease. A recent study of 100 programs that reduced high-risk behavior among teens indicated that young people need more than good medical information, they also need training in how to stand up to peer pressure. Other reports indicate that each at-risk group has different needs. For example, heterosexual teenagers need to understand that they are not immune just because they're straight. Gay teens, on the other hand, need special support as they cope with accepting their sexuality and the possibility of disease. Dr. June Osborn, chair of the National Commission on AIDS, says that kids want frank answers from someone who is not judgmental or condemnatory. "They know their peers are sexually active and they know there's something out there they don't know enough about," she says. "They know the adult world is quarreling about condoms, and they are terribly eager to ask questions."

But getting those questions answered has not been simple—even in supposedly "liberal" areas of the country where AIDS among adults is openly discussed. For example, New York leads the nation in the number of AIDS cases among teenagers and the state's schools and health facilities have pioneered approaches to AIDS education. Since 1987, all public schools in New York have been required to include HIV/AIDS instruction as part of their sex-education and family-planning programs. And last fall, New York City became the first major city to begin giving out free condoms to high-school students despite pressure from religious groups and others opposed to the program.

But last May, after 92 of the city's 120 high schools had implemented condom-distribution plans, the city school board voted to bar a state-approved video and city-produced pamphlet used in the schools. The board members said the materials did not place enough emphasis on abstinence, and they required all AIDS educators to devote "substantially" more time and attention

AIDS also kills dreams.

At 18, Kaye Brown was ready for the world. The bubbly honor student was looking forward to life in the army. Last March, she signed up at a recruiting office in Houston and took a mandatory AIDS test. A week later she learned she was HIV-positive, and the world was no longer a sure thing. "I was really, really angry," she says. "My career had been snatched away from me."

Though doctors estimated that she had contracted the virus recently, they recommended that she get in touch with anyone she had had sex with in the previous year. The list was long. "It was easy for me to list the guys I had slept with," she says, "but when I counted 24, I was like, gosh!" Brown chose to tell them personally. One former partner said, "But you don't look like you're that way." Brown shot back, "What is that way? HIV doesn't mean that I'm dirty or low. It just means I made a mistake." Her boyfriend couldn't cope with the news, and they split up. Not one man was willing to be tested. "They were too scared," Brown says.

Brown blames only herself; she never insisted on condoms. "It makes me angry that I allowed this to happen," she says. "Choices I made have stolen away the choices that I might have had in the future." Now she's turning her anger to good use by working at the AIDS Foundation Houston Inc., talking to teens. "Kids see people who have HIV as bad," she says. "I'm out there to prove that it does happen to good, everyday people." Most teenagers, says Brown, won't practice safe sex unless someone really close to them becomes ill. HIV, she tells them, "doesn't discriminate. It doesn't care how old you are or who you are." She refuses to put her life on hold, and next fall she'll attend Texas Southern University. She gobbles up romance novels ("If you can't live it, read it," she jokes) and lives a day at a time: "That way, worry won't kill me before HIV does." AIDS, she says, has given her a purpose: "I feel responsible for educating other young people. That's my big mission; that's why I'm here."

to abstinence than to other methods of prevention. The restrictions went even further, requiring outside AIDS groups working with the schools to abide by the rules as well. The board's actions have been challenged by the New York Civil Liberties Union; to date, there has been no ruling. In the meantime, the city's AIDS educators complain that they can't work under censorship. "This is a disaster for us," says Cydelle Berlin, coordinator of the adolescent AIDS-prevention program at Mount Sinai Medical Center. "We're talking life and death. We can't submit our work to the sex police."

Sessions at clinics like Berlin's go far beyond technical descriptions of the virus—and discussions of abstinence seem beside the point. On one recent afternoon, 20-year-old Jerome Bannister held up a pink plastic penis for a group of inner-city teens. "Anybody wanna touch this?" he asked. "His name is Johnson." Bannister's 20-year-old partner, Diana Hernandez, flicked open a

15

flesh-colored condom. "We've got a little friend here," she said. Bannister went next. "You wanna put a little jelly inside," he said, gesturing toward the condom. "There are a lot of nerve endings in the penis. That way you get that wet, hot feeling when it's in the vagina where it's warm. But lubrication's not only for that warm feeling. It's also a backup. If you use nonoxynol-9, it can kill the sperm—and the HIV virus." Many experts believe that nonoxynol-9 helps prevent transmission. Bannister and Hernandez then demonstrated exactly how to slip the condom on the penis. The team went through equally detailed descriptions of dental dams and the new female condom, which is inserted like a diaphragm. Their audience took the session very seriously, asking questions about where to buy condoms and grabbing handfuls of free samples.

Buying condoms isn't enough; kids also need help persuading partners to use them. Many AIDS programs focus on role-playing, giving teens practical strategies for dealing with social pressure. "All these kids want to do is fit in with their peers," says Dr. Marvin Belzer of Children's Hospital in Los Angeles. "If a young woman thinks she'll lose her boyfriend if she insists on condoms, and feels that he is the only reason she is somebody, she's not going to use them." There are mixed cultural messages to deal with, too. A boy who is told that having sex with multiple partners is dangerous is also being told that more sexual conquests make him more of a man. "In this society, if we want to make a difference, we have to stop the mixed message between parental and community values versus the values portrayed in the media," says Belzer.

Straight teens have a difficult time sorting out conflicting values; gay teens have even fewer resources—and they have to contend with cultural prejudices and their own mixed emotions about their emerging sexual identity. "Nobody wants to talk about male-to-male sex in the teen population," says Rene Durazzo of the San Francisco AIDS Foundation. AIDS experts say that prevention campaigns designed for older gay men don't help teenagers. "Education efforts to date assume youths have choices and are free agents," says Barry Lawlor of the Haight Ashbury Free Clinic in San Francisco. "Many youths do not have choices . . . They're new to sexual behavior and they can be exploited." The likelihood of exploitation increases among runaways who are desperate for money. "On the streets, when a teen says he's not going to have sex without a condom and the other guy says he'll pay $20 more if he does, that's a lot of pressure," Lawlor says. But even teens still at home take risks when they know they shouldn't. The need for love and affection overwhelms the fear of getting sick. Scott Miller, 24, of San Francisco, discovered he was HIV-positive in college. He says that when he was a teenager, his sense of self-worth was low; witnessing a particularly violent gay-bashing incident made him feel even more vulnerable. "Unsafe behavior was OK if it would make you my friend," he says. "If this person wouldn't want me because I wanted to use a condom, well, I'd rather have him like me."

> *Getting a driver's license was a liberating experience for 16-year-old Wally Hansen, who grew up in a household so "normal [it was] almost like 'Leave It to Beaver'." He and some buddies in suburban Pinole, Calif., would cut classes and drive to the woods near a gay beach in San Francisco, where they would "frolic" with each other and the men they met there. Hansen never considered using a condom—this was the mid '80s, when safe sex meant not getting caught by your parents.*
>
> *Hansen eventually joined the air force. But in 1987, he was discharged after the service discovered he was a homosexual. Routine exit exams revealed the presence of the AIDS virus. Hansen, now 24, is almost certain he was first exposed to HIV during his hooky-playing days. Had he known about the growing epidemic, he says, he might have altered his behavior. He is convinced that education is the key to stopping the spread of AIDS among young people. The effort, he says, should begin in junior high. And since teenagers "are going to have sex no matter what," it's important, "especially in high school, to hand out condoms, anything." Hansen, an administrative assistant at the Bay Area Reporter, a gay paper in San Francisco, is active in the AIDS war. For two years he was a driver for Rubbermen, an organization that donates condoms to city bars, and now volunteers at AIDS fund raisers.*
>
> *But when it comes to his own health—and sometimes that of others— Hansen is reckless. He says he has used speed intermittently for two years. Though he knows that unprotected sex brings the risk of more infections with more strains of the AIDS virus, he doesn't always use a condom. He admits that many of his peers who are HIV-positive don't always inform their partners of their condition, on the assumption that they are infected, too. Some may see it as the behavior of the doomed, but to Hansen, "it basically comes down to what you think it's worth." He insists he wouldn't be happy if he restricted his activities. "I can only think positively. I do anything I want. I feel like I'd do more damage to myself by stressing my system out of worry." His family has taken his illness in stride. "My mom and dad told me they may not love the things I do," says Hansen, "but they love me." And that, sad to say, makes him luckier than many.*

Gay teens who discover they are HIV-positive must tell their parents— often in the same conversation—that they're gay and that they're infected. Sue Beardsley, a volunteer with Rest Stop, a San Francisco support center for people with AIDS, still remembers the phone call she got from 16-year-old David on the last night of his life. His family was thousands of miles away and he didn't want to be alone. She rushed to his hospital room; a few hours later he died in her arms. Beardsley telephoned David's mother to tell her that her son was gone. "My son David doesn't exist," the mother said. "He died a year ago." That was when David had told his mother he was gay.

18

In the fall of 1990, Krista Blake was 18 and looking forward to her first year at Youngstown State University in Ohio. She and her boyfriend were talking about getting married. Her life, she says, was "basic, white bread America." Then she went to the doctor, complaining about a backache, and found out she had the AIDS virus.

Blake had been infected with HIV, the virus that causes AIDS, two years earlier by an older boy, a hemophiliac. "He knew that he was infected, and he didn't tell me," she says. "And he didn't do anything to keep me from getting infected, either." When she first heard the diagnosis, Blake felt as though she had just walked into a brick wall. Suddenly, she couldn't envision her future. She found herself thinking things like "There are 50 states out there. I don't want to just live and die in Ohio." Her doctor sent her to University Hospital in Cleveland, 90 minutes from home, for treatment. She has taken AZT and is now on the new antiviral DDI. Although she needed frequent transfusions to counteract the effects of AZT, she is relatively healthy. "I am living with AIDS, not dying from AIDS," she says. "I do all of the same things I used to do. That doesn't mean I can run the Boston Marathon, but my mind is still 20." She reads everything from Danielle Steel to "Life 101," a popular advice book. She makes a point of going out at least once every day even if it's just down to the park to watch a softball game. "It gets those juices moving," she says.

Still, she doesn't know how long her good health will last—a month, a year, five years. She doesn't make longterm commitments. Blake and her fiancé broke off their engagement, because, she says, "I love him enough that I want him to have his options for a life open." However, they are still very good friends. Blake also dropped out of school. "A bachelor's degree wouldn't do much for me," she says with a rueful laugh.

Since the spring of 1991, Blake has spent as many as four or five days a week doing the one thing she believes is really important—talking to other teens about HIV and how to avoid infection. The first thing the kids ask about is her sex life. "I don't have a sex life," she tells them, "but that's because I don't have any energy to have a sex life." The kids usually start laughing. Then she says: "I have just so much energy and I have to decide, do I come out here and talk to you, or do I have sex? I pick what's important, and you won." After one presentation, a student came up to Blake and told her: "I had an uncle who came home at Easter one year, and he had AIDS. This was in 1988. My mom was afraid. We didn't go see him. She wouldn't let us go. He died the next year, at Easter. I never got to say goodbye to my uncle. Would it be OK if I came up and gave you a hug?"

Lucille Beachy

Fear of such rejection compels many gay teens to keep both their sexual   *19*
identity and their HIV status a secret. They're desperate for a "safe place"
where they can talk freely. One such place is Bay Positives in San Francisco, a
peer support group for HIV-positive young people. Jim Neiss, 21, a Bay Positives member, says that even though his family is behind him, he needs the
group as well. "In the middle of the night, if I'm really upset or traumatized
about something, I don't hesitate to call a member." They share a tragic bond:
confronting the prospect of an unnaturally early death before they have even
embarked on their adult lives. Support groups for adult AIDS sufferers often
seem irrelevant because the adult agenda is so different. In adult groups,
says therapist Julie Graham, a founder of Bay Positives, "People talk about
stuff . . . they'll never have. Like wills. Young people with HIV often don't
have enough material possessions to need a will. Or relationships. Young
people with HIV feel like they're never going to get the chance to have a
relationship."

Knowing that life will be short gives other HIV-positive young people a   *20*
special sense of purpose. Amy Dolph grew up in the quintessential small town
of Katy, Texas. In the spring of 1987, she seemed to be just a typical all-
American girl: blond, blue-eyed, with nothing more serious on her mind than
going steady and heading for college in the fall. But when she donated blood
to help her ailing great-grandmother, she found out that the second man she
slept with had given her HIV. She was shocked and confused. The last of her
friends to lose her virginity, she didn't sleep around. "Every one of my dreams
was shattered, blown away," she says. To this day she isn't sure how the man
who infected her contracted the virus; she knew that he had been sexually
active at an early age and had experimented with drugs. Later she found out
that he was also bisexual. She is past the stage of blaming him but says she
wishes she had known more and had understood that she could be at risk.
"Back then we were always reading that you're only at high risk if you're this
group, this group or this group," she says. "And you're at low risk if you're a
sexually active heterosexual. And everyone saw that 'low risk' as 'no risk'."

Dolph, now 23, works with the AIDS Foundation Houston Inc. in its   *21*
education program, traveling to urban and rural high schools and junior highs
to talk about AIDS. She's trying to give the kids something she never got—a
warning. She tells teenagers that they shouldn't allow their sex partners, no
matter how close they are to them, to have control over when they're going
to die. "Do you want to put your life in that other person's hands? Is that boy
or girl worth dying for? I doubt it." Dolph doesn't dwell on the past and she
doesn't look too far ahead into the future. Her present is full—and, for the
moment, that has to be enough.

Barbara Kantrowitz with Mary Hager in Washington, Geoffrey Cowley
and Lucille Beachy in New York, Melissa Rossi in Seattle, Brynn Craffey
in San Francisco, Peter Annin in Houston, Rebecca Crandall in Los An-
geles and bureau reports

Topics for Discussion and Writing

1. This article states that Wally Hansen is reckless and doesn't always use a condom despite his disease. "I do anything I want. I feel like I'd do more damage to myself by stressing my system out of worry." With a group of classmates discuss his attitude. When is "unsafe sex" acceptable?

2. On September 25, 1992, Magic Johnson resigned from the National Commission on AIDS because he said George Bush was fighting the disease with "lip service and photo opportunities" (*Washington Post* 26 Sept. 1992). What role should the Clinton administration take with regard to AIDS education and research? With regard to the support of AIDS patients and their families?

3. It has been stated that although teens recognize the problem of sex linked to AIDS, they are less likely to worry about themselves "because it can't happen to me." How did the people in this selection show this attitude? In what other ways do teenagers take unreasonable risks?

4. Compare the tone of the stories represented here. How would you characterize the mood of these pieces? Underline the words or phrases that convey that tone to you.

MARTHA BARRON BARRETT
from *Invisible Lives*

>"The secretary that I had for eight years when I was teaching watched an *ABC* documentary and, as I came into the office, asked, 'Did you see that *ABC News* Closeup last night?' I said, 'Yeah, I did,' and I was about to say I thought parts of it were really good, when she said, 'I turned it right off. It made me nauseous. I wanted to throw up. I'd never be around those lesbian/ gay people. They're sick.' And I was standing there. I almost said, 'Lou, I'm one of them.'"

>Martha Barron Barrett was born in Pittsburgh, Pennsylvania, and received degrees in the social sciences from the University of Maine and the University of Pennsylvania. She taught in Philadelphia for 13 years. She has written two novels: Maggie's Way *(1981)* and God's Country *(1987)*. Invisible Lives: The Truth About Millions of Women Loving Women *was published in 1989.*

>Martha Barron Barrett lives on the coast of Maine and winters in New Hampshire.

Before and as You Read

1. Recall a situation in which you felt you could not be yourself. What were the circumstances? How did you act? Why? Were you alone in that situation? Were you afraid? Angry? What did you learn from your experience?

2. Define the word *stereotype*. With this definition in mind, list as many groups as you can that you have heard stereotyped. Write a character sketch of a fictional person from one of those groups. Deliberately use stereotypes. What nationality is this person? What is his or her race? Religious affiliation? What does this person look like? How does she or he speak? What level of education has this person attained? Describe where this person lives and his or her close friends and plans for the future.

   Review what you have written and identify phrases that are generalizations. Does your sketch dehumanize your character?

   Now write about the same person without the stereotyping. Illustrate this person's unique qualities as a human being. Draw out his or her personal traits that are counter to the generalizations of the first sketch you wrote. Does your treatment of the second character change your feelings for him or her? Why is it dangerous to use stereotypes when referring to people?

3. In your journal, discuss your feelings about homosexuality. How did you reach your opinions? Have your views changed at any time? If so, how and why?

4. As you read this selection, note how the author makes her presence felt throughout. Give examples of this. Why do you suppose Barrett decided

to interject her presence rather than just record the dialogue among the women as it occurred? As a writer, how would you have presented this piece? Does the author's presence enhance it? Detract from it?

2: LIVING TWO LIVES

TAYLOR, SIX feet tall with an athlete's body, a competent manner   1
and a gentle voice, has lived in Spokane, Washington, all of her adult life. Short, dusty-blond hair curls around her face, glasses frame blue eyes. "What really tears me up inside is their ignorance. The straight world just doesn't understand. If I had the guts, I could help, but there's that part of me that doesn't want to shed my blood to be the sacrificial lamb for the women in the year 2040 to be out. I'm ashamed of that. But I have to live.

"The secretary that I had for eight years when I was teaching watched   2
an ABC documentary and, as I came into the office, asked, 'Did you see that ABC News *Closeup* last night?' I said, 'Yeah, I did,' and I was about to say I thought parts of it were really good, when she said, 'I turned it right off. It made me nauseous. I wanted to throw up. I'd never be around those lesbian/gay people. They're sick.' And I was standing there. I almost said, 'Lou, I'm one of them.'

"She really likes me, and it would throw her into shock, but after she   3
thought about it . . . I kept thinking, 'You're so ignorant. I'm right here. I'm in the flesh. You go out drinking with me. We've shared a room together during Special Olympics.'"

For the past twelve years Taylor, who is thirty-seven, has lived in an   4
older suburban neighborhood of modest houses and has created a private backyard world by building a deck, an enclosure for a hot tub, and a high fence around the yard. On this July night her long, tan legs are stretched toward where Kate, her partner for three years, sits with her slender body carefully composed, her hazel eyes alert, her long black hair loose around her shoulders. Tara, delicate, bubbly, and Lisa, grave and watchful, a pixielike couple who have been together less than a year, share a lounge chair. Tara is twenty-five, Kate and Lisa twenty-nine; all are natives of Spokane. Their names, including Taylor's, are fictitious.

The women exchange stories about the raw edges where the lesbian and   5
heterosexual worlds meet. A straight woman traveling with longtime lesbian friends hears the motel maid say she is sorry she forgot to put extra blankets for both beds in their room. With surprise and anger she realizes that her friends pretend to sleep in separate beds.

Taylor nods and adds, "When Kate and I were in Hawaii, we got up   6
every morning and jumped around on the beds to make it look like they had both been slept in. You just do this constantly."

Tara leans forward. "It wasn't like that when I traveled with Lisa. She   7
made all the reservations by phone, and I heard her say, 'No. Two women.
One bed.' 'Lisa, what are you doing!' I yelled. She's determined. But we don't
have any less service. I walk around like this"—Tara shields one side of her
face with her hand—"but we're fine."

Lisa, who acknowledged her lesbian sexuality only eight months ago, is   8
fighting not to lose self-respect, not to treat or be treated by the world any
differently. "Every time you make reservations, you have to go through this,
and it makes me mad. When we show up, it doesn't seem as though anyone
stares at us strangely, but we look alike in a way, and maybe they think we're
sisters." She describes the assumptions of heterosexuality that assault and invade
her from store windows, billboards, and movies, then adds, "Tara will say,
'God, sometimes I just feel ripped off.'"

Kate was married for three and a half years, and Taylor is the first woman   9
she has been with. Her entire family lives in Spokane. "Ever since Taylor and
I have been together, there's been a distance between my mother and me. We
used to be very, very close, and I'd talk to her about my relationships. I never
pretend I'm interested in guys—that's just not happening. I can't lie to my
mother, but I can't just go up and tell her. I'm too afraid to tell her. It would
make it much easier if my mother would just come out and say, 'I'm okay
with it.'"

The pretense of having separate bedrooms angers Kate, but "at this point   10
it's something I need to do in order to stay in this relationship and to stay on
the same terms that I want to with my family."

"Her mother's gotten to know me," Taylor says. "Not that that would   11
help . . ." Everyone laughs. "But she used to call and just ask for Kate; now
she talks to me for twenty, thirty minutes."

Kate explains that any sadness she feels about being lesbian "is because I   12
feel separated from my parents. It feels like they don't really know who I am.
There's a big part of me that's not connecting with them. I'd like them to see
that part of me—to know that I'm healthy and everything is okay with me."

"The most important person in my world," Taylor says, "is Kate. And to   13
not be able to share the most important thing in the world with your family
hurts. I apologized once to my father, told him the only reason I was sad I
wasn't married was because I couldn't give him a grandchild. 'You don't have
to worry about that,' he said. 'But your mother and I are very happy, and our
happiness in our life has been our marriage, and that's why we want you to be
married.' I say, 'I am happy,' and he says, 'That's fine, then.' But there's this
piece of them that is always waiting for me to call and say, 'Sit down, I've got
something to tell you,' and tell them I'm going to get married."

Taylor speaks about her childhood: "My brother hates violence, hates the   14
military, hates sports, hates TV, plays music, identifies flowers, and catches bees.
He's a wonderful human being, but he's so different from your stereotypic
macho male. And then here comes me, and I was in training for the Olympics. . . ." She pauses, then whispers, "It was my swim coach who raped me."

Lisa and Tara sit wide-eyed, biting their lips; Kate, whose pose all eve-   15
ning has been arms close to her sides, hands in her lap, reaches toward her
lover. Taylor shifts in her chair and says, "So that ended my career. On my
tenth birthday. It was my present from him. But we don't need to dwell
on that.

"Anyway, I did everything that my brother should have done. My dad   16
paid him to play Little League, and I cried tears because they wouldn't let girls
play. And I was better than any of the guys on the team. I never, ever felt like
I could please my dad. I broke my neck doing the things I heard him wanting
my brother to do so that I would feel good."

Tara says, "Even in my circumstances, where people are so accepting of   17
me, who like me and love me"—Tara has nine supportive siblings including
two stepsisters who are gay, and a very understanding mother—"it was quite
difficult to come out. Because of our society and how shameful it is. I am
very happy with who I am, and yet I still go through those cycles of 'What is
going on?' But they're getting shorter and shorter."

"The main reason I don't tell my parents," Taylor says, "is fear of rejec-   18
tion, which would be like saying, 'I just won't acknowledge your presence.'
Like you're dead."

Lisa echoes, "Like you're dead," and Taylor continues. "An interesting   19
thing that goes along with that is that every time I go home—except the last
two times when Kate has gone with me—toward the end of my visit I lie in
bed at night questioning, 'Why am I lesbian?'" A murmur of "Mm-hmms"
accompanies her as she speaks. "Maybe I should . . . maybe if I was . . . maybe
if I tried harder. . . . And I shake my head and I say, 'No, you don't have to
try harder, you're fine.'

"Because at home I lose an identity, question myself, I go for short   20
periods, never longer than seven days. But when I'm home—back here—
there is no question in my mind that I'm happy. It always shakes me up because
I am so at ease, so happy with who I am, but all I have to do is go home
without another lesbian person around. Five days and I'm frantic."

Lisa assumed that she "would be like your average person, end up with   21
a man, be as happy as anyone around me." Her voice grows firm as she speaks
of her work. "I've wanted to be a fiction writer since I was twelve, and here
all of a sudden I was going to be a *gay* fiction writer, and that just scared the
pants off me. So much of my identity is wrapped up in writing fiction. I'm
working on a lesbian novel that I hope straight people can read and understand
me and people like me. It doesn't begin with the trauma—right now I want
to deal with the joy."

"We need writers," Tara says, "writing about women who are being   22
women, not women who are being men-women, women who want to do
everything better than anyone else as if the worst insult is just being a woman,
being feminine."

Kate works, as Tara does, with mentally disturbed adolescents, but she is   23
also an artist. "I know there was a time when I felt that feminist art—breaking
away from what I had grown up to be—was a statement of me. But lesbian

art that outwardly supports lesbianism—no, I've never done that." She speaks of a nude self-portrait. "The way I saw it was strength rather than—sexxxxx," and adds that she was married then and not consciously aware of her attraction to women.

Before Lisa realized her attraction, it was evident to others who read the manuscript of her first novel. "The first-person narrator had no conflict at all that she might be gay, but her descriptions of another woman were really, really erotic. I had no idea. It's like I was totally blind. When I finally came out to a writer friend who had read it, she said, 'Yeah. I saw it all over your book and I was wondering when you'd become aware of it. I was so embarrassed. How come I didn't see it?" She speaks to Kate. "So perhaps with that painting you were becoming aware of your sexuality."   24

Kate, who has the high-cheekboned face of a model, frowns. "Maybe. I loved the guy I was married to and I was happy, but a part of me was dissatisfied. We mutually decided we were happier apart. It was after that that I began to talk to my counselor about my feelings for women. The idea of a relationship with a woman in this town just freaked me out, but I went to a dinner of professional women who were lesbians because I had heard about"—blushing, she motions toward Taylor—"her."   25

The two women tell their love story in day-by-day detail, agreeing that an approach/avoidance situation existed between them for a long time. They would go out and drive and talk until two or three in the morning, not wanting to say goodnight, yet not acknowledging their sexual attraction. Taylor admits, "In a lot of things I'm really assertive, but when it comes to women I'm not."   26

"Unless Kate's in the hot tub," someone suggests.   27

Taylor laughs. "That's a whole different thing."   28

Kate says that sexual attraction for her is based more on the person than on the gender. "And that's a hard thing for me, because my radical lesbian friends do not understand that."   29

Lisa agrees that it is person with her; Tara says gender, adding, "I have just never been attracted on a sexual level to men. I have intimate platonic relationships with them."   30

Taylor believes that for her a continuum expresses it best. "I think, given a certain time and space, it might be gender; given a certain time and space, it might be person. I personally feel more like Tara and I don't know why. I try not to ask myself the question, Had I never been raped, would I be with men? I don't know.   31

"I could beat myself silly trying to figure that out, and it's not going to make any difference. I'm just not attracted to men at all if you are talking sexually. I don't find any beauty in men's bodies. I'm madly in love with my boss—I'd do almost anything for him—but that's an emotional love and respect. And I have other men I really love, so it's not a hate thing. Yet I don't get turned on when I look at women either. I need to say that. I think they're beautiful, but—"   32

Kate interrupts. "When you first came out, didn't you do the little   33
adolescent thing, you know, everybody is a possible—"

"Yes!" Tara shouts. "And I thought, 'No wonder men look at women   34
like that!' And it just hit me, 'I'm a pervert, too!'"

Lisa murmurs, "Yeah. No wonder men like it. God . . ."   35

"Yeah. The lust—"   36

Taylor interrupts Kate. "But that's faded away for me. I *look* at the real   37
beauties, the tens, but I'm *attracted* to women who are the threes and twos.
But sexual doesn't happen for me until I know them." Taylor is, however,
emphatically monogamous. "Kate could go away for ten years, and I wouldn't
mess with anybody." She grabs Kate's hand. "But don't! I would have to end
it with Kate before I could ever act on a sexual attraction for another woman.
See, I'm real old-fashioned that way." Lisa and Tara have a verbal contract to
preserve their openness with each other and the monogamy they both believe in.

Taylor recalls the deep excitement, the validation she experienced the   38
first time she was with a group of lesbians and heard their coming-out stories.
"The most support we have in Spokane is ourselves, sitting and talking. It's a
rush for me to be around lesbians because I spend over half my life pretending
not to be who I am. That is something that is sad to me. I have a heterosexual
life and I have a lesbian life. When I'm at work, I talk hetero, and when I
come home, I love to walk through that door, because then I can relax. I'm a
pro at this double life."

She doesn't associate with her co-workers outside the office. Several   39
years ago she told two people she was lesbian, and they responded by saying it
was "okay with them," but Taylor hasn't seen them socially since.

Lisa tells of coming out to a straight friend at work who talked con-   40
stantly about her boyfriend. "The woman looked blank and said, 'What do
you want from me?'" Lisa lowers her voice, "'I want your body.'" After the
laughter subsides she continues. "No. I said, 'I want you to be as understanding
of my relationship with Tara as I have been of yours.' And she got tears in her
eyes. And what I imagined she was thinking was that she couldn't be. She
realized that she did not have that capacity and she felt badly. So she doesn't
talk about him anymore. So not much at all is left. It's sad."

"When the weekend comes," Taylor says, "I'm exhausted. I've spent a   41
whole week being a hetero and I want to be able to sit and touch this person
if I want to and not be playing that game. This separates lesbians, it makes us
more a minority, but it is unifying for us."

"I don't realize," Lisa says, "how much I need validation until I get it. I   42
don't go to bars and I'm not in any of these lesbian circles—these are my only
two lesbian friends. But when I am at a lesbian party, there is something special
and empowering about being able to express your love and your relationship
in public. I feel myself beaming and I'm proud and I'm happy. I don't miss it
until I have it, and then there *I am in the middle and I want it all the time. That's
what I wish the world understood.*"

Spokane, the women say, is a very conservative town—"The only place   43
that you can wake up and believe Eisenhower is still president." The white-
supremacy Aryan Nation headquarters are in Idaho, an hour's drive away; the
gay Metropolitan Community Church has been invaded by disruptive funda-
mentalists and TV cameras; abortion centers are harassed. It is rumored that
the local Presbyterian College conducted a witch-hunt and fired five lesbians.
Taylor has seen windows of friends' cars, which were parked outside a gay bar,
smashed and police who simply cruised past. People with whom she used to
work would urge her to come to the bars on Fridays, their amusement being
"to sit and watch the gays and lesbians come in."

Spokane has many college students, away from their homes, exuberant   44
in discovering their sexuality. All four women believe the students do not
realize that their loud openness in public jeopardizes the lesbians who live and
work in Spokane. "They scare me," Kate says.

Kate describes what she feels is another threat. Her former boss—whose   45
attitude toward her and two of her lesbian co-workers was, "Damnit, you
have a right to be what you want to be!"—told a man who worked for the
state child-protective services, "There're three lesbians out there and they're
just doing a fine job."

Kate's back is very straight as she says, "One of the radical women saw   46
nothing wrong with that, but I felt he had no right to reveal information
about us that we did not give him permission to. We're talking about a state
worker who can make decisions about people's jobs. My boss didn't see what
living this life actually poses. What he saw was, 'Well, everybody out there
ought to feel okay about it, and I'm going to see that they know that I feel
okay about it.' I believe it's my personal life and it's up to me to tell people."

Taylor agrees. "It's more appropriate to talk about yourself. It's a lot easier   47
to go spouting off about other people, showing how cool you are."

Kate declares, "We need to look out for ourselves. To see the realities of   48
how society is going to take it."

Taylor, who acknowledges, "It's real difficult living two lives," firmly   49
concludes, "I would choose this life and whatever you want to call it—
oppression, living a double life—fifty times over trying to live a straight life. I
would never get married to a man. I couldn't do it, just to do it. So my
choices are to be single and not have a relationship with a woman and be okay
to talk about anything I want to, or to live like this. I'd take this a million
times versus going the other way—which is certainly easier in some ways.

"It's like what Lisa said and Tara said about things fitting. When I finally   50
realized that I was gay, everything came together for me. I've certainly had my
ups and downs since then, but I am terribly happy. I feel fulfilled. What was
missing is there."

Topics for Discussion and Writing

1. The four women in this selection discuss their fears and frustrations about being lesbian in our society. Do you think their fears are well founded? In a journal entry, write about how you would feel if these women lived next door to you.

2. Part of how we think as a population is influenced by the media. How do the media portray homosexuals? If you could change this portrayal by the media, would you do so? How?

3. In what ways are all these women courageous? In what ways are they not? What toll does this "invisible" behavior take on their lives?

4. At the beginning of this selection, Taylor recounts her secretary's negative feelings about homosexuals. Taylor remarked, "I almost said, 'Lou, I'm one of them.'" Write a dialogue between Taylor and Lou in which Taylor tells her that she is a lesbian. What does Lou say? What does Taylor respond? Does this signal the end to their friendly relationship? Compare your dialogue with those of others in your class.

MARY BETH WHITEHEAD

from *A Mother's Story*

"... I drove to Planned Parenthood in Red Bank and got the blood test. It came back positive. That night, as a surprise for Bill, Betsy decorated their bathroom with signs that said, 'SHE'S PREGNANT.' The excitement and fulfillment that I felt during those early months of pregnancy were so strong and deep that I barely stopped to wonder what it all meant."

Shortly after her daughter entered kindergarten, Mary Beth Whitehead responded to an ad in the Asbury Park Press asking for women to become surrogate mothers. "It was," she said, "a way for me to help someone less fortunate, by doing what I was born to do." The subsequent birth of a daughter for the couple, William and Betsy Stern, resulted in the highly publicized "Baby M" trial when Whitehead refused to relinquish the baby.

Before and as You Read

1. Refresh your memory about the Baby M case by doing some research in the library. How did the media portray Mary Beth Whitehead? The Sterns? Write a short character sketch of these three people.
2. Make a list of the pros and cons of surrogate motherhood. What are your personal feelings regarding this issue? Might it be a good idea in some cases? Why or why not?
3. Mary Beth Whitehead was a pioneer "in spite of herself." What does this mean? Do you think that she enjoyed being in the national spotlight? Why or why not?
4. It might be said that our consciences wrestle with the crises that science creates. Comment. Should humans impose limitations on certain types of research, such as transplants of fetal tissue and genetic engineering? Who should decide?

3: THE LOSS

Probably the most stressful and anxiety-provoking act in human existence is the separation of a woman from her newborn infant. The response to this, which humans share with most of the animal kingdom, is an overwhelming combination of panic, rage, and distress.

Who can dare judge the psychological acts and responses of a woman put to such a test? In the present-day United States, what psychologist can claim to have experience with women subject to that experience?

—A. P. Ruskin, M.D., in The New York Times, *April 20, 1987*

(letter to the editor)

O N THE evening of Sara's birth, the Sterns came to my hospital room. They seemed cold and standoffish. They offered no congratulations; they brought no flowers. It seemed as though they just wanted to take my baby, leave, and forget that I existed. Later, the Sterns claimed they were deliberately hiding their excitement because no one at the hospital knew of our arrangement. Now, with a nurse at my side, I went with the Sterns and all my other visitors down to the nursery window to look at Sara. The baby was crying, so I went into the nursery and picked her up. I comforted her and then I held her up to the window. 1

Tuesday was there. For weeks her classmates had been asking her if the baby had been born yet and what we were going to name it. Tuesday had tried to pretend that nothing was wrong, but as she looked at the baby I could see what she was going through. In one sense it was no different from any other child looking at a new baby sister—except that the love was more intense. At the age of ten, Tuesday was more ready than a child of three or four to accept a baby. Younger children often feel jealous when they are brought to the hospital to see a new baby; they have missed their mothers and want to be the focus of attention themselves. Suddenly, Tuesday's eyes filled with tears. She looked at me as if to say, "Mom, don't do this. Don't give my sister away. Don't sell her. Don't do it." 2

Everyone was commenting on how much she looked like Tuesday. Everybody was excited and bubbling over. The Sterns were just looking. They didn't smile or laugh or say how beautiful she was. I thought she was gorgeous, but they just stood in the shadows. I felt as though they were vultures waiting to move in for the kill, waiting to claim my treasure. Maybe they were offended because she looked like *my* baby. She wasn't supposed to be mine. But [she] *was* my child. She had my bracelet on her wrist, and I had her bracelet on mine, and I was the only person who was allowed to go into the nursery and get her. 3

Actually, except for visiting hours, she was rooming in. I only put her in the nursery when I was taking a shower or something of that sort. She didn't like the nursery; she didn't want to be there. She would cry, so I kept her with me day and night. I held her hour after hour, and it was like holding Tuesday again after ten years. 4

At that point, I thought, What a mistake I've made. I did not want to make the mistake real. I wanted to pretend that it hadn't happened, that this was just my baby and we would share a normal life together. On one level, I felt guilty because of the obligation I believed I had to the Sterns and I was worried about their feelings, but now I also felt a strong obligation to the baby, as any mother would to her child. I think that young girls who give their babies up for adoption often think that the baby will be better off, but I knew my baby wouldn't be better off. My God, I thought, how is she going to feel when she finds out that she was sold for $10,000? She's going to feel like the slaves did. 5

On Saturday morning, my roommate was getting ready to go home. Her 6 baby was jaundiced and the doctor didn't know if she could take her home that day. She was crying, and she was upset, as any mother would be. And there I was, thinking, How can I be doing this?

In the next room, a fourteen-year-old unmarried girl had just delivered a little boy and she was keeping him. God, this girl is fourteen, I said to myself. She is keeping her baby. I'm twenty-nine years old and this is *my* baby and these people want to take her away.

Noel Keane had called me a surrogate mother, but now I clearly understood that I was the natural, biological mother. Bill Stern had supplied the sperm, so genetically he was the father, but Rick was my husband and my lover. He was there for the delivery. He watched that baby be born. He was delighted with her, just as he was with Ryan and Tuesday.

I now wonder about the whole concept of what makes someone a father, and how he feels when he sees his child. Do men look at their children and love them because they are a product of their sperm or because they are a part of their wives? Are we to believe that it is just sperm that makes a man a father? And if that is so, then why have we decided that if a married woman is artificially inseminated under usual circumstances, the baby is her husband's child, not the sperm donor's? Is this different because of intent? Because Bill Stern didn't intend to make a donation? Does that change the law and make him a father?

Bill Stern wasn't there when I couldn't get out of bed. He wasn't there when I was throwing up over a toilet bowl on Christmas morning. Rick was. Rick didn't promise to come into the bathroom and put his arms around me when I was throwing up. Rick didn't promise to help me get out of bed or shave my legs or put on my sneakers and tie them. Rick didn't make these promises. Neither did Bill Stern. So either I would have walked around with my sneakers untied and been throwing up in the bathroom by myself or Rick would have been there—and Rick was there. He was the one who was there when I got into bed at night and the baby was kicking and moving and would kick right through my stomach to his back. He was the one who felt that, not Bill Stern.

As I said, I don't know what makes a father, but at that point on that Saturday in April, I knew that I just didn't want to leave the hospital and come home and give my daughter away. I wanted that hospital stay to last forever. My friends were calling and I couldn't pretend anymore. I would just say, "I don't want to talk about it"; "I can't do it"; "I don't know what I'm going to do." So at that point, everybody knew. Slowly but surely, the news was starting to circulate that Mary Beth had made a terrible mistake and was probably going to keep the baby.

When my roommate left on Saturday, I let down my wall. That was when everything came out. I called Rick at work and asked him to come right away. I asked him not to go home first because I needed him now. When I hung up with Rick, the phone rang. It was Betsy Stern. She said that the

Infertility Center had messed up, and in order for me to get my $10,000 they had to bring a notary to the hospital. I didn't want the $10,000; I didn't want the notary. I just wanted my baby. I was crying as I said, "Betsy, I don't want the ten thousand dollars. I don't want to talk about this," and I hung up.

The nurse came in. I had the baby lying on my chest, sleeping. I was   *13*
sobbing. She thought it was the blues, the baby blues. She looked at me and said, "That's okay, cry. It's good to get it out. Don't worry about it."

When Rick came in, I was weeping. Rick sat on the bed with me.   *14*
"What can I do?" He shook his head and said, "I don't know what we're going to do." Then he put his arms around me. I was looking to him for answers, and he didn't know what they were. I kept crying and repeating, "What can I do? I can't give her away. I can't give her up." And if I said it once, I said it a hundred times.

That night, the Sterns came back. I wanted them to say, "Mary Beth,   *15*
we can't take your baby away from you," but they didn't say it. They wouldn't say it. I wanted to make them realize that this was my baby and I couldn't give her up. I couldn't give her away or sell her. I told them I didn't think I could go through with it, and Betsy said, "You can visit. You will be like a sister." "I don't want to be the baby's sister," I explained through my tears. "I want to be the baby's mother, which I am. You're asking me to do something that I know isn't right. It's unnatural and I know it's something that I shouldn't be doing."

At that point the Sterns offered me more money. They said, "You keep   *16*
the money for the delivery." My insurance company was supposed to reimburse me, and I was going to give the money to them. I thought their offer was very generous, but it didn't sway me one bit from wanting to keep my baby. Actually, one side of me thought it was touching, and the other side was almost insulted that they thought they could offer me more money for my child. That wasn't why I was doing the whole thing to begin with.

I looked at Betsy Stern and thought to myself, "Betsy, I'm not selling   *17*
this child. I started this when I actually believed it *wasn't* my child. Everyone had convinced me that it was your child, but going through the pregnancy and the pain of labor, and then seeing the baby has made me realize that this is *my* baby, not yours, mine." But I didn't say anything. I just burst into tears.

We left the hospital on Easter Sunday morning. My mother had bought   *18*
the baby an outfit to come home in. Sara wore a pink and white bunting, a white eyelet hat, and an Easter bunny blanket. Everything fit her perfectly and the nurse took her and paraded her around the hospital and everybody was thrilled. She was the center of attention because of the Easter bunnies all over her outfit.

They wheeled me down to the car in a wheelchair. I was holding the   *19*
baby. Rick had taken all the flowers and gifts down in a cart because there were so many. We got into the car. The sun was shining. It was eleven o'clock, and the Sterns were coming to our home to take her away at two.

On the way home, I spontaneously decided to stop and show Sara to 20 my brothers, who were living together on a farm nearby. I wanted them to be able to see her because I was afraid that none of us would ever see her again. The Sterns were coming in less than three hours, and the deadline was ripping at me all the way home. When I got out of the car, I saw how excited my sister-in-law and two nephews were to see the baby. I had never expected that. I didn't realize that anyone would think of Sara as my baby. But my nephew, who was only three years old, knew it was his cousin. My sister-in-law took her. I was crying. My brother put his arms around me and said, "Oh, Mary, I knew you couldn't do it. What are you going to do?"

When we got home, my neighbor Sue, her husband, my niece, Joei, and 21 my sister-in-law, Sherri, were there. Tuesday and her best friend, Dana, were also there. Everyone wanted to hold the baby. They all thought they were never going to see her again. It was as if I were sentencing her to death or to be banished. Everybody just couldn't hold her enough. We didn't want to put her down. We just didn't want to be without her.

My friend Sue was taking roll after roll of pictures. Tuesday was kissing 22 the baby and playing with her and changing her and I was just numb. I was going to let two strangers take my daughter simply because I couldn't bear to hurt them. I still kept hoping and praying they were going to walk in and say, "We can't do it. We can't take your baby away from you. As much as we want her, as much as she may be a part of Bill, she is also a part of you, and we can't take your child. You deserve to keep her, if that's what you want to do."

But that's not what they did. They came in, they sat on the couch, they 23 didn't know how to hold her, and they couldn't wait to get out of there. They just wanted to take my child. I had refused the money, but they still wanted to take what they had planned to buy and leave. It was as if they were at a car dealership and they were saying, "Just give us the merchandise and we're leaving." I knew it wasn't the right thing, and I knew in my heart I would never get over it. But they were trying to make me feel as though something was wrong with me for wanting to keep my child.

They got up to leave. I went with them to the door. "I always knew the 24 day would come when you would be left empty-handed," Bill admitted sadly. I watched as he put Sara in a baby seat in the back of the car. I looked at her alone in the seat, all curled up like a little rubber ball. Then, as I stood at the door, they drove away.

I collapsed on my front steps. Rick practically carried me into the house. 25 My friend Sue put her arms around me and urged me to come next door to her house for Easter dinner. She thought it would take my mind off the baby. I was trying to pull myself together, and I went over there. But every time I looked at anybody, I burst into tears.

Sue's in-laws were there. They told me I had done a beautiful thing and 26 I would be okay. I just kept crying because I knew it wasn't a beautiful thing for me to give away my baby. I tried to eat, but I couldn't put even a mouthful of food in my mouth. I left and went home. I was upsetting everyone.

Tuesday stayed and spent the night there. I didn't want Tuesday to see me so upset. She knew something was really wrong. She knew a really unnatural thing had taken place. She didn't want to be a part of it. *27*

Rick tried to comfort me. He tried everything he knew. Nothing worked. I didn't want to talk. I didn't want to live. I didn't think Rick felt good about putting his arms around me, even though he was trying to comfort me, because the reason he was trying to comfort me was the wrong reason. You don't comfort somebody who is giving away her child. *28*

Everybody said, "You have two other children." It wasn't as if my baby were dead. My child was alive, and I had given her to two strangers. How could anyone feel that giving away my child was the right thing? I can't imagine that. I just can't. *29*

The Sterns and the Infertility Center had told me I was doing a beautiful thing, but I wasn't. All the way through my pregnancy, I had tried to believe it. I had suppressed the reality; I had denied my feelings. I had not allowed myself to deal with it. *30*

But now I couldn't pretend anymore. I just didn't want to be a party to it, no matter how much it was going to disappoint them. I couldn't bear to be a woman who gave away her child. I didn't want Rick to love me, or Tuesday and Ryan to love me, or even my dogs to love me, because I knew I wasn't worth loving. I wanted to go back to being Mary Beth Whitehead, the person I was before I got involved in this thing. If I gave away my baby, my life wasn't worth anything, and as far as Tuesday and Ryan went, I was no longer worthy of being their mother. *31*

There wasn't anything left, not in my eyes. I knew I was out of control, but I think anyone having her newborn baby taken away from her would be out of control. I wanted to be in control. I wanted to be able to do it. It wasn't that I wouldn't. I *couldn't*. *32*

I began to feel angry and defensive. My body, my soul, my heart, my breathing, my everything had gone into making this baby. What had Bill Stern done? Put some sperm in a cup. What had Betsy done? Bought some clothes, a box of diapers, and a case of formula. That's not having a child. *33*

My sister Joanne had tried to comfort me by telling me about the baby she had lost. Her baby was dead, mine was alive. I couldn't pretend she was dead. She was alive and living with strangers two and a half hours from my house. How could I be at peace, not knowing when she needed me, not knowing when she was crying? *34*

There are a whole lot of things that you don't know when you leave your child. If you are gone for two hours, the first thing you do when you come home is to say, "Was she okay, did she cry?" I wasn't going to be allowed to do that. Everything was meaningless if I couldn't be there for her. It was all gone. *35*

All I did was sob and cry. I just couldn't stop crying. It just kept coming, and the emptiness that I felt was something I never want to feel again. *36*

Eventually I fell asleep. Suddenly I opened my eyes. The room was dark, and I was lying in a pool of milk. The sheets were full of milk. I knew it was time to feed my baby. I knew she was hungry, but I could not hear her crying. The room was quiet as I sat up in the bed, alone in the darkness, with the milk running down my chest and soaking my nightgown. I held out my empty arms and screamed at the top of my lungs, "Oh God, what have I done—I want my baby!"

———————

Topics for Discussion and Writing

1. What do you think is Whitehead's primary message to her audience? Jot down words or phrases that illustrate this message. Can you name several reasons why she may have decided to write a book about her experience?
2. Go back to your list of the pros and cons of surrogate motherhood. After having read the selection, what else might you add to your list? What changes in opinion, if any, have you made?
3. One might look upon the Baby M trial as a trial between the classes: one side representing the working class, with limited education and few resources—hence, limited choices—the other representing the professional upper middle class with wealth to spend on any desire, even a child. Who do you believe would be the best parents for Baby M? Defend your choice.
4. Mary Beth Whitehead Gould has been declared Melissa Stern's legal mother and has extended visitation privileges. What problems do you anticipate this child will have as she grows up?

———————

WILLIAM CARLOS WILLIAMS

from *The Doctor Stories*

> *"But without science, without pituitrin, I'd be here 'till noon or maybe—what? Some others wouldn't wait so long but rush her now. A carefully guarded shot of pituitrin—ought to save her at least much exhaustion—if not more. But I don't want anything to happen to her."*
>
> *William Carlos Williams was a poet, playwright, novelist, essayist, and physician in private practice from 1910 to 1951.*
>
> *He worked, lived, and died in his hometown of Rutherford, New Jersey. His writing, he said, was inspired by his patients. They gave him the subject matter and the energy to write.*
>
> *Williams, who died in 1963 at the age of 80, was called "the most important literary doctor since Chekhov." The following selection, "A Night in June," is taken from his collection of essays* The Doctor Stories.

Before and as You Read

1. One might call Williams a writer who practiced medicine rather than a doctor who wrote. What is the specific distinction between these two descriptions? How strange is this combination of professions? How might a doctor who writes short stories be different from a doctor who writes only medical comments related to his job?

2. While reading, take notes on the many ways that this selection is different from the others. How does Williams use imagery? Why and how does he use the dream sequence to battle his conscience? Exchange ideas in a class discussion.

3. In the introduction to *The Doctor Stories,* Robert Coles states, "Williams knew the special weakness we all have for those who have a moral hold on us, for those who attend us in our life-and-death times. Williams knew, too, that such a vulnerability prompts gullibility, and abject surrender of one's personal authority. . . . arrogance is the other side of eager acquiescence. Presumptuousness and self-importance are the wounds that this life imposes upon those privy to the wounds of others."

   Explain what this statement means. How is it illustrated in "A Night In June"? As you read, list passages that suggest the laboring woman's "surrender of her authority" to Williams. What passages hint at the "arrogance" or "self-importance" felt by Williams during this woman's labor? In contrast, what passages convey his love and respect for her?

4. Williams once stated, "Often after I have gone into my office harassed by personal perplexities of whatever sort, fatigued physically and mentally, after two hours of intense application to the work [his writing], I came out at the finish completely rested . . . ready to smile and to laugh as if the day were just starting."

Talk about a time when you have used writing to reduce stress, for example, making a journal entry, firing off a letter to the editor, or writing to a friend or your family. Be specific in your assessment of how writing works for you.

A NIGHT IN JUNE

I WAS a young man then—full of information and tenderness. It was   *1*
her first baby. She lived just around the corner from her present abode, one room over a small general store kept by an old man.

It was a difficult forceps delivery and I lost the child, to my disgust;   *2*
though without nurse, anesthetist, or even enough hot water in the place, I shouldn't have been overmuch blamed. I must have been fairly able not to have done worse. But I won a friend and I found another—to admire, a sort of love for the woman.

She was slightly older than her husband, a heavy-looking Italian boy.   *3*
Both were short. A peasant woman who could scarcely talk a word of English, being recently come from the other side, a woman of great simplicity of character—docility, patience, with a fine direct look in her grey eyes. And courageous. Devoted to her instincts and convictions and to me.

Sometimes she'd cry out at her husband, as I got to know her later, with   *4*
some high pitched animalistic sound when he would say something to her in Italian that I couldn't understand and I knew that she was holding out for me.

Usually though, she said very little, looking me straight in the eye with   *5*
a smile, her voice pleasant and candid though I could scarcely understand her few broken words. Her sentences were seldom more than three or four words long. She always acted as though I must naturally know what was in her mind and her smile with a shrug always won me.

Apart from the second child, born a year after the first, during the   *6*
absence of the family from town for a short time, I had delivered Angelina of all her children. This one would make my eighth attendance on her, her ninth labor.

Three A.M., June the 10th, I noticed the calendar as I flashed on the   *7*
light in my office to pick up my satchel, the same, by the way, my uncle had given me when I graduated from Medical School. One gets not to deliver women at home nowadays. The hospital is the place for it. The equipment is far better.

Smiling, I picked up the relic from where I had tossed it two or three   *8*
years before under a table in my small laboratory hoping never to have to use it again. In it I found a brand new hypodermic syringe with the manufacturer's name still shiny with black enamel on the barrel. Also a pair of curved scis-

sors I had been looking for for the last three years, thinking someone had stolen them.

I dusted off the top of the Lysol bottle when I took it from the shelf and quickly checking on the rest of my necessities, I went off, without a coat or necktie, wearing the same shirt I had had on during the day preceding, soiled but—better so.   *9*

It was a beautiful June night. The lighted clock in the tower over the factory said 3:20. The clock in the facade of the Trust Company across the track said it also. Paralleling the railroad I recognized the squat figure of the husband returning home ahead of me—whistling as he walked. I put my hand out of the car in sign of recognition and kept on, rounding the final triangular block a little way ahead to bring my car in to the right in front of the woman's house for parking.   *10*

The husband came up as I was trying to decide which of the two steep cobbled entry-ways to take. Got you up early, he said.   *11*

Where ya been? his sister said to him when we had got into the house from the rear.   *12*

I went down to the police to telephone, he said, that's the surest way.   *13*

I told you to go next door, you dope. What did you go away down there for? Leaving me here alone.   *14*

Aw, I didn't want to wake nobody up.   *15*

I got two calls, I broke in.   *16*

Yes, he went away and left me alone. I got scared so I waked him up anyway to call you.   *17*

The kitchen where we stood was lighted by a somewhat damaged Welsbach mantel gaslight. Everything was quiet. The husband took off his cap and sat along the wall. I put my satchel on the tubs and began to take things out.   *18*

There was just one sterile umbilical tie left, two, really, in the same envelope, as always, for possible twins, but that detail aside, everything was ample and in order. I complimented myself. Even the Argyrol was there, in tablet form, insuring the full potency of a fresh solution. Nothing so satisfying as a kit of any sort prepared and in order even when picked up in an emergency after an interval of years.   *19*

I selected out two artery clamps and two scissors. One thing, there'd be no need of sutures afterward in this case.   *20*

You want hot water?   *21*

Not yet, I said. Might as well take my shirt off, though. Which I did, throwing it on a kitchen chair and donning the usual light rubber apron.   *22*

I'm sorry we ain't got no light in there. The electricity is turned off. Do you think you can see with a candle?   *23*

Sure. Why not? But it was very dark in the room where the woman lay on a low double bed. A three-year-old boy was asleep on the sheet beside her. She wore an abbreviated nightgown, to her hips. Her short thick legs   *24* had, as I knew, bunches of large varicose veins about them like vines. Every-thing was clean and in order. The sister-in-law held the candle. Few words were spoken.

I made the examination and found the head high but the cervix fully dilated. Oh yeah. It often happens in women who have had many children; pendulous abdomen, lack of muscular power resulting in a slight misdirection of the forces of labor and the thing may go on for days. 25

When I finished, Angelina got up and sat on the edge of the bed. I went back to the kitchen, the candle following me, leaving the room dark again. 26

Do you need it any more? the sister-in-law said, I'll put it out. 27

Then the husband spoke up, Ain't you got but that one candle? 28

No, said the sister. 29

Why didn't you get some at the store when you woke him up; use your head. 30

The woman had the candle in a holder on the cold coal range. She leaned over to blow it out but misdirecting her aim, she had to blow three times to do it. Three or four times. 31

What's the matter? said her brother, getting weak? Old age counts, eh Doc? he said and got up finally to go out. 32

We could hear an engineer signaling outside in the still night—with short quick blasts of his whistle—very staccato—not, I suppose, to make any greater disturbance than necessary with people sleeping all about. 33

Later on the freights began to roar past shaking the whole house. 34

She doesn't seem to be having many strong pains, I said to my compan-ion in the kitchen, for there wasn't a sound from the labor room and hadn't been for the past half hour. 35

She don't want to make no noise and wake the kids. 36

How old is the oldest now? I asked. 37

He's sixteen. The girl would have been eighteen this year. You know the first one you took from her. 38

Where are they all? 39

In there, with a nod of the head toward the other room of the apart-ment, such as it was, the first floor of an old two-story house, the whole thing perhaps twenty-five feet each way. 40

I sat in a straight chair by the kitchen table, my right arm, bare to the shoulder, resting on the worn oil cloth. 41

She says she wants an enema, said the woman. O.K. But I don't know how to give it to her. She ain't got a bed-pan or nothing. I don't want to get the bed all wet. 42

Has she had a movement today? 43

Yeah, but she thinks an enema will help her. 44

Well, have you got a bag? 45

Yeah, she says there's one here somewhere. 46

Get it. She's got a chamber pot here, hasn't she? 47

Sure.   *48*

So the woman got the equipment, a blue rubber douche bag, the rubber   *49*
of it feeling rather stiff to the touch. She laid it on the stove in its open box
and looked at it holding her hands out helplessly. I'm afraid, she said.

All right, you hold the candle. Mix up a little warm soapy water. We'll   *50*
need some vaseline.

The woman called out to us where to find it, having overheard our   *51*
conversation.

Lift up, till I put these newspapers under you, said my assistant. I don't   *52*
want to wet the bed.

That's nothing, Angelina answered smiling. But she raised her buttocks   *53*
high so we could fix her.

Returning ten minutes later to my chair, I saw the woman taking the   *54*
pot out through the kitchen and upstairs to empty it. I crossed my legs, crossed
my bare arms in my lap also and let my head fall forward. I must have slept,
for when I opened my eyes again, both my legs and my arms were somewhat
numb. I felt deliciously relaxed though somewhat bewildered. I must have
snored, waking myself with a start. Everything was quiet as before. The peace
of the room was unchanged. Delicious.

I heard the woman and her attendant making some slight sounds in the   *55*
next room and went in to her.

Examining her, I found things unchanged. It was about half past four.   *56*
What to do? Do you mind if I give you the needle? I asked her gently. We'd
been through this many times before. She shrugged her shoulders as much as
to say, It's up to you. So I gave her a few minims of pituitrin to intensify the
strength of the pains. I was cautious since the practice is not without danger.
It is possible to get a ruptured uterus where the muscle has been stretched by
many pregnancies if one does not know what one is doing. Then I returned
to the kitchen to wait once more.

This time I took out the obstetric gown I had brought with me, it was   *57*
in a roll as it had come from the satchel, and covering it with my shirt to make
a better surface and a little more bulk, I placed it at the edge of the table and
leaning forward, laid my face sidewise upon it, my arms resting on the table
before me, my nose and mouth at the table edge between my arms. I could
breathe freely. It was a pleasant position and as I lay there content, I thought
as I often do of what painting it was in which I had seen men sleeping
that way.

Then I fell asleep and, in my half sleep began to argue with myself—or   *58*
some imaginary power—of science and humanity. Our exaggerated ways will
have to pull in their horns, I said. We've learned from one teacher and neglected another. Now that I'm older, I'm finding the older school.

The pituitary extract and other simple devices represent science. Science,   *59*
I dreamed, has crowded the stage more than is necessary. The process of
selection will simplify the application. It touches us too crudely now, all new-
ness is over-complex. I couldn't tell whether I was asleep or awake.

But without science, without pituitrin, I'd be here till noon or maybe— 60
what? Some others wouldn't wait so long but rush her now. A carefully
guarded shot of pituitrin—ought to save her at least much exhaustion—if not
more. But I don't want to have anything happen to her.

Now when I lifted my head, there was beginning to be a little light 61
outside. The woman was quiet. No progress. This time I increased the dose
of pituitrin. She had stronger pains but without effect.

Maybe I'd better give you a still larger dose, I said. She made no demur. 62
Well, let me see if I can help you first. I sat on the edge of the bed while the
sister-in-law held the candle again glancing at the window where the daylight
was growing. With my left hand steering the child's head, I used my ungloved
right hand outside on her bare abdomen to press upon the fundus. The
woman and I then got to work. Her two hands grabbed me at first a little
timidly about the right wrist and forearm. Go ahead, I said. Pull hard. I
welcomed the feel of her hands and the strong pull. It quieted me in the way
the whole house had quieted me all night.

This woman in her present condition would have seemed repulsive to 63
me ten years ago—now, poor soul, I see her to be as clean as a cow that calves.
The flesh of my arm lay against the flesh of her knee gratefully. It was I who
was being comforted and soothed.

Finally the head began to move. I wasn't sorry, thinking perhaps I'd have 64
to do something radical before long. We kept at it till the head was born and
I could leave her for a moment to put on my other glove. It was almost light
now. What time is it? I asked the other woman. Six o'clock, she said.

Just after I had tied the cord, cut it and lifted the baby, a girl, to hand it 65
to the woman, I saw the mother clutch herself suddenly between her thighs
and give a cry. I was startled.

The other woman turned with a flash and shouted, Get out of here, 66
you damned kids! I'll slap your damned face for you. And the door through
which a head had peered was pulled closed. The three-year-old on the bed
beside the mother stirred when the baby cried at first shrilly but had not
wakened.

Oh yes, the drops in the baby's eyes. No need. She's as clean as a beast. 67
How do I know? Medical discipline says every case must have drops in the
eyes. No chance of gonorrhoea though here—but—Do it.

I heard her husband come into the kitchen now so we gave him the 68
afterbirth in a newspaper to bury. Keep them damned kids out of here, his
sister told him. Lock that door. Of course, there was no lock on it.

How do you feel now? I asked the mother after everything had been 69
cleaned up. All right, she said with the peculiar turn of her head and smile by
which I knew her.

How many is that? I asked the other woman. Five boys and three girls, 70
she said. I've forgotten how to fix a baby, she went on. What shall I do? Put a
little boric acid powder on the belly button to help dry it up?

Topics for Discussion and Writing

1. When Williams says, "The flesh of my arm lay against the flesh of her knee gratefully. It was I who was being comforted and soothed." What do you think he means? What does such a statement reveal about his feelings toward women in general and toward this woman specifically?

2. This story was written from the doctor's point of view. Write a story about the same incident from the mother's viewpoint. What kind of person do you imagine her to be? How does she regard men? What is her relationship with her husband? With Dr. Williams? What are her fears in labor? What are her feelings about having another child? (If you prefer, write a story from the father's perspective.)

3. Reread the passages that capture the baby's birth. Why, do you think, did Williams not emphasize the moment of birth, skipping over it to the cutting of the cord and the handing of the newborn to the sister-in-law? Is this merely an omission, or did he do this for a specific effect?

4. There is an old saying: "There's nothing worse than a doctor who isn't busy." What does this tongue-in-cheek statement mean? How do you think Williams would respond? Answer using specific illustrations from "A Night In June."

KAREN BROWNE
"To My Daughter: June 16, 1988"

> *"My choices were narrow: . . . have an abortion, or have a baby. I debated for a few days whether to tell anyone, and my first thought was not to say a word, but rather to have an abortion and move on with my life. Something, however, prevented me from going through with this, and rather than take any action, I pushed it to the back of my head again, waiting for it to somehow magically take care of itself."*
>
> *The selection you are about to read is from an article submitted by the author as a part of course-assigned work in independent writing, taught by Professor Ellen Nunnally, at George Mason University in July 1992. Karen Browne is a pseudonym.*

Before and as You Read

1. Examine your feelings about adoption. Have you had any personal or secondhand experience with someone who chose to give up a child for adoption? What might be some of the problems encountered by couples wishing to adopt? What might be some of the problems for teenagers making the decision to put their babies up for adoption?
2. As you read Karen's story, write down questions that she doesn't address or fully answer for you. What would you like to know about her home life, school life, social life, and relationship with her friends during this time?
3. In your journal write about a situation in which you had to make a difficult revelation to your parents. Recall the event and the circumstances. How did it make you feel? What was their reaction? Did the incident change your relationship in any way? How? (If you wish, write about a time when you learned something of significance about one or both of your parents. Describe that event, the circumstances, how you felt, and how it changed your relationship.)
4. Why did Karen choose to write her story in the form of a letter? In class discuss different genres of writing that she might have used and how her story would change if she structured it differently.

YOU ENTERED my life on June 16, 1988, at 8:51 a.m. I remember   *1*
waking up earlier than usual with bad stomach cramps, but thinking nothing of it. I got dressed and went into my parent's bedroom to sit down and talk with my mother. Just being near her always made everything feel O.K. I hope this is the same feeling that you have with your mother. My dad was still in the bathroom getting ready, so it must have been much earlier than I thought because my dad usually got up at around 5:30. Mom and I were

talking, and all of a sudden I felt a cutting pain rip across my back and I gasped for air. Immediately, Mom knew what was going on and called my father out of the bathroom—I was going into labor.

My mother called Dr. Jackson, my obstetrician and gynecologist, and told him what had happened. She then put me in the car to take me to the hospital. My father was going to call John (he was up at William and Mary taking a summer course in Anthropology) and after he got in touch with him, he was going to meet us at the hospital.

I was so scared that I didn't know what to do. I had known that this day would come, but had not prepared myself for it. All I kept thinking was "Mom and Dad, please don't hate me for all that I am putting you through." I also prayed, probably for the first true time in my life, that everything would be okay: I prayed that you would be a healthy baby with ten fingers and ten toes. I also kept wondering if I was really going to be able to go through with the adoption. Actually, that was all I had thought about since we had decided on that route.

The hospital was about thirty minutes away, and I can remember getting sick on the way there. Morning sickness had, luckily, not been a regular part of my pregnancy, but today was different. I think that it was fear more than anything, but what it was didn't matter. I just didn't want to get sick in Mom's car, her new car. When I began to feel nauseous, my first response was to roll down the window. When this didn't help, I broke down and told Mom that I didn't feel well. Luckily, she had a ziploc freezer bag in the car door to hold her pantyhose, and she yanked the hose out and handed me the bag. She handed it to me just in time. I cried the whole way to the hospital, but I cried to myself, again not wanting to hurt my mother more than I had already. I was too scared to do anything else. I stared out of the window the entire ride to the hospital so that I wouldn't have to face her. And yet, during the entire ride she held my hand and didn't let go except to put on her turn signal or to wipe the tears from her own eyes.

When we got to the hospital, I was put in a wheelchair and taken to my room. Dr. Jackson was already there waiting for me and kept telling me over and over that everything was going to be all right. I trusted and believed in him. After I was in my hospital gown and lying down on my bed, my mother, Dr. Jackson, and I were joined by a nurse who prepped me for delivery. She inserted the I.V. needle into my arm and took my vital signs. I suppose she was trying to make light conversation when she told me that she had been in labor with her first child for thirty-six hours, but all I wanted to do was punch her lights out. I didn't speak to her the rest of the time she was with me.

While all of this was happening, the cutting pain in my back was still there, but it was every so often joined by a cramp that felt like all of the organs were being sucked out of my body. I just wanted it to end.

An hour and a half after I started having pains, Dr. Jackson was on my left side rolling me into the delivery room, and my mother was on my right side. All I could see were her eyes and the tears that filled them, and I knew that they were her way of saying, "I love you, Sweetie. And if I could take it all away from you, I would." She was still holding my hand.

The delivery room was cold. As they wheeled me in, I could feel goose- *8* bumps crawling up my arms and legs. All that I could see from my angle was the tiled ceiling and a bright light above me. Then I heard a voice.

"O.K., Karen. I want you to start counting backwards from a hundred." *9* A strange voice whispered to me from behind my range of sight.

"100, 99, 98, 97, 96, 95, 94 . . ." *10*

I had been anesthetized because Dr. Jackson knew that it would be *11* impossible for me to relax voluntarily. While I was semiconscious during the delivery, I have no clear memories of what happened. The only thing I re-member is my mother telling me that everything would be all right.

When they took me back to my room my father was there waiting for *12* me and told me that he loved me. I knew that while I had probably caused him a lot of pain, this was proof that he would always be there for me, and from that day forward I have felt even closer to him. I guess what they say is true: good things come from bad situations. Then he took hold of my hand. He told me that he had called John and that he was on his way. I was ex-hausted; I just wanted to sleep.

John walked in a few minutes after I had closed my eyes, and I could tell *13* that he felt very awkward with my parents being there. . . . My mother sug-gested to my father that they leave, . . .

"How are you doing?" *14*

"Fine." I lied. *15*

"I saw her. She had on a little pink hat." *16*

"I thought you had decided you didn't want to see her." *17*

"Yeah, well, I couldn't resist." *18*

"John, I can't do this. It hurts so much." The tears began to flow. John *19* came over and sat down on the bed with me. He, too, began to cry.

I thought for a brief period—for that moment of time when John and *20* I were sitting alone in my hospital room—that somehow everything would work out and we would get to stay together and become a family. Maybe it was just a dream, but something inside of me saw a future, a happy future, one that would last.

I am glad that your father got to see you. I think that it would have *21* been much harder for him to deal with the situation had he not seen you were "real."

Later, after John and my parents had left . . . the nurse called on the *22* intercom and asked if I wanted to feed you your lunch. I don't think she realized the situation, but rather than tell her, I said "Yes" and waited for you to arrive.

When she brought you in, you were wearing the little pink hat that John *23* had seen you in. The nurse handed you to me, handed me your bottle, and then left. You and I were all alone for the first time in our lives.

You were so perfect. You had these big, beautiful, blue eyes, and you 24
were trying to soak up everything you saw with them.

I was sitting up in the bed and had you propped up on my knees so that 25
I could look straight at you, and you at me. You were so precious. I couldn't
believe that I had given birth to such a beautiful baby. It was the one thing I
had done right in my life.

Half an hour after she brought you in, the nurse returned to take you 26
to the nursery for your nap. I, too, was tired, but sleep was the farthest thing
from my mind. I had to go back over everything again and be sure I made the
right decision—for both of us . . .

I had gotten pregnant sometime in September of 1987, which was the 27
first month of my last year of high school. I had only been in school for a
few weeks when I realized I might be pregnant, and even knowing there was
a possibility, I was so wrapped up in everything that was going on in my life
that I ignored that possibility. My weeks were spent researching colleges and
doing my homework, and my weekends were spent up at college with John.

Early October came, and with it . . . my last Homecoming, and I again 28
found myself too busy to think about being pregnant. . . . Every day after
school we would all go to a friend's house to work on our float. Our class
float had won three years in a row and we did not intend to be beat in our
senior year. . . . It was as if my mind had voluntarily shut itself off from
thinking that there might be a problem during what was supposed to be one
of the best years of my life. . . .

When I finally realized what was going on (I can remember it so 29
clearly—I was driving to school on Interstate 460 when the realization struck),
something came over me, and I began to change. Actually, I began to grow
up. I realized that I was in a situation that my father could no longer get me
out of, as he had done so many times before. I knew that I had gotten myself
into the situation, and only I could get myself out of it.

What was I going to do? I didn't want to tell my parents because, while 30
I knew they would support me through anything and love me unconditionally
regardless of what I did with my life, I was afraid. At the time I didn't realize
what I was afraid of; I have since come to understand that my biggest fear was
of letting them down. From the time I was born, my parents have done
everything they knew how to prevent me from being hurt, and they have
always given me anything I wanted. While this, to some, may sound wonderful, it can also be detrimental. You see, with all of that protection and love
there was this condition attached that felt as if it were smothering itself around
my body and preventing me from doing a lot of things I would love to have
done, but did not do solely because of the thought that it might disappoint
my parents. I'm sure all children worry about disappointing their parents, but
my worry was almost suffocating. Everything I did had to be perfect or I felt
as if I had let them down. Not that they ever made me feel that way, it was
just a sensation I got that I was never able to shake.

My choices were narrow: . . . have an abortion, or have a baby. I debated *31* for a few days whether to tell anyone, and my first thought was not to say a word, but rather to have an abortion and move on with my life. Something, however, prevented me from going through with this, and rather than take any action, I pushed it to the back of my head again, waiting for it to somehow magically take care of itself.

When the day arrived that I realized there were no miracles to be found *32* in my corner, I decided to tell John and hope that he would provide the miracle that I was so desperately seeking. Every night when we talked, however, I was never able to get up the courage to tell him, . . . so . . . I decided to write him a letter. . . .

John's response to my news was, "Let's get married." For almost three *33* years, those had been the words I had gone to bed at night praying he would say to me, and yet, now that I was hearing them, I did not know how to respond. My heart was screaming "Yes. Let's get married," but my head was saying "No, Karen. You have to get married for the right reasons, not the wrong ones." . . . I told John that I needed some time to think about things and that when I had decided what to do I would let him know. Looking back, I suppose that was selfish, but I didn't care. I knew that I had to do what was right for me and you, and I knew that no one would be able to decide that but me. Unfortunately, I didn't do a very good job of making that decision.

The phone rang at around 3:00 p.m. and my heart jumped up into my *34* throat. It was a Saturday and my mother and I were usually shopping all day on Saturdays, but we had gotten home earlier than usual. Still, I thought, Dr. Jackson wouldn't call this late in the day. He's always at the golf course on Saturday. I was wrong. My mother answered the call and she was on the line less than a minute. I knew when she hung up the receiver that he wasn't playing golf. I had been to see him the day before, March 9th, for my annual exam, and he had become the first person besides John and me to find out that I was pregnant. . . .

As my mother stood in front of me with tears streaming down her face, *35* it dawned on me that everything was not going to be all right and that I was beginning to hurt more people. Hurting John was bad enough; I never intended to hurt my parents as well. . . .

My mother called my father at work and after he came home, we all sat *36* down to decide what we were going to do. I was so embarrassed. I just wanted to crawl into a hole and die. My mother was on the phone with Dr. Jackson and my father was sitting next to me on the sofa. The silence was the worst. I wanted him to yell or throw something, anything to indicate his anger; the silence only indicated his hurt.

My mother came over to the sofa after she was off the phone for the *37* second time and told us that Dr. Jackson had estimated I was six months pregnant.

"Is that right, honey?" She took hold of my hand; I had lost one of my weapons to combat the tears that were trying to escape. 38

I nodded my head. 39

"Well, what do you want to do?" I was waiting for the screams: Why didn't you tell us? What were you going to do? I couldn't say anything. 40

"What did Dr. Jackson say we should do?" My father was talking over my head as if I were not there. 41

"He said it was too late to have an abortion here, but he knows of a clinic in Atlanta that performs up through the end of the second trimester, if that's what she wants." 42

They didn't seem to understand that the reason things had come this far along was because I didn't know what I wanted. They didn't seem to realize that I could have easily had an abortion months before and no one ever would have known anything. But whether or not they understood this, I knew that it was abortion that they wanted, so I would do it. 43

We entered into a mass of whiteness. There was no color on the wall, no paintings, not even a plant in the corner. The doors were white and so were the window sills. The only thing that caught the eye were the steel doorknobs that jutted out from the wall every few feet. The air conditioner was on and the building was cold; the doorknobs were freezing to the touch. I didn't like this building; I hated it. I hated it for what it represented and what it was trying to do to my life. I just wanted out of there. 44

The waiting room was full of young girls who fidgeted in their seats, their feet barely touching the floor, mixed with older women who looked familiar with their surroundings, almost comfortable. Other than my father, there were no men; other than me, everyone was there all alone. For a brief moment, I wished I was alone as well. 45

After the routine of filling out paperwork and waiting, I was led away by a nurse, at least I think she was a nurse, to another cold, white room. She told me to take off my clothes, put on a gown, and give her a urine sample. I obeyed. 46

She then told me to sit on the bed and she left. I looked around the room, but the only other thing to look at besides the bed I was on was a giant, steel contraption in the corner that looked like a weapon from *Terminator*. It had fixtures and gadgets poking out of all sides that looked like they would swing out and strike me at any moment. I closed my eyes and waited for the nurse to return. 47

"Miss Browne," she was back. "Is there somebody here to drive you home?" 48

"Yes. My parents are waiting for me." 49

"O.K. I'll be back in a moment." 50

I assumed she was going out there to tell them when I'd be ready to go home. I thought of Mom and Dad sitting in that waiting room, blaming themselves for what was happening, and wishing they could right the wrong. If only they didn't love me so much . . . 51

Click. The door opened. It was the nurse, only she was not alone. My 52
parents were behind her, and for the third time that day I could see tears in
my mother's eyes. She was squeezing my father's hand so tightly her knuckles
were white. She came over and took my hand. I knew something was wrong.

"Miss Browne, I just explained to your parents that we are not going to 53
be able to give you an abortion because according to both of our tests, you
are already in your third trimester."

My mother began to cry, actually it was more of a whimper. I could tell 54
that she was trying to keep it in for my sake, but that wasn't what I wanted. I
wanted her to get it out of her system, regardless of how she went about
doing it. Yet, she was still trying to be the protector, and she was doing a
good job.

After my parents and the nurse left, I started to get dressed. It must have 55
taken me a long time because the nurse came and knocked on the door to see
if I was all right. I pulled myself together and went out to meet my parents.
We had a long trip ahead of us, and a lot to discuss when we got home.

It's getting hard to write. Of course, it makes sense that it would be 56
difficult to write when I can't see through my tears. All of this writing brings
back so much pain; I hope you are still reading. As difficult and as long as this
may be to get through, I chose not to leave anything out so that you wouldn't
have any misconceptions about me. I hope that you will continue to read, as
I continue to write.

July 25, 1992

My Darling Daughter,

People can come into your life for a brief period of time and be no 57
more a part of your memory than your first step. Other people can come into
your life for a brief period of time and remain with you always. I will always
remember Audrey Williams. You should remember her, at least in name, as well.

Once my parents and I realized, and accepted, that having an abortion 58
was an impossibility due to the lateness in my pregnancy, my choices were
even narrower. I knew that I was going to have you, but I had to decide
whether I was going to keep you or put you up for adoption.

I think I had convinced myself that I could take care of you, but I knew 59
that these convictions were based on fantasy and not reality. John and I had
spent many a night discussing how we could make it as a family: there were as
many different possibilities as there were days. But something inside of me
knew that the odds were against us. I knew that I wanted to spend the rest of
my life with John, but I also knew that getting married because of a pregnancy
immediately put a strain on things, and I didn't want us to get off on the
wrong foot.

I hope that you are not taking any of this in the wrong way. I am having 60
such a hard time writing as I want to. I just want you to know what was going
through my mind, and how tough my decision was.

Since I had less than two months to decide what I was going to do, my 61 mother gave me the phone number for an adoption agency: Catholic Family Services.

I am not sure what religious denomination you are, but I was baptized 62 Catholic at the request of my maternal grandmother. Much to her chagrin, my parents never attended church, so neither did my sister and I. Although I was not practicing, I knew enough about the Catholic faith to know that the words Catholic and Unwed Mother do not exactly go hand in hand. I assumed my mother had intentionally given me this number to lay a guilt trip on me. Then I realized that she had every right to make me feel guilty—not only had I lied to her, but I had put her through a living hell as well. I decided to go once, just to satisfy her.

When I first pulled up to the building, it was so dirty and shady looking 63 that I almost turned around and drove home. The windows were covered with a gray film that I knew caused the people inside looking out of them to think that it was overcast everyday. I just wanted to get myself in and out of there as soon as possible; I had no intention of returning.

The actual office of CFS was no better. The smell that permeated the 64 room was of staleness. The woman who greeted me at the front desk was a throwback from the seventies. Her blue plaid suit was too small, and she was wearing brown leather high-heeled boots that zipped up the side.

"Hi. Who are you here to see?" Her gum smacked in my ears. 65

"Audrey Williams. I'm Ka . . ." 66

"Hold on." She swiveled her chair. "Audrey, your next one's here." 67

Next one, I thought. *Next what? Oh God, please get me out of here. Please* 68 *don't make me do this.*

There was a breath on my neck. "Hi. You must be Karen. . . . Come on 69 into my office and we can talk."

Sure, I thought, *let's talk. Let's sit here and I can tell you, a total stranger, how* 70 *I ended up pregnant at seventeen and on your doorstep. Then you can tell me that everyone makes mistakes and we can chalk this one up to experience.*

But for the next hour, I talked about my hobbies and interests, what 71 kinds of books I liked, what kind of food I liked, I talked about everything except the pregnancy which was all I had talked about for weeks to my parents, and for months to John. I didn't know what the point of the meeting was, but I didn't really care; I was having a normal conversation that was virtually stress free for the first time in months.

When my "hour" was up and I got up to leave, Audrey put her hand on 72 my shoulder and said, "You see, Karen, there's a wonderful, intelligent person in there who has absolutely nothing to be ashamed of." That was, as you can expect, the last thing I expected to hear from a representative of the Catholic Church. I had prepared myself to be accosted by a priest, if not The Pope himself, and thrown into a room to watch a video entitled Sinners in Hell that would be all about my life. Instead, I made a new friend.

Appearance-wise, Audrey was plain, very plain. Standing about 5'8", she 73
was, I'm assuming, in her mid-to-late forties and had a graying, bob haircut.
Her clothes were all L.L. Bean staples—denim and khaki skirts, pink oxfords,
and belts with tiny whales or turtles running across them. Her husband was
military and had been stationed in Southern Virginia for a few years. She had
two sons, both of whom were close to my age. Oddly enough, she didn't
have any family pictures on her desk—all mothers have pictures on their
desks—so I began to wonder if the whole story hadn't been a fabrication for
conversation. Then one day I asked her.

"So, do you have any pictures of your sons here?" 74

"No, I share this desk with two other counselors and we decided it 75
would be too cluttered if we all had family pictures up. Here, I have some in
my wallet."

Great, I thought, *she is perfect.* 76

When we finally began to talk about you and what I wanted to do, 77
Audrey tried to, and did, make everything as easy for me as possible. She knew
immediately that I was not entirely settled about whether or not I was going
to give you up, so we went through all of my options in great detail.

Anybody who has never had to give a child up for adoption can ever 78
begin to know or understand the pain that accompanies the process. And
adoption is a process. It is never an easy decision, and I can truthfully say that
it was the hardest decision I have ever had to make. There are so many factors
that I had consider when, essentially, I was planning your future. There were
certain things that I knew I wanted you to have—boundless love, an opportunity to learn and grow, and a lifetime of happiness. These were the things
that I knew I could provide for you, but there was so much more I had to
consider. I wanted stability for you; I wanted security for you. Yet I was never
able to convince myself that I could provide these for you to the degree I
desired.

My struggle was endless. Every time I decided that we should be to- 79
gether no matter what, doubt would begin to creep into my mind and I would
question my ability to successfully raise a child. You see, I was, in my eyes, still
a child myself.

I felt as if I was being pulled in so many different directions by so many 80
different people—my parents, John, my friends; everybody had their own
opinion about what was best for me. All this did was to further cloud my own
decision.

I suppose I made my final decision as a result of my many meetings with 81
Audrey. During one of my appointments, she began to ask me specifics, and
I was forced to respond.

"O.K. Karen, do you care where the baby lives?" 82

Of course, I thought. *Just because I'm giving her up for adoption doesn't mean* 83
I don't love her and want the absolute best for her.

"Not really. But I'd like her to stay in Virginia, I think. Southern   84
Virginia."

"Do you want the mother to work?"   85

No, I don't want either of them to work. I want them to stay at home with her   86
24 hours a day and give her everything she wants.

"I'd rather she not work, but if she has to, I don't want her to work   87
until the baby enters school. And then I want her there when she gets home."

"O.K. Is there anything else you can think of?"   88

Yes, I want her to be told every day how very much I love her and how hard this   89
was for me to do, but that it was the right thing for everyone involved and that I'll
always be here if she needs me. Oh, and I want you to give her my phone number
so she can call if she ever needs to, and my address so she can come find me more
easily, and . . .

"No, not that I can think of right now. Can I let you know if anything   90
else comes up?"

"Sure, and take your time. We've got a while to get this taken care of."   91

These and many other questions forced me to recognize that my ability   92
to raise you was limited, and I wanted so much more for you. My only other
insecurities now were of the lucky family that was going to be able to call
you their daughter. I wanted them to be perfect. Anytime I thought of something else I wanted in your life, I would call Audrey and let her know. If she
wasn't there, I would leave a message. It must have sounded like we were
working undercover.

"Is Audrey Williams there?"   93

"No she's not. May I take a message?"   94

"Yes. Tell her that Karen Browne called and she wants one older brother   95
and a large back yard. Thanks!"

The day you were finally born—June 16, 1988—Audrey was there to   96
see me as soon as I got out of recovery. She didn't mention the adoption, she
just came to make sure we were both O.K., and I'm sure she knew how much
I needed support. . . .

A few weeks after I was out of the hospital, Audrey arranged for me to   97
see you, by myself, at her office. . . . She . . . went to your foster home . . .
and brought you to the office. There was a room at CFS with a rocking chair
and bassinet in it for occasions like these, I suppose. We were able to be alone
for a short while, and it was the most sad and wonderful moment in my life.
You were wearing a pink snap-on suit and had already grown several inches.
John is 6'3" and my father is over 6'5", so I figured you'd be pretty tall. Are
you? The blanket they had for you was very soft and had pink, blue, and
yellow sheep on it. Your fingernails were long, so long that they softly
scratched me. All I wanted to do was take you and run. But I knew that this
was an impossibility. And I knew that you were in good hands—Audrey had
made sure of that. . . . I took some pictures of you. . . . They are the only
tangible reminder I have of you, those and the pink bracelet they gave me to
wear with your weight and time of birth. Not many people know about the

pictures; I'm not even sure if I told my family about them. They are here in front of me as I'm writing this letter to you. I keep them close to me wherever I go.

July 27, 1992

To My Daughter,

There it is: my story, my life, how you came to be adopted. I cannot speak for you, but I know that for me, writing this all down has made me a little more convinced that my decision was the right one. Not only that, but it is now on paper, for whenever you desire to look over it. 98

I'm sure there are things I have left out; it is impossible to remember all that happened four years ago. What, if anything, I remember from now on, can simply be added for you to read. And I hope that you do read it. 99

There are many days when I wish you were mine. Yes, I know that you are in some ways mine, but you are not the here-by-my-side mine that I so desperately long for. It's on days like today that I wish I could take you to the park and show you the elephants. It's on days like today that I wish you could come crawl in bed with me and fall asleep watching cartoons. And it's on days like today that I wish I could tell you through actions rather than through words on paper, how very much I love you. 100

But most of all, it's on days like today that I hope and pray you will one day find it in your heart to forgive me. That is, if there is anything to forgive. 101

Topics for Discussion and Writing

1. Both Karen and Mary Beth Whitehead were faced with difficult decisions that only they could make on behalf of their children. Although their circumstances are very different, think about ways that these two women are alike.

2. Karen mentions her parents a number of times, yet the picture of them is not entirely clear. What was her relationship with her parents before she became pregnant? What do you think were her feelings about how they responded to her situation? What does Karen leave unwritten? List phrases or sentences that illustrate how Karen tries to protect her parents in the story.

3. Compare this essay to the following one by Maya Angelou. What similarities do they share? List the ways in which they are different.

4. John and Audrey Williams play important roles in this story. What is Karen's relationship with these two people? How does she show her love for them? With their help, how does Karen become an adult?

MAYA ANGELOU

from *I Know Why the Caged Bird Sings*

"No one had helped me endure the sickly gray months. I had had help in the child's conception, but no one could deny that I had had an immaculate pregnancy."

Maya (Marguerite) Angelou is the best-selling author of I Know Why the Caged Bird Sings, Gather Together in My Name, *and* Heart of a Woman. *She has also published five collections of poetry and produced, directed, and starred in* Cabaret for Freedom, *in collaboration with Godfrey Cambridge.*

At the request of Dr. Martin Luther King, Jr., Angelou became the northern coordinator for the Southern Christian Leadership Conference. President Jimmy Carter appointed her to the National Commission on the Observance of the International Women's Year, and she also served on the American Revolution Bicentennial Advisory Council.

Angelou is on the board of trustees of the American Film Institute, and is currently Reynolds Professor at Wake Forest University.

Before and as You Read

1. Think about some of the issues facing a teenage mother in our society. How does this responsibility interfere with her growth into adulthood? On the other hand, what reasons can you find in favor of a teenage parent keeping and raising a baby, perhaps with the help of her parents? Discuss the benefits and disadvantages of a teenage couple marrying to raise their child.

2. A writer can begin a story in an infinite number of places. How does this selection open? What expectations are raised in you by the first sentence? By the first paragraph? Find another part of this essay that might make a suitable beginning. How would this change your expectations?

   Write several beginnings, no more than a sentence or two, for a story about an event in your life. Observe how the different first sentences determine where you'll go next.

3. As Angelou explains her actions, try to determine why she behaved so recklessly. In recalling your own past behavior, can you empathize with her actions in any way?

4. Maya Angelou was asked by President Clinton to read an original poem at his 1993 inauguration, the first poet to do so in 32 years. As you read the following, what traits can you identify that might have contributed to her long and respected writing career?

W<small>HAT</small> I needed was a boyfriend. A boyfriend would clarify my 1
position to the world and, even more important, to myself. A
boyfriend's acceptance of me would guide me into that strange and exotic
land of frills and femininity.

Among my associates, there were no takers. Understandably the boys of 2
my age and social group were captivated by the yellow- or light-brown-
skinned girls, with hairy legs and smooth little lips, and whose hair "hung
down like horses' manes." And even those sought-after girls were asked to
"give it up or tell where it is." They were reminded in a popular song of the
times, "If you can't smile and say yes, please don't cry and say no." If the
pretties were expected to make the supreme sacrifice in order to "belong,"
what could the unattractive female do? She who had been skimming along on
life's turning but never-changing periphery had to be ready to be a "buddy"
by day and maybe by night. She was called upon to be generous only if the
pretty girls were unavailable.

I believe most plain girls are virtuous because of the scarcity of oppor- 3
tunity to be otherwise. They shield themselves with an aura of unavailableness
(for which after a time they begin to take credit) largely as a defense tactic.

In my particular case, I could not hide behind the curtain of voluntary 4
goodness. I was being crushed by two unrelenting forces: the uneasy suspicion
that I might not be a normal female and my newly awakening sexual appetite.

I decided to take matters into my own hands. (An unfortunate but apt 5
phrase.)

Up the hill from our house, and on the same side of the street, lived 6
two handsome brothers. They were easily the most eligible young men in the
neighborhood. If I was going to venture into sex, I saw no reason why I
shouldn't make my experiment with the best of the lot. I didn't really expect
to capture either brother on a permanent basis, but I thought if I could hook
one temporarily I might be able to work the relationship into something more
lasting.

I planned a chart for seduction with surprise as my opening ploy. One 7
evening as I walked up the hill suffering from youth's vague malaise (there was
simply nothing to do), the brother I had chosen came walking directly into
my trap.

"Hello, Marguerite." He nearly passed me. 8

I put the plan into action. "Hey." I plunged, "Would you like to have a 9
sexual intercourse with me?" Things were going according to the chart. His
mouth hung open like a garden gate. I had the advantage and so I pressed it.

"Take me somewhere." 10

His response lacked dignity, but in fairness to him I admit that I had left 11
him little chance to be suave.

He asked, "You mean, you're going to give me some trim?" 12

I assured him that that was exactly what I was about to give him. Even 13
as the scene was being enacted I realized the imbalance in his values. He

thought I was giving him something, and the fact of the matter was that it was my intention to take something from him. His good looks and popularity had made him so inordinately conceited that they blinded him to that possibility.

We went to a furnished room occupied by one of his friends, who understood the situation immediately and got his coat and left us alone. The seductee quickly turned off the lights. I would have preferred them left on, but didn't want to appear more aggressive than I had been already. If that was possible.

I was excited rather than nervous, and hopeful instead of frightened. I had not considered how physical an act of seduction would be. I had anticipated long soulful tongued kisses and gentle caresses. But there was no romance in the knee which forced my legs, nor in the rub of hairy skin on my chest.

Unredeemed by shared tenderness, the time was spent in laborious gropings, pullings, yankings and jerkings.

Not one word was spoken.

My partner showed that our experience had reached its climax by getting up abruptly, and my main concern was how to get home quickly. He may have sensed that he had been used, or his disinterest may have been an indication that I was less than gratifying. Neither possibility bothered me.

Outside on the street we left each other with little more than "Okay, see you around."

Thanks to Mr. Freeman nine years before, I had had no pain of entry to endure, and because of the absence of romantic involvement neither of us felt much had happened.

At home I reviewed the failure and tried to evaluate my new position. I had had a man. I had been had. I not only didn't enjoy it, but my normalcy was still a question.

What happened to the moonlight-on-the-prairie feeling? Was there something so wrong with me that I couldn't share a sensation that made poets gush out rhyme after rhyme, that made Richard Arlen brave the Arctic wastes and Veronica Lake betray the entire free world?

There seemed to be no explanation for my private infirmity, but being a product (is "victim" a better word?) of the Southern Negro upbringing, I decided that I "would understand it all better by-and-by." I went to sleep.

Three weeks later, having thought very little of the strange and strangely empty night, I found myself pregnant.

The world had ended, and I was the only person who knew it. People walked along the streets as if the pavements hadn't all crumbled beneath their feet. They pretended to breathe in and out while all the time I knew the air had been sucked away in a monstrous inhalation from God Himself. I alone was suffocating in the nightmare.

The little pleasure I was able to take from the fact that if I could have a   *26*
baby I obviously wasn't a lesbian was crowded into my mind's tiniest corner
by the massive pushing in of fear, guilt and self-revulsion.

For eons, it seemed, I had accepted my plight as the hapless, put-upon   *27*
victim of fate and the Furies, but this time I had to face the fact that I had
brought my new catastrophe upon myself. How was I to blame the innocent
man whom I had lured into making love to me? In order to be profoundly
dishonest, a person must have one of two qualities: either he is unscrupulously
ambitious, or he is unswervingly egocentric. He must believe that for his ends
to be served all things and people can justifiably be shifted about, or that he is
the center not only of his own world but of the worlds which others inhabit.
I had neither element in my personality, so I hefted the burden of pregnancy
at sixteen onto my own shoulders where it belonged. Admittedly, I staggered
under the weight.

I finally sent a letter to Bailey, who was at sea with the merchant marines.   *28*
He wrote back, and he cautioned me against telling Mother of my condition.
We both knew her to be violently opposed to abortions, and she would very
likely order me to quit school. Bailey suggested that if I quit school before
getting my high school diploma I'd find it nearly impossible to return.

The first three months, while I was adapting myself to the fact of   *29*
pregnancy (I didn't really link pregnancy to the possibility of my having a
baby until weeks before my confinement), were a hazy period in which days
seemed to lie just below the water level, never emerging fully.

Fortunately, Mother was tied up tighter than Dick's hatband in the weave   *30*
of her own life. She noticed me, as usual, out of the corner of her existence.
As long as I was healthy, clothed and smiling she felt no need to focus her
attention on me. As always, her major concern was to live the life given to
her, and her children were expected to do the same. And to do it without too
much brouhaha.

Under her loose scrutiny I grew more buxom, and my brown skin   *31*
smoothed and tight-pored, like pancakes fried on an unoiled skillet. And still
she didn't suspect. Some years before, I had established a code which never
varied. I didn't lie. It was understood that I didn't lie because I was too proud
to be caught and forced to admit that I was capable of less than Olympian
action. Mother must have concluded that since I was above out-and-out lying
I was also beyond deceit. She was deceived.

All my motions focalized on pretending to be that guileless schoolgirl   *32*
who had nothing more wearying to think about than mid-term exams.
Strangely enough, I very nearly caught the essence of teenage capriciousness
as I played the role. Except that there were times when physically I couldn't
deny to myself that something very important was taking place in my body.

Mornings, I never knew if I would have to jump off the streetcar one   *33*
step ahead of the warm sea of nausea that threatened to sweep me away. On
solid ground, away from the ship-motioned vehicle and the smell of hands

coated with recent breakfasts, I regained my balance and waited for the next trolley.

School recovered its lost magic. For the first time since Stamps, information was exciting for itself alone. I burrowed myself into caves of facts, and found delight in the logical resolutions of mathematics. 34

I credit my new reactions (although I didn't know at the time that I had learned anything from them) to the fact that during what surely must have been a critical period I was not dragged down by hopelessness. Life had a conveyor-belt quality. It went on unpursued and unpursuing, and my only thought was to remain erect, and keep my secret along with my balance. 35

Midway along to delivery, Bailey came home and brought me a spun-silver bracelet from South America, Thomas Wolfe's *Look Homeward, Angel,* and a slew of new dirty jokes. 36

As my sixth month approached, Mother left San Francisco for Alaska. She was to open a night club and planned to stay three or four months until it got on its feet. Daddy Clidell was to look after me but I was more or less left on my own recognizance and under the unsteady gaze of our lady roomers. 37

Mother left the city amid a happy and cheerful send-off party (after all how many Negroes were in Alaska?), and I felt treacherous allowing her to go without informing her that she was soon to be a grandmother. 38

Two days after V-Day, I stood with the San Francisco Summer School class at Mission High School and received my diploma. That evening, in the bosom of the now-dear family home I uncoiled my fearful secret and in a brave gesture left a note on Daddy Clidell's bed. It read: *Dear Parents, I am sorry to bring this disgrace on the family, but I am pregnant. Marguerite.* 39

The confusion that ensued when I explained to my stepfather that I expected to deliver the baby in three weeks, more or less, was reminiscent of a Molière comedy. Except that it was funny only years later. Daddy Clidell told Mother that I was "three weeks gone." Mother, regarding me as a woman for the first time, said indignantly, "She's more than any three weeks." They both accepted the fact that I was further along than they had first been told but found it nearly impossible to believe that I had carried a baby, eight months and one week, without their being any the wiser. 40

Mother asked, "Who is the boy?" I told her. She recalled him, faintly. 41

"Do you want to marry him?" 42

"No." 43

"Does he want to marry you?" The father had stopped speaking to me during my fourth month. 44

"No." 45

"Well, that's that. No use ruining three lives." There was no overt or subtle condemnation. She was Vivian Baxter Jackson. Hoping for the best, prepared for the worst, and unsurprised by anything in between. 46

Daddy Clidell assured me that I had nothing to worry about. That   47
"women been gittin' pregnant ever since Eve ate that apple." He sent one of
his waitresses to I. Magnin's to buy maternity dresses for me. For the next two
weeks I whirled around the city going to doctors, taking vitamin shots and
pills, buying clothes for the baby, and except for the rare moments alone,
enjoying the imminent blessed event.

After a short labor, and without too much pain (I decided that the pain   48
of delivery was overrated), my son was born. Just as gratefulness was confused
in my mind with love, so possession became mixed up with motherhood. I
had a baby. He was beautiful and mine. Totally mine. No one had bought him
for me. No one had helped me endure the sickly gray months. I had had help
in the child's conception, but no one could deny that I had had an immaculate
pregnancy.

Totally my possession, and I was afraid to touch him. Home from the   49
hospital, I sat for hours by his bassinet and absorbed his mysterious perfection.
His extremities were so dainty they appeared unfinished. Mother handled him
easily with the casual confidence of a baby nurse, but I dreaded being forced
to change his diapers. Wasn't I famous for awkwardness? Suppose I let him
slip, or put my fingers on that throbbing pulse on the top of his head?

Mother came to my bed one night bringing my three-week-old baby.   50
She pulled the cover back and told me to get up and hold him while she put
rubber sheets on my bed. She explained that he was going to sleep with me.

I begged in vain. I was sure to roll over and crush out his life or break   51
those fragile bones. She wouldn't hear of it, and within minutes the pretty
golden baby was lying on his back in the center of my bed, laughing at me.

I lay on the edge of the bed, stiff with fear, and vowed not to sleep all   52
night long. But the eat-sleep routine I had begun in the hospital, and kept up
under Mother's dictatorial command, got the better of me. I dropped off.

My shoulder was shaken gently. Mother whispered, "Maya, wake up.   53
But don't move."

I knew immediately that the awakening had to do with the baby. I   54
tensed. "I'm awake."

She turned the light on and said, "Look at the baby." My fears were so   55
powerful I couldn't move to look at the center of the bed. She said again,
"Look at the baby." I didn't hear sadness in her voice, and that helped me to
break the bonds of terror. The baby was no longer in the center of the bed.
At first I thought he had moved. But after closer investigation I found that I
was lying on my stomach with my arm bent at a right angle. Under the tent
of blanket, which was poled by my elbow and forearm, the baby slept touching my side.

Mother whispered, "See, you don't have to think about doing the right   56
thing. If you're for the right thing, then you do it without thinking."

She turned out the light and I patted my son's body lightly and went   57
back to sleep.

Topics for Discussion and Writing

1. Write your definition of the word *freedom* in all the senses in which you feel it applies. Consider Maya Angelou's lack of freedom when she secretly carried the knowledge of her baby within her. Think of a time when you held an important secret. How did that lack of freedom affect you? How difficult would it be to carry such a burden as she did without the counsel of a trusted relative or friend?

2. Why do you suppose that Angelou seems so matter-of-fact? Does she appear mature beyond her years? Could this be a defense mechanism?

3. As a child, you may have heard the story of the three blind men who were asked to describe an elephant. One touched the trunk, one touched the tail, and one touched an ear. All the descriptions were different, but all were correct. Imagine William Carlos Williams, Maya Angelou, and Karen Browne talking about childbirth. Write your impression of such a conversation.

4. Maya Angelou ends *I Know Why the Caged Bird Sings,* the autobiography of her early years, with this selection. Why might this be an appropriate place to end such a book?

For Further Thought

1. Have any of your opinions regarding sexuality, birth, or personal relationships changed since you began reading this chapter? Have any of your convictions grown deeper? In what way?

2. Although childbirth is certainly an issue that affects both men and women, no one could deny the unique role that nature has given to women. What might women do, with the support of their male peers, to change the American way of childbirth and make it more sensitive to the needs of the family? What might be done to change our view of childbirth as a medical condition to the view that it is the beginning of a family? How would society benefit from this new focus?

3. There is no question that our society could benefit from improvement of our medical health insurance system. Interview friends, parents, and colleagues about their opinions of this hot topic and then write to your representative or senators with your views on this subject.

4. Become better informed about the abortion issue. Read literature published by both prolife and prochoice groups, as well as articles in news magazines that try to evaluate these positions fairly. If possible, interview representatives from both sides. Use the information to write a balanced report. Share your report with others who have done this assignment, then collaborate

with several others to write a revised report that incorporates information from each person.

5. Write an account of your own birth from your perspective as a baby. Make it serious or humorous, but be aware of what you are feeling through your senses. Who was there? What was happening to you? Were you happy? Scared? Confused? Curious? Read your account to a group of your fellow students.

6. Write an article on a sexuality issue for your local newspaper. Interview appropriate people for this venture. Throughout your writing, keep your mind on the audience you are trying to reach.

7. Much can be said about a society by how it treats its helpless citizens. Think about the infant mortality rate in this country. Should the public demand a solution to this problem? What are some of the suggestions you would make if you had the ear of your governor or president?

CHAPTER EIGHT

War

18 October, 1945

Position occupied or duty being performed at time of loss to United States military control:

"On 26 Nov 43 while performing duty as Flight Leader on a bomb mission on a target at Bremen, Germany, my plane was hit by fighters and severely damaged. I bailed out, landing in enemy held territory, and evaded capture for 22 days. I was aided by the Underground of Holland, but later one of the members, [a] Nazi-sympathizer, turned me over to the Luftwaffe. Later I was taken to Stalag Luft I, where I performed the duty of Flight Leader in my Squadron for approximately 1 year."

The preceding was the memo written by 1st Lt. Virgil H. Jeffries, a B-17 pilot in the United States 8th Air Force, recalling what would have been his final mission before going back to the United States to train pilots for the rest of World War II. Unlike many others, Jeffries and his crew of nine made it to that final, 25th mission, but they were unable to return that final time to the relative safety of their air field at Thurleigh, England.

November 26, 1943, did not begin well. Bad weather delayed the Bremen mission: a common occurrence for all crews stationed in England. For Lt. Jeffries and his crew, their flight would be complicated by more than just weather. A mechanical problem forced Lt. Jeffries to shut down one of the four engines of his B-17 before arriving at the target. Flying with three engines reduced speed considerably, so that after the bombs were dropped, the plane could not keep up with the squadron returning to England.

Shortly after they turned to make that final trip back to base, the tail gunner announced on the interphone that they were in luck—three escort planes were coming to give them safe passage home. As the planes came closer, however, the crew realized that the planes were Luftwaffe fighters. The struggling B-17 battled the fighters for 20 minutes, while Lt. Jeffries flew the plane under the worst of conditions. When the German flyers shot out a second engine, the B-17 lost control and Lt. Jeffries called for a bailout. Standing between the pilot and copilot seats, he flew the craft as straight as he could with one hand and held a cable to keep the bomb bay doors open with the other so that his crew could jump to safety. When the final crewman was out, Lt. Jeffries followed through the bomb bay doors, but as the plane was falling with him, his parachute got caught on the wing and he started to go down with it. For several horrible seconds Jeffries' life hung in the balance, until the chute came free from the falling plane.

Although the day ended without the celebration at Thurleigh of that rare 25th mission, and although he faced the next 18 months as a prisoner of war, Jeffries still believes that the day ended well. And we agree. For had fortune not been with this B-17 pilot on that Friday in November, one of the authors of this book would not have been born. Thus does war reach deeply into the lives of many generations.

This chapter is about the women and men like Lt. Jeffries and his crew, for whom such an account is an expected part of a day's work. It would be in error, however, to assume that each individual who serves *wants* to do what he or she is doing. Danger and death are the constants faced by all in battle. Dealing on a daily basis with your own mortality, and that of your compatriots, is business of the most sobering nature. Soldiers also face the realities of their destruction, not only of those trying to destroy them, but also of the ever-present innocent.

In this chapter we will read the story of a man who made sacrifices to avoid military service for reasons that he held supremely important. We will also remember the victims of war, as well as those whose daily lives have been shaped by ideologies imposed to limit political, social, educational, and religious freedoms.

Although wars in history books or on the nightly news may appear remote to some, the injustices and pain of war experienced by each individual affect all of us. More than a moment's thought should be given to humankind's seeming inability to learn from the past and find alternatives to appease our differences.

Thinking about the Issues

1. In your own words define the following: *war, enemy, hero, coward, conscientious objector, patriot, traitor,* and *tyrant.*
2. As a class, name as many wars or conflicts as you can: domestic and foreign, historic and modern. What are some of the reasons these wars began?
3. From question 1 above, develop your definition of war into an essay. Examine your personal views about humanity in conflict. Does the use of military arms always define war, that is, can there be a war without the use of weapons? Is war ever a good thing? When?
4. How would you define *cold war*? How did the cold war begin? How did it affect the United States? How did it affect you and your family as individual citizens? How do you expect to see life in the United States changing as a result of the ease in this tension?

ADOLF HITLER

from *Mein Kampf*

"*Our own painful struggle for existence destroys our feeling for the misery of those who have remained behind. . . . Hence today I believe that I am acting in accordance with the will of the Almighty Creator:* by defending myself against the Jew, I am fighting for the work of the Lord."

Adolf Hitler was born in 1889 in Braunau-am-Inn, Austria. As a youth he wanted to study fine arts and architecture, but his father was adamant in his refusal to allow him to pursue this field of study. Hitler defied his father but could not make a go of it financially, eventually giving up art to work as a day laborer to support himself.

After the death of his mother, Hitler moved to Vienna; and it was of this time that he says, "I owe it to that period that I grew hard and am still capable of being hard. And even more, I exalt it . . . for hurling me, despite all resistance, into a world of misery and poverty, thus making me acquainted with those for whom I was later to fight."

He was a corporal in World War I, and after the war he joined a new political group, the German Workers' Party. He became a charismatic speaker and began his crusade for power. In 1920 he began his own political party, the National Socialist German Workers' Party (NAZI). Shortly thereafter, he formed his own army, called the storm troopers. In three years Hitler gained enough power to attempt a takeover of Munich in what is known as the "beer hall putsch." Hitler was captured, tried, and sentenced to five years in jail. He served only nine months of that sentence, but it was enough time for him to write Mein Kampf *(My Struggle), the autobiography in which he revealed his plans to control Germany and the world.*

Germany's economy had been in depression since World War I—the same economic collapse that would hit the United States in 1929—and the Nazis gained strength as Hitler promised jobs to the people. In 1933 Hitler was appointed chancellor, and shortly thereafter the German parliament gave him the powers of dictator. He soon became both chancellor and president; he took for himself the title Führer (leader).

Total power was Hitler's goal. On September 1, 1939, Germany invaded Poland, and World War II began. For over five years, the German armies battled for more territory across Europe. But Hitler wanted more than land. At home, as well as in the countries that he conquered, he undertook "ethnic cleansing"—the systematic annihilation of all he felt to be undesirable people. At Hitler's behest many millions of people, including six million of the Jewish faith, were tortured and killed.

In 1945, as the Russian army attacked Berlin, Hitler and his wife, Eva Braun, committed suicide.

Before and as You Read

1. Few names stir emotions more than that of Adolf Hitler. In your journal write your feelings about the man and his legacy to the world. How has your life been personally touched by the fact that this man was born and commanded the Third Reich?

2. Among the most compelling questions with which history has challenged us are how Hitler gained the power that he did and why so many trusted him so completely. According to Konrad Heiden, who wrote the introduction to the 1943 English translation of *Mein Kampf,* "For years *Mein Kampf* stood as proof of the blindness and complacency of the world. For in its pages Hitler announced—long before he came to power—a program of blood and terror in a self-revelation of such overwhelming frankness that few among its readers had the courage to believe it. Once again it was demonstrated that there was no more effective method of concealment than the broadest publicity. . . . That such a man could go so far toward realizing his ambitions, and—above all—could find millions of willing tools and helpers, that is a phenomenon the world will ponder for centuries to come."

   Study books and articles on Germany before and during the early days of the Third Reich. What possibilities do you speculate may account for this society's looking to and supporting a leader like Adolf Hitler? How could such an unimposing and obscure little man end up with such absolute power? What "danger signals" would make *you* wary of a man seeking such power? What could and would you do? Discuss within your class the difficulties people face when confronted with a megalomaniac like Hitler, and what a society can do to protect itself from dictatorial rule.

3. Define *Holocaust.* What do you believe that the world has learned from this experience? In what ways do you see evidence around the world that we have not learned from our past?

4. Few works can be found in which a writer states more precisely or systematically how he has reached his philosophy of life than in *Mein Kampf.* Not surprisingly, however, this book is filled with blatant ironies that can be understood only by comparing his sentiments to his later behavior. As you read the following excerpt, list all the ironies you find; for example, "When at the age of fourteen the young man is discharged from school, it is hard to decide what is stronger in him: his incredible stupidity as far as any real knowledge and ability are concerned, or the corrosive insolence of his behavior, combined with an immorality, even at this age, which would make your hair stand on end." Compare your findings with those of your class about what these ironic statements mean to you.

IDO NOT know what horrified me most at that time: the economic   *1*
misery of my companions, their moral and ethical coarseness, or the
low level of their intellectual development.

How often does our bourgeoisie rise in high moral indignation when   *2*
they hear some miserable tramp declare that it is all the same to him whether
he is a German or not, that he feels equally happy wherever he is, as long as
he has enough to live on!

This lack of "national pride" is most profoundly deplored, and horror at   *3*
such an attitude is expressed in no uncertain terms.

How many people have asked themselves what was the real reason for   *4*
the superiority of their own sentiments?

How many are aware of the infinite number of separate memories of   *5*
the greatness of our national fatherland in all the fields of cultural and artistic
life, whose total result is to inspire them with just pride at being members of
a nation so blessed?

How many suspect to how great an extent pride in the fatherland de-   *6*
pends on knowledge of its greatness in all these fields?

Do our bourgeois circles ever stop to consider to what an absurdly small   *7*
extent this prerequisite of pride in the fatherland is transmitted to the
"people"?

Let us not try to condone this by saying that "it is no better in other   *8*
countries," and that in those countries the worker avows his nationality "notwithstanding." Even if this were so, it could serve as no excuse for our own
omissions. But it is not so; for the thing that we constantly designate as "chau-
vinistic" education, for example among the French people, is nothing other
than extreme emphasis on the greatness of France in all the fields of culture,
or, as the Frenchman puts it, of "civilization." The fact is that the young
Frenchman is not brought up to be objective, but is instilled with the most
subjective conceivable view, in so far as the importance of the political or
cultural greatness of his fatherland is concerned.

This education will always have to be limited to general and extremely   *9*
broad values which, if necessary, must be engraved in the memory and feeling
of the people by eternal repetition.

But to the negative sin of omission is added in our country the positive   *10*
destruction of the little which the individual has the good fortune to learn in
school. The rats that politically poison our nation gnaw even this little from
the heart and memory of the broad masses, in so far as this has not been
previously accomplished by poverty and suffering.

Imagine, for instance, the following scene: *11*

In a basement apartment, consisting of two stuffy rooms, dwells a worker's family of seven. Among the five children there is a boy of, let us assume,
three years. This is the age in which the first impressions are made on the
consciousness of the child. Talented persons retain traces of memory from this
period down to advanced old age. The very narrowness and overcrowding of
the room does not lead to favorable conditions. Quarreling and wrangling will

very frequently arise as a result. In these circumstances, people do not live with one another, they press against one another. Every argument, even the most trifling, which in a spacious apartment can be reconciled by a mild segregation, thus solving itself, here leads to loathsome wrangling without end. Among the children, of course, this is still bearable; they always fight under such circumstances, and among themselves they quickly and thoroughly forget about it. But if this battle is carried on between the parents themselves, and almost every day in forms which for vulgarity often leave nothing to be desired, then, if only very gradually, the results of such visual instruction must ultimately become apparent in the children. The character they will inevitably assume if this mutual quarrel takes the form of brutal attacks of the father against the mother, of drunken beatings, is hard for anyone who does not know this milieu to imagine. At the age of six the pitiable little boy suspects the existence of things which can inspire even an adult with nothing but horror. Morally poisoned, physically undernourished, his poor little head full of lice, the young "citizen" goes off to public school. After a great struggle he may learn to read and write, but that is about all. His doing any homework is out of the question. On the contrary, the very mother and father, even in the presence of the children, talk about his teacher and school in terms which are not fit to be repeated, and are more inclined to curse the latter to their face than to take their little offspring across their knees and teach them some sense. All the other things that the little fellow hears at home do not tend to increase his respect for his dear fellow men. Nothing good remains of humanity, no institution remains unassailed; beginning with his teacher and up to the head of the government, whether it is a question of religion or of morality as such, of the state or society, it is all the same, everything is reviled in the most obscene terms and dragged into the filth of the basest possible outlook. When at the age of fourteen the young man is discharged from school, it is hard to decide what is stronger in him: his incredible stupidity as far as any real knowledge and ability are concerned, or the corrosive insolence of his behavior, combined with an immorality, even at this age, which would make your hair stand on end.

What position can this man—to whom even now hardly anything is   12
holy, who, just as he has encountered no greatness, conversely suspects and knows all the sordidness of life—occupy in the life into which he is now preparing to emerge?

The three-year-old child has become a fifteen-year-old despiser of all   13
authority. Thus far, aside from dirt and filth, this young man has seen nothing which might inspire him to any higher enthusiasm.

But only now does he enter the real university of this existence.   14

Now he begins the same life which all along his childhood years[1] he has   15
seen his father living. He hangs around the street corners and bars, coming home God knows when; and for a change now and then he beats the broken-

---

1. 'die Jahre der Kindheit entlang.'

down being which was once his mother, curses God and the world, and at length is convicted of some particular offense and sent to a house of correction.

There he receives his last polish.   16

And his dear bourgeois fellow men are utterly amazed at the lack of   17
"national enthusiasm" in this young "citizen."

Day by day, in the theater and in the movies, in backstairs literature and   18
the yellow press, they see the poison poured into the people by bucketfuls, and then they are amazed at the low "moral content," the "national indifference," of the masses of the people.

As though trashy films, yellow press, and such-like dung[1] could furnish   19
the foundations of a knowledge of the greatness of our fatherland!—quite aside from the early education of the individual.

What I had never suspected before, I quickly and thoroughly learned in   20
those years:

The question of the "nationalization" of a people is, among other things, primarily a question of creating healthy social conditions as a foundation for the possibility of educating the individual. For only those who through school and upbringing learn to know the cultural, economic, but above all the political, greatness of their own fatherland can and will achieve the inner pride in the privilege of being a member of such a people. And I can fight only for something that I love, love only what I respect, and respect only what I at least know.

. . . Today it is difficult, if not impossible, for me to say when the word   21
"Jew" first gave me ground for special thoughts. At home I do not remember having heard the word during my father's lifetime. I believe that the old gentleman would have regarded any special emphasis on this term as cultural backwardness. In the course of his life he had arrived at more or less cosmopolitan views which, despite his pronounced national sentiments, not only remained intact, but also affected me to some extent.

Likewise at school I found no occasion which could have led me to   22
change this inherited picture.

At the *Realschule,* to be sure, I did meet one Jewish boy who was treated   23
by all of us with caution, but only because various experiences had led us to doubt his discretion and we did not particularly trust him; but neither I nor the others had any thoughts on the matter.

Not until my fourteenth or fifteenth year did I begin to come across the   24
word "Jew," with any frequency, partly in connection with political discussions. This filled me with a mild distaste, and I could not rid myself of an unpleasant feeling that always came over me whenever religious quarrels occurred in my presence.

At that time I did not think anything else of the question.   25

There were few Jews in Linz. In the course of the centuries their   26

---

1. *'ähnliche Jauche.'* In the second edition this is toned down to *'ähnliches'* (the like).

outward appearance had become Europeanized and had taken on a human look; in fact, I even took them for Germans. The absurdity of this idea did not dawn on me because I saw no distinguishing feature but the strange religion. The fact that they had, as I believed, been persecuted on this account sometimes almost turned my distaste at unfavorable remarks about them into horror.

Thus far I did not so much as suspect the existence of an organized opposition to the Jews. 27

Then I came to Vienna. 28

Preoccupied by the abundance of my impressions in the architectural field, oppressed by the hardship of my own lot, I gained at first no insight into the inner stratification of the people in this gigantic city. Notwithstanding that Vienna in those days counted nearly two hundred thousand Jews among its two million inhabitants, I did not see them. In the first few weeks my eyes and my senses were not equal to the flood of values and ideas. Not until calm gradually returned and the agitated picture began to clear did I look around me more carefully in my new world, and then among other things I encountered the Jewish question. 29

I cannot maintain that the way in which I became acquainted with them struck me as particularly pleasant. For the Jew was still characterized for me by nothing but his religion, and therefore, on grounds of human tolerance, I maintained my rejection of religious attacks in this case as in others. Consequently, the tone, particularly that of the Viennese anti-Semitic press, seemed to me unworthy of the cultural tradition of a great nation. I was oppressed by the memory of certain occurrences in the Middle Ages, which I should not have liked to see repeated. Since the newspapers in question did not enjoy an outstanding reputation (the reason for this, at that time, I myself did not precisely know), I regarded them more as the products of anger and envy than the results of a principled, though perhaps mistaken, point of view. 30

I was reinforced in this opinion by what seemed to me the far more dignified form in which the really big papers answered all these attacks, or, what seemed to me even more praiseworthy, failed to mention them; in other words, simply killed them with silence. 31

I zealously read the so-called world press (*Neue Freie Presse, Wiener Tageblatt,* etc.) and was amazed at the scope of what they offered their readers and the objectivity of individual articles. I respected the exalted tone, though the flamboyance of the style sometimes caused me inner dissatisfaction, or even struck me unpleasantly. Yet this may have been due to the rhythm of life in the whole metropolis. 32

Since in those days I saw Vienna in that light, I thought myself justified in accepting this explanation of mine as a valid excuse. 33

But what sometimes repelled me was the undignified fashion in which this press curried favor with the Court. There was scarcely an event in the Hofburg which was not imparted to the readers either with raptures of enthusiasm or plaintive emotion, and all this to-do, particularly when it dealt with 34 the "wisest monarch" of all time, almost reminded me of the mating cry of a mountain cock.

To me the whole thing seemed artificial. 35

In my eyes it was a blemish upon liberal democracy. 36

To curry favor with this Court and in such indecent forms was to sacri- 37
fice the dignity of the nation.

This was the first shadow to darken my intellectual relationship with the 38
"big" Viennese press.

As I had always done before, I continued in Vienna to follow events in 39
Germany with ardent zeal, quite regardless whether they were political or
cultural. With pride and admiration, I compared the rise of the Reich with
the wasting away of the Austrian state. If events in the field of foreign politics
filled me, by and large, with undivided joy, the less gratifying aspects of internal life often aroused anxiety and gloom. The struggle which at that time was
being carried on against William II did not meet with my approval. I regarded
him not only as the German Emperor, but first and foremost as the creator of
a German fleet. The restrictions of speech imposed on the Kaiser by the
Reichstag angered me greatly because they emanated from a source which in
my opinion really hadn't a leg to stand on, since in a single session these
parliamentarian imbeciles gabbled more nonsense than a whole dynasty of
emperors, including its very weakest numbers, could ever have done in
centuries.

I was outraged that in a state where every idiot not only claimed the 40
right to criticize, but was given a seat in the Reichstag and let loose upon the
nation as a "lawgiver," the man who bore the imperial crown had to take
"reprimands" from the greatest babblers' club of all time.

But I was even more indignant that the same Viennese press which made 41
the most obsequious bows to every rickety horse in the Court, and flew into
convulsions of joy if he accidentally swished his tail, should, with supposed
concern, yet, as it seemed to me, ill-concealed malice, express its criticisms of
the German Kaiser. Of course it had no intention of interfering with conditions within the German Reich—oh, no, God forbid—but by placing its
finger on these wounds in the friendliest way, it was fulfilling the duty imposed
by the spirit of the mutual alliance, and, conversely, fulfilling the requirements
of journalistic truth, etc. And now it was poking this finger around in the
wound to its heart's content.

In such cases the blood rose to my head. 42

It was this which caused me little by little to view the big papers with 43
greater caution.

And on one such occasion I was forced to recognize that one of the 44
anti-Semitic papers, the *Deutsches Volksblatt*, behaved more decently.

Another thing that got on my nerves was the loathsome cult for France 45
which the big press, even then, carried on. A man couldn't help feeling
ashamed to be a German when he saw these saccharine hymns of praise to
the "great cultural nation." This wretched licking of France's boots more than

once made me throw down one of these "world newspapers." And on such occasions I sometimes picked up the *Volksblatt,* which, to be sure, seemed to me much smaller, but in these matters somewhat more appetizing. I was not in agreement with the sharp anti-Semitic tone, but from time to time I read arguments which gave me some food for thought.

At all events, these occasions slowly made me acquainted with the man 46 and the movement, which in those days guided Vienna's destinies: Dr. Karl Lueger[1] and the Christian Social Party.

When I arrived in Vienna, I was hostile to both of them. 47

The man and the movement seemed "reactionary" in my eyes. 48

My common sense of justice, however, forced me to change this judg- 49 ment in proportion as I had occasion to become acquainted with the man and his work; and slowly my fair judgment turned to unconcealed admiration. Today, more than ever, I regard this man as the greatest German mayor of all times.

How many of my basic principles were upset by this change in my 50 attitude toward the Christian Social movement!

My views with regard to anti-Semitism thus succumbed to the passage 51 of time, and this was my greatest transformation of all.

It cost me the greatest inner soul struggles, and only after months of 52 battle between my reason and my sentiments did my reason begin to emerge victorious. Two years later, my sentiment had followed my reason, and from then on became its most loyal guardian and sentinel.

At the time of this bitter struggle between spiritual education and cold 53 reason, the visual instruction of the Vienna streets had performed invaluable services. There came a time when I no longer, as in the first days, wandered blindly through the mighty city; now with open eyes I saw not only the buildings but also the people.

Once, as I was strolling through the Inner City, I suddenly encountered 54 an apparition in a black caftan and black hair locks. Is this a Jew? was my first thought.

For, to be sure, they had not looked like that in Linz. I observed the 55 man furtively and cautiously, but the longer I stared at this foreign face, scrutinizing feature for feature, the more my first question assumed a new form: Is this a German?

As always in such cases, I now began to try to relieve my doubts by 56 books. For a few hellers I bought the first anti-Semitic pamphlets of my life. Unfortunately, they all proceeded from the supposition that in principle the reader knew or even understood the Jewish question to a certain degree. Besides, the tone for the most part was such that doubts again arose in me, due in part to the dull and amazingly unscientific arguments favoring the thesis.

1. Karl Lueger (1844–1910). In 1897, as a member of the anti-Semitic Christian Social Party, he became mayor of Vienna and kept the post until his death. At first opposed by the Court for his radical nationalism and anti-Semitism, toward the end of his career he became more moderate and was reconciled with the Emperor.

I relapsed for weeks at a time, once even for months. 57

The whole thing seemed to me so monstrous, the accusations so bound- 58
less, that, tormented by the fear of doing injustice, I again became anxious
and uncertain.

Yet I could no longer very well doubt that the objects of my study were 59
not Germans of a special religion, but a people in themselves; for since I had
begun to concern myself with this question and to take cognizance of the
Jews, Vienna appeared to me in a different light than before. Wherever I went,
I began to see Jews, and the more I saw, the more sharply they became
distinguished in my eyes from the rest of humanity. Particularly the Inner City
and the districts north of the Danube Canal swarmed with a people which
even outwardly had lost all resemblance to Germans.

And whatever doubts I may still have nourished were finally dispelled by 60
the attitude of a portion of the Jews themselves.

Among them there was a great movement, quite extensive in Vienna, 61
which came out sharply in confirmation of the national character of the Jews:
this was the *Zionists.*

It looked, to be sure, as though only a part of the Jews approved this 62
viewpoint, while the great majority condemned and inwardly rejected such a
formulation. But when examined more closely, this appearance dissolved itself
into an unsavory vapor of pretexts advanced for mere reasons of expedience,
not to say lies. For the so-called liberal Jews did not reject the Zionists as non-
Jews, but only as Jews with an impractical, perhaps even dangerous, way of
publicly avowing their Jewishness.

Intrinsically they remained unalterably of one piece. 63

In a short time this apparent struggle between Zionistic and liberal Jews 64
disgusted me; for it was false through and through, founded on lies and scarcely
in keeping with the moral elevation and purity always claimed by this people.

The cleanliness of this people, moral and otherwise, I must say, is a point 65
in itself. By their very exterior you could tell that these were no lovers of
water, and, to your distress, you often knew it with your eyes closed. Later I
often grew sick to my stomach from the smell of these caftan-wearers. Added
to this, there was their unclean dress and their generally unheroic appearance.

All this could scarcely be called very attractive; but it became positively 66
repulsive when, in addition to their physical uncleanliness, you discovered the
moral stains on this "chosen people."

In a short time I was made more thoughtful than ever by my slowly 67
rising insight into the type of activity carried on by the Jews in certain fields.

Was there any form of filth or profligacy, particularly in cultural life, 68
without at least one Jew involved in it?

If you cut even cautiously into such an abscess, you found, like a maggot 69
in a rotting body, often dazzled by the sudden light—a kike![1]

---

1. *Sowie man nur vorsichtig in eine solche Geschwulst hineinschnitt, fand man, wie die Made im faulenden
Leibe, oft ganz geblendet vom plötzlichen Lichte, ein Jüdlein.*

What had to be reckoned heavily against the Jews in my eyes was when   70
I became acquainted with their activity in the press, art, literature, and the
theater. All the unctuous reassurances helped little or nothing. It sufficed to
look at a billboard, to study the names of the men behind the horrible trash
they advertised, to make you hard for a long time to come. This was pestilence,
spiritual pestilence, worse than the Black Death of olden times, and the people
was being infected with it! It goes without saying that the lower the intellectual
level of one of these art manufacturers, the more unlimited his fertility will
be, and the scoundrel ends up like a garbage separator, splashing his filth in
the face of humanity. And bear in mind that there is no limit to their number;
bear in mind that for one Goethe Nature easily can foist on the world ten
thousand of these scribblers who poison men's souls like germ-carriers of the
worse sort, on their fellow men.

It was terrible, but not to be overlooked, that precisely the Jew, in tre-   71
mendous numbers, seemed chosen by Nature for this shameful calling.

Is this why the Jews are called the "chosen people"?   72

I now began to examine carefully the names of all the creators of un-   73
clean products in public artistic life. The result was less and less favorable for
my previous attitude toward the Jews. Regardless how my sentiment might
resist, my reason was forced to draw its conclusions.

The fact that nine tenths of all literary filth, artistic trash, and theatrical   74
idiocy can be set to the account of a people, constituting hardly one hun-
dredth of all the country's inhabitants, could simply not be talked away; it was
the plain truth.

And I now began to examine my beloved "world press" from this point   75
of view.

And the deeper I probed, the more the object of my former admiration   76
shriveled. The style became more and more unbearable; I could not help
rejecting the content as inwardly shallow and banal; the objectivity of exposition now seemed to me more akin to lies than honest truth; and the writers
were—Jews.

A thousand things which I had hardly seen before now struck my notice,   77
and others, which had previously given me food for thought, I now learned
to grasp and understand.

I now saw the liberal attitude of this press in a different light; the lofty   78
tone in which it answered attacks and its method of killing them with silence
now revealed itself to me as a trick as clever as it was treacherous; the transfigured raptures of their theatrical critics were always directed at Jewish writers,
and their disapproval never struck anyone but Germans. The gentle pinpricks
against William II revealed its methods by their persistency, and so did its
commendation of French culture and civilization. The trashy content of the
short story now appeared to me as outright indecency, and in the language I
detected the accents of a foreign people; the sense of the whole thing was so
obviously hostile to Germanism that this could only have been intentional.

But who had an interest in this?   79

Was all this a mere accident? 80

Gradually I became uncertain. 81

The development was accelerated by insights which I gained into a 82
number of other matters. I am referring to the general view of ethics and
morals which was quite openly exhibited by a large part of the Jews, and the
practical application of which could be seen.

Here again the streets provided an object lesson of a sort which was 83
sometimes positively evil.

The relation of the Jews to prostitution and, even more, to the white- 84
slave traffic, could be studied in Vienna as perhaps in no other city of Western
Europe, with the possible exception of the southern French ports. If you
walked at night through the streets and alleys of Leopoldstadt,[1] at every step
you witnessed proceedings which remained concealed from the majority of
the German people until the War gave the soldiers on the eastern front occasion to see similar things, or, better expressed, forced them to see them.

When thus for the first time I recognized the Jew as the cold-hearted, 85
shameless, and calculating director of this revolting vice traffic in the scum of
the big city, a cold shudder ran down my back.

But then a flame flared up within me. I no longer avoided discussion of 86
the Jewish question; no, now I sought it. And when I learned to look for the
Jew in all branches of cultural and artistic life and its various manifestations, I
suddenly encountered him in a place where I would least have expected to
find him.

When I recognized the Jew as the leader of the Social Democracy, the 87
scales dropped from my eyes. A long soul struggle had reached its conclusion.

Even in my daily relations with my fellow workers, I observed the amaz- 88
ing adaptability with which they adopted different positions on the same question, sometimes within an interval of a few days, sometimes in only a few
hours. It was hard for me to understand how people who, when spoken to
alone, possessed some sensible opinions, suddenly lost them as soon as they
came under the influence of the masses. It was often enough to make one
despair. When, after hours of argument, I was convinced that now at last I
had broken the ice or cleared up some absurdity, and was beginning to rejoice
at my success, on the next day to my disgust I had to begin all over again; it
had all been in vain. Like an eternal pendulum their opinions seemed to swing
back again and again to the old madness.

All this I could understand: that they were dissatisfied with their lot and 89
cursed the Fate which often struck them so harshly; that they hated the
employers who seemed to them the heartless bailiffs of Fate; that they cursed
the authorities who in their eyes were without feeling for their situation; that
they demonstrated against food prices and carried their demands into the
streets: this much could be understood without recourse to reason. But what

---

1. Second District of Vienna, separated from the main part of the city by the Danube Canal.
Formerly the ghetto, it still has a predominantly Jewish population.

inevitably remained incomprehensible was the boundless hatred they heaped upon their own nationality, despising its greatness, besmirching its history, and dragging its great men into the gutter.

This struggle against their own species, their own clan, their own home- *90* land, was as senseless as it was incomprehensible. It was unnatural.

It was possible to cure them temporarily of this vice, but only for days *91* or at most weeks. If later you met the man you thought you had converted, he was just the same as before.

His old unnatural state had regained full possession of him. *92*

I gradually became aware that the Social Democratic press was directed *93* predominantly by Jews; yet I did not attribute any special significance to this circumstance, since conditions were exactly the same in the other papers. Yet one fact seemed conspicuous: there was not one paper with Jews working on it which could have been regarded as truly national, according to my education and way of thinking.

I swallowed my disgust and tried to read this type of Marxist press *94* production, but my revulsion became so unlimited in so doing that I endeav- ored to become more closely acquainted with the men who manufactured these compendiums of knavery.

From the publisher down, they were all Jews. *95*

I took all the Social Democratic pamphlets I could lay hands on and *96* sought the names of their authors: Jews. I noted the names of the leaders; by far the greatest part were likewise members of the "chosen people," whether they were representatives in the Reichsrat or trade-union secretaries, the heads of organizations or street agitators. It was always the same gruesome picture. The names of the Austerlitzes, Davids, Adlers, Ellenbogens, etc., will remain forever graven in my memory. One thing had grown clear to me: the party with whose petty representatives I had been carrying on the most violent struggle for months was, as to leadership, almost exclusively in the hands of a foreign people; for, to my deep and joyful satisfaction, I had at last come to the conclusion that the Jew was no German.

Only now did I become thoroughly acquainted with the seducer of our *97* people.

A single year of my sojourn in Vienna had sufficed to imbue me with *98* the conviction that no worker could be so stubborn that he would not in the end succumb to better knowledge and better explanations. Slowly I had be- come an expert in their own doctrine and used it as a weapon in the struggle for my own profound conviction.

Success almost always favored my side. *99*

The great masses could be saved, if only with the gravest sacrifice in *100* time and patience.

But a Jew could never be parted from his opinions. *101*

At that time I was still childish enough to try to make the madness of *102* their doctrine clear to them; in my little circle I talked my tongue sore and my throat hoarse, thinking I would inevitably succeed in convincing them how ruinous their Marxist madness was; but what I accomplished was often the opposite. It seemed as though their increased understanding of the destructive effects of Social Democratic theories and their results only reinforced their determination.

The more I argued with them, the better I came to know their dialectic. *103* First they counted on the stupidity of their adversary, and then, when there was no other way out, they themselves simply played stupid. If all this didn't help, they pretended not to understand, or, if challenged, they changed the subject in a hurry, quoted platitudes which, if you accepted them, they immediately related to entirely different matters, and then, if again attacked, gave ground and pretended not to know exactly what you were talking about. Whenever you tried to attack one of these apostles, your hand closed on a jelly-like slime which divided up and poured through your fingers, but in the next moment collected again. But if you really struck one of these fellows so telling a blow that, observed by the audience, he couldn't help but agree, and if you believed that this had taken you at least one step forward, your amazement was great the next day. The Jew had not the slightest recollection of the day before, he rattled off his same old nonsense as though nothing at all had happened, and, if indignantly challenged, affected amazement; he couldn't remember a thing, except that he had proved the correctness of his assertions the previous day.

Sometimes I stood there thunderstruck. *104*

I didn't know what to be more amazed at: the agility of their tongues *105* or their virtuosity at lying.

Gradually I began to hate them. *106*

All this had but one good side: that in proportion as the real leaders or *107* at least the disseminators of Social Democracy came within my vision, my love for my people inevitably grew. For who, in view of the diabolical craftiness of these seducers, could damn the luckless victims? How hard it was, even for me, to get the better of this race of dialectical liars! And how futile was such success in dealing with people who twist the truth in your mouth, who without so much as a blush disavow the word they have just spoken, and in the very next minute take credit for it after all.

No. The better acquainted I became with the Jew, the more forgiving I *108* inevitably became toward the worker.

In my eyes the gravest fault was no longer with him, but with all those *109* who did not regard it as worth the trouble to have mercy on him, with iron righteousness giving the son of the people his just deserts, and standing the seducer and corrupter up against the wall.

Inspired by the experience of daily life, I now began to track down the *110* sources of the Marxist doctrine. Its effects had become clear to me in individual cases; each day its success was apparent to my attentive eyes, and, with some exercise of my imagination, I was able to picture the consequences. The only remaining question was whether the result of their action in its ultimate form had existed in the mind's eye of the creators, or whether they themselves were the victims of an error.

I felt that both were possible.   *111*

In the one case it was the duty of every thinking man to force himself   *112* to the forefront of the ill-starred movement, thus perhaps averting catastrophe; in the other, however, the original founders of this plague of the nations must have been veritable devils; for only in the brain of a monster—not that of a man—could the plan of an organization assume form and meaning, whose activity must ultimately result in the collapse of human civilization and the consequent devastation of the world.

In this case the only remaining hope was struggle, struggle with all the   *113* weapons which the human spirit, reason, and will can devise, regardless on which side of the scale Fate should lay its blessing.

Thus I began to make myself familiar with the founders of this doctrine,   *114* in order to study the foundations of the movement. If I reached my goal more quickly than at first I had perhaps ventured to believe, it was thanks to my newly acquired, though at that time not very profound, knowledge of the Jewish question. This alone enabled me to draw a practical comparison between the reality and the theoretical flim-flam of the founding fathers of Social Democracy, since it taught me to understand the language of the Jewish people, who speak in order to conceal or at least to veil their thoughts; their real aim is not therefore to be found in the lines themselves, but slumbers well concealed between them.

For me this was the time of the greatest spiritual upheaval I have ever   *115* had to go through.

I had ceased to be a weak-kneed cosmopolitan and become an anti-   *116* Semite.

Just once more—and this was the last time—fearful, oppressive thoughts   *117* came to me in profound anguish.

When over long periods of human history I scrutinized the activity of   *118* the Jewish people, suddenly there rose up in me the fearful question whether inscrutable Destiny, perhaps for reasons unknown to us poor mortals, did not with eternal and immutable resolve, desire the final victory of this little nation.

Was it possible that the earth had been promised as a reward to this   *119* people which lives only for this earth?

Have we an objective right to struggle for our self-preservation, or is this   *120* justified only subjectively within ourselves?

As I delved more deeply into the teachings of Marxism and thus in   *121* tranquil clarity submitted the deeds of the Jewish people to contemplation, Fate itself gave me its answer.

The Jewish doctrine of Marxism rejects the aristocratic principle of   *122* Nature and replaces the eternal privilege of power and strength by the mass of numbers and their dead weight. Thus it denies the value of personality in man, contests the significance of nationality and race, and thereby withdraws from humanity the premise of its existence and its culture. As a foundation of the universe, this doctrine would bring about the end of any order intellectually conceivable to man. And as, in this greatest of all recognizable organisms, the result of an application of such a law could only be chaos, on earth it could only be destruction for the inhabitants of this planet.

If, with the help of his Marxist creed, the Jew is victorious over the   123
other peoples of the world, his crown will be the funeral wreath of humanity and this planet will, as it did thousands[1] of years ago, move through the ether devoid of men.

Eternal Nature inexorably avenges the infringement of her commands.   124

Hence today I believe that I am acting in accordance with the will of   125
the Almighty Creator: *by defending myself against the Jew, I am fighting for the work of the Lord.*

Topics for Discussion and Writing

1. Who do you believe was Hitler's intended audience? What is his method of weaving arguments to persuade? How would you "grade" him as a writer? A politician?
2. *Mein Kampf* was first published in 1925 and 1927, then again in 1943. Discuss with your class how you might have reacted if you had read this material in Germany in 1939.
3. Assume the character of a student in Germany in early 1939. In your journal you will write a letter to your family back in Austria telling them about life in Berlin. You tell them about a public rally that you attended on Sunday in which Adolf Hitler spoke. What did he say? How was it received by the crowd? How did you feel about his speech? (Assume that you have already read the complete *Mein Kampf.*) After the speech, you and some other students and a few teachers met for supper and discussion. What was the talk that evening regarding Hitler's leadership and the direction he was leading Germany? Conclude your letter by telling your family what you believe the future holds.
4. Interview someone who has had—or whose family has had—personal experience with Hitler's Third Reich. What is his or her story? How was this person and his or her family's life changed? How did she or he learn to cope during and after the war? How is life for this person today? If this person could leave a message to be heeded by future citizens of the world, what would that message be?

---

1. Changed to "millions" in second edition.

ANNE FRANK

from *The Diary of Anne Frank*

> *"And in the evening, when I lie in bed and end my prayers with the words, 'I thank you, God, for all that is good and dear and beautiful,' I am filled with joy."*
>
> *Anne Frank was born June 12, 1929, in Frankfurt, Germany. Shortly after she turned 13, she and her family went into hiding in an attempt to escape capture by the Gestapo, Hitler's secret police. The hiding place, or "Secret Annexe" as she called it, was an attic apartment above her father's place of business in the city of Amsterdam.*
>
> *Anne, her family, and another family of three were in hiding from July 6, 1942, until August 4, 1944 (during this time they were joined by another person seeking shelter). On that August day the Gestapo raided the Secret Annexe and deported all the occupants to various concentration camps. Among the rifled belongings left strewn on the floors of the hiding place was Anne's diary, found and saved by two friends.*
>
> *Only Anne's father, Otto Frank, returned after the war. Anne died in the concentration camp at Bergen-Belsen in March 1945, two months before the liberation of Holland.*

Before and as You Read

1. Find the 1959 film *The Diary of Anne Frank* (frequently found in the "classics" section of video stores). As you watch it, keep in mind that it was made only 14 years after her death. What impresses you about the way these people lived?

2. Make a list of the factors that required people like the Franks to go into hiding. What was the crime for which Hitler and his followers felt that these people must be punished? Are there any current situations in which people are living with the same fear for survival?

3. Anne Frank states in her diary that some day she hopes to be a journalist. As you read this selection, how does Anne make it clear to you that she loves writing? Comment on her style, her use of imagery, narrative details, and so on. What does she teach you about journal writing?

4. One of the surest ways to become a more proficient writer is to read the published works of others. Before you read the following selections from Anne's diary, make a journal entry about life in your home. Describe your living quarters and the people with whom you live. After you read the selection, rewrite your journal entry with the new insights into your own life and writing style that you may have gained.

5. As you read, pay particular attention to the intelligence and civility of Anne, her family, and the people with whom she lived. Contrast this humanity with the outside world and the brutality that they were trying to escape. What ironies do you perceive in Anne Frank's world?

Sunday, 14 June, 1942

ON FRIDAY, June 12th, I woke up at six o'clock and no wonder; 1
it was my birthday. But of course I was not allowed to get up at
that hour, so I had to control my curiosity until a quarter to seven. Then I
could bear it no longer, and went to the dining room, where I received a
warm welcome from Moortje (the cat).

Soon after seven I went to Mummy and Daddy and then to the sitting 2
room to undo my presents. The first to greet me was *you,* possibly the nicest
of all. Then on the table there were a bunch of roses, a plant, and some
peonies, and more arrived during the day.

I got masses of things from Mummy and Daddy, and was thoroughly 3
spoiled by various friends. Among other things I was given *Camera Obscura,* a
party game, lots of sweets, chocolates, a puzzle, a brooch, *Tales and Legends of
the Netherlands* by Joseph Cohen, *Daisy's Mountain Holiday* (a terrific book),
and some money. Now I can buy *The Myths of Greece and Rome*—grand!

Then Lies called for me and we went to school. During recess I treated 4
everyone to sweet biscuits, and then we had to go back to our lessons.

Now I must stop. Bye-bye, we're going to be great pals! 5

Saturday, 20 June, 1942

I haven't written for a few days, because I wanted first of all to think 6
about my diary. It's an odd idea for someone like me to keep a diary; not only
because I have never done so before, but because it seems to me that neither
I—nor for that matter anyone else—will be interested in the unbosomings of
a thirteen-year-old schoolgirl. Still, what does that matter? I want to write,
but more than that, I want to bring out all kinds of things that lie buried deep
in my heart.

There is a saying that "paper is more patient than man"; it came back to 7
me on one of my slightly melancholy days, while I sat chin in hand, feeling
too bored and limp even to make up my mind whether to go out or stay at
home. Yes, there is no doubt that paper is patient and as I don't intend to
show this cardboard-covered notebook, bearing the proud name of "diary," to
anyone, unless I find a real friend, boy or girl, probably nobody cares. And
now I come to the root of the matter, the reason for my starting a diary: it is
that I have no such real friend.

Let me put it more clearly, since no one will believe that a girl of 8
thirteen feels herself quite alone in the world, nor is it so. I have darling
parents and a sister of sixteen. I know about thirty people whom one might
call friends—I have strings of boy friends, anxious to catch a glimpse of me
and who, failing that, peep at me through mirrors in class. I have relations,
aunts and uncles, who are darlings too, a good home, no—I don't seem to
lack anything. But it's the same with all my friends, just fun and joking,
nothing more. I can never bring myself to talk of anything outside the

common round. We don't seem to be able to get any closer, that is the root of the trouble. Perhaps I lack confidence, but anyway, there it is, a stubborn fact and I don't seem to be able to do anything about it.

Hence, this diary. In order to enhance in my mind's eye the picture of the friend for whom I have waited so long, I don't want to set down a series of bald facts in a diary like most people do, but I want this diary itself to be my friend, and I shall call my friend Kitty. No one will grasp what I'm talking about if I begin my letters to Kitty just out of the blue, so, albeit unwillingly, I will start by sketching in brief the story of my life.   *9*

My father was thirty-six when he married my mother, who was then twenty-five. My sister Margot was born in 1926 in Frankfort-on-Main, I followed on June 12, 1929, and, as we are Jewish, we emigrated to Holland in 1933, where my father was appointed Managing Director of Travies N.V. This firm is in close relationship with the firm of Kolen & Co. in the same building, of which my father is a partner.   *10*

The rest of our family, however, felt the full impact of Hitler's anti-Jewish laws, so life was filled with anxiety. In 1938 after the pogroms, my two uncles (my mother's brothers) escaped to the U.S.A. My old grandmother came to us, she was then seventy-three. After May 1940 good times rapidly fled: first the war, then the capitulation, followed by the arrival of the Germans, which is when the sufferings of us Jews really began. Anti-Jewish decrees followed each other in quick succession. Jews must wear a yellow star,[1] Jews must hand in their bicycles, Jews are banned from trams and are forbidden to drive. Jews are only allowed to do their shopping between three and five o'clock and then only in shops which bear the placard "Jewish shop." Jews must be indoors by eight o'clock and cannot even sit in their own gardens after that hour. Jews are forbidden to visit theaters, cinemas, and other places of entertainment. Jews may not take part in public sports. Swimming baths, tennis courts, hockey fields, and other sports grounds are all prohibited to them. Jews may not visit Christians. Jews must go to Jewish schools, and many more restrictions of a similar kind.   *11*

So we could not do this and were forbidden to do that. But life went on in spite of it all. Jopie used to say to me, "You're scared to do anything, because it may be forbidden." Our freedom was strictly limited. Yet things were still bearable.   *12*

Granny died in January 1942; no one will ever know how much she is present in my thoughts and how much I love her still.   *13*

In 1934 I went to school at the Montessori Kindergarten and continued there. It was at the end of the school year, I was in form 6B, when I had to say good-by to Mrs. K. We both wept, it was very sad. In 1941 I went, with my sister Margot, to the Jewish Secondary School, she into the fourth form and I into the first.   *14*

1. To distinguish them from others, all Jews were forced by the Germans to wear, prominently displayed, a yellow six-pointed star.

So far everything is all right with the four of us and here I come to the   15
present day.

Wednesday, 8 July, 1942

Dear Kitty,

Years seem to have passed between Sunday and now. So much has hap-   16
pened, it is just as if the whole world had turned upside down. But I am still
alive, Kitty, and that is the main thing, Daddy says.

Yes, I'm still alive, indeed, but don't ask where or how. You wouldn't   17
understand a word, so I will begin by telling you what happened on Sunday
afternoon.

At three o'clock (Harry had just gone, but was coming back later) some-   18
one rang the front doorbell. I was lying lazily reading a book on the veranda
in the sunshine, so I didn't hear it. A bit later, Margot appeared at the kitchen
door looking very excited. "The S.S. have sent a call-up notice for Daddy,"
she whispered. "Mummy has gone to see Mr. Van Daan already." (Van Daan is
a friend who works with Daddy in the business.) It was a great shock to me,
a call-up; everyone knows what that means. I picture concentration camps and
lonely cells—should we allow him to be doomed to this? "Of course he won't
go," declared Margot, while we waited together. "Mummy has gone to the
Van Daans to discuss whether we should move into our hiding place tomorrow. The Van Daans are going with us, so we shall be seven in all." Silence.
We couldn't talk any more, thinking about Daddy, who, little knowing what
was going on, was visiting some old people in the Joodse Invalide; waiting for
Mummy, the heat and suspense, all made us very overawed and silent.

Suddenly the bell rang again. "That is Harry," I said. "Don't open the   19
door." Margot held me back, but it was not necessary as we heard Mummy
and Mr. Van Daan downstairs, talking to Harry, then they came in and closed
the door behind them. Each time the bell went, Margot or I had to creep
softly down to see if it was Daddy, not opening the door to anyone else.

Margot and I were sent out of the room. Van Daan wanted to talk to   20
Mummy alone. When we were alone together in our bedroom, Margot told
me that the call-up was not for Daddy, but for her. I was more frightened than
ever and began to cry. Margot is sixteen; would they really take girls of that
age away alone? But thank goodness she won't go, Mummy said so herself;
that must be what Daddy meant when he talked about us going into hiding.

Into hiding—where would we go, in a town or the country, in a house   21
or a cottage, when, how, where . . . ?

These were questions I was not allowed to ask, but I couldn't get them   22
out of my mind. Margot and I began to pack some of our most vital belongings into a school satchel. The first thing I put in was this diary, then hair
curlers, handkerchiefs, schoolbooks, a comb, old letters; I put in the craziest
things with the idea that we were going into hiding. But I'm not sorry,
memories mean more to me than dresses.

At five o'clock Daddy finally arrived, and we phoned Mr. Koophuis to   *23*
ask if he could come around in the evening. Van Daan went and fetched
Miep. Miep has been in the business with Daddy since 1933 and has become
a close friend, likewise her brand-new husband, Henk. Miep came and took
some shoes, dresses, coats, underwear, and stockings away in her bag, promising to return in the evening. Then silence fell on the house; not one of us felt
like eating anything, it was still hot and everything was very strange. We let
our large upstairs room to a certain Mr. Goudsmit, a divorced man in his
thirties, who appeared to have nothing to do on this particular evening; we
simply could not get rid of him without being rude; he hung about until ten
o'clock. At eleven o'clock Miep and Henk Van Santen arrived. Once again,
shoes, stockings, books, and underclothes disappeared into Miep's bag and
Henk's deep pockets, and at eleven-thirty they too disappeared. I was dog-
tired and although I knew that it would be my last night in my own bed, I fell
asleep immediately and didn't wake up until Mummy called me at five-thirty
the next morning. Luckily it was not so hot as Sunday; warm rain fell steadily
all day. We put on heaps of clothes as if we were going to the North Pole,
the sole reason being to take clothes with us. No Jew in our situation would
have dreamed of going out with a suitcase full of clothing. I had on two vests,
three pairs of pants, a dress, on top of that a skirt, jacket, summer coat, two
pairs of stockings, lace-up shoes, woolly cap, scarf, and still more; I was nearly
stifled before we started, but no one inquired about that.

Margot filled her satchel with schoolbooks, fetched her bicycle, and rode   *24*
off behind Miep into the unknown, as far as I was concerned. You see I still
didn't know where our secret hiding place was to be. At seven-thirty the door
closed behind us. Moortje, my little cat, was the only creature to whom I said
farewell. She would have a good home with the neighbors. This was all written in a letter addressed to Mr. Goudsmit.

There was one pound of meat in the kitchen for the cat, breakfast things   *25*
lying on the table, stripped beds, all giving the impression that we had left
helter-skelter. But we didn't care about impressions, we only wanted to get
away, only escape and arrive safely, nothing else. Continued tomorrow.

Yours, Anne

Thursday, 9 July, 1942

Dear Kitty,

So we walked in the pouring rain, Daddy, Mummy, and I, each with a   *26*
school satchel and shopping bag filled to the brim with all kinds of things
thrown together anyhow.

We got sympathetic looks from people on their way to work. You could   *27*
see by their faces how sorry they were they couldn't offer us a lift; the gaudy
yellow star spoke for itself.

Only when we were on the road did Mummy and Daddy begin to tell   *28*
me bits and pieces about the plan. For months as many of our goods and
chattels and necessities of life as possible had been sent away and they were

sufficiently ready for us to have gone into hiding of our own accord on July 16. The plan had had to be speeded up ten days because of the call-up, so our quarters would not be so well organized, but we had to make the best of it. The hiding place itself would be in the building where Daddy has his office. It will be hard for outsiders to understand, but I shall explain that later on. Daddy didn't have many people working for him: Mr. Kraler, Koophuis, Miep, and Elli Vossen, a twenty-three-year-old typist who all knew of our arrival. Mr. Vossen, Elli's father, and two boys worked in the warehouse; they had not been told.

I will describe the building: there is a large warehouse on the ground floor which is used as a store. The front door to the house is next to the warehouse door, and inside the front door is a second doorway which leads to a staircase (A). There is another door at the top of the stairs, with a frosted glass window in it, which has "Office" written in black letters across it. That is the large main office, very big, very light, and very full. Elli, Miep, and Mr. Koophuis work there in the daytime. A small dark room containing the safe, a wardrobe, and a large cupboard leads to a small somewhat dark second office. Mr. Kraler and Mr. Van Daan used to sit here, now it is only Mr. Kraler.

1st FLOOR   2nd FLOOR   3rd FLOOR

One can reach Kraler's office from the passage, but only via a glass door which can be opened from the inside, but not easily from the outside.

From Kraler's office a long passage goes past the coal store, up four steps *30* and leads to the showroom of the whole building: the private office. Dark, dignified furniture, linoleum and carpets on the floor, radio, smart lamp, everything first-class. Next door there is a roomy kitchen with a hot-water faucet and a gas stove. Next door the W.C. That is the first floor.

A wooden staircase leads from the downstairs passage to the next floor *31* (B). There is a small landing at the top. There is a door at each end of the landing, the left one leading to a storeroom at the front of the house and to the attics. One of those really steep Dutch staircases runs from the side to the other door opening on to the street (C).

The right-hand door leads to our "Secret Annexe." No one would ever *32* guess that there would be so many rooms hidden behind that plain gray door. There's a little step in front of the door and then you are inside.

There is a steep staircase immediately opposite the entrance (E). On the *33* left a tiny passage brings you into a room which was to become the Frank family's bed-sitting-room, next door a smaller room, study and bedroom for the two young ladies of the family. On the right a little room without windows containing the washbasin and a small W.C. compartment, with another door leading to Margot's and my room. If you go up the next flight of stairs and open the door, you are simply amazed that there could be such a big light room in such an old house by the canal. There is a gas stove in this room (thanks to the fact that it was used as a laboratory) and a sink. This is now the kitchen for the Van Daan couple, besides being general living room, dining room, and scullery.

A tiny little corridor room will become Peter Van Daan's apartment. *34* Then, just as on the lower landing, there is a large attic. So there you are, I've introduced you to the whole of our beautiful "Secret Annexe."

Yours, Anne

Friday, 14 August, 1942

Dear Kitty,

I have deserted you for a whole month, but honestly, there is so little *35* news here that I can't find amusing things to tell you every day. The Van Daans arrived on July 13. We thought they were coming on the fourteenth, but between the thirteenth and sixteenth of July the Germans called up people right and left which created more and more unrest, so they played for safety, better a day too early than a day too late. At nine-thirty in the morning (we were still having breakfast) Peter arrived, the Van Daans' son, not sixteen yet, a rather soft, shy, gawky youth; can't expect much from his company. He brought his cat (Mouschi) with him. Mr. and Mrs. Van Daan arrived half an hour later, and to our great amusement she had a large pottie in her hat box. "I don't feel at home anywhere without my chamber," she declared, so it was the first thing to find its permanent resting place under her divan. Mr. Van Daan did not bring his, but carried a folding tea table under his arm.

From the day they arrived we all had meals cozily together and after   *36*
three days it was just as if we were one large family. Naturally the Van Daans
were able to tell us a lot about the extra week they had spent in the inhabited
world. Among other things we were very interested to hear what had happened to our house and to Mr. Goudsmit. Mr. Van Daan told us:

"Mr. Goudsmit phoned at nine o'clock on Monday morning and asked   *37*
if I could come around. I went immediately and found G. in a state of great
agitation. He let me read a letter that the Franks had left behind and wanted
to take the cat to the neighbors as indicated in the letter, which pleased me.
Mr. G. was afraid that the house would be searched so we went through all
the rooms, tidied up a bit, and cleared away the breakfast things. Suddenly I
discovered a writing pad on Mrs. Frank's desk with an address in Maastricht
written on it. Although I knew that this was done on purpose, I pretended to
be very surprised and shocked and urged Mr. G. to tear up this unfortunate
little piece of paper without delay.

"I went on pretending that I knew nothing of your disappearance all   *38*
the time, but after seeing the paper, I got a brain wave. 'Mr. Goudsmit'—I
said—'it suddenly dawns on me what this address may refer to. Now it all
comes back to me, a high-ranking officer was in the office about six months
ago, he appeared to be very friendly with Mr. Frank and offered to help him,
should the need arise. He was stationed in Maastricht. I think he must have
kept his word and somehow or other managed to get them into Belgium and
then on to Switzerland. I should tell this to any friends who may inquire.
Don't, of course, mention Maastricht.'

"With these words I left the house. Most of your friends know already,   *39*
because I've been told myself several times by different people."

We were highly amused at the story and, when Mr. Van Daan gave us   *40*
further details, laughed still more at the way people can let their imagination
run away with them. One family had seen the pair of us pass on bicycles very
early in the morning and another lady knew quite definitely that we were
fetched by a military car in the middle of the night.

Yours, Anne

Friday, 9 October, 1942

Dear Kitty,

I've only got dismal and depressing news for you today. Our many Jewish   *41*
friends are being taken away by the dozen. These people are treated by the
Gestapo without a shred of decency, being loaded into cattle trucks and sent
to Westerbork, the big Jewish camp in Drente. Westerbork sounds terrible:
only one washing cubicle for a hundred people and not nearly enough lava-
tories. There is no separate accommodations. Men, women, and children all
sleep together. One hears of frightful immorality because of this; and a lot of
the women, and even girls, who stay there any length of time are expecting
babies.

It is impossible to escape; most of the people in the camp are branded   *42*
as inmates by their shaven heads and many also by their Jewish appearance.

If it is as bad as this in Holland whatever will it be like in the distant   43
and barbarous regions they are sent to? We assume that most of them are
murdered. The English radio speaks of their being gassed.

Perhaps that is the quickest way to die. I feel terribly upset. I couldn't   44
tear myself away while Miep told these dreadful stories; and she herself was
equally wound up for that matter. Just recently for instance, a poor old crippled Jewess was sitting on her doorstep; she had been told to wait there by the
Gestapo, who had gone to fetch a car to take her away. The poor old thing
was terrified by the guns that were shooting at English planes overhead, and
by the glaring beams of the searchlights. But Miep did not dare take her in;
no one would undergo such a risk. The Germans strike without the slightest
mercy. Elli too is very quiet: her boy friend has got to go to Germany. She is
afraid that the airmen who fly over her home will drop their bombs, often
weighing a million kilos, on Dirk's head. Jokes such as "he's not likely to get a
million" and "it only takes one bomb" are in rather bad taste. Dirk is certainly
not the only one who has to go: trainloads of boys leave daily. If they stop at
a small station en route, sometimes some of them manage to get out unnoticed
and escape; perhaps a few manage it. This, however, is not the end of my bad
news. Have you ever heard of hostages? That's the latest thing in penalties for
sabotage. Can you imagine anything so dreadful?

Prominent citizens—innocent people—are thrown into prison to await   45
their fate. If the saboteur can't be traced, the Gestapo simply puts about five
hostages against the wall. Announcements of their deaths appear in the papers
frequently. These outrages are described as "fatal accidents." Nice people, the
Germans! To think that I was once one of them too! No, Hitler took away
our nationality long ago. In fact, Germans and Jews are the greatest enemies
in the world.

Yours, Anne

Wednesday, 13 January, 1943

Dear Kitty,

Everything has upset me again this morning, so I wasn't able to finish a   46
single thing properly.

It is terrible outside. Day and night more of those poor miserable people   47
are being dragged off, with nothing but a rucksack and a little money. On the
way they are deprived even of these possessions. Families are torn apart, the
men, women, and children all being separated. Children coming home from
school find that their parents have disappeared. Women return from shopping
to find their homes shut up and their families gone.

The Dutch people are anxious too, their sons are being sent to Germany.   48
Everyone is afraid.

And every night hundreds of planes fly over Holland and go to German   49
towns, where the earth is so plowed up by their bombs, and every hour
hundreds and thousands of people are killed in Russia and Africa. No one is
able to keep out of it, the whole globe is waging war and although it is going
better for the Allies, the end is not yet in sight.

And as for us, we are fortunate. Yes, we are luckier than millions of 50
people. It is quiet and safe here, and we are, so to speak, living on capital. We
are even so selfish as to talk about "after the war," brighten up at the thought of
having new clothes and new shoes, whereas we really ought to save every penny,
to help other people, and save what is left from the wreckage after the war.

The children here run about in just a thin blouse and clogs; no coat, no 51
hat, no stockings, and no one helps them. Their tummies are empty, they
chew an old carrot to stay the pangs, go from their cold homes out into the
cold street and, when they get to school, find themselves in an even colder
classroom. Yes, it has even got so bad in Holland that countless children stop
the passers-by and beg for a piece of bread. I could go on for hours about all
the suffering the war has brought, but then I would only make myself more
dejected. There is nothing we can do but wait as calmly as we can till the
misery comes to an end. Jews and Christians wait, the whole earth waits; and
there are many who wait for death.

Yours, Anne

Sunday, 13 June, 1943

Dear Kitty,

My birthday poem from Daddy is too good to keep from you. As Pim 52
usually writes verses in German, Margot volunteered to translate it. Judge for
yourself whether Margot didn't do it brilliantly. After the usual summary of
the events of the year, this is how it ran:

Though youngest here, you are no longer small,
But life is very hard, since one and all
Aspire to be your teacher, thus and thus:
"We have experience, take a tip from us."
"We know because we did it long ago."
"Elders are always better, you must know."
At least that's been the rule since life began!
Our personal faults are much too small to scan
This makes it easier to criticize
The faults of others, which seem double size.
Please bear with us, your parents, for we try
To judge you fairly and with sympathy.
Correction sometimes take against your will,
Though it's like swallowing a bitter pill,
Which must be done if we're to keep the peace,
While time goes by till all this suffering cease.
You read and study nearly all the day,
Who might have lived in such a different way.
You're never bored and bring us all fresh air.
Your only moan is this: "What can I wear?
I have no knickers, all my clothes are small,
My vest might be a loincloth, that is all!

To put on shoes would mean to cut off toes,
Oh dear, I'm worried by so many woes!"

There was also a bit about food that Margot could not translate into *53*
rhyme, so I shall leave it out. Don't you think my birthday poem is good? I
have been thoroughly spoiled in other ways and received a lot of lovely things.
Among other things a fat book on my pet subject—the mythology of Greece
and Rome. I can't complain of a shortage of sweets either—everyone has
broken into their last reserves. As the Benjamin of the family in hiding, I am
really more honored than I deserve.

Yours, Anne

Tuesday, 11 April, 1944

Dear Kitty,

My head throbs, I honestly don't know where to begin. *54*

On Friday (Good Friday) we played Monopoly, Saturday afternoon too.
These days passed quickly and uneventfully. On Sunday afternoon, on my
invitation, Peter came to my room at half past four; at a quarter past five we
went to the front attic, where we remained until six o'clock. There was a
beautiful Mozart concert on the radio from six o'clock until a quarter past
seven. I enjoyed it all very much, but especially the "Kleine Nachtmusik." I
can hardly listen in the room because I'm always so inwardly stirred when I
hear lovely music.

On Sunday evening Peter and I went to the front attic together and, in *55*
order to sit comfortably, we took with us a few divan cushions that we were
able to lay our hands on. We seated ourselves on one packing case. Both the
case and the cushions were very narrow, so we sat absolutely squashed together,
leaning against other cases. Mouschi kept us company too, so we weren't
unchaperoned.

Suddenly, at a quarter to nine, Mr. Van Daan whistled and asked if we *56*
had one of Dussel's cushions. We both jumped up and went downstairs with
cushion, cat, and Van Daan.

A lot of trouble arose out of this cushion, because Dussel was annoyed *57*
that we had one of his cushions, one that he used as a pillow. He was afraid
that there might be fleas in it and made a great commotion about his beloved
cushion! Peter and I put two hard brushes in his bed as a revenge. We had a
good laugh over this little interlude!

Our fun didn't last long. At half past nine Peter knocked softly on the *58*
door and asked Daddy if he would just help him upstairs over a difficult
English sentence. "That's a blind," I said to Margot, "anyone could see through
that one!" I was right. They were in the act of breaking into the warehouse.
Daddy, Van Daan, Dussel, and Peter were downstairs in a flash. Margot,
Mummy, Mrs. Van Daan, and I stayed upstairs and waited.

Four frightened women just have to talk, so talk we did, until we heard *59*
a bang downstairs. After that all was quiet, the clock struck a quarter to ten.
The color had vanished from our faces, we were still quiet, although we were

afraid. Where could the men be? What was that bang? Would they be fighting the burglars? Ten o'clock, footsteps on the stairs: Daddy, white and nervous, entered, followed by Mr. Van Daan. "Lights out, creep upstairs, we expect the police in the house!"

There was no time to be frightened: the lights went out, I quickly grabbed a jacket, and we were upstairs. "What has happened? Tell us quickly!" There was no one to tell us, the men having disappeared downstairs again. Only at ten past ten did they reappear; two kept watch at Peter's open window, the door to the landing was closed, the swinging cupboard shut. We hung a jersey round the night light, and after that they told us: 60

Peter heard two loud bangs on the landing, ran downstairs, and saw there was a large plank out of the left half of the door. He dashed upstairs, warned the "Home Guard" of the family, and the four of them proceeded downstairs. When they entered the warehouse, the burglars were in the act of enlarging the hole. Without further thought Van Daan shouted: "Police!" 61

A few hurried steps outside, and the burglars had fled. In order to avoid the hole being noticed by the police, a plank was put against it, but a good hard kick from outside sent it flying to the ground. The men were perplexed at such impudence, and both Van Daan and Peter felt murder welling up within them; Van Daan beat on the ground with a chopper, and all was quiet again. Once more they wanted to put the plank in front of the hole. Disturbance! A married couple outside shone a torch through the opening, lighting up the whole warehouse. "Hell!" muttered one of the men, and now they switched over from their role of police to that of burglars. The four of them sneaked upstairs, Peter quickly opened the doors and windows of the kitchen and private office, flung the telephone onto the floor, and finally the four of them landed behind the swinging cupboard. 62

End of Part One

The married couple with the torch would probably have warned the police: it was Sunday evening, Easter Sunday, no one at the office on Easter Monday, so none of us could budge until Tuesday morning. Think of it, waiting in such fear for two nights and a day! No one had anything to suggest, so we simply sat there in pitch-darkness, because Mrs. Van Daan in her fright had unintentionally turned the lamp right out; talked in whispers, and at every creak one heard "Sh! sh!" 63

It turned half past ten, eleven, but not a sound; Daddy and Van Daan joined us in turns. Then a quarter past eleven, a bustle and noise downstairs. Everyone's breath was audible, otherwise no one moved. Footsteps in the house, in the private office, kitchen, then . . . on our staircase. No one breathed audibly now, footsteps on our staircase, then a rattling of the swinging cupboard. This moment is indescribable. "Now we are lost!" I said, and could see us all being taken away by the Gestapo that very night. Twice they rattled at the cupboard, then there was nothing, the footsteps withdrew, we 64 were saved so far. A shiver seemed to pass from one to another, I heard someone's teeth chattering, no one said a word.

There was not another sound in the house, but a light was burning on our landing, right in front of the cupboard. Could that be because it was a secret cupboard? Perhaps the police had forgotten the light? Would someone come back to put it out? Tongues loosened, there was no one in the house any longer, perhaps there was someone on guard outside. . . . 65

Talk, whispers, fear, stink, flatulation, and always someone on the pot; then try to go to sleep! However, by half past two I was so tired that I knew no more until half past three. I awoke when Mrs. Van Daan laid her head on my foot. 66

"For heaven's sake, give me something to put on!" I asked. I was given something, but don't ask what—a pair of woolen knickers over my pajamas, a red jumper, and a black skirt, white oversocks and a pair of sports stockings full of holes. Then Mrs. Van Daan sat in the chair and her husband came and lay on my feet. I lay thinking till half past three, shivering the whole time, which prevented Van Daan from sleeping. I prepared myself for the return of the police, then we'd have to say that we were in hiding; they would either be good Dutch people, then we'd be saved, or N.S.B.-ers,[1] then we'd have to bribe them! 67

"In that case, destroy the radio," sighed Mrs. Van Daan. "Yes, in the stove!" replied her husband. "If they find us, then let them find the radio as well!" 68

"Then they will find Anne's diary," added Daddy. "Burn it then," suggested the most terrified member of the party. This, and when the police rattled the cupboard door, were my worst moments. "Not my diary; if my diary goes, I go with it!" But luckily Daddy didn't answer. 69

There is no object in recounting all the conversations that I can still remember; so much was said. I comforted Mrs. Van Daan, who was very scared. We talked about escaping and being questioned by the Gestapo, about ringing up, and being brave. 70

"We must behave like soldiers, Mrs. Van Daan. If all is up now, then let's go for Queen and Country, for freedom, truth, and right, as they always say on the Dutch News from England. The only thing that is really rotten is that we get a lot of other people into trouble too." 71

Mr. Van Daan changed places again with his wife after an hour, and Daddy came and sat beside me. The men smoked non-stop, now and then there was a deep sigh, then someone went on the pot and everything began all over again. 72

Four o'clock, five o'clock, half past five. Then I went and sat with Peter by his window and listened, so close together that we could feel each other's bodies quivering; we spoke a word or two now and then, and listened attentively. In the room next door they took down the blackout. They wanted to call up 73

1. The Dutch National Socialist Movement.

Koophuis at seven o'clock and get him to send someone around. Then they wrote down everything they wanted to tell Koophuis over the phone. The risk that the police on guard at the door, or in the warehouse, might hear the telephone was very great, but the danger of the police returning was even greater.

The points were these: 74

Burglars broken in: police have been in the house, as far as the swinging cupboard, but no further.

Burglars apparently disturbed, forced open the door in the warehouse and escaped through the garden.

Main entrance bolted, Kraler must have used the second door when he left. The typewriters and adding machine are safe in the black case in the private office.

Try to warn Henk and fetch the key from Elli, then go and look round the office—on the pretext of feeding the cat.

Everything went according to plan. Koophuis was phoned, the type- 75 writers which we had upstairs were put in the case. Then we sat around the table again and waited for Henk or the police.

Peter had fallen asleep and Van Daan and I were lying on the floor, when 76 we heard loud footsteps downstairs. I got up quietly: "That's Henk."

"No, no, it's the police," some of the others said. 77

Someone knocked at the door, Miep whistled. This was too much for 78 Mrs. Van Daan, she turned as white as a sheet and sank limply into a chair; had the tension lasted one minute longer she would have fainted.

Our room was a perfect picture when Miep and Henk entered, the table 79 alone would have been worth photographing! A copy of *Cinema and Theater,* covered with jam and a remedy for diarrhea, opened at a page of dancing girls, two jam pots, two started loaves of bread, a mirror, comb, matches, ash, cigarettes, tobacco, ash tray, books, a pair of pants, a torch, toilet paper, etc., etc., lay jumbled together in variegated splendor.

Of course Henk and Miep were greeted with shouts and tears. Henk 80 mended the hole in the door with some planks, and soon went off again to inform the police of the burglary. Miep had also found a letter under the warehouse door from the night watchman Slagter, who had noticed the hole and warned the police, whom he would also visit.

So we had half an hour to tidy ourselves. I've never seen such a change 81 take place in half an hour. Margot and I took the bedclothes downstairs, went to the W.C., washed, and did our teeth and hair. After that I tidied the room a bit and went upstairs again. The table there was already cleared, so we ran off some water and made coffee and tea, boiled the milk, and laid the table for lunch. Daddy and Peter emptied the potties and cleaned them with warm water and chlorine.

At eleven o'clock we sat round the table with Henk, who was back by 82 that time, and slowly things began to be more normal and cozy again. Henk's story was as follows:

Mr. Slagter was asleep, but his wife told Henk that her husband had 83 found the hole in our door when he was doing his tour round the canals, and that he had called a policeman, who had gone through the building with him. He would be coming to see Kraler on Tuesday and would tell him more then. At the police station they knew nothing of the burglary yet, but the policeman had made a note of it at once and would come and look round on Tuesday. On the way back Henk happened to meet our greengrocer at the corner, and told him that the house had been broken into. "I know that," he said quite coolly. "I was passing last evening with my wife and saw the hole in the door. My wife wanted to walk on, but I just had a look in with my torch; then the thieves cleared at once. To be on the safe side, I didn't ring up the police, as with you I didn't think it was the thing to do. I don't know anything, but I guess a lot."

Henk thanked him and went on. The man obviously guesses that we're 84 here, because he always brings the potatoes during the lunch hour. Such a nice man!

It was one by the time Henk had gone and we'd finished doing the 85 dishes. We all went for a sleep. I awoke at a quarter to three and saw that Mr. Dussel had already disappeared. Quite by chance, and with my sleepy eyes, I ran into Peter in the bathroom; he had just come down. We arranged to meet downstairs.

I tidied myself and went down. "Do you still dare to go to the front 86 attic?" he asked. I nodded, fetched my pillow, and we went up to the attic. It was glorious weather, and soon the sirens were wailing; we stayed where we were. Peter put his arm around my shoulder, and I put mine around his and so we remained, our arms around each other, quietly waiting until Margot came to fetch us for coffee at four o'clock.

We finished our bread, drank lemonade and joked (we were able to 87 again), otherwise everything went normally. In the evening I thanked Peter because he was the bravest of us all.

None of us has ever been in such danger as that night. God truly pro- 88 tected us; just think of it—the police at our secret cupboard, the light on right in front of it, and still we remained undiscovered.

If the invasion comes, and bombs with it, then it is each man for himself, 89 but in this case the fear was also for our good, innocent protectors. "We are saved, go on saving us!" That is all we can say.

This affair has brought quite a number of changes with it. Mr. Dussel 90 no longer sits downstairs in Kraler's office in the evenings, but in the bathroom instead. Peter goes round the house for a checkup at half past eight and half past nine. Peter isn't allowed to have his window open at nights any more. No one is allowed to pull the plug after half past nine. This evening there's a carpenter coming to make the warehouse doors even stronger.

Now there are debates going on all the time in the "Secret Annexe." 91 Kraler reproached us for our carelessness. Henk, too, said that in a case like that we must never go downstairs. We have been pointedly reminded that we are in hiding, that we are Jews in chains, chained to one spot, without any rights, but with a thousand duties. We Jews mustn't show our feelings, must be brave and strong, must accept all inconveniences and not grumble, must do what is within our power and trust in God. Sometime this terrible war will be over. Surely the time will come when we are people again, and not just Jews.

Who has inflicted this upon us? Who has made us Jews different from   92
all other people? Who has allowed us to suffer so terribly up till now? It is God that has made us as we are, but it will be God, too, who will raise us up again. If we bear all this suffering and if there are still Jews left, when it is over, then Jews, instead of being doomed, will be held up as an example. Who knows, it might even be our religion from which the world and all peoples learn good, and for that reason and that reason only do we have to suffer now. We can never become just Netherlanders, or just English, or representatives of any country for that matter, we will always remain Jews, but we want to, too.

Be brave! Let us remain aware of our task and not grumble, a solution   93
will come, God has never deserted our people. Right through the ages there have been Jews, through all the ages they have had to suffer, but it has made them strong too; the weak fall, but the strong will remain and never go under!

During that night I really felt that I had to die, I waited for the police, I   94
was prepared, as the soldier is on the battlefield. I was eager to lay down my life for the country, but now, now I've been saved again, now my first wish after the war is that I may become Dutch! I love the Dutch, I love this country, I love the language and want to work here. And even if I have to write to the Queen myself, I will not give up until I have reached my goal.

I am becoming still more independent of my parents, young as I am, I   95
face life with more courage than Mummy; my feeling for justice is immovable, and truer than hers. I know what I want, I have a goal, an opinion, I have a religion and love. Let me be myself and then I am satisfied. I know that I'm a woman, a woman with inward strength and plenty of courage.

If God lets me live, I shall attain more than Mummy ever has done, I   96
shall not remain insignificant, I shall work in the world and for mankind!

And now I know that first and foremost I shall require courage and   97
cheerfulness!

Yours, Anne

Friday, 21 July, 1944

Dear Kitty,

Now I am getting really hopeful, now things are going well at last. Yes,   98
really, they're going well! Super news! An attempt has been made on Hitler's life and not even by Jewish communists or English capitalists this time, but by a proud German general, and what's more, he's a count, and still quite young. The Führer's life was saved by Divine Providence and, unfortunately, he managed to get off with just a few scratches and burns. A few officers and generals who were with him have been killed and wounded. The chief culprit was shot.

Anyway, it certainly shows that there are lots of officers and generals   *99*
who are sick of the war and would like to see Hitler descend into a bottomless
pit. When they've disposed of Hitler, their aim is to establish a military dictator, who will make peace with the Allies, then they intend to rearm and start
another war in about twenty years' time. Perhaps the Divine Power tarried on
purpose in getting him out of the way, because it would be much easier and
more advantageous to the Allies if the impeccable Germans kill each other
off; it'll make less work for the Russians and the English and they'll be able to
begin rebuilding their own towns all the sooner.

But still, we're not that far yet, and I don't want to anticipate the glorious   *100*
events too soon. Still, you must have noticed, this is all sober reality and that
I'm in quite a matter-of-fact mood today; for once, I'm not jabbering about
high ideals. And what's more, Hitler has even been so kind as to announce to
his faithful, devoted people that from now on everyone in the armed forces
must obey the Gestapo, and that any soldier who knows that one of his
superiors was involved in this low, cowardly attempt upon his life may shoot
the same on the spot, without court-martial.

What a perfect shambles it's going to be. Little Johnnie's feet begin   *101*
hurting him during a long march, he's snapped at by his boss, the officer,
Johnnie grabs his rifle and cries out: "You wanted to murder the Führer, so
there's your reward." One bang and the proud chief who dared to tick off
little Johnnie has passed into eternal life (or is it eternal death?). In the end,
whenever an officer finds himself up against a soldier, or having to take the
lead, he'll be wetting his pants from anxiety, because the soldiers will dare to
say more than they do. Do you gather a bit what I mean, or have I been
skipping too much from one subject to another? I can't help it; the prospect
that I may be sitting on school benches next October makes me feel far too
cheerful to be logical! Oh, dearie me, hadn't I just told you that I didn't want
to be too hopeful? Forgive me, they haven't given me the name "little bundle
of contradictions" all for nothing!

Yours, Anne

Tuesday, 1 August, 1944

Dear Kitty,

"Little bundle of contradictions." That's how I ended my last letter and   *102*
that's how I'm going to begin this one. "A little bundle of contradictions," can
you tell me exactly what it is? What does contradiction mean? Like so many
words, it can mean two things, contradiction from without and contradiction
from within.

The first is the ordinary "not giving in easily, always knowing best,   *103*
getting in the last word," *enfin,* all the unpleasant qualities for which I'm
renowned. The second nobody knows about, that's my own secret.

I've already told you before that I have, as it were, a dual personality.   *104*
One half embodies my exuberant cheerfulness, making fun of everything, my
high-spiritedness, and above all, the way I take everything lightly. This includes

not taking offense at a flirtation, a kiss, an embrace, a dirty joke. This side is usually lying in wait and pushes away the other, which is much better, deeper and purer. You must realize that no one knows Anne's better side and that's why most people find me so insufferable.

Certainly I'm a giddy clown for one afternoon, but then everyone's had   *105* enough of me for another month. Really, it's just the same as a love film is for deep-thinking people, simply a diversion, amusing just for once, something which is soon forgotten, not bad, but certainly not good. I loathe having to tell you this, but why shouldn't I, if I know it's true anyway? My lighter superficial side will always be too quick for the deeper side of me and that's why it will always win. You can't imagine how often I've already tried to push this Anne away, to cripple her, to hide her, because after all, she's only half of what's called Anne: but it doesn't work and I know, too, why it doesn't work.

I'm awfully scared that everyone who knows me as I always am will   *106* discover that I have another side, a finer and better side. I'm afraid they'll laugh at me, think I'm ridiculous and sentimental, not take me seriously. I'm used to not being taken seriously but it's only the "lighthearted" Anne that's used to it and can bear it; the "deeper" Anne is too frail for it. Sometimes, if I really compel the good Anne to take the stage for a quarter of an hour, she simply shrivels up as soon as she has to speak, and lets Anne number one take over, and before I realize it, she has disappeared.

Therefore, the nice Anne is never present in company, has not appeared   *107* one single time so far, but almost always predominates when we're alone. I know exactly how I'd like to be, how I am too . . . inside. But, alas, I'm only like that for myself. And perhaps that's why, no, I'm sure it's the reason why I say I've got a happy nature within and why other people think I've got a happy nature without. I am guided by the pure Anne within, but outside I'm nothing but a frolicsome little goat who's broken loose.

As I've already said, I never utter my real feelings about anything and   *108* that's how I've acquired the name of chaser-after-boys, flirt, know-all, reader of love stories. The cheerful Anne laughs about it, gives cheeky answers, shrugs her shoulders indifferently, behaves as if she doesn't care, but, oh dearie me, the quiet Anne's reactions are just the opposite. If I'm to be quite honest, then I must admit that it does hurt me, that I try terribly hard to change myself, but that I'm always fighting against a more powerful enemy.

A voice sobs within me: "There you are, that's what's become of you: *109* you're uncharitable, you look supercilious and peevish, people dislike you and all because you won't listen to the advice given you by your own better half." Oh, I would like to listen, but it doesn't work; if I'm quiet and serious, everyone thinks it's a new comedy and then I have to get out of it by turning it into a joke, not to mention my own family, who are sure to think I'm ill, make me swallow pills for headaches and nerves, feel my neck and my head to see whether I'm running a temperature, ask if I'm constipated and criticize me for being in a bad mood. I can't keep that up: if I'm watched to that extent, I start by getting snappy, then unhappy, and finally I twist my heart round again, so that the bad is on the outside and the good is on the inside and keep on trying to find a way of becoming what I would so like to be, and what I could be, if . . . there weren't any other people living in the world.

Yours, Anne

Epilogue

Anne's diary ends here. On August 4, 1944, the Grüne Polizei made a raid on the "Secret Annexe." All the occupants, together with Kraler and Koophuis, were arrested and sent to German and Dutch concentration camps.

The "Secret Annexe" was plundered by the Gestapo. Among a pile of old books, magazines, and newspapers which were left lying on the floor, Miep and Elli found Anne's diary. Apart from a very few passages, which are of little interest to the reader, the original text has been printed.

Of all the occupants of the "Secret Annexe," Anne's father alone returned. Kraler and Koophuis, who withstood the hardships of the Dutch camp, were able to go home to their families.

In March 1945, two months before the liberation of Holland, Anne died in the concentration camp at Bergen-Belsen.

Topics for Discussion and Writing

1. Miep, Henk, Elli, Mr. Koophuis, and Mr. Kraler (pseudonyms Anne used to protect her friends) were among those who risked their lives so that their friends might have a chance to live. Put yourself in the place of these people in 1942. Would you do what they did to help the Franks? Why or why not? (Remember that the possible punishment for anyone aiding a Jew at that time was death.)

2. Write a letter from the Secret Annexe to a friend on the outside. Tell him or her about your living conditions, a typical day, and how you pass your time. Who brings you food? What do you eat? How do you feel about having to go into hiding? What are your fears, your hopes? What do you think of Hitler and his attempt to take over Europe? Who are the people around you and what do you think of them? How do you stay sane amid such uncertainty? (Remember that you cannot give out any information that will give away your location should your letter get into the wrong hands. Also remember to instruct your friend to burn your letter after reading.)

3. We know that in the spring of 1944 Anne began to revise her diary in the hopes of its future publication. However, when she began writing in 1942, Anne had no intention that her diary would be read by anyone, let alone that it should be acclaimed by the world. Indeed, what would be the chances that this Jewish teenager's thoughts would ever be published and be of interest to anyone? And yet her writing turned out to be one of the finest documents that was written about World War II. Focus on your own

writing. Imagine that something you have written has found its way into a time capsule that will be opened in the future. What would you want future generations to know about you and your way of life? How would you try to change your writing if you knew that those in the future would read it and learn from it? What would you want them to learn?

4. In her diary, Anne stated, "I believe in the good of man." She made this statement knowing what the Nazis were doing to the Jews and many others. Anne continued to find reasons to hope and be grateful during the days in hiding. Write a dialogue between Anne Frank and Adolph Hitler. Where do they meet? What does he say to her? How would she respond to him?

BEIRNE LAY, JR.

"I Saw Regensburg Destroyed"

> *"I knew that I was going to die, and so were a lot of others. What I didn't know was that the real fight, the Anschluss of Luftwaffe 20-mm. cannon shells, hadn't really begun. The largest and most savage fighter resistance of any war in history was rising to stop us at any cost, and our group was the most vulnerable target."*
>
> *Beirne Lay, Jr. was born September 1, 1909, in Berkeley Springs, West Virginia. He based his novel,* Twelve O'Clock High, *and the screenplays,* Jet Pilot *and* Strategic Air Command, *on his experiences as a World War II pilot. Lay was shot down over France and wrote about his experience in* Presumed Dead *and* I've Had Enough. *He died in 1982.*

Before and as You Read

1. As you read the following account, be mindful of how Lay tells his story. How does he engage his readers? How does he use imagery and detail to bring you aboard this B-17? Does it surprise you that he was a screenwriter? Why or why not? What other forms might this story have taken?

2. This article appeared in the November 6, 1943, issue of *The Saturday Evening Post*. Whom does Lay write for? Why? If you were a reader at that time, what would your reaction be? What questions, thoughts, and feelings would be foremost in your mind?

3. Beirne Lay had two careers: one as a military officer and pilot and one as a writer. Think of other endeavors that would combine well with the talents of a writer. Consider how your career choice or plans might stimulate a successful writing career as well. For whom would you like to write? What would you like to publish?

4. Talk to a soldier who served during World War II. What experiences does this person recall? How did he or she feel about serving during that time? How was this person received when she or he came home? With a 50-year perspective, how does she or he feel about war in general? Vietnam? Desert Storm? Share your interview with your class. (If you do not have a personal acquaintance to interview, check with your library regarding local military associations that may be able to put you in touch with a group of veterans.)

IN THE briefing room, the intelligence officer of the bombardment group pulled a cloth screen away from a huge wall map. Each of the 240 sleepy-eyed combat-crew members in the crowded room leaned forward. There were low whistles. I felt a sting of anticipation as I stared at the red string on the map that stretched from our base in England to a pin point deep in Southern Germany, then south across the Alps, through the Brenner Pass to the coast of Italy, then past Corsica and Sardinia and south over the Mediterranean to a desert airdrome in North Africa. You could have heard an oxygen mask drop.

"Your primary," said the intelligence officer, "is Regensburg. Your aiming point is the center of the Messerschmitt One Hundred and Nine G aircraft-and-engine-assembly shops. This is the most vital target we've ever gone after. If you destroy it, you destroy thirty per cent of the Luftwaffe's single-engine-fighter production. You fellows know what that means to you personally."

There were a few hollow laughs.

After the briefing, I climbed aboard a jeep bound for the operations office to check up on my Fortress assignment. The stars were dimly visible through the chilly mist that covered our blacked-out bomber station, but the weather forecast for a deep penetration over the Continent was good. In the office, I looked at the crew sheet, where the line-up of the lead, low and high squadrons of the group is plotted for each mission. I was listed for a copilot's seat. While I stood there, and on the chance suggestion of one of the squadron commanders who was looking over the list, the operations officer erased my name and shifted me to the high squadron as copilot in the crew of a steady Irishman named Lieutenant Murphy, with whom I had flown before. Neither of us knew it, but that operations officer saved my life right there with a piece of rubber on the end of a pencil.

At 5:30 A.M., fifteen minutes before taxi time, a jeep drove around the five-mile perimeter track in the semi-darkness, pausing at each dispersal point long enough to notify the waiting crews that poor local visibility would postpone the take-off for an hour and a half. I was sitting with Murphy and the rest of our crew near the Piccadilly Lily. She looked sinister and complacent, squatting on her fat tires with scarcely a hole in her skin to show for the twelve raids behind her. The postponement tightened, rather than relaxed, the tension. Once more I checked over my life vest, oxygen mask and parachute, not perfunctorily, but the way you check something you're going to have to use. I made sure my escape kit was pinned securely in the knee pocket of my flying suit, where it couldn't fall out in a scramble to abandon ship. I slid a hunting knife between my shoe and my flying boot as I looked again through my extra equipment for this mission: water canteen, mess kit, blankets and English pounds for use in the Algerian desert, where we would sleep on the ground and might be on our own from a forced landing.

Murphy restlessly gave the Piccadilly Lily another once-over, inspecting ammunition belts, bomb bay, tires and oxygen pressure at each crew station. Especially the oxygen. It's human fuel, as important as gasoline, up where we operate. Gunners field-stripped their .50-calibers again and oiled the bolts. Our top-turret gunner lay in the grass with his head on his parachute, feigning sleep, sweating out his thirteenth start.

We shared a common knowledge which grimly enhanced the normal   7
excitement before a mission. Of the approximately 150 Fortresses who were
hitting Regensburg, our group was the last and lowest, at a base altitude of
17,000 feet. That's well within the range of accuracy for heavy flak. Our
course would take us over plenty of it. It was a cinch also that our group
would be the softest touch for the enemy fighters, being last man through the
gantlet. Furthermore, the Piccadilly Lily was leading the last three ships of the
high squadron—the tip of the tail end of the whole shebang. We didn't relish
it much. Who wants a Purple Heart?

The minute hand of my wrist watch dragged. I caught myself thinking   8
about the day, exactly one year ago, on August 17, 1942, when I watched a
pitifully small force of twelve B-17's take off on the first raid of the 8th Air
Force to make a shallow penetration against Rouen, France. On that day it
was our maximum effort. Today, on our first anniversary, we were putting
thirty times that number of heavies into the air—half the force on Regensburg and half the force on Schweinfurt, both situated inside the interior of
the German Reich. For a year and a half, as a staff officer, I had watched the
8th Air Force grow under Maj. Gen. Ira C. Eaker. That's a long time to watch
from behind a desk. Only ten days ago I had asked for and received orders
to combat duty. Those ten days had been full of the swift action of partici-
pating in four combat missions and checking out for the first time as a four-
engine pilot.

Now I knew that it can be easier to be shot at than telephoned at. That   9
staff officers at an Air Force headquarters are the unstrung heroes of this war.
And yet I found myself reminiscing just a little affectionately about that desk,
wondering if there wasn't a touch of suicide in store for our group. One thing
was sure: Headquarters had dreamed up the biggest air operation to date to
celebrate its birthday in the biggest league of aerial warfare.

At 7:30 we broke out of the cloud tops into the glare of the rising sun.   10
Beneath our B-17 lay English fields, still blanketed in the thick mist from
which we had just emerged. We continued to climb slowly, our broad wings
shouldering a heavy load of incendiary bombs in the belly and a burden of
fuel in the main and wing-tip Tokyo tanks that would keep the Fortress afloat
in the thin upper altitudes eleven hours.

From my copilot's seat on the right-hand side, I watched the white   11
surface of the overcast, where B-17's in clusters of six to the squadron were
puncturing the cloud deck all about us, rising clear of the mist with their glass
noses slanted upward for the long climb to base altitude. We tacked on to one
of these clutches of six. Now the sky over England was heavy with the weight
of thousands of tons of bombs, fuel and men being lifted four miles straight
up on a giant aerial hoist to the western terminus of a 20,000-foot elevated
highway that led east to Regensburg. At intervals I saw the arc of a sputtering
red, green or yellow flare being fired from the cabin roof of a group leader's
airplane to identify the lead squadron to the high and low squadrons of each
group. Assembly takes longer when you come up through an overcast.

For nearly an hour, still over Southern England, we climbed, nursing the   *12*
straining Cyclone engines in a 300-foot-per-minute ascent, forming three
squadrons gradually into compact group stagger formations—low squadron
down to the left and high squadron up to the right of the lead squadron—
groups assembling into looser combat wings of two to three groups each along
the combat-wing assembly line, homing over predetermined points with radio
compass, and finally cruising along the air-division assembly line to allow the
combat wings to fall into place in trail behind Col. Curtis E. Le May in the
lead group of the air division.

Formed at last, each flanking group in position 1000 feet above or below   *13*
its lead group, our fifteen-mile parade moved east toward Lowestoft, point of
departure from the friendly coast, unwieldly, but dangerous to fool with. From
my perch in the high squadron in the last element of the whole procession,
the air division looked like huge anvil-shaped swarms of locusts—not on dress
parade, like the bombers of the Luftwaffe that died like flies over Britain in
1940, but deployed to uncover every gun and permit maneuverability. Our
formation was basically that worked out for the Air Corps by Brig. Gen. Hugh
Knerr twenty years ago with eighty-five-mile-an-hour bombers, plus refine-
ments devised by Colonel Le May from experience in the European theater.

The English Channel and the North Sea glittered bright in the clear   *14*
visibility as we left the bulge of East Anglia behind us. Up ahead we knew
that we were already registering on the German RDF screen, and that the
sector controllers of the Luftwaffe's fighter belt in Western Europe were busy
alerting their *Staffeln* of Focke-Wulfs and Messerschmitts. I stole a last look
back at cloud-covered England, where I could see a dozen spare B-17's, who
had accompanied us to fill in for any abortives from mechanical failure in the
hard climb, gliding disappointedly home to base.

I fastened my oxygen mask a little tighter and looked at the little ball in   *15*
a glass tube on the instrument panel that indicates proper oxygen flow. It was
moving up and down, like a visual heartbeat, as I breathed, registering normal.

Already the gunners were searching. Occasionally the ship shivered as   *16*
guns were tested with short bursts. I could see puffs of blue smoke from the
group close ahead and 1000 feet above us, as each gunner satisfied himself that
he had lead poisoning at his trigger tips. The coast of Holland appeared in
sharp black outline. I drew in a deep breath of oxygen.

A few miles in front of us were German boys in single-seaters who were   *17*
probably going to react to us in the same way our boys would react, emotionally, if German bombers were heading for the Pratt & Whitney engine factory
at Hartford or the Liberator plant at Willow Run. In the making was a death
struggle between the unstoppable object and the immovable defense, every
possible defense at the disposal of the Reich, for this was a deadly penetration
to a hitherto inaccessible and critically important arsenal of the *Vaterland*.

At 10:08 we crossed the coast of Holland, south of The Hague, with   *18*
our group of Fortresses tucked in tightly and within handy supporting distance
of the group above us, at 18,000 feet. But our long, loose-linked column

looked too long, and the gaps between combat wings too wide. As I squinted into the sun, gauging the distance to the barely visible specks of the lead group, I had a recurrence of that sinking feeling before the take-off—the lonesome foreboding that might come to the last man about to run a gantlet lined with spiked clubs. The premonition was well founded.

At 10:17, near Woensdrecht, I saw the first flak blossom out in our vicinity, light and inaccurate. A few minutes later, at approximately 10:25, a gunner called, "Fighters at two o'clock low." I saw them, climbing above the horizon ahead of us to the right—a pair of them. For a moment I hoped they were P-47 Thunderbolts from the fighter escort that was supposed to be in our vicinity, but I didn't hope long. The two FW-190's turned and whizzed through the formation ahead of us in a frontal attack, nicking two B-17's in the wings and breaking away in half rolls right over our group. By craning my neck up and back, I glimpsed one of them through the roof glass in the cabin, flashing past at a 600-mile-an-hour rate of closure, his yellow nose smoking and small pieces flying off near the wing root. The guns of our group were in action. The pungent smell of burnt cordite filled the cockpit and the B-17 trembled to the recoil of nose and ball-turret guns. Smoke immediately trailed from the hit B-17's, but they held their stations. 19

Here was early fighter reaction. The members of the crew sensed trouble. There was something desperate about the way those two fighters came in fast right out of their climb, without any preliminaries. Apparently, our own fighters were busy somewhere farther up the procession. The interphone was active for a few seconds with brief admonitions: "Lead 'em more." . . . "Short bursts." . . . "Don't throw rounds away." . . . "Bombardier to left waist gunner, don't yell. Talk slow." 20

Three minutes later the gunners reported fighters climbing up from all around the clock, singly and in pairs, both FW-190's and Me-109-G's. The fighters I could see on my side looked like too many for sound health. No friendly Thunderbolts were visible. From now on we were in mortal danger. My mouth dried up and my buttocks pulled together. A co-ordinated attack began, with the head-on fighters coming in from slightly above, the nine and three o'clock attackers approaching from about level and the rear attackers from slightly below. The guns from every B-17 in our group and the group ahead were firing simultaneously, lashing the sky with ropes of orange tracers to match the chain-puff bursts squirting from the 20-mm. cannon muzzles in the wings of the jerry single-seaters. 21

I noted with alarm that a lot of our fire was falling astern of the target— particularly from our hand-held nose and waist guns. Nevertheless, both sides got hurt in this clash, with the entire second element of three B-17's from our low squadron and one B-17 from the group ahead falling out of formation on fire, with crews bailing out, and several fighters heading for the deck in flames or with their pilots lingering behind under the dirty yellow canopies that distinguished some of their parachutes from ours. Our twenty-four-year-old 22 group leader, flying only his third combat mission, pulled us up even closer to the preceding group for mutual support.

As we swung slightly outside with our squadron, in mild evasive action, I got a good look at that gap in the low squadron where three B-17's had been. Suddenly I bit my lip hard. The lead ship of that element had pulled out on fire and exploded before anyone bailed out. It was the ship to which I had been originally assigned. 23

I glanced over at Murphy. It was cold in the cockpit, but sweat was running from his forehead and over his oxygen mask from the exertion of holding his element in tight formation and the strain of the warnings that hummed over the interphone and what he could see out of the corners of his eyes. He caught my glance and turned the controls over to me for a while. It was an enormous relief to concentrate on flying instead of sitting there watching fighters aiming between your eyes. Somehow, the attacks from the rear, although I could see them through my ears via the interphone, didn't bother me. I guess it was because there was a slab of armor plate behind my back and I couldn't watch them, anyway. 24

I knew that we were in a lively fight. Every alarm bell in my brain and heart was ringing a high-pitched warning. But my nerves were steady and my brain working. The fear was unpleasant, but it was bearable. I knew that I was going to die, and so were a lot of others. What I didn't know was that the real fight, the *Anschluss* of Luftwaffe 20-mm. cannon shells, hadn't really begun. The largest and most savage fighter resistance of any war in history was rising to stop us at any cost, and our group was the most vulnerable target. 25

A few minutes later we absorbed the first wave of a hailstorm of individual fighter attacks that were to engulf us clear to the target in such a blizzard of bullets and shells that a chronological account is difficult. It was at 10:41, over Eupen, that I looked out the window after a minute's lull, and saw two whole squadrons, twelve Me-109's and eleven FW-190's climbing parallel to us as though they were on a steep escalator. The first squadron had reached our level and was pulling ahead to turn into us. The second was not far behind. Several thousand feet below us were many more fighters, their noses cocked up in a maximum climb. Over the interphone came reports of an equal number of enemy aircraft deploying on the other side of the formation. 26

For the first time I noticed an Me-110 sitting out of range on our level out to the right. He was to stay with us all the way to the target, apparently radioing our position and weak spots to fresh *Staffeln* waiting farther down the road. 27

At the sight of all these fighters, I had the distinct feeling of being trapped—that the Hun had been tipped off or at least had guessed our destination and was set for us. We were already through the German fighter belt. Obviously, they had moved a lot of squadrons back in a fluid defense in depth, and they must have been saving up some outfits for the inner defense that we didn't know about. The life expectancy of our group seemed definitely 28 limited, since it had already appeared that the fighters, instead of wasting fuel trying to overhaul the preceding groups, were glad to take a cut at us.

Swinging their yellow noses around in a wide U turn, the twelve-ship squadron of Me-109's came in from twelve to two o'clock in pairs. The main event was on. I fought an impulse to close my eyes, and overcame it. 29

A shining silver rectangle of metal sailed past over our right wing. I recognized it as a main-exit door. Seconds later, a black lump came hurtling through the formation, barely missing several propellers. It was a man, clasping his knees to his head, revolving like a diver in a triple somersault, shooting by us so close that I saw a piece of paper blow out of his leather jacket. He was evidently making a delayed jump, for I didn't see his parachute open. 30

A B-17 turned gradually out of the formation to the right, maintaining altitude. In a split second it completely vanished in a brilliant explosion, from which the only remains were four balls of fire, the fuel tanks, which were quickly consumed as they fell earthward. 31

I saw blue, red, yellow and aluminum-colored fighters. Their tactics were running fairly true to form, with frontal attacks hitting the low squadron and rear attackers going for the lead and high squadrons. Some of the jerries shot at us with rockets, and an attempt at air-to-air bombing was made with little black time-fuse sticks, dropped from above, which exploded in small gray puffs off to one side of the formation. Several of the FW's did some nice deflection shooting on side attacks from 500 yards at the high group, then raked the low group on the breakaway at closer range with their noses cocked in a side slip, to keep the formation in their sights longer in the turn. External fuel tanks were visible under the bellies or wings of at least two squadrons, shedding uncomfortable light on the mystery of their ability to tail us so far from their bases. 32

The manner of the assaults indicated that the pilots knew where we were going and were inspired with a fanatical determination to stop us before we got there. Many pressed attacks home to 250 yards or less, or bolted right through the formation wide out, firing long twenty-second bursts, often presenting point-blank targets on the breakaway. Some committed the fatal error of pulling up instead of going down and out. More experienced pilots came in on frontal attacks with a noticeably slower rate of closure, apparently throttled back, obtaining greater accuracy. But no tactics could halt the close-knit juggernauts of our Fortresses, nor save the single-seaters from paying a terrible price. 33

Our airplane was endangered by various debris. Emergency hatches, exit doors, prematurely opened parachutes, bodies and assorted fragments of B-17's and Hun fighters breezed past us in the slip stream. 34

I watched two fighters explode not far beneath, disappear in sheets of orange flame; B-17's dropping out in every stage of distress, from engines on fire to controls shot away; friendly and enemy parachutes floating down, and, on the green carpet far below us, funeral pyres of smoke from fallen fighters, marking our trail. 35

On we flew through the cluttered wake of a desperate air battle, where   36
disintegrating aircraft were commonplace and the white dots of sixty parachutes in the air at one time were hardly worth a second look. The spectacle
registering on my eyes became so fantastic that my brain turned numb to the
actuality of the death and destruction all around us. Had it not been for the
squeezing in my stomach, which was trying to purge, I might easily have been
watching an animated cartoon in a movie theater.

The minutes dragged on into an hour. And still the fighters came. Our   37
gunners called coolly and briefly to one another, dividing up their targets,
fighting for their lives with every round of ammunition—and our lives, and
the formation. The tail gunner called that he was out of ammunition. We sent
another belt back to him. Here was a new hazard. We might run out of .50-
caliber slugs before we reached the target.

I looked to both sides of us. Our two wing men were gone. So was the   38
element in front of us—all three ships. We moved up into position behind the
lead element of the high squadron. I looked out again on my side and saw a
cripple, with one prop feathered, struggle up behind our right wing with his
bad engine funneling smoke into the slip stream. He dropped back. Now our
tail gunner had a clear view. There were no more B-17's behind us. We were
last man.

I took the controls for a while. The first thing I saw when Murphy   39
resumed flying was a B-17 turning slowly out to the right, its cockpit a mass
of flames. The copilot crawled out of his window, held on with one hand,
reached back for his parachute, buckled it on, let go and was whisked back
into the horizontal stabilizer of the tail. I believe the impact killed him. His
parachute didn't open.

I looked forward and almost ducked as I watched the tail gunner of a   40
B-17 ahead of us take a bead right on our windshield and cut loose with a
stream of tracers that missed us by a few feet as he fired on a fighter attacking
us from six o'clock low. I almost ducked again when our own top-turret
gunner's twin muzzles pounded away a foot above my head in the full forward
position, giving a realistic imitation of cannon shells exploding in the cockpit, while I gave an even better imitation of a man jumping six inches out of
his seat.

Still no letup. The fighters queued up like a bread line and let us have   41
it. Each second of time had a cannon shell in it. The strain of being a clay
duck in the wrong end of that aerial shooting gallery became almost intolerable. Our Piccadilly Lily shook steadily with the fire of its .50's, and the air
inside was wispy with smoke. I checked the engine instruments for the thou-
sandth time. Normal. No injured crew members yet. Maybe we'd get to that
target, even with our reduced fire power. Seven Fortresses from our group had
already gone down and many of the rest of us were badly shot up and short-
handed because of wounded crew members.

Almost disinterestedly I observed a B-17 pull out from the group pre-   42
ceding us and drop back to a position about 20 feet from our right wing tip.

His right Tokyo tanks were on fire, and had been for a half hour. Now the smoke was thicker. Flames were licking through the blackened skin of the wing. While the pilot held her steady, I saw four crew members drop out the bomb bay and execute delayed jumps. Another bailed from the nose, opened his parachute prematurely and nearly fouled the tail. Another went out the left-waist-gun opening, delaying his opening for a safe interval. The tail gunner dropped out of his hatch, apparently pulling the ripcord before he was clear of the ship. His parachute opened instantaneously, barely missing the tail, and jerked him so hard that both his shoes came off. He hung limp in the harness, whereas the others had shown immediate signs of life, shifting around in their harness. The Fortress then dropped back in a medium spiral and I did not see the pilots leave. I saw the ship, though, just before it trailed from view, belly to the sky, its wing a solid sheet of yellow flame.

Now that we had been under constant attack for more than an hour, it 43 appeared certain that our group was faced with extinction. The sky was still mottled with rising fighters. Target time was thirty-five minutes away. I doubt if a man in the group visualized the possibility of our getting much farther without 100 per cent loss. Gunners were becoming exhausted and nerve-tortured from the nagging strain—the strain that sends gunners and pilots to the rest home. We had been aiming point for what looked like most of the Luftwaffe. It looked as though we might find the rest of it primed for us at the target.

At this hopeless point, a young squadron commander down in the low 44 squadron was living through his finest hour. His squadron had lost its second element of three ships early in the fight, south of Antwerp, yet he had consistently maintained his vulnerable and exposed position in the formation rigidly in order to keep the guns of his three remaining ships well uncovered to protect the belly of the formation. Now, nearing the target, battle damage was catching up with him fast. A 20-mm. cannon shell penetrated the right side of his airplane and exploded beneath him, damaging the electrical system and cutting the top-turret gunner in the leg. A second 20-mm. entered the radio compartment, killing the radio operator, who bled to death with his legs severed above the knees. A third 20-mm. shell entered the left side of the nose, tearing out a section about two feet square, tore away the right-hand-nose-gun installations and injured the bombardier in the head and shoulder. A fourth 20-mm. shell penetrated the right wing into the fuselage and shattered the hydraulic system, releasing fluid all over the cockpit. A fifth 20-mm. shell punctured the cabin roof and severed the rudder cables to one side of the rudder. A sixth 20-mm. shell exploded in the No. 3 engine, destroying all controls to the engine. The engine caught fire and lost its power, but eventually I saw the fire go out.

Confronted with structural damage, partial loss of control, fire in the air 45 and serious injuries to personnel, and faced with fresh waves of fighters still rising to the attack, this commander was justified in abandoning ship. His crew, some of them comparatively inexperienced youngsters, were preparing to bail out. The copilot pleaded repeatedly with him to bail out. His reply at this critical juncture was blunt. His words were heard over the interphone and had a magical effect on the crew. They stuck to their guns. The B-17 kept on.

Near the initial point, at 11:50, one hour and a half after the first of at least 200 individual fighter attacks, the pressure eased off, although hostiles were still in the vicinity. A curious sensation came over me. I was still alive. It was possible to think of the target. Of North Africa. Of returning to England. Almost idly, I watched a crippled B-17 pull over to the curb and drop its wheels and open its bomb bay, jettisoning its bombs. Three Me-109's circled it closely, but held their fire while the crew bailed out. I remembered now that a little while back I had seen other Hun fighters hold their fire, even when being shot at by a B-17 from which the crew were bailing. But I doubt if sportsmanship had anything to do with it. They hoped to get a B-17 down fairly intact.

And then our weary, battered column, short twenty-four bombers, but still holding the close formation that had brought the remainder through by sheer air discipline and gunnery, turned in to the target. I knew that our bombardiers were grim as death while they synchronized their sights on the great Me-109 shops lying below us in a curve of the winding blue Danube, close to the outskirts of Regensburg. Our B-17 gave a slight lift and a red light went out on the instrument panel. Our bombs were away. We turned from the target toward the snow-capped Alps. I looked back and saw a beautiful sight—a rectangular pillar of smoke rising from the Me-109 plant. Only one burst was over and into the town. Even from this great height I could see that we had smeared the objective. The price? Cheap. 200 airmen.

A few more fighters pecked at us on the way to the Alps and a couple of smoking B-17's glided down toward the safety of Switzerland, about forty miles distant. A town in the Brenner Pass tossed up a lone burst of futile flak. Flak? There had been lots of flak in the past two hours, but only now did I recall having seen it, a sort of side issue to the fighters. Colonel Le May, who had taken excellent care of us all the way, circled the air division over a large lake to give the cripples, some flying on three engines and many trailing smoke, a chance to rejoin the family. We approached the Mediterranean in a gradual descent, conserving fuel. Out over the water we flew at low altitude, unmolested by fighters from Sardinia or Corsica, waiting through the long hot afternoon hours for the first sight of the North African coast line. The prospect of ditching, out of gasoline, and the sight of other B-17's falling into the drink seemed trivial matters after the vicious nightmare of the long trial across Southern Germany. We had walked through a high valley of the shadow of death, not expecting to see another sunset, and now I could fear no evil.

With red lights showing on all our fuel tanks, we landed at our designated base in the desert, after eleven hours in the air. I slept on the ground near the wing and, waking occasionally, stared up at the stars. My radio headset was back in the ship. And yet I could hear the deep chords of great music.

Topics for Discussion and Writing

1. Most crews of the 8th Air Force were between the ages of 18 and 24. The night before leaving for Regensburg, August 16, 1943, you are writing to your parents. What can you tell them about the dangers you live with every time you "go to work"? Tell them how you deal with the day-to-day tension. Mention how you cope with the fact that after every mission some of your friends do not come back. How do you get to sleep at night? How do you feel about the job you are doing? How do you feel about those who started this war?

2. Continue to imagine yourself as a crew member aboard Lay's B-17. What are your feelings as you take off? During the hours of constant fighting? As your comrades in the planes around you are shot down? As you drop your bombs on target? As you arrive safely at your destination in the North African desert?

3. What does Lay mean when he says the following:

   "Even from this great height I could see that we had smeared the objective. The price? Cheap. 200 airmen."

   "Colonel Le May, who had taken excellent care of us all the way, circled the air division over a large lake. . . ."

   "I slept on the ground near the wing and, waking occasionally, stared up at the stars. My radio headset was back in the ship. And yet I could hear the deep chords of great music."

4. Lay tells us that he was a staff officer at his base who volunteered for combat duty ten days before the Regensburg mission. On the flight he says that he wondered "if there wasn't a touch of suicide in store for our group." Why do you suppose Lay asked for combat duty? In your opinion, what did he hope to gain by choosing to fly when he didn't have to? What do you think his feelings were after the mission when he realized he would have been killed had it not been for the "piece of rubber on the end of a pencil"?

HENRY BERRY

from *Hey, Mac, Where Ya Been?*

> *"And, you know, as I was looking for a good hole to jump into, I quickly decided to do something I'd been thinking of for the last day or so. I'd stick my hand under my body in such a way that when I jumped, I'd be sure to break it. We'd heard they were evacuating our wounded by air. If I did this, I might even get home and see my wife and new son. . . . I'm not the slightest bit ashamed of thinking about it. Ask any guy who's been in combat. You're bound to think that way at one time or another. But in the long run, most guys don't do it. After all, you have to live with yourself."*
>
> Henry Berry, *a Marine who served in the Pacific in World War II, has published two other works of oral war history:* Make the Kaiser Dance *and* Semper Fi, Mac. *He is also the author of* A Baseball Century *and* The Boston Red Sox, *and is currently working on* This Is Not A Drill, *an oral history of Pearl Harbor.*

Before and as You Read

1. Read books and articles on the origins of the Korean War. Why did the United States get involved? How? When? What was our leaders' goal? Was it achieved? How did the war end? When?

2. Look up a map of Korea at the time of the Korean conflict. Compare this map with a map of the region today. What changes do you see? What accounts for these changes?

3. The Korean conflict has been called the "forgotten war" by some in the United States. In Berry's introduction, he writes about the reaction of U.S. veterans to their reception when they returned from the war: "First they'd tell me how they didn't mind not having a parade when they came home, and how they weren't greatly upset at their country's forgetting about them so fast. . . . 'Look,' one said, 'we don't mind those Vietnam vets squawking. God knows they've been abused, but what about us? At least they built a wall for them down in Washington.'

   'Yeah,' said the other man, 'they didn't even build an outhouse for us!'"

   Comment on these statements.

4. What is an oral history? As you read this selection, make note of how it differs in tone from others in this chapter. What accounts for those differences? Compare this piece with Beirne Lay's "I Saw Regensburg Destroyed."

SERGEANT JOHN SADDIC: 11TH MARINES

WHEN I went down to Parris Island in '42, I was only seventeen   1
years old. Some of the men in my platoon were twenty-five,
twenty-six years of age, with a couple of them even older. I looked at these
guys as old men, everyone my age did. We even called a couple of them Pop.
I'd look at them and say to myself, Okay, you guys have had your shot. Most
of you are fathers; you've already produced someone to carry on your name.
But what about me? I've had nothing!

Oh, I'd bumped up against a few girls, but as far as having a lasting   2
relationship, zero. I felt that if I'd gotten killed then, I would have been
cheated. Let those old guys get killed, not me.

Then, after I was called back for Korea, *I* was the twenty-five, twenty-   3
six-year-old guy. I had a wife—still have her—and a baby boy. The shoe was
on the other foot, Right?

Now, the seventeen-year-old kid, he has no responsibilities. Right? If I   4
get killed, who will take care of my wife and kid? Let those seventeen-year-
old kids get killed, not me.

You figure that out.   5

Okay. New Year's Eve, 1949. I had gone to a party with my wife   6
and my oldest boyhood friend and his wife. We had knocked down several
drinks when the conversation turned toward the Corps. My friend had a
brainstorm.

"John," he said, "you know I'm in the Marine Corps Reserves. We meet   7
down at the Philadelphia Navy Yard. There are several of your buddies from
the 6th Marine Division down there, and they're always asking for you. Why
don't you join up? We have one hell of a time. We get paid thirty dollars a
month for doing almost nothing. It'll be a snap for you."

"Jeez," I said, "that sounds great! It'll give me a night out with the boys."   8

So that's how I got back in the Corps. Everybody thought it was great,   9
except my wife. She always was smart as a whip.

"Are you off your rocker? Haven't you had enough of all that killing?   10
There's bound to be another war, and you'll be the first one called up."

"Oh no, not with all my experience," I told her, "me, a Purple Heart   11
machine gunner. I'll spend the war training kids."

Well, I trained kids, all right. On the ship going to Korea we had some   12
machine gunners who had never fired a machine gun. We tied a wooden duck
to a line we had hanging off the fantail. I showed these kids the score off the
ass end of our ship. And it was the same with the mortar men. We must have
scared the hell out of the fish.

Well, June 21, 1950, was the happiest day of my life. My wife presented   13
me with a son. I was still on cloud nine when those bastards crossed over into
South Korea. I didn't think much about it, but my wife did. She was still in
the hospital, but she gave me the word.

"John, you better get ready because you're going to go. I just know you   *14*
are going to go."

Well, just like that, our unit is called up. My wife was right; so what else   *15*
is new?

Now I'm beginning to panic. Hell, I had no dough then. I was going to   *16*
Villanova on the GI Bill. Who was going to support my wife and son? She
couldn't very well work, with the baby and all.

You see, at this time you had to be a sergeant or above to get a family   *17*
allowance. I was just a corporal. So I went over to welfare to state my case.

"Do you own a car?" they asked me.   *18*

"No."   *19*

"How about furniture?"   *20*

"Yes."   *21*

"Sell it."   *22*

Sell it? I thought they'd gone bananas. Here I am with a brand-new baby   *23*
and they want me to sell my furniture. What the hell's going on?

My next step was to go to the Red Cross. And you know what they   *24*
told me? "Go to welfare; we can't help you."

Oh, for Christ's sake, talk about the runaround, I was getting it in spades.   *25*

Then I got a brainstorm. I decided to call the *Philadelphia Inquirer* and   *26*
ask for the editorial department. They'd usually eat up a human-interest story
like this.

"Look," I said to this editor, "I'm a World War II Purple Heart veteran   *27*
of the Pacific. My unit has been called up over this police action in Korea. I'll
go, all right, but I'll be a sonofabitch if I'm going while my wife and child are
begging on the street. I've called both welfare and the Red Cross and they
gave me the brush-off."

Oh, did this guy get excited!   *28*

"What's the matter with those idiots?" he said. "I'll call you back within   *29*
the hour." He did.

"Call the Red Cross; I think you'll get a better reception now. Ask for   *30*
Mrs. What's-her-face."

So I called the Red Cross and it turns out Mrs. What's-her-face is the   *31*
same broad I talked to earlier. Now she's singing a different tune.

"Oh, Mr. Saddic, of course we'll help you out. We didn't realize the full   *32*
story, blah, blah, blah . . ." She's falling all over me.

About three months later, Congress got into the act. Now you didn't   *33*
have to be a sergeant or above to get a family allowance. So the Corps took
over from the Red Cross.

But a year or so later I've been to Korea and have been sent home with   *34*
frozen feet, I got a call from the Red Cross. They want to know when I'm
going to pay back the loan they had given my family a year before. I think it
was fifteen dollars a week for three months. Now they've really got me pissed
off, but I kept my cool.

"Gee," I said, in my altar-boy voice, "the man at the *Inquirer* didn't say *35*
anything to me about a loan. I'll have to call him and check this out." *In-*
quirer—I'd said the magic word. You know, like Groucho Marx used to say on
his television show, the magic word.

"Oh," this guy said, "if you didn't know it was a loan, forget it. Glad to *36*
have you back in Philadelphia."

Ah, the power of the press. *37*

Back to June of 1950. And, by the way, if you remember 1950, here's *38*
something else for you to think about. For years they had been kicking our
Philadelphia Phillies around. But by 1950 they'd come up with a team they
called the Whiz Kids. Our group didn't want to go to war. We wanted to go
to Shibe Park.

Anyway, we went down to Camp Lejeune in Jacksonville, North Caro- *39*
lina. Here they told us we would have extensive training before leaving for the
West Coast. But it soon became very apparent this was bad dope. The scuttlebutt had us going to Camp Pendleton out in Oceanside, California, as soon as
possible. I called my wife, Linda, and told her she better get down to Lejeune
in a hurry if she wanted to see me. So she got ahold of a mutual friend and
down they came. It was a pretty crummy drive from Philly, but they arrived
on a Friday. We later figured out that she arrived at the camp gate at about
the same time our troop train was leaving for the West Coast. That's how fast
they were moving us. I didn't see Linda again until I got back from Korea.

After we got to Oceanside, we were told once again that we would have *40*
a lot of time to train and organize our outfit. All I knew was, I was a machine
gunner in the 11th Marines, the artillery regiment of the 1st Division. I was a
squad leader in a group that was set up to guard the guns from a charging enemy.

Well, once again we'd be given a lot of bullshit. Now they've changed *41*
our plans again. We were to leave for Japan as soon as possible. They'd set up
a camp over there with the terrain quite similar to Korea. It was in Japan we
were to become a real fighting division.

Now, can you believe this? Japan ended up being more of the same. I *42*
should have known this when we were still at sea. If we were really slated for
a long stay in Japan, why not wait for our machine-gun practice there?

Okay. We land in Japan. The first thing they do is give out port and *43*
starboard liberty. I was starboard. As we were going down the gangplank, this
gyrene taps me on the shoulder.

"If we're going to train a lot in Japan, why the hell are they loading all *44*
those ships?"

Christ, he was right! We no sooner got back on board than we headed *45*
for the assault on Inchon. Many of those who made that landing may have
still have had hangovers. The short time we were ashore, a lot of the guys
tried to drink Japan dry.

After all, it was only ten weeks earlier that a good many of the Marines *46*
who went into Inchon were civilians, serving in reserve units not only in
Philadelphia but throughout the country. During those ten weeks they'd been

hustled all over the lot. There was no real camaraderie like we had in World War II. I guess the main reason they did so well was their pride in the Corps.

But bitch, my God, did we bitch! Many of the men in my unit had learned to gripe in World War II, and I mean they already had degrees in bitching before Korea. It got so bad our captain figured he'd better call a meeting. His talk to us was a classic.

"Look, you guys," he said, "I know you're pissed off about being here. So am I." (He was also a World War II vet, a tall, lanky guy from Texas.) "But we're here and that's it.

"Now," he continued, "let me tell you something. Let's say you're back in the States and you want to get laid." (As you can imagine, this broke the guys up.) "You go to a cathouse and you pick out some broad. You give her the three or five dollars, whatever the going rate calls for, and go upstairs.

"Okay. Did you ever think that maybe the whore doesn't want to get laid at that point? Maybe she's tired or sore, something like that. But she's taken your money, so she spreads her legs and makes believe she loves it. She makes you think you're the greatest lover since Errol Flynn.

"So that's exactly the position we're in. We're getting fucked, just like the hooker in the cathouse. And, like her, we can't do anything about it. So, relax, do the best job you can, and, for Christ's sake, remember you're Marines!"

Jeez, you should have heard the laughter and the cheering. The men loved the way he put things. From then on, especially up in the Chosin, when we were freezing our nuts off, every time we'd see the captain, we'd push our heads back, put both hands behind our heads, and moan, "Oh, Captain, oh, oh, I love it, I love it!" He'd just smile and utter some brilliant remark like "Attaboy."

So, after Inchon and all that vicious fighting around Seoul, they stuck us aboard LSTs. The scuttlebutt is really flying. The rumor we all loved was that the war was almost over and we were headed home, which brings me around to one of my favorite bitches about Korea.

In World War II we normally had a pretty good idea about what was going on. The company commander, the platoon leaders, even the sergeants, someone would keep the troops apprised of what the score was. Not in Korea. Here's what I mean.

When we were up in the Reservoir in late November, we'd been seeing Chinese for several days, but I had no idea of their involvement in the war. It wasn't until I saw all these planes dropping supplies to us that I knew something was screwed up. Why had gear stopped coming to us via the road from the south? I asked one of our sergeants what was going on.

"Hell," he said, "don't you know? The road's cut off. We've got these fuckin' chinks on all sides, thousands of them."

That's the way it was in Korea. You didn't know what was going on until it happened.

Well, we left Inchon sometime in October. Much to our surprise, the

LSTs we were on were crewed by Japanese, that's right, the guys who were shooting at us just five or six years before. Remember, the original Marines in Korea had a tremendous amount of World War II men in their ranks. One of these vets, he must have been about six foot three, goes over to one of these Japs.

"Look, you little sonofabitch," he roars at the little Nip, "a few years ago you were probably shooting at me. I'm about to toss your ass overboard. Let the sharks have their dinner." 59

Of course, the Jap doesn't speak English. All he knows is that the rest of us are laughing our heads off. So he starts laughing too, and bobbing his head up and down. To top it off, the little guy has thick glasses and buck teeth. He looks just like the Japs we used to see in the cartoons during World War II. Then he starts saying something like, "Ah so, ah so." 60

All this was too much for the big Marine. He also burst out laughing. We never did find out if he was going to throw the Jap over the side or not, but it's a good thing he didn't. After all, the Japanese were our host. 61

Well, we headed out from Inchon not really knowing where we were going. No more rumors about going home. We knew we were heading for another combat landing. 62

Then we got a pleasant surprise. The landing was a lark. Hell, we just walked in. It was at a place called Wonsan, over on the east coast of North Korea—no combat whatsoever. But when we started out for the Chosin, things were going to change—my God, how they changed! 63

Can you imagine a situation like this? The thermometer is beginning to drop, yet we continue to go north. By the time the Chinese hit us, it was below zero. I've been told that before we got back to Hungnam, it was thirty below zero. All I know is, it was colder than a witch's heart. 64

When we'd march, our body fluids would be working and our feet would be sweating. We couldn't change our socks—we'd be wearing two or three pairs, and they'd freeze to our feet. The chinks would be wearing rubber sneakers. They're better in the cold. 65

And, by the way, the worst thing was trying to take a leak. You're trying to find your pecker through six inches of clothing. You know what happens to it in frigid weather? It shrinks so it feels like it's gone into your belly. That's tough. And when you take a crap—well, you don't read any newspapers. Boom, boom, it's over. You try to clean yourself off and get your pants back on. I can't remember much diarrhea. Maybe it's because we were strictly on rations. But, I'll tell you, those bodily functions were murder as it was. 66

Okay, let's go back to Philadelphia. A month or two before we were called up, my wife and I went to a fortune-teller, one of those gypsy women you had a lot of in those days. She told me that my lucky day was going to be November 29. We both laughed. I told my wife maybe I'd make a big killing at the track that day. 67

Back to Korea. It's November 29, my lucky day. The Chinese start to zero in on us with mortars. Everyone was trying to find a hole to dive in. I 68 spotted this cart, so I jumped under it. This guy in our outfit, can't remember his name, but he was from Texas, sees me and yells over, "Hey, asshole, don't you know you're under a cart full of land mines?"

Oh, for Christ's sake, *this* is my lucky day? I hightailed it out of there 69 and jumped into the first hole I could find.

And, you know, as I was looking for a good hole to jump into, I quickly 70 decided to do something I'd been thinking of for the last day or so. I'd stick my hand under my body in such a way that when I jumped, I'd be sure to break it. We'd heard they were evacuating our wounded by air. If I did this, I might even get home and see my wife and new son.

Ya know, at the last second I couldn't do it. Don't ask me why. One 71 shell that had wounded me in World War II had killed five of my buddies. I'd done my share. There were millions of guys back in the States who hadn't done a fuckin' thing. Let them come to Korea!

And I'll tell you something else. I'm not the slightest bit ashamed of 72 thinking about it. Ask any guy who's been in combat. You're bound to think that way at one time or another. But in the long run, most guys don't do it. After all, you have to live with yourself.

Well, speaking of those planes that were coming in to get our wounded 73 out, they were one of the reasons we were able to fight our way down to Hungnam. All day long we'd have complete control of the air. Our Marine Corsairs were kicking the hell out of those Chinese. We loved watching it.

You see, in a situation like we were in, with the miserable weather and 74 all those gooks, we were always looking for anything that would take our minds off our problems. Give me a pencil and I'll show you what we did.

If a Corsair would come in like this and get rid of its bombs, napalm, 75 or start strafing,

$$\diagdown\underline{X}\diagup$$

we figured he was a married man.

If he came in like this,

$$\diagdown\underline{}\diagdown\,X\diagup\underline{}\diagup$$

hell, this guy was a bachelor!

Anyway, we'd cheer like hell every time they came over. These guys 76 were keeping the gooks off our ass. We were all for them.

But the cheers were few and far between. That Chosin campaign was 77 one mess after another. There was one I'll never forget. It was horrible.

It happened one morning when we'd been trying to keep the gooks off 78 our back. We started following this trail of blood. You could see where the blood increased, and you could tell by the footprints that the guy was staggering and that he was a Marine. We were afraid of what we'd find, and we found it. There was this young Marine propped up against a tree. You know how guys will push back their helmets, like the guys in the cigarette ads? That's what this kid looked like, just like he was resting, only of course he was dead. I thought of myself in World War II. This kid had just begun to live. I thought of the telegram that would go out to his parents. What a waste!

There was one bright spot on the road down that did give me a tremendous ego trip. We ran into some British Marines who were brewing some coffee. Jeez, did it smell good! One of the Brits called us over.

"Hey, Yanks," he said, "want some good coffee?"

We jumped at the chance. That joe wasn't going to stay hot long, but while it did, it was great. Well, there I was, sitting on the tripod of a 105, when I heard this whirring noise. There's a guy with a camera and he's centered right in on me. There I am, with a canteen filled with coffee, and this guy has shown up out of nowhere and he's taking a motion picture of me. The only thing I could do was give him a big shit-eating grin.

Now get this, that picture was shown in the news all over the country. My wife later told me she got several phone calls from guys who had known me in World War II, wanting to know if it was me.

Then, in 1967, a firm called Wolpert made a documentary film on the Korean War. The narrator was a man named Richard Basehart, you know, the guy who played a submarine captain. Well, I'm sitting there, watching this Korean War film, half asleep, when my wife yells, "John, there you are, drinking your coffee!"

Jeez, this gives me a jolt. She's right; there am I on the TV screen with that shit-eating grin. Hell, you'd think I was on a movie lot.

Then, to top it off, when they list all the people at the end of the show, the producer and all that crap, they have a still shot of me drinking that coffee. You'd think I was John Wayne or someone like that. It was great!

Of course, this all happened years *after* the Chosin. I wasn't thinking about anything but that coffee—as a matter of fact, the Brits did give me a refill—and how good it was, when the picture was taken.

Okay, we did finally get to Hungnam and the sea, but we were beat down to our socks. My dogs were killing me. I was scared to death that I'd develope gangrene and they'd have to chop them off. The whole outfit was like that.

Of course, they tried to tell us what a glorious thing we'd done, advancing to the rear through all those Chinese and all that baloney. Bullshit! We knew we'd had the hell kicked out of us, no matter how many chinks we'd killed and no matter how badly we'd been outnumbered.

By now it's sometime around the middle of December. Our morale is pretty low. This chaplain comes over to us and starts to tell us that the Chinese are evil and that we are the best fighting men in the world, that we are fighting for the good, blah, blah, blah.

Oh, he gets no answer from any of us. I mean, I'm worrying about losing my feet and this guy is giving us a pep talk like a high school coach gives between halves. The next thing we expected was to be told to go out and win one for the Gipper.

So, what does this clown do next but say something about it getting close to Christmas and we should all start singing Christmas carols. 91

Can you believe this? The guy is certifiable. He thinks it's a Hollywood war. We'd just gone through all this crap and he wants us to sing Christmas carols. He starts off with "Oh, Come All Ye Faithful," but he's the only one singing. Christ, is he frustrated! 92

Then he starts to chew our asses out, but we just stare at him. Finally he looks disgusted and leaves. So much for that rah-rah crap. 93

Shortly after that, a doctor comes over and looks at my feet. One look, that's all, and he orders me aboard a hospital ship out in the harbor. I'm hobbling aboard when I spot this guy I knew during World War II. We exchange glances. We called each other the same thing, no "hello" or "how are you," just "dumb sonofabitch." Then we smiled. 94

Topics for Discussion and Writing

1. What does Saddic mean when he says: "Ah, the power of the press"? Why did this decorated soldier of World War II find no help for his family situation until those who were in a position to help were threatened? What do you believe the United States owes its men and women who give distinguished military service?

2. From a writer's perspective, what is the purpose of the profanity, the crude language, and the graphic descriptions in this piece? What kind of a man would you expect Saddic to be if you met him?

3. You are a journalist on special assignment from the *New York Times.* You are at a M.A.S.H. interviewing wounded Chinese soldiers (with the help of an interpreter). Your job is to bring a human face to the enemy. What do the Chinese soldiers think of this war? How do they see themselves as soldiers? What are they fighting for? How do they feel about the treatment they have received from American doctors and nurses? What do they think of the United States?

4. The foundation of many Americans' knowledge of the Korean War was formulated by the television show, "MASH." Why do you think that this show was so popular? Why do you think that we have not seen a television comedy set in Vietnam? Are we likely to see one in the near or distant future?

PHUNG THI LE LY HAYSLIP AND JAY WURTS

from *When Heaven and Earth Changed Places*

> *"Because we had to appease the allied forces by day and were terrorized by Viet Cong at night, we slept as little as you did. We obeyed both sides and wound up pleasing neither. We were people in the middle. We were what the war was all about."*

(Phung Thi) Le Ly Hayslip was 12 when American aircraft first bombed her village on the central coast of Vietnam in the mid-60s, but for generations earlier her rural people had been caught in the battleground between contending forces: Japanese, Chinese, French, Khmer, and factions within Vietnam itself. When Heaven and Earth Changed Places *(1989) is the autobiography (written with Jay Wurts) of this child of war, who eventually fled her country for the United States, then returned to Vietnam in 1986 to search for those she had left behind. In 1987, with the help of Vietnamese and American organizations, Le Ly Hayslip began the California-based East Meets West Foundation, "an agency to help my brothers and sisters in Vietnam while helping my brothers and sisters in the United States come back from their wartime experience."*

Coauthor Jay Wurts, a writer and editor, served as an Air Guard pilot in the Vietnam War.

The following excerpt from When Heaven and Earth Changed Places *includes the Prologue and a portion of Chapter Two, "Fathers and Daughters."*

Before and as You Read

1. Interview two or more relatives or friends who would have been of at least high school age during the Vietnam War and who lived in the United States at that time. Ask them to recall, among other things, (1) what they were told were our troops' reasons for being there, (2) how they learned about the war day by day, and (3) what they saw of and imagined about the Vietnamese people. Did they ever hear or read the thoughts of Vietnamese people during the war?

2. Study newspaper files from 1965–68, the years of the largest buildup of U.S. forces in Southeast Asia. (Large public libraries and college libraries have micro-fiche or computer database files of such papers as the *New York Times, Chicago Tribune,* and *Christian Science Monitor.*) How do newspaper reports refer to Vietnamese people? How do maps depict the disputed territory? Do these reports concern the perspectives of Vietnamese people? Which people are quoted or paraphrased?

3. Imagine that you are a person living in the midst of a war-torn disputed area. Write in your journal about the life that you lead on a typical day. Share your entry with others doing this exercise.

4. As you read the following selection, observe how Le Ly Hayslip makes explicit the readers she is trying to reach. Note techniques she uses to try to win the confidence of these readers. How would you as a writer contend with such a challenge?

PROLOGUE: DEDICATION TO PEACE

FOR MY first twelve years of life, I was a peasant girl in Ky La, now called Xa Hoa Qui, a small village near Danang in Central Vietnam. My father taught me to love god, my family, our traditions, and the people we could not see: our ancestors. He taught me that to sacrifice one's self for freedom—like our ancient kings who fought bravely against invaders; or in the manner of our women warriors, including Miss Trung Nhi Trung Trac who drowned herself rather than give in to foreign conquerors—was a very high honor. From my love of my ancestors and my native soil, he said, I must never retreat.

From my mother I learned humility and the strength of virtue. I learned it was no disgrace to work like an animal on our farm, provided I did not complain. "Would you be less than our ox," she asked, "who works to feed us without grumbling?" She also taught me, when I began to notice village boys, that there is no love beyond faithful love, and that in my love for my future husband, my ancestors, and my native soil, I must always remain steadfast.

For my next three years of life, I loved, labored, and fought steadfastly for the Viet Cong against American and South Vietnamese soldiers.

Everything I knew about the war I learned as a teenaged girl from the North Vietnamese cadre leaders in the swamps outside Ky La. During these midnight meetings, we peasants assumed everything we heard was true because what the Viet Cong said matched, in one way or another, the beliefs we already had.

The first lesson we learned about the new "American" war was why the Viet Cong was formed and why we should support it. Because this lesson came on the heels of our war with the French (which began in 1946 and lasted, on and off, for eight years), what the cadre leaders told us seemed to be self-evident.

First, we were taught that Vietnam was *con rong chau tien*—a sovereign nation which had been held in thrall by Western imperialists for over a century. That all nations had a right to determine their own destiny also seemed beyond dispute, since we farmers subsisted by our own hands and felt we owed nothing to anyone but god and our ancestors for the right to live as we saw fit. Even the Chinese, who had made their own disastrous attempt to rule

Vietnam in centuries past, had learned a painful lesson about our country's zeal for independence. "Vietnam," went the saying that summarized their experience, "is nobody's lapdog."

Second, the cadres told us that the division of Vietnam into North and South in 1954 was nothing more than a ploy by the defeated French and their Western allies, mainly the United States, to preserve what influence they could in our country. 7

"*Chia doi dat nuoc?*" the Viet Cong asked, "Why should outsiders divide the land and tell some people to go north and others south? If Vietnam were truly for the Vietnamese, wouldn't we choose for ourselves what kind of government our people wanted? A nation cannot have *two* governments," they said, "anymore than a family can have two fathers." 8

Because those who favored America quickly occupied the seats of power formerly held by the French, and because the North remained pretty much on its own, the choice of which side best represented independence was, for us, a foregone conclusion. In fact, the Viet Cong usually ended our indoctrination sessions with a song that played on our worst fears: 9

> Americans come to kill our people,
> Follow America, and kill your relatives!
> The smart bird flies before it's caught.
> The smart person comes home before Tet.
> Follow us, and you'll always have a family.
> Follow America, and you'll always be alone!

After these initial "lessons," the cadre leaders introduced us to the two Vietnamese leaders who personified each view—the opposite poles of our tiny world. On the South pole was President Ngo Dinh Diem, America's staunch ally, who was Catholic like the French. Although he was idolized by many who said he was a great humanitarian and patriot, his religion alone was enough to make him suspicious to Buddhists on the Central Coast. The loyalty we showed him, consequently, was more duty to a landlord than love for a founding father. Here is a song the Republican schoolteachers made us learn to praise the Southern president: 10

> In stormy seas, Vietnam's boat rolls and pitches.
> Still we must row; our President's hand upon the helm.
> The ship of state plows through heavy seas,
> Holding fast its course to democracy.
> Our President is celebrated from Europe to Asia,
> He is the image of philanthropy and love.
> He has sacrificed himself for our happiness.
> He fights for liberty in the land of the Viet.
> Everyone loves him earnestly, and behind him we will march
> Down the street of freedom, lined with fresh flowers,
> The flag of liberty crackling above our heads!

In the North, on the other pole, was Ho Chi Minh, whom we were 11
encouraged to call *Bac Ho*—Uncle Ho—the way we would refer to a trusted
family friend. We knew nothing of his past beyond stories of his compassion
and his love for our troubled country—the independence of which, we were
told, he had made the mission of his life.

Given the gulf between these leaders, the choice of whom we should 12
support again seemed obvious. The cadre leaders encouraged our natural prejudices (fear of outsiders and love of our ancestors) with stirring songs and
tender stories about Uncle Ho in which the Communist leader and our ancient heroes seemed to inhabit one congenial world. Like an unbroken thread,
the path from our ancestors and legends seemed to lead inevitably to the
Northern leader—then past him to a future of harmony and peace.

But to achieve that independence, Ho said, we must wage total war. His 13
cadremen cried out "We must hold together and oppose the American empire.
There is nothing better than freedom, independence, and happiness!"

To us, these ideas seemed as obvious as everything else we had heard. 14
Freedom meant a Vietnam free of colonial domination. *Independence* meant one
Vietnamese people—not two countries, North and South—determining its
own destiny. *Happiness* meant plenty of food and an end to war—the ability,
we assumed, to live our lives in accordance with our ancient ways. We wondered: how can the Southerners oppose these wonderful things? The answer
the Viet Cong gave us was that the Republicans prized Yankee dollars more
than the blood of their brothers and sisters. We did not think to question with
our hearts what our minds told us must be true.

Although most of us thought we knew what the Viet Cong meant by 15
freedom, independence, and happiness, a few of us dared to ask what life the
Northerners promised when the war was over. The answer was always the
same: "Uncle Ho promises that after our victory, the Communist state will
look after your rights and interests. Your highest interest, of course, is the
independence of our fatherland and the freedom of our people. Our greatest
right is the right to determine our own future as a state." This always brought
storms of applause from the villagers because most people remembered what
life was like under the French.

Nonetheless, despite our vocal support, the Viet Cong never took our 16
loyalty for granted. They rallied and rewarded and lectured us sternly, as the
situation demanded, while the Republicans assumed we would be loyal because we lived south of a line some diplomats had drawn on a map. Even
when things were at their worst—when the allied forces devastated the countryside and the Viet Cong themselves resorted to terror to make us act the
way they wanted—the villagers clung to the vision the Communists had
drummed into us. When the Republicans put us in jail, we had the image of
"Communist freedom"—freedom from war—to see us through. When the
Viet Cong executed a relative, we convinced ourselves that it was necessary to
bring "Communist happiness"—peace in the village—a little closer. Because
the Viet Cong encouraged us to voice our basic human feelings through

patriotic songs, the tortured, self-imposed silence we endured around Republicans only made us hate the government more. Even on those occasions when the Republicans tried to help us, we saw their favors as a trick or sign of weakness. Thus, even as we accepted their kindness, we despised the Republicans for it.

As the war gathered steam in the 1960s, every villager found his or her little world expanded—usually for the worse. The steady parade of troops through Ky La meant new opportunities for us to fall victim to outsiders. Catholic Republicans spurned and mistreated Buddhists for worshiping their ancestors. City boys taunted and cheated the "country bumpkins" while Vietnamese servicemen from other provinces made fun of our funny accents and strange ways. When the tactics on both sides got so rough that people were in danger no matter which side they favored, our sisters fled to the cities where they learned about liquor, drugs, adultery, materialism, and disrespect for their ancestors. More than one village father died inside when a "stranger from Saigon" returned in place of the daughter he had raised. *17*

In contrast to this, the Viet Cong were, for the most part, our neighbors. Even though our cadre leaders had been trained in Hanoi, they had all been born on the Central Coast. They did not insult us for our manners and speech because they had been raised exactly like us. Where the Republicans came into the village overburdened with American equipment designed for a different war, the Viet Cong made do with what they had and seldom wasted their best ammunition—the goodwill of the people. The cadremen pointed out to us that where the Republicans wore medals, the Viet Cong wore rags and never gave up the fight. "Where the Republicans pillage, rape, and plunder," they said, "we preserve your houses, crops, and family"; for they knew that it was only by these resources—our food for rations, our homes for hiding, our sons and brothers for recruits—that they were able to keep the field. *18*

Of course, the Viet Cong cadremen, like the Republicans, had no desire (or ability, most of them) to paint a fairer picture. For them, there could be no larger reason for Americans fighting the war than imperialist aggression. Because we peasants knew nothing about the United States, we could not stop to think how absurd it would be for so large and wealthy a nation to covet our poor little country for its rice fields, swamps, and pagodas. Because our only exposure to politics had been through the French colonial government (and before that, the rule of Vietnamese kings), we had no concept of democracy. For us, "Western culture" meant bars, brothels, black markets, and *xa hoi van minh*—bewildering machines—most of them destructive. We couldn't imagine that life in the capitalist world was anything other than a frantic, alien terror. Because, as peasants, we defined "politics" as something other people did someplace else, it had no relevance to our daily lives—except as a source of endless trouble. As a consequence, we overlooked the power that lay in our hands: our power to achieve virtually anything we wanted if only we acted together. The Viet Cong and the North, on the other hand, always recognized and respected this strength. *19*

We children also knew that our ancestral spirits demanded we resist the   20
outsiders. Our parents told us of the misery they had suffered from the invad-
ing Japanese ("small death," our neighbors called them) in World War II, and
from the French, who returned in 1946. These soldiers destroyed our crops,
killed our livestock, burned our houses, raped our women, and tortured or
put to death anyone who opposed them—as well as many who did not. Now,
the souls of all those people who had been mercilessly killed had come back
to haunt Ky La—demanding revenge against the invaders. This we children
believed with all our hearts. After all, we had been taught from birth that
ghosts were simply people we could not see.

There was only one way to remove this curse. Uncle Ho had urged the   21
poor to take up arms so that everyone might be guaranteed a little land on
which to cultivate some rice. Because nearly everyone in Central Vietnam was
a farmer, and because farmers must have land, almost everyone went to war:
with a rifle or a hoe; with vigilance to give the alarm; with food and shelter
for our fighters; or, if one was too little for anything else, with flowers and
songs to cheer them up. Everything we knew commanded us to fight. Our
ancestors called us to war. Our myths and legends called us to war. Our
parents' teachings called us to war. Uncle Ho's cadre called us to war. Even
President Diem had called us to fight for the very thing we now believed he
was betraying—an independent Vietnam. Should an obedient child be less
than an ox and refuse to do her duty?

And so the war began and became an insatiable dragon that roared around   22
Ky La. By the time I turned thirteen, that dragon had swallowed me up.

In 1986, after living for sixteen years in America and becoming a U.S.   23
citizen, I went back to Vietnam—to find out what had happened to my family,
my village, my people, and to the man I loved who had given me my first
son. I went with many memories and many questions. This book is the story
of what I remember and what I found.

It is dedicated to all those who fought for their country, wherever it may   24
be. It is dedicated, too, to those who did not fight—but suffered, wept, raged,
bled, and died just the same. We all did what we had to do. By mingling our
blood and tears on the earth, god has made us brothers and sisters.

If you were an American GI, I ask you to read this book and look into   25
the heart of one you once called enemy. I have witnessed, firsthand, all that
you went through. I will try to tell you who your enemy was and why almost
everyone in the country you tried to help resented, feared, and misunderstood
you. It was not your fault. It could not have been otherwise. Long before you
arrived, my country had yielded to the terrible logic of war. What for you
was normal—a life of peace and plenty—was for us a hazy dream known only
in our legends. Because we had to appease the allied forces by day and were
terrorized by Viet Cong at night, we slept as little as you did. We obeyed both
sides and wound up pleasing neither. We were people in the middle. We were
what the war was all about.

Your story, however, was different. You came to Vietnam, willingly or   *26*
not, because your country demanded it. Most of you did not know, or fully
understand, the different wars my people were fighting when you got here.
For you, it was a simple thing: democracy against communism. For us, that
was not our fight at all. How could it be? We knew little of democracy and
even less about communism. For most of us it was a fight for independence—
like the American Revolution. Many of us also fought for religious ideals, the
way the Buddhists fought the Catholics. Behind the religious war came the
battle between city people and country people—the rich against the poor—a
war fought by those who wanted to change Vietnam and those who wanted
to leave it as it had been for a thousand years. Beneath all that, too, we had
vendettas: between native Vietnamese and immigrants (mostly Chinese and
Khmer) who had fought for centuries over the land. Many of these wars go
on today. How could you hope to end them by fighting a battle so different
from our own?

The least you did—the least any of us did—was our duty. For that we   *27*
must be proud. The most that any of us did—or saw—was another face of
destiny or luck or god. Children and soldiers have always known it to be
terrible. If you have not yet found peace at the end of your war, I hope you
will find it here. We have important new roles to play.

In the war many Americans—and many more Vietnamese—lost limbs,   *28*
loved ones, and that little light we see in babies' eyes which is our own hope
for the future. Do not despair. As long as you are alive, that light still burns
within you. If you lost someone you love, his light burns on in you—so long
as you remember. Be happy every day you are alive.

If you are a person who knows the Vietnam war, or any war, only by   *29*
stories and pictures, this book is written for you too. For you see, the face of
destiny or luck or god that gives us war also gives us other kinds of pain: the
loss of health and youth; the loss of loved ones or of love; the fear that we
will end our days alone. Some people suffer in peace the way others suffer in
war. The special gift of that suffering, I have learned, is how to be strong
while we are weak, how to be brave when we are afraid, how to be wise in
the midst of confusion, and how to let go of that which we can no longer
hold. In this way, anger can teach forgiveness, hate can teach us love, and war
can teach us peace.

CHAPTER TWO, FATHERS AND DAUGHTERS

. . . ."Father—why are you smiling?" my mother snapped. "Your daugh-   *30*
ter was almost killed today by Americans. The propellers could have chewed
her up and spat her all the way to Danang. What's wrong with you?"

My father put down his bowl. Little rice grains stuck to his chin. "I'm   *31*
smiling because I'm told we have a brave woman warrior in our house—

although she'd better be more careful if she wants to be around for New Year's, eh?" He mussed the stringy black hair on my head.

"What are you talking about?" my mother asked. 32

"Oh, haven't you heard the news? It's the talk of Ky La: How little Bay 33 Ly stood her ground against the enemy's *may bay chuong-chuong cua My huy.* She didn't budge an inch!"

"That's what the neighbors are saying?" My mother couldn't believe that 34 her lazy, absentminded daughter could have done anything so grand.

I didn't have the heart to tell them it was awe, not courage, that nailed 35 my feet to the ground when the Americans landed. In time, we all would learn the wisdom of standing still at the approach of Americans—the way one learns to stand still in the face of an angry dog. Before long, any Vietnamese who ran from American gunships would be considered Viet Cong and shot down for the crime of fear.

Although Americans had been in the village before and now came more 36 frequently to Ky La, we children never got used to them. Because they had blue eyes and always wore sunglasses, a few of us thought they were blind. We called them *mat meo*—cat eyes—and "long nose" to their backs and repeated every wild story we heard about them. Because the Viet Cong, when they captured them, always removed the Americans' boots (making escape too painful for their soft, citified feet), we thought we could immobilize the Americans by stealing both their sunglasses and their shoes. How can a soldier fight, we reasoned, if he's not only blind but lame?

Still, the arrival of the Americans in ever-increasing numbers meant the 37 new war had expanded beyond anyone's wildest dreams. A period of great danger—one we couldn't imagine at the time—was about to begin.

The Viet Cong, too, sensed this grave development and stepped up their 38 activities. In our midnight meetings, which were now held more often, they told us how to act when the Americans and their Republican "lap dogs" were around.

"What will you do when the enemy sleeps in your house?" the cadre 39 leader asked.

"Steal his weapons!" we answered in chorus. "Steal his medicine! Steal 40 his food!"

"And what will you do with what you steal?" 41

"Give it to you!" The village children laughed happily and applauded 42 our own correct answers. Whenever we turned something in to the Viet Cong—even something as small as a mess kit or pocketknife—we were rewarded like heroes. Handmade medals were pinned to our shirts and our names were entered on the Blackboard of Honor.

My name quickly rose on the list because the Republicans in our house 43 were so careless. We lived on a rise of ground near the fields and swamps and because it was easy to see in all directions, the soldiers there would relax. A few of us stole firearms—automatic rifles and pistols—but the Viet Cong seldom used them because the ammunition was different from the kind they received from the North. What they really wanted were hand grenades and first aid kits—things any fighter could use—things that were in perilously short supply. Once, I stole a hand grenade and hid it in a rice container that also held *man cau* fruit, which looks just like pineapples. My father discovered it by chance and his mouth fell open when one "fruit" he grabbed weighed so much more than the others. He buried it in a secret place and lectured me sternly about taking such chances, but I didn't care and promptly stole another one as soon as I had the chance. We kids used to laugh when a careless Republican got chewed out by his superior for losing such equipment. The fact that those things might lead to new deaths on both sides, including women and children in our own village, never occurred to us. For us, the new war was a game for earning medals and an honored place on lists—ideas we had been taught to honor for years in the government's own school.

Of course, every once in a while, one of us would get caught. If the stolen thing was a bit of food or clothing, the soldiers would just box our ears and take it back. But if it was a weapon or a piece of expensive equipment, the child would be arrested and taken away, to be tortured if she did not tell the soldiers what she knew about the Viet Cong. One friend of mine—a girl named Thi, whose parents "went north" when the war began—was about two years older than I was and very clever. Because she lived with her grandmother and there were no men around, the Republicans often used her house as a base and were very careless with their gear. One afternoon, she stole not only several hand grenades, but a large Republican machine gun. Unfortunately for her, she was caught when the soldiers found her struggling with a box of heavy ammunition and was spirited out of town in the officer's jeep. The Republicans never publicized these arrests because they were ashamed to admit that so many peasants in our village were against them. It was easier for the suspect to "just disappear," like the wayward equipment itself. 44

The cadre leaders were very clear about how we were supposed to act if we were threatened with capture. Because we knew where many secret tunnels were hidden, we were told to hide in them until the Viet Cong could help us. If they could not, we were expected to commit suicide—using, if need be, the weapon or explosives we had just stolen. Our deaths would mean nothing if they came after torture; only by dying in battle or by our own little hands would we be immortalized as heroes. This had been programmed into us by the Viet Cong and our own ancient, heroic legends, so we never questioned it for an instant. We didn't realize the Viet Cong were more concerned about terrified children giving away their secrets than guaranteeing our places in history. Loyalty was something the Viet Cong always worried about—more than battles or American bombs—and I would one day find out just how dangerous these worries could make them. 45

Eventually, the children my age and older went to fight for the Viet Cong. As you would expect, few parents approved of this, even the ones who hated the Republicans and Americans the most. Many parents, including my own, begged to have their children excused but few exceptions were made. 46

Fortunately, because I was my parents' last daughter (my brother Sau Ban, by this time, was away in Saigon working with the youth construction brigade) and because my father had worked so diligently to build bunkers and tunnels for the Viet Cong in our village, and because my eldest brother Bon Nghe had gone to Hanoi, and because I had already proved my loyalty and steadfastness on other occasions—including the arrival of the American helicopters— I was allowed to remain at home and perform other duties. In a solemn ceremony, I was inducted into the secret self-defense force and told I would be responsible for warning the Viet Cong about enemy movements in my village. After a battle, I was to help the nurses tend our wounded and report on enemy casualties. Although I was disappointed that I could not join my friends in combat, I was proud to be doing a job so similar to that of brother Bon Nghe.

My main assignment was to keep an eye on the stretch of jungle that 47 ran between Ky La and the neighboring village. As usual, my father played an important role in keeping me safe and alive. He would stand on the high ground behind our house—the same ground on which he had first instructed me about my duty to Vietnam—and relay my signal to the Viet Cong sentinels at the far edge of the forest. If Republicans or Americans were inside the village, he would take off his hat and fan himself three times. If the enemy was approaching the village, he would fan himself twice. If the coast was clear, and no enemy troops were around, he would fan himself once. This system, my father told me, had been used by the Viet Minh and was very effective. It allowed me to stay near the village where I would be safer and less suspect, and permitted the adult, my father in this case, to take most of the risk by giving the signal himself. If the system went wrong and some Viet Cong were killed, he assured me that his, not mine, would be the next body found on the road to Danang. Similarly, if the Republicans figured out the signals, he would also be killed—but only after being tortured for information. Although I was still blinded by my young girl's vision of glory, I began to see dimly what a terrible spot the war had put him in. For me and most other children, the new war was still an exciting game. For my father, it was a daily gamble for life itself.

As the war around Ky La dragged on, the Viet Cong established regular 48 tasks for the villagers. One week, our family would cook rations for them— although the Viet Cong never asked for anything special and refused to take food if it meant we would have nothing ourselves. The next week, it might be our duty to sew clothes: to repair old uniforms or make new ones— sometimes with the parachute silk taken from captured fliers or from the wreckage of an American plane. As standing orders, young girls like me were supposed to make friends with the Republicans and steal their toothpaste, cigarettes, and other sundries that were welcomed in the jungle. To make sure these false friendships didn't blossom into real ones, we were reminded during our midnight meetings of the differences between our liberation soldiers and the Republicans and Americans who fought them.

"The imperialists and their running dogs," the cadre leader said, shaking   *49*
his fist in the air and showering spit on those nearest him, "have aircraft and
bombs and long-range artillery and ten men for every one of ours. We have
only rags and rifles and those supplies we carry on our backs. When the
Republicans and Americans come to your village, they trample your crops,
burn your houses, and kill your relatives just for getting in the way. We respect
your homes and the shrines of your ancestors and execute only those who are
traitors to our cause. President Diem gives you foreign invaders while Ho Chi
Minh promises you a free Vietnam. The Republicans fight for pay, like mer-
cenaries, while we fight only for your independence."

As much as we disliked the wartime dangers, we could not argue with   *50*
what the leader said. For every American who yielded the right of way to us
on the road, many more bullied us like cattle. For every Republican whose
politeness reminded us of our sons and brothers, there were others who acted
like pirates. Whenever it was safe to do so, we organized demonstrations
and walked from village to village in our area, waving the Viet Cong flag and
shouting slogans to our neighbors. We cursed the "Republican lapdogs" and
told the safely distant Americans to get out of our country. It was helpless
rage that drove us, but it made us feel better and seemed to even the odds, if
only in our hearts. Unfortunately, on one occasion, those terrible odds—and
the awful reality of the war—finally caught up with me.

It was during one of these demonstrations, on a hot windless night, that   *51*
a Viet Cong runner came up and told us the Republicans were about to
bombard the area. Everyone ran to the roadside trenches and the Viet Cong
themselves disappeared into the jungle.

At first, the shells hit far away, then the explosions came toward us. Flares   *52*
drifting down on parachutes lit up the sky and threw eerie, wavering shadows
across my trench. The bombardment seemed to go on for hours, and as I lay
alone in my hiding place, flinching with each explosion, I began to worry
about my family. I had a terrifying vision of my house and parents coming
apart as they rose high on a ball of flame. I had a powerful urge to run home,
but somehow I overcame it. Leaving the trench before the shelling stopped
would have been suicide—even silly young farm girls knew that.

When the explosions stopped, I stretched out from my embryonic coil   *53*
and poked my head out of the trench. The night air smelled terrible—like
burning tires—and splintered trees and rocks lay all over the road. From the
direction of Ky La, a big force of Republicans were coming up the road,
rousting civilians from the trenches. It was illegal to be outside after dark, even
in your own village. To be away from your local area on top of that was all
but a confession of being a Viet Cong.

I lay in my burrow and tried to decide what to do. All I could think of   *54*
was our two neighbors, sisters named Tram and Phat, whose two brothers had
gone to Hanoi while a third had stayed in Ky La. The Ky La brother was
arrested and tortured by Republicans because of his connections to the North.
When he was released, the first thing he did was kiss his family good-bye and

slash his wrists. This so shocked and angered the sisters that they became staunch supporters of the Viet Cong. When the Republicans came back to arrest them, the sisters let it be known they were hiding in their family bunker, too afraid to come out. The soldiers, of course, went in after them. When they crawled inside the bunker, they saw the sisters sitting together, calm as can be, each holding a grenade without its pin. Their small hands were clasped around the safety handle, ready to release it should either of them be bothered. The soldiers, fearing to shoot them and thus set off the grenades, scrambled to get out. But the sisters released the grenades anyway and perished with three of their enemies. The next day, their mother buried what was left of her daughters beside her son and went out to work in the fields. The Republicans followed her and, fearing to get too close to the last member of such a dangerous, desperate family, shot her down from behind the dikes.

I did not have a weapon, but it would be easy enough to goad the 55 soldiers into shooting me, or, for that matter, to grab the barrel of one rifle and pull it against my chest. Still, I did not want my own mother to die because of my heroism or bad luck. Over and over in my head I repeated her advice for just this situation: *If you're too smart or too dumb, you'll die—so play stupid, eh? That shouldn't be too hard for a silly girl who lets herself get caught! Act like you don't know anything because you are young and stupid. That goes for either side, no matter who's asking the questions. Play stupid, eh? Stupid, stupid child!*

When the soldiers finally lifted me from the trench, muttering and cov- 56 ered with dirt, they must have thought I was simpleminded or shell-shocked by the explosions. Instead of questioning me or beating me or shooting me on the spot, as they had done with some others, they tied my hands behind my back and pushed me into a truck with other people from the parade and drove us all to the nearest jail.

From the truck we were led to a room with no furniture and told to 57 wait silently. One by one, the guards took people to another room for inter- rogation. I was the fifth or sixth to be taken, and until that time, no one before me had come back. Because I hadn't heard shots, I was foolish enough to think they had been released.

When my turn came, the guards hustled me down a corridor to a win- 58 dowless cell with a single electric light bulb hanging from the ceiling. A young Vietnamese soldier with many stripes and decorations made me squat in the middle of the floor and began to ask simple questions like "What is your name? Where are you from? Who is in your family?" and, most importantly, "What were you doing so far from your home in the middle of the night?" I answered each question like a terrified little girl, which, as my mother had promised, was not difficult. I said I sneaked away from home to follow what sounded like a feast-day parade. The people in the parade said we were going down the road to see a play. I told the soldier I was always getting into trouble like this and asked him to please not tell my parents because my father would whip me and my mother would—

The soldier's blow stopped my clever story and almost knocked me out. 59 The next thing I remember I was being jerked up by my hair with my face pointed up at the light bulb. The interrogator asked again, in a rougher voice, what I had been doing away from my village. Sobbing, I answered again that I had heard a parade and followed it to see a play. I didn't mean any harm to anyone. I only wanted to see the play and have fun—

The guard behind me lifted me by my hair and I yelped and he kicked 60 the small of my back—once, twice, three times—with his heavy boots. I now screamed as loud as I could—no acting!—but he kept me dangling and kicked me some more, my scalp and back on fire. Each time I tried to support myself, the soldier kicked my legs out from under me so the more I struggled the worse it hurt. Finally I went limp and the guard dumped me on the floor. The interrogator screamed his questions again, but I could only cry hysterically. He hit me a few more times, then pulled me up by my tied hands and shoved me out the door. The guard took me down the hall and into a big room that had been divided by bamboo bars into a dozen tiny cages. They thrust me into one of them—a space not big enough for even a small girl like me to stand up or stretch out in—and padlocked the door.

For a long time I simply lay sobbing on the cage's bamboo floor. My 61 tears stung the welts rising on my face and my back was beginning to throb. With my hands still tied behind me, I rolled upright against the bars. The room smelled like a sewer and when I focused my eyes I saw that a single drain at its center was used as the toilet for the cages. At once I recognized some people from the demonstration, although nobody was from my village. What we all had in common, though, was the badge of interrogation: purple eyes, puffed foreheads, mouths and noses caked with blood, teeth chipped or missing behind split lips and broken jaws. Like the interrogation cell, the dingy room had but a single unblinking light bulb from which even closed eyes offered no relief.

I began to feel desperate pain now in my lower back and bladder. Afraid 62 I would wet my pants, I hiked down my trousers and relieved myself shamelessly on the floor. I watched the stream of frothy liquid tinged with red meander down the drain and I almost fainted. I had never seen blood in my urine before, and assumed it meant I was dying. Still, the painful river inside me flowed on, blood or no blood, and my little girl's bottom sank to the bars and I sat there shivering, peeing, and crying—careless of anyone—wanting only my mother and my bed and an end to this terrible nightmare.

After crying myself out, I went to sleep. The next thing I knew the 63 door of my cage banged open and strong hands dragged me by the ankles toward the door. I was put on my feet and shoved down the hall toward the interrogation cell, which, just by my seeing its door, almost made me vomit. By the hazy light at the end of the hall I knew that the sun had come up— perhaps to mock my misery—on a beautiful summer day.

Inside the airless cell, however, everything was midnight—except for the 64 harsh, unsleeping bulb. But a different, older soldier greeted me now and, to my astonishment, he ordered the guard to untie me. My little joints popped as I stretched out my arms and rubbed the welts on my wrists.

"*Con an com chua?*" (Have you eaten?), the soldier asked politely. 65

I didn't know how to answer. The question might have been what it 66 seemed—a jailer's inquiry about the status of an inmate. But the question was also the formal greeting made between peasants from the earliest mists of time in a land where food was always scarce. I chose the most traditional, politest answer possible.

"*Da con an com roi*" (I have already eaten, thank you), and cast my eyes 67 down at the filthy floor. It seemed to satisfy him, although he said nothing more about my breakfast.

"Sergeant Hoa tells me you were most uncooperative last night." The 68 soldier circled me slowly, inspecting my wounds, gauging, perhaps, which weeping cut or puffy bruise would render pain—and therefore answers—most quickly. He paused, as if expecting me to dispute Sergeant Hoa, then said, "Anyway, all that's in the past. Others have told us everything we want to know about last night. All you need do is confirm a few details, then we can get you cleaned up and back to your family—perhaps in time for lunch, eh? You'd like that, wouldn't you, Le Ly?"

My heart leaped at the sound of my name spoken kindly on this strange 69 man's lips—as well as at the prospect of seeing my family. As my surprised and hopeful face looked up, I saw he was reading a piece of paper—perhaps Sergeant Hoa's report from the night before. Possibly, it contained a good deal more.

"Yes, I would like to go home," I said meekly. 70

"Good. Well now, Le Ly, let's talk a moment about the Viet Cong hiding 71 places around Binh Ky. We know about their tunnels beneath the haystacks and their rooms behind the artillery shelter south of the village—" He trailed off, hoping, perhaps, that I would add some other places to his list. "By the way, why *were* you in the trenches last night?"

"I jumped in to escape the explosions." 72

"Of course. And why were you outside at all?" 73

"I woke up and saw a parade pass our house. I joined it without waking 74 my parents and was told we were going to see a play. We were almost to the playhouse when the explosions began. I got scared and jumped in a trench. I was too afraid to go home because I thought my parents would spank me."

"I see. And what was the play about?" 75

I was quiet a moment, then said, "I don't know. I didn't see it." 76

"Just so. And who was to be in the play?" 77

"I—I don't know that either." 78

"Tell me, Le Ly, do you know this song? 79

We are so cheerful and happy,
We act and sing and dance,
Vietnam's stage is in sunlight,
Because Uncle Ho fills us with joy.

"I know that song," I replied, "but you sang the wrong words. The song   *80*
I know goes:

> We are so cheerful and happy,
> We act and sing and dance,
> Vietnam's stage is in sunlight,
> Because Ngo Dinh Diem fills us with joy.

My little girl's voice, choked with fear and bruises, must have sounded   *81*
funny because the soldiers in the room laughed loudly. Perhaps I was the first
peasant girl they'd met whose father knew two versions of every political song.

"Do the Viet Cong ever come to your village, Le Ly?"   *82*

"Yes."   *83*

"And what do they look like?"   *84*

"They look like you—except they wear black uniforms."   *85*

The soldier lit a cigarette. He was quiet for such a long time that I   *86*
thought he was going to hit me. Instead he said, "We'll talk again, Le Ly." He
nodded and the guard took me back to my cage.

I stayed in the cage two more days. Every morning, a prison worker   *87*
would splash water on the fetid floor and every evening we were given one
bowl of rice with a few greens or pork fat mixed in to sustain us. We were
allowed to drink three dippers of water each day and had a few minutes every
afternoon to walk around in the compound. Prisoners were forbidden to
speak, even in the cages, because the soldiers feared we would coordinate our
stories or make plans for breaking out. Given our pathetic condition and the
many soldiers and guns that surrounded us, I had trouble imagining how
anyone could fear us. Of course, that was exactly why the soldiers worried.
The Viet Cong were famous for turning innocent situations into danger for
their enemies. Because of our reputation and the countermeasures it demanded, neither jailers nor inmates could relax.

Each night I was taken back for interrogation with Sergeant Hoa and   *88*
each time he asked fewer questions and beat me longer and with more fury.
Each morning I was taken to the cell where the second soldier—always kindly
and fatherly and good-natured—would show horror at my wounds and ask
me different questions about the Viet Cong and life around Ky La. Compared
with Sergeant Hoa and the endless hours in the stinking bamboo cage, these
sessions were almost pleasant and I found it harder and harder to play dumb
and avoid telling him about my family, whom I now missed very much.

On the third day, after a particularly bad beating the night before, I was   *89*
summoned for what I thought would be my morning interrogation, but instead was led down the hall toward the shaft of daylight where I found my
mother and my sister Ba's husband, Chin, who worked for the government
police force in Danang. Despite the toughness I tried to cultivate in prison, I
ran weeping to my mother while Chin talked to a soldier about my release.
My poor mother, who looked ten years older for my absence, inspected my
oozing wounds distastefully—like a shopper sizing up a bad melon. Although

I could see she was in almost as much pain as I was, she said nothing, but kept a grim straight face for the soldiers. If I had fooled my jailers into thinking that I was just a naughty, runaway child, my mother's hard look must have convinced them that the beatings I suffered in jail would be nothing compared with the punishment I would get from this heartless woman at home.

Outside, Chin gave me a nasty look and departed on his bicycle. When we got on the bus that would take us near our village and had ridden about a mile, my mother could contain herself no longer and wept as I had done that first night in my cell. She told me Chin was angry at having been disturbed to help his country in-laws, especially since his own house might now be watched and his loyalties questioned because of his shadowy relatives. Although I felt sorry for him, I was so happy to be free that his future troubles— or even my own—just didn't seem to matter.

90

Topics for Discussion and Writing

1. Compare Hayslip's explanation of the views of her people with the perspectives you discovered in your interviews ("Before and As You Read" topic 1) or newspaper search (topic 2). How do you account for the differences? What in her account of the war and warriors helps explain why her perspective might not have been reported to or understood by U.S. audiences?

2. As you read Le Ly Hayslip's work, what current conflicts in the world are brought to mind? As you listen to and read the news, let your "inner ear" hear the perspective of those who are not represented by the media and are therefore voiceless. What does this do for your perspective of the situation?

3. Take on the role of one of the characters either described or alluded to (such as U.S. soldiers) in the excerpt. Tell the story of the shelling of the village from the perspective of that character. What happened? Why did it happen? What will happen next? Share your narrative.

4. Compare Le Ly Hayslip's story and reflections with those of Lily Jean Lee Adams in the following selection. What aspects of the personalities and styles of the two come across in your reading? Draft an imagined conversation about the war between these two people now, so many years later. What might each try to explain to the other?

KEITH WALKER

from *A Piece of My Heart*

"... *my thoughts on the flight home were, 'Wait until I tell everybody what happened, how we really helped our guys and all the wonderful things that we did as medical people.' But then things began to make sense to me. In the bus terminal, people were staring at me and giving me dirty looks. I expected the people to smile, like, 'Wow, she was in Vietnam, doing something for her country—wonderful.' I felt like I had walked into another country, not my country. So I went into the ladies room and changed [out of my uniform]."*

Keith Walker, who lives in Oakland, California, is a painter, filmmaker, and writer who served during the Korean war. He states that his interest in the Vietnam War was prompted by his own need to examine his feelings and "reconcile the conflicting emotions that I still carried with me." After being introduced to Rose Sandecki, director of the Veterans Outreach Center in Concord, California, his interest in learning about the women who served in Vietnam grew. "I was amazed that fifteen thousand women had been in Vietnam and yet I had heard nothing about them in the aftermath of the war." Walker's desire to learn about and give a voice to those women led him to write A Piece of My Heart. *The following selection is a taped recollection by Lily Jean Lee Adams who served in the 12th Evac. Hospital, Cu Chi, Vietnam, from October 1969 to October 1970.*

Lily has served on the National Board of Directors of Vietnam Veterans of America and has chaired its Special Committee on Women Veterans. As a consultant on Vietnam veterans, she has counseled, lectured, and shared resources and referrals.

Lily lives in Atlanta, Georgia. She is married to a Vietnam veteran and has two children.

Before and as You Read

1. What images does the word *Vietnam* stir in you? As a student of history, what do you think that the Vietnam War has taught us? Might these lessons help the United States avoid another such tragedy in the future? Has that avoidance in any way already occurred? Defend your answer.

2. According to the U.S. government, Korea and Vietnam were "unofficial wars." Look up the definitions of *police action* and *military action*, terms that were used for these conflicts. Why did the United States not make these wars official?

3. Lily Adams speaks with great emotion. She talks of her fear, bitterness, sense of betrayal, anger, and depression. As you read, identify the experiences she has had that resulted in these emotions. How was she twice betrayed? What did she fear? Why was she angry? Bitter? Depressed? How did she show bravery? Pride? Love?

4. This selection is a spoken interview. List ways that you can tell that this piece was an oral narrative rather than a written account of Adams's story. How is this selection like that of John Saddic? How is it different?

IT WAS in my junior year of nursing school when an Army recruiter was invited to give us a little sales pitch on joining the Army. She was dressed in her uniform and showed us this wonderful film on being an Army nurse. She showed us the various hospitals and all the modern equipment (which we were lacking at the nursing school I was going to), so I was very impressed. After the film I asked her, "Do nurses have to go to Vietnam?" And she said, "No. Women volunteer to go to Vietnam. The Army does not send us; we have to volunteer to go." I talked to some of the other girls in my class, and they were saying I was crazy. There were two others that were willing to sign up at any minute, and I thought about it. I wanted to get out of New York City. I was born and raised there, hated it, and I saw this as an opportunity of getting out. I had always wanted to go to San Francisco, always, and figured that would be the quickest way of going. I also wanted to go to Hawaii. I'm Eurasian—half Chinese, half Italian—and had gone through a lot of discrimination in New York. I wanted to go to a place where everybody was like me. I thought, well, the Army sounds adventurous—I'd be meeting people from all over the country, it would be a very interesting life for me, and it is only two years out of my life.

I was antiwar. I wasn't a protester because I was so involved with nursing school that I wasn't really aware of the political aspect that was going on in the country, but I didn't think it was fair to send young men to Vietnam, and I wanted to do something for them in some way. I felt when they came back from Nam I could take care of them. Then there was Kennedy: "What can you do for your country?" I was part of that era, of that generation, and I thought, "This is perfect. I can serve my country, I can express my feelings about the war, I can get out of New York, and there's a lot of adventure. Plus it pays for my last year of nursing school." So I thought, "What the heck." I signed up.

During officer basic training I started to notice that every class concentrated a lot on Vietnam, so I approached the major who was head of the program and asked, "Why are you always concentrating on Vietnam?" She said, "Well, you will probably go; eventually you will go." I said, "No, I'm not. I'm stateside." She said, "Oh, my dear, no. More than likely you will go to Vietnam." I said, "Look, my recruiter told me that women have to volunteer to go to Vietnam." She said, "Oh my, she must have made a mistake. Maybe she was misinformed." I was fit to be tied. We graduated and I was assigned to Fort Ord, California. I drove from Fort Sam to California, and when I hit Monterey, I thought, "Am I in heaven or what? This is God's country!"

I was assigned to orthopedics and learned that as a lowly second lieutenant I didn't get to work day shifts too often. On evening shift I covered two wards, which was the equivalent of sixty guys, give or take. I had to prep them for surgery and then took care of them post-operatively. I would say 50 percent were from Vietnam that had repeat orthopedic surgery. They were on what was called "medical hold" before they could be discharged to civilian life. The other half were men who were injured during basic, because there was a lot of basic training going on at Fort Ord. I took care of two patients who had a pact, who didn't want to go to Vietnam. One guy put his leg up on a chair, and the other stomped on it, ruined his knee for life.

The guys who had just come back from Vietnam were the most critical psychologically. You would think they were on speed, they were so high and so hyper. They would sit by my desk and talk the whole night long. At five in the morning the cannon goes off—it's reveille. I'd watch the time for them, because after a while I realized that these guys really freaked out when they heard the cannon—it sounds like a mortar attack. I'd say, "In five minutes the cannon is going to go off. Now take it easy, it's just a cannon." But it didn't matter, they would hit the floor and just shake. Night shift seemed to be the worst shift. I'd hear some screaming and a lot of funny noises in the ward, and it would be the guys having nightmares. I'd sit with them and talk to them, and they'd tell me war stories and how they'd come home and find out their wives were cheating on them, or they'd come home and their family wouldn't want anything to do with them. In the morning when I had to wake them for rounds, I'd have to go to the foot of the bed, grab their big toe, and shake it a little bit, because if you get too close to them or shake them by the shoulders, they would have their hands around your neck within two seconds . . . they were so combat-ready. And it took them a really long time to come down from that.

One afternoon my roommate came in looking really down in the dumps. She said, "Lily, I have some bad news." I said, "You got orders." And she said, "*We* got orders." In the beginning I wanted to fight it. I learned you could do what one nurse did—she made believe she had swallowed a bunch of Librium and played the game of being half-crazy and suicidal, and they discharged her. Another one got pregnant. Various women were doing various things so they wouldn't have to go to Nam. . . . I didn't want to do any of that; I didn't feel right doing that. I remember going to work the next day, and the chief nurse, who was a really nice lady, came down and put her arm around me, and we walked down the ward. She said, "I'm really sorry. We've got a shortage of nurses as it is. They really need nurses in Vietnam, more than they need them here at stateside." I appreciated the fact that she saw me as an individual, she understood how I felt about the war, and she did try to do something. So I accepted it. I went to New York, back home, just to kind of hold on to my roots. Met a couple of people who had gone to Woodstock—I had missed Woodstock by two days—and regretted not being a part of it, but I was very excited because of what was going on in the country. Things were happening, and I was part of the generation, even though I was in the military. This was before the military was a negative concept in the eyes of the country.

So . . . I got to Travis AFB. The flight was at four o'clock in the after- 7 noon—it is amazing how I remember such details—and there was a group of women that I recognized from Fort Sam. There must have been about ten of them. I got very angry because I was thinking, "It's not only me; there are others that are going too." I went down the row, "Did your recruiter tell you that you didn't have to go to Vietnam unless you volunteered?" "Yes." Every single one of them.

We were all getting brave and ready to go when they announced that 8 something was wrong with the plane, they were going to ship us to a motel. So we go into the motel, and there is this one room where everybody is having a big party. We went over thinking that we might as well join the party, had a couple of drinks, and decided we'd better get a good night's sleep. Another woman and I shared one room and were in our pajamas getting ready for bed when this guy walks into our room and sits on the bed. He's talking to me, and I said, "Excuse me for a minute." And we walked out. We went next door, where there were two other women. The four of us against one, you know. After about half an hour of deciding how we are going to do it, we all went back, and the guy was gone. Apparently he got the message that we weren't interested. And that was basically my first introduction to "Well, you are an Army nurse aren't you? I mean, don't you get laid all the time?"

We arrived in Hawaii, the place I had wanted to go since I was a kid— 9 very ironic. Had a cup of coffee, and we all go to the ladies room. I am thinking, "Right now I could walk out. Even though I'm in uniform, I could still do that—I could desert." I learned when I asked the stewardess if she would get me a pillow that she could care less about the women on board. We got the same chicken dinner five times going across the world. Then we look out the window, and there is this beautiful country, Vietnam. It was green and lush, and I couldn't comprehend that there could be a war in such a beautiful place. The plane lands, and I'm one of the first to get out—after seventeen hours I just wanted to get away from the plane. They opened the door, and I could smell this awful smell and feel the high humidity and heat. I backed off! I didn't want to go out there. . . . It was just instinct. So we go down the stairs of the plane, and I heard the roar of a crowd. I looked over and there are all these guys, and they seemed aged. They didn't look like nineteen or twenty; they looked about forty. That is the first thing I noticed. Our plane was their Freedom Bird for home, and that was what had caused the roar.

We got into an area called 90th Replacement. There was Gayle, who 10 was in the same platoon as me at Fort Sam, and Sue, who had this red hair and was engaged to a paraplegic who had been one of her patients. The three of us became kind of chummy, and we were hoping to be assigned to the same area. The guys back at Fort Ord had said, "Ask for Vung Tau. It's on the beach—you'll love it." But it seemed every place I asked for, the chief nurse said they didn't need nurses there. "We need three nurses for Cu Chi." And I had a funny feeling that she was sizing us up, but right away Gayle, Sue, and I say, "Hey, let's go, and we'll stay together." So we volunteered, so to speak, for Cu Chi.

The next day we got on a C-130. Gayle, Sue, myself, and a couple of guys we had met at 90th Replacement. I had become friends with one man who was married with a kid; we had talked a lot, and we were happy to be stationed in the same area. On the way, I asked him what his insignia was. He said, "We are responsible for spraying areas to kill off weeds so that Charlie can't hide in the jungle." I thought, "What an awful assignment. . . . You go to Vietnam to kill weeds?" All of a sudden I see all the troops on the floor, and I'm going, "What's going on?" He says, "We've just been hit." I thought, "I didn't even know. . . . The Army never taught me how to take care of myself. God, I could be killed so easily without this knowledge." I was very angry realizing that these guys on the floor had a better chance of living than I did because I didn't know anything. I'm thinking, "Yeah, Lily, you are in the war." *11*

At Cu Chi we were asked by the chief nurse, "Where do you want to be assigned?" I said, "Intensive care" because I'd had a taste of intensive care at Fort Ord and I just loved it. ICU was a challenge for me. She said, "It looks like we may be able to send you to ICU, but we are going to put you on orientation. You are going to spend a few days in the emergency room, then we'll send you to recovery room ICU, and then we'll put you in ICU." They wanted to give us a feel for what a patient goes through from the minute they land in the ER to when they leave. *12*

So I go to the emergency room and they orient you to where all the equipment is, and it's getting confusing because there is so much to remember. But they don't expect you to do too much, just observe. I hear a chopper land, it becomes very windy, and they bring in a couple of stretchers. One guy I remember has no legs; they are blown off from the thigh down. I'm standing there looking at this, and I'm totally freaked out. I see a lot of blood, I see mud, his green fatigues all soaked, and I'm seeing a lot of action. The doctors and nurses are doing, like, ten thousand things at one time. One is cutting off his uniform, another is starting up an IV, another asking his name, rank, serial number, that business. Blood is going up, and all this is happening at one time. I couldn't even look to see what was going on in the second stretcher because what I was seeing was so horrifying to me that I was, like, in a hysteria. You know, here I am, the nurse and shit—I couldn't even do anything; I was frozen there. I thought, "The next group that comes in, I'm going to do something. I'm going to prove to them that I'm just as good a nurse as they are, and I'm going to prove to myself that I can get over this shit and do it." Well, they bring in two or three more stretchers, and I'm still in *13* shock—and ready to cry, thinking, "This isn't me. I'm usually the active one." So I'm doing a lot of in-fighting within myself, saying, "What's wrong with you?" And my other half saying, "Jesus Christ, look at this!" All of a sudden I hear a doctor say, "I need someone to hold his head." Everybody's busy, and he repeats, "I need someone to hold his head." I just walked in there—because he defined to me what was needed—and positioned his head while the doctor did manual resuscitation with the bag. After that I was able to finally get in and function. So I felt that I had taken a big step.

I was sent to recovery ICU and reported to the head nurse. She said, *14* "We've got this POW over there. I want you to take care of him. He's got real low blood pressure, has lost a lot of blood." . . . I was angry that they would assign me to someone as low as an NVA. I thought, "I'm not over here to take care of a POW!" I took the vital signs and took over from the nurse that was taking care of him. He was so sick that he had a nurse assigned just to him. I remember that nurse was a male nurse, and he gave me the report. They were using a CVP, which measured the spinal pressure, and that was fairly new to me. The Aramine, which was the medication to regulate the blood pressure, I was familiar with. He told me how much he was dripping, and then he picked up on my anger or uncomfortableness and said, "Do you feel comfortable enough to take care of the patient?" I said, "Yeah, I'm okay as far as the nursing aspects of it, but I didn't come here to take care of gooks." He said to me, "I know how you feel, but just look at it this way: this is a North Vietnamese POW. He's got lots of information, and if you can keep him alive long enough to be able to talk to our interrogators, you're probably saving hundreds of men—there is that possibility. We think that this guy is really important." So I thought, "Well, I can deal with this guy now." I took his blood pressure and I'm working on him for two or three hours, and I start becoming attached to him, like any nurse gets attached to her patient. I'm with him for maybe six or eight hours when Intelligence comes in. I'm thinking, "If they start slapping him around, I'm going to start slapping them around, because I worked my ass off to keep this guy alive." They are interrogating him in Vietnamese, and I'm watching this kid—he is nineteen years old, answering everything. I said to the interrogator, "Oh, come on, he must be lying to you." And he says, "No, this story goes along with that POW over on the other side of the ward. This guy knows that we caught both of them, and if they lie, we will know it." I was listening to all these questions, kind of enjoying learning more about my patient. Then I said to the interrogator, "Would you do me a favor? Would you ask him a question from me?" And he said, "Sure, what is it?" I said, "He doesn't have to answer if if he doesn't want to, but I'd like to know how he feels about the war." The interpretation was—and he looked straight at me when he said it—"If I could march in Hanoi, like you are marching in Washington, D.C., I would be doing it."

After orientation they assigned me to the new ward, which was half *15* burn patients and half amputations. Some men had second-degree burns from sunburn. Most of the guys didn't wear shirts, as it was so hot out there, and I remember one guy who got an Article 15 for having a sunburn. We got in guys that had phosphorous burns, which, if you don't neutralize, will go straight through your body. So you have to keep their wounds neutralized, which was really hard to keep up with when you had other patients. The head nurse used to sit on her butt and do nothing. The ward master was in and out, and if you asked him, he would help you move the patient, but the guy was always on his way somewhere, so he was no help. We had a Vietnamese woman who set fire to herself with gasoline when she learned that her GI boyfriend was going home without her after he promised that he would take her with him. Took care of some Vietnamese kids with phosphorous burns, that had urine that was as red as wine. . . .

The other half of the ward was amputations with complications. If you were a clean amputee, you were off to Japan in no time flat, but if you had complications you needed to stay in the evac hospital until you were stable enough to go. One guy had lost one leg, and this night he was in tears. I said, "What's going on? Let's talk about it." He said, "I'm engaged to get married, and I don't know if my girlfriend is going to want to marry me." I was in a dilemma. I didn't know what to say to him. Sue was on duty with me, and I told her about it. She said, "Just tell him that if his girlfriend is as wonderful as he says she is, she will probably go ahead and marry him." I said, "Sue, do me a favor. You talk to him. You are there—you can vouch for her." So she went over and talked to him. He wrote her a letter about a month later, and she said, "Yes, he managed to not only get married, but he walked down the aisle on his prosthesis, without any crutches!" *16*

I remember another GI, with both legs gone, and he'd say, "My legs hurt." And I'd explain to him about the "phantom leg," about the nerve endings. I would lift the sheets and say, "The legs are not there." You have to get them to acknowledge that, because they get psychotic after a while. He would look straight at the TV set and totally ignore me and tell me his legs hurt. He needed a lot of encouragement and love, so I spent a lot of time with him. I'd tell him, "As soon as you get home, they are going to make you do exercises and things with your stumps. You'll get prostheses, and you will be able to walk upright on them. You will be able to do a lot of special things on them, like skiing and parachuting. There is a lot to look forward to." It must have been about two weeks later, not very long, and I get a letter from this guy. He is doing really well; he is thanking me and telling me all of his plans. I realized that even though I wasn't getting any feedback from him at the time, I didn't fail him; I managed to succeed. And that kept me going. *17*

I worked there about four months and found myself getting more and more depressed, because I'd learn that these guys would have a girlfriend at home; I would learn that they were married and had a two-month-old baby at home, that their mother was sick. All this information I was picking up from my patients was getting me down. I decided that I had to get out of there and thought, "emergency room," because you only deal with them a few minutes and out the door they go. But then, Sue had this plan to go to Hawaii, *18* meet her boyfriend and get married, and then ask to get out of Nam. She thought being married would help her to get a transfer. She needed support so I went with her to Hawaii. She got married the next day, and I spent the rest of the week by myself. I sat there two days in a row, just watching people being ordinary people: no rifles, no war, no noises.

I bought a Hawaiian ring that I had seen while I was hanging out at Ala   19
Moana shopping center. I asked the lady, "What do you usually engrave on this kind of ring?" She said, "It's basically a wedding ring, and people put their names on them. You can put anything you want on it." So I said, "Peace and Love." And she said, "Oh, that's very beautiful." She asked why it was so important to me, and I told her about myself. She said, "You must come to dinner. Here is my name and phone number; call me when you have some time." I was very impressed by that, but I never called her because I felt embarrassed that I had poured my troubles out to her. She'd heard enough about Vietnam.

I was at Fort Derussy and a fire engine went by, and I hit the dirt—it   20
sounded like the red alert siren—and then I thought, "Oh shit! How embarrassing." I get up and am brushing myself off, and here are two guys laughing hysterically, and I'm really angry at them. They were laughing because they were enjoying the scene—they had been in Vietnam. So they asked me if I had seen Oahu yet, and they gave me a Cook's tour: "You deserve it." They drove me around the island and then stopped at the Crouching Lion restaurant and said, "We want to treat you to dinner." We had a delicious dinner, and they told me about their time in Nam and how somehow they were lucky enough to get out after four months. They told me how they had had one huge party when they got to Hawaii, dancing in the streets and celebrating, and I was enjoying their joy at being out of the war zone. I told them that I didn't want to go back to Vietnam. They were saying, "We know it's not the safest place to be, but those guys need you." They were building me up to go back. I was saying, "You know, I could desert." The next day they called and asked if I was still thinking about deserting and promised they would write to me and told me, "Just keep the faith." At the airport I'm thinking, "All I have to do is turn around and go to the ticket office and get the hell out of here." And there is a captain who is eyeing me. I'm thinking, "Does he know what I'm thinking? Am I producing a profile?" He kept his eye on me till I got on the plane. I thought, "I wonder if there are people like me that show it right outside that we don't want to go back—that we are thinking twice about it." Sue cried the whole way back. She wrote to her senator and left two months before me—off she went. . . . She was gone.

When I was first in Nam I had met a guy from one of the wards who   21
had an arm in a cast. One day he came in and said, "Come out for a minute." I got out, and before me are about ten guys in jeans and shirts and hats, as if they had just walked off the plane from Woodstock. I was going, "I can't believe my eyes. Who are you?" I learned that they were in a dog scout unit and they lived on the other side of the compound. "You've gotta come over

to our place—black lights and day-glo posters, just like home." People are walking down the ramp, medical people, giving a second look, saying, "Where the hell did you come from?" They got that response from everybody and got a little joy out of it. It was like a little bit of home. So this guy says, "When is your next day off?" I say, "In two or three days." He said, "I'll pick you up at seven o'clock, walk you over and back. Don't worry about it—we'll take good care of you." I wanted to take advantage of this opportunity to get out of the hospital area. These guys were sensitive to my feelings; they were saying the right words, and their actions seemed sincere enough to me, so I thought, "Well, why not take a chance?"

He shows up on my day off, and I'm in jeans and T-shirt. He's going, "Wow, you look a hell of a lot better in those clothes." We walked across the compound, about a fifteen-minute walk. I learn he's from New Hampshire and we like the same music, and I'm getting more comfortable. We go into the hooch. There are posters all over the ceilings and walls, and all these guys are dressed in their civilian clothes again. Led Zeppelin is going as loud as it can go—it was party time. Everybody moves over for me to sit down, and I'm just hypnotized looking at all the posters. The guys aren't talking about the war; they are talking about the stupid stuff: harassment, funny things, food, and music. Plus they were talking about home, what was going on—it was wonderful. I was away from the people that talk medicine. I would go there and be very depressed and exhausted, and they would start talking about everything but Vietnam, and within an hour or two I was feeling as good as they were. I continued to go there for four or five months until everybody got short enough that they were all going home. And when they left, I thought I was going to die.

Another part of Vietnam was the chief nurse, "the Virgin Mary," who came around to harass me because I was fraternizing with EMs and I should be dating officers. I told her I was going to date anybody that I damn well please—it was none of her business who I was dating. Then years later, looking back, I realized she could have used that precious time to help me out with the patients. But no, she's got to come around and harass me about who I am dating. She harassed me because my love beads were showing, because I put ribbons in my hair, because I was out of uniform. We knew that our guys appreciated women. To prove a point: you get these guys with their legs blown off and in agony and in fear, and in the middle of all this they stop and look at you and say, "God, you smell so good." And they said it to me all of the time. So I made a point to wear perfume. Or, "God, you look beautiful." And I would think, "Yeah, that is important to them." Here some of these guys were dying, and in the middle of it they'd say, "Oh, you smell good!" A lot of the women went out of their way to look good for their patients, just because they wanted to do that much more for them.

Well, I think I have covered enough about Vietnam. I still haven't decided which was worse: my experience in Vietnam or my experience coming home. We landed at Travis AFB, and from there we were sent out to the real world through Oakland Army Base. I spent the evening there, and the next day we were processed out. They gave us our pay, and that was it. They didn't provide transportation; they dropped us like a hot potato.

I had a friend in Monterey that I got in contact with, who was expecting   25
me to come home. We decided to spend some time together, and I wanted to do that because Monterey was like home base for me. I took a bus to San Francisco and called my friend in Monterey, who knew some people that could give me a ride down there. So I called them, and we decided to meet at the bus depot. He asked me to describe myself, and I said, "I'm in this green uniform." He said, "You're what?" I said, "Yeah, I just got in from Vietnam." "Oh, shit . . . you're at the bus terminal, right?" "Right." He said, "Why don't you go into the ladies room and change." And I am not understanding it because my thoughts on the flight home were, "Wait until I tell everybody what happened, how we really helped our guys and all the wonderful things that we did as medical people." But then things began to make sense to me. In the bus terminal, people were staring at me and giving me dirty looks. I expected the people to smile, like, "Wow, she was in Vietnam, doing something for her country—wonderful." I felt like I had walked into another country, not my country. So I went into the ladies room and changed.

When I got to Monterey I took the uniform out of my suitcase, threw   26
it to my friend and said, "Burn it." My friend said, "What about your medals? Don't you want to save your medals?" I said, "Fuck my medals." Now I regret it. Not that I want the medals, but it's something, you know, something that I was proud of, and nobody has the right to take that pride away. . . . That's what happened. The attitude took the pride away. I'm changing my feelings about it now; I am proud of having been over there, and I'm not afraid to admit that now—and I'm sorry I don't have that jacket.

I applied for work at the VA hospital. I remember I wanted to be around   27
Vietnam veterans. The director of nurses was impressed with my résumé, that I was an Army nurse in Vietnam, and I expected her to ask what nursing was like over there. Instead, she wanted to know about the dope addicts, and I'm saying, "What dope addicts?" She said, "Well, we understood there has been a lot of dope addiction in Vietnam—there is heroin, you know, and people are taking it like water." It hadn't hit my brain yet what was going on—that they were making a big deal about dope addicts in Vietnam. They weren't talking about the guys that had their legs blown off, you know, the guys that had their faces blown off—no, they're talking about dope addicts. Dope addicts were, like, a real small percentage. The media made a big deal about it, and the people needed that reason to attack the war even more. I was really angry. I had to have a physical exam before starting work, and the woman who was doing the EKG said to me, "We don't like working here. They are all old men, and it's very depressing. You don't want a job here." And I don't know why this woman said that to me, but I was so lost and confused that I thought, "Well, there must be some reason for this. Okay, I will take her advice." So I didn't take the job.

Instead, I went to another hospital, a large hospital in San Francisco. I   *28*
was interviewed by the director of nurses, who again was impressed by the
résumé, and who again asked me about the dope addicts. I took the job and
was in charge of about thirty-five patients. I had one aide, who was not
allowed to write in the charts, so I had to do her charts and my charts.
Sometimes, if I was lucky, I'd get an LVN, who was allowed to write in the
charts and save me some time, but her hands were tied on other things that
my corpsmen could have done in Vietnam. I was the type of nurse that, when
a patient was going into surgery the next day, I felt it was very important to
sit down and talk to them and educate them, as well as alleviate their fears.
That was my belief as a nurse. I was always behind in my work, and I said to
a nurse after about two months, "This place is overworking me. I'm not
getting the cooperation and staff I should be getting, and I'll be damned if
I'm going to give poor nursing care." So I quit.

I had some money saved from Vietnam and thought I could live off   *29*
that. Around that time I was starting to hit the bars, looking for Vietnam vets,
drinking a lot, and doing things that weren't really me. I was caught up in the
bar scene. It was better than sitting home and crying all the time. If you are
an attractive woman, you can go into a bar and there will always be somebody
to talk to. You can depend on it. And that's what I needed, another human
being to talk to.

I had met a GI in Hong Kong when I was on leave, and we became   *30*
chummy. He came to see me a few times in Vietnam, and it was a nice
friendship. Around Christmastime I sent him a card, 'cause I could remember
how it was at Christmas in Vietnam. In fact, even today, Christmas is depressing for me. Our letters became serious, and we agreed to continue our friendship when he came home four months later. Then I thought maybe the
full-time job had been too much for me right off the bat, maybe I needed to
just take a part-time job. So I went to work at a blood bank, taking plasma.
Most of the donors were alcoholics and deadbeats out of the Tenderloin
district. I really got attached to the guys, and looking back on it, it was like
being around Vietnam vets, 'cause they were guys dealing with a very depressing situation, being very lighthearted and joking around just like the guys did
in Vietnam. And when I'd walk through Union Square on my way to work,
all the drunks would go, "Hey, Lily, how are you?" They were all my guys
from the blood bank.

My friend came back from Nam, and we decided we would stick to-   *31*
gether. We thought the same way, saw the world the same way, and we became
very supportive of each other. He went back to the company he worked for
before he was drafted, and they said they had no job for him in California,
but would he go to Houston, Texas. He asked me, "How would you like to
go to Houston?" and I said, "All my life I've wanted to be in San Francisco,
and now we're going to Houston?" But I thought, "What the hell, I'm killing
myself in San Francisco.". . . . I had this gut instinct that this guy was going
to keep me going. So we went to Houston. Considering all the crazy things

that were going on, our relationship was very sound, and we went ahead and got married.

My husband was pretty well settled in his job, and I decided to work at the Texas Medical Center with Dr. Cooley, the famous heart surgeon. They were impressed by my background and put me into the recovery room ICU, which is similar to Vietnam's recovery ICU. There was a lot of action; I liked it. But I started to realize that it wasn't like Vietnam. There was a lot of competition between doctors and nurses, doctors and doctors, et cetera. There would be a cardiac arrest, and everybody would want to be in on it. In Nam, if someone was under cardiac arrest, whoever was there with the patient did it. And whoever was good at it. . . . For example, there was a sergeant there who was good at heart massage, and he was so good at it, that everyone would move out of his way so he could do it. . . . There wasn't the hierarchy. I was going to classes to learn more about the EKG monitor, and I wasn't able to retain anything new. I became very self-conscious of my nursing skills; I was losing my confidence. I would know this person was going into cardiac arrest and yet not be sure. . . . In Nam, you know, if I said, "Something's wrong with this patient—I'm not feeling right about him," the doctor would work on him until we figured out what it was. A lot of it was gut feeling, and we all trusted each other's gut feelings. Yet here, in intensive care, I'd say, "Something's wrong. I can't pinpoint it, but something is wrong." And I'd get, "Well, I haven't got time to check this out. If you can't figure out what it is . . ." This was the attitude that I couldn't understand. 32

I'd wake up in the morning and cry. I didn't want to go to work. My husband would say, "Well, go find another job." I'd say, "No, I've gotta work at this job until I figure out why I can't do what I could do in Nam." I thought maybe I should get out of intensive care and find something simpler. So I worked for a small hospital as a float nurse, and I got along fine at that job; it helped my ego. When people heard that I had lasted for eight months at the other place, they were saying, "How could you last eight months? The usual rotation is about three." So I started to feel a little bit better. 33

My husband was transferred back to San Francisco, and I got another job as a float nurse there. I found myself getting bored after a while because I was perfecting each floor: I was dying for a challenge. I was finding that I wasn't happy with nursing anymore; it was different. 34

I decided to get pregnant, and when I was seven and a half months pregnant, I had toxemia of pregnancy. Went into the hospital, found out I was carrying twins, and one died in uterus. They did an emergency c-section because I was having water in the lungs and my kidneys shut down. I had high blood pressure—something like 280 over 180. They told me the twins died because they had a problem among themselves, that my problem was unrelated to theirs. They did autopsies and found that one twin had some liver damage so . . . we accepted that. I went into a heavy depression. I felt that life was really against me, and for eight months did nothing but sleep twenty-one hours a day. My husband couldn't get me out of it. A neighbor of mine who 35 had had a miscarriage started to bang on the door and made me get out of bed. Then she would come in and dance all around and make me get dressed and drag me outside and tell me that life is really beautiful . . . "Look at the sunshine and the flowers." . . . and she got me out of it.

My husband and I put our heads together, and he encouraged me to go to school. I had the GI Bill. At the same time, we found out that I was pregnant with my daughter Erika. I went to junior college and discovered that I loved it. I loved geology, art, all the subjects that had nothing to do with nursing. I had a lot of fun, got good grades, and decided that psychology might be an interesting subject to get involved in—it appealed to me a lot. I went to San Francisco State University and decided to get my master's in psychology. Got pregnant again with my son, Daniel. He was okay when he was born, but we started having problems with him when we started putting him on solid food at four months. At eight months he had to have a temporary colostomy; 50 percent of his intestines did not have nerve cells. When he was twelve months old, he had 50 percent of his large intestine removed and had what you call a pull-through, with the good intestine pulled down and attached to his rectum. . . . We are still having medical problems with him. His surgeon explained that this condition was familial, but we could not find anyone in either of our families that suffered from this defect. A geneticist friend of mine explained that this condition was genetic. It wasn't until later that I realized the key to this problem could be Agent Orange.

Around that time, my husband had a job change and we were transferred to Hawaii. I thought it was a good omen, because Hawaii would be a real healthy place for Daniel, and I needed a change in geography. And Hawaii has been a healthy place for my son. We moved there during the Iranian crisis, the summer of 1980. Within a few months there were three or four helicopters flying around where we lived, and we didn't live near the military bases. They started to freak me out. I'd run outside, and my kids would run out with me to find out where Mommy was going. I found myself figuring out if it was going to be a good case or a bad case, how to be ready, then realizing after a while that they weren't going to land because I wasn't in Nam. . . . I had seen the ads about the vet center, so I called them, and a guy answered and I felt, "If he rejects me, I don't know what I'm going to do." But this guy said to me, "You're a woman vet—we've been looking for you!" That made me feel really good. So he connects me to a woman, and I said, "Are you a Vietnam vet?" She said, "No, I'm a psychologist and I work here." I said, "I want to talk to a Vietnam vet that knows what I'm talking about." I felt insulted. But then she was saying the right things to me, and I started explaining that we had just moved there and the choppers were getting to me . . . and she had me crying, and I was becoming hysterical on the phone. It was the first time I allowed myself to do that type of thing. She said, "Come down." I said, "Well, I have a child." She said, "You can bring him down, come down." . . . And I said, okay, but I didn't. Then the helicopters would come around, and

36

37

I'd call and talk to her some more. It took five phone calls before I felt comfortable enough to go down.

Around this time the whole issue of the hostages quieted down, and they were coming home. I remember seeing them getting into cars and seeing all the yellow ribbons and the wonderful reception they got, and I was really happy for them. Then, in the middle of all this, I said, "Wait a minute. What the fuck did they do? They sat around for four hundred and some odd days reading magazines, and I worked my ass off three hundred and sixty-five days saving lives. . . . They are getting this homecoming, and I got beat up, psychologically beat up." I was so angry! I found out that a lot of other vets were flipping out too, and that I was one of many that were going to the vet center on account of the incident.   38

That is when I got some one-to-one counseling and talked into doing a rap group. They promised that they would make it safe so that the men would understand where I was coming from. The men were very understanding. It's just that when it came time for me to talk about my experiences, they tended to change the subject. I just got the sense that they couldn't deal with it. Because you've got to understand, these guys would see their buddies all messed up in the field, and they'd say good-bye to them on the helicopter and not know what happened to them. I ended up taking care of the end results. . . . And I don't think they wanted to know about that.   39

It was around the same time—it was a coincidence, or I think that sometimes things are supposed to happen—there was an article in *Ms* magazine. "Please write to Lynda Van Devanter. She is interested in research on women veterans." I didn't have the time to write her a letter, you know, with these two kids running around, and there was so much I had to say, so I did a tape. I told her a little story here and a little story there and basically about what it was like to be a woman in Nam. About a week or so later I got a call, and it was Lynda calling from Washington, D.C. She said, "I got your tape, and I could have done the same exact tape." We talked and talked, and I started to realize that it wasn't me, wasn't my personality, I wasn't getting crazy, it was something that was happening to other people and that it was a reaction to our experience in Nam. I was getting validation that what I had gone through was real heavy shit, no matter what the combat vets said, and my reaction to it was normal. Then she said, "Well, how is your health?" And I said, "Oh, okay, I guess. I had acne and a breast tumor a couple of years after I came back. I had a couple of twins that died, and my son was born with a birth defect." She says, "Have you ever heard about Agent Orange?" I thought, "Oh, my God, that's the answer to all this stuff. Now it makes sense to me."   40

Then I read in the newspaper how a bill in Texas had been passed to create research in Agent Orange and to provide genetic counseling. I thought, "This is what we need," so I sent the article to the representative of our state. She wrote me this beautiful letter back. She had, in fact, just come back from   41

Texas, had met Representative Shaw, who was the person who had pushed the bill through, and she was very interested in it. She got a powerful senator to introduce the bill. I was introduced to another powerful person, who said, "Do you know what you are doing?" And I said, "No, I don't know what I am doing. . . . Lobby, what is that?" I thought, "Write a letter to your representative, they introduce the bill, and that was it." I didn't know anything. Apparently it was a very important bill to this man too, because he sat with me and told me what to do and who to see. I lobbied people, and he kind of helped out. . . . Apparently I was able to convince a lot of people to support the bill. I had wonderful support from representatives and senators I had lobbied with—not promising me anything, but really looking into things. After hearing my testimony—I talked about the health problems, about my knee joint pains and how I've yet to find a doctor that can help that out: I can't climb stairs, I can't hike or bike, and my family is so used to stopping at the top of a flight of stairs to wait for me, they just automatically do it now. And about how Daniel got adhesions and one third of his small bowel was removed, and he almost died on us—the bill passed.

It was very hard for me. There was a lot of stress, but there were a lot 42 of people that helped me out and kept me going. And my husband supported me the most—he was just wonderful. The governor signed the bill, and I had a chat with him—changed his view about Vietnam vets, and he told me that. I got involved with other vets and coordinated a ceremony at the National Cemetery at Punchbowl on Memorial Day for all those killed or missing in Vietnam. Found myself getting very involved with the issues and feeling good about it. Then the governor's office got in contact with me. They had received a letter about the national salute for Vietnam veterans to be held in November. He asked me to be the state coordinator. I said, "I'd love it, because I'm thinking about going and I don't want to be in that parade by myself."

I remember the first night at the salute in Washington, D.C. The dele- 43 gation arrived, and I said, "Let's go see the memorial." A couple of guys said, "Yeah, let's go," and this was twelve midnight, but everybody was just so up and excited about being there and having the salute happen to us. We went to the Wall and found two candles burning, reflecting off of it, and it was just beautiful. The next day we went down to Arlington Cemetery, and there were Vietnam vets all over the place. They were all in jeans and fatigues and beards, and it felt wonderful to be there. Jan Scruggs got up, and we were all cheering (this was supposed to be a solemn ceremony). We were getting dirty looks from the World War II vets. Then Weinberger got up and said, "If we have to get into another war, we are going to make sure the country backs its soldiers." And everyone went nuts again. I remember thinking, "It's starting to happen. . . . Good stuff is starting to happen." Then they had the twenty-one-gun salute, and everybody was hitting the bushes, and we were all laughing because part of the humor of it was the fact that everybody else was doing the same thing.

That night at the Wall was interesting for me. I looked at it and thought, 44

"I don't know any of the names except one." It was too dark, and I thought, "I'll never find his name." Then I did a real strange thing. I rubbed my hand along the memorial and ran from one side of it to the other, and by the time I got to the other end I was totally hysterical and crying. I realized I hurt for *all* of them. . . . I felt I took care of *all* of them. I got so much out. It was dark, and nobody could see me. It was the first time I really got the mourning, the grief, out. I bought a big candle and brought it back for my friend that died over there. I found some women's names. I saw people leaving things at the memorial, pictures and what have you. So it was really up and down for me. I did want to meet someone that served with me at the 12th Evac, I wanted that. I wanted to find someone from the dog scout unit, just to say, "If it wasn't for you, I would have gone insane those first few months." And I wanted to run into some patients of mine who were amputees to see how they were doing. And my wishes came true. I was hanging around VVA for a while with Lynda, answering phones. It was totally crazy, and who gets on the phone but this woman that I had known at the 12th Evac, Sharon. I said, "Please come up." And she said, "Well, I was thinking about it, but now that you are there, I'm going to come." I was so happy to see her!

When we had the unit reunions at the hotel, there were Vietnam vets 45 all over the place. Various men would come up to me and say, "Hey, you're a nurse!" They'd give me this big hug and say, "I love what you did for me. It doesn't matter if you were my nurse or not; I loved you!" We were getting all of this positive feedback, meeting people who knew what it was all about, and I was in seventh heaven. Then this guy comes up to me and says, "Where were you at?" I said, "The Twelfth Evac." And he said, "When?" I said, "Sixty-nine and seventy." He said, "I got hit in seventy. I knew that I knew you!" And I said, "I just don't remember you." He said, "I know you, I know you! You took care of me!" I said, "Well, maybe I did." So we talked for a while, and then he put his cane down and said, "Watch this," and he walks down the hallway. I'm looking at him and thinking, "So, he's walking." He turned around and came towards me, and I said, "Are you a double amp?" He said, "Yes, ma'am." And he told me his story. And I hugged him and said, "You are beautiful!" This whole scene was going on between us like a love scene. Even though I didn't remember him, I thought, "It really doesn't matter. I need this guy, and he needs me. . . . Just enjoy it." He had this half-dead rose in his boonie hat, and he took it off and said, "This is for you." I still have it. It is something one of my patients gave me. A gift back. Then he pulled out an apple and cut some slices off, and I guess it was the best-tasting apple I ever ate. And we didn't want to part. It was wonderful.

Toward the end of the celebration, everybody was going home, and I 46 thought, "I have yet to find a dog scout," and I was a little disappointed. So I went back to the memorial for one last visit. I walked along, then stopped, and there was a picture of a dog scout with his dog, a big color picture. I just sat there and cried. This was the one I wanted. . . . It wasn't a live human being, but it was my connection, and I got that. I knew that this guy was here, and I wrote down the panel number, so that the next time I go there I can pay my respects to him for the way his unit took care of me.

Then I came home, and my husband and my kids met me. My husband   47 said, "Welcome home," which, I found out later on, was a common response. And I said, "Yeah, I'm finally coming home." They each had a lei. My daughter had a red flower lei, my son had a white flower lei, and my husband, a blue one: red, white, and blue leis . . . So I guess that's . . . I want to end on a happy note.

Questions and Assignments

1. Interview a Vietnam veteran. Learn from this person his or her perspective on the war: When did she or he serve? Where (bring a map of Vietnam to the interview)? For how long? What role did she or he play? What are his or her feelings about the war and about those who protested? How was she or he received when the tour of duty was over? What was the hardest adjustment when he or she returned home? Share your interview with your class.
2. What does Adams mean when she says, "The attitude took the pride away."
3. Describe Adams's homecoming and her view of the homecomings of other Vietnam veterans. Contrast this with the homecoming of Desert Storm troops. Why was there a difference? Are Vietnam veterans justified in feeling bitter about the lack of support this country appeared to offer? Why or why not?
4. Compare Adams's experience during and after the war with the story of the Vietnam veteran that you interviewed. How are their stories similar? Different? What new insights have these two people given you regarding that time in our history?

SHERRY GERSHON GOTTLIEB
from *Hell No, We Won't Go!*

> *"Who is this descendant of the slave masters to order a descendant of slaves to fight other people in their own country?"*—Muhammad Ali
>
> *Sherry Gershon Gottlieb became interested in the subject of draft evasion while she was in college in the late sixties. Over the years she gathered stories of men who resisted the Vietnam draft and decided to put them into a book in 1986. In the preface Gottlieb states, "The reader has the right to know the perspective of the guide as this volume does not present all views on draft evasion during the Vietnam War. I do not pretend to be objective on the subject. I have been a pacifist since childhood, a position that, in some cases, I have found intellectually indefensible, yet morally imperative. War will cease when Mankind refuses to fight."*
>
> *Sherry Gershon Gottlieb lives in Santa Monica, California.*

Before and as You Read

1. Talk with a person who protested against the Vietnam War. What were the reasons behind the protest? What did this person do? Did he or she encounter any danger while protesting? How does she or he feel about those actions today?
2. Examine your feelings about people who resist being drafted. What accommodations should governments make, if any, for those who choose not to serve in the military when they are called to do so? Why would governments resist making such accommodations?
3. Ali says, ". . . this is the biggest victory of my life. I've won something that's worth whatever price I have to pay." As you read the following, make note of what he believes that victory to be. Is there more than one victory?
4. Just like the work of Berry and Walker, Gottlieb's work is an oral history "written" with a tape recorder. Why did these authors choose to edit and organize their material in the way that they did? What benefits does such a work have for the reader? What are some of the drawbacks?

WHY AM I resisting? My religion, of course, but what a politician told me in Chicago is true: I won't be barred from the Nation of Islam if I go into the Army. "Who are you to judge?" he had asked. All my life I've watched White America do the judging. But who is to judge now? Who is to say if this step I'm about to be asked to take is right or wrong? If not me, who else? I recall the words of the Messenger: "If you feel what you have decided to do is right, then be a man and stand up for it. . . . Declare the truth and die for it."

The lieutenant has finished with the man on my left and everybody seems to brace himself. The room is still and the lieutenant looks at me intently. He knows that his general, his mayor, and everybody in the Houston induction center is waiting for this moment. He draws himself up straight and tall.   *2*

Something is happening to me. It's as if my blood is changing. I feel fear draining from my body and a rush of anger taking its place.   *3*

I hear the politician again: "Who are you to judge?" But who is this white man, no older than me, appointed by another white man, all the way down from the white man in the White House? Who is he to tell me to go to Asia, Africa, or anywhere else in the world, to fight people who never threw a rock at me or America? Who is this descendant of the slave masters to order a descendant of slaves to fight other people in their own country?   *4*

Now I am anxious for him to call me. "Hurry up!" I say to myself. I'm looking straight into his eyes. There's a ripple of movement as some of the people in the room edge closer in anticipation.   *5*

"Cassius Clay—Army!"   *6*

The room is silent. I stand straight, unmoving. Out of the corner of my eye I see one of the white boys nodding his head at me, and thin smiles flickering across the faces of some of the blacks. It's as if they are secretly happy to see someone stand up against the power that is ordering them away from their homes and families.   *7*

The lieutenant stares at me a long while, then lowers his eyes. One of the recruits snickers and he looks up abruptly, his face beet-red, and orders all the other draftees out of the room. They shuffle out quickly, leaving me standing alone.   *8*

He calls out again: "Cassius Clay! Will you please step forward and be inducted into the Armed Forces of the United States?"   *9*

All is still. He looks around helplessly. Finally, a senior officer with a notebook full of papers walks to the podium and confers with him a few seconds before coming over to me. He appears to be in his late forties. His hair is streaked with gray and he has a very dignified manner.   *10*

"Er, Mr. Clay . . ." he begins. Then, catching himself, "Or Mr. Ali, as you prefer to be called."   *11*

"Yes, sir?"   *12*

"Would you please follow me to my office? I would like to speak privately with you for a few minutes, if you don't mind."   *13*

It's more of an order than a request, but his voice is soft and he speaks politely. I follow him to a pale-green room with pictures of Army generals on the walls. He motions me to a chair, but I prefer to stand. He pulls some papers from his notebook and suddenly drops his politeness, getting straight to the point.   *14*

"Perhaps you don't realize the gravity of the act you've just committed. Or maybe you do. But it is my duty to point out to you that if this should be your final decision, you will face criminal charges and your penalty could be five years in prison and ten thousand dollars fine. It's the same for you as it   *15* would be for any other offender in a similar case. I don't know what influenced you to act this way, but I am authorized to give you an opportunity to reconsider your position. Regulations require us to give you a second chance."

"Thank you, sir, but I don't need it." 16

"It is required." 17

I follow him back into the room. The lieutenant is still standing behind 18
the rostrum, ready to read the induction statement.

"Mr. Cassius Clay," he begins again, "you will please step forward and 19
be inducted into the United States Army." Again, I don't move.

"Cassius Clay—Army," he repeats. He stands in silence, as though he 20
expects me to make a last-minute change. Finally, with hands shaking, he gives
me a form to fill out. "Would you please sign this statement and give your
reasons for refusing induction?" His voice is trembling.

I sign quickly and walk out into the hallway. The officer who originally 21
ordered me to the room comes over. "Mr. Clay," he says with a tone of respect
that surprises me, "I'll escort you downstairs."

I keep walking with the officer who leads me to a room where my 22
lawyers are waiting. "You are free to go now," he tells us. "You will be contacted later by the United States Attorney's office."

I step outside and a huge crowd of press people rush towards me, pushing 23
and shoving each other and snapping away at me with their cameras.
Writers from two French newspapers and one from London throw me a
barrage of questions, but I feel too full to say anything. My lawyer, Hayden
Covington, gives them copies of a statement I wrote for them before I left
Chicago. In it, I cite my ministry and my personal convictions for refusing to
take the step, adding that "I strongly object to the fact that so many newspapers
have given the American public and the world the impression that I have only
two alternatives in taking this stand—either I go to jail or I go into the Army.
There is another alternative, and that is justice."

By the time I get to the bottom of the front steps, the news breaks. 24
Everyone is shouting and cheering. Some girls from Texas Southern run over
to me, crying, "We're glad you didn't go!" A black boy shouts out, "You don't
go, so I won't go!"

I feel a sense of relief and freedom. For the first time in weeks, I start 25
to relax. I remember the words of a reporter at the hotel: "How will you act?"
Now it's over, and I've come through it. I feel better than when I beat the
eight-to-ten odds and won the World Heavyweight title from Liston.

"You headin' for jail. You headin' straight for jail." I turn and an old 26
white woman is standing behind me, waving a miniature American flag. "You
goin' straight to jail. You ain't no champ no more. You ain't never gonna be
champ no more. You get down on your knees and beg forgiveness from God!"
she shouts in a raspy tone. I start to answer her, but Covington pulls me inside
a cab. She comes over to my window. "My son's in Vietnam, and you no
better'n he is. He's there fightin' and you here safe. I hope you rot in jail. I
hope they throw away the key."

The judge who later hears my case reflects the same sentiment. I receive   27
a maximum sentence of five years in prison and ten thousand dollars fine. The
prosecuting attorney argues, "Judge, we cannot let this man get loose, because
if he gets by, all black people will want to be Muslims and get out for the
same reasons."

Four years later, the Supreme Court unanimously reverses that decision,   28
8–0, but now this is the biggest victory of my life. I've won something that's
worth whatever price I have to pay. It gives me a good feeling to look at the
crowd as we pull off. Seeing people smiling makes me feel that I've spoken for
them as well as myself. Deep down, they didn't want the World Heavyweight
Champion to give in, and in the days ahead their strength and spirit will keep
me going. Even when it looks like I'll go to jail and never fight again.

"They can take away the television cameras, the bright lights, the money,   29
and ban you from the ring," an old man tells me when I get back to Chicago,
"but they can't destroy your victory. You have taken a stand for the world and
now you are the people's champion."

MUHAMMAD ALI

*Muhammad Ali refused induction on April 28, 1967. On that day, he
was stripped of the title of World Heavyweight Champion and was barred
from fighting in the United States. He was sentenced to five years in prison.
Free on bond, he appealed to the United States Supreme Court, which
reversed his conviction in 1971.*

Topics for Discussion and Writing

1. Write a lively dialogue between John Saddic (interviewed by Henry Berry
   in *Hey, Mac, Where Ya Been?*) and Muhammad Ali. Be sure not to overlook
   the points that they have in common. Can these men respect one another?
   Defend your answer with evidence from their stories.

2. How did Ali set the stage for the drama to unfold? List some of the phrases
   that he uses to capture his listener's imagination. Think about a dramatic
   incident in your life that you can describe in a two- or three-page essay.
   Focus on language and descriptive details to heighten the drama of the
   moment. Share your work.

3. Why do you suppose that Muhammad Ali was offered only two choices:
   military service or jail? Why was he not granted the alternative of conscientious objector with alternative service? Why was it important for the
   government and media to make an example of him? What purpose did it
   serve the government? What purpose did it serve the media?

4. On January 21, 1977, President Carter issued a blanket pardon for draft
   resisters. Why was this action important? Why was the date of this action
   so significant?

ANDREW MYERS

"What I Did on My Summer Vacation"

". . . I was soaked and exhausted and if I squinted my eyes just right I thought I could see Death riding shotgun on a pale horse."

Andrew Myers was an undergraduate student in Professor Patricia Snell's advanced composition class at George Mason University when this essay was written about his summer of 1990.

Before and as You Read

1. Why did Myers choose this title for this piece?
2. The experiences that we accept for ourselves are not always pleasant or without some pain. As you read this selection consider what Myers is gaining by going through boot camp. Do you think that what he is gaining is worth what he is suffering? Does *he* think that what he is gaining is worth what he is suffering?
3. As you read, mark examples of how Myers uses irony and humor to engage his readers. How does this enhance his essay?
4. As you read, write down your impressions of Myers's boot camp. What is the reasoning behind this type of training? Would you be willing to join? Why or why not?

IT WAS the summer of 1990, for reasons that escape me I found myself in Marine Corps boot camp, not liking it one bit.

I guess I never realized the extent of the danger I was in until the day my Senior drill instructor tried to break me. Suffice it to say, he never really did like me. Senior drill instructor Staff Sergeant Wilkins* was certifiably crazy, crazy like a fox. We were scared of him, 5'10", polished boots, pressed cammies, shaved head and an evil glint in his eyes. He heard, saw, smelled and perceived everything. No sooner did "crazy bastard" roll through your head than you felt a jackslap across the back of your bare skull enough to slosh your brain around. Our Senior was a walkin' talkin' goddamned jerk on speed. The other drill instructors were meaner and scarier to be sure. But it was your Senior that you had to please and when he was unhappy everybody was.

The other DIs would pick out a recruit for special "attention" and dog the hell out of him and it usually involved ME and whoever else had been stupid, careless, sleepy or not scared enough. But usually it was just business, they weren't doing it for personal pleasure unless you really pissed them off. Normal procedure would be to send you running to the pit or the quarterdeck

*pseudonym

and just have you jump up and down until you lay in a pool of your own sweat. Grovelling just made them madder. I became very familiar with the pit and the quarterdeck, both were places for punishment and education. The pit was a large square of hateful sand that clung to your body in every crevice after rolling in it for a while. The quarterdeck was just a space of concrete stained dark with sweat, situated in front of the DI's office. The Senior usually only pitted us when he was mad at us or to prove a point. As I began to say, I will never forget the day I was singled out for focused attention. Though there have been many days before and since when I have been extremely uncomfortable, never have I gone so close to the edge and turned back.

Dawn was many hours yet when we awoke to the vehement urging of   4
our drill instructors. The hated sun rose over Parris Island, Marine Corps Recruit Depot to find us humping along to our new home. Having completed about a third of its training the platoons of 1104–09 were now shifting to the barracks of the rifle range. At a leisurely pace (running speed) we carried every object that we owned and a few we didn't. A mere hundred pounds tends to cut off circulation badly in the shoulders and tends to cause pain. The powers that be decided that the distance between our barracks and the range wasn't sufficient on such a beautifully thick summer morning. It was decided that we should circle the Island first. Needless to say I was soaked and exhausted and if I squinted my eyes just right I thought I could see Death riding shotgun on a pale horse. Was it too much to ask to be left alone for a glorious rest of ten minutes or so? Apparently yes.

I have spent some time in afterthought wondering. I believe the reasons   5
for the rest of the day were as follows: (a) We were in a new barracks and they did not want us to get soft, loose or undisciplined; (b) It was the beginning of rifle training and it was their last chance to physically debilitate us without affecting rifle qualification scores; or (c) sheer malice. I believe a bit of all three with lots of (c).

So the circus of pain began. They had people pushing everywhere. "You   6
can't make a rack in ten seconds? Good. Good. Get on my quarterdeck now. Push ups, sidestraddle hops, push ups, run in place, push ups" . . . for hours. I lost track of time. I tried keeping track of the puddles of sweat I left as I moved position. I was no longer human, just some sort of battered piece of meat. The time came when I could do no more. I pushed up, muscles quivering, failing, no longer responding to my desperate orders. "Oh you don't want to do anymore do ya? You stinkin' friggin nasty thing. You just want to fuck your Senior Drill Instructor don't ya?" The Senior being gone, they took his campaign cover and put it under me." Go ahead, crush the Senior's cover, go ahead thing. Say it, fuck you Sir, Say it, Say it. NoSir! What? I can't hear you thing. NoSir!.". . . . and so it went for eternity.

That is until the Senior came back. He came to find the DIs playing   7
with their favorite toy and he could not resist the game. "So you want to fuck me and your platoon. Low crawl up the squadbay now," he said thrusting the

Guidon at me. The Guidon being a big stick with a flag on it, we held this in great reverence mainly because we'd get whacked with it if we didn't.

This is what I consider the bad part, whatever fate has in store for me the rest of my life it can not touch me for I have these moments. 8

So I crawled up and down the squadbay dragging the Guidon on the deck. With every lunge I yell "I am a buddy fucker. I am a back stabber." Shame and pain mixing in a virulent poison. "I am a buddy fucker, I am a backstabber." Leaving a snail trail of sweat on the cold, well-scrubbed deck. "I am a buddy fucker I am a back stabber." My platoon busy making racks on both sides stealing surreptitious embarrassed glances at me. "Glad it's not me. What did he do?" It went on forever and then it was over. I was back on line trying to perfect my rack, and keep out of trouble. I was still me, I had passed through the flames and survived. Later in life when my friends died and my ex-girlfriend had my daughter, nothing fazed me. I found I could deal with anything, for I had seen the elephant. 9

Topics for Discussion and Writing

1. Write a brief character sketch of Myers. What do you suppose made him join the marines? Does he seem to be ill-suited to what he is doing? If so, give examples. Is he a marine today? Why or why not?
2. Write a brief character sketch of the senior drill instructor. What personality characteristics would you expect such a man to have? Who is he? What is his background? Describe his family life. What are his fears? Does he feel guilty about anything? Does he enjoy his job? Explain.
3. How alike are Myers and John Saddic (in Henry Berry's *Hey, Mac, Where Ya Been?*) as Marines? As storytellers?
4. What does Myers mean when he says, "Later in life . . . nothing fazed me. I found I could deal with anything, for I had seen the elephant."

For Further Thought

1. Research a war that is not represented in this chapter. Try to find first-person accounts of that time. As we have done in this chapter, seek the perspectives of combatants, civilians, or representatives of different sides. What similarities do you note when you compare your research with the selections represented here?
2. It has been said that "Old men make wars that young men die in." Think about all possible ways that war might be averted between nations in crisis. What strategies might be put to use that would make peace a more attractive alternative? (You might discuss, for example, the Cuban Missile Crisis

of 1962, the Israeli Palestinian accords of 1993, or other peace negotiations occurring in various places in the world today.)

3. Obtain a biography of Mohandas Gandhi, Martin Luther King, Jr., or another pacifist. What was this person's philosophy? How did the person live his or her beliefs? How did she or he influence followers? Is this person's influence felt anywhere in the world today? Where? If the person is dead, when, how, and why did this person meet death?

4. Prepare with your class to debate a major issue of war. Some examples: What are the rights of conscientious objectors? Should women serve in combat? How much should the Pentagon cut its budget, and what levels of personnel, equipment, and so forth do we need to maintain necessary military strength? How might the military be conceived other than as a force to wage war?

CHAPTER NINE

What I Learned in School

Every chapter and every selection in this book concerns education. Everyone who speaks in this book proclaims what life in its myriad expressions has taught them. But we wish here to give special attention to that place in most societies where people, especially in their youth, are sent for the specific purpose of learning: school. That schools teach us "values," few would dispute, but there is much conflict over what values they are "supposed" to teach. Not only do schools frequently fail to define the values they purport to teach, they also often teach us very different lessons from what they intend. Sometimes people deliberately reject schools and their values; instead they seek "school" in other, less conventional places.

We have included diverse schools in this chapter: among them, public elementary and high schools, a school at home, private and religious schools, a university, and schools without walls—schools formed by students' search for wisdom and by those, old and young, who teach them. As everywhere in *A Sense of Value,* we present these places through the words of those who have learned, been transformed by the experience, and been moved to write their lives for many readers.

Thinking about the Issues

1. Write about your earliest school experience. (Your writing should help uncover "forgotten" memories.) What stands out for you? Why do you feel this event made such a powerful impression on you? In what ways do you feel that this early schooling shaped the person you are today?

2. If you are a student at present, write about your current schooling. Find in particular any statements of goals or guiding principles published by the school you attend (and by the teachers you currently have). In what ways do you feel that the school and the classes you take live up to those stated values? In what ways do they fall short? Explore your current school

experience for other values that are unstated but nonetheless taught by your current school experience.

3. Put the shoe on the other foot: Write about your own teaching of others. If you have taught in any setting, formal or informal (such as coaching, tutoring, or teaching a child), consider what you said you were trying to accomplish. Consider also what you did not say, but that your actions and attitude taught. If you had a chance to teach in that situation over again, what would you try to do differently?

HARVEY ARDEN

from *Wisdomkeepers*

> *"We went out two journalists after a good story. We came back two 'runners'*
> *from another world, carrying an urgent message from the Wisdomkeepers."*
>
> *So writes Harvey Arden, who has written articles for* National Geo-
> graphic *for 24 years, and who currently serves as one of* Geographic's *senior*
> *writers. In 1990, Arden and noted photographer Steve Wall published* Wis-
> domkeepers: Meetings with Native American Spiritual Elders, *from*
> *which we reprint the Foreword, one brief chapter, and the Epilogue.*

Before and as You Read

1. Have you ever encountered a stranger who influenced you so strongly that
   you decided to follow this person's example or obey this person's request
   rather than pursue what you had thought were your goals? Reflect on this
   question and write about such an experience. If you have not had such an
   experience, try to recall another person who has. What did this person say
   to you? What was your reaction to this person's words? As you read these
   excerpts from *Wisdomkeepers,* pay particular attention to what Arden writes
   about his meeting with "the Gatekeeper."

2. If you are a Native American, write about the idea of the elder. If you
   have met an elder, write about those meetings. How are this person's values
   different from those of most others you know? In what situations is this
   person held in respect? Are there situations in which this person is not
   respected?

3. If you are not Native American, what is your experience of Native Americans? Be sure to distinguish in your thinking between your direct experience and anything you might have read, heard, or seen about Native
   Americans. Note that since *Native American* and *American Indian* are terms
   that encompass many peoples, and since these peoples are as diverse in
   appearance as the rest of the population, it's likely that you know more
   Native Americans than you are probably aware of.

       For more information, read the selections by Katsi Cook and Mari
   Sandoz in chapter 5 and the selection by N. Scott Momaday in this chapter.

4. Contemplate the future. When you visualize the future, what do you see?
   In particular, whom do you see? Do you think of yourself, in the decisions
   you make, as living for those in the future? Write about this idea. Have
   you made any recent decisions that show your concern for those who will
   come after you? As you read this selection, attend to ways in which the
   people who speak in these pages regard the future. How is their decision
   making different from and similar to yours?

FOREWORD

JUST OFF the map, beyond the Interstates, out past the power lines   *1*
and the shopping malls, up that little side road without a sign on it,
lies the land of the Wisdomkeepers. Hidden from the mainstream of contemporary life, these living treasures of traditional Native America are revered among their people as the Elders, the Old Ones, the Grandfathers and the Grandmothers—the fragile repositories of ancient ways and sacred knowledge going back millenniums. They don't preserve it. They live it.

We knew little about such things when the man we now call the Gate-   *2*
keeper approached us in late 1981. We were in western North Carolina, working on an unrelated magazine article, and found ourselves talking to a local landowner in his horse pasture one afternoon. We'd just asked him if he knew any interesting local "characters" for the article, and he mentioned an Indian, a Cherokee medicine man, whom he thought we might find interesting. Even as he was speaking, the Cherokee slid his battered blue pickup to a halt in front of us, emerged from the billowing dust, and with surprising nimbleness for a full-bellied man vaulted the barbed-wire fence to present his outstretched hand in greeting.

At first, in spite of his smiles and outward good humor, there seemed   *3*
something vaguely menacing about him. His smile had a way of fading suddenly, revealing an underlying expression that was half angry, half sad. Not much was said at that first meeting. We found ourselves avoiding his eyes. Drawing back, we exchanged pleasantries and said goodbye, not expecting to see him again. But, then, wherever we went over the next few days, it seemed he was already there—or would turn up shortly after we had arrived—always friendly, always ready to talk. His appearances were uncanny. Eventually we got over our inhibitions, our inner uncertainties. This man wasn't looking for small talk. He had something on his mind—and in some unfathomable way, we two unlikely white journalists had something to do with it. What was bothering him finally surfaced.

He was a "middle-level" medicine man, primarily an herbalist. He had   *4*
studied with two famous modern medicine men—Amonyeeta Wolf Sequoyah of the Cherokee and Josie Billie of the Seminole. Both, alas, had died in recent months. He recalled that Amonyeeta, just before his death, had invited him to become a disciple, so he could pass on everything he knew—but, feeling inadequate, he had declined. When Amonyeeta abruptly died, the Gatekeeper was swept by a wave of remorse. As a kind of penance, he took it upon himself to make a journey—a spirit-journey—to the Grandfathers and Grandmothers of other Indian nations around the country. He would sit at their knees and learn from them whatever they cared to share.

"I'm no photographer or writer. I believe you two guys have been   *5*
chosen to do it." The Cherokee's words, like seeds, took root in us, and the idea was born of a journey into Native America in search of the Grandfathers and Grandmothers—the Wisdomkeepers. At first we thought the Cherokee

himself would lead us into that mystic labyrinth, but we were wrong. Yes, he would be going on such a spirit-journey, he told us, but he would be going alone, going down his own path. For us, he was only the Gatekeeper, not the Guide. He had shown the Way. It was up to us to follow it.

So began an odyssey that continues to this day. Traveling across the land for nearly ten years now, we have sought out the spiritual Elders of more than a score of Native American nations: Lakota, Iroquois, Seminole, Ojibway, Hopi, Ute, Pawnee, Shinnecock, Hoh, Lumbee, and others. We have met them on their sacred soil, entered their homes and lives, and discovered the infinite riches of their friendship. Not being "Indian experts" may have been our greatest strength. Had we been anthropologists or sociologists or, heaven help us, "ethnohistorians," we would likely have been thrown out on our ears more than a few times. We asked for no "secrets," only for whatever they cared to share with us. Quite beyond our expectations, they revealed their inmost thoughts and feelings, their dreams and visions, their healing remedies and apocalyptic prophecies, and, above all, their humanity—which shines through every page of *Wisdomkeepers.*   6

What began as a journalistic project became a mission. Each Wisdom-keeper bestowed on us some special gift of understanding, some indelible experience. From each we came back enriched. Wisdomkeepers, we learned, are not necessarily "old." Several of the acknowledged spiritual or political leaders of their people are still in their forties and fifties. Others even younger are coming after them. We learned that our Cherokee Gatekeeper had been wrong in one thing: The Grandfathers and Grandmothers may be dying—as inevitably they must—but they are emphatically *not* dying out. As we learned from Eddie Benton-Banai, fourth-level Midewiwin priest of the Ojibway, "The Grandfathers and the Grandmothers are in the children—whose faces are coming from beneath the ground!"   7

We are changed. We have been seized and shaken. We went out two journalists after a good story. We came back two "runners" from another world, carrying an urgent message from the Wisdomkeepers.   8

This book is that message.   9

LEILA FISHER: HOH

After a two-hour drive through the misty, darkly beautiful rain forest of Washington State's Olympic Peninsula, we come to the Hoh Indian reservation—a mere 443 acres perched at the edge of the Pacific. Just before the two-lane blacktop gives out onto the beach, we stop and knock at the door of a small frame house. "Come on in!" calls a woman's voice. Within, in the sparsely furnished living room, Hoh Elder Leila Fisher sits in a well-worn armchair, her fingers deftly weaving one of the straw baskets she's noted for.   10

She can't imagine why two strangers would want to talk to her, and she suggests we go out on the beach where a feast and powwow has just begun. Through the open windows we can hear the sound of a faraway drum and distant voices singing.

"They're singing songs of the earth," Leila says. "I'm too weak to go out *11* there with them, but I love hearing the children's voices sing those songs. I helped teach them, you know. They're my children. All children are my children. I teach them the songs and whatever else I can. That's what Grandmothers are for—to teach songs and tell stories and show them the right berries to pick and roots to dig. And also to give them all the love they can stand. No better job in the world than being a Grandmother! Now you boys get out there before the food's all gone—but before you go I'll tell you just one little story. It's one of my favorites—and it's true."

How Wisdom Comes

"Did you ever wonder how wisdom comes?" Without taking her hands *12* from her weaving or even looking up to see if we're listening, she continues: "There was a man, a postman here on the reservation, who heard some of the Elders talking about receiving objects that bring great power. He didn't know much about such things, but he thought to himself that it would be a wonderful thing if he could receive such an object—which can only be bestowed by the Creator. In particular, he heard from the Elders that the highest such object a person can receive is an eagle feather. He decided that was the one for him. If he could just receive an eagle feather he would have all the power and wisdom and prestige he desired. But he knew he couldn't buy one and he couldn't ask anyone to give him one. It just had to come to him somehow by the Creator's will."

"Day after day he went around looking for an eagle feather. He figured *13* one would come his way if he just kept his eyes open. It got so he thought of nothing else. That eagle feather occupied his thoughts from sunup to sundown. Weeks passed, then months, then years. Every day the postman did his rounds, always looking for that eagle feather—looking just as hard as he could. He paid no attention to his family or friends. He just kept his mind fixed on that eagle feather. But it never seemed to come. He started to grow old, but still no feather. Finally, he came to realize that no matter how hard he looked he was no closer to getting the feather than he had been the day he started."

"One day he took a break by the side of the road. He got out of his *14* little jeep mail-carrier and had a talk with the Creator. He said: 'I'm so tired of looking for that eagle feather. Maybe I'm not supposed to get one. I've spent all my life thinking about that feather. I've hardly given a thought to my family and friends. All I cared about was that feather, and now life has just about passed me by. I've missed out on a lot of good things. Well, I'm giving up the search. I'm going to stop looking for that feather and start living.

Maybe I have time enough left to make it up to my family and friends. Forgive me for the way I have conducted my life.'"

"Then—and only then—a great peace came into him. He suddenly felt   15
better inside than he had in all these years. Just as he finished his talk with the Creator and started getting back in his jeep, he was surprised by a shadow passing over him. Holding his hands over his eyes, he looked up into the sky and saw, high above, a great bird flying over. Almost instantly it disappeared. Then he saw something floating down ever so lightly on the breeze—a beautiful tail feather. It was his eagle feather! He realized that the feather had come not a single moment before he had stopped searching and made his peace with the Creator.

"That postman is still alive and he's a changed person. People come to   16
him for wisdom now and he shares everything he knows. Even though now he has the power and the prestige he searched for, he no longer cares about such things. He's concerned about others, not himself. So now you know how wisdom comes."

Epilogue: Unto the Seventh Generation

Our journey into Native America began with a heavy burden of mis-   17
conceptions and stereotypes—gleaned from history books, movie Westerns, and popular myths ingrained in the psyche from an earlier "Manifest Destiny" mentality. What we thought we were going out to "discover" turned out to be far different from what we found. We uncovered no "secrets," no soul-bewitching gurus, no miraculous healers, no hitherto unknown sacred ceremonies. Life itself, we learned, is a sacred ceremony. From the Wisdomkeepers we learned a different way of thinking, which profoundly affected our views about the Earth, about sovereignty, about family and community, and about the future.

The future, we learned, was not some abstract, untouchable "Beyond"   18
far out there somewhere, beyond our ken. Rather, the Wisdomkeepers taught us, the future is with us here today, in the Now and Here. It's coming up, in fact, right behind us. Over and over we were told: Turn around and look, there they are, the Seventh Generation—they're coming up right behind you. "Look over your shoulder," Tadodaho Leon Shenandoah told us.

This immediate and compassionate approach to the future was a revela-   19
tion to us, moving us from a mental position to which we can never return. We came to realize that we ourselves, in all of our decisions—individually and collectively—are responsible for, and to, the generations "whose faces are coming from beneath the ground." They will soon be walking the same earthly path we walk today, and we must ensure that there is a path to walk. We hope that we'll leave a better path than the one left to us.

Contrary to the popular notion that the traditional circle is dying away,   *20*
we saw emerging Wisdomkeepers in action. Spiritual Elder Leila Fisher of the
Hoh died in 1986. During a recent kitchen-table conversation that lasted into
the wee hours of the morning and took us through many cups of strong black
coffee, Leila's daughter, Mary Leitka, spoke of her mother.

"Mom always told me I would have to prepare myself, and she said she   *21*
would help me. But when she died it seemed she'd never really gotten around
to properly instructing me. She knew so much and I know so little. Yet I'm
hearing her words over and over in my thoughts. She said there are two ways
to go: the way of the Black Face—a society within our culture—or another
way that is more personal—like going and bathing in the river every morning,
sitting and meditating at a special place. 'Merge into Nature,' she would say.
'Merge into the spirit of the river, of the eagle, of the salmon.' This way
would lead me to my power, or 'Help,' as we say."

During the funeral and the burning of all of Leila Fisher's personal   *22*
belongings (as is the custom of the Hoh so that there is nothing to hold the
one who has passed away to this world), Mary was told by the few remaining
family Elders that she was the one to sing her mother's song during the
proceedings. Mary adds, "It was my grandfather's song, and he passed it to my
mother. Pansy Hudson, an Elder, told me that I was to have the family song
after Mom died."

"Now everyone looks to me. I don't know why, and it's very hard on   *23*
me. They don't know where to turn, so they come to me like I'm supposed
to know what to do. I have seven children and all their friends come here.
Everyone is calling me 'Auntie.' They're welcome—but it's so hard. I'm at a
crossroads. I see what's happening, and I wish so much that Mom was here."

Before passing, Leila told Mary, "Take care of my grandchildren, all of   *24*
them." Today Mary is teaching the youth the ancient songs and dances, passing
along the stories of the Hoh which she learned in her own childhood. She
says, "Maybe it boils down to my accepting the idea that Mom really gave me
something and did prepare me all along through my life without my knowing
what she was doing."

One bright June day an entire Oneida clan climbed a hill near their   *25*
community in upstate New York. There was the Elder leading the way, and
behind him were his children, nieces and nephews, followed by grandchildren
and grandnieces and grandnephews—generation by generation, down to the
infants in traditional baby boards. Atop the hill they posed for a photograph
by "making circle," a traditional activity in which family members honor the
Elder by recognizing his or her central position in the family. Throughout our
travels in search of the Wisdomkeepers we kept seeing aspects of that same
sacred circle or sacred hoop—one of the fundamental symbols of Native
American culture.

There's the cycle or circle of the seasons, the circle of the ceremonies,   *26*
the family circle, the circle of the community, the circle of Elders, the cycle

of the generations, and the circle of all life, of which mankind is only one aspect—all things *one*.

Yes, we are changed. 27

Topics for Discussion and Writing

1. Reflect on the significance in *Wisdomkeepers* of the "seventh generation." For how many generations into the past do you have knowledge of members of your family? What decisions made by the earliest ancestor of which you have any knowledge have influenced the life you live today? If you consider U.S. history back "seven generations" (roughly 175 years), how is the American present the legacy of that time? Write in your journal in response to this question and share your speculations with others in your class.

2. What were Arden and Wall looking for? What did they find? When they say, "Yes, we are changed," what do you think they mean? What details in *Wisdomkeepers* help you answer these questions?

3. The book from which we have drawn this selection is a combination of writings and photographs. Obviously, we have reprinted only words. Review the text to find passages that you feel provide a good verbal "picture" of the people, places, or events. Also note passages that you wish were more visually described. Choose one such passage and add a description of how you imagine this person, place, or event. Compare your description with those of others who have done this assignment. What surprises you in their descriptions?

4. Note all the ways in which *teaching* and *learning* occur in this selection. Has education of the kinds portrayed here been important in your life? Explain.

5. Reread the sentence spoken by Leila Fisher's daughter that begins, "Merge into Nature. . . ." Try to imagine living one day of your life with the kind of consciousness that she describes in that sentence. How might your thinking change? What mental images that currently guide your thinking would have to be replaced if you were to think as she does?

N. SCOTT MOMADAY
from *The Names*

> *"When I turn my mind to my early life, it is the imaginative part of it that comes first and irresistibly into reach, and of that part I take hold."*
>
> *Born in 1934 in the Great Plains, Natachee Scott Momaday, a Kiowa Indian, grew up listening to the stories and songs of his grandparents and great-grandparents. To them and to his parents he gives credit for his own love of language, a love that has shown forth in such works as the novel* House Made of Dawn, *which won the Pulitzer Prize for 1968,* The Way to Rainy Mountain *(folktales),* The Gourd Dancer *(poems), and* The Names *(1976), his memoir of his early years. In* The Names, *from which we have reprinted portions of the Prologue and the final chapter, plus the Epilogue, Momaday writes what he calls "imaginative" autobiography, wherein he recounts the lives of his forebears as well as his own growing up in the Plains and in the desert Southwest.*

Before and as You Read

1. Consider the significance of names in your life. By what names, including nicknames or "pet" names, are you known to different people? Has anyone ever given you a name that you feel characterizes you best? Do you have a name that you feel imposes on you definite responsibilities? Write about these questions and discuss them with others. As you read the following excerpt, regard the significance of names in Momaday's memoir.
2. Consider the role of ritual in your life and in the life of the community. Focus on one family practice that has the status of ritual in your life. Describe it. Why is it important to you and others? What sacrifices do members make to fulfill this family ritual? Whom do you regard as the leader of the ritual? Now focus on a communal ritual in which you take part. Why do you participate? How would you feel if you did not? Specifically, what does this communal ritual teach you?
3. Momaday calls this memoir "an act of imagination." Before you read this selection, consider the role of your imagination in the autobiographical writing you have done as you've worked through this book. Has your imagination helped you achieve a stronger sense of reality as you've written? Find a writing of yours that you consider particularly "imaginative." Why do you regard it so?
4. As you read the following selection, watch for "turning points" in Momaday's experience. How does Momaday write about these influences on his life? When he says late in the selection, ". . . for some of them I have the names," what do you feel he means?
5. Observe that Momaday constructs his work as a series of stories of varying lengths, rather than as a single story with a smooth chronological flow from event to event. Note also that he does not often tell the reader what he

feels the story "means," but expects the reader to enter into the narrative just as he entered into the events he describes.

My name is Tsoai-talee. I am, therefore, Tsoai-talee; therefore I am.

The storyteller Pohd-lohk gave me the name Tsoai-talee. He believed that a man's life proceeds from his name, in the way that a river proceeds from its source.

In general my narrative is an autobiographical account. Specifically it is an act of the imagination. When I turn my mind to my early life, it is the imaginative part of it that comes first and irresistibly into reach, and of that part I take hold. This is one way to tell a story. In this instance it is my way, and it is the way of my people. When Pohd-lohk told a story he began by being quiet. Then he said Ah-keah-de, *"They were camping," and he said it every time. I have tried to write in the same way, in the same spirit. Imagine: They were camping.*

PROLOGUE

You know, everything had to begin, and this is how it was: the Kiowas came one by one into the world through a hollow log. They were many more than now, but not all of them got out. There was a woman whose body was swollen up with child, and she got stuck in the log. After that, no one could get through, and that is why the Kiowas are a small tribe in number. They looked all around and saw the world. It made them glad to see so many things. They called themselves **Kwuda,** *"coming out."*

Kiowa folk tale

THEY WERE stricken, surely, nearly blind in the keep of some primordial darkness. And yet it was their time, and they came out into the light, one after another, until the way out was lost to them. Loss was in the order of things, then, from the beginning. Their emergence was a small thing in itself, and unfinished. But it gave them to know that they were and who they were. They could at last say to themselves, "We are, and our name is *Kwuda*."   1

. . . The events of one's life take place, *take place*. How often have I used this expression, and how often have I stopped to think what it means? Events do indeed take place; they have meaning in relation to the things around them. And a part of my life happened to take place at Jemez. I existed in that landscape, and then my existence was indivisible with it. I placed my shadow   2 there in the hills, my voice in the wind that ran there, in those old mornings and afternoons and evenings. It may be that the old people there watch for me in the streets; it may be so.

Late in February the people of Jemez turned out to clear the irrigation ditches. The sun appeared at a notch on the skyline; beyond that there was no sign of the spring; the snow was old and frozen fast on the north sides of the dunes, and in the air you could tell of more snow to come. And at dawn there was a foot race. The race was run over a long distance, towards the town, on the old San Ysidro road. I saw the runners pass in front of the day school in the cold gray morning, running evenly, their breath visible on the dark air, stripped to their waists. They ran without effort, or the ordinary effort had been translated into extraordinary terms; the running was ceremonial, emphatic, and was itself the measure of time. There were long successions in it, the runners again and again bearing down upon the little cottonwood kick-stick, to place it on the broad, moccasined foot, to kick it high and away, wobbling in long arcs, running after it, not in a straight line along the road, but in zigzag lines across the road, back and forth; it is the way water rushes and dips, swirling along in the channels.

One day when the wind had got up and the weather had turned warm and the water was running fast I walked along the river, talking to myself and throwing stones against the bank opposite. After a time I was surprised to see many people coming from the village, in wagons, on horseback, and walking. I watched them come down to the crossing, a little way upstream from where I was standing, and I could not imagine what was going on. Then I saw my friend Eddie Loretto coming towards me on his horse. He pulled up and said to me, "Let's go; come with us." "Well, where?" I wanted to know. "Oh, we are going out to work. Come, help us." It was all right with me—I had nothing better to do, and I was very curious—and I climbed up on the horse behind Eddie and we followed after the others. We went out to the far fields below the west mesa, and there, in two large rectangles of freshly turned earth, we planted corn and melons, working all together, hard, like a great lot of ants. Soon the work was finished, and we sat down to eat in a cottonwood grove nearby. There was plenty of good food, and it was of a kind that I did not ordinarily see on the feast days. The main dish was a rabbit stew which was especially tasty. At first I sat down with Eddie and the members of his family, but in a little while Joe Baca, who held as I recall the office of war captain that year, came to me and invited me to sit with him and some other men who were seated in a circle at the center of the whole group. It was clear to me that I must accept this invitation, but I was reluctant and self-conscious, for it seemed to me that everyone was looking on in amusement. For a time I was ill at ease among those men whom I did not know. But they were very gracious to me and went out of their way to make me comfortable. There is a great gift for hospitality in the Jemez people; welcome is intrinsic in them,

3

4

and they judge others, I believe, by what is best in themselves. It happened after all that I was very pleased to talk and eat with these men, to laugh with them, to be alive in their company. And only later did I learn that I had been a highly honored, though unwitting, guest, that I had sat among the chief dignitaries of the town: the cacique, the governor, the lieutenant governor, and the war captain. Indeed, I had taken part in the ceremonial planting of the cacique's fields. The cacique, the chief of the tribe, presides over the matters of the pueblo, great and small, until he dies, and his position is one of singular honor and importance. Every year the people of Jemez plant and harvest his fields for him, and they give him a choice portion of the food which they obtain by means of hunting.

    . . . Lupe Lucero was a wizened child. He was very small and swarthy, with glittering black eyes and a shock of coarse black hair on his head. He was bandy-legged and much animated; something of the rooster Thaddeus Waring was in him, some wise and wary notion of the world. There was a slight deformity in the right side of his face, a thing which gave to him the grave look of a man who must deal with God before breakfast, the scowl of a theologian. And it suited him, I believe; it is the expression he would have chosen for himself, had there been a choice. It was in his nature, who could not himself have been taken by surprise, to take others by surprise, and all the time. He was of a mind to hold the world precisely at bay and in a delicate balance between delight and disdain. When he first came to the day school as a beginner he could speak only the Jemez language, but he was highly intelligent, and he learned very quickly. One day on the playground, when I was watching him (for he bore watching), the governor of the village came to the fence and asked Lupe in his native tongue where my father might be found. And after due consideration, Lupe replied, "I am sorry, my friend, but we speak only English here." 5

I did not and do not know his name. He was an old man who appeared at Jemez one winter. He was said to have come from one of the other pueblos, Zia, maybe, or San Felipe. He had a strong, heroic face, broad and dark and expressive—but expressive of what, exactly, I do not know. The talk of the village had it that he was *muy loco,* and perhaps it was so, but I was never convinced of it. His behavior was extraordinary, to be sure; he did things that other people in general did not think of doing. But I rather liked that in this old man and thought of it as his own business, after all. In any case I felt no compunction to account for him either to myself or to anyone else; he seemed to get on well enough in his particular way. He came to the day school on several occasions, walked right into our home without knocking, and stood for long moments before the fire, warming his gnarled hands, saying nothing to anyone; or else he spoke out loudly, almost urgently, in a tongue that none of us knew or had ever heard before. And at such times he closed his eyes. I believe that he looked then inward upon his mind and saw there, and there only, such things as were real to him. One morning, when I stepped out into 6 the raw January weather on my way to school, a truck sped by on the road in front of me, and in the bed of the truck were several young men laughing, jeering, and gesturing wildly. And in the dust in their wake rode the old man on a paint horse. He was standing in the stirrups and holding out both his arms in the attitude of Christ on the Cross, his face contorted in a scream and his long gray hair lying out flat on the wind, and the horse was running at full speed, bolting after the truck. It was a strange and breath-taking sight, some-thing upon which to found a faith, it may be, a faith in the apparent, often beautiful, aberrations of this world.

The old man Francisco Tosa's daughter-in-law, Sefora, came every day   7
to the day school for water, and her husband, Joe, brought wood from the mountains for our fires. Sefora was a beautiful woman, with fine pueblo fea-tures and a remarkably composed, gentle disposition. She was not jolly, as were many of the good women of Jemez; rather, she was very quiet and shy and sweet. The old ethnic reserve, which in others of her race, especially the men, made for a kind of formidable and exclusive nature, appeared in her as a soft and serene good will, a rich dignity and grace like beauty; indeed, beauty. She lived with her family directly across the river road, on the north side of the day school, and we could not have wished for a better neighbor. Very often she brought us the delicacies of her table, hot tortillas and beans, chili and tamales; and when she baked bread, she never failed to bring us one or two hot loaves. Joe, who was an excellent hunter, provided us with fresh venison, and sometimes bear meat. In the course of years my mother, especially, and Sefora Tosa became very close friends. When after all—after the good days and bad, the weathers and harvests of twenty-six years, the coming and going of children at the day school—it was time for my parents to leave, it was hard for the two women to say goodbye. They must have seen much in each other's eyes. After I had been away for a long time and had become a man I returned to Jemez and called on Sefora Tosa. Her son Tony, whom I had known as a little boy at the day school, had only a few days before been killed in Vietnam. She wept softly to see me, and she thanked me for coming. I wanted to tell her how good it was to know her, to have known who and what she was to me through that past, pastoral time of my growing up in the neighborhood between us, the good realm in which we had come close together in our lives, but in that formal quiet of her grief I did not say it. And I want to say it now, that it may be said well, in love and remembrance.

. . . There was at Jemez a climate of the mind in which we, my parents   8
and I, realized ourselves, understood who we were, not perfectly, it may be, but well enough. It was not our native world, but we appropriated it, as it were, to ourselves; we invested much of our lives in it, and in the end it was the remembered place of our hopes, our dreams, and our deep love.

My father looked after the endless paper work that came down from the   9
many levels of the Bureau of Indian Affairs. In innumerable ways he worked

with the people of the village and was their principal contact with the Government of the United States. When a boy or girl wanted to apply for admission to the Santa Fe Indian School or the Albuquerque Indian School, or when a man wanted to find work, or a woman to use the telephone to talk to her daughter in California, it was to my father that the petition was made. But first of all he was the man of the family. It was he who got up before daylight and went out to get wood and coal for the fires on winter mornings; it was he who dealt with the emergencies, great and small, of those years; and it was he who taught me such responsibilities as I learned then. One of these was to myself, and it was to dream. On winter evenings before the fire, or on summer nights on the porch, our home of Jemez was a place to dream, and my father dreamed much of his youth. He told me the stories of the coming-out people, of Mammedaty and of Guipagho, of Saynday, who wandered around and around. And very softly, as to himself, he sang the old Kiowa songs. And in all he went on with his real work, the making of paintings. He saw wonderful things, and he painted them well.

My mother has been the inspiration of many people. Certainly she has 10 been mine, and certainly she was mine at Jemez, when inspiration was the nourishment I needed most. I was at that age in which a boy flounders. I had not much sense of where I must go or of what I must do and be in my life, and there were for me moments of great, growing urgency, in which I felt that I was imprisoned in the narrow quarters of my time and place. I wanted, needed to conceive of what my destiny might be, and my mother allowed me to believe that it might be worthwhile. We were so close, she and I, when I was growing up that even now I cannot express the feelings between us. I have great faith in words, but in this there are no words at last; there is only a kind of perfect silence—the stillness of a late autumn afternoon in the village and the valley—in which I listen for the sound of her voice. In a moment she will speak to me; she will speak my name.

One day my mother burned her hand. In a way it was my fault, for I 11 had got in her way when she was carrying a hot pan to the table. It was a strange moment. She made a little cry, and I looked to see what was the matter. I stepped out of the way at once, but her hand was already burned. My mother said nothing about it—that was what seemed strange to me—but I had seen the pain in her face.

Many times she called me to the kitchen window to see something of 12 interest—horses running on the road, a hen with new chicks in the Tosa's garden, a storm gathering in San Diego Canyon, a sunset. At night we talked about innumerable things at the kitchen table, the innumerable things of our world and of our time. We laughed often together, and we saw eye to eye on the larger issues of our lives. The words we had were the right ones; we were easy and right with each other, as it happened, natural, full of love and trust.

"Look," one of us would say to the other, "here is something new, something that we have not seen together." And we would simply take delight in it.

... I sometimes think of what it means that in their heyday—in 1830, *13* say—the Kiowas owned more horses *per capita* than any other tribe on the Great Plains, that the Plains Indian culture, the last culture to evolve in North America, is also known as "the horse culture" and "the centaur culture," that the Kiowas tell the story of a horse that died of shame after its owner committed an act of cowardice, that I am a Kiowa, that therefore there is in me, as there is in the Tartars, an old, sacred notion of the horse. I believe that at some point in my racial life, this notion must needs be expressed in order that I may be true to my nature.

It happened so: I was thirteen years old, and my parents gave me a horse. *14* It was a small nine-year-old gelding of that rare, soft color that is called strawberry roan. This my horse and I came to be, in the course of our life together, in good understanding, of one mind, a true story and history of that large landscape in which we made the one entity of whole motion, one and the same center of an intricate, pastoral composition, evanescent, ever changing. And to this my horse I gave the name Pecos.

On the back of my horse I had a different view of the world. I could *15* see more of it, how it reached away beyond all the horizons I had ever seen; and yet it was more concentrated in its appearance, too, and more accessible to my mind, my imagination. My mind loomed upon the farthest edges of the earth, where I could feel the full force of the planet whirling into space. There was nothing of the air and light that was not pure exhilaration, and nothing of time and eternity. Oh, Pecos, *un poquito mas!* Oh, my hunting horse! Bear me away, bear me away!

It was appropriate that I should make a long journey. Accordingly I set *16* out one early morning, traveling light. Such a journey must begin in the nick of time, on the spur of the moment, and one must say to himself at the outset: Let there be wonderful things along the way; let me hold to the way and be thoughtful in my going; let this journey be made in beauty and belief.

I sang in the sunshine and heard the birds call out on either side. Bits of *17* down from the cottonwoods drifted across the air, and butterflies fluttered in the sage. I could feel my horse under me, rocking at my legs, the bobbing of the reins to my hand; I could feel the sun on my face and the stirring of a little wind at my hair. And through the hard hooves, the slender limbs, the supple shoulders, the fluent back of my horse I felt the earth under me. Everything was under me, buoying me up; I rode across the top of the world. My mind soared; time and again I saw the fleeting shadow of my mind moving about me as it went winding upon the sun.

When the song, which was a song of riding, was finished, I had Pecos *18* pick up the pace. Far down on the road to San Ysidro I overtook my friend

Pasqual Fragua. He was riding a rangy, stiff-legged black and white stallion, half wild, which horse he was breaking for the rancher Cass Goodner. The horse skittered and blew as I drew up beside him. Pecos began to prance, as he did always in the company of another horse. "Where are you going?" I asked in the Jemez language. And he replied, "I am going down the road." The stallion was hard to manage, and Pasqual had to keep his mind upon it; I saw that I had taken him by surprise. "You know," he said after a moment, "when you rode up just now I did not know who you were." We rode on for a time in silence, and our horses got used to each other, but still they wanted their heads. The longer I looked at the stallion the more I admired it, and I suppose that Pasqual knew this, for he began to say good things about it: that it was a thing of good blood, that it was very strong and fast, that it felt very good to ride it. The thing was this: that the stallion was half wild, and I came to wonder about the wild half of it; I wanted to know what its wildness was worth in the riding. "Let us trade horses for a while," I said, and, well, all right, he agreed. At first it was exciting to ride the stallion, for every once in a while it pitched and bucked and wanted to run. But it was heavy and raw-boned and full of resistance, and every step was a jolt that I could feel deep down in my bones. I saw soon enough that I had made a bad bargain, and I wanted my horse back, but I was ashamed to admit it. There came a time in the late afternoon, in the vast plain far south of San Ysidro, after thirty miles, perhaps, when I no longer knew whether it was I who was riding the stallion or the stallion who was riding me. "Well, let us go back now," said Pasqual at last. "No. I am going on; and I will have my horse back, please," I said, and he was surprised and sorry to hear it, and we said goodbye. "If you are going south or east," he said, "look out for the sun, and keep your face in the shadow of your hat. *Vaya con Dios.*" And I went on my way alone then, wiser and better mounted, and thereafter I held on to my horse. I saw no one for a long time, but I saw four falling stars and any number of jackrabbits, roadrunners, and coyotes, and once, across a distance, I saw a bear, small and black, lumbering in a ravine. The mountains drew close and withdrew and drew close again, and after several days I swung east.

Now and then I came upon settlements. For the most part they were dry, burnt places with Spanish names: Arroyo Seco, Las Piedras, Tres Casas. In one of these I found myself in a narrow street between high adobe walls. Just ahead, on my left, was a door in the wall. As I approached the door was flung open, and a small boy came running out, rolling a hoop. This happened so suddenly that Pecos shied very sharply, and I fell to the ground, jamming the thumb of my left hand. The little boy looked very worried and said that he was sorry to have caused such an accident. I waved the matter off, as if it were nothing; but as a matter of fact my hand hurt so much that tears welled up in my eyes. And the pain lasted for many days. I have fallen many times from a horse, both before and after that, and a few times I fell from a running horse on dangerous ground, but that was the most painful of them all.

19

In another settlement there were some boys who were interested in   20
racing. They had good horses, some of them, but their horses were not so
good as mine, and I won easily. After that, I began to think of ways in which
I might even the odds a little, might give some advantage to my competitors.
Once or twice I gave them a head start, a reasonable head start of, say, five or
ten yards to the hundred, but that was too simple, and I won anyway. Then it
came to me that I might try this: we should all line up in the usual way, side
by side, but my competitors should be mounted and I should not. When the
signal was given I should then have to get up on my horse while the others
were breaking away; I should have to mount my horse during the race. This
idea appealed to me greatly, for it was both imaginative and difficult, not to
mention dangerous; Pecos and I should have to work very closely together.
The first few times we tried this I had little success, and over a course of a
hundred yards I lost four races out of five. The principal problem was that
Pecos simply could not hold still among the other horses. Even before they
broke away he was hard to manage, and when they were set running nothing
could hold him back, even for an instant. I could not get my foot in the
stirrup, but I had to throw myself up across the saddle on my stomach, hold
on as best I could, and twist myself into position, and all this while racing at
full speed. I could ride well enough to accomplish this feat, but it was a very
awkward and inefficient business. I had to find some way to use the whole
energy of my horse, to get it all into the race. Thus far I had managed only
to break his motion, to divert him from his purpose and mine. To correct this
I took Pecos away and worked with him through the better part of a long
afternoon on a broad reach of level ground beside an irrigation ditch. And it
was hot, hard work. I began by teaching him to run straight away while I ran
beside him a few steps, holding on to the saddle horn, with no pressure on
the reins. Then, when we had mastered this trick, we proceeded to the next
one, which was this: I placed my weight on my arms, hanging from the saddle
horn, threw my feet out in front of me, struck them to the ground, and
sprang up against the saddle. This I did again and again, until Pecos came to
expect it and did not flinch or lose his stride. I sprang a little higher each time.
It was in all a slow process of trial and error, and after two or three hours both
Pecos and I were covered with bruises and soaked through with perspiration.
But we had much to show for our efforts, and at last the moment came when
we must put the whole performance together. I had not yet leaped into the
saddle, but I was quite confident that I could now do so; only I must be sure
to get high enough. We began this dress rehearsal then from a standing position. At my signal Pecos lurched and was running at once, straight away and
smoothly. And at the same time I sprinted forward two steps and gathered
myself up, placing my weight precisely at my wrists, throwing my feet out and
together, perfectly. I brought my feet down sharply to the ground and sprang
up hard, as hard as I could, bringing my legs astraddle of my horse—and
everything was just right, except that I sprang too high. I vaulted all the way
over my horse, clearing the saddle by a considerable margin, and came down

into the irrigation ditch. It was a good trick, but it was not the one I had in mind, and I wonder what Pecos thought of it after all. Anyway, after a while I could mount my horse in this way and so well that there was no challenge in it, and I went on winning race after race.

I went on, farther and farther into the wide world. Many things happened. And in all this I knew one thing: I knew where the journey was begun, that it was itself a learning of the beginning, that the beginning was infinitely worth the learning. The journey was well undertaken, and somewhere in it I sold my horse to an old Spanish man of Vallecitos. I do not know how long Pecos lived. I had used him hard and well, and it may be that in his last days an image of me like thought shimmered in his brain. *21*

4

At Jemez I came to the end of my childhood. There were no schools within easy reach. I had to go nearly thirty miles to school at Bernalillo, and one year I lived away in Albuquerque. My mother and father wanted me to have the benefit of a sound preparation for college, and so we read through many high school catalogues. After long deliberation we decided that I should spend my last year of high school at a military academy in Virginia. *22*

The day before I was to leave I went walking across the river to the red mesa, where many times before I had gone to be alone with my thoughts. And I had climbed several times to the top of the mesa and looked among the old ruins there for pottery. This time I chose to climb the north end, perhaps because I had not gone that way before and wanted to see what it was. It was a difficult climb, and when I got to the top I was spent. I lingered among the ruins for more than an hour, I judge, waiting for my strength to return. From there I could see the whole valley below, the fields, the river, and the village. It was all very beautiful, and the sight of it filled me with longing. *23*

I looked for an easier way to come down, and at length I found a broad, smooth runway of rock, a shallow groove winding out like a stream. It appeared to be safe enough, and I started to follow it. There were steps along the way, a stairway, in effect. But the steps became deeper and deeper, and at last I had to drop down the length of my body and more. Still it seemed convenient to follow in the groove of rock. I was more than halfway down when I came upon a deep, funnel-shaped formation in my path. And there I had to make a decision. The slope on either side was extremely steep and forbidding, and yet I thought that I could work my way down on either side. The formation at my feet was something else. It was perhaps ten or twelve feet *24* deep, wide at the top and narrow at the bottom, where there appeared to be a level ledge. If I could get down through the funnel to the ledge, I should be all right; surely the rest of the way down was negotiable. But I realized that there could be no turning back. Once I was down in that rocky chute I could not get up again, for the round wall which nearly encircled the space there was too high and sheer. I elected to go down into it, to try for the ledge directly below. I eased myself down the smooth, nearly vertical wall on my back, pressing my arms and legs outward against the sides. After what seemed a long time I was trapped in the rock. The ledge was no longer there below me; it had been an optical illusion. Now, in this angle of vision, there was nothing but the ground, far, far below, and jagged boulders set there like teeth. I remember that my arms were scraped and bleeding, stretched out against the walls with all the pressure that I could exert. When once I looked down I saw that my legs, also spread out and pressed hard against the walls, were shaking violently. I was in an impossible situation: I could not move in any direction, save downward in a fall, and I could not stay beyond another minute where I was. I believed then that I would die there, and I saw with a terrible clarity the things of the valley below. They were not the less beautiful to me. It seemed to me that I grew suddenly very calm in view of that beloved world. And I remember nothing else of that moment. I passed out of my mind, and the next thing I knew I was sitting down on the ground, very cold in the shadows, and looking up at the rock where I had been within an eyelash of eternity. That was a strange thing in my life, and I think of it as the end of an age. I should never again see the world as I saw it on the other side of that moment, in the bright reflection of time lost. There are such reflections, and for some of them I have the names.

EPILOGUE

I entered into the Staked Plains and turned north. At some point in my journey it became clear to me that I was moving against the grain of time. 25

I came to a great canyon in the plain and descended into it. It was a very beautiful place. There was clear water and high green grass. A great herd of buffalo was grazing there. I moved slowly among those innumerable animals, coming so close to some that I could touch them, and I did touch them, and the long, dusty hair of their hides was crinkled and coarse in my fingers. In among them they were so many that I could not see the ground beneath them; they seemed a great, thick meadow of dark grain, and their breathing was like the sound of a huge, close swarm of bees. Guadal-tseyu and I, we picked our way, going very slowly, and the buffalo parted before us—it was like the careful tearing of a seam, stitch by stitch—and otherwise they paid us no mind. We were a long time in their midst, it seemed, a long time passing 26 through. And farther on there were tipis, some of them partly dismantled, and little fires gone and going out, embers smoldering, and many things were strewn about, as if a people were breaking camp. But there were no people; the people had gone away. And for a long time after that I followed their tracks.

And one day the earth turned red and the plains began to roll, and *27* Guadal-tseyu bore me into the Wichita Mountains. And in the night I saw again some falling stars, and the next day it rained at Rainy Mountain, and I came upon the cemetery there and stood for a time among the stones. I heard the wind running, and there were magpies huddled away in the shadows.

There were old people in the arbor, and they were all very glad to see *28* me, and they called me by my Indian name. And to each one, face to face, weeping, I spoke his name: *Mammedaty, Aho, Pohd-lohk, Keahdinekeah, Kau-au-ointy.* I saw the old woman Ko-sahn, who was my grandmother's close friend, who told me many things. She seemed to know of everything that had happened to us, to the coming-out people, from the beginning. She was very old, and I loved the age in her; it was a thing hard to come by, great and noble in itself. I remained there for many days, I believe. Guadal-tseyu ran with my grandfather's horses in the north pasture. From the arbor, in the early mornings and late afternoons I saw him there, how the low sun shone upon the rare red color of his hide. In the evenings we told stories, the old people and I.

When it was time to go on I rode north and west a long way, across *29* many rivers, across the Washita, across the Canadian and the North Canadian, across the Arkansas and the Smoky Hill and the Republican, across the Platte and the Niobrara. There was no end to the land, and the land was wild and beautiful, and always there was a wind like music on the land.

In the Black Hills I breathed deeply among the trees, looking down *30* from a hundred summits upon the deep swing of the plains to the sky. And when suddenly and at last I beheld Tsoai, it was the color of iron and it loomed above the earth, the far crest roving upon eternity. This strange thing, this Tsoai, I saw with my own eyes and with the eyes of my own mind, how in the night it stood away and away and grew up among the stars.

I bore westward across the Powder River and the Bighorn Mountains, *31* and after many days I took leave of the plains. The way was rocky then and steep, and it seemed that my horse was bearing me up to the top of the world. All the rivers ran down from that place, and many times I saw eagles in the air under me. And then there were meadows full of wildflowers, and a mist roiled upon them, the slow, rolling spill of the mountain clouds. And in one of these, in a pool of low light, I touched the fallen tree, the hollow log there in the thin crust of the ice.

Topics for Discussion and Writing

1. This selection begins with the name Tsoai-talee, given Momaday by his ancient relative Pohd-lohk. From your reading of the selection, what do

you feel *Tsoai-talee* might mean? Justify your speculation by citing details from the selection. Compare your speculation with those of others.

2. How is this selection about Momaday's schooling? Even though the selection does not talk about Momaday's formal education, as most of us know it, what roles in this story do schools play? What seems to you to be the relationship between the school his parents administer and his own education, as represented here?

3. Focus on one of the people whom Momaday describes. In telling us his story of this person, what values or principles do you feel he is trying to communicate? When he says, for example, that his sight of the "old man" might be "something on which to found a faith," what would be the characteristics of that faith?

4. Study Momaday's Epilogue. How does it connect with the rest of the selection? Write a story about a journey that you might take, as Momaday says here, "against the grain of time." Where would you go? Who might accompany you? What about yourself, including your "real name," would you want to communicate in that story?

5. Tell the story of an important event from your childhood. Imagine the event vividly and try to describe it as strongly as you imagine it. Like Momaday, do not try to explain to your reader what you feel the event means.

MAXINE HONG KINGSTON

from *The Woman Warrior*

> *"My silence was thickest—total—during the three years that I covered my school paintings with black paint. I painted layers of black over houses and flowers and suns, and when I drew on the blackboard, I put a layer of chalk on top."*

Born in 1940, Maxine Hong Kingston grew up in a Chinese community in Stockton, California, where she struggled to adjust to the often conflicting demands of the two cultures of which she was a part. Her autobiography of her youth, The Woman Warrior: Memories of a Girlhood Among Ghosts *(1976), demonstrates her success in achieving mastery in her new language, even as it describes the difficulties of the cultural task for the immigrant. In addition to* The Woman Warrior, *which has become in the United States one of the most widely read books by a Chinese-American, Kingston is also known for her books* China Men *(1980) and* Tripmaster Monkey *(1989). She teaches at the University of California, Berkeley.*

We have reprinted here the portion of The Woman Warrior *that contrasts Kingston's earliest American and Chinese schools.*

Before and as You Read

1. Silence, particularly the inability to speak under pressure, is a subject of the selection. Consider silence. In your school experience, how has silence been regarded? When is it a virtue; when is it a flaw? Have you ever, in school or out, been taught ways to use silence (for example, in meditation)? Do you feel that American popular culture encourages or discourages silence?

2. Write reflectively about times when you were unable to speak when called upon, or when you wished you'd had the courage to speak. Tell one such story. Why did you remain silent? Conversely, write about a time when you did speak, even though you were afraid to. What happened? Did the incident increase or decrease your confidence?

3. As you read the following excerpt, attend to how Kingston organizes the information. Watch particularly how she moves from paragraph to paragraph. What seems to you to be the relationship of one paragraph to the next? Mark places where the connection is not clear to you. If a connection is not clear, how do you as a reader "fill in the silence" in the writing?

4. As you read the selection, try to ascertain Kingston's attitude toward the different schools. Does she seem to be saying that one school is better than the other? Does she seem to be finding fault with her own behavior and that of others? If you do see a critical purpose in her writing, try to find passages that are explicitly critical. If you do not see her purpose as primarily critical, what do you feel is her purpose in the writing? Discuss your responses with others.

L ONG AGO in China, knot-makers tied string into buttons and frogs,   1
and rope into bell pulls. There was one knot so complicated that it
blinded the knot-maker. Finally an emperor outlawed this cruel knot, and the
nobles could not order it anymore. If I had lived in China, I would have been
an outlaw knot-maker.

Maybe that's why my mother cut my tongue. She pushed my tongue up   2
and sliced the frenum. Or maybe she snipped it with a pair of nail scissors. I
don't remember her doing it, only her telling me about it, but all during
childhood I felt sorry for the baby whose mother waited with scissors or knife
in hand for it to cry—and then, when its mouth was wide open like a baby
bird's, cut. The Chinese say "a ready tongue is an evil."

I used to curl up my tongue in front of the mirror and tauten my frenum   3
into a white line, itself as thin as a razor blade. I saw no scars in my mouth. I
thought perhaps I had had two frena, and she had cut one. I made other
children open their mouths so I could compare theirs to mine. I saw perfect
pink membranes stretching into precise edges that looked easy enough to cut.
Sometimes I felt very proud that my mother committed such a powerful act
upon me. At other times I was terrified—the first thing my mother did when
she saw me was to cut my tongue.

"Why did you do that to me, Mother?"   4
"I told you."   5
"Tell me again."   6
"I cut it so that you would not be tongue-tied. Your tongue would be   7
able to move in any language. You'll be able to speak languages that are
completely different from one another. You'll be able to pronounce anything.
Your frenum looked too tight to do those things, so I cut it."

"But isn't 'a ready tongue an evil'?"   8
"Things are different in this ghost country."   9
"Did it hurt me? Did I cry and bleed?"   10
"I don't remember. Probably."   11
She didn't cut the other children's. When I asked cousins and other   12
Chinese children whether their mothers had cut their tongues loose, they said,
"What?"

"Why didn't you cut my brothers' and sisters' tongues?"   13
"They didn't need it."   14
"Why not? Were theirs longer than mine?"   15
"Why don't you quit blabbering and get to work?"   16
If my mother was not lying she should have cut more, scraped away the   17
rest of the frenum skin, because I have a terrible time talking. Or she should
not have cut at all, tampering with my speech. When I went to kindergarten
and had to speak English for the first time, I became silent. A dumbness—a
shame—still cracks my voice in two, even when I want to say "hello" casually,
or ask an easy question in front of the check-out counter, or ask directions of
a bus driver. I stand frozen, or I hold up the line with the complete, gram-
matical sentence that comes squeaking out at impossible length. "What did

you say?" says the cab driver, or "Speak up," so I have to perform again, only weaker the second time. A telephone call makes my throat bleed and takes up that day's courage. It spoils my day with self-disgust when I hear my broken voice come skittering out into the open. It makes people wince to hear it. I'm getting better, though. Recently I asked the postman for special-issue stamps; I've waited since childhood for postmen to give me some of their own accord. I am making progress, a little every day.

My silence was thickest—total—during the three years that I covered   18
my school paintings with black paint. I painted layers of black over houses and flowers and suns, and when I drew on the blackboard, I put a layer of chalk on top. I was making a stage curtain, and it was the moment before the curtain parted or rose. The teachers called my parents to school, and I saw they had been saving my pictures, curling and cracking, all alike and black. The teachers pointed to the pictures and looked serious, talked seriously too, but my parents did not understand English. ("The parents and teachers of criminals were executed," said my father.) My parents took the pictures home. I spread them out (so black and full of possibilities) and pretended the curtains were swinging open, flying up, one after another, sunlight underneath, mighty operas.

During the first silent year I spoke to no one at school, did not ask   19
before going to the lavatory, and flunked kindergarten. My sister also said nothing for three years, silent in the playground and silent at lunch. There were other quiet Chinese girls not of our family, but most of them got over it sooner than we did. I enjoyed the silence. At first it did not occur to me I was supposed to talk or to pass kindergarten. I talked at home and to one or two of the Chinese kids in class. I made motions and even made some jokes. I drank out of a toy saucer when the water spilled out of the cup, and everybody laughed, pointing at me, so I did it some more. I didn't know that Americans don't drink out of saucers.

I liked the Negro students (Black Ghosts) best because they laughed the   20
loudest and talked to me as if I were a daring talker too. One of the Negro girls had her mother coil braids over her ears Shanghai-style like mine; we were Shanghai twins except that she was covered with black like my paintings. Two Negro kids enrolled in Chinese school, and the teachers gave them Chinese names. Some Negro kids walked me to school and home, protecting me from the Japanese kids, who hit me and chased me and stuck gum in my ears. The Japanese kids were noisy and tough. They appeared one day in kindergarten, released from concentration camp, which was a tic-tac-toe mark, like barbed wire, on the map.

It was when I found out I had to talk that school became a misery, that   21
the silence became a misery. I did not speak and felt bad each time that I did not speak. I read aloud in first grade, though, and heard the barest whisper with little squeaks come out of my throat. "Louder," said the teacher, who scared the voice away again. The other Chinese girls did not talk either, so I knew the silence had to do with being a Chinese girl.

Reading out loud was easier than speaking because we did not have to   22
make up what to say, but I stopped often, and the teacher would think I'd
gone quiet again. I could not understand "I." The Chinese "I" has seven
strokes, intricacies. How could the American "I," assuredly wearing a hat like
the Chinese, have only three strokes, the middle so straight? Was it out of
politeness that this writer left off strokes the way a Chinese has to write her
own name small and crooked? No, it was not politeness; "I" is a capital and
"you" is lowercase. I stared at the middle line and waited so long for its black
center to resolve into tight strokes and dots that I forgot to pronounce it. The
other troublesome word was "here," no strong consonant to hang on it, and
so flat, when "here" is two mountainous ideographs. The teacher, who had
already told me every day how to read "I" and "here" put me in the low
corner under the stairs again, where the noisy boys usually sat.

When my second grade class did a play, the whole class went to the   23
auditorium except the Chinese girls. The teacher, lovely and Hawaiian, should
have understood about us, but instead left us behind in the classroom. Our
voices were too soft or nonexistent, and our parents never signed the permission slips anyway. They never signed anything unnecessary. We opened the
door a crack and peeked out, but closed it again quickly. One of us (not me)
won every spelling bee, though.

I remember telling the Hawaiian teacher, "We Chinese can't sing 'land   24
where our fathers died.'" She argued with me about politics, while I meant
because of curses. But how can I have that memory when I couldn't talk? My
mother says that we, like the ghosts, have no memories.

After American school, we picked up our cigar boxes, in which we had   25
arranged books, brushes, and an inkbox neatly, and went to Chinese school,
from 5:00 to 7:30 P.M. There we chanted together, voices rising and falling,
loud and soft, some boys shouting, everybody reading together, reciting together and not alone with one voice. When we had a memorization test, the
teacher let each of us come to his desk and say the lesson to him privately,
while the rest of the class practiced copying or tracing. Most of the teachers
were men. The boys who were so well behaved in the American school played
tricks on them and talked back to them. The girls were not mute. They
screamed and yelled during recess, when there were no rules; they had fist-
fights. Nobody was afraid of children hurting themselves or of children hurting school property. The glass doors to the red and green balconies with the
gold joy symbols were left wide open so that we could run out and climb the
fire escapes. We played capture-the-flag in the auditorium, where Sun Yat-sen
and Chiang Kai-shek's pictures hung at the back of the stage, the Chinese flag
on their left and the American flag on their right. We climbed the teak ceremonial chairs and made flying leaps off the stage. One flag headquarters was
behind the glass door and the other on stage right. Our feet drummed on
the hollow stage. During recess the teachers locked themselves up in their office with the shelves of books, copybooks, inks from China. They drank tea

and warmed their hands at a stove. There was no play supervision. At recess we had the school to ourselves, and also we could roam as far as we could go—downtown, Chinatown stores, home—as long as we returned before the bell rang.

At exactly 7:30 the teacher again picked up the brass bell that sat on his desk and swung it over our heads, while we charged down the stairs, our cheering magnified in the stairwell. Nobody had to line up.   26

Not all of the children who were silent at American school found voice at Chinese school. One new teacher said each of us had to get up and recite in front of the class, who was to listen. My sister and I had memorized the lesson perfectly. We said it to each other at home, one chanting, one listening. The teacher called on my sister to recite first. It was the first time a teacher had called on the second-born to go first. My sister was scared. She glanced at me and looked away; I looked down at my desk. I hoped that she could do it because if she could, then I would have to. She opened her mouth and a voice came out that wasn't a whisper, but it wasn't a proper voice either. I hoped that she would not cry, fear breaking up her voice like twigs underfoot. She sounded as if she were trying to sing through weeping and strangling. She did not pause or stop to end the embarrassment. She kept going until she said the last word, and then she sat down. When it was my turn, the same voice came out, a crippled animal running on broken legs. You could hear splinters in my voice, bones rubbing jagged against one another. I was loud, though. I was glad I didn't whisper. There was one little girl who whispered.   27

. . . How strange that the emigrant villagers are shouters, hollering face to face. My father asks, "Why is it I can hear Chinese from blocks away? Is it that I understand the language? Or is it they talk loud?" They turn the radio up full blast to hear the operas, which do not seem to hurt their ears. And they yell over the singers that wail over the drums, everybody talking at once, big arm gestures, spit flying. You can see the disgust on American faces looking at women like that. It isn't just the loudness. It is the way Chinese sounds, chingchong ugly, to American ears, not beautiful like Japanese sayonara words with the consonants and vowels as regular as Italian. We make guttural peasant noise and have Ton Duc Thang names you can't remember. And the Chinese can't hear Americans at all; the language is too soft and western music unhearable. I've watched a Chinese audience laugh, visit, talk-story, and holler during a piano recital, as if the musician could not hear them. A Chinese-American, somebody's son, was playing Chopin, which has no punctuation, no cymbals, no gongs. Chinese piano music is five black keys. Normal Chinese women's voices are strong and bossy. We American-Chinese girls had to whisper to make ourselves American-feminine. Apparently we whispered even more softly than the Americans. Once a year the teachers referred my sister and me to speech therapy, but our voices would straighten out, unpredictably normal, for the therapists. Some of us gave up, shook our heads, and said nothing, not one word. Some of us could not even shake our heads. At times shaking my   28 head no is more self-assertion than I can manage. Most of us eventually found some voice, however faltering. We invented an American-feminine speaking personality.

Topics for Discussion and Writing

1. On the basis of your reading of this selection, how do you account for Kingston's "silence" in the American school? Cite passages that support your view. Be sure to include her description of her and her sister's recitations in the Chinese school as you consider this question.
2. What surprises you in this selection? Write in your journal about ways in which information given here conflicts with your prior views of Chinese culture. Are you surprised also by the opinions expressed about the "ghosts" by the American-Chinese parents and children?
3. Compare your early school experiences with those related by Kingston. With which of her experiences can you identify? Write about one school event that her narrative reminds you of. Conversely, which of the experiences she relates seem most foreign to your own schooling? Why do you feel that your experience did not include something similar to this?
4. This selection includes a brief dialogue between the young Kingston and her mother about an event that occurred to Kingston as a baby. Note the writer's use of dialogue as a technique both to "bring characters to life" and to explore an issue more deeply. In your journal create an imagined dialogue between you and a parent (or between you and an influential teacher) about an event in your childhood that has had great meaning for you. What happens to your thinking as you compose the dialogue?

MALCOLM X AND ALEX HALEY

from *The Autobiography of Malcolm X*

"Then the bell rang and we came out of our corners. I knew I was scared, but I didn't know, as Bill Peterson told me later on, that he was scared of me, too. He was so scared that I was going to hurt him that he knocked me down fifty times if he did once."

Malcolm X was born Malcolm Little in 1925. When he was six, his father, a minister known for his courage in speaking out against racial injustice, was mysteriously murdered. Three years later, his mother, unable any longer to endure the terrible difficulties of raising eight children on little income, was committed to a mental hospital and her children were dispersed to relatives and foster families. Chapter Two of The Autobiography of Malcolm X, *which we reprint here, recounts his school years from age 12 to 14, after which time Malcolm moved to Boston and later to New York, where he became involved in the criminal activity that led to his imprisonment.*

While in prison, Malcolm became an avid, eclectic reader and a student of the teachings of Elijah Muhammad, leader of the Nation of Islam. When he was released from prison, Malcolm, renamed Malcolm X, became a powerful figure in the Black Muslims, as the Nation of Islam was popularly known; he was widely regarded as the movement's most eloquent, persuasive speaker. His speeches brought him to national prominence in the early 60s; he became identified by the media—wrongly, as his autobiography attests—as an advocate of violent racial protest, and so an object of fear and anger for many.

A pilgrimage to Mecca in 1964, made out of his intense interest in Islam, led him to regard as unacceptable some of the teachings of Elijah Muhammad (the journey also led him to take on a new name, El-Hajj Malik El-Shabazz). When he thus broke with the Nation of Islam on moral and philosophical grounds, the number of his enemies increased. With his life the subject of constant threats, his assassination on February 21, 1965, while he spoke to a gathering in Harlem, surprised no one. Nevertheless, the forces behind his murder remain a mystery to this day.

The Autobiography of Malcolm X, *first published in 1964, is a remarkable document, not only because it was written by an embattled public figure under constant threat of assassination, but also because it brought into a working relationship Malcolm X and Alex Haley, whose writings about black experience have had perhaps greater impact on white America than those of any other writer in this century, with the possible exception of Martin Luther King, Jr. Haley, who died in February 1992, had been a career officer in the Coast Guard for 20 years before embarking on a career as a free-lance writer and historian. Haley's articles on the Muslims and on Malcolm X appeared in* The Reader's Digest, The Saturday Evening Post, *and* Playboy *before he and Malcolm X began the autobiography. Haley's Epilogue to the book recounts his working relationship with the political leader and has become in itself a classic. Haley's even more famous work,* Roots, *is both Haley's own story of his search for his African ancestors and an archetypal rendering of black experience in America into the 20th century.*

We recommend that you read the entire book of which this selection is just one chapter, because we feel that this chapter, though rich in itself, loses much by being taken out of its context in The Autobiography. *(This is also true, but we feel to a lesser extent, of other excerpts we have drawn from longer books.) We also recommend that you read the entire* Autobiography *because of the great amount of distortion that the image of Malcolm X has suffered.*

Before and as You Read

1. Think about your earlier school experience in terms of social hierarchies and codes of behavior. What were the unwritten rules of appearance and behavior, of who could talk with whom, of who could date whom, and so on? How did teachers and administrators back up these rules? Do you recall people, either students or teachers, who addressed these codes and perhaps challenged them? How were those people treated?

2. What did you learn in your earlier schooling about relations between people of different racial and ethnic groups? Did your teachers or textbooks address this issue? If so, what do you recall? Within the school community, how did people of different ethnic and linguistic backgrounds treat one another? As you read the following selection, compare your own school experiences with those reported by Malcolm X and Alex Haley. If people followed racial stereotypes or used racist language, why do you think they did so? Attend to Malcolm X's explanation of why the whites spoke of blacks as they did.

3. Can you recall an experience that changed dramatically your ideas about a group of people—that taught you the narrowness or inadequacy of your former view? Write about this. Compare your writing with that of Malcolm X and Haley about Malcolm's half sister.

4. If you are familiar with the reputation or the work of Malcolm X, write about what you have heard of him and from whom. Consider the reliability of your sources. Compare your image of Malcolm X with those of others doing this assignment. What do these images share? How do you account for the similarity?

CHAPTER TWO: MASCOT

ON JUNE twenty-seventh of that year, nineteen thirty-seven, Joe Louis knocked out James J. Braddock to become the heavyweight champion of the world. And all the Negroes in Lansing, like Negroes every-where, went wildly happy with the greatest celebration of race pride our generation had ever known. Every Negro boy old enough to walk wanted to be the next Brown Bomber. My brother Philbert, who had already become a pretty good boxer in school, was no exception. (I was trying to play basketball. I was gangling and tall, but I wasn't very good at it—too awkward.) In the fall of that year, Philbert entered the amateur bouts that were held in Lansing's Prudden Auditorium.

He did well, surviving the increasingly tough eliminations. I would go down to the gym and watch him train. It was very exciting. Perhaps without realizing it I became secretly envious; for one thing, I know I could not help seeing some of my younger brother Reginald's lifelong admiration for me getting siphoned off to Philbert.

People praised Philbert as a natural boxer. I figured that since we belonged to the same family, maybe I would become one, too. So I put myself in the ring. I think I was thirteen when I signed up for my first bout, but my height and raw-boned frame let me get away with claiming that I was sixteen, the minimum age—and my weight of about 128 pounds got me classified as a bantamweight.

They matched me with a white boy, a novice like myself, named Bill Peterson. I'll never forget him. When our turn in the next amateur bouts came up, all of my brothers and sisters were there watching, along with just about everyone else I knew in town. They were there not so much because of me but because of Philbert, who had begun to build up a pretty good following, and they wanted to see how his brother would do.

I walked down the aisle between the people thronging the rows of seats, and climbed in the ring. Bill Peterson and I were introduced, and then the referee called us together and mumbled all of that stuff about fighting fair and breaking clean. Then the bell rang and we came out of our corners. I knew I was scared, but I didn't know, as Bill Peterson told me later on, that he was scared of me, too. He was so scared I was going to hurt him that he knocked me down fifty times if he did once.

He did such a job on my reputation in the Negro neighborhood that I practically went into hiding. A Negro just can't be whipped by somebody white and return with his head up to the neighborhood, especially in those days, when sports and, to a lesser extent show business, were the only fields open to Negroes, and when the ring was the only place a Negro could whip a white man and not be lynched. When I did show my face again, the Negroes I knew rode me so badly I knew I had to do something.

But the worst of my humiliations was my younger brother Reginald's attitude: he simply never mentioned the fight. It was the way he looked at me—and avoided looking at me. So I went back to the gym, and I trained—hard. I beat bags and skipped rope and grunted and sweated all over the place. And finally I signed up to fight Bill Peterson again. This time, the bouts were held in his hometown of Alma, Michigan.

The only thing better about the rematch was that hardly anyone I knew was there to see it; I was particularly grateful for Reginald's absence. The moment the bell rang, I saw a fist, then the canvas coming up, and ten seconds later the referee was saying "*Ten!*" over me. It was probably the shortest "fight" in history. I lay there listening to the full count, but I couldn't move. To tell the truth, I'm not sure I wanted to move.

That white boy was the beginning and the end of my fight career. A lot of times in these later years since I became a Muslim, I've thought back to that fight and reflected that it was Allah's work to stop me: I might have wound up punchy.

Not long after this, I came into a classroom with my hat on. I did it deliberately. The teacher, who was white, ordered me to keep the hat on, and to walk around and around the room until he told me to stop. "That way," he said, "everyone can see you. Meanwhile, we'll go on with class for those who are here to learn something."

I was still walking around when he got up from his desk and turned to the blackboard to write something on it. Everyone in the classroom was looking when, at this moment, I passed behind his desk, snatched up a thumbtack and deposited it in his chair. When he turned to sit back down, I was far from the scene of the crime, circling around the rear of the room. Then he hit the tack, and I heard him holler and caught a glimpse of him spraddling up as I disappeared through the door.

With my deportment record, I wasn't really shocked when the decision came that I had been expelled.

I guess I must have had some vague idea that if I didn't have to go to school, I'd be allowed to stay on with the Gohannas' and wander around town, or maybe get a job if I wanted one for pocket money. But I got rocked on my heels when a state man whom I hadn't seen before came and got me at the Gohannas' and took me down to court.

They told me I was going to go to a reform school. I was still thirteen years old.

But first I was going to the detention home. It was in Mason, Michigan, about twelve miles from Lansing. The detention home was where all the "bad" boys and girls from Ingham County were held, on their way to reform school—waiting for their hearings.

The white state man was a Mr. Maynard Allen. He was nicer to me than most of the state Welfare people had been. He even had consoling words for the Gohannas' and Mrs. Adcock and Big Boy; all of them were crying. But I wasn't. With the few clothes I owned stuffed into a box, we rode in his car to Mason. He talked as he drove along, saying that my school marks showed that if I would just straighten up, I could make something of myself. He said that reform school had the wrong reputation; he talked about what the word "reform" meant—to change and become better. He said the school was really a place where boys like me could have time to see their mistakes and start a new life and become somebody everyone would be proud of. And he told me that the lady in charge of the detention home, a Mrs. Swerlin, and her husband were very good people.

They were good people. Mrs. Swerlin was bigger than her husband, 17 I remember, a big, buxom, robust, laughing woman, and Mr. Swerlin was thin, with black hair, and a black mustache and a red face, quiet and polite, even to me.

They liked me right away, too. Mrs. Swerlin showed me to my room, 18 my own room—the first in my life. It was in one of those huge dormitory-like buildings where kids in detention were kept in those days—and still are in most places. I discovered next, with surprise, that I was allowed to eat with the Swerlins. It was the first time I'd eaten with white people—at least with grown white people—since the Seventh Day Adventist country meetings. It wasn't my own exclusive privilege, of course. Except for the very troublesome boys and girls at the detention home, who were kept locked up—those who had run away and been caught and brought back, or something like that—all of us ate with the Swerlins sitting at the head of the long tables.

They had a white cook-helper, I recall—Lucille Lathrop. (It amazes me 19 how these names come back, from a time I haven't thought about for more than twenty years.) Lucille treated me well, too. Her husband's name was Duane Lathrop. He worked somewhere else, but he stayed there at the detention home on the weekends with Lucille.

I noticed again how white people smelled different from us, and how 20 their food tasted different, not seasoned like Negro cooking. I began to sweep and mop and dust around in the Swerlins' house, as I had done with Big Boy at the Gohannas'.

They all liked my attitude, and it was out of their liking for me that I 21 soon became accepted by them—as a mascot, I know now. They would talk about anything and everything with me standing right there hearing them, the same way people would talk freely in front of a pet canary. They would even talk about me, or about "niggers," as though I wasn't there, as if I wouldn't understand what the word meant. A hundred times a day, they used the word "nigger." I suppose that in their own minds, they meant no harm; in fact they probably meant well. It was the same with the cook, Lucille, and her husband, Duane. I remember one day when Mr. Swerlin, as nice as he was, came in from Lansing, where he had been through the Negro section, and said to Mrs. Swerlin right in front of me, "I just can't see how those niggers can be so happy and be so poor." He talked about how they lived in shacks, but had those big, shining cars out front.

And Mrs. Swerlin said, me standing right there, "Niggers are just that 22 way. . . ." That scene always stayed with me.

It was the same with the other white people, most of them local politi- 23 cians, when they would come visiting the Swerlins. One of their favorite parlor topics was "niggers." One of them was the judge who was in charge of me in Lansing. He was a close friend of the Swerlins. He would ask about me when he came, and they would call me in, and he would look me up and down, his expression approving, like he was examining a fine colt, or a pedigreed pup. I knew they must have told him how I acted and how I worked.

What I am trying to say is that it just never dawned upon them that I   *24*
could understand, that I wasn't a pet, but a human being. They didn't give me
credit for having the same sensitivity, intellect, and understanding that they
would have been ready and willing to recognize in a white boy in my position.
But it has historically been the case with white people, in their regard for black
people, that even though we might be *with* them, we weren't considered *of*
them. Even though they appeared to have opened the door, it was still closed.
Thus they never did really see *me*.

This is the sort of kindly condescension which I try to clarify today, to   *25*
these integration-hungry Negroes, about their "liberal" white friends, these
so-called "good white people"—most of them anyway. I don't care how nice
one is to you; the thing you must always remember is that almost never does
he really see you as he sees himself, as he sees his own kind. He may stand
with you through thin, but not thick; when the chips are down, you'll find
that as fixed in him as his bone structure is his sometimes subconscious conviction that he's better than anybody black.

But I was no more than vaguely aware of anything like that in my   *26*
detention-home years. I did my little chores around the house, and everything
was fine. And each weekend, they didn't mind my catching a ride over to
Lansing for the afternoon or evening. If I wasn't old enough, I sure was big
enough by then, and nobody ever questioned my hanging out, even at night,
in the streets of the Negro section.

I was growing up to be even bigger than Wilfred and Philbert, who had   *27*
begun to meet girls at the school dances, and other places, and introduced me
to a few. But the ones who seemed to like me, I didn't go for—and vice versa.
I couldn't dance a lick, anyway, and I couldn't see squandering my few dimes
on girls. So mostly I pleasured myself these Saturday nights by gawking around
the Negro bars and restaurants. The jukeboxes were wailing Erskine Hawkins'
"Tuxedo Junction," Slim and Slam's "Flatfoot Floogie," things like that. Sometimes, big bands from New York, out touring the one-night stands in the
sticks, would play for big dances in Lansing. Everybody with legs would come
out to see any performer who bore the magic name "New York." Which is
how I first heard Lucky Thompson and Milt Jackson, both of whom I later
got to know well in Harlem.

Many youngsters from the detention home, when their dates came up,   *28*
went off to the reform school. But when mine came up—two or three
times—it was always ignored. I saw new youngsters arrive and leave. I was
glad and grateful. I knew it was Mrs. Swerlin's doing. I didn't want to leave.

She finally told me one day that I was going to be entered in Mason   *29*
Junior High School. It was the only school in town. No ward of the detention
home had ever gone to school there, at least while still a ward. So I entered
their seventh grade. The only other Negroes there were some of the Lyons
children, younger than I was, in the lower grades. The Lyons and I, as it
happened, were the town's only Negroes. They were, as Negroes, very much
respected. Mr. Lyons was a smart, hardworking man, and Mrs. Lyons was a

very good woman. She and my mother, I had heard my mother say, were two of the four West Indians in that whole section of Michigan.

Some of the white kids at school, I found, were even friendlier than some of those in Lansing had been. Though some, including the teachers, called me "nigger," it was easy to see that they didn't mean any more harm by it than the Swerlins. As the "nigger" of my class, I was in fact extremely popular—I suppose partly because I was kind of a novelty. I was in demand, I had top priority. But I also benefited from the special prestige of having the seal of approval from that Very Important Woman about the town of Mason, Mrs. Swerlin. Nobody in Mason would have dreamed of getting on the wrong side of her. It became hard for me to get through a school day without someone after me to join this or head up that—the debating society, the Junior High basketball team, or some other extracurricular activity. I never turned them down.

And I hadn't been in the school long when Mrs. Swerlin, knowing I could use spending money of my own, got me a job after school washing the dishes in a local restaurant. My boss there was the father of a white classmate whom I spent a lot of time with. His family lived over the restaurant. It was fine working there. Every Friday night when I got paid, I'd feel at least ten feet tall. I forget how much I made, but it seemed like a lot. It was the first time I'd ever had any money to speak of, all my own, in my whole life. As soon as I could afford it, I bought a green suit and some shoes, and at school I'd buy treats for the others in my class—at least as much as any of them did for me.

English and history were the subjects I liked most. My English teacher, I recall—a Mr. Ostrowski—was always giving advice about how to become something in life. The one thing I didn't like about history class was that the teacher, Mr. Williams, was a great one for "nigger" jokes. One day during my first week at school, I walked into the room and he started singing to the class, as a joke, "'Way down yonder in the cotton field, some folks say that a nigger won't steal." Very funny. I liked history, but I never thereafter had much liking for Mr. Williams. Later, I remember, we came to the textbook section on Negro history. It was exactly one paragraph long. Mr. Williams laughed through it practically in a single breath, reading aloud how the Negroes had been slaves and then were freed, and how they were usually lazy and dumb and shiftless. He added, I remember, an anthropological footnote on his own, telling us between laughs how Negroes' feet were "so big that when they walk, they don't leave tracks, they leave a hole in the ground."

I'm sorry to say that the subject I most disliked was mathematics. I have thought about it. I think the reason was that mathematics leaves no room for argument. If you made a mistake, that was all there was to it.

Basketball was a big thing in my life, though. I was on the team; we traveled to neighboring towns such as Howell and Charlotte, and wherever I showed my face, the audiences in the gymnasiums "niggered" and "cooned" me to death. Or called me "Rastus." It didn't bother my teammates or my coach at all, and to tell the truth, it bothered me only vaguely. Mine was the same psychology that makes Negroes even today, though it bothers them down inside, keep letting the white man tell them how much "progress" they are making. They've heard it so much they've almost gotten brainwashed into believing it—or at least accepting it.

After the basketball games there would usually be a school dance. When- *35* ever our team walked into another school's gym for the dance, with me among them, I could feel the freeze. It would start to ease as they saw that I didn't try to mix, but stuck close to someone on our team, or kept to myself. I think I developed ways to do it without making it obvious. Even at our own school, I could sense it almost as a physical barrier, that despite all the beaming and smiling, the mascot wasn't supposed to dance with any of the white girls.

It was some kind of psychic message—not just from them, but also from *36* within myself. I am proud to be able to say that much for myself, at least. I would just stand around and smile and talk and drink punch and eat sand- wiches, and then I would make some excuse and get away early.

They were typical small-town school dances. Sometimes a little white *37* band from Lansing would be brought in to play. But most often, the music was a phonograph set up on a table, with the volume turned up high, and the records scratchy, blaring things like Glenn Miller's "Moonlight Serenade"—his band was riding high then—or the Ink Spots, who were also very popular, singing "If I Didn't Care."

I used to spend a lot of time thinking about a peculiar thing. Many of *38* these Mason white boys, like the ones at the Lansing school—especially if they knew me well, and if we hung out a lot together—would get me off in a corner somewhere and push me to proposition certain white girls, sometimes their own sisters. They would tell me that they'd already had the girls them- selves—including their sisters—or that they were trying to and couldn't. Later on, I came to understand what was going on: If they could get the girls into the position of having broken the terrible taboo by slipping off with me somewhere, they would have that hammer over the girls' heads, to make them give in to them.

It seemed that the white boys felt that I, being a Negro, just naturally *39* knew more about "romance," or sex, than they did—that I instinctively knew more about what to do and say with their own girls. I never did tell anybody that I really went for some of the white girls, and some of them went for me, too. They let me know in many ways. But anytime we found ourselves in any close conversations or potentially intimate situations, always there would come up between us some kind of a wall. The girls I really wanted to have were a couple of Negro girls whom Wilfred or Philbert had introduced me to in Lansing. But with these girls, somehow I lacked the nerve.

From what I heard and saw on the Saturday nights I spent hanging *40* around in the Negro district I knew that race-mixing went on in Lansing. But strangely enough, this didn't have any kind of effect on me. Every Negro in Lansing, I guess, knew how white men would drive along certain streets in the black neighborhoods and pick up Negro streetwalkers who patrolled the area. And, on the other hand, there was a bridge that separated the Negro and Polish neighborhoods, where white women would drive or walk across and pick up Negro men, who would hang around in certain places close to the bridge, waiting for them. Lansing's white women, even in those days, were famous for chasing Negro men. I didn't yet appreciate how most whites accord to the Negro this reputation for prodigious sexual prowess. There in Lansing, I never heard of any trouble about this mixing, from either side. I imagine that everyone simply took it for granted, as I did.

41   Anyway, from my experience as a little boy at the Lansing school, I had become fairly adept at avoiding the white-girl issue—at least for a couple of years yet.

42   Then, in the second semester of the seventh grade, I was elected class president. It surprised me even more than other people. But I can see now why the class might have done it. My grades were among the highest in the school. I was unique in my class, like a pink poodle. And I was proud; I'm not going to say I wasn't. In fact, by then, I didn't really have much feeling about being a Negro, because I was trying so hard, in every way I could, to be white. Which is why I am spending much of my life today telling the American black man that he's wasting his time straining to "integrate." I know from personal experience. I tried hard enough.

43   "Malcolm, we're just so *proud* of you!" Mrs. Swerlin exclaimed when she heard about my election. It was all over the restaurant where I worked. Even the state man, Maynard Allen, who still dropped by to see me once in a while, had a word of praise. He said he never saw anybody prove better exactly what "reform" meant. I really liked him—except for one thing: he now and then would drop something that hinted my mother had let us down somehow.

44   Fairly often, I would go and visit the Lyons, and they acted as happy as though I was one of their children. And it was the same warm feeling when I went into Lansing to visit my brothers and sisters and the Gohannas'.

45   I remember one thing that marred this time for me: the movie "Gone with the Wind." When it played in Mason, I was the only Negro in the theater, and when Butterfly McQueen went into her act, I felt like crawling under the rug.

46   Every Saturday, just about, I would go into Lansing. I was going on fourteen, now. Wilfred and Hilda still lived out by themselves at the old family home. Hilda kept the house very clean. It was easier than my mother's plight, with eight of us always under foot or running around. Wilfred worked wherever he could, and he still read every book he could get his hands on. Philbert was getting a reputation as one of the better amateur fighters in this part of the state; everyone really expected that he was going to become a professional.

47   Reginald and I, after my fighting fiasco, had finally gotten back on good terms. It made me feel great to visit him and Wesley over at Mrs. Williams'. I'd offhandedly give them each a couple of dollars to just stick in their pockets, to have something to spend. And little Yvonne and Robert were doing okay, too,

over at the home of the West Indian lady, Mrs. McGuire. I'd give them about a quarter apiece; it made me feel good to see how they were coming along.

None of us talked much about our mother. And we never mentioned   48
our father. I guess none of us knew what to say. We didn't want anybody else to mention our mother either, I think. From time to time, though, we would all go over to Kalamazoo to visit her. Most often we older ones went singly, for it was something you didn't want to have to experience with anyone else present, even your brother or sister.

During this period, the visit to my mother that I most remember was   49
toward the end of that seventh-grade year, when our father's grown daughter by his first marriage, Ella, came from Boston to visit us. Wilfred and Hilda had exchanged some letters with Ella, and I, at Hilda's suggestion, had written to her from the Swerlins'. We were all excited and happy when her letter told us that she was coming to Lansing.

I think the major impact of Ella's arrival, at least upon me, was that she   50
was the first really proud black woman I had ever seen in my life. She was plainly proud of her very dark skin. This was unheard of among Negroes in those days, especially in Lansing.

I hadn't been sure just what day she would come. And then one after-   51
noon I got home from school and there she was. She hugged me, stood me away, looked me up and down. A commanding woman, maybe even bigger than Mrs. Swerlin, Ella wasn't just black, but like our father, she was jet black. The way she sat, moved, talked, did everything, bespoke somebody who did and got exactly what she wanted. This was the woman my father had boasted of so often for having brought so many of their family out of Georgia to Boston. She owned some property, he would say, and she was "in society." She had come North with nothing, and she had worked and saved and had invested in property that she built up in value, and then she started sending money to Georgia for another sister, brother, cousin, niece or nephew to come north to Boston. All that I had heard was reflected in Ella's appearance and bearing. I had never been so impressed with anybody. She was in her second marriage; her first husband had been a doctor.

Ella asked all kinds of questions about how I was doing; she had already   52
heard from Wilfred and Hilda about my election as class president. She asked especially about my grades, and I ran and got my report cards. I was then one of the three highest in the class. Ella praised me. I asked her about her brother, Earl, and her sister, Mary. She had the exciting news that Earl was a singer with a band in Boston. He was singing under the name of Jimmy Carleton. Mary was also doing well.

Ella told me about other relatives from that branch of the family. A   53
number of them I'd never heard of; she had helped them up from Georgia. They, in their turn, had helped up others. "We Littles have to stick together," Ella said. It thrilled me to hear her say that, and even more, the way she said it. I had become a mascot; our branch of the family was split to pieces; I had just about forgotten about being a Little in any family sense. She said that

different members of the family were working in good jobs, and some even had small businesses going. Most of them were homeowners.

When Ella suggested that all of us Littles in Lansing accompany her on a visit to our mother, we all were grateful. We all felt that if anyone could do anything that could help our mother, that might help her get well and come back, it would be Ella. Anyway, all of us, for the first time together, went with Ella to Kalamazoo. ⁵⁴

Our mother was smiling when they brought her out. She was extremely surprised when she saw Ella. They made a striking contrast, the thin near-white woman and the big black one hugging each other. I don't remember much about the rest of the visit, except that there was a lot of talking, and Ella had everything in hand, and we left with all of us feeling better than we ever had about the circumstances. I know that for the first time, I felt as though I had visited with someone who had some kind of physical illness that had just lingered on. ⁵⁵

A few days later, after visiting the homes where each of us were staying, Ella left Lansing and returned to Boston. But before leaving, she told me to write to her regularly. And she had suggested that I might like to spend my summer holiday visiting her in Boston. I jumped at that chance. ⁵⁶

That summer of 1940, in Lansing, I caught the Greyhound bus for Boston with my cardboard suitcase, and wearing my green suit. If someone had hung a sign, "HICK," around my neck, I couldn't have looked much more obvious. They didn't have the turnpikes then; the bus stopped at what seemed every corner and cowpatch. From my seat in—you guessed it—the back of the bus, I gawked out of the window at white man's America rolling past for what seemed a month, but must have been only a day and a half. ⁵⁷

When we finally arrived, Ella met me at the terminal and took me home. The house was on Waumbeck Street in the Sugar Hill section of Roxbury, the Harlem of Boston. I met Ella's second husband, Frank, who was now a soldier; and her brother Earl, the singer who called himself Jimmy Carleton; and Mary, who was very different from her older sister. It's funny how I seemed to think of Mary as Ella's sister, instead of her being, just as Ella is, my own half-sister. It's probably because Ella and I always were much closer as basic types; we're dominant people, and Mary has always been mild and quiet, almost shy. ⁵⁸

Ella was busily involved in dozens of things. She belonged to I don't know how many different clubs; she was a leading light of local so-called "black society." I saw and met a hundred black people there whose big-city talk and ways left my mouth hanging open. ⁵⁹

I couldn't have feigned indifference if I had tried to. People talked casually about Chicago, Detroit, New York. I didn't know the world contained as many Negroes as I saw thronging downtown Roxbury at night, especially on Saturdays. Neon lights, nightclubs, poolhalls, bars, the cars they drove! Restaurants made the streets smell—rich, greasy, down-home black ⁶⁰ cooking! Jukeboxes blared Erskine Hawkins, Duke Ellington, Cootie Williams, dozens of others. If somebody had told me then that some day I'd know them all personally, I'd have found it hard to believe. The biggest bands, like these, played at the Roseland State Ballroom, on Boston's Massachusetts Avenue—one night for Negroes, the next night for whites.

I saw for the first time occasional black-white couples strolling around 61 arm in arm. And on Sundays, when Ella, Mary, or somebody took me to church, I saw churches for black people such as I had never seen. They were many times finer than the white church I had attended back in Mason, Michigan. There, the white people just sat and worshiped with words; but the Boston Negroes, like all other Negroes I had ever seen at church, threw their souls and bodies wholly into worship.

Two or three times, I wrote letters to Wilfred intended for everybody 62 back in Lansing. I said I'd try to describe it when I got back.

But I found I couldn't. 63

My restlessness with Mason—and for the first time in my life a restless- 64 ness with being around white people—began as soon as I got back home and entered eighth grade.

I continued to think constantly about all that I had seen in Boston, and 65 about the way I had felt there. I know now that it was the sense of being a real part of a mass of my own kind, for the first time.

The white people—classmates, the Swerlins, the people at the restaurant 66 where I worked—noticed the change. They said, "You're acting so strange. You don't seem like yourself, Malcolm. What's the matter?"

I kept close to the top of the class, though. The topmost scholastic 67 standing, I remember, kept shifting between me, a girl named Audrey Slaugh, and a boy named Jimmy Cotton.

It went on that way, as I became increasingly restless and disturbed 68 through the first semester. And then one day, just about when those of us who had passed were about to move up to 8-A, from which we would enter high school the next year, something happened which was to become the first major turning point of my life.

Somehow, I happened to be alone in the classroom with Mr. Ostrowski, 69 my English teacher. He was a tall, rather reddish white man and he had a thick mustache. I had gotten some of my best marks under him, and he had always made me feel that he liked me. He was, as I have mentioned, a natural-born "advisor," about what you ought to read, to do, or think—about any and everything. We used to make unkind jokes about him: why was he teaching in Mason instead of somewhere else, getting for himself some of the "success in life" that he kept telling us how to get?

I know that he probably meant well in what he happened to advise me 70 that day. I doubt that he meant any harm. It was just in his nature as an American white man. I was one of his top students, one of the school's top students—but all he could see for me was the kind of future "in your place" that almost all white people see for black people.

He told me, "Malcolm, you ought to be thinking about a career. Have   71
you been giving it thought?"

The truth is, I hadn't. I never have figured out why I told him, "Well,   72
yes, sir, I've been thinking I'd like to be a lawyer." Lansing certainly had no
Negro lawyers—or doctors either—in those days, to hold up an image I might
have aspired to. All I really knew for certain was that a lawyer didn't wash
dishes, as I was doing.

Mr. Ostrowski looked surprised, I remember, and leaned back in his   73
chair and clasped his hands behind his head. He kind of half-smiled and said,
"Malcolm, one of life's first needs is for us to be realistic. Don't misunderstand
me, now. We all here like you, you know that. But you've got to be realistic
about being a nigger. A lawyer—that's no realistic goal for a nigger. You need
to think about something you *can* be. You're good with your hands—making
things. Everybody admires your carpentry shop work. Why don't you plan on
carpentry? People like you as a person—you'd get all kinds of work."

The more I thought afterwards about what he said, the more uneasy it   74
made me. It just kept treading around in my mind.

What made it really begin to disturb me was Mr. Ostrowski's advice to   75
others in my class—all of them white. Most of them had told him they were
planning to become farmers. But those who wanted to strike out on their
own, to try something new, he had encouraged. Some, mostly girls, wanted
to be teachers. A few wanted other professions, such as one boy who wanted
to become a county agent; another, a veterinarian; and one girl wanted to be
a nurse. They all reported that Mr. Ostrowski had encouraged what they had
wanted. Yet nearly none of them had earned marks equal to mine.

It was a surprising thing that I had never thought of it that way before,   76
but I realized that whatever I wasn't, I *was* smarter than nearly all of those
white kids. But apparently I was still not intelligent enough, in their eyes, to
become whatever *I* wanted to be.

It was then that I began to change—inside.   77

I drew away from white people. I came to class, and I answered when   78
called upon. It became a physical strain simply to sit in Mr. Ostrowski's class.

Where "nigger" had slipped off my back before, wherever I heard it   79
now, I stopped and looked at whoever said it. And they looked surprised that
I did.

I quit hearing so much "nigger" and "What's wrong?"—which was the   80
way I wanted it. Nobody, including the teachers, could decide what had come
over me. I knew I was being discussed.

In a few more weeks, it was that way, too, at the restaurant where I   81
worked washing dishes, and at the Swerlins'.

One day soon after, Mrs. Swerlin called me into the living room, and   82
there was the state man, Maynard Allen. I knew from their faces that something was about to happen. She told me that none of them could understand
why—after I had done so well in school, and on my job, and living with them,

and after everyone in Mason had come to like me—I had lately begun to make them all feel that I wasn't happy there anymore.

She said she felt there was no need for me to stay at the detention home   83 any longer, and that arrangements had been made for me to go and live with the Lyons family, who liked me so much.

She stood up and put out her hand. "I guess I've asked you a hundred   84 times, Malcolm—do you want to tell me what's wrong?"

I shook her hand, and said, "Nothing, Mrs. Swerlin." Then I went and   85 got my things, and came back down. At the living room door I saw her wiping her eyes. I felt very bad. I thanked her and went out in front to Mr. Allen, who took me over to the Lyons'.

Mr. and Mrs. Lyons, and their children, during the two months I lived   86 with them—while finishing eighth grade—also tried to get me to tell them what was wrong. But somehow I couldn't tell them, either.

I went every Saturday to see my brothers and sisters in Lansing, and   87 almost every other day I wrote to Ella in Boston. Not saying why, I told Ella that I wanted to come there and live.

I don't know how she did it, but she arranged for official custody of me   88 to be transferred from Michigan to Massachusetts, and the very week I finished the eighth grade, I again boarded the Greyhound bus for Boston.

I've thought about that time a lot since then. No physical move in my   89 life has been more pivotal or profound in its repercussions.

If I had stayed on in Michigan, I would probably have married one of   90 those Negro girls I knew and liked in Lansing. I might have become one of those state capitol building shoeshine boys, or a Lansing Country Club waiter, or gotten one of the other menial jobs which, in those days, among Lansing Negroes, would have been considered "successful"—or even become a carpenter.

Whatever I have done since then, I have driven myself to become a   91 success at it, I've often thought that if Mr. Ostrowski had encouraged me to become a lawyer, I would today probably be among some city's professional black bourgeoisie, sipping cocktails and palming myself off as a community spokesman for and leader of the suffering black masses, while my primary concern would be to grab a few more crumbs from the groaning board of the two-faced whites with whom they're begging to "integrate."

All praise is due to Allah that I went to Boston when I did. If I hadn't,   92 I'd probably still be a brainwashed black Christian.

Topics for Discussion and Writing

1. Note how Malcolm X characterizes the various authorities (Mrs. Swerlin, Mr. Ostrowski, and so on) described in this chapter. Describe his tone. Observe how he strives to characterize his younger self in his dealings with and attitudes toward them. Do you feel that he is not fair enough, fair, or too fair in his characterizations of them and of himself? Explain.

2. Reflect on the conversation between Malcolm Little and Mr. Ostrowski. Recall similar "advice" conferences in your own life. How might Malcolm have reacted to Ostrowski had he not met Ella and visited her in Boston before his talk with the English teacher? How have your subsequent experiences given you a different perspective on the "advice about your future" that you received in earlier years?

3. Take on the roles of three of the people, other than Malcolm, important in this chapter. In the form of diary or notebook entries, have each of these people write about Malcolm: their concerns for him, their appraisal of him, their expectations for his future. Share your drafts with others who have read the chapter and perhaps written their own role plays. After discussion, revise your drafts.

DONTÉ CORNISH

"A Reaction and Retrospective"

"The time has come to confront societal ills such as blame and the desire to dominate. These are issues of greater significance than pigmentation."

The following essay was written by Donté Cornish for Professor Robert Karlson's class in dimensions of literature at George Mason University. The class read The Autobiography of Malcolm X *as part of an annual program at George Mason called "Text and Community," in which a single book is chosen to be discussed and written about in classes across campus.*

Cornish's essay was one of three winners in an essay contest held as part of the program.

Before and as You Read

1. Write about a time when reading or hearing a person's own words changed your views of that person. On what evidence had your earlier opinion been based? What features of the person's own words caused you to change your point of view? After your views changed, how did you feel about your former perspective?

2. One basic purpose of schools has been to bring people together to share their knowledge of and ideas about mutual concerns. In what ways do you feel that your education has fulfilled this purpose? In what ways has your education not promoted the ideals of sharing knowledge and ideas among students? Can you imagine one or two ways in which your current school could encourage this sharing?

3. As you read Donté Cornish's essay, note how he creates a sense of the communities of which he is a part. How would you define these communities? Mark passages that demonstrate that the reading of this book is genuinely important to him.

4. Read the preceding selection from *The Autobiography of Malcolm X.* What in the selection is new information to you? How do your feelings about Malcolm X after you have read the selection compare with any earlier impressions you might have had of this controversial figure? Write your reflections on this question and compare your views with those of Donté Cornish.

As FOR reading *The Autobiography of Malcolm X, as told to Alex Haley,* 1
I am apprehensive. The historical merit of his life is often overlooked because most people think of Malcolm X as inflammatory. People usually respond to the controversial aspects of his life more than to his contri-

butions. It is difficult to get beyond how the press portrays Malcolm X, even for people like myself who try to maintain objectivity.

His thoughts and rhetoric are still relevant and warrant examination in a 1990s context. "The white man knows his actions have been those of a devil!" (Haley 257). However, this sort of idea divides camps and draws battle lines. Therefore, the timing of such an endeavor on this campus seems askew, given the recent racial tension. I believe that concentrating on a figure who possessed an uncanny ability to raise people's ire will elicit a negative reaction from the community.

I'm aware of the goal in choosing to focus on Malcolm X. Here was a man who lived an extraordinary life and ultimately came to advocate peace among all human beings: "True Islam taught me that it takes all of the religious, political, economic, psychological, and racial ingredients, or characteristics, to make the Human Family and the Human Society complete" (375). Yet, I still think that distortions of the whole story presented to the community won't be enough to realize his transformation. Most will only see the provoking influence of a resurgent Left-wing perspective: a perspective created by the crisis-hungry popular press. That bothers me.

I don't mean to say that if an issue is controversial we should avoid it. Neither do I believe as a black man that black communities should accept whatever circumstances are thrust upon them.

The spirit of Malcolm X's beliefs were nurtured by The Nation of Islam. He rightfully shared those beliefs with his community because they were his true convictions. No one can deny that they were authentic and genuine. Far be it for me to undermine the liberation from social, economic and political captivity that he desired and strove to accomplish for black people all over the country. "Awakening this brainwashed black man and telling this arrogant, devilish white man the truth about himself, Betty understands, is a full time job" (233).

Despite the racial harmony that Malcolm X sought, people attempted to disgrace his efforts. Some said that he was motivated by self-interest, his critics tried to discourage his growing allegiance—and they did so by printing lies. That fact has a profoundly obscuring effect. Anyone inclined to believe lies in the past still harbors some of those lies. When I heard that much of the campus would be reading his autobiography, I, without realizing it, perpetrated some of that obscuring of the facts. Joking with a friend who admires Malcolm X, I said, "You know, he never led a march or registered a voter." This was my attitude toward Malcolm X—formulated from whatever I learned through the popular press. It was a view that allowed me to dismiss Malcolm X as a man with a tremendous ego, a man of no action. Upon reading the book, however, I realized that the statements I took to be truth were, in fact, lies.

Malcolm X did lead a march when his Muslim brother was brutalized by the Police. "A high Police official came up to me saying 'get those people out of there.' I told him that our brothers were standing peacefully, disciplined perfectly, and harming no one" (234). Furthermore, he definitely believed that by creating a united vote, black people could wield tremendous influence. "Whether you use bullets or ballots, you've got to aim well . . ." (416).

So, why was my first instinct to say that Malcolm X was inflammatory? 8 Perhaps it's because I came from a small town on the Eastern Shore of Maryland where Blacks and Whites smile in one another's faces. Even though race often pervades the thoughts of people in that town, many choose to ignore the issue. That is the easy way to avoid the difficult process of change. With respect to improving race relations in our communities, to re-examine racism through the same lens that was so volatile in the 1960s would only recapitulate hackneyed tensions. The complexities of race have always gone beyond skin color. However, they are rarely viewed from any perspective other than that of skin color. The time has come to confront societal ills such as blame and the desire to dominate. These are issues of greater significance than pigmentation. Malcolm X's autobiography has made me realize that we have two options: as a society blanketed by latent hatred, we can either rehash the malaise of old—or create a fundamental understanding about the human experience.

"Most of us adults are so afraid, so cautious, so 'safe,' and therefore so 9 shrinking and rigid and afraid that it is why so many humans fail" (411). In deep-seated fear is where racism gets its start. Malcolm X witnessed the devastating effects of that fear as a child: the brutalization of his father by white racists; his mother's committal to an asylum. So, associating race with hatred later in life is often a result of our childhood experiences. For example, in the third grade I tended to be a "bully." One day a little boy in my class upset one of my friends. I proceeded to chase him around the room. That is when he said, "Get your cotton pickin' paws off me!" My perception of that comment was not as scathing as he intended. For all I knew, he meant that my hands were on him; he didn't appreciate it and thus used a phrase that I didn't know in referring to my hands.

Had I realized his anger was a result of all the wretched things his parents 10 may have expressed to him about the vile nature of black people, I might have hurt him. If I was aware of the allusion he made to the bent and tortured Negroes who labored in the fields, I might have strangled him with my "cotton pickin' paws." It's hard for me to believe that young boy's anger was all his own.

Perhaps to be ignorant of such hatred would give young people the 11 freedom to develop a wholesome respect for anyone with a different color skin. I didn't hate that little boy because he was white. I hated him because I feared a lack of respect from my peers. It was important that they see me as superior to him. "Children have a lesson adults should learn . . ." (411).

William Blake once said, "The road of excess leadeth to the palace of 12 wisdom." Malcolm X's life was definitely one of excess. In the final chapter of his book he mentions his penchant for devotion, especially to Elijah Muhammed. So thorough a sense of commitment was perhaps a need to belong ultimately to something he could trust. ". . . America could offer a society where rich and poor could truly live like human beings" (371).

Despite his outward condemnation of white America, I can gather from   *13*
Malcolm X's transformation, after he went to the Holy Land, that he truly wanted to be at peace with his fellow humans. "Truly a paradise could exist where material progress and spiritual values could be properly balanced" (349).

After reading *The Autobiography of Malcolm X* and writing this response, I   *14*
wonder why my friend with whom I joked about Malcolm X's inaction didn't explain to me that I was suffering from an unfortunate delusion: a delusion that comes from hearing what I wanted to hear and believing what I wanted to believe—instead of seeking the truth. I hope it is not because my friend underestimated my ability to comprehend Malcolm X's transformation. For, if that is the case, then she committed the same crime against humanity that I did. It is foolish to believe that the community can't realize the enlightening effects of being exposed to Malcolm X.

Topics for Discussion and Writing

1. Think about Cornish's initial reaction to the choice of the *Autobiography* for the "Text and Community" program. Can you identify with his concern about the impact of a specific book on his community? Can you recall a school experience in which a piece of literature created controversy among students, teachers, and others in the community. Describe this incident. If you cannot recall such an experience, how do you account for the lack of controversy?

2. Based on your reading of this essay and other evidence you cite, write about the value of school programs that promote discussion of controversial works. How do you feel such discussions should be handled? If you could choose a book to be discussed in your school community, what would it be? What do you feel the benefits of the reading and discussion of this book would be?

3. From your reading of this essay, what would you imagine to be Cornish's goals for the communities of which he is a part? (See "Before and as You Read" topic 3.) Note statements in his essay that express his goals and values. If certain values are only implied in the essay, which passages lead you to infer these values?

4. This essay was written as a college assignment and later submitted to an essay contest. One can assume that the essay was written for the teacher and for the writer himself. Do you perceive other audiences to whom Cornish is speaking? Who are these readers? If you could imagine one of your school papers being published in a book such as this one, with a national readership, how might that change your perspective as a writer?

VICTOR VILLANUEVA, JR.

"Whose Voice Is It Anyway?"

> *". . . as far as I knew, I spoke something close to the standard dialect in the classroom. We thought ourselves Americans, assimilated."*
>
> Victor Villanueva, Jr. (born 1948) wrote the following essay in response to a speech by Richard Rodriguez given at an annual convention for elementary, middle, high school, and college English teachers. Beginning with a summary of Rodriguez's speech—in which the author of Hunger of Memory argues against the concept of "bilingual education"—Villanueva goes on to describe his own childhood and schooling, distinct from Rodriguez's in important ways.
>
> Originally from New York City, Villanueva now teaches English at Northern Arizona University.

Before and as You Read

1. Richard Rodriguez's popular autobiography, *Hunger of Memory* (Boston: Godine, 1982), has been widely excerpted in anthologies. Though Villanueva summarizes Rodriguez's argument, you may wish to read *Hunger of Memory* before reading "Whose Voice Is It Anyway?"

2. One point of Villanueva's essay is that while immigrants know that they are not part of the culture of their new countries, minorities (such as Blacks, Puerto Ricans, and American Indians in the United States) often wrongly assume that they are part of the mainstream. Write about a time in your life when, for whatever reason, you were surprised to discover that something you had assumed that "everybody does" was actually just common to a smaller group of people, including yourself. How did you feel when you realized this? Did you change your behavior in order to be included? If not, why?

3. How important do you feel it is for people living in the United States to learn to speak and write "standard" English? What have been your parents' attitudes on this question? Have you found differing views on this among your teachers? In what ways have the schools you've attended ranked students on the basis of how well they know the "standard" dialect?

4. Unlike many of the selections in this book, "Whose Voice Is It Anyway?" explicitly sets out to prove one point of view in opposition to another. As you read the essay, mark the different types of evidence Villanueva uses. What evidence impresses you most? Which least? Why?

D‌URING THE 1986 annual conference of the NCTE (National Council of Teachers of English) I attended a luncheon sponsored by the secondary section. Richard Rodriguez, author of *Hunger of Memory,* was the guest speaker. He spoke of how he came to be an articulate speaker of this standard dialect, and he spoke of the conclusions concerning language learning that his experiences had brought him to. He was impressive. I was taken by his quiet eloquence. His stage presence recalled Olivier's Hamlet. He spoke well. But for all his eloquence and his studied stage presence, I was nevertheless surprised by the audience's response, an enthusiastic, uncritical acceptance, marked by a long, loud standing ovation. I was surprised because he had blurred distinctions between language and culture, between his experiences and those more typical of the minority in America, between the history of the immigrant and that of the minority, in a way that I had thought would raise more than a few eyebrows. Yet all he raised was the audience to its feet.

In retrospect, I think I can understand the rave reception. The message   2
he so softly delivered relieved us all of some anxiety. Classroom teachers' shoulders stoop under the weight of the paper load. They take 150 students through writing and grammar, spelling and punctuation. Within those same forty-five-minute spurts they also work on reading: drama, poetry, literature, the great issues in literature. After that, there's the writers' club or the school paper or the yearbook, coaching volleyball or producing the school play. And throughout it all, they are to remain sensitive to the language of the nonstandard or non-English speaker. They are not really told how—just "be sensitive," while parents, the media, sometimes it seems the whole world, shake their fingers at them for not doing something about America's literacy problems. Richard Rodriguez told the teachers to continue to be sensitive but to forget about doing anything special. The old ways may be painful, but they really are best. There is a kind of violence to the melting pot, he said, but it is necessary. He said that this linguistic assimilation is like alchemy, initially destructive perhaps but magical, creating something new and greater than what was. Do as you have always done. And the teachers sighed.

Richard Rodriguez is the authority, after all: a bilingual child of immi-   3
grant parents, a graduate of two of the nation's more prestigious schools, Stanford and Berkeley, an English teacher, the well-published author of numerous articles and a well-received, well-anthologized book. He knows. And he says that the teachers who insisted on a particular linguistic form can be credited with his fame. But what is it, really, that has made him famous? He is a fine writer; of that there can be no doubt. But it is his message that has brought him fame, a message that states that the minority is no different than any other immigrant who came to this country not knowing its culture or its language, leaving much of the old country behind to become part of this new one, and in becoming part of America subtly changing what it means to be American. The American who brought his beef and pudding from England became the American of the frankfurter, the bologna sandwich, pizza. Typically American foods—like typical Americans—partake of the world.

At the luncheon, Richard Rodriguez spoke of a TV ad for Mexican-   4
style Velveeta, "the blandest of American cheeses," he called it, now speckled

with peppers. This cultural contrast, said Rodriguez, demonstrated how Mexico—no less than England or Germany—is part of America.

But I think it shows how our times face a different kind of assimilation.   5
Let's put aside for the moment questions as to why, if Mexicans really are being assimilated, they have taken so much longer than other groups, especially since Mexicans were already part of the West and Southwest when the West and Southwest became part of America. Let's look, rather, at the hyphen in Mexican-Velveeta. Who speaks of a German-American sausage, for instance? It's a hot dog. Yet tacos remain ethnic, sold under a mock Spanish mission bell or a sombrero. You will find refried beans under "ethnic foods" in the supermarket, not among other canned beans, though items as foreign-sounding as sauerkraut are simply canned vegetables. Mexican foods, even when as Americanized as the taco salad or Mexican-Velveeta, remain distinctly Mexican.[1]

And like the ethnic food, some ethnic minorities have not been assimi-   6
lated in the way the Ellis Islanders were. The fires of the melting pot have cooled. No more soup. America's more a stew today. The difference is the difference between the immigrant and the minority, a difference having to do with how each, the immigrant and the minority, came to be Americans, the difference between choice and colonization. Those who emigrated from Europe chose to leave unacceptable conditions in search of better. Choice, I realize, is a tricky word in this context: religious persecution, debtor's prison, potato famine, fascism, foreign takeover, when compared with a chance at prosperity and self-determination doesn't seem to make for much of a choice; yet most people apparently remained in their homelands despite the intolerable, while the immigrants did leave, and in leaving chose to sever ties with friends and families, created a distance between themselves and their histories, cultures, languages. There is something heroic in this. It's a heroism shared by the majority of Americans.

But choice hardly entered into most minorities' decisions to become   7
American. Most of us recognize this when it comes to Blacks or American Indians. Slavery, forcible displacement, and genocide are fairly clear-cut. Yet the circumstances by which most minorities became Americans are no less clear-cut. The minority became an American almost by default, as part of the goods in big-time real estate deals or as some of the spoils of war. What is true for the Native American applies to the Alaska Native, the Pacific Islander (including the Asian), Mexican-Americans, Puerto Ricans. Puerto Rico was part of Christopher Columbus' great discovery, Arawaks and Boriquens among his "Indians," a real-estate coup for the Queen of Spain. Then one day in 1898, the Puerto Ricans who had for nearly four hundred years been made

---

1. Mexican food is not the only ethnic food on the market, of course. Asian and Mediterranean foods share the shelves. But this too is telling, since Asians alone had had restricted access to the US before the country ended its Open Door Immigration Policy. When the US closed its doors in 1924, it was to regulate the flow of less desirable "new immigrants"—the Eastern and Southern Europeans who remain "ethnic" to this day. See Oscar Handlin's *Race in American Life,* New York: Anchor, 1957.

proud to be the offspring of Spain, so much so that their native Arawak and Boricua languages and ways were virtually gone, found themselves the property of the United States, property without the rights and privileges of citizenship until—conveniently—World War I. But citizenship notwithstanding, Puerto Rico remains essentially a colony today.[1]

One day in 1845 and in 1848 other descendants of Spain who had all but lost their Indian identities found themselves Americans. These were the long-time residents and landowners of the Republic of Texas and the California Republic: the area from Texas to New Mexico, Arizona, Utah, and California. Residents in the newly established US territories were given the option to relocate to Mexico or to remain on their native lands, with the understanding that should they remain they would be guaranteed American Constitutional rights. Those who stayed home saw their rights not very scrupulously guarded, falling victim over time to displacement, dislocation, and forced expatriation. There is something tragic in losing a long-established birthright, tragic but not heroic—especially not heroic to those whose ancestors had fled their homelands rather than acknowledge external rule.

The immigrant gave up much in the name of freedom—and for the sake of dignity. For the Spanish-speaking minority in particular, the freedom to be American without once again relinquishing one's ancestry is also a matter of dignity.

This is not to say that Richard Rodriguez forfeited his dignity in choosing not to be Ricardo. The Mexican's status includes not only the descendants of the West and Southwest, Spanish-speaking natives to America, but also immigrants and the descendants of immigrants. Richard Rodriguez is more the immigrant than the minority. His father, he told us, had left his native Mexico for Australia. He fell in love along the way, eventually settling with wife and family in Sacramento. America was not his father's first choice for a new home perhaps, but he did choose to leave his homeland in much the same way European immigrants had. The Rodriguezes no doubt felt the immigrants' hardships, the drive to assimilate, a drive compounded perhaps by the association in their and others' minds between them and the undocumented migrant worker or between them and the minority.

And it is this confusion of immigrant and minority in Richard Rodriguez with which we must contend. His message rings true to the immigrant heritage of his audience because it happens to be the immigrant's story. It is received as if it were a new story because it is confused with this story of the minority. The complexities of the minority are rendered simple—not easy—but easily understood.

Others tell the story of the minority. I think, for instance, of Piri Thomas and Tato Laviera, since theirs are stories of Puerto Ricans. My own

---

1. Nor is it a simple matter of Puerto Rico's deciding whether it wants to remain a commonwealth, gaining statehood, or independence. The interests of US industry, of the US military, and the social and economic ramifications of Puerto Rico's widespread poverty complicate matters.

parents had immigrated to New York from Puerto Rico, though not in the way of most. My mother, an American, a US citizen like all Puerto Ricans, fair-skinned, and proud of her European descent, had been sold into servitude to a wealthy Chicago family. My father, recently discharged from the US Army, followed my mother, rescued his sweetheart, and together they fled to New York. I was born a year later, 1948.

My mother believed in the traditional idea of assimilation. She and my father would listen to radio shows in English and try to read the American newspapers. They spoke to me in two languages from the start. The local parochial school's tuition was a dollar a month, so I was spared PS 168. Rodriguez tells of nuns coming to his home to suggest that the family speak English at home. For Rodriguez this was something of a turning point in his life; intimacy lost, participation in the public domain gained. A public language would dominate, the painful path to his assimilation, the path to his eventual success. A nun spoke to my parents, too, when I was in kindergarten. I spoke with an accent, they were told. They should speak to me in English. My mother could only laugh: my English was as it was *because* they spoke to me in English. The irony reinforced our intimacy while I continued to learn the "public language."

There is more to assimilating than learning the language. I earned my snacks at the Saturday matinee by reading the credits on the screen. I enjoyed parsing sentences, was good at it too. I was a Merriam-Webster spelling bee champ. I was an "A" student who nevertheless took a special Saturday course on how to do well on the standardized test that would gain me entry to the local Catholic high school. I landed in the public vo-tech high school, slotted for a trade. Jarapolk, whose parents had fled the Ukraine, made the good school; so did Marie Engels, the daughter of German immigrants. Lana Walker, a Black girl whose brains I envied, got as far as the alternate list. I don't recall any of the Black or Puerto Rican kids from my class getting in. I never finished high school, despite my being a bright boy who knew the public language intimately.

I don't like thinking minorities were intentionally excluded from the better school. I would prefer to think minorities didn't do as well because we were less conscious than the immigrants of the cultural distances we had to travel to be truly Americans. We were Americans, after all, not even seeing ourselves as separated by language by the time most of us got to the eighth grade. I spoke Spanglish at home, a hybrid English and Spanish common to New York Puerto Ricans; I spoke the Puerto Rican version of Black English in the streets, and as far as I knew, I spoke something close to the standard dialect in the classroom. We thought ourselves Americans, assimilated. We didn't know about cultural bias in standardized tests. I still don't do well on standardized tests.

A more pointed illustration of the difference between the minority and the immigrant comes by way of a lesson from my father. I was around ten. We went uptown one day, apartment hunting. I don't recall how he chose the

13

14

15

16

place. He asked about an apartment in his best English, the sounds of a Spanish speaker attempting his best English. No vacancies. My father thanked the man, then casually slipped into the customary small talk of the courteous exit. During the talk my father mentioned our coming from Spain. By the end of the chat a unit became available. Maybe my father's pleasing personality had gained us entry. More likely, Puerto Rican stereotypes had kept us out. The immigrant could enter where the minority could not. My father's English hadn't improved in the five minutes it had taken for the situation to change.

Today I sport a doctorate in English from a major university, study and teach rhetoric at another university, do research in and teach composition, continue to enjoy and teach English literature. I live in an all-American city in the heart of America. And I know I am not quite assimilated. In one weekend I was asked if I was Iranian one day and East Indian the next. "No," I said. "You have an accent," I was told. Yet tape recordings and passing comments throughout the years have told me that though there is a "back East" quality to my voice, there isn't much of New York to it anymore, never mind the Black English of my younger years or the Spanish of my youngest. My "accent" was in my not sounding midwestern, which does have a discernable, though not usually a pronounced, regional quality. And my "accent," I would guess, was in my "foreign" features (which pale alongside the brown skin of Richard Rodriguez). *17*

Friends think I make too much of such incidents. Minority hypersensitivity, they say. They desensitize me (and display their liberal attitudes) with playful jabs at Puerto Ricans: greasy hair jokes, knife-in-pocket jokes, spicy food jokes (and Puerto Ricans don't even eat hot foods, unless we're eating Mexican or East Indian foods). If language alone were the secret to assimilation, the rate of Puerto Rican and Mexican success would be greater, I would think. So many Mexican-Americans and Puerto Ricans remain in the barrios—even those who are monolingual, who have never known Spanish. If language alone were the secret, wouldn't the secret have gotten out long before Richard Rodriguez recorded his memoirs? In fact, haven't we always worked with the assumption that language learning—oral and written—is the key to parity, even as parity continues to elude so many? *18*

I'm not saying the assumption is wrong. I think teachers are right to believe in the potential power of language. We want our students to be empowered. That's why we read professional journals. That's why we try to accommodate the pronouncements of linguists. That's why we listen to the likes of Richard Rodriguez. But he spoke more of the English teacher's power than the empowerment of the student. "Listen to the sound of my voice," he said. He asked the audience to forget his brown skin and listen to his voice, his "unaccented voice." "This is your voice," he told the teachers. Better that we, teachers at all levels, give students the means to find their own voices, voices that don't have to ask that we ignore what we cannot ignore, voices that speak of their brown or yellow or red or black skin with pride and without need for bravado or hostility, voices that can recognize and exploit *19* the conventions we have agreed to as the standards of written discourse—without necessarily accepting the ideology of those for whom the standard dialect is the language of home as well as commerce, for whom the standard dialect is as private as it is public, to use Rodriguez' terms.

Rodriguez said at the luncheon that he was not speaking of pedagogy as much as of ideology. He was. It is an ideology which grew out of the memoirs of an immigrant boy confronting contrasts, a child accommodating his circumstances. He remembers a brown boy in a white middle-class school and is forced to say no to bilingual education. His classmates were the descendants of other immigrants, the products of assimilation, leading him to accept the traditional American ideology of a multiculturalism that manifests as one new culture and language, a culture and language which encompasses and transcends any one culture. I remember a brown boy among other brown boys and girls, blacks, and olives, and variations on white, and must agree with Richard that bilingualism in the classroom would have been impractical. But my classmates were in the process of assimilation—Polish, German, Ukrainian, and Irish children, the first of their families to enter American schools; my classmates were also Black and Puerto Rican. It seemed to this boy's eyes that the immigrants would move on but the minority would stay, that the colonized do not melt. Today I do not hear of the problems in educating new immigrants, but the problems of Black literacy continue to make the news. And I hear of an eighty per cent dropout rate among Puerto Ricans in Boston, of Mexicans in the Rio Grande Valley, where the dropout rate exceeds seventy per cent, of places where English and the education system do not address the majority—Spanish speakers for whom menial labor has been the tradition and is apparently the future. I must ask how *not* bilingual education in such situations. One person's experiences must remain one person's, applicable to many others, perhaps, but not all others. Simple, monolithic, universal solutions simply can't work in a complex society.

When it comes to the nonstandard speaker, for instance, we are torn between the findings of linguists and the demands of the marketplace. Our attempts at preparing students for the marketplace only succeed in alienating nonstandard speakers, we are told. Our attempts at accommodating their nonstandard dialects, we fear, only succeed in their being barred from the marketplace. So we go back to the basics. Or else we try to change their speech without alienating them, in the process perhaps sensing that our relativism might smack of condescension. Limiting the student's language to the playground and home still speaks of who's right and who's wrong, who holds the power. I would rather we left speaking dialects relatively alone (truly demonstrating a belief in the legitimacy of the nonstandard). The relationship between speaking and writing is complex, as the debate sparked by Thomas Farrell has made clear. My own research and studies, as well as my personal experiences, suggest that exposure to writing and reading affects speaking. My accent changes, it seems, with every book I read. We don't have to give voices

20

21

to students. If we give them pen and paper and have them read the printed page aloud, no matter what their grade, they'll discover their own voices.

And if we let the printed page offer a variety of world views, of ideol- 22
ogies, those voices should gather the power we wish them to have. Booker T. Washington, Martin Luther King, Jr., W. E. B. DuBois all wrote with eloquence. Each presents a different world view. Maxine Hong Kingston's "voice" resounds differently from Frank Chin's. Ernesto Galarza saw a different world than Richard Rodriguez. Rodriguez' is only one view, one voice. Yet it's his voice which seems to resound the loudest. Rodriguez himself provided the reason why this is so. He said at the luncheon that the individual's story, the biography or autobiography, has universal appeal because it strikes at experiences we have in common. The immigrant's story has the most in common with the majority.

Rodriguez implied that he didn't feel much kinship to minority writers. 23
He said he felt a special bond with D. H. Lawrence. It seems appropriate that Rodriguez, who writes of his alienation from family in becoming part of the mainstream, would turn to Lawrence. Lawrence, too, was a teacher turned writer. Lawrence, too, felt alienated from his working-class background. It was Lawrence who argued, in "Reflections on the Death of the Porcupine," that equality is not achievable; Lawrence who co-opted, left the mastered to join the masters. Is this what we want for our minority students? True, Lawrence's mastery of the English language cannot be gainsaid. I would be proud to have a Lawrence credit me with his voice, would appreciate his acknowledging my efforts as a teacher, and would surely applaud his accomplishment. But I would rather share credit in a W. B. Yeats, Anglo and Irish, assimilated but with a well-fed memory of his ancestry, master of the English language, its beauty, its traditions—and voice of the colony.

Topics for Discussion and Writing

1. Closely review the essay to define the ways in which Villanueva distinguishes between *immigrant* and *minority*. Do you find this a useful distinction? How might this distinction change your views of yourself and of others? Write in your journal about this possible change.

2. What does Villanueva mean by *assimilation*? Into what is the immigrant being assimilated? Learning theorists and sociologists frequently mention a process that is the opposite of assimilation. Called accommodation, it is a process in which the old changes to accept the new. As you observe American culture, what changes in standard views or practices have you seen? Focus in particular on changes brought about by the influence of the peoples named by Villanueva.

3. Based on your reading and experience, and taking into account differing views such as those of Rodriguez and Villanueva, would you support a U.S. constitutional amendment, such as some have proposed at various

times, to make English the official language of the country? What might be the purposes, benefits, and drawbacks of such a law? Discuss your thoughts with others who have also thought about this question; brainstorm ways to collect the data you would need to make an informed decision.

4. Villanueva does not describe his own practices as a teacher, but based on the principles he espouses here, write your speculations about an English class he'd teach at his university. What would be his objectives? What assignments might he make? If you were a student in his class, what features of your writing would he comment on?

KENDALL HAILEY

from *The Day I Became An Autodidact*

"Perhaps if what my classmates were facing now was life and not just another year of high school, they would share my excitement. I have a feeling it is conventional choices that lead to unconventional stimulants."

"With steno pad in hand," Kendall Hailey (born 1966) set out to record in her journal the day-by-day results of a most unconventional choice: not to return to high school for her senior year, not to go to college, and not to get a job, but to teach herself at home by "getting a head start on reading everything ever published." The choice was not only tolerated but also encouraged by her parents, novelist Elizabeth Forsythe Hailey and playwright Oliver Hailey. Following in their footsteps as a publishing writer, Kendall Hailey turned her journal into autobiography: The Day I Became an Autodidact: and the Advice, Adventures, and Acrimonies That Befell Me Thereafter *was published by* Delacorte Press in 1988.

We have reprinted excerpts of the book in which she reflects on her choice and on the differences of her life from those of others. Since the book is loosely organized as a series of observations from her daily writing, we feel that we can provide glimpses, as it were, into her story without doing violence to the overall structure.

Before and as You Read

1. To what degree are you an autodidact? Write about important learning that you have initiated and carried out on your own. What problems did you face? How did you attempt to deal with them?

2. Use your library to track down information on the history of formal education in the United States. How old are the first laws for mandatory public education? How common was it for a person to go to college, or even to high school in, say, 1900? How does the information you find influence your feelings about your own years of formal schooling?

3. Consider the personal characteristics that you feel would be necessary for a person to succeed as an autodidact. Do you feel that most people are capable of teaching themselves or that rare talent is required? Compare your ideas with those of others.

4. Remember that journal or diary writing, because it often captures a person's first thoughts about an event or idea, is likely to appear unformed, not fully thought out. As you read the selection, look for passages that have the "I just thought of this idea" quality. Does this quality appeal to you in any way? Where do you feel it succeeds? Where would you suggest careful reconsideration?

STARING AT the list today's mail brought, I made a solemn vow (my *1* very first solemn vow, I believe—I'm only fifteen). I am going to become an autodidact. I am never going back to school.

Of course, as bad luck would have it, I have only just finished the tenth *2* grade. But as soon as I can extricate myself from high school, it's over between me and formal education. And all because of that list.

As I opened the envelope from my school, I was already suspicious of *3* what school would have to say to me during the summer. And what I saw made me shudder. A mandatory (my least favorite word) summer reading list.

I read (rarely skimming) everything school tells me to from the middle *4* of September to the middle of June, but the summer is mine. And being told what to read during the summer suddenly made me realize that I don't really like being told what to read during the fall, winter, and spring either.

I cannot wait to tell Mom and Dad what I am becoming. Though I *5* wonder if they'll know what an autodidact is. I discovered the word thanks to the writer Jessica Mitford. Once asked on a forbidding form to list her degrees and not having any, she wrote "autodidact"—a swell word for one who is self-taught. It is nice indeed to have parents who, though they might not know what an autodidact is until I explain, will still welcome one into the family.

Just to be on the safe side (there's always the possibility they could turn *6* on a word they don't know), I took the most erudite approach I could manage. I said Milton's family had supported him for five years while he educated himself (I did not mention this was after his graduation from Cambridge—though perhaps I should have. Go to Cambridge and you still have to educate yourself). I was asking for only one year.

They said to take ten. But as it only took five to send Milton on the *7* road to blindness, I said I'd stick to one for now. Of course I can't really become a full-time autodidact until I finish high school, but I can start practicing this summer. And make sure I like this word I've taken for my life. Though I know I will.

Thinking of Milton sitting in his family's country home reading every- *8* thing ever published, I know that's what I want to do. And if I need glasses later on, then that's not too much of a price to pay.

FIFTY-SEVEN DAYS TILL SCHOOL

———

What I Hope To Do:
Get a Head Start on Reading Everything Ever Published.

———

IT'S THE beginning of summer and the morning of the first day of   9
my self-education. Actually, it's the middle of July and a little past
noon, but it feels like the beginning and the morning.

I've said something pleasant to every member of my family, almost, so   10
now I can ignore them for a while in favor of literature. And it is Leo Tolstoy
who is giving me the eye. No, not *War and Peace*. I'm not that brave this early.
But I do think I have enough courage for *Anna Karenina*.

Great books rarely make their way into daily conversation (or at least my   11
daily conversation), but I remember my father saying once that he disagreed
with the first sentence of *Anna Karenina*. Unlike Tolstoy, Dad thinks all unhappy families are alike, and every happy family is happy in its own way. I hate
to disagree with Tolstoy so early in our relationship, and yet I do trust Dad.
But to put them both in their place, I can't imagine finding a family that could
manage to be always happy or always unhappy, hard though they might try.

I have begun *Anna,* and this is my favorite sentence yet about families: 12

> Every person in the house felt that there was no sense in their
> living together, and that the stray people brought together by chance
> in any inn had more in common with one another than they . . .

It would be hard to find an honest family member who would not admit   13
to that thought crossing his mind several times a day. I love my family, but I
do sometimes wonder what I would think of them had I not started out
loving them and then gotten to know them.

We are an odd bunch. A father, a mother (not too odd yet), a younger   14
sister (getting odder), a grandmother (approaching the bend), and an uncle
(and round it).

It was my uncle who sparked my first battle with formal education. He   15
had infantile paralysis when he was ten years old, and one day when I was in
kindergarten I decided to paint a picture of his wheelchair. My teacher looked
at it and said it was the most depressing picture she'd ever seen because it was
all gray. And wouldn't it be nice to put some yellow in it? At the age of five,
I did my best to explain that the painting was a true rendering of my uncle's
wheelchair, not a comment on my life.

And that was the only trouble my uncle Thomas's being in a wheelchair   16
ever caused me. When we went to Europe as a break from kindergarten, I
rode in his lap across the continent. There is little better in life than a moveable
lap. In Paris, I had a nightmare—Thomas had learned to walk. And there had
gone my lap.

And so if sometimes I wonder how I ever got to know my family, I am   17
almost always glad I did. The great gift of family life is to be intimately
acquainted with people you might never even introduce yourself to, had life
not done it for you.

I have great autodidact news.   18

At sixteen, Tolstoy entered the University of Kazan but was hopelessly 19
disappointed (I confess the encyclopedia did not actually say "hopelessly")
and returned to his estate to conduct his own education. (Little did I know
what a big role country homes and estates played in literary life. I've got to
get one.)

I shared this information with all available family members, and when I 20
returned to the encyclopedia was very glad I had not read them the next
phrase, which said that he did not achieve much success.

Of course, now that I think about it, that's wonderful. It turns out that 21
to be a great literary genius, not only do you not have to go to college, you
don't even have to be very good at educating yourself.

I always like to begin a new phase of life on a comforting note. 22

I've finished *Anna Karenina*. My favorite characters were Levin and Kitty, 23
though I loved Anna too. I never cared much for Vronsky.

As it turns out, Levin and Kitty are based on Tolstoy and his wife. Which 24
just confirms my suspicion that the best writing is about what you know.
However, the happiness Levin finds at the end of the book was soon lost by
Tolstoy, who spent much of his life in confusion and agony.

His novel has aroused in me many doubts about how we can hope to do 25
good things. I dreamed last night that the only way I wouldn't feel guilty
spending my life being a writer would be to cure cancer first—and even then
I would still feel a little guilty.

A little exhausted from having read every one of *Anna*'s nine hundred 26
fifty pages, I have started the four-hundred-page and larger print *Madame
Bovary* (I wonder if Flaubert ever thought his book would be described like
that). Despite the print size, I like *Anna Karenina* better, and I was very disappointed to hear from Mom that the distinguishing characteristic of Flaubert's
work is his desire to choose exactly the right word. A gift I wonder if I'll ever
be able to appreciate because when it comes to French, my gift is choosing
exactly the wrong one.

Discovery: After failing his law examinations, Flaubert was allowed to 27
remain at home devoting himself to literature.

I have new respect for the man and his parents. . . . 28

I wonder if it will prove harder to be an individual when not surrounded 29
by other people. Having never succumbed to peer pressure, I hope I won't be
affected by life pressure.

Mom told me this morning that she'd discovered the key to peer pres- 30
sure. She said it was the fault of parents who by excluding children from their
world force them into a world dominated by their so-called peers. I agreed
with her and thanked her for giving me a perfect life so far.

But for a little while longer, it is nice to be near the dangerous world of 31 peer pressure. For a few last weeks, before I become an independent dot, it is nice to be part of a circle.

My friends and I were discussing the future today. I do find it a little 32 disconcerting that they can all answer when asked where they want to go to college, but so few have a response when asked what they want to do with their lives.

Of course, I am too harsh a judge because I have always had a response 33 when asked what I wanted to do. I grew up watching my father do everything in life with a steno pad in his left hand and a pen in his right. It seemed an ideal way to live and so I decided that I too would live that way. However, the fact that he never set down a specific time to write, but instead wrote while waiting in line at the post office, while pulling weeds, while talking, while walking, while even driving a car, led to my greatest childhood misconception.

I did not really understand that writing was his profession. I assumed he 34 was kind of a waiter-in-line-at-post-offices/weed puller/talker/walker/driver. And he, as I assumed everyone did, wrote while doing all his jobs. I thought that was the way everyone lived. They had these odd jobs and, of course, always wrote. When I envisioned my future life, it was usually as a farmer (I preferred the profession of farmer to that of waiter-in-line-at-post-offices/ weed puller/talker/walker/driver), but of course I would always be writing a new play while feeding the sheep. A great melancholy accompanied the realization that not everyone in the world carried a steno pad. And I still feel that perhaps secretly they all do.

So I urge all my friends to be writers. But none have listened. They are 35 waiting for college to find out what they want to do with their lives. But is that what college should be used for? I thought its main use was for the consumption of knowledge. Yet I have met very few people of any age who recommend higher education for anything but the experience of it. One frank friend of my mother's told me: "I only went to college to lose my virginity and I had to take a year abroad to do that."

I do concede that college is very useful for becoming a doctor, a lawyer, 36 an architect, an engineer, or Madame Curie. But for people without such definite ambitions, college seems more a passageway from childhood to adulthood than a place to learn. And as rites of passage go, it would be hard to find a more expensive one. In general, the parents of my friends are going to be shelling out close to twenty thousand dollars a year. With plane trips home and all the items necessary to make a home away from home feel like a real one, I suspect in a few years an education at a private university will cost somewhere very near a hundred thousand dollars per child. Whereas being an autodidact is open to everyone.

I remember when I was little, watching a program on television (I have 37 found the only surefire rule of bringing up a wonderful child is never to limit the amount of television consumed) that mentioned how much college could cost, and I was suddenly so afraid I might not be able to go (college being, at that tender age, my main ambition).

Yesterday I read that the fear of escalating college costs has made some   *38*
states adopt a system whereby new parents give the state a certain sum of
money at their child's birth, and the state, in exchange, guarantees the child a
college education in eighteen years.

What happens if they've raised an autodidact? Why must college be the   *39*
only choice after high school? I think I am the only one of my graduating
class not choosing it, but also the only one whose parents have not limited the
choices to college or getting a job.

So many parents seem perfectly willing to shell out all that money for an   *40*
education, but so unwilling just to provide food and shelter and allow their
children the opportunity to educate themselves. Or to get a head start on their
chosen careers. Without the pressure to show immediate monetary gain. Or just
time to take a look at this life we have been tested on so furiously for so long.

Did you know that the eighteen-year-old leaving for the first semester of   *41*
college has the highest incidence of suicide among teenagers? We are so terrified that the decisions we make now will decide the rest of our lives. And we
feel as if we have to decide everything by tomorrow. That shouldn't be what
tomorrow is for. The point of tomorrow is it's a chance to change our minds.

A girl in my class has had to leave school because she has leukemia. All   *42*
this time I have been thinking I was so much braver than anyone I knew
because I was going to be facing life while they were just going to school.
And in my all-encompassing self-concern, I had not even realized she was ill.

It was strange in the sense that the news came during a period when I   *43*
have been obsessed by the fear of losing my grandmother or my dog—my
two oldest living relatives.

At school, after I heard the news, I went in the bathroom and cried. I   *44*
said a few rather clichéd lines like why did it have to happen to her—all of
which I meant very deeply—their truth has made them clichés.

I told both my parents what had happened but avoided telling Nanny   *45*
and Thomas because I thought it would make them so sad. However, as I was
telling Nanny good night, I remembered I had to borrow a stamp from her,
and Nanny (who is loathe to part with a stamp without a reason) asked whom
I had written. I told her I was writing a friend who had to leave school because
of leukemia. And she said, "Oh, Kendall, I'm so glad you're writing her.
Maybe if you tell her what's happening in school, she won't miss it." I kissed
her good night, assuring her Mallory was much too bright to miss school.

And as I was walking to my room, I suddenly realized that in writing   *46*
the letter today (something I want to do every day), school had validity to me
for the first time. At last the fact that my English teacher shakes the hands of
people who say brilliant things in class and that I have never gotten my hand
shook (thank God) seemed important because it might amuse Mallory.

Mom got a letter today from a woman saying she thought *Life Sentences*   *47*
had saved her life. A few weeks after reading the novel, she, like the book's

heroine, was raped. She said the novel was in the back of her mind, so she tried to react as the heroine did and she felt that was what saved her life.

I guess that's about the zenith when it comes to the effect a novel can   48 have on a life. And how right that *Life Sentences* should save a life since it is a book that makes me want so much to live. And to live so much.

And, heaven knows, it has already begun to make me live more. It was   49 because of *Life Sentences* and the book tour that I had to leave drama, which would have required my presence at rehearsals, and take up painting, which is a more portable art.

And painting has been the great gift of school to me. With a teacher so   50 marvelous I would go to college if I could expect to find more like her. But I'm afraid she's a rarity—an art teacher who does not impose her vision on her students. She saves it for her own paintings.

And thanks to her beautiful introduction to the art, I'll want to paint all   51 my life. As my five-year-old self would have said, I'm changing my profession from farmer to painter, but of course I'll always have a steno pad in hand.

. . . I guess George Bernard Shaw was right when he said anyone can   52 write a first act. Not that my twelve pages really qualify as a first act, but you should see my second act. Seven pages and I've already run out of things to say. But then I don't seem to be able to do anything twice. I started a second painting tonight (I think of the self-portrait as my first real painting). And I think I made a big mistake painting to the strains of Handel. His music is so alive and vibrant I became convinced my painting was as good as his music. Until the record ended. I only paint to dirges from now on.

Today I told Dad I now trusted him totally and asked where he kept *The*   53 *Green Hills of Africa,* but he suggested I begin with *A Farewell to Arms.*

As for Henry James, I know there will be more of him in my future,   54 but I feel guilty sticking to one author when there are so many left unexplored.

And I admit a little verbal economy will be refreshing. Several readers   55 were reported lost for years in a Henry James sentence.

I just got home from seeing the 1950s television show *Together with Music*   56 starring Mary Martin and Noel Coward. Watching them perform made me want to so much. You would think talent like that would give one an inferiority complex, but I think it's usually the inept who make one feel inept. Greatness and timelessness seem so easy when you watch Noel and Mary.

I'm afraid it must say something about Henry James that I felt guilty at   57 the mere thought of reading another of his books immediately. Yet directly after finishing *A Farewell to Arms,* I went right to Hemingway's *A Moveable Feast.* Forgive me, Henry.

It is the purple dawn. I'm not being fancy (I wouldn't dare after reading   58 Hemingway), it really is purple.

I had some social contact today, but finding out how little my friends   *59*
have read this summer has had the opposite effect I supposed—I couldn't wait
to get back to Ernest, but that may be more a credit to him than a reflection
on my illiterate acquaintances.

These people have lived a whole summer and what do they have to   *60*
show for it? They are going to return for their senior year tomorrow without
having learned a thing.

Julie Reich is one of my closest friends and the most literary of the   *61*
whole class (proof positive of this is that the only thing she ever submitted to
our school literary magazine was turned down). Her total reading for the
summer consisted of the first five pages of *Pride and Prejudice.* Not being able
to get involved stopped her from reaching the sixth.

It takes only the first sentence to get involved in *Pride and Prejudice.* ("It   *62*
is a truth universally acknowledged, that a single man in possession of a good
fortune, must be in want of a wife.") And after reading the second ("However
little known the feelings or views of such a man may be on his first entering
a neighbourhood, this truth is so well fixed in the minds of the surrounding
families, that he is considered as the rightful property of some one or other
of their daughters."), I should think anyone of sound mind would want to
follow Miss Austen anywhere.

I did my best to bolster Jane's sagging reputation (it hit its nadir at this   *63*
gathering), but I seriously doubt whether any of these people will ever see
the sixth page of any of her six novels.

Perhaps I am underestimating them reading-wise, but I think I've been   *64*
overestimating them life-wise.

One girl whom I thought I knew well mentioned casually tonight that   *65*
she was still recovering from getting stoned two days ago. I was shocked, but
then I am shocked too easily to be taken too seriously. How naive can a person
be? I suppose I should consider the word "very."

I realize I have always overlooked the use of drugs, alcohol, and sex by   *66*
my classmates in an attempt not to feel odd man out.

Why are there so few of us who find life exciting enough not to need   *67*
to hallucinate? Perhaps if what my classmates were facing now was life and
not just another year of high school, they would share my excitement. I have
a feeling it is conventional choices that lead to unconventional stimulants.

———

What I Did:
*923 pages of Charles Dickens, 196 pages of Henry James, 458 pages of Ernest
Hemingway, and 19 pages of my own.*

———

UNCONVENTIONAL CHOICES

———————

What I hope To Do:
Make as many as possible.

———————

Though it is no longer a part of my life, I suppose it should be noted   *68*
that formal education began again today. I have not had one moment of
regret. A fact that stuns me. But I seem to have a knack for life decisions. It is
certainly a wonderful thing to go all summer and not worry about school or
have cardiac arrest when "Back to School" ads start appearing. Yet I remember
school very fondly, which must be proof I left at the right time.

Autodidacts do not get the same respect householdwise that students of   *69*
formal education do. When school started, Nanny began making up Brooke's
bed. I waited for that seventy-eight-year-old to make her way into my room
to do mine, but she never came. I followed her to her room and asked if she
didn't think autodidacts should get their beds made? She said she didn't. I was
offended educationally, but I'm just writing it off to the terrible seventy-eights.

Actually, I rather like making my bed (though I like to save doing it till   *70*
early evening—you never know when Nanny might change her mind, and I'd
hate for the bed to be made the morning she did).

I started my second act for a second time and now all is going swim-   *71*
mingly. I so enjoy writing my play. The thing is, before I write any more of
it I must decide what the plot is—not that I necessarily want one, but it does
help to give the chatter a direction.

I have decided I like writing at night. I look forward to it all day. It is   *72*
something to build to. I just hope I'm not taking myself too catastrophically
seriously.

I am in awe of autumn. I just stand outside and stare at trees—and keep   *73*
a lookout for other members of the family who might very well have me
committed. But now that I'm no longer in school, I finally have time to enjoy
my favorite season. It is all so beautiful. I feel a bit like Wordsworth walking
near Tintern Abbey. I can finally understand how those poets felt.

You know, now that I think about it, it defies understanding to teach   *74*
the Romantics in a classroom. Sitting in that room, pulling up my knee socks
(Brooke has given up on me fashion-wise) and trying to get comfortable at
my desk, I had no feeling for any of them.

Though I'm not going to read any of the Romantics right this minute   *75*
and disprove my wonderful theory, I do feel closer to them in spirit.

An unproductive day ended with me going to bed chanting, "You're a 76
failure, you're a failure"—which produced a curiously comforting effect.

The first acrimony of an autodidact: the fact that there is a barrier to 77
break down every day with Brooke because I have not had to sit through
seven and a half hours of school. She hates me a little bit for it. But usually if
I approach her very nicely after she's had something to eat, then all is forgiven.

Tomorrow I'm going with Dad to pick her up at school. I have been 78
avoiding doing this because I hate to get so close to formal education again.
And I will have to sit on the floorboard to avoid acquaintances and questions
about just what I am doing with my life. But I'll risk it to see Brooke that
much sooner.

You know, I'm actually lonely for that child when she's at school. I think 79
this is retribution for the way I treated her when she was little. I was always
busy doing homework and kept wishing she'd just say hello, then leave me
alone. I had an image of the perfect little sister, who would come in, give me
a kiss, then leave with our relationship still in a state where I could smile after
her—as opposed to her demanding my attention and then crying and screaming and yelling when she didn't get it. I never thought the sins against the little
sister could catch up with me.

Just three minutes ago I was in such an indecisive mood about what to 80
read next. But the solution has just come in the form of *The Brothers Kara-
mazov.* I am very excited because, first and most important, it is so much
shorter than I expected.

Tonight I went with Dad to the playwrights' group he leads. About 81
thirty playwrights meet every week and read scenes from their works in progress. It all sounded very interesting when I was in school and Dad would come
home and tell us about the scenes. Sitting through some of them is a different
matter. I suppose I was rather superior and nasty in the car going home (the
only people who are ever superior are the people who have no right to be)
and we had a small argument, but today he has forgiven and forgotten all (and,
worst of all, I may have to go again!).

. . . . I am watching fields whizzing by and imagining myself on a horse 82
riding through them. We are on a train to Chicago to see a production of one
of my father's plays.

As I sit here watching the moving fields and thinking how much they 83
look like process shots, I am trying to think up something to write. I read that
Ben Hecht wrote the script for *Nothing Sacred,* a great Carole Lombard screw-
ball comedy I have yet to see, on a four-day train trip across the country. Well,
I've got a two-day train trip across half the country twice. Which does add up
to four days and one country. If only I added up to Ben Hecht.

I am actually thinking of writing a sequel to the Thin Man films. With 84
Nick and Nora aged appropriately. Of course, William Powell is now ninety-

one years old. But Myrna Loy is just seventy-nine. The awful truth is I was born about fifty years too late. Sixty-one to be exact. Of course, Nanny was born in 1905, my ideal year of birth, and she wasn't ever buddies with Myrna Loy. You can even be born in the right time and still miss the right life.

. . . . This trip to Chicago is the first time I have been introduced to a 85 lot of new people since I left school. I hadn't realized how much more difficult it would be to answer the question, "What grade are you in?" Eleventh certainly was an easier reply.

Now I let Brooke respond first and hope they'll just forget to ask me. 86 But after she says eighth, I have no choice but to take a deep breath and say as quickly as I can, "Well, actually, I've decided to take a year off between high school and college."

What has amazed me is that the response to this quickly sputtered state- 87 ment is so positive. Nine out of ten think it's a wonderful choice. The only trouble is, I haven't learned how to argue with the disagreeing tenth. I find myself so politely agreeing with them that you'd think I'd be spending the next day begging colleges to Federal Express me their catalogues. Of course, I don't really think there's much point in arguing with the closed-minded. I have found that no one I truly respect ever disagrees with me. Of course that makes sense, as I decide after a person agrees or disagrees with me whether or not I truly respect them.

The play opens tonight, but we boarded the train this morning. We 88 don't like to stay in a city after the critics have come out of their caves.

We saw a beautiful last performance. I keep trying to imagine what it 89 would be like to walk into a theatre and see one of my father's plays without having grown up alongside them. I can't help thinking I would be overwhelmed with the feeling that I had found all I was looking for in the mind of one man.

I always so hate to leave a theatre in which one of Dad's plays has lived 90 for a while. I doubt if there are any friendships that grow faster than those connected with a play. Yet once the play is in perfect working order, they seem to end. Or perhaps not so much end as be put on hold until a new play.

As a very well-planned present of fate to cheer us up, we met the 91 sweetest taxi driver, who drove us back to our hotel after the play. He liked us the minute he found out we were not from Chicago. For some unknown reason, he hates all Chicagoans. He asked if we could guess where he was from, and Dad guessed Egypt and hit it right on the nose, and the relationship was sealed. He said he would be at the hotel this morning to take us to the train station, adding his only regret is that he did not meet us earlier so he could have introduced us to his pet snake (the most current in a long line of pet snakes—they keep running away from home, he says, but I think he is getting his revenge on the people of this city).

We woke up this morning to a Chicago looking beautiful but half 92 buried from an overnight blizzard. The usually packed cab stand was deserted, except for our beloved Chicago-hating Egyptian. As we approached, a woman was begging him to let her have the cab. We were within earshot when she made her fatal mistake:

"But I'm a native Chicagoan," she pleaded.   93

"That is the best reason yet for not letting you in my cab."   94

He drove us to the station without turning on his meter. He said he   95
wanted no money for the ride. We were friends. He is going to school, getting
a master's degree (the first pedant I've liked), and Dad said it was his education
that was important and forced the money on him. He mourned again that we
would not be meeting his pet snake and drove away. Perhaps the best friendships are the impermanent ones. My first lesson of the year. . . .

Today I finished painting my background for my new painting of Mom,   96
and tomorrow I'm starting on Mom. Dad said tonight, "It's going so well why
don't you just leave your mother out of it?" Encouragement, encouragement,
encouragement.

At the moment I am at odds with my father. Mom is now rewriting her   97
new novel. And though Dad has a lot of ideas, he always says that finally she
must follow her own vision.

Then, directly after telling her that, he runs down here to tell me how   98
to paint my painting, even using a throw rug to cover parts of the canvas he
feels should be banned from human sight forever.

It's different in writing. I listen to everything he says in that area, but the   99
man has no firsthand experience with painting. And I'm not even sure I want
to paint the "masterpieces" he wants me to paint. I like to paint to capture the
way I saw us and that may not always lead to a masterpiece.

I've discovered the sweetest writer—Saki (the pen name of the Scottish   100
writer, H. H. Munro). We met in the most roundabout way.

Dad came running down at about 11:15 last night, saying there was a   101
great *Alfred Hitchcock Presents* on. It was indeed—with Hermione Gingold, Pat
Hitchcock, and such a dear story.

The credits at the end said it was based on a story by Saki, and today   102
Dad found another of his stories, "The Lumber Room," for me in a collection. It was full of truth and laughter. When I read the notes on Saki at the
back of the collection, I saw that one of his books of short stories is entitled
Beasts and Superbeasts, and suddenly I remembered reading Cole Lesley's book
about Noel Coward and writing down that very title because Noel Coward
loved Saki so much. I was in school then, so I never followed up on it, but I
am so glad I didn't lose Saki a second time.

I keep worrying that there are so many people I miss. Education is, I   103
think, the meeting of kindred souls. I am kindred with Terence (his *Phormio*
certainly makes for a fun evening), can get nowhere with Lucretius, and buddies with Saki. Tomorrow I sink my teeth into Catullus. An overflowing life.

Topics for Discussion and Writing

1. What are Kendall Hailey's complaints against high school and college? Have you voiced similar complaints at any time? Since it is probably universal for students to complain about school, why is it so novel for a person to make the sort of choice Hailey did?

2. Compare Hailey with at least two other persons featured in this chapter who for one reason or another left conventional schools at an early age and sought learning on their own. How is she like them? How is she different? Is it more or less surprising to you that a Kendall Hailey would leave school than, say, a Malcolm Little or a Leila Fisher (other persons featured in this chapter)? Why?

3. For many years states and localities have fought the desires of some parents to teach their children at home, outside formal public or private schools. (These battles are recorded in the works of John Holt and in the newsletter he founded, *Growing without Schooling*.) Consult your local school officials about the laws, policies, and procedures governing home schooling in your area. What arguments do school officials use against home education? How would a Kendall Hailey argue in rebuttal?

4. Talk with faculty and admissions officials at your local college about the chances for acceptance of a student without the formal educational background most applicants present. How do, or would, officials evaluate such a student? Interview local professional employers as well. How do they, or would they, regard job applications in their fields from an autodidact?

For Further Thought

1. Review your writing in response to any of the "Thinking about the Issues" questions at the start of this chapter. Revise your writing based on your work with the selections.

2. Use the concept of the Wisdomkeepers (see the selection by Harvey Arden) to think about people who have taught you important lessons. Write a personal essay about one such person and his or her influence on you. Try to recreate the person and yourself at that time as vividly as possible. Note techniques that the writers you've studied in this chapter use to create vivid scenes and characters.

3. The essays in this chapter describe schools as places and as relationships among people. Design what for you would be an ideal school. Consider both these dimensions. What will be the goals of your school? How would the physical place help you achieve them? What would students do in your school? How would people work with one another? Visualize yourself as both teacher and student in your ideal school. Express your design in words and other media, such as drawings or dramatized scenes, that can help others understand it. Share your ideas with others in your current school environment; discuss with them ways in which your school might be modified to begin to realize the ideals you've presented.

CHAPTER TEN

The Artist's Calling

> *"A not unsuccessful man with an Oscar told me that when he is out of work an inertia so great overwhelms him that he is practically catatonic. He could not leave his home during one period for over three months. 'Why?' I asked. 'Fear,' he said."*
>
> Frank Langella, *"Actors' Demons,"* Screen Actor *Fall 1990:2.*

Art touches our lives in different ways. Almost all of us found some expression, as we grew up, through song or poetry, acting or drawing, dancing or musicianship. And who among us has not enjoyed the fruits of those who dedicate their lives to artistic expression?

The *American Heritage Dictionary* defines art as "The conscious production or arrangement of sounds, colors, forms, movements, or other elements in a manner that affects the sense of beauty. . . ." Such a definition provides the barest skeleton of understanding, as art is difficult to define apart from the artist. The "consciousness" of art involves an occupation more difficult to assess than the surgeon's perfect incision or the accountant's balanced ledger. Each incision or ledger can be judged as correct or even perfect. We do not know art that easily.

For the artist who hopes that his or her talent will provide a decent living, art proves to be a callous employer, demanding the artist's best years, but giving no guarantees and little security. For those who perform, art is a fickle lover—always pursuing someone younger, more talented, lither, better looking, or more versatile. Few professions require so much of one's personal life as the arts. And few exact such a personal toll.

So why do people give themselves to the struggle of the artist? Why, instead, does one not sell insurance policies, or fix plumbing, or make donuts? To quote one artist, "There was never any choice in the matter. I didn't choose acting, acting chose me."

This chapter will help you think about the complicated issues that define artists and their world. Perhaps you share the concerns and lifestyles of those represented here, or you know someone who does. The only certainty is that art is not a frivolous pastime for the idle. Humans cannot survive for long without trying to make sense of their world. And it is through art that the human soul reaches out to embrace the universe.

Thinking about the Issues

1. Recall your very first childhood encounter with the arts. What impressed you? In your journal try to reconstruct that experience. Remember the place, whom you were with, the sounds, the smells, the colors, the light. What did you carry away with you that day? How were you affected?

2. In the middle of a blank sheet of paper write the word *Artist*. For at least five minutes, write down any word or phrase that this word sparks in you. (You might use the clustering exercise described in chapter 2, pp. 22.) Use the associations you have made to write several definitions of what you perceive an artist to be.

3. In your journal write about your own artistic work. Describe it in some detail. Do you feel that your audience has appreciated what you have done? How important is an audience's approval to you?

4. Discuss with your class what is meant by *inspiration*. What role might inspiration play in the work of an artist? How do you compare the inspiration of the artist with that of the inventor or scientist? How do you contrast the three?

5. Why do you suppose some artists appear to lead unstable lives? What is it about Mozart or Monroe, Beethoven or Booth, Hugo or Hendrix that makes happiness so elusive? Is their pain different from the pain of their peers? Or are they simply less able to cope? Should they be judged by different standards in life? After death?

ANNIE DILLARD

from *The Writing Life*

> *A shoe salesman—who is doing others' tasks, who must answer to two or three bosses, who must do his job their way, and must put himself in their hands, at their place, during their hours—is nevertheless working usefully. Further, if the shoe salesman fails to appear one morning, someone will notice and miss him. Your manuscript, on which you lavish such care, has no needs or wishes; it knows you not. Nor does anyone need your manuscript; everyone needs shoes more.*

> *Annie Dillard's* The Writing Life *(1986) is this prolific artist's autobiographically written advice to those who would follow her calling. For more on Dillard's life and work, see our introduction to the selection from her nonfiction book* Pilgrim at Tinker Creek *that we have included in chapter 3.*

Before and as You Read

1. Do you have a "writing ritual"? What do you do before you settle down to work? One college student we know cannot write a paper until her room is in perfect order; she says that she can't think clearly in a messy environment. Another student cannot work without classical music playing softly. Yet another needs chips and dip and a coke by the word processor.

    What do you do to prepare yourself to work? Are you one of those lucky writers who can lasso the muse in almost any environment and at almost any time? For those who use them, what purpose do personal "writing rituals" serve?

2. Do some research on your favorite writer. (One good source on current, established writers is *Contemporary Authors,* available on the reference shelves of the library.) You might also look for autobiographical or biographical sources that reveal what this writer feels about the art of writing. What did you learn about this person that you never knew? Does the new knowledge of your favorite writer change your view of him or her?

3. As you read this selection, make a note of the many metaphors that Dillard uses. Write down those that you consider particularly eloquent or insightful. Why does she use metaphor? Why doesn't she "just say it"? Does the use of metaphor enhance her communication with us? Can you think of historic figures who are famous for their metaphors? Why are metaphors memorable?

4. When you consider that Annie Dillard won a Pulitzer Prize for her first book, *Pilgrim at Tinker Creek,* you might be daunted by her talent. Yet it may prove comforting to learn that she has many of the same difficulties that we all do when faced with a blank page or a blank screen. What does this tell you about writing? What does this tell you about your personal experience as a writer? Discuss these ideas with members of your class.

WHEN YOU are stuck in a book; when you are well into writing 1
it, and know what comes next, and yet cannot go on; when every
morning for a week or a month you enter its room and turn your back on it;
then the trouble is either of two things. Either the structure has forked, so the
narrative, or the logic, has developed a hairline fracture that will shortly split
it up the middle—or you are approaching a fatal mistake. What you had
planned will not do. If you pursue your present course, the book will explode
or collapse, and you do not know about it yet, quite.

In Bridgeport, Connecticut, one morning in April 1987, a six-story 2
concrete-slab building under construction collapsed, and killed twenty-eight
men. Just before it collapsed, a woman across the street leaned from her window and said to a passerby, "That building is starting to shake." "Lady," he said,
according to the Hartford *Courant*, "you got rocks in your head."

. . . . To find a honey tree, first catch a bee. Catch a bee when its legs 3
are heavy with pollen; then it is ready for home. It is simple enough to catch
a bee on a flower: hold a cup or glass above the bee, and when it flies up, cap
the cup with a piece of cardboard. Carry the bee to a nearby open spot—best
an elevated one—release it, and watch where it goes. Keep your eyes on it as
long as you can see it, and hie you to that last known place. Wait there until
you see another bee; catch it, release it, and watch. Bee after bee will lead
toward the honey tree, until you see the final bee enter the tree. Thoreau
describes this process in his journals. So a book leads its writer.

You may wonder how you start, how you catch the first one. What do 4
you use for bait?

You have no choice. One bad winter in the Arctic, and not too long 5
ago, an Algonquin woman and her baby were left alone after everyone else in
their winter camp had starved. Ernest Thompson Seton tells it. The woman
walked from the camp where everyone had died, and found at a lake a cache.
The cache contained one small fishhook. It was simple to rig a line, but she
had no bait, and no hope of bait. The baby cried. She took a knife and cut
a strip from her own thigh. She fished with the worm of her own flesh
and caught a jackfish; she fed the child and herself. Of course she saved the
fish gut for bait. She lived alone at the lake, on fish, until spring, when she
walked out again and found people. Seton's informant had seen the scar on
her thigh.

It takes years to write a book—between two and ten years. Less is so 6
rare as to be statistically insignificant. One American writer has written a
dozen major books over six decades. He wrote one of those books, a perfect
novel, in three months. He speaks of it, still, with awe, almost whispering.
Who wants to offend the spirit that hands out such books?

Faulkner wrote *As I Lay Dying* in six weeks; he claimed he knocked it 7
off in his spare time from a twelve-hour-a-day job performing manual labor.
There are other examples from other continents and centuries, just as albinos,
assassins, saints, big people, and little people show up from time to time in

large populations. Out of a human population on earth of four and a half billion, perhaps twenty people can write a book in a year. Some people lift cars, too. Some people enter week-long sled-dog races, go over Niagara Falls in barrels, fly planes through the Arc de Triomphe. Some people feel no pain in childbirth. Some people eat cars. There is no call to take human extremes as norms.

Writing a book, full time, takes between two and ten years. The long poem, John Berryman said, takes between five and ten years. Thomas Mann was a prodigy of production. Working full time, he wrote a page a day. That is 365 pages a year, for he did write every day—a good-sized book a year. At a page a day, he was one of the most prolific writers who ever lived. Flaubert wrote steadily, with only the usual, appalling, strains. For twenty-five years he finished a big book every five to seven years. My guess is that full-time writers average a book every five years: seventy-three usable pages a year, or a usable fifth of a page a day. The years that biographers and other nonfiction writers spend amassing and mastering materials are well matched by the years novelists and short-story writers spend fabricating solid worlds that answer to immaterial truths. On plenty of days the writer can write three or four pages, and on plenty of other days he concludes he must throw them away.   *8*

Octavio Paz cites the example of "Saint-Pol-Roux, who used to hang the inscription 'The poet is working' from his door while he slept."   *9*

The notion that one can write better during one season of the year than another Samuel Johnson labeled, "Imagination operating upon luxury." Another luxury for an idle imagination is the writer's own feeling about the work. There is neither a proportional relationship, nor an inverse one, between a writer's estimation of a work in progress and its actual quality. The feeling that the work is magnificent, and the feeling that it is abominable, are both mosquitoes to be repelled, ignored, or killed, but not indulged.   *10*

The reason to perfect a piece of prose as it progresses—to secure each sentence before building on it—is that original writing fashions a form. It unrolls out into nothingness. It grows cell to cell, bole to bough to twig to leaf; any careful word may suggest a route, may begin a strand of metaphor or event out of which much, or all, will develop. Perfecting the work inch by inch, writing from the first word toward the last, displays the courage and fear this method induces. The strain, like Giacometti's penciled search for precision and honesty, enlivens the work and impels it toward its truest end. A pile of decent work behind him, no matter how small, fuels the writer's hope, too; his pride emboldens and impels him. One Washington writer—Charlie Butts—so prizes momentum, and so fears self-consciousness, that he writes fiction in a rush of his own devising. He leaves his house on distracting errands, hurries in the door, and without taking off his coat, sits at a typewriter and retypes in a blur of speed all of the story he has written to date.   *11*

Impetus propels him to add another sentence or two before he notices he is writing and seizes up. Then he leaves the house and repeats the process; he runs in the door and retypes the entire story, hoping to squeeze out another sentence the way some car engines turn over after the ignition is off, or the way Warner Bros.' Wile E. Coyote continues running for several yards beyond the edge of a cliff, until he notices.

The reason not to perfect a work as it progresses is that, concomitantly, *12* original work fashions a form the true shape of which it discovers only as it proceeds, so the early strokes are useless, however fine their sheen. *Only when a paragraph's role in the context of the whole work is clear can the envisioning writer direct its complexity of detail to strengthen the work's ends.*

Fiction writers who toss up their arms helplessly because their characters *13* "take over"—powerful rascals, what is a god to do?—refer, I think, to these structural mysteries that seize any serious work, whether or not it possesses fifth-column characters who wreak havoc from within. Sometimes part of a book simply gets up and walks away. The writer cannot force it back in place. It wanders off to die. It is like the astonishing—and common—starfish called the sea star. A sea star is a starfish with many arms; each arm is called a ray. From time to time a sea star breaks itself, and no one knows why. One of the rays twists itself off and walks away. Dr. S. P. Monks describes one species, which lives on rocky Pacific shores:

"I am inclined to think that *Phataria* . . . always breaks itself, no matter *14* what may be the impulse. They make breaks when conditions are changed, sometimes within a few hours after being placed in jars. . . . Whatever may be the stimulus, the animal can and does break of itself. . . . The ordinary method is for the main portion of the starfish to remain fixed and passive with the tube feet set on the side of the departing ray, and for this ray to walk slowly away at right angles to the body, to change position, twist, and do all the active labor necessary to the breakage." Marine biologist Ed Ricketts comments on this: "*It would seem that in an animal that deliberately pulls itself apart we have the very acme of something or other.*"

The written word is weak. Many people prefer life to it. Life gets your *15* blood going, and it smells good. Writing is mere writing, literature is mere. It appeals only to the subtlest senses—the imagination's vision, and the imagination's hearing—and the moral sense, and the intellect. This writing that you do, that so thrills you, that so rocks and exhilarates you, as if you were dancing next to the band, *is barely audible to anyone else.* The reader's ear must adjust down from loud life to the subtle, imaginary sounds of the written word. An ordinary reader picking up a book can't yet hear a thing; it will take half an hour to pick up the writing's modulations, its ups and downs and louds and softs.

An intriguing entomological experiment shows that a male butterfly will *16* ignore a living female butterfly of his own species in favor of a painted cardboard one, if the cardboard one is big. If the cardboard one is bigger than he is, bigger than any female butterfly ever could be. He jumps the piece of cardboard. Over and over again, he jumps the piece of cardboard. Nearby, the real, living female butterfly opens and closes her wings in vain.

Films and television stimulate the body's senses too, in big ways. A nine-foot handsome face, and its three-foot-wide smile, are irresistible. Look at the long legs on that man, as high as a wall, and coming straight toward you. The music builds. The moving, lighted screen fills your brain. You do not like filmed car chases? See if you can turn away. Try not to watch. Even knowing you are manipulated, you are still as helpless as the male butterfly drawn to painted cardboard.   17

That is the movies. That is their ground. The printed word cannot compete with the movies on their ground, and should not. You can describe beautiful faces, car chases, or valleys full of Indians on horseback until you run out of words, and you will not approach the movies' spectacle. Novels written with film contracts in mind have a faint but unmistakable, and ruinous, odor. I cannot name what, in the text, alerts the reader to suspect the writer of mixed motives; I cannot specify which sentences, in several books, have caused me to read on with increasing dismay, and finally close the books because I smelled a rat. Such books seem uneasy being books; they seem eager to fling off their disguises and jump onto screens.   18

Why would anyone read a book instead of watching big people move on a screen? Because a book can be literature. It is a subtle thing—a poor thing, but our own. In my view, the more literary the book—the more purely verbal, crafted sentence by sentence, the more imaginative, reasoned, and deep—the more likely people are to read it. The people who read are the people who like literature, after all, whatever that might be. They like, or require, what books alone have. If they want to see films that evening, they will find films. If they do not like to read, they will not. People who read are not too lazy to flip on the television; they prefer books. *I cannot imagine a sorrier pursuit than struggling for years to write a book that attempts to appeal to people who do not read in the first place.*   19

Topics for Discussion and Writing

1. Make a journal entry about a group called The Struggling Writers Society. Since writing is in some ways a solitary endeavor, how might the members of such a society help each other? Write about yourself and your classmates as writers in a positive way. In such a community, what would you consider to be helpful when you begin a writing assignment? What role would your instructors play in this community? What role would you play?
2. Write a short essay on any topic of your choice. Use Annie Dillard's style. Draw concrete images with your words. Mobilize metaphors. Is it easier to write when you have a style to imitate?
3. In your journal write a newspaper article about you, the latest *New York Times* best-selling author. Describe your work. Write a glowing review. (Be bold! Be proud!)

4. What would you like to achieve as a writer? Think of all the possibilities. Ask your writing instructor for guidance in setting goals and seeking out the various writing resources available to you through your school and community. Establish a plan that you can follow throughout the year, and document your progress in your writing journal. Always remember that problems with writing are only dangerous if they make you stop writing.

5. Find a copy of the *American Heritage Dictionary of the English Language*. Read the Introduction by the editor. Read about the editorial staff, the contributors, and the consultants. Write what you believe it takes to publish a dictionary. How are dictionaries designed to help writers? What is in the mind of the writers that contribute to such an endeavor?

JEFFRIES THAISS
"Reflections on an Actor's Journal"

>   *"My experience as an actor in training has been that as you become an actor you move past, or rather, completely devour, stage fright, and it becomes something more profound . . . , a fear, or self-consciousness, that lives with you night and day."*
>
>   *Jeffries Thaiss (born 1971) was a senior in the drama program at the North Carolina School of the Arts in Winston-Salem when he wrote this essay for* A Sense of Value. *With professional experience on television and the stage since age 12, he plans a career as an actor. He lives in New York City*

Before and as You Read

1. Think about some embarrassing moments in your life. What happened? Why were you embarrassed? How did you cope with the humiliation so that it did not continue to affect your spirits?
2. Write frankly about some "performance anxiety" or "stage fright" that you currently feel. Is there some art that you'd like to express but are afraid to because you fear failure? Write also about a kind of performance that you are not afraid to do, but that you know others do fear. How do you account for your confidence?
3. Observe the writer using the journal as a tool to deal with perceived failure and fear. Note how the writing flows emotionally and how each part of an entry relates to the part immediately before it.
4. As you read Jeffries Thaiss's "Reflections on the Journal," think about the audience he is trying to reach. Who is his audience in the first section?

Wednesday, September 30, 1992

O N THE twentieth anniversary of Roberto Clemente's last hit, I feel   *1*
like I have acted my last moment on stage—although my departure from the profession will be a little less spectacular than the great Puerto Rican's.

   Ugh. Romeo and Juliet. West Side Story. Love's Labour's Lost. I expe-   *2*
rienced an incredible actor's soup tonight. After rehearsing LLL for four hours (after having studied it all day and rehearsing it the night before) I walked into the first tech of my R&J and WSS balcony scenes. Ugh. Nothing I did worked. Where was I? Not singing or acting, just screwing up. Godammit! It won't get any better. I am frustrated. What to do. This is silly. Ha Ha.

   Okay, what am I doing? Okay, I need to clear my head. Yesterday it was   *3*
really good. Really good. Why was it different? Well, I was in the theatre

tonight. That does change things—or at least they always say it does. Well, I didn't feel like that was the reason. I'm so tired. I don't know. Right now I don't feel I can think. It seemed like it was going so slow. The scenes were crawling. Very embarrassing. My partners were both terrific. Am I being too hard on myself, or did I really stink that bad? Well, I was singing off key and acting like an idiot. Okay, enough. I can do it. Time for sleep. Or something. I have so much damn work to do. Gerry is great. Thank God.

Thursday, October 1, 1992

George Brett, last night, notched his 3,000th hit, paralleling Clemente's 4 feat twenty years to the day. Tonight, my feelings of frustration and embarrassment parallel those I had last night. But worse: the WSS and R&J scenes were seen by an audience tonight, it being dress before the big gala event on Saturday. Also, since I've sucked two nights in a row—but have I? Okay—I felt bad about my singing, especially as compared to my Maria, who has a voice to end all voices. Nobody would give me the time of day afterward, as if they were too embarrassed to. Oh my God. I know I was flat on some notes. I wonder if I was just way off in outer space. Why is this happening? The scenes were going so well! I hate this! What the hell is going on? I did a lot of good, invigorating, freeing work on it today—not heavy, brainy, tense stuff, but various Barney exercises to open it up. I feel they worked for the R&J. I actually feel good about the R&J. But MY GOD! WHAT THE HELL! My singing must have sucked. I must have been way off key. And Gerry is such a positive person, I fear he would think, "If I tell him, it'll just get worse."

C'mon—I'm not THIS bad. I mean—I got that feeling one gets when 5 someone knows an awful secret about you, or something awful has happened, and no one wants to say a word. They still like and respect you, but GEEZ! have you got problems now!

WHAT THE HELL! I HATE THIS! THIS SUCKS! COULD I HAVE 6 BEEN THAT BAD? WHO CAN I TALK TO? NOBODY. MY PARA- NOIA IS TOO INTENSE, MY INSECURITY TOO GREAT TO BE ABLE TO BELIEVE ANY PRAISE OR WITHSTAND ANY CRITI- CISM. THIS IS MOST upsetting because I want to be a really great singer. I want to be Mandy Patinkin, and think I can be. I just need to train consistently and not be afraid. This is a great opportunity to defeat fear and go on in courage, but screw opportunities—I want to be great. Shit. I'll think of something. Maybe. WHAT THE HELL? In case you haven't noticed, I'm amazed at this.

Saturday, October 3, 1992

It is three in the afternoon. I've just finished rehearsing the Russian 7 dance in LLL with Felix. I came home, showered, made out a shopping list, meditated and will go to Gianni Final dress in twenty minutes. I feel better about my scenes. I'm just timid about my voice. I have to enjoy it and let it fly. I'm holding back because I'm scared. This won't be my best work, but, well, we've just slapped this thing together, what do you want. I'm sure the Gianni people will love it.

Yesterday I got some confidence boosters from people I respect, so   *8*
I'm ready to roll. It'll all be over tonight at 10:30, at which time I can begin to concentrate almost solely on LLL—I must be off book by Monday. After Gianni this afternoon, I'll write out a schedule for Sunday and balance my checkbook. I've let all money concerns slide into the toilet the last couple weeks.

Sunday, October 4, 1992

It's all over. After it ended—I was sad. I had a good time. I got compli-   *9*
ments here and there from people, which leads me to believe I wasn't that bad after all. We were given a standing O (all of the scenes—at the end of the presentation). I think we served our purpose well. And I didn't feel particularly embarrassed about what happened. Now I can concentrate full time on *Love's Labour's Lost,* on which I have a bundle of work to do by tomorrow afternoon. I am getting frustrated. I have to learn to let go. I really don't want to talk about it, other than to say that I have to be a bit easier on my self from now on.

Reflections on the Journal, December 1992

Reflecting on my journal entry of twelve weeks ago, I am struck with   *10*
both how painful it is to read and how familiar I am with these feelings.

The two scenes I speak of, the balcony scenes from *West Side Story,*   *11*
and *Romeo and Juliet,* were part of a presentation that my school, the North Carolina School of the Arts, was giving in honor of one of the founding fathers. At the same time, my class and I were beginning rehearsals for *Love's Labour's Lost.*

Most everyone is familiar with stage fright, or at least with the nerves   *12*
that accompany public speaking. Usually after you get started with your presentation, you get comfortable; the fear goes away. My experience as an actor in training has been that as you *become* an actor you move past, or rather, completely devour stage fright, and it becomes something more profound (it certainly has in my case), a fear, or self-consciousness, that lives with you night and day.

The process of actor training is peculiar, as I believe, indeed, is acting,   *13*
in the public's perception. Because our "instrument" is our bodies, voices, minds, and souls, and the form of our art is very nearly congruous with our everyday and "real" selves, and because it is very difficult for the individual actor to know how he or she is being perceived (as it's difficult to know that

in our everyday existences as well), it is necessary for actors to be ultra-aware of how others see them. In my experience, you either muster up enough courage to confront, accept, and challenge very basic and habitual elements of yourself, or you ignore them. The former is painfully embarrassing and requires a lot of patience, but, hopefully, eventually leads to a more dynamic and effective instrument. The latter is easier, but keeps you from progressing in the field you love, and you know it.

I think it boils down to the old axiom: "to do what you want to do, you 14 must first do what you don't want to do." As you become aware of your idiosyncracies (i.e., your particular posture, vocal quality, recurring vocal or physical mannerisms, predictable emotional responses to certain stage situations, etc.), and begin working on expanding or stretching your instrument, it's easy to become highly defensive about them, knowing that they are on display.

My journal is an exhibition of one of my more defensive moments. As 15 I became more sensitive to how I was being perceived by those watching, I became less and less occupied with being present *in the scene,* which led to my being more and more aware that I wasn't doing as good work as I like to, which became more and more embarrassing.

I have found that acting well requires a tremendous amount of faith. 16 Because you can't really know how you look ("are they laughing at me or at something else? Did they shift in their seats because I'm bad, or is it something else?"), I believe that you must have faith that you have the basic natural ability to do anything on the stage well, that you have the knowledge and tools to build and correct any specific scene or moment, and that if you are true to what you as the character want, and not what you as the actor are scared of, everything will turn out well.

You have to accept that you're not perfect, and appreciate that nobody 17 expects you to be, either; that some audience members will like you no matter what, and some will hate you no matter what (it's your problem or theirs). As cryptic as that sounds, it's very comforting to be able to look at this art form from a distance and know that it's a lot more than a popularity contest, and, if you're accepting of yourself as mortal, a lot easier to win.

Topics for Discussion and Writing

1. Compare the two sections of the selection. How are they different? Mark passages or words that convey these differences. Try rewriting a paragraph of each section so that it conveys the tone of the other section of the work.

2. What do you feel Thaiss means by "looking at this art form from a distance"? Does this statement appear ironic to you? Can you relate to his feeling? How can a performer be both, as Thaiss states, "present in the scene" and "distant"?

3. Study the journal and the reflection for Thaiss's explicit and implicit beliefs about what audiences expect from actors. What do you expect from the actors you watch? How does Thaiss's work affect your perceptions about the difficulty and skill of the actor?

4. Think about the role of actors, and of drama in general, in shaping the values and beliefs of a culture. Write about at least one performance or work that has helped shape your convictions. Identify at least one performer whom you respect as a spokesperson for a political cause or point of view. Why do you feel that performers have this power?

ROBERT HENRI

from *The Art Spirit*

> "It is often said, 'The public does not appreciate art!' Perhaps the public is dull, but there is just a possibility that we are also dull, and that if there were more motive, wit, human philosophy, or other evidences of interesting personality in our work the call might be stronger."

> Robert Henri (1865–1929) was known both as a great painter and as a great teacher. Born in Cincinnati and raised in Denver, Henri's talent and desire as a painter led him to the Philadelphia Academy of Fine Art at age 18, and then—after a year spent painting pictures on clam shells for tourists at Atlantic City to earn the money—to Europe to continue his study and practice.

> While not nearly so famous as the French Impressionists, who were his somewhat older contemporaries, Henri became an important interpreter of impressionist art, translating the revolutionary freedom of these painters into a distinctive American style. His influence came both through his painting and through his New York school for artists. At the incessant urging of his students, he compiled his lecture notes, thoroughly revised by Henri himself, into the collection titled The Art Spirit (1923), now a classic of the discipline. We have reprinted two brief sections of the book.

Before and as You Read

1. Visit an art gallery or museum. Take notes as you observe the art work. What media and which works evoke the strongest reaction from you? Why? How would you describe your favorite works from the collection for others?

2. Try some sketches of scenes or objects from your daily life. What are you attempting to show? What are you deliberately leaving out? What does your attempt to draw teach you about what you are drawing?

3. Think about something manufactured that you consider to be visually beautiful, but that some others do not appreciate to the degree that you do. How do you account for the difference in perceptions? Conversely, think about something manufactured that you do not find beautiful but that appeals to others. Again, why do you think your tastes differ? Write these observations in your journal. Do you believe in the old saying, "Beauty is in the eye of the beholder," or does your thinking lead you to believe that all beautiful objects have some characteristics in common?

4. *The Art Spirit* is a collection of Henri's notes, plus bits of lectures and speeches and informal talks with students. Though to some extent fragmented and separate, do these pieces seem to have coherence, an idea or "spirit" that joins them? As you read, consider the pieces fit together. Develop a statement that begins "According to Robert Henri, good art is. . . ." Compare your statement with those drafted by others. Discuss the similarities and the differences.

THE APPRECIATION of art should not be considered as merely a *1* pleasurable pastime. To apprehend beauty is to work for it. It is a mighty and an entrancing effort, and the enjoyment of a picture is not only in the pleasure it inspires, but in the comprehension of the new order of construction used in its making.

Get up and walk back and judge your drawing. Put the drawing over *2* near the model, or on the wall, return to your place and judge it. Take it out in the next room, or put it alongside something you know is good. If it is a painting put it in a frame on the wall. See how it looks. Judge it. Keep doing these things and you will have as you go along some idea of what you are doing.

I once met a man who told me that I always had an exaggerated idea of *3* things. He said, "Look at me, I am never excited." I looked at him and he was not exciting. For once I did not overappreciate.

There are painters who paint their lives through without ever having any *4* great excitements. One man said to me, "I lay it in in the morning, then I have luncheon and I take a nap, after which I finish." Certainly a well regulated way for a quiet gentleman and quite unlike the procedure of an idea-mad enthusiast who works eighteen hours at a stretch.

One of the reasons that exhibitions of pictures do not attract a larger *5* public is that so many pictures placidly done, placidly conceived, do not excite to imagination. The pictures which do not represent an intense interest cannot expect to create an intense interest.

It is often said "The public does not appreciate art!" Perhaps the public *6* is dull, but there is just a possibility that we are also dull, and that if there were more motive, wit, human philosophy, or other evidences of interesting personality in our work the call might be stronger.

A public which likes to hear something worth while when you talk *7* would like to understand something worth while when it sees pictures.

If they find little more than technical performances, they wander out *8* into the streets where there are faces and gestures which bear evidence of the life we are living, where the buildings are a sign of the effort and aspiration of a people.

It may be that the enthusiast does not exaggerate and that an excited *9* state is only an evidence of the thrill one has in really seeing.

When the motives of artists are profound, when they are at their work *10* as a result of deep consideration, when they believe in the importance of what they are doing, their work creates a stir in the world.

The stir may not be one of thanks or compliment to the artist. It may *11* be that it will rouse two kinds of men to bitter antagonism, and the artist may be more showered with abuse than praise, just as Darwin was in the start, because he introduced a new idea into the world.

The complaint that "the public do not come to our exhibitions—they *12* are not interested in art!" is heard with a bias to the effect that it is *all* the public's fault, and that there could not possibly be anything the matter with art. A thoughtful person may ponder the question and finally ask if the fault is totally on the public's side.

There are two classes of people in the world: students and non-students. 13 In each class there are elements of the other class so that it is possible to develop or to degenerate and thus effect a passage from one class to the other.

The true character of the student is one of great mental and spiritual 14 activity. He arrives at conclusions and he searches to express his findings. He goes to the market place, to the exhibition place, wherever he can reach the people, to lay before them his new angle on life. He creates a disturbance, wins attention from those who have in them his kind of blood—the student blood. These are stirred into activity. Camps are established. Discussion runs high. There is life in the air.

The non-student element says it is heresy. Let us have "peace!" Put the 15 disturber in jail.

In this, we have two ideas of life, motion and non-motion. 16

If the art students who enter the schools today believe in the greatness 17 of their profession, if they believe in self-development and courage of vision and expression, and conduct their study accordingly, they will not find the audience wanting when they go to the market place with expressions of their ideas.

They will find a crowd there ready to tear them to pieces; to praise them 18 and to ridicule them.

Julian's Academy, as I knew it, was a great cabaret with singing and huge 19 practical jokes, and as such, was a wonder. It was a factory, too, where thousands of drawings of human surfaces were turned out.

It is true, too, that among the great numbers of students there were 20 those who searched each other out and formed little groups which met independently of the school, and with art as the central interest talked, and developed ideas about everything under the sun. But these small groups of true students were exceptional.

An art school should be a boiling, seething place. And such it would be 21 if the students had a fair idea of the breadth of knowledge and the general personal development necessary to the man who is to carry his news to the market place.

When a thing is put down in such permanent mediums as paint or stone 22 it should be a thing well worthy of record. It must be the work of one who has looked at all things, has interested himself in all life.

Art has relations to science, religions and philosophies. The artist must 23 be a student.

The value of a school should be in the meeting of students. The art 24 school should be the life-centre of a city. Ideas should radiate from it.

I can see such a school as a vital power; stimulating without and within. 25 Everyone would know of its existence, would feel its hand in all affairs.

I can hear the song, the humor, of such a school, putting its vitality into 26
play at moments of play, and having its say in every serious matter of life.

Such a school can only develop through the will of the students. Some 27
such thing happened in Greece. It only lasted for a short time, but long
enough to stock the world with beauty and knowledge which is fresh to
this day.

Schools have transformed men and men have transformed schools. 28

When Wagner came into the world it was very different from when he 29
left it, and he was one of the men who made the changes.

Such people are very disturbing. They often create trouble, we can't 30
sleep when they are around.

If the art galleries of the future are to be crowded with spectators it will 31
depend wholly on the students.

If there had been no such disturbers as Wagner, auditoriums would not 32
now be filled with listeners.

When a drawing is tiresome it may be because the motive is not worth 33
the effort.

Be willing to paint a picture that does not look like a picture. 34

The mere copying, without understanding, of external appearances can 35
hardly be called drawing. It is a performance and difficult, but—

Every movement, every evidence of search is worthy of the considera- 36
tion of the student.

The student must look things squarely in the face, know them for what 37
they are worth to him.

Join no creed, but respect all for the truth that is in them. 38
The battle of human evolution is going on. 39
There must be investigations in all directions. 40
Do not be afraid of new prophets or prophets that may be false. 41
Go in and find out. The future is in your hands. 42

You can learn much by a cool study of the living eye. Examine it closely 43
and record in your mind just what and where its parts are. In pictures eyes
should fascinate, arrest, haunt, question, be inscrutable, they should invite into
depths. They must be remarkable. You must have your anatomical knowledge
so that you can use it without consciously thinking of it, and your technique
must be positive and swift. Eyes express human sensitiveness and they must be
wonderfully done.

I am sure there are many people—and there are artists—who have never 44
seen a whole head. They look from feature to feature. You can't draw a head
until you see it whole. It's not easy. Try it. When I first realized this it seemed
that I had to stretch my brain in order to get it around a whole head. It seemed
that I could go so far, but it was a feat to comprehend the whole. No use

trying to draw a thing until you have got all around it. It is only then that you comprehend a unity of which the parts can be treated as parts.

_____

Topics for Discussion and Writing

1. Review and summarize what Henri says about the relationship of the artist and the viewing public. Do you agree with him, or do you agree with those who decry public lack of interest?
2. What does Henri say here about what the artist should strive to do? What does he say the artist should not do? Identify an artist who seems to you to have followed the philosophy of art Henri expresses here. Write as much as you know about this artist and how the public received his or her work. Find additional information on this person.
3. Based on what you read here of Henri's views, describe subjects, styles, and examples of art that he would probably praise (including very modern work). Then locate some examples of Henri's own painting. In what ways does the work match his philosophy? In what ways does it seem not to conform with what he says?
4. Consider Henri's statement "Art has relations to science, religions, and philosophies. The artist must be a student." Relate this statement to your own experience as an artist or as an appreciator of art. Can you imagine an art without relations to other disciplines such as those he names?
5. Do you perceive any dangers in the philosophy of art expressed here? Explain. Can you cite examples from history? How might Henri argue with those who prefer a less "spirited" purpose for art?

_____

GELSEY KIRKLAND AND GREG LAWRENCE
from *Dancing on My Grave*

> "*I was not born a ballerina. I did not emerge from the womb on pointe, nor did I wear a tutu instead of diapers. I was a baby pudgeball, with a head like a tulip bulb and belly to match.*"

> *Thus Gelsey Kirkland (born 1952 in Bucks County, Pennsylvania) begins her autobiography,* Dancing on My Grave *(1986). We have reprinted a portion of Chapter Two, "Cat's Cradle," which explores her early years in ballet and her early success with the School of American Ballet in New York, the school directed by the legendary George Balanchine. The autobiography goes on to recount both her rise to stardom with the American Ballet Theatre and the chronic depression and drug addiction that almost ended her career.*

> *Kirkland's coauthor and husband, Greg Lawrence, has written book reviews and has been a story analyst for the Twentieth Century Fox film studio. A sequel to* Dancing on My Grave, The Shape of Love, *also coauthored by Kirkland and Lawrence, appeared in 1990.*

Before and as You Read

1. Write about yourself as a dancer. Even if you don't normally consider yourself a dancer, define the concept of dance in a way that includes you, for example, "purposeful, organized physical movement." Think about related concepts such as grace and agility. When do you feel graceful or agile or dexterous? When do you feel awkward or clumsy? How important to you is the feeling of physical competence?

2. Write what you know about classical ballet. Where have your knowledge or your impressions of the discipline come from? Identify several questions you have about classical ballet and use library resources such as dance encyclopedias and histories to help answer your questions.

3. Think about the role of dance in American cultures. In your cultural background, what forms of dance were encouraged? What forms discouraged? Were girls and boys treated differently in this regard? If you have knowledge of different cultures, either in the United States or elsewhere, how is dance viewed differently from culture to culture? (Read, for example, the selection by Katsi Cook from *New Voices from the Longhouse* in chapter 5.)

4. To what extent is physical grace and coordination part of your sense of what is "good"? This may at first seem to you to be a strange connection, but think about it. In what ways is moral or immoral behavior, as you regard it, defined by how a person moves and gestures? Cite specific examples.

CHAPTER TWO: CAT'S CRADLE

DURING THOSE early days, when my sister and I shared a bedroom   *1*
and attended ballet school together, we sometimes amused ourselves with a game called "cat's cradle." By tying the ends of a string, we
constructed a circular loop, and by manipulating the loop between the fingers
of both hands, we fashioned a cradle that could be passed back and forth
between us. With each pass, the complexity of design increased, as did the
challenge of manual dexterity. After witnessing this birth of form many times,
we discovered, almost without knowing it, the principles that determined the
pattern of the string.

Playing by myself, I contrived cradles of amazing intricacy. Lying on my   *2*
bed with my legs in the air, I could transfer the twisted string from my hands
to my feet. I heard somewhere that Houdini was able to tie knots with his
toes; I did him one better, sprawled on my back, stringing a web from toe to
toe. Placing the elaborate mesh between my hands, I tested its design by
holding it up between my face and the mirror. Crossing my eyes, I was startled
to see that the left side of my face did not match the right side. The symmetry
of the string accentuated my facial lines, reminding me that I was not
beautiful.

My fascination with the string became an obsession. I spent hours play-   *3*
ing the game, long after my sister lost interest. One evening, waiting for
Johnna to come to bed, I fell asleep. When she finally arrived to turn in, she
found me, still asleep, trespassing on her side of the curtain. Having already
ransacked the room, I was rifling the trash can. Johnna woke me as I was
saying, "I gotta find the string." I repeated the phrase over and over. When my
sister finally forced me to admit that I had been sleepwalking, I accepted
responsibility for the rampage. But I could not remember why I was looking
for the string. After returning to bed, I found it under my pillow; I must have
fallen asleep with the cradle in my hands.

I can now imagine a cat's cradle large enough to cover the entire floor   *4*
of the stage upon which I dance. By extending the imaginary grid into three
dimensions, I create a mental image of the space within which the dancer
performs. Within the holy circle of the stage, geometrical principles are used
to organize physical energy so that the beauty of the human form reveals
a web of drama and truth—that is the essence of dance as I have come to
know it.

I entered ballet school the same year that my mother embarked on a   *5*
new professional career with *Sports Illustrated*. That was 1960, the beginning
of a decade that I would experience, for the most part, from the inside of a
ballet studio. As my father's royalties had dwindled, my mother sought employment to help support the family. The expenses included, until we received
scholarships, the considerable cost of sending two daughters to the School of

American Ballet. To contribute to the cause, I acquiesced to a brief stint as a child model.

I recall the day that my father collected me early from Professional Children's School to attend a photographic session. I was outraged that I would have to miss my ballet class. I refused to smile for the photographer and finally burst into tears to end the session. The photographs were used by a painter for a children's wear advertisement. There was no false modesty in my dismay at seeing myself immortalized on a page of the New York *Times Magazine*. I recognized the painted smile for the lie that it was. Altering the facial lines had falsified what I had experienced.

When my father said the picture was beautiful, I exploded. How could he call me beautiful when he was aware of the fraud that had been committed? Perhaps, with the fantastic simplicity of a child's logic, I knew that beauty somehow depended on truth. My denials were vehement, but I could not look my father in the eye.

Our domestic life degenerated over the years of his addiction. His dependence on alcohol was never acknowledged by spoken word. Consequently, I had no explanation for either his behavior or my animosity. There were many times I hated him. He seemed to be drunk more than he was sober. I was so intimidated by his presence that I tiptoed through the house trying to avoid him.

When I returned home between classes in the late morning, I would find him stumbling out of bed, hung over. His first act of the day was to throw up in the bathroom that he shared with Mother. Then he proceeded to his coffee, cigarettes, newspaper, and soap operas. When he was absorbed by the TV set in the kitchen, I would try to sneak around him, creeping through the rooms. The apartment was too cramped to elude him. Hearing me, he would holler, "What's the matter? You're not going to give your father a kiss?" My submission to this ritual was a violation of the heart. After the kiss, I always wanted to wipe my lips.

The high point of my father's day was his afternoon visit to Sardi's. Dressed without fail in a stylish suit and tie, he made a regular appearance at the bar with his drinking buddies, mostly theatre types. Seeing him leave and return hours later, I knew his mood had changed. He usually came home in time to listen to my mother's stories about her day in the office. While she prepared the evening meal and poured out her heart to him, he sat nearby with his drink.

After dinner, he drank himself into a stupor. I frequently heard him snore when he fell asleep on the couch. Following a brief nap, he arose to read paperbacks until the early hours of the morning, when more alcohol and a sleeping pill would put him temporarily out of his misery. His condition shamed me so much that I almost never brought friends to our home.

I sometimes witnessed him break down my mother. Their lives together seemed to be over except for the dinner hour, the quiet times when my mother would say he was a good listener. There were other times, more and more frequent, when he used his cynical wit to browbeat her. I dared intervene only once. At the age of twelve, I came to my mother's defense.

They had come to a standoff in the living room. His shouting made 13 my hair stand on end. I could see that my mother was trembling and trying to hide her tears. I scrambled between them and faced my father. Thrusting my chin forward, I spit out my words. "I know who pays for the groceries around here!"

I had touched his masculine pride. There was a terrible silence as my 14 mother disappeared out the door. I watched my father go into the kitchen and open a drawer. He pulled out a knife and turned toward me, saying, "You little . . ."

The expression on his face was as terrifying as the knife. As he came at 15 me, I rushed behind the dining room table. He hesitated. Maybe he had second thoughts. I didn't wait to find out. I was quick enough to beat him out the door of the apartment.

After my escape, I raced to catch up with my mother. She reacted with 16 mute anguish as I told her of my father's attack. She took me under her arm and led me to the local market. We returned to the scene of the crime with the very groceries that began the dispute. My mother told me that my father had paid for them.

We ate our dinner at the same table around which he had chased me 17 only hours before. While she tried to make believe that nothing had happened, he and I exchanged wounded looks and kept our distance. The incident was never mentioned again, nor was it forgotten.

Ballet provided a convenient way to avoid my father and escape from 18 home. It also gave me a creative arena in which to vent my rage. Over the years, my anger was transformed into a more complicated response to ballet itself, but the passion of my commitment can be traced to the turmoil of my childhood. If I was not able to control my social world, I could at least begin to coordinate the movements of my own body. By devoting myself to the discipline of dance, I was able to establish a measure of control that was otherwise lacking in my life, or so it seemed.

I was hurt when my father made wisecracks that told me he thought 19 ballet was a frivolous pastime. During my first couple of years of ballet school, I enjoyed telling my mother how much I admired my teachers, Madame Tumkovsky, who had auditioned me, and Helene Dudin, another Russian woman. Their classes were an absorbing challenge, the most complicated game of monkey-see-monkey-do that I had ever played. I loved wrestling with myself, grappling with problems. The exercises demanded an investment of energy and produced results that I could see. The reward was not so much the feeling of outward accomplishment, but the inner sense that something had clicked, that a light had been turned on in my little brain. This was serious stuff as far as I was concerned.

I felt more secure as I began to understand the structure of the school, 20 the ladder of annual progress that started with First Division, proceeded by numbers for the first five years, then changed to letters. I was climbing toward an unknowable future, but each rung was a new class that promised more exciting challenges where the rules seemed more complex. I knew that was so because I snuck in to watch my sister's advanced classes. She was already wearing pointe shoes.

. . . Pleasure and pain were inextricably connected and integral to the study of dance. When I think of how much pain and how little pleasure were involved in the next few years of ballet school, I marvel at my perseverance and clarity of purpose. What distinguished me from other students was my early refusal to allow ideas to be imposed upon me without question. In my effort to fashion myself as a dancer, I adopted an instinctual strategy of passive resistance. *21*

My early demands for autonomy came into conflict with one of the operative metaphors of the classroom. I was told to imagine a string that extended from my head to the ceiling, as if I were a puppet. This was intended to correct the line of the upper body. However, pulling myself up along this axis only prevented me from coordinating my entire body along the vertical line through my spinal cord, neck, and head. The primary impulse for movement was placed outside my "physical instrument" and, therefore, outside the sphere of my control. *22*

I frequently received verbal corrections addressed to each part of my body in isolation, figuratively dismembering me and dispelling any semblance of grace. It was as if separate strings were arbitrarily attached to my head, arms, and legs; the teacher seemed to pull each without regard to the others, usually ignoring the torso entirely. Nevertheless, I forced my body to absorb the spastic effect of each correction. *23*

My swayback and narrow hips might have been assets if I had been allowed to pursue my passion for riding horses. Instead, I found myself saddled with a set of physical impediments that had to be overcome. I was long-legged, but not pretty or sleek enough to fit the image of a "Balanchine ballerina." So I set about to alter my natural shape. *24*

During a session of locker-room gossip, one of my classmates, Sasha, told me about an operation that was performed on a dancer to change the line of her foot. By surgically breaking the arch, the bones could be realigned to enhance the dancer's pointe. At the time, I thought the idea ghastly, but I understood the impulse to bring about a cosmetic miracle, to improve upon the imperfections of nature. *25*

In order to circumvent the limitations of my own anatomy, I became a contortionist. With the help of my best friend, Meg Gordon, I undertook a regimen of torture worthy of the Marquis de Sade. By turning a bed into a makeshift rack, I stretched myself out like a victim of medieval abuse. Assuming various positions that forced my extension beyond its natural limit, I told Meg to hold me down no matter how much I might beg for release. She sat on me, disregarding my groans, allowing her body weight to restrain me until *26* the pain became so excruciating that I collapsed into tears. This scene was repeated many times. Its effect would prove ultimately disastrous.

At this awkward stage of my development, I was especially challenged 27 by the technical imperative known as "turn-out," one of the fundamentals of ballet. With the heels together and feet splayed at an angle approaching 180 degrees, the dancer rotates the thighs so as to effect a pose that is turned out to the audience.

The eighteenth-century choreographer Jean-Georges Noverre was one 28 of the first to note the expressive advantages offered by dancing from a turned-out position: "In order to dance well, nothing is so important as the turning out of the thigh . . . A dancer with his limbs turned inward is awkward and disagreeable. The contrary attitude gives ease and brilliancy, it invests steps, position, and attitude with grace." According to modern medical science, early training to achieve turn-out is critical because the femur bone must be taught slowly to adjust within its socket. If this does not occur, aided by a sustained program of physical therapy, the dancer will compensate by twisting the ankles and feet into a dangerous parody of the desired effect.

Nobody told me any of this at the time. Years later I read Balanchine's 29 views on the importance of proper training. In his 1945 essay, "Notes on Choreography," he certainly recognized the physical vulnerability of the child:

> Even with eight- or nine-year-old children, we must always keep in mind the fact that their bones are still soft and their muscles (particularly the ones around the knee) are still unformed. For this reason one should never force the feet of children to attain perfect ballet positions, nor insist on their making an effort to turn out their legs.

However, in actual practice, Balanchine and his teachers unwittingly encouraged young dancers to self-destruct, rationalized as part of the sacrifice that must be made to the art. The speed and shortcuts that he built into the training process called for physical cheating in which the dancer distorted the body to deliver the position or step that Balanchine demanded. The risk of injury was ignored. I watched many of my friends become casualties and fall by the wayside. I thought they were either unlucky or unsuited.

As turn-out was compulsory, I had no choice but to subject myself to 30 chronic strain. They would bend my body but not my will. I have a vivid memory of one of the teachers stopping me in the middle of class to demand that I turn out my feet. There was no regard for the knees or hips, which in my case were distorted to the breaking point. The teacher refused to continue the class until I complied with her wishes.

After giving her a look that I hoped would maim if not kill, I cranked 31 myself into an impossibly exaggerated position, with my feet literally pointing backward. Pretending innocence, I asked, "You mean like this?" I got off with a warning, but the physical problems which had begun to plague me could not be evaded so easily.

During my third year of training, I was introduced to toe shoes, the 32 standard footwear for all ballerinas since the mid-nineteenth century. With its tapered toe, the shoe is designed to complete the line that runs along the top of the instep and through the ankle, knee, and hip. In going up on pointe, some constriction of the foot is unavoidable, creating yet another stress that works against proper placement and coordination.

Before I began pointe class, I borrowed an oversized pair of toe shoes   33
that belonged to my sister and staged an informal exhibition in our living room. Encouraged by Johnna and her friends, I hopped about on one foot, amazing them with my ability to hold my balance. Yet there was something about their appreciative laughter that made me uncomfortable. Thereafter, withdrawing to my bedroom, I spent hours alone, practicing spins and turns, adjusting my visual focus to avoid getting dizzy. Perhaps I was already anticipating the great feat of the evil swan, Odile, who performs thirty-two consecutive fouettés, those one-legged spins that have been the downfall of so many ballerinas, in the third act of *Swan Lake.*

Misguided and caught between excessive demands for turn-out and   34
pointe, my feet had already begun to deform. At the age of eleven, I came down with a severe case of bunions. Many of the teachers had the same malady, caused from years of strain placed on the foot. It was said that Balanchine cherished the aberration of line induced by bunions, that they contributed to the impression of winged feet.

I was initially pleased with the swollen bulge just below the joint of the   35
big toe, but the discomfort soon became so crippling that I was forced to see a doctor. By the time I visited Dr. William Liebler, an orthopedic surgeon at Lenox Hill Hospital, my feet had turned purple from inflammation. A specialist in sports medicine, he was quite familiar with the problem and recommended the only reliable form of treatment. He advised me to quit ballet.

Ignoring his advice and keeping my distress secret from my mother, I   36
danced through the pain and compensated as well as I could. At age twelve, the tendons in my ankles became acutely inflamed. I tried to inure myself to the aches and twinges. This became the standard operating procedure for all injuries throughout my early career. At the School of American Ballet, no viable alternative existed.

For whatever reasons, Mr. B seemed to favor me, and I was determined   37
to prove myself worthy of his affection. During the fourth year of my training, he assembled a number of the teachers in the school for a review of my class. Accompanied by piano, he demonstrated a combination of steps across the floor of the studio and asked the students to follow his example in a line. His special instructions called for us to perform the steps with "energy," one of his pet concepts. When my turn arrived, I took off with such speed and exuberance, so anxious was I to please, that I took a nasty spill. With the resounding tumble of my body on the wood, the music stopped and all eyes glared at me, as if I had interrupted a church service with some blasphemous utterance. The exception was Balanchine.

In the midst of my terrible embarrassment, he alone applauded, saying,   *38*
"You see, everybody, this girl is the only one who understood. I ask for energy, and all of you others were lazy, lazy, lazy. But Gelsey, she has it—energy!"

With his characteristic nasal inflection, he ordered me to repeat the   *39*
exercise. I was astonished, uncertain whether or not he had just mocked me with his praise. I dutifully repeated the steps, this time without falling down. Shortly after that eventful class, I was informed that I would skip a year to the next level of instruction.

Ten years later, observing a ballet class in Russia, I experienced an epi-   *40*
sode of déjà vu in which I was reminded of that afternoon with Mr. B. At the Kirov School in Leningrad, an elderly Russian ballet teacher had arranged her students according to her estimation of their abilities, with the most talented at the front of the line. At the end of the class, she approached the little girl whose talents were deemed most promising. The teacher hugged and praised her in front of the others. I recognized the expressions of the other girls as those I had seen on the faces of my former classmates when Balanchine lauded my own potential. My heart went out to all those who had been overlooked.

Topics for Discussion and Writing

1. In what ways does the cat's cradle work as a metaphor for the entire excerpt? Why do you think Kirkland and Lawrence use this anecdote to begin the chapter? Write your ideas in response to these questions and share them in discussion. As a next step, take one of your journal entries about a personal experience and try to find in it an image or metaphor that characterizes your experience. Revise the journal entry to emphasize this important image or metaphor.
2. Focus on what Kirkland says about her motivation to proceed in ballet. Do you think that these statements capture all the aspects of her motivation? From your reading of the excerpt, can you identify other motives that she has not made explicit?
3. This selection shares with many in *A Sense of Value* a concern with physical risk and danger. Do you feel that what Kirkland was attempting to achieve made the risk worthwhile? Do you feel that she should have taken the advice to "quit ballet"? Explore this issue in writing and discussion. To gain perspective, you might compare this piece with others in this book, such as those by Diane Ackerman, Bo Jackson, and Elisabeth Bumiller.
4. In what ways does this selection enhance your appreciation of ballet and of the ballet dancer? Write about the different kinds of information you could learn about ballet from a personal history like this versus what you might learn from a technical source such as a textbook or a dance review.

GORDON PARKS

from *Voices in the Mirror*

> "When the newsreel ended, a voice boomed over the intercom. 'And here he is—the photographer who shot this remarkable footage!' Norman Alley, the cameraman, had leaped onto the stage to rousing cheers. And I was carried away by his bravery and dedication to his job. From that moment I was determined to become a photographer."
>
> Born in 1912 to a sharecropping family in Kansas, Gordon Parks received from his courageous, hard-working parents a deep faith and hopefulness that pervade the pages of his 1990 autobiography, Voices in the Mirror. The excerpt we have reprinted focuses on the birth of his interest in photography, the art that eventually brought him international recognition. A truly versatile artist, Parks has also been internationally honored for his painting, has published 12 books of poetry, fiction, and nonfiction, has directed films, and has written the music and libretto of the opera Martin (1990), based on the life of Martin Luther King, Jr.
>
> Though he never finished high school, Parks has received over 50 honorary doctorates and awards, including the U.S. National Medal of Art in 1988.

Before and as You Read

1. Write about yourself as a photographer. Considering that photographic and video technology has advanced so rapidly that millions of Americans easily record complex images on tape, film, and disk, what differences do you perceive between the everyday home photographer and the photographic artist? Do you believe that the technology enables you to achieve a higher level of skill in these arts than in others we have represented in this chapter?

2. Find several photographs, from any source, that you admire as works of art. Define the qualities that inspire your admiration. What has the artist made you see that you otherwise would not have seen?

3. Use library resources to locate collections of works by well-known photographers such as Gordon Parks, Annie Liebowitz, Margaret Bourke-White, Ansel Adams, and Diane Arbus. What makes the work of each artist distinctive? If each were given the same subject, how would each handle it?

4. As you read this selection, watch closely how Parks, the writer, with the well-trained eye of Parks, the photographer, uses language to create vivid scenes. Underline passages that particularly strike you. Try to create some of your own.

O N QUIETER runs, in between meals, when the wealthy passengers   *1*
were either sleeping or consuming alcohol in the lounge cars, I
read every magazine I could get my hands on. In one that had been left behind
by a passenger I found a portfolio of photographs that I would never forget.
They were of migrant workers. Dispossessed, beaten by storms, dust and
floods, they roamed the highways in caravans of battered jalopies and wagons
between Oklahoma and California, scrounging for work. Some were so poor
that they traveled on foot, pushing their young in baby buggies and carts.
They lived in shanties with siding and roofs of cardboard boxes, the inside
walls dressed with newspapers. There was a man with two children running
through a dust storm to their shanty. The names of the photographers stuck
in my mind—Arthur Rothstein, Russell Lee, Carl Mydans, Walker Evans, Ben
Shahn, John Vachon, Jack Delano and Dorothea Lange. They all worked for
the Farm Security Administration, a government agency set up by President
Roosevelt to aid submarginal farmers. These stark, tragic images of human
beings caught up in the confusion of poverty saddened me. I took the magazine home and studied it for weeks. Meanwhile I read John Steinbeck's *In
Dubious Battle* and Erskine Caldwell and Margaret Bourke-White's *You Have
Seen Their Faces.* These books stayed in my mind. During layovers in Chicago,
I began visiting the Art Institute on Michigan Avenue, spending hours in this
large voiceless place, studying paintings of Monet, Renoir and Manet.

I might have remained a waiter on the *North Coast Limited* forever, but   *2*
two incidents changed my course. At a Chicago movie house I watched a
newsreel of the bombing of the United States gunboat *Panay* by Japanese
fighter planes. Courageously the cameraman had stayed at his post, shooting
the final belch of steam and smoke that rose when the boat sank in the
Yangtze River. When the newsreel ended, a voice boomed over the intercom.
"And here he is—the photographer who shot this remarkable footage!" Nor-
man Alley, the cameraman, had leaped on the stage to rousing cheers. And I
was carried away by his bravery and dedication to his job. From that moment
I was determined to become a photographer. Three days later I bought my
first camera at a pawnshop for $7.50. It was a Voightlander Brilliant. Not
much of a camera, but a great name to toss around. I had bought what was
to become my weapon against poverty and racism.

The second incident, one that forever banished me from that superior   *3*
train, recorded itself rather harshly several months after the pawnshop purchase. The dining car steward I worked under, a Mr. Barnes, became terribly
unhappy with "black boys" who spent time between meals reading books and
fancy magazines. He was considerably more at ease with those who shot craps
or lolled around up in the bunk car behind the noisy locomotive. "Parks," he
quipped one afternoon, "you must be studyin' up on becoming the first Nigra
president of the United States." The look I gave him, when I half rose from
my seat, sent him scurrying from the dining car in unusual haste. We were
serving dinner, and approaching home that same night, when he provoked me
with a vicious bump in the back as I was placing a bowl of hot soup before a

woman passenger. The soup went in her lap as I chased Barnes to the pantry, picked up a bread knife and put it to his throat. Two waiters grabbed me from behind, urging me to give them the knife. I did. Barnes got off with a kick in the shins. It was ten below zero outside and Christmas was coming. It would be a sorrowful holiday; I knew I was through. I went to the bunk car, dressed and lay across a bunk and waited for the train's arrival in St. Paul.

    . . . Two weeks later the problems of work had also backed off when I   4
got a porter's job on the *400,* a fast train that ran between Minneapolis and Chicago. Hope had a way of blooming, exhausting itself, then blooming again. Hold on to the dreams. Barnes and others, in trying to rob me of them, had only hardened my determination.

    The new camera had helped dispel my gloom. The first few rolls I had   5
taken with it were earning respect from the Eastman Kodak Company. The manager of its Minneapolis branch showed surprise when he found out they were my very first attempt, and he emphatically assured me that they were very good. Too, he promised me a showing in their window gallery if I kept progressing. Dubious, I thanked him, smiled and told him I would hold him to his promise. After that hardly a thing faced my Voightlander that I didn't attempt to glorify—sunsets, beaches, boats, skies, even an elaborate pattern of pigeon droppings on the courthouse steps. I wasn't rushing to the bank with proceeds from those first efforts but experience was mounting, giving me a sense of direction. The gentleman at Eastman lived up to his promise; six months later he had my photographs placed in the company's show windows.

    The *400* allowed me layovers in Chicago. There, visual imagery multi-   6
plied tenfold, with skyscrapers, boats plying Lake Michigan, bridges and the inner-city canals. But before long I realized that such imagery, although it was fine for the family album, was hardly the kind to put steak and potatoes on my family's table. A beautiful sunset over the lake was just a beautiful sunset— no more. Natural instinct had served to aim my sights much higher, and those Farm Security photographs with all their power were still pushing my thoughts around. Before long I had deserted the waterfronts, skyscrapers and canals for Chicago's south side—the city's sprawling impoverished black belt. And there among the squalid, rickety tenements that housed the poor, a new way of seeing and feeling opened up to me. A photograph I made of an ill-dressed black child wandering in a trash-littered alley and another of two aged men warming themselves at a bonfire during a heavy snowfall pleased me more than any I had made. They convinced me that even the cheap camera I had bought was capable of making a serious comment on the human condition. Subconsciously I was moving toward the documentary field, and Chicago's south side was a remarkably pitiful place to start. The worst of it was like bruises on the face of humanity.

    I increased my visits to Chicago and to its Southside Art Center, which   7
sat formidably in the heart of the black belt. Once a stately mansion owned

by the rich, it was now a haven for struggling black artists, sculptors and writers. The gallery walls were usually weighted with the work of well-known painters who used their art to encourage protest from the underprivileged and dispossessed. How effective they were remains questionable, but for me, at the time, their approach to art seemed commensurate with the people they were attempting to serve. A large impressive painting by Isaac Soyer displayed in the front window had pulled me into the art center. The painting was of a building that brought memories of Mrs. Haskins's old place back in Harlem. Before going in I had stood looking at it for several moments, wondering if Mrs. Haskins's old gray stone tenement was still standing; if the grimy stone was even grimier, and the unwashed windows still unwashed. I had entered the art center's doors glancing to see if some young man sat now on the stoop where I had sat by garbage cans, enclosed in a world I was trying to forget. Soyer's painting had been staring at me from another block of time that I was glad to have survived.

On exhibit inside were the works of Soyer, Charles White, Ben Shahn, Max Weber and Alexander Brook, along with the merciless satires of William Gropper and Jack Levine. Oppression was their subject matter. With paint, pencil and charcoal, they had put down on canvas what they had seen, and what they had felt about it. Quite forcefully they were showing me that art could be most effective in expressing discontent, while suggesting that the camera—in the right hands—could do the same. They had forsaken the lovely pink ladies of Manet and Renoir, the soft bluish-green landscapes of Monet that hung several miles north at Chicago's Art Institute. To me these classicists were painters who told far different tales, and for several weeks the difference between the two schools—one classical, the other harshly documentary— would expand the possibilities of the artistic directions I could take. *8*

Vogue was one of the magazines left behind by passengers. Along with its fashion pages I studied the names of its famous photographers—Steichen, Blumenfeld, Horst, Beaton, Hoyningen-Huené, thinking meanwhile that my own name could look quite natural among them. Spring was in the air and I was back in St. Paul feeling aggressive. Energy pulsed through me, urged me toward the impossible as I walked the business area. Suddenly something propelled me toward Frank Murphy's fashionable store for women—rich women. I can't explain what took over when I reached the imposing entrance; but I walked in boldly and asked for Frank Murphy. The tall, elegantly attired man I had approached observed me with smileless eyes. "I'm Frank Murphy," he said sharply. "What can I do for you?" For a disquieting moment I wondered about that myself. *9*

"I would like to photograph some fashions for your store." I had, without forethought, voiced a fantasy—but not an outright lie—and he had all but walked me out the door when his wife turned from a customer. "What does the young man want, Frank?" *10*

He gestured hopelessly. "To shoot fashions." *11*

Madeline Murphy looked me over quickly. "Well, Frank, maybe he can. 12
Have him wait. I'll talk to him." Frank Murphy looked at his wife as though
she had lost her wits. The customer left and she walked over to me. "Have
you samples of your work?"

"No, ma'am, I don't." 13

Frank cut in. "Our clothes are photographed out East." My heart sank. 14

"Quiet, Frank. Can you really photograph fashion?" 15

"Yes, ma'am," I lied. 16

Madeline Murphy gave me a long, hard look. "All right, you'll have the 17
chance. How many gowns do you want?"

"Ah—ah—six." 18

"And how many models?" 19

"Three—three will be enough." 20

"Can you be here tomorrow after we close at six?" 21

"Yes, ma'am—I'll be here." 22

"Fine. I'll have the models and dresses ready." 23

I was stunned. I didn't have an appropriate camera, lights or film, but I 24
was suddenly plumped up with courage.

I arrived at the appointed time—with the camera and lighting equip- 25
ment lent to me by a noble-hearted fellow, Harvey Goldstein, who had a
camera store near the Minnesota campus and let me have film on credit. He
always told me I would amount to something. "And when you do," he would
say, "let it be known that I was your godfather." The camera was a 4 × 5
Speed Graphic, and as Harvey drove me to the store, he tried to show me
how to use it, but being intimidated by Frank Murphy's prestigious store, he
dumped me and the equipment at the door and fled. The dresses and models
were indeed beautiful and, surprisingly, I did a good job of lighting them
while Frank Murphy watched with a skeptical eye.

The big blow fell at exactly two o'clock in the morning, when I devel- 26
oped the film. With the exception of one negative, I had double-exposed the
entire lot. My wife got out of bed when she heard my head bumping against
the wall. The whole universe had collapsed. How could I bear to face Madeline Murphy? She had been so impressed with watching the session that she
had asked me to shoot sport clothes at her country club the following day.

"I'd blow up the good one and show it to her," Sally suggested as she 27
went back to bed. I sat moaning for an hour before her remark sank in, and
early the next morning I got Harvey out of bed to make that print. And it
was a big one. When the Murphys arrived, there it was—elegantly framed and
standing on an easel at the entrance to the club.

"My dear boy," Mrs. Murphy exclaimed. "It's exquisite. Where are the 28
others? I can't wait to see them!"

I was tempted to concoct a lie of some sort, but she deserved the truth, 29
so I mobilized my scruples and gave her the truth—the whole truth. Madeline
Murphy didn't bat an eye. "Would they all have been that good?" she asked.

"Oh, by all means. The one there is the worst of the lot." 30

"Then we do it all over tomorrow evening," she said. You could have   *31*
heard Frank's groan a block away.

Shortly after, my photographs filled Frank Murphy's windows. I passed   *32*
those windows many times during that first week—and spent a lot of time
staring at them and smiling.

Fortunes have a way of feeding on one another. My photographs in   *33*
Frank Murphy's windows caught the eye of Marva Louis, the wife of Joe
Louis, the heavyweight champion. Fashion coursed through her blood and
she urged me to move to her city, Chicago, where she would assure me of
beautiful fashions and women to photograph. That combined with an offer
from the Southside Art Center to use its studio and darkroom facilities led me
to pack up my family, which now included our daughter, Toni, and move to
that big city in 1940. Somehow I had survived those icy Minnesota winters,
but many other manipulative things lay in wait to confuse the geography of
the approaching months. I didn't know what lay before me, but I was moving
ahead—at least, I thought so, and that was enough. For a long time I had been
inclined to believe that fate moved me with its own persuasions. Now I suspected it was backing off for a spell, and it was time to take things into my
own hands. By doing so I hoped that fate was becoming more compliant with
my dreams. In any case, I had decided to help shape my own destiny.

It makes me think back to a close friend, Jasper Caldwell, who after one   *34*
of his numerous failures, would always say, "Look, man, everything turned
out as it was meant to be. Nothing I could do about it." Jasper departed this
planet without trying to do much about anything. His philosophy became his
excuse. In looking back at those days that died before he did, he failed to
realize that they expired without help from him; that his neglect of them had
a lot to do with what he failed to accomplish. I sensed the danger in misleading myself into thinking I did my best by those efforts that came to nothing.
One's memory can be deceptive. To placate you it often refuses to remember
things as they really were, preferring to see them as *you* want them to be. That
is always a good time to listen to the mirror.

Chicago welcomed me cautiously, offering me a few society matrons to   *35*
photograph along with its devastated black area on the south side with its
storefront Bethels, God in Christs, African Methodists and Pilgrim Baptists—
all kept going with the pennies, nickels and dimes of poor black people.
Chicago offered me many things that first year, but not many of the golden
arms Marva Louis had promised. During that first year there my family learned
to spell *suffer*. But just when food and money hit the zero mark, fate resur-
rected my hopes. A collection of photographs I had taken in the impoverished
area of the black belt came to the attention of the Julius Rosenwald Fund, a
cultural foundation established by its namesake to aid promising blacks and
Southern whites. Writers, painters, sculptors and scholars had been recipients
of fellowships—but never a photographer. I was considered to be promising, so
my work was sent to be judged by a jury of Chicago's most esteemed white photographers and, to a man, they turned thumbs down. To allow my application

yet another chance, my work was then sent to a jury composed of painters and sculptors. While I awaited their decision, time crawled ever so slowly. Worry set in. The postman arrived with nothing but bills. After three weeks the jury was still out, still feeding my anxiety and sleepless nights. The fourth week an envelope, with the fund's masthead, appeared in the small pack of mail. I was fearful of opening it; it seemed to be shaped with rejection. I handed it to Sally so that she might read the bad news. She tore the envelope open, read its contents and smiled weakly. "You *are* a Julius Rosenwald Fellow."

It was the first time I ever saw my wife weep. Perhaps I too would have wept, but I was too numb with happiness. Now we could look forward to the sum of two hundred dollars each month. To celebrate our good fortune, we planned a party on Gordon Jr.'s birthday: December 7, 1941—fourteen years after I departed my father's house back in Kansas.   36

Then suddenly bombs were dropping on Pearl Harbor. The news was astonishing. For me other staggering news was to come shortly after. Through the prodding of the fund, I was to serve out my fellowship with the Farm Security Administration; with those same photographers whose work had beckoned to me when I was a waiter on the *North Coast Limited*. It was an extravagant moment as we began packing, and for the next two years Washington, D.C., would be our home.   37

Topics for Discussion and Writing

1. Mark statements in which Parks comments on the events of his life. Would you say from your reading that Parks sees his life primarily as a random series of events directed by some benevolent force greater than himself, or as an organized progression controlled by his own thinking and will? Share your perceptions with others who have read the selection.

2. What roles do other people play in Parks's story? How does he describe their influence?

3. Note the many different kinds of things Parks tells us that he photographed in his early days as a photographer. How did he choose his subjects? What does he say about his sense of purpose as a photographer? How do his purposes change? Why? Pay particular attention to the motives of earning money and promoting social change. Do you find these motives conflicting or working together in his narrative?

4. Write about a person in your family, or another person you know well, who is devoted to taking photographs. Take this person seriously as an artist; explain to a reader who has not seen this person's photographs your perception of the motives and the style of this photographer. How does this photographer work? What are his or her tools? Are there characteristic features of this person's best work? End your writing with a statement of the contribution that you feel this person has made to the family or other community she or he has recorded.

For Further Thought

1. Choose an artist whom you admire. Research this person's life. At what point did this person consider him- or herself to be an artist? What were some of the financial, social, emotional, and other obstacles that this person encountered in life? Share your biographical findings with your class.

2. Attend a live performance such as a recital, poetry reading, or play. After the performance, introduce yourself to the artist. Try to engage this person in a conversation about his or her work. Does this person seem different in a one-on-one conversation than he or she did on stage? In what way?

3. In your journal write a composite sketch of an artist based on the people you have encountered in this chapter. This new character will have at least one characteristic from each writer. Give your character life. Where was she or he born? Where did she or he grow up? What is this person's marital status? What, if any, is his or her religious affiliation? Political ties? Charity involvement? What are his or her hopes, dreams, and insecurities? How is this person different from you? How is this person the same?

4. How has AIDS affected the artistic community around the world? Do you think that our government's response to the growing threat of this disease would have been more far-reaching much earlier had the gay community not been one of the initial populations affected? Since many artists are gay or lesbian, what does this response in the face of such peril tell us about ourselves? Recall from history another time when the arts and politics clashed.

5. Refer to your responses to any of the topics or questions at the beginning of this chapter. On the basis of your readings and writings as you worked through the chapter, revise your responses to those topics and questions.

ACKNOWLEDGMENTS

DIANE ACKERMAN, from *The Moon by Whale Light.* Copyright © 1991 by Diane Ackerman. Reprinted by permission of Random House, Inc.

KEN ADELMAN, "There Ought to be a Law." Reprinted by permission of *The Washingtonian.*

LYLE ALZADO, "I'm Sick and I'm Scared." Reprinted courtesy of *Sports Illustrated* from the July 8, 1991 issue. Copyright © 1991, Time, Inc.

RUDOLFO ANAYA, "The Censorship of Neglect," *English Journal.* Copyright 1992 by the National Council of Teachers of English. Reprinted with permission.

MAYA ANGELOU, *I Know Why the Caged Bird Sings.* Copyright © 1970 by Maya Angelou. Reprinted by permission of Random House, Inc.

HARVEY ARDEN, *Wisdomkeepers.* Copyright © 1990, Steve Wall and Harvey Arden from the book *Wisdomkeepers*, Beyond Words Publishing, Inc., Hillsboro, Oregon.

JOAN BENOIT, "Childhood of a Long-Distance Runner" from *Running Tide.* Copyright © 1989 by Joan Benoit Samuelson. Reprinted by permission of Alfred A. Knopf, Inc.

MARTHA BARRON BARRETT, *Invisible Lives.* Copyright © by Martha Barron Barrett. By permission of William Morrow & Company, Inc.

HENRY BERRY, from the book *Hey Mac, Where Ya Been?* Copyright © 1988 by Henry Berry. Reprinted with permission from St. Martin's Press, Inc., New York, NY.

ELISABETH BUMILLER, "At the Peak of Her Profession, The Japanese Climber, Conquering Mountains Real and Cultural." Copyright © 1991, The Washington Post. Reprinted with permission.

KAREN BROWNE, "A Letter to My Daughter." Reprinted by permission of the author.

KATSI COOK, "The Women's Dance, 1986. Reprinted with permission of Akwe:kon Press, Cornell University, Ithaca, NY.

DONTÉ CORNISH, *"The Autobiography of Malcolm X:* Reaction and Retrospective." Reprinted by permission of the author.

ANNIE DILLARD, "Seeing" from *Pilgrim at Tinker Creek.* Copyright © 1974 by Annie Dillard. Pages 9, 12–19 from *The Writing Life.* Copyright © 1989 by Annie Dillard. Reprinted by permission of HarperCollins Publishers Inc.

FREDERICK DOUGLASS, *My Bondage and My Freedom.* Reprinted by permission of Dover Publications, Inc.

BARBARA FERRARO AND PATRICIA HUSSEY, *No Turning Back.* Copyright © 1990 by Barbara Ferraro & Patricia Hussey. Reprinted by permission of Poseidon Press, a division of Simon & Schuster, Inc.

DAVID FLORY, "One Day, South Africa." Reprinted by permission of the author.

LINDA BIRD FRANCKE, "I Didn't Want My Child to Die" from *The Ambivalence of Abortion.* Reprinted by permission of Random House, Inc. Copyright © 1978 by Linda Bird Francke.

ANNE FRANK, *Anne Frank: The Diary of a Young Girl.* Copyright 1952 by Otto H. Frank. Used by permission of Doubleday, a division of Bantam Doubleday Dell Publishing Group, Inc.

MIKE FREEMAN, "In NFL's Fight Against Steroids, New Technology Is Half the Battle." Copyright © 1991, *The Washington Post.* Reprinted with permission.

606

INDEX BY TECHNIQUE AND GENRE

All good non-fiction writing shows writers using a variety of techniques and forms (or genres) in order to meet their purposes and move their readers. Some techniques, such as careful **description** of people, objects, or scenes, are so basic to successful essay writing that almost any good piece of nonfiction can be used as a model for the writer trying to improve his or her descriptive ability. Likewise, the genre of the **essay,** with its blending of the "story" and the "point" (or claim), is so widespread and encompasses so many types of writing that it says little about a piece to label it an "essay." (See chapter 2 on the "personal essay" for ideas on how to write in this form.)

On the other hand, some techniques, such as the use of **dialogue,** and some genres within the essay, such as the **interview, memoir,** or **interpretation of reading,** are more specialized. We have categorized the essays in *A Sense of Value* according to some of the techniques and genres that the writers have employed. You'll note that all of the pieces demonstrate more than one genre or technique; indeed, any essay uses a wide array of techniques and falls into several genres, some of which we have chosen to label, some of which we have not, because we want this index to be useful, but not cumbersome.

Letter

Vision or Dream

Survey Report

Analysis of News Events

Interpretation of Reading, Oral Language, or Art

Self-Analysis or Memoir

Close Observation

Editorial or Formal Argument

Description

Comparison/Contrast

Every selection

Narrative

Every selection

SUBJECT INDEX